American Entrepreneur

THE FASCINATING STORIES OF THE PEOPLE WHO DEFINED BUSINESS IN THE UNITED STATES

Larry Schweikart, Ph.D.
Lynne Pierson Doti, Ph.D.

⋅AMACOM

AMERICAN MANAGEMENT ASSOCIATION

New York • Atlanta • Brussels • Chicago • Mexico City • San Francisco
Shanghai • Tokyo • Toronto • Washington, D.C.

Special discounts on bulk quantities of AMACOM books are available to corporations, professional associations, and other organizations. For details, contact Special Sales Department, AMACOM, a division of American Management Association, 1601 Broadway, New York, NY 10019.

Tel: 800-250-5308. Fax: 518-891-2372.

E-mail: specialsls@amanet.org

Website: www.amacombooks.org/go/specialsales

To view all AMACOM titles go to: www.amacombooks.org

This publication is designed to provide accurate and authoritative information in regard to the subject matter covered. It is sold with the understanding that the publisher is not engaged in rendering legal, accounting, or other professional service. If legal advice or other expert assistance is required, the services of a competent professional person should be sought.

Although this book does not always specifically identify trademarked names, AMACOM uses them for editorial purposes only, with no intention of trademark violation. A list of trademarks appearing in this book begins on page iv.

Library of Congress Cataloging-in-Publication Data
Schweikart, Larry.
    American entrepreneur : the fascinating stories of the people who defined business in the United States / Larry Schweikart, Lynne Pierson Doti.
        p. cm.
    Includes index.
    ISBN-13: 978-0-8144-1411-8 (hardcover)
    ISBN-10: 0-8144-1411-7 (hardcover)
1. Entrepreneurship—United States—History. I. Doti, Lynne Pierson. II. Title.

    HB615.S377 2010
    338.0973—dc22   2009009842

Portions of this book were previously published under the title *The Entrepreneurial Adventure* in 1999.

Printing number
10 9 8 7 6 5 4 3 2 1

3 9547 00329 1262

CONTENTS

Trademarked Terms Appearing in *American Entrepreneur*

A&P
ABC
Adams Express Company
AIG
Air Jordan
Amazon
American Airlines
American Bridge
    Company
American Express
American Greetings
American Institute of
    Steel Construction
Anaheim Ducks
Anheuser-Busch
AOL
APAC
Apple
Arizona Diamondbacks
AT&T
Atari
AutoNation
Avon

Bank of America
Barbie
Barnes & Noble
Barnum & Bailey Circus
Batten, Barton, Durstine
    & Osborn (BBD&O)
Bayou Steel
Beanie Babies
Bear Stearns
Beatrice International
Bebe
Bell Laboratories
Birds Eye
BlackBerry
Blockbuster
BMW
Boeing
Border Steel
Borland
BP

Broadcom
Brown & Sharpe
Budweiser
Buick
Burger King
Burpee

Cadbury
Cadillac
Campbell's
Caterpillar
CBS
Chevrolet
Chevron
Chicago Bulls
Chrysler
Chuck E. Cheese
Circus Circus Hotel and
    Casino
Cisco
Cisco Systems Inc.
Citibank
CNN
Coca-Cola
Cocoa Pebbles
Colt
Comcast
Compaq
ConocoPhillips
Continental Airlines
Corning Inc.
Costco
C-SPAN

Dallas Cowboys
Datsun
Dayton Power and
    Light Co.
Deere & Company
Dell
Delmonico's Restaurant
Delta Air Lines

Detroit Lions
Disney
Disneyland
Dodge
Dole Food Company
DuPont

Eagle Iron Works
eBay
Electric Boat
Epcot
Excalibur
Excite
Exxon Mobil

Famous Amos
Fannie Mae
Federal Express
Federal Steel
Ferrari
Fleetwood
Florida Marlins
Florida Panthers
Florida Steel
Food Network
Ford Motor Company
Four Seasons
Fox
Freddie Mac
Freon
Fuller Brush Company

Garrett
General Electric
General Motors
Gerber
Gillette
Godfather's Pizza
Goldman Sachs
Goodyear
Google

Grand Ole Opry
Grape-Nuts
Green Bay Packers
Greenpeace
Grunder Landscaping
GTE
Gulf Oil

Hallmark
Hasbro
HBO
Heelys, Inc.
Heinz
Herbal Life
Hewlett-Packard
Hitachi
Holiday Inn
Holidome
Hollywood Video
Home Shopping Network
Honda
Horizon
Hurricane Industries

IBM
ImClone
Intel
International Harvester
International Paper
iPhone
ITT
Ivory Soap

J. C. Penney Company
Jack Daniel's
JPMorgan Chase
JVC

Kansas City Royals
Kelly Services
Kimberly-Clark
Kmart
Kodak
Kraft
Kroger

Lands' End
Level 3 Communications
Libby
Lincoln
Lionel Train
Listerine
Little Caesars
Lockheed Martin
Lord & Taylor
Lucent
Luxor
Luxottica Group
Lycos

Maersk
Magnavox
Martin Marietta
Mary Kay
Mattel
McCall Pattern Company
McDonald's
MCI
Mercedes
Merrill Lynch
Metro-Goldwyn-Mayer
MGM Grand Hotel
Miami Dolphins
Michelob
Microchip Technology
Microsoft
Microsoft Windows
Milken Institute
Minute Maid
Mirage
Mitsubishi
Mobil
ModBargains
Monopoly
Montgomery Ward
Motorola
Mozilla
Mr. Potato Head

Nabisco
Nathan's Famous
National Tube Supply
    Company
Navistar

NBC
NCR
Nestlé
Netscape
Nike
Nikon
Nintendo
Nissan
Nucor Steel

Oakley, Inc.
Odd Ball Cabaret
Oreo O's
Otis Elevator Company

Pabst
Panasonic
Paramount Pictures
Parker Bros.
Patti-Maids
PCs Limited
Pepsi
Philadelphia Cream
    Cheese
Philip Morris
Phoenix Suns
Piggly Wiggly
Pillsbury
PlayStation
Pontiac
Post Cereals
PowerPoint
Pratt & Whitney
Procter & Gamble

Quaker Oats
Qwest

Radio America
RadioShack
RCA
Remington Arms
    Company

(continued on next page)

RKO
Rockwell

Safeway
Salvation Army
Santander Bank
Sanyo
Scott Paper Company
Seabrook Farms
Sears, Roebuck,
   and Company
SeaWorld
SEGA
SEMATECH
Sharp
Shell
Sheraton
Silicon Graphics Inc.
Singer
Six Flags
Snapple
Sony
Southwest Airlines
Spago
St. Louis Cardinals
Stanley Home Products
Staples

Steinway & Sons
Sun Microsystems
SunCoast Video

Taco Bell
Target
Technicolor
TeleTech
Texaco
Texas Instruments
Ticketmaster
Time Warner
Toshiba
Toyota
Toys "R" Us
Trailer Bridge Inc.
TransWave
TWA
Twitter
Tyco International

United Airlines
United Artists
Universal Studios
UPS
U.S. Airways
U.S. Steel Corporation
uWink

Volkswagen

Waffle House
Wal-Mart
Walt Disney World
Warner Bros.
Waste Management Inc.
Welch's
Wells Fargo
Western Union
Westinghouse Electric
   Company
Weyerhaeuser Company
Wii
Willys-Overland
Wurlitzer

Xbox
Xerox

Yahoo!
YMCA/YWCA

Zenith

PREFACE

Few, if any, books attempt to combine a comprehensive business history of the United States with basic economic history. Moreover, those that do approach either business or economic history do so from an "institutional" perspective, focusing on big corporations and, oddly, government actions. In *American Entrepreneur*, our aim is not only to combine business and economic history, but to tell it in an entertaining and informative way by focusing on the individuals who made America's economy the greatest in the world.

This sweeping story begins with the logical and yet exceptional development of early merchants such as Thomas Hancock, who then became owners of textile mills and other established businesses. Those mill owners—people like Samuel Slater and Francis Cabot Lowell—soon needed financing, giving rise to America's early banks. Bankers and politicians, seeing the need for "internal improvements," provided the infrastructure for such marvels as the Erie Canal, but also the opportunity for extraordinary businessmen like Cornelius Vanderbilt. "The Commodore," as Vanderbilt was called, soon stretched his steamship lines across the oceans, and then began linking American cities by rail. With the advent of the railroads, business in the United States entered a "managerial revolution" where professional managers began to make the key decisions in major companies.

As the railroads grew, they became intertwined with other large-scale industries, such as Andrew Carnegie's steel company, John D. Rockefeller's refining business, and, of course, the banking businesses of J. P. Morgan. At the turn of the century, the owner-operated firm was disappearing, replaced by "managerial hierarchies." This form of business brought new advantages, including the ability to expand almost limitlessly, and risk reduction through diversification. But it also brought a certain stagnation, as managers became more conservative than the radical entrepreneurs—the business barons—they replaced. The Great Depression not only winnowed out the number of businesses, but President Franklin D. Roosevelt's New Deal placed onerous burdens on the survivors. Those burdens were not lifted until World War II, when America again turned to its "capitalist folk heroes," and men like Andrew Jackson Higgins and Henry Kaiser rose to the challenge.

In the postwar era, American business stood atop the world. Yet many of the companies—now firmly in the hands of the managers— were already losing their competitive edge, while new entrepreneurs in hotels (Kemmons Wilson), fast food (Ray Kroc), and music (Berry Gordy) were quietly rising. Following two decades of internal mismanagement and external government regulation, American business entered a renaissance in the 1980s and unveiled the most important invention of the late-twentieth century, the personal computer. More than ever, entrepreneurs such as Bill Gates and Steve Jobs, who led the personal computer revolution, and Jeff Bezos, who created an entirely new business to take advantage of Internet-connected computers, demonstrated the necessity of risk takers. Despite the dot-com recession and the 9/11 attacks, American business rebounded to again lead the world in productivity and innovation in the early twenty-first century—with an entirely new cast of entrepreneurs. Then, yet another challenge appeared as the mortgage, banking, and auto industries all faltered in the first decade of the twenty-first century. Would American entrepreneurs again triumph? That remains in the future. The lessons of the past suggest that America's innovators and industrialists, inventors and businesspeople have the capacity to come back yet again.

Larry Schweikart, Ph.D.
Lynne Pierson Doti, Ph.D.

CHAPTER 1

Entrepreneurs:
The Essence of Enterprise

Sometime in 2001, shoppers began to see an odd sight: Kids in malls would appear to walk a few steps and then strangely seem to glide on their heels. A closer look revealed they were wearing "Heelys," athletic shoes with wheels in the heels. Heelys are the brainchild of Roger Adams, who invented the shoes while taking time off with "a midlife crisis."[1] Adams was a manager who was constantly on call and "totally burned out," and he was on vacation at Huntington Beach, California, in 1998 when he saw kids going up and down the sidewalk on their inline skates. Suddenly Adams had the idea for a combination shoe and skate—a shoe that could roll on command when the wearer shifted body weight. He cut up some Nike running shoes, put some skateboard wheels in the back, and a prototype was born. Adams started his company in December 2000, went public in 2006, and sold out his stock in hours. In June 2007, Heelys, Inc., was worth $800 million and was number one on *BusinessWeek*'s list of "Hot Growth Companies."[2] Just getting to that point was a journey of its own: On his way to Texas to meet with an investor, his car was rear-ended and caught fire. His prototype, his business plan, and even his clothes were in that car. A short time later, however, the son of a patent attorney showed Adams's promotional film to a friend, whose father was a venture capitalist. Impressed, the father backed Heelys. The product had "arrived" when former Los Angeles Lakers star Shaquille O'Neal ordered a pair of the shoes in size 22 and R & B star Usher appeared in a music video wearing a pair.

Business historians will look back at the introduction of Heelys and ask why they were developed. While the answer may seem obvious to some people (okay, some young people), historians often make the obvious complex. For example, Adams claimed that he harkened back to the fun of his childhood, but did he contrive the recollections of his youth as a justification after the fact? Did vast, sweeping social forces make 2000 "the right time" for such an invention? Did Adams perceive great profits and leave other, unrelated work to create his product? In short, does the economy operate from entrepreneurs upward or from large invisible forces downward? And what is the role of success in creating, and sustaining, business?

To understand how success and failure, birth and death are essential to the entrepreneurial process, it is necessary to ask yet another set of questions. What is it that entrepreneurs do? How do they differ from managers who oversee an existing business? How do other people, even others around the world who have no awareness of entrepreneurs' efforts or specific businesses, benefit from entrepreneurs' successes? Perhaps more important, how do those same people benefit from entrepreneurs' failures?

This book, while tracing the history of American business from its European origins to contemporary times, will examine these questions through a focus on entrepreneurs. To a considerable extent, this book is a celebration of entrepreneurs and entrepreneurship. We do not intend to delve deeply into the contributions of labor or on the social forces that shaped labor movements. Instead, the entrepreneur, and those forces that directly affect entrepreneurs, will receive central treatment. At the same time, defining entrepreneurship has proved more difficult for economists and business historians than might appear at first glance, and that definition has expanded or changed over time. We have therefore chosen to examine the context in which the concept of entrepreneurship appeared in a comprehensive framework. It begins not with a businessman, but with a professor at the University of Glasgow, Adam Smith.

ADAM SMITH, ECONOMICS, AND ENTREPRENEURSHIP

The essence of entrepreneurship is capitalism, an economic system elaborated by Adam Smith in his famous book written in 1776, *An Inquiry into the Nature and Causes of the Wealth of Nations*.[3] Smith did not invent the market system: He only laid out in a systematic form an explanation of economic practices as old as time itself. But Smith is worth examining in detail at this early point for two reasons. First, his theory is as valid today as it was in 1776. Challengers still remain, but increasingly they have retreated into debating the effects of capitalism on spiritual grounds, where proof is impossible and faith is essential. Second, Smith's explanation of human behavior is particularly important to the point of this book: entrepreneurs and their contributions.

Adam Smith explained economic wealth creation as a process of making products or providing services with the goal of personal gain. For most people, gain means material gain. It must be remembered that in the eighteenth century, most people had so little that material gain often meant survival for yourself and your family. In that context, aside from those dedicated individuals on the planet entirely motivated by religious, ideological, or artistic factors (Mother Teresa or Tibetan monks come to mind), people operate to a substantial degree out of concern for material gain. Even for Mother Teresa or Tibetan monks, Smith's "rational self-interest" could be a motivation. After all, if you are absolutely certain that there are rewards to come in heaven or in the next life, wouldn't a few more "good deeds" be worked into your schedule? (Of course, in some poor countries, becoming a monk can be a path to a better material life, too.) Certainly some individuals crave power instead of wealth, but usually the trappings of power include most material goods, including houses, transportation, food, and personal assistants. Other people want fame, but fame, too, usually produces wealth as a by-product, making it difficult to separate a desire for one from the other. Whatever the case, a good rule of thumb for life is that when people say they are "not in it for themselves," watch out! They are in it precisely "for themselves." Smith understood that rational self-interest was the most important motivating force in the world under normal conditions. More important to Smith, he observed that society as a whole benefited and improved materially as individuals pursued self-interest.

Critics of capitalism have viewed this as a paradox: How can society thrive if the key economic tenet is self-interest? Perhaps it cannot; but Smith never equated self-interest with selfishness. Instead, he saw capitalism as a moral system. Smith was a man consumed by moral questions. His previous book, *A Theory of Moral Sentiments* (1764), established his view that self-interest was a guide for empathetic humans who could not know what was best for others, because they did not have access to "the big picture." The market system, or prices, ensured that individuals, each person acting according to this internal mechanism, would behave in a way that would ensure the outcome best for all. Although Smith sought to explain the overall functioning of the economy—really, as a capstone to his broader discussion of morality—he did so through analysis of individual markets and examples. Thus his famous quotation: "It is not from the benevolence of the butcher, the brewer, or the baker that we can expect our dinner, but from their regard to their own interest."[4] People are "encouraged" to serve others in a market system. Because he already had written extensively on morality, Smith assumed that the reader already would have grasped the spiritual elements of his economic theory. Thus, the references in *Wealth of Nations* to "self-interest" were intended to describe an element of human psychology that ensured people would respond to the needs of others.

Smith thus began his investigation with the "natural wants" of people, and noted that the range of human wants made people dependent on the labor of others. This resulted in a division of labor that made capitalism especially vibrant. Any person, he theorized, could perform almost any labor to one degree or another. As he put it, "By nature a philosopher is not in genius and disposition half so different from a street porter, as is a mastiff from a greyhound."[5] However "no one ever saw a dog make a fair and deliberate exchange with another dog," in spite of the obvious advantages the above-mentioned dogs might have in joining their resources to increase their consumption possibilities.[6] To Smith, then, it did not seem logical for every person to try to do everything (farm, build, philosophize, and so on), but rather to specialize in what the person did best, to maximize the return, allowing others to do those tasks they did better. This resulted in more total production, but also made people dependent on others. Self-interest was what made people pay attention to the desires of others and ensured that that dependency could not be ignored.

But while division of labor was a key element in capitalism, Smith's theory consisted of far more. He observed that self-interest created competition between people, either to produce goods and supply services on one side of the equation, or to acquire goods and services on the other. Human nature meant that people thought highly of themselves, regardless of religious training or government suasion. Individuals therefore tended to ask for as much payment as possible for their own labor and sought to purchase goods made by others for as little as possible. Or, in Smith's vernacular, "sell dear, buy cheap." Smith realized, however, that everyone could not "sell dear" and "buy cheap" simultaneously. This observance eventually led to exploration of the role of the entrepreneur. Instead of pursuing that concept, Smith went on to explore the nature of value and price. Smith noted that because all sellers wanted high prices and buyers wanted low prices, it caused competition to appear, creating a market wherein all goods and services would reach a specific price. Thus, he introduced the supply-and-demand model now considered so essential to economic understanding.

When explaining "price," Smith did not use the notions of "just price" developed by the Catholic Church.[7] Instead, a price was a piece of information about the availability of a good or service, plus the difficulty in producing it or attaining it, combined with the desire of people to acquire that good or service and their ability to pay for it. In fact, there can be no such thing as a "just price" or a "fair price" any more than there can be a "just" or "fair" report of a basketball score or a cake recipe. Information is information: Data is either accurate or not, but has no inherent moral value. It is as absurd to talk about a "fair price" as it is to insist that it is "unfair" that only a Chevrolet car key will start a Corvette, or that an airplane will fly only when it attains greater thrust than it has drag. Smith—again, concerned with morality—instead noted that if a price is "unfair" or "unjust," no one will pay it (excluding, of course, situations where government is able through force to exclude competitors or to restrict supply, or in other situations where consumers have no genuine choice). It also should be obvious that, as information, prices cannot be controlled by governments. Have governments ever successfully controlled information? Some command economies with access to extensive secret police networks and torture have kept the lid on certain types of information temporarily. However, no major state has controlled information and maintained a vibrant economy, as the former Soviet Union demonstrated. Even China, a communist nation, realized that it must permit widespread operation of the free market in many sectors of its economy and did not interfere with the vigorous market economy of Hong Kong, which it took over in 1997. A decade later, large areas of China are developing market economies, with the blessing of the communist government.

Smith understood that competition among suppliers and competition among buyers occurred simultaneously; that innumerable business decisions stood behind any single transaction (or exchange, as he called it); and that no single individual or group could possibly have access to all the necessary information about availability or desirability of a particular good or service. Only the market, which represented the cumulative information of all the sellers and buyers, could reflect that information through a price.

For all its genius, Smith's explanation was unduly dependent in its discussion on large, impersonal forces, such as markets and competition. Although he mentioned the butcher and the baker, Smith de-emphasized—and outright ignored—the role of entrepreneurs. The seeds of that recognition were there, for example, when he pointed out the need of people to buy cheap and sell dear. For most things, one has to spend money to buy cheap with only the expectation that one can later sell dear. Economists wrestled with that "profit" issue for another 100 years, trying to make the price of goods equal some combination of the price of the land, labor, and capital that went into their making. In spite of this effort, there was recognition of a disturbing fact: that in every commercial venture, as Frank Knight put it in his path-breaking work *Risk, Uncertainty, and Profit* (1921), "the profit is in the future and uncertain when the decision is made and hence it is the *prospect* or *estimated* probability of profit" that "moves men's wills."[8]

In 1912, Joseph Schumpeter published *Theory of Economic Development.* In this work the entrepreneur was credited as the driving force in economic progress. The entrepreneur is an "innovator," not an inventor, who leads the economy forward into a new paradigm. This individual is a "change agent" driving an often-reluctant society into more efficient use of its resources. The entrepreneur doesn't necessarily invent anything, but "innovates," as Schumpeter puts it. This innovation can be a way to "buy cheap," as in making a product with less expensive (perhaps more abundant) resources, or it can be a way to "sell dear" by making a better product than anything currently available. By lowering costs or raising price, the entrepreneur creates space for profit, for the entrepreneur's own reward. It is in Schumpeter's book that our entrepreneur emerges.

While Schumpeter provides the emergence of the railroad industry as an example of how entrepreneurs replaced the horse and wagon with a superior form of transportation, the economists, in their theoretical expositions, do not provide any single case study of how one person became an entrepreneur or succeeded in a specific business. But one has to look no further than the *Forbes* 400 list of the richest Americans to find entrepreneurs who have incrementally moved the United States to minor and major new ways of doing things. In a recent list, we see many entrepreneurs:[9]

- Michael Ilitch, the son of Macedonian immigrants, played shortstop for pro baseball's Detroit Tigers farm team. He opened the first Little Caesars pizza and now owns the Detroit Tigers as well as pro hockey's Detroit Red Wings. Net worth: $1.5 billion.

- H. Ty Warner was a salesman's son who dropped out of college and took to the road selling plush toys. The line of stuffed animals he developed in 1986, Beanie Babies, ruled the lunch-box set for years. Net worth: $4.5 billion.

- Manny Mashouf, an Iranian-born immigrant, ran a steakhouse before opening a women's boutique, Bebe, in San Francisco in 1976. Net worth: $1.5 billion.

- Pierre M. Omidyar is a French-born immigrant who launched online auction giant eBay in 1995; today, eBay lets consumers buy and sell everything from real estate to kitsch. Net worth: $7.7 billion.

- Bill Gates and Paul Allen left college to make software that would make personal computers more accessible. Their development (not invention) of Microsoft Windows undeniably changed the world. Net worth for Gates: $46 billion, Allen: $21 billion. Big changes create more wealth!

Certainly, we could also find on the Forbes list many who inherited wealth. All the Walton kids are there, but Dad (Sam Walton) made them rich by starting a store that focused on selling low-cost items using an innovative inventory system now standard for all "big-box" stores. Some highly successful individuals, such as Chris Gardner, whose life was captured in the movie *The Pursuit of Happyness*, state emphatically that they deliberately balanced making more money with family life and are proud of the fact they aren't on the list. But excluding women who inherited wealth from their husbands or fathers, the *Forbes* list features many, if not more, billionaires who created their wealth from entrepreneurial activity than it does people who inherited their fortunes. The entrepreneurial life is not easy. Remember, it is based on the *prospect* of profit. Many entrepreneurs declared bankruptcy—some two or three times—and several had no college education. But they all had one thing in common: They took a leap of faith, either on savings or borrowed funds, to pursue a vision. Whether in bingo or video, cat chow or catheters, garbage or great buildings, the fruits of those entrepreneurs have improved all our lives. They also shared another characteristic in that they stepped out on faith with total and complete dedication. That total dedication came at great personal cost: More than a few of the *Forbes* entrepreneurs were divorced, some many times, reflecting the demands of their quest. Other entrepreneurs, as we will see in later chapters, have clashed with the federal government, occasionally at the expense of their companies or private fortunes. Still others—Howard Hughes comes to mind—captivated the public with their exploits but never successfully developed a business that remained a legacy. One final quality is visible in the lives of entrepreneurs—namely, that every businessman or woman must identify a need or desire on the part of others for that product. Likewise with service businesses, every service must serve someone. Successful entrepreneurs are better than others at identifying and meeting the needs and desires of others, and it therefore should be obvious that— far from concentrating on their own needs and wants—successful entrepreneurs focus on others.

It also should be obvious from the above examples that entrepreneurs come from all walks of life and backgrounds—from Harvard MBAs to penniless immigrants—and defy any capsule definition. And since the nature of entrepreneurship is creating something beneficial to others—which can take almost any form—no clear model of entrepreneurship or path for entrepreneurial success exists. Despite the appearance of dozens of courses in entrepreneurship blossoming around the country, business success requires small doses of talent and knowledge, but large doses of attitude. Indeed, not all entrepreneurial success is related to formal education: As late as the 1990s, the *Forbes* 400 featured ten people who never finished high school, and sixty-four of the 304 who went to college never graduated. Still others attended school after the fact to enhance their already-prospering commercial ventures.

Most theorists have accepted a definition of the entrepreneur as "one who takes the risk to start a business," a phrase generally attributed to Jean-Baptiste Say, a French writer (accounting for the French origins of the word) who first defined production as composed of three factors: land, labor, and capital.[10] After the emergence of the modern corporate structure in the mid-1800s, some scholars argued that the definition of an entrepreneur needed to be broadened to include managers or even executives in nonprofit and government sectors. That approach led economic historians such as Jonathan R. T. Hughes to count as entrepreneurs religious leaders such as William Penn and Brigham Young, as well as employees of the federal bureaucracy in his classic study of business leaders, *The Vital Few.*[11] Individuals within corporations, nonprofit organizations, the military, and government can operate with great independence and autonomy, but one should not carry this line of thinking too far: Entrepreneurship still requires an element of *personal* risk—the individual must stand to lose or gain financially and personally. Consider the position of a U.S. Air Force officer placed in charge of a procurement program for new aircraft. The Air Force invests the officer with considerable institutional authority and provides a large budget. The officer might even use cutting-edge managerial techniques or innovative business strategies to acquire the aircraft. Yet, if the aircraft program is an abysmal flop, the officer loses none of his own money, although a worse assignment might be in store. In short, little personal capital has been risked. One should not confuse using entrepreneurial methods with entrepreneurship. It is also not entrepreneurial to merely invest in a new venture to qualify as an entrepreneur. Both innovation and risk must be part of the venture.

For our purposes, then, our definition of an entrepreneur is "the person who takes the risk to create material wealth in the economic realm." For the most part, such a definition excludes individuals such as Lee Iacocca or Walter Wriston because they made their marks as executives within larger corporations. It excludes bureaucrats, such as the former Secretary of Housing and Urban Development, Jack Kemp, because no matter how innovative his programs, he personally assumed none of the risk. And it excludes William Penn or Brigham Young, counted as entrepreneurs by Jonathan R. T. Hughes, because they did not concern themselves primarily with creating material wealth in the economic realm. Nor would it include modern ministers such as "FaithDome" Pastor Frederick K. C. Price. Although his messages encourage investment, sacrifice, and other pro-business attitudes, and he personally signed for the entire $9 million loan on the Los Angeles FaithDome, Price is not primarily concerned with material wealth. But while Penn, Young, or Price have concerned themselves with creating value in the spiritual realm, it is critical to realize that the process of creating material wealth involves the spiritual as much as the physical. George Gilder has argued that for entrepreneurs to develop a business idea, that "creative thought requires an act of faith [for which] commitment can create its own confirmation."[12] Thus, creative activity itself is in a sense spiritual, involving a "personal and psychological drama" that decides whether an entrepreneur will borrow money to launch a new business in the face of statistics that show that close to two-thirds of all new businesses fail within five years.

THE SPIRITUAL SIDE OF CAPITALISM

Publication of Gilder's *Wealth and Poverty* and, later, his work on *Recapturing the Spirit of Enterprise* brought renewed emphasis to capitalism's spiritual side.[13] Gilder's writings, along with Michael Novak's *The Spirit of Democratic Capitalism,* provided a desperately needed counter to the almost century-long trend of casting capitalism in a morally negative light.[14] But Gilder's books also unfortunately implied that Adam Smith had ignored spiritual aspects of capitalism, suggesting that Smith concerned himself more with technical factors of supply, demand, and price. Such a misperception seeped into the work of writers of all political stripes, resulting in critics of capitalism from the Left (Michael Harrington and Robert Heilbroner) and from the Right (Irving Kristol and Richard Weaver) charging that material progress occurred only at the expense of individual dignity or of society's spiritual values.[15] Were such claims true?

Smith explained that individual self-interest required a person to serve his fellow man to obtain a return. Whatever the motivation, the individual must focus on the desires and needs of others, address those needs, and provide a good or service *before* receiving any recompense. Another way to look at those activities is as service: A person must first serve others before demanding a return. Determining how much value the service has is fraught with problems if one leaves it to an arbitrary source, such as a government board or commission. Market economies typically use money as a measure, or symbol, of how much service one individual has provided to others. Economist Walter Williams has detailed on several occasions how the process works in daily life. A woman sits down in a restaurant and orders a meal (which represents the accumulated efforts of farmers, shippers, meat packers, the restaurant owner, the waiter, and others); but in order to pay for the meal, she must have money. Her money represents her own service to others that she has performed in her clothing business and the value that others have placed on her service to them. Money acts as a type of "accumulated service to others"—proof that the holder has served others, and to what degree.

Assume that an entrepreneur starts a hamburger stand. In doing so, he invests time, energy, and talent procuring products, facilities, and employees. Before earning a single dime, he has served others by making these investments of time, talent, and energy. The entrepreneur still has not received any personal return, which comes from meeting his customers' culinary needs or desires. What if he provides terrible food? Or what if the food is good, but he is abusive and crabby to his customers? In either case, he will soon be out of business: He has not served his fellow man, nor has he met any need or fulfilled any desire. Note that despite working hard, he has not benefited others! Consequently, labor itself is not sufficient as a measure of value. Indeed, unwanted labor is economically useless in one economic sense, in that it allows a single person to consume scarce resources without returning anything to society. Rather, labor that does not serve others (in a market sense) is actually consumption, not production. All economic activity can then be summarized with a question—"How have you served your fellow man?"—and an imperative—"Prove it!"

Smith thought that most people were naturally inclined to such service, but that they naturally overestimated the value of their own labor and underestimated that of others. Consequently, the only reliable measure that could adjust for the individual misperceptions of millions of people in the market was the crucial price mechanism. Prices forced on everyone a reality check, so they could not overestimate their own service or undervalue that of others. For that reason, he warned about any distortions of prices brought about by anything other than the market itself. His warning extends to business combinations (monopolies, in current jargon) or businesses obtaining special privileges from governments.

Indeed, it is important to realize that any economic activity not solely derived from market effects can produce negative results. Charity, for example, generates its own economic implications. If individuals, churches, community groups, or governments provide for nothing (or at artificially lower cost) what others in the market would charge to provide, that free service will have an impact on the price and affect the market. Labor unions have long resisted efforts to have prisoners perform work, contending that "slave labor" undermines the price of "free labor," and they are correct. If a farmer simply gave food away—for whatever moral motive—it would have the effect of driving down the price of food everywhere, essentially telling other farmers that their service is worth less than it really is. Artists, musicians, writers, and actors have long faced the grim reality that their love of their craft means that they would paint, act, write, or play music if no one paid them, which has had the effect of driving down the price of all art. In short, all activity—even charity—has economic outcomes that affect prices. Giving goods away creates another problem: Gift givers don't always choose what the recipient wants. This is so obvious to the reader that we will leave it to you to contemplate the last gift-giving occasion in your life for examples.

A final point alludes to one of our earlier questions, namely, how do others benefit from the failure of entrepreneurs? First, when entrepreneurs fail, they provide critical information about the wants and needs of others. The collapse of a RadioShack in Amish country may suggest the location is wrong. But it might also be that the product is too expensive, or that the Amish have other things to do. One thing is certain: Other aspiring RadioShack-type businesses will think twice before venturing into that location. Second, failure of a business frees up resources for the use of other businesses. The former location of the RadioShack store may be the perfect location for a feed store. Third, not only do other businesses benefit from failed enterprises, but consumers profit, too. The new feed store adds price competition and convenience. In fact, some of America's greatest success stories resulted from abject failure. Automaker Henry Ford, banker A. P. Giannini, and department store founder Sam Walton all declared bankruptcy, had their first enterprises fail miserably, or were unceremoniously kicked out of companies they created before they attained ultimate success. In other cases, entrepreneurs have made fortunes or founded thriving businesses in services or with products that few would find lucrative. Yet no matter what path a particular entrepreneur took, each had a single characteristic in common: a willingness to take a risk.

The element of risk taking by entrepreneurs—which, again, constitutes an act of faith and not reason—sets them apart from managers and paid employees. No element of business enterprise is risk free, and certainly management and labor have seen periods of mass layoffs. Ultimately, the only source of a job is one's own talent and labor: The worker's ability, in essence, creates his own employment demand. But in general, companies in capitalist societies offer a far higher level of income security and, whenever possible, extended employment to managers and employees than typical entrepreneurs ever attain. In most small businesses, employees receive pay even if there is not enough left for the owner at the end of the week. Many small-business owners have reported not taking a paycheck for years, plowing every cent back into the business. At larger companies (barring the most calamitous circumstances), even when the stock plunges and the stockholders lose huge amounts of money, employees are retained—and paid—until quarterly reports appear and the company can restructure.

ENTREPRENEURIAL BUSINESSES

Capitalism's spiritual side is most clearly seen in the activities of entrepreneurs who constantly must act on faith. Ultimately, they must believe that their idea, product, service, or business will succeed. While larger firms also take risks and make investments based on their convictions that a demand exists for their products, the number of managerial "filters" through which decisions must pass weakens and dilutes the connection between action and faith in large corporations. Big companies recognize this barrier and take steps to encourage their employees to behave as entrepreneurs, with very mixed success. On the other hand, entrepreneurial faith is clearly visible in the millions of new businesses launched each year.

Most of these businesses are small (although more than 100,000 of them started in 2004 had more than 500 employees). People still have daily contact with small businesses—usually grocery stores, bookstores, restaurants, or service businesses—but for much of American history, the most common small business was the family farm. On the fringes of the early frontier, the family farm truly put entrepreneurial faith to the test: If the farmer failed to plant enough, or failed to plant the right type of crops, or did not take precautions against flooding or fire, he and his family literally faced starvation. Between 1850 and 1900, the urbanization of America shifted the majority of entrepreneurial activity into cities, and typical small businesses included foundries, tool shops, general stores, and producers of a vast spectrum of other goods and services. The advent of the personal computer and of desktop publishing in the late 1970s and 1980s sparked yet another transition among sole proprietorships, reducing the size of the average small business and making it more mobile. For the first time in American history, many small businesses had a genuine opportunity to tap into national, if not world, markets. Entrepreneurs appreciated the chance that had appeared: In 1950, small business start-ups numbered 93,000 annually. That number surged to more than 450,000 by 1980, and by 1995, the number of start-ups had almost doubled the 1980 figure, exceeding 800,000.[16]

Far more influential are the large companies most people identify with the word *corporation*: the large, multi-unit business enterprise with hundreds (if not thousands) of employees. Every year, *Fortune* magazine lists the largest companies in the United States. In 2007, ranked by revenue (which for that year reflects high oil prices), the top five were Wal-Mart, Exxon Mobil, General Motors, Chevron, and ConocoPhillips. The United States had Phillips, plus 162 of the world's largest companies. In 2004, more than half the employees in the United States worked for a company with more than 500 employees.[17] Large companies are certainly important to the economy. However, the presence of small businesses, and particularly start-ups, is widely acknowledged to keep the larger businesses competitive.

In fact, it is common for larger companies acquiring smaller, entrepreneurial businesses to make the type of arrangement that Luxottica Group made in 2007 when it bid to acquire Oakley, Inc., the innovative sports accessory company started by Jim Jannard. "As 'chief mad scientist and leader of the rogue state,' Jim will continue to play a crucial role in Oakley's product design, continuing to push the blending of technology, performance, and innovation, as he's been [doing] since day one [as] Oakley's chief visionary," said a spokesperson for Luxottica. If Jannard decides to leave the company, a five-year noncompete clause will keep him from developing new products similar to those offered by Oakley.[18] Does Jannard care? The company he started with $300 sold for $1.2 billion, and if he gets bored, he once said, "Everything in the world can and will be made better. The only questions are, 'when and by whom?'"[19]

IS THERE AN ENTREPRENEURIAL CHARACTER?

In his corporate headshot, Jim Jannard wears goggles, a leather helmet, and is smoking a cigar; not the typical suit-and-tie-clad executive. What is the typical entrepreneur like? Defining an entrepreneur as "someone who assumes risk" hardly narrows the search for characteristics that identify entrepreneurs. Is there an entrepreneurial character one can point to that all businesspeople possess? Do certain cultures, or backgrounds, lend themselves to entrepreneurship? Max Weber thought so. In the early 1900s, he argued in *The Protestant Ethic and the Spirit of Capitalism* that Protestants, particularly those who derived their teachings from John Calvin, adopted certain practices (frugality, investment, hard work) that they believed reflected their status with the divine.[20] Material prosperity, they assumed, was an indication of heavenly blessings. Rather than wait for such prosperity—which might never come—they instead created it themselves, leading Weber to contend that Protestants substantially accelerated capitalism.

Weber's thesis ignored the phenomenal success by Italian Catholic bankers, such as the Medici, the Bardi, and the Frescobaldi, not to mention the entrepreneurial spirit of the great Catholic explorers such as

Columbus. Studies by "public choice" economists have taken a much more favorable view of the Church's appreciation for the market.[21] Economist Thomas Sowell has detailed the vitality of entrepreneurship among such groups as the Lebanese, Jews, Chinese, and West Indians, often even as those peoples immigrated to other nations as minorities.[22] In South America, Jewish minorities carved out thriving businesses as middlemen; in Malaya, Chinese minorities have dominated commercial business despite government programs designed to impede them at the expense of native Malays.[23] Immigrant experiences of non-Protestants in America have looked much the same. Studies of business in Atlanta, Georgia, showed that Lebanese and Koreans achieved inordinate success in retailing and groceries, while Vietnamese immigrants in Texas carved out a share of the fishing industry on the Gulf Coast. Several non-Christian cultures worldwide over time have witnessed pockets of capitalism, and simple entrepreneurship has existed since the earliest stages of human life. Given this evidence, it seems that all Weber managed to do was to identify certain traits of entrepreneurship—thrift, diligence, hard work, honesty—that Protestants happened to share with other entrepreneurs from other faiths and other nations.

Conversely, religion can act as a deterrent to business success. Some Christian denominations, for example, have treated wealth creation and accumulation as evil or sinful, citing passages in the Bible that either imply rich people fell short of Heaven or that, conversely, the wealthy gave away their possessions when they took their religion seriously. Christianity is hostile to neither wealth nor entrepreneurship, and there is substantial biblical evidence that Jesus and the disciples were far from being poor, homeless vagabonds.[24] Under Judaism, wealth was an outward sign of God's blessings. God prospered Abraham so much that he and Lot could not graze their herds on the same hills, and when the Jews gave gifts to build the Tabernacle, they provided gold, silver, and precious gems in such vast abundance that Moses had to tell them to stop giving! Clearly, Old Testament Jews had wealth in abundance to permit them to give in such quantities. The New Testament Christians maintained that they were the rightful heirs of Abraham, and that his blessings were their blessings. Jesus's disciple Matthew held a feast in his house so large that all of the "publicans" (government employees, tax collectors, and, in general, "sinners") in the city could fit inside. Paul apparently came from a wealthy family, as indicated by the fact that Felix held him for ransom, expecting a payment.[25] Other evidence abounds that many New Testament Christians had productive jobs and material wealth.

In the Middle Ages, the Church possessed exceptional amounts of wealth and land, and the Catholic hierarchies lived in luxury in apparent contradiction to their vows of poverty. At one point, the Church held one-third of all the land in Europe, leaving kings to "raid Church revenues to survive," and financing King John of England's campaigns against Wales, Scotland, and Ireland.[26] The Church's ability to expand its resources, at a time when peasants complained about their own deplorable conditions and landlessness, constituted a serious challenge to the allegiance of the masses to the Christian religion. Whether deliberate or not, the gradual emergence of an emphasis on "the meek inheriting the Earth" certainly provided theological grounds for the masses to accept their lot in life. Moreover, individuals who deliberately sought wealth—which was a gift from God, given for a moral purpose to improve the welfare of everyone—risked committing the sin of avarice. Or, as Christine Rider summarizes the situation, "Poverty was of divine origin…. Wealth was justified: It enabled the wealthy to fulfill the obligations imposed on them by Divine Providence."[27] Commercial activities, however, which involved the active pursuit of wealth, constituted sin and were excoriated from the pulpit.

The Catholic Church had a long philosophical strain that established such concepts as "just price," which in its original use accounted for scarcity and applied centrally to instances of emergency. Over time, however, the notion was secularized and broadened to apply to any "undo" profit. Further interpretations of prices devolved from early variants of the Labor Theory of Value, made famous later by Karl Marx. Theologians such as Saint Augustine argued that human existence involved man's mixing his labor with land, thus lending value to all work. Prices and wages had to be "just," a concept ultimately left to the definition of the religious or political leader at the time. Any activity that did not involve a visible exchange of goods or services—and thus anything requiring a middleman, due to distance or insufficient funds—represented a potential immoral transaction because it could not be seen, although the Church did allow for clearly documented "transaction costs" to be included in the price. Thus, over a period of 1,000 years, religious interpretations of Scripture related to the material world had substantially inverted the notion that "faith is the evidence of things not seen" (Hebrews 11:1). Economic growth required faith in exactly those things "not seen" because the investment had to appear first—as an act of faith. At any rate, the methods designed by the feudal societies to maintain the social ethic, and in the process regulate the social order, proved impossible to enforce outside of the individual's compliance.

IS THERE AN ENTREPRENEURIAL "LIFE PATTERN"?

It is clear that the entrepreneurial spirit is not limited to any one religion. Other attempts to characterize a typical entrepreneur can produce abject futility when considering the life stories of numerous entrepreneurs. P. T. Barnum did not found the Barnum & Bailey Circus until he was seventy years old. "Jerry and David's Guide to the World Wide Web" was started by two graduate students who wanted to keep track of their favorite websites. In just a few years their company, Yahoo!, had a $1.5 million IPO.[28] Famous Amos built his million-dollar cookie empire using a recipe from the back of the Nestlé's chocolate bag available to every baker and housewife in the nation. Sandra Lee, who risked everything on home-show demonstrations, finally got her own accessories line and a Food Network cooking show. Frederick Tudor made a fortune by selling the free ice from ponds and lakes around his home. A dentist, Dr. Thomas B. Welch, an ardent opponent of "demon rum," created a nonalcoholic beverage that tasted like wine for use in Communion. Hall of Fame pitcher Albert Spalding is better known today for the special baseball glove he designed and produced. Dr. John Harvey Kellogg, a Seventh-Day Adventist who ran a health sanitarium, provided specialized cereal products for his patients in Battle Creek, Michigan. It was there that a sick cowboy who had lost his fortune in real estate scams, C. W. Post, got the idea for his own cereal company that would later compete with Kellogg's company.[29]

Many entrepreneurs grew up impoverished. Andrew Carnegie went from a "bobbin boy," a child laborer in a textile mill, to one of the richest men to ever live in the United States.[30] By contrast, J. P. Morgan sampled all the luxuries of his era in his youth, and his successful father arranged for his first job. He, too, amassed one of the largest fortunes in U.S. history.[31] Some families even have a tradition of entrepreneurship. John W. Nordstrom started a Seattle shoe store in 1902 after his adventures in the Klondike gold mines. His three sons expanded the operation into the country's largest independently owned shoe store chain. The next generation—John, Jim, and Bruce Nordstrom—took the company public as one of the most successful and admired clothing and shoe stores anywhere.[32]

Perhaps the most amazing thing about these individuals, and thousands of other entrepreneurs, is that they have no life pattern: The old, the young, the idealistic, the pragmatic, the inventors, the innovators, the driven, the greedy, the compassionate—all characterize different entrepreneurs. Every successful entrepreneur, however, does have one characteristic in common with the others. The entrepreneur has faith and vision, in essence a driving motivation that infuses the individual's commitment to at least one idea or product (and often more). For the true entrepreneur, challenges represent opportunities. Indeed, it seems that entrepreneurs do not even see challenges in the same way others do. Consciously or subconsciously, entrepreneurs diminish the size of the hurdle to be cleared, or possibly some of them do not even perceive obstacles as existing at all. If anything, the traditional juxtaposition of the "glass half full" and the "glass half empty" does not apply to entrepreneurs at all, because to them, the half-full glass is already full!

Entrepreneurs do recognize serious threats to their concepts or businesses, but they seem to have an innate ability to separate genuine from perceived threats, which leads them to focus always on the most important issues. In turn, they pay little attention to competitors, especially in the early stages of their businesses. Most entrepreneurs concentrate so intently on their own product, idea, or operations that they have no time to worry about the actions of competitors. At some point, virtually every successful person—and certainly every entrepreneur—has been told "You can't," "It won't work," or "There are enough of those already." If Arnold Schwarzenegger had listened to critics who said that he could never succeed in acting with his accent, some of the biggest box-office hits in the world never would have been made. If Louis L'Amour had heeded any of the first 100 rejection letters he received, he never would have become the best-read novelist of all time of classic Western stories. And if a fourteen-year-old Tennessean named Jack Daniels had listened to his neighbors who insisted he be satisfied with the local moonshining, one of the best-known names in whiskey never would have existed.

While those people had persistence and determination, more than just hard work or a good idea is required to achieve success. A structural foundation must exist that ensures human liberty and a society based on law. Such notions as property protections, contract enforcement, copyrights, and other mainstays of free capitalist societies made it possible for Schwarzenegger, Daniels, and virtually all of the other entrepreneurs discussed above to take advantage of their own talents and abilities.

THE FOUNDATIONS OF AMERICAN CAPITALISM

In *The Wealth and Poverty of Nations*, David S. Landes addresses the question of why some countries are richer than others. He reviews the issues of geography and climate and also religious culture, in particular views on hard work, progress, and domination over nature. He concludes: "In the last analysis, however, I would stress the market." He notes that in Europe, "innovation worked and paid, and rulers and vested interests were limited in their ability to prevent or discourage innovation. Success bred imitation and emulation; also a sense of power that would in the long run raise men almost to the level of gods." The public was fascinated. Economists yawned.[33]

Several factors permitted entrepreneurship to flourish in America and thus encourage economic growth. The mainspring of any capitalist system is the presence of private property, or more specifically, the very clear definition of ownership. This right serves as an incentive to acquisition and development. Because one can retain the fruits of one's own labors, an individual is motivated to work all the harder. In the United States, the right to property is so basic that it is formally guaranteed to all in the Constitution. The Fifth Amendment explicitly forbids arbitrary interference from the federal government by the command that no person "be deprived of life, liberty, or property, without due process of law" and that no "private property be taken for public use, without just compensation." Interference by state governments is prohibited both by the Fourteenth Amendment and by the clause in Article I, Section 10, which prevents any state from enacting a "law impairing the obligation of contracts." And the Constitution's property protections even extend to a specific manufactured item, guns.

A second permanent feature of the U.S. system is its economic freedom. It includes freedom of enterprise, which is the right of individuals and firms to enter any markets (with some exceptions) they choose and to conduct their own operations as successfully as their abilities, resources, and even luck allow them. Conversely, consumers have the freedom to buy the products they prefer and to reject those they do not, if they have the money to pay for their purchases. Similarly, employees are free to pick the employment they find most suitable, if they are adequately qualified for it and willing to accept the wages offered.

Another element of the U.S. economy is its reliance upon competition instead of government planning as the primary means of allocating resources. This allocation takes place in the marketplace, where the exchange of privately owned goods and/or services occurs. There an economic unit, such as an individual or a firm, offers to supply goods or services in exchange for the products or services of others, or as is more likely in a complex society, for their equivalent value in money, with the monetary value being established by the price (i.e., the information) of the item. Whereas at one time markets involved hand-to-hand transactions, as one might see at a supermarket, modern markets span the globe, involving billions of transactions every hour.

The debate over the proper role and scope of government has never ended in the United States. The 1980s experienced a privatization movement, in which government agencies "outsourced" certain activities to private industry. City governments have handed over large segments of work, such as garbage collection in Ohio, education in New England, or fire protection in Arizona, to the private sector. There was also a "deregulation" movement. Trucking and airlines, for example, were allowed to set their own routes and rates for the first time in the late 1970s and early 1980s; some banking functions were deregulated in the 1980s and early 1990s.[34]

On the national level, however, the United States federal government has moved slowly in yielding power. By 1985, U.S. government expenditures absorbed 23.9 percent of gross national product (GNP).[35] The bad news was that that number represented a peacetime high—it had dropped to under 23 percent by 1989 through economic growth. By whatever measure—GNP or GDP—American government expenditures of national income and wealth remained far below that of almost all developed countries. In 1994, the Republican Party's "Contract with America," signed by all of the victorious Republican members of the House of Representatives, contained numerous provisions for scaling down government's role in all aspects of American life. And in his 1996 State of the Union message, even Democratic President Bill Clinton admitted "the era of big government is over."

That attitude did not last long. Government spending was 19 percent of GDP in 2006. After 9/11, American domestic spending rapidly expanded as both Republicans and Democrats rushed to add massive new entitlement programs to the federal trough. In terms of both total debt (in the trillions of dollars), total unfunded obligations (trillions more), and debt-to-GNP, the United States was rapidly entering uncharted waters. In 2009, the U.S. economy was in recession and massive increase in government spending characterized both the end of the George W. Bush presidency and the beginning of the Barack Obama presidency. With a few exceptions, regardless of the role of government, American business continued to prosper. Some sectors, particularly automotives and steel, have declined dramatically, while others, such as information technology, entertainment, biomedicine, and aviation, have continued to dominate world markets. American capitalism has retained most—if not all—of the characteristics that were in place when the first colonists arrived. Although capitalism as an economic system was not instituted until the eighteenth century, many of the fundamentals of capitalism, especially private property rights, were already well established when the first colonists landed at Jamestown in 1607. Because their arrival owed much to the economic beliefs prevalent in Europe and England that predated Smith's exposition on capitalism, that is where our focus will turn.

CHAPTER 2

European Settlement and Business Enterprise in the New World

In the 1300s, Europe languished under a succession of famines and poor harvests—complicated by the Black Death, which killed one-third of the population (England suffered an even sharper decline of 40 percent). The demographic crisis spawned a period of lawlessness, as bandits and pirates inhibited commerce and discouraged investment. Nevertheless, the so-called "Dark Ages" had left a foundation for entrepreneurial success in the form of the monastic farms, which demonstrated division of labor and specialization; the free farm—unseen in the Islamic world; and the rational process of inquiry, enhanced by dozens of universities that dotted Europe. By the 1400s, though, trade had revived as nation-states established order and as merchants devised new tools for facilitating the exchange of goods and services, not the least of which was the *bill of exchange.* Until bills of exchange appeared, the only money accepted by most merchants, especially at long distances from the purchaser's home, was gold or silver coin. The heavy weight of coins, however, made this money difficult and unsafe to carry. As early as the 1100s, Italian trading cities pioneered paper promissory notes that the seller accepted from the purchaser and then converted into gold or silver upon demand at the purchaser's city. These bills of exchange carried a future date, after which the seller could present the notes for collection. Over time, merchants extended the bills' payment date for a small fee (still hesitating to call it "interest" for fear of being labeled "usurers" by the Catholic Church).

Armed with the bills of exchange, an early banking establishment emerged in Italian cities, led by families such as the Bardi, the Ricardi, the Peruzzi, the Frescobaldi, and the Medici. Italian influence spread as far north as England, with traders following the papal tax collectors to gain a virtual monopoly over wool trade there by 1300. Italian traders had the benefit of good port cities—particularly Venice—and a central location in the Mediterranean, then the nexus of most seaborne commerce. But Italian merchants, especially in England, also had the good sense to provide generous loans to English royalty, leaving them in a protected position until the Hundred Years' War, when they failed to extend further credit to the king.[1] The Italian merchants also pioneered another business innovation, *dual entry bookkeeping*, developed in the 1300s. The foundation for all modern accounting, wherein transactions are arranged into credits and debits, dual entry bookkeeping owed much to Luca Pacioli, an Italian who in 1494 wrote one of the earliest texts on accounting.[2]

When the British Crown evicted the Italians from England, English businesses filled the vacuum. In the early 1300s, a group of wool merchants formed the Company of the Staple to compete with the Mediterranean houses. Although lacking in most of the characteristics associated with modern corporations—unlimited life and limited liability—the Company of the Staple illustrated how rapidly European business institutions adapted and innovated. Other English merchants formed consortia, particularly businessmen in Bristol, who managed to enlist the entire town in their enterprise. The Bristol merchants rapidly stretched their routes and diversified their products from wool and clothing to fish, coal, wine, and iron.

EXPLORATION AND ENTREPRENEURS

Several historical forces combined to make overseas exploration more profitable and desirable. First, new technologies, as well as European breakthroughs, led to advances in sailing. The astrolabe—a circular device with a pivoted limb that measured a beam of sunlight, establishing the sun's altitude above the horizon—was introduced through trade with the Arabs in the 800s and soon made its way to Spain.[3] The Vikings introduced new hull construction, enabling the vessels to withstand violent ocean storms. In the Baltic States, the Hanseatic League experimented with larger ships capable of carrying heavy cargoes and utilizing sternpost rudders for better control; triangular and lateen sails were incorporated after the Crusades, making it possible to sail a vessel at an angle. Improved ships, however, would have had difficulty reaching new destinations without the appearance of accurate maps generated by the Arabs and Italians—and accelerated by the inquisitive character of the Renaissance and the scientific foundation of reason provided by Christianity.[4]

Second, political changes coincided with the search for treasure and advances in shipbuilding technologies. After ambitious European monarchs had started to consolidate their possessions into cohesive dynastic states, the funding available to expeditions increased and military protection (in the form of soldiers aboard the ships) was provided free to investors. Capital, combined with the improved sailing technology, made it possible for Europeans to consider voyages of much longer duration, stimulating a new generation of explorers who found that monarchs would support more expensive undertakings that integrated the monarch's interests with economic reward.[5] At the same time, the acceleration of the "Western Way of War," using more sophisticated technology, meant that increasingly smaller numbers of Western soldiers or marines could protect larger areas of conquered territory or ships at sea.[6]

Third, by the 1500s, the Protestant Reformation had fostered a fierce, and often bloody, competition between Catholic and Protestant countries, as well as among Protestant countries themselves, for power and territory that reinforced the infant nationalism. Therefore, even in the face of marginal economic or political gains for discovery and colonization, strong religious incentives spurred monarchs to open their royal treasuries.

Those three factors explained the sudden burst of exploratory fervor that swept the European nations in the period from 1400 to 1600. Portugal took an early lead, thanks to the efforts of Prince Henry the Navigator, an eccentric who lived as a recluse in Sagres, where he trained navigators and mapmakers.[7] Henry's Portuguese explorers concentrated on finding routes around Africa to the East, unlike the

Genoese explorer Christopher Columbus, who persuaded Spanish royalty to outfit a three-ship expedition to sail westward in 1492. Columbus embodied the best traits of the new generation of navigators: He had resilience, fearlessness, vision, and courage to demand obedience when all other leadership skills failed. To be sure, Columbus sought glory, and as a religious man, he was "earnestly desirous of taking Christianity to heathen lands."[8] Yet Columbus was also an entrepreneur who persuaded investors to support his mission. Risking his reputation as a sailor and even his life at the hands of a mutinous crew, Columbus put on his managerial hat at sea, allocating scarce resources and maintaining efficiency within his small fleet.[9]

Sir Walter Raleigh was among the first to see the potential returns of colonization. He received a royal charter in 1584 to plant a settlement in Roanoke, North Carolina. Using the marketing methods of the day, Raleigh enlisted Richard Hakluyt, whose *Discourse Concerning Western Planting* (1584) lured investors with promises of acquiring the Spanish West Indies trade, eliminating Spanish middlemen. That Raleigh's colony, planted in 1587, and all of its settlers vanished, leaving only the cryptic message "Croatoan" carved into a tree, did not deter adventurers from arriving in the New World.

FOUNDATIONS FOR BUSINESS SUCCESS IN THE NEW WORLD

Even as Raleigh's Roanoke colony failed, England had laid the foundations for business success in the New World. Fifty years after the first British colonies were established, they equaled any Spanish, Portuguese, or French colony in the Americas. Why?

While it is conceivable that English colonies prospered simply due to luck, the dominance of Europe in general and England in particular—a tiny island with few natural resources—suggests that specific factors can be identified as the reasons for the rise of an English-Atlantic civilization, including the appearance of new business practices and structures and the presence of a widespread attitude that encouraged risk taking and innovation.[10]

One of the most obvious areas in which England surpassed other nations was in its business practices. The threat of incurring substantial losses during the establishment of the English colonies in the Americas could have strangled most of the early efforts if not for another innovation of business (and law), the *joint-stock company*. Sole proprietorships and partnerships both suffered from a common problem, that of unlimited liability. The individual was liable to creditors for all the debts of the business, even to the extent that personal assets were subject to confiscation by creditors for debts owed. Likewise, even a minor partner was liable for the debts of a majority partner if a business collapsed. In either case, potential investors often shied away from any but the most secure investments, and middle-class investors avoided putting their personal assets at risk in any involvement in a business that might sour. But joint-stock companies allowed investors to spread their risk among many owners, although at first each remained liable for the debts of the entire operation.

Joint-stock companies also achieved a degree of permanence because they did not end with the death of the proprietor. Instead, shares of stock, and the liabilities of the venture, simply changed hands. Thus the joint-stock company solved simultaneously the problems faced by overseas expeditions of raising capital and ensuring stability over time. A number of joint-stock companies formed between 1500 and 1600, including the Levant Company (1592) and the Dutch East India Company (1600), facilitating a burst of overseas trade and colonization.

A second factor, a social climate receptive to risk taking, contributed to the early success of the West in general and the English colonies in particular. Joel Mokyr has argued that "political and mental diversity combined to create an ever-changing panorama of technologically creative societies."[11] While that climate permeated all of Europe, it reached its most advanced state in England. It is important to note that key inventions and technologies appeared in non-Western countries first; yet they were seldom, if ever, employed in such a way as to change society dramatically until applied by the Western societies. The stirrup, for example, was known as early as AD 400–500 in the Middle East. But it took until 730, when Charles Martel's mounted knights used the stirrup while engaged in cavalry charges and thus changed combat on a permanent basis.[12] Something other than mere invention was at work. As one economic historian put it, "The West did not overtake the East merely by becoming more efficient at making bridles and stirrups, but by developing steam engines... [and] by taking unknown risks on novelty."[13] Stability of the state, the rule of law, and a willingness to accept new or foreign ideas, rather than ruthlessly suppressing them, proved vital to entrepreneurship, invention, and technical innovation. In societies dominated by the state, scientists risked their lives if they arrived at unacceptable answers.

Finally, by the 1600s, property rights had become so firmly established as a basis for English economic activities that its rules sifted through to the lowest classes in society. The combination of freedom (from royal retribution in science and technology) and the right to retain the fruit of one's labor—even intellectual property—gave England a substantial advantage in the colonization process over rivals that had more than a century head start.[14]

An appreciation for competition played a central role in the drive by various European states to surpass each other. The multitude of small city-states, especially in Italy, led to the adoption of a "free market" of ideas, and any planner or merchant who could improve the lot of the city was rewarded. As economist E. L. Jones notes, "The general explanation of change lies at the intersection of technological change, increasing market size, and the ambitions of a system of nation-states."[15] Jones credits the "organizational change associated with the growth of the market," combined with the nation-states' establishment of "stable conditions necessary for expanding development and growth, for the diffusion of the best practices in technology and commerce, and in several countries for the actual founding of manufactories where there only had been handicrafts."[16] Both concepts—state competition and private markets—had deeply ingrained themselves into the English psyche by the age of colonization.

MERCANTILISM: THE MERGER OF BUSINESS AND GOVERNMENT

The rapid appearance of the joint-stock companies, which received their charters from the king, fit well with the new economic doctrine of *mercantilism*. Spain and Portugal had practiced mercantilism since the early 1500s, but not until 1620, when Thomas Mun elaborated the theory, was it applied by England. Mercantilism rested on the premise that the individual entrepreneur existed to serve the needs of the state.

It contained three basic concepts: 1) All wealth in the world was limited or fixed, because wealth consisted only of gold, silver, and precious gems; 2) for a nation to improve its position among other nations, it had to obtain gold and silver, preferably through a "favorable balance of trade"; and 3) the government should regulate the nation's production and investment through a series of tariffs and subsidies that were enforced at ports and harbors by having all goods travel (in Mun's case) in British ships. With wealth fixed, as Mun suggested, all economic activities resulted in a "zero sum game," with a winner and loser—a concept that made even Mun uncomfortable.

Monarchs, naturally, approved of mercantilism, and where they achieved "total control over the nobility… and where the commercial class remained weak, mercantilism remained in its earliest phase."[17] They needed cash to maintain the military forces that were the basis of their power. The means of obtaining cash varied. Spain and Portugal engaged in little more than resource extraction from Mexico and Latin America. In England and Holland, however, business simply moved beyond the ability of the government to direct all its activities. Although the search for gold and silver still dominated the agendas of English colonies in the New World, new incentives for exploration in North America appeared, including a rising demand for furs, particularly beaver fur for hats. Eleven English joint-stock companies formed between 1606 and 1630, most of them with the aim of establishing a fur (and, of secondary importance, fishing) trade in Canada and northeastern North America.

ENGLISH BUSINESS IN COLONIAL AMERICA

The most significant of the English joint-stock companies in the New World, the Virginia Company, was established in 1606 after receiving a grant from King James I for land in North America. Two subsidiary companies emerged: the London Company, based in Bristol, and the Plymouth Company, located in Plymouth, each with its own grant of land from the Virginia Company. Territory under the grant to the London Company received the name "Virginia" in honor of Queen Elizabeth (the "Virgin Queen"), while the Plymouth Company's grant encompassed New England. The London Company organized its expedition first, sending three ships and 144 settlers to establish a trading colony designed to live off the land and extract wealth for shipment back to England. In April 1607, twenty-six-year-old Captain John Smith piloted the fleet fifty miles up the James River, where the settlers established the triangle-shaped "James Forte," or Jamestown, on low-lying, swampy land.

Jamestown's investors, who stayed in England, quickly learned that they had misread the opportunities for business in America. Rather than producing profits, the colony produced starvation. It had few of the advantages found in the established Asian port cities, which had served as the model for the London investors, and none of the Far Eastern existing markets for trade. Worse, the settlers had come from the ranks of adventurers who drifted into endless searches for precious metals and refused any agricultural work until provisions dwindled. By then, it was too late. Fewer than forty of the settlers saw the second winter, and so few survived that Smith noted the living "were scarce able to bury the dead." Burdened with soldiers and gold-seekers, Smith pleaded with the London Company to send "thirty carpenters, husbandmen, gardeners, fishermen, blacksmiths, masons, and diggers up of trees ... [instead of] a thousand of such as we have...."[18] Smith saved the colony by imposing military-style discipline, issuing the biblical edict that "he who will not work will not eat," with the resulting society briefly resembling a regiment more than a commune.

Had tobacco not come along, Jamestown would have disappeared. Instead, the colony stumbled onto perhaps the product perfectly suited to the warm, moist climate. A market already existed. Columbus had reported Cuban natives rolling tobacco leaves, lighting them on fire, and sticking them in a nostril. By 1612, when John Rolfe cured tobacco, the English had refined the custom by using a pipe or smoking the tobacco directly by mouth. King James, demonstrating that smoking was no more popular with government officials then as it is today, described it as a "vile and stinking ... custom," but tobacco smoking continued to gain wider popularity in England, chiefly through the promotions of Walter Raleigh. Jamestown and the London Company had a product and a market. What they did not have was a labor force.

After the "starving time" of 1609–10, when the colonists, barricaded within James Forte, ate dogs, cats, rats, toadstools, horsehides, and anything else they could, a new influx of settlers arrived. Many of them had received stock from the company as an incentive to migrate to

Virginia. Free passage, in the form of "indentures," awaited anyone willing to work for seven years upon reaching the New World. By 1617, however, the London Company needed still more laborers, and it offered a grant of 100 acres of land to any freeman who would migrate to America. The company also shipped more than 100 young women to the colony as potential wives, seeking to make the men "more settled."

Within a short time, the policy of giving land to encourage immigration, called *headright*, not only offered every head of a household fifty acres for himself, but also an additional fifty acres for every adult family member or servant who came with the male family head. Immediately, market incentives spurred productivity gains and overcame the labor shortages, ending America's first brush with communalism. The headright policy, which enticed laborers to migrate in return for land, had the ironic effect of liberating the new immigrants, leaving them in a position to demand higher wages. If employers chose not to pay, laborers could always just start their own farms. Increasingly, planters turned to the importation of labor. They turned, therefore, to slavery.[19]

At a penny a pound, rice was almost as profitable as tobacco when shipped in large quantities, but the location of the coastal paddies and its oppressive climate in the summer caused many of the planters to reside further inland and leave the administration of the slaves to overseers. As for tobacco, the monopolies on the English market granted to the colonial planters ensured success and substantial wealth. Production soared, from half a million pounds annually in 1627 to 15 million pounds by 1670. Despite thirty years of stagnant tobacco prices, production of tobacco hovered at approximately 28 million pounds per year in the late 1600s. Then prices took off again, and by 1750, tobacco accounted for almost half of "the total value of colonial commodity exports in 1750."[20]

Rice and tobacco planters constituted the backbone of the early Southern economy, although these growers often had a wide range of business interests beyond agriculture. Tobacco grower William Byrd, for example, had substantial estates by 1700, but he also had commercial activities including trade with the Indians, an import/export business, and a labor-supply service that employed a slaver. His son, William Byrd II, was not a pure entrepreneur. Well educated, he chose to abandon formal schooling as an apprentice in a Dutch business house, where he studied commercial exchanges and international trade. He inherited his father's estate in 1704 and simply could have retired on the wealth he received, had he sold the Virginia properties. Instead, he went to America to run the plantation.

There, he plunged into daily management of the estate that produced corn, wheat, hay, fruits, vegetables, livestock, and lumber.[21] Byrd's estate, like other early plantations, was self-sufficient. Located on—or close to—rivers, the early tobacco growers received regular visits from merchant ships that bought their products and sold utensils and basic supplies. Byrd, however, did not passively preside over his manor; instead, he worked the business daily, rising at five or six o'clock to start his management rounds, caring for sick slaves, investigating the condition of the crops, testing the soil, and bargaining with tobacco factors or merchants. As his letter books make clear, Byrd knew his business well. But in addition to his estate-related activities, Byrd engaged in land surveying and sales, which involved exploring a tract of territory in North Carolina and eventually acquiring 20,000 acres. In another transaction, he received a grant of 105,000 acres tax free on the condition that he populate it with at least one family per 1,000 acres. Colonists in his territories might, "with the help of Moderate Industry, pass their time very happily.... Besides grazing and Tillage, which would abundantly compensate their Labour, they might plant Vineyards upon the Hills," as well as "Hemp, Flax, and Cotton, in what quantity they pleas'd." In short, he astutely observed, "Every thing will grow plentifully here to supply either the Wants or Wantonness of Man."[22]

Despite their ostentatious mansions and expansive tracts, some of the Southern planters lived on the verge of bankruptcy, dependent on the English subsidies on tobacco, rice, and indigo to sustain them. Even more common, many of them became land speculators. Between 1743 and 1760, for example, Virginia awarded 3 million acres of land in its Appalachian West to individual speculators and to others organized in joint-stock companies. Certainly no one epitomized the planter/land speculator better than George Washington, whose Mount Vernon plantation generated a romantic legend but yielded a slight income for its master. Washington branched out into a variety of activities: He was a tobacco middleman; he exported flour, imported and sold finished goods, ran a fishery, and, of course, bought and sold land in the West. At times, Washington even operated a ferryboat service and a distillery.[23]

Agricultural businesses such as indigo and rice production required extensive contacts with intermediaries from other cities, regions, and even abroad. Middlemen for tobacco, then later cotton, known as "factors," soon appeared. Perceptions that factors took more than their "fair share" spurred planters to assume many financial functions—including what were later called banking functions.[24]

COLONIZATION AND BUSINESS IN THE NORTH

The other famous settlement in North America resulted from the efforts of a group of Protestants called Puritans. After moving to Holland to escape religious intolerance, the Puritans arranged a joint-stock company that was partly financed by investors. Under the arrangement, the Puritans would work on the investors' land for five days a week and on their own land for two. The original agreement was modified several times before the adventure began. In September 1620, fifty or so Puritans and an equal number of other passengers embarked on the *Mayflower* for America.[25] In November 1620, they entered Provincetown Harbor and signed an agreement to "enact, constitute, and frame such just and equal laws, ordinances, acts, constitutions, and offices, from time to time, as shall be thought most meet and convenient for the general good of the colony, unto which we promise all due submission and obedience."[26] Thus, in what would be known as Plymouth, they established the rule of law, not individual, that would be a key element in the success of this New World.

In both the Plymouth colony and a subsequent colony of Puritans who arrived in 1629 under the auspices of the Massachusetts Bay Company, political rights stemmed from shares of ownership in the trading company. In 1640, investors withdrew and all rights of ownership were ceded to the free residents of the colony.[27] Although both investors and residents sought religious freedom in the New World, they also intended to produce goods. That situation starkly differed from that of the Virginia Company, where the stockholders had remained in England, and it produced enough friction that the early immigrants complained about the interference of English business owners who did not understand the conditions in North America.[28] Every colonist had an economic stake in the performance of the company. Also unlike the Virginia settlers, the Puritans prospered at the outset, possibly because they, as stockholders, *were* the entrepreneurs. They took advantage of the area's natural timber, fishing, and abundant furs as well as, of course, farming. Fishing represented one of the first, and most natural, occupations in colonies along the North Atlantic. In 1631, the Puritan leader and governor of the Massachusetts Bay Colony, John Winthrop, had launched the first colonial-made fishing vessel. New England fishermen rapidly established themselves as formidable competitors, developing techniques that allowed them to preserve cod and mackerel with salt for export to Europe. Although the business was seasonal, it produced a reliable source of gold and silver coin, providing a mainstay of American colonial enterprise. By the time of the Revolution, fishing comprised up to 90 percent of Massachusetts' exports to Europe and represented 10 percent of all American exports.

A similarly labor-intensive industry, whaling, developed in Nantucket and New Bedford. Wampanoag Indians on Nantucket butchered whales that drifted onto the beach, and they retained the rights to this activity even after selling their land to the English.[29] Whale oil was the cheapest and most popular fuel for interior lamps. Massachusetts colonists were making oil from beached whales by 1635.[30] Dominated at first by the early Puritan fishermen, whaling eventually became the province of Quakers. In the early eighteenth century, whalers developed the ability to catch whales in deep water. Catching the leviathans was not easy, however, as Herman Melville explained in his classic adventure tale, *Moby Dick*. Lacking the powerful harpoon guns of later years, colonial whalers had to approach the mammal in a small boat, heave a harpoon into the animal, and hang on for dear life as the whale ran or flailed about, depending on the accuracy of the throw. Many a whaler went on a "Nantucket sleigh ride," in which a whale dragged a tiny boat and a handful of terrified men across the water at breakneck speed or, if they were unlucky, took them down with a fatal dive.

Whaling fortunes were common in the 1700s. Thomas Hancock dealt in whalebone and oil starting in 1731, eventually creating a fortune that allowed his nephew and adopted son, John, a less effective trader, to devote himself to politics. Obadiah Brown (whose family later founded Brown University) developed the technique for making fine candles from sperm whale oil and built candle works in Providence, Rhode Island, in 1753. He swaddled his tapers in blue tissue and nestled them in boxes with labels engraved in English and

French. Benjamin Franklin praised this new type of candle, commenting that they "afford a clear white Light; may be held in the Hand, even in hot Weather, without softening; that their Drops do not make Grease Spots like those from common Candles; that they last much longer."[31]

The challenge of the candle-making industry was that there were few barriers to competition. By 1760, eight of the largest candle makers formed a trust in an attempt to keep the price of the oil low and the price of candles high. As with most trusts, it was unsuccessful. Oil prices continued to climb and candle prices changed little. The Rotch family, successful whalers, got into candle making in 1761, joining the then twenty-four other members of the trust.

In the 1770s, America dominated the whaling industry. An average of 360 ships embarked from New England ports over the period from 1771 to 1774. The Revolution nearly killed the industry, however. In the 1770s, the Rotch family had started whaling operations in New Bedford. When the Revolution interfered with their business, they moved their operations to the Falkland Islands, then France. By the 1780s, the 150 ships based in Nantucket had dropped to thirty and probably a thousand seamen were missing, killed, or imprisoned. Britain's taxes on American whale oil impeded recovery. It wasn't until after the War of 1812 that the U.S. whaling industry began to recover, until it experienced unparalleled growth, again dominating the world industry.[32]

Whaling and fishing generated a boom in ship construction, making the American maritime fleet the third largest in the world by 1776.[33] British competitors grew alarmed at the sudden rise in the merchant sea power of the colonies, commissioning a study of American shipping after the Revolutionary War called *Observation in the Commerce of the American States* (1784) by John Lord Sheffield. American shipyards, Sheffield maintained, had cut into English marine construction. In 1769 alone, they built 113 ships with topsails and 274 sloops or schooners. Massachusetts alone launched forty ships with topsails that same year, as well as ninety-seven sloops or schooners.

With the expansion in ship construction, seagoing trade expanded, opening other lucrative early business opportunities for the New Englanders. Exports of wood products made up the fourth largest category of exported items by 1768, reflecting the fact that the industry had expanded from simply cutting and shipping trees to making a wide assortment of furniture and finished wooden goods. Skilled artisans appeared in cities and towns, becoming small-business owners. To facilitate sales abroad, colonial merchants became adept at international trade in woodcraft, ironworks, copper and tin products, and other finished goods. American middlemen learned the foreign markets, identified the most profitable regions, cultivated the best customers, and took note of the most important competitors.

Despite the impressive expansion in maritime activities, most New Englanders earned their living from the land instead of the ocean, thanks to falling freight rates that encouraged farmers to ship to increasingly distant markets.[34] Even the small farms, which represented the dominant business activity in the North, looked outside their region for consumers.

Northerners developed a variety of practices and laws that secured property ownership and enhanced equality over time. Pennsylvania, under the proprietorship of William Penn, established rules that, while feudal in nature, extended landownership to individuals on a liberal basis. His use of "quit rents," in which landowners received their holdings for a payment, after which they were "quit and free" of further obligations to the proprietor, made Penn "history's most enlightened feudal lord."[35] Inheritance laws in the North also contributed to a culture that encouraged small farms. Most northern colonies established traditions of dividing the patriarch's land among the living sons. That meant that an estate of 400 acres would be divided into four 100-acre estates if four sons survived the father. Compare that with the South, where the legal tradition of *primogeniture* prevailed. In that case, the entire estate went to the eldest son upon the father's death, leaving other sons to move or become landless employees of the eldest boy. Most tended to move westward, putting constant pressure on Indian tribes and on colonial authorities to restrain them. But even in the North, there was a limit to the division and subdivision of property—forty to fifty acres was considered the minimum needed for a self-sufficient family farm—forcing sons with small amounts of land to sell their inheritance and move to cities for employment.

Consequently, each region took on a distinct business culture related in no small measure to the land policies it adopted. Large plantations appeared in the South; smaller farms emerged in the North, with the resulting expansion of northern towns and their hubs of commercial activity and scores of mechanics and artisans. The availability of slaves and the profitability of tobacco, then rice and cotton—large "cash crops" grown in vast quantities—further supported the differences between the regions over time. And while Southern towns had their share of cobblers, barrel makers, ironworkers, tinsmiths, and other artisans, they did not exist in comparable numbers or concentrations as in New England towns.

Wherever they conducted their business, however, the artisans (or "mechanics," as they were called) included chandlers, tanners, shipwrights, tailors, and coach makers. We can gain a glimpse into the world of those early small businessmen, thanks to Richard Walsh's essay examining Charleston mechanics. Walsh located an army of painters, glaziers, iron wrights, rope makers, and other independent business owners in the city, some of which dealt with problems scarcely different from those existing today. Even in the 1760s, it appears, businesses had to cope with government environmental regulation, as Charleston candle makers found themselves presented before grand juries on charges that the noxious fumes produced from boiling tallow constituted a threat to the health of local residents. Most made living wages, and some grew rich, including a cooper whose business expanded to the point that he employed thirty other workers. The wills of several tanners, shoemakers, and other entrepreneurs revealed that they attained substantial wealth from their enterprises.[36] Whether cabinetmakers or silversmiths, the careers of the mechanics were characterized by a high degree of mobility—both upward and downward—on the ladder of wealth. Much of that mobility arose from the fact that licenses or other regulations did not inhibit ambitious men from expanding their business. Carpenters often entered the ranks of architects; housepainters entered teaching and otherwise instructed in art; and so on.

COLONIAL MERCHANTS: THOMAS HANCOCK AND PAUL REVERE

Alongside the mechanics and artisans, a second business group began to emerge in the 1700s: the colonial merchants. Sometimes the lines between the two groups blurred, as in the case of Paul Revere. At other times, the merchant led a distinctly nonartisan life, as with Thomas

Hancock. Those two men, therefore, serve as examples of the variety of entrepreneurial experience in colonial America.

After the 1690s, England reestablished its authority over New England, which to that point had operated with considerable independence under Puritan governors. Until that time, the clergy represented not only the most respected members of society politically, but also the upper strata within the economy. Not surprisingly, then, the quintessential colonial merchant, Thomas Hancock (1703–64), was the second son of a Lexington, Massachusetts, clergyman named John Hancock. Unable to afford a Harvard education for his younger boy, Reverend Hancock placed Thomas in an apprenticeship in Boston with a bookseller. At age 21, after a seven-year apprenticeship in which he learned printing, bookbinding, sales, and other business skills, Thomas established his own small business, importing his volumes from England and Europe. To acquire books, he purchased and resold maritime products, particularly whale oil, bone, and related products, abroad.

Although he expanded from his book business, Hancock did not ignore it. Instead, he solidified his place in the Boston book trade, selling a diverse mix of wares in his stores, acquiring some products on consignment and others in payment for books or other debts. One could find clothes (which constituted more than half his total sales by the 1750s), knives, buttons, and swords, as well as tea, pepper, salt, and other food items. Bins of coal sat next to reams of paper; cloth jackets were draped near leather belts or fur pelts; and ship's compasses and bells hung above the ever-present books. Hancock found that many of his customers needed credit, and as he started to supply other merchants, he routinely offered them goods with up to one year to repay with interest. Hancock and other American shop owners also understood that money—especially gold and silver coin—was scarce, making it imperative that businesses deal in credit, consignment, or barter on a regular basis. Hancock's firm used bills of exchange, which circulated domestically in the colonies to allow merchants to draw funds on a business in another section of the country, and which also allowed merchants with limited access to gold or silver to acquire products around the world.[37] Hancock's rags-to-riches story was not unique among American colonists.[38]

Equally famous, but seldom recognized as an entrepreneur, was Paul Revere (1735–1818), who made himself into the premier silver- and goldsmith in the colonies. His hardware store bought and sold

English and American goods, but with a difference: Paul Revere also manufactured the iron, the "hinges of Brass," "Sley Bells," "Truck Bells," copper, and silver products he sold.[39] At age 65, when many modern working Americans think about retirement, Revere embarked on one of the riskiest ventures of his life. He built a rolling mill to produce sheet copper, calling the project "a great undertaking [that] will require every farthing which I can rake or scrape."[40] Using $25,000 of his savings (a fortune in modern dollars) and a loan of money and 19,000 pounds of copper from the United States government, Revere began making rolled sheet copper to plate the sides of the USS *Constitution* in 1803. "Old Ironsides," which ironically resisted cannonballs because it had green, flexible wood, was coated with copper! One hundred years later, a Navy lieutenant who was conducting a repair of the *Constitution* identified the very bolts Revere manufactured and proudly reported that they had been "stretched [so that] the elastic limit of the metal had been reached" and, although it went unstated, not exceeded. The bolts held.[41] Revere's casting and foundries were unmatched in their craftsmanship and quality. For that reason, Paul Revere received numerous government contracts for items ranging from plates to bells and cannon. And while Paul Revere was exceptional, the "career path" he followed was not. Rather than resisting change, colonial artisans themselves had started to change their crafts through innovations and inventions that allowed America to industrialize. Both Hancock and Revere aggressively pursued diversification and innovation. Throughout the northeastern seaboard, especially in the cities such as Philadelphia, the promise of social mobility and the prod of economic adversity encouraged local entrepreneurs to adopt new products and strategies whenever possible. In the port cities, "under the insistent, reckless, often ruthless urging of merchants and manufacturers, a backward agricultural economy was pushed into the onrushing currents of the Industrial Revolution."[42]

THE LADDER OF WEALTH

Not only did merchants' relentless competition improve the material conditions of the entire society by propelling it into industrialism, it resulted in a highly stratified merchant community in which new entrants into the business rose quickly to wealth while older, less adaptable traders drifted to the bottom. But traders at the top found they could not freeze out new entrepreneurs on the bottom, and therefore to remain successful merchants had to stay on the cutting edge of technology and management. Or, as historian Thomas Doerflinger put it, in port areas "opportunity, enterprise, and adversity reinforced each other. A young businessman could borrow money and move into trade, challenging the commercial position of older, more established merchants. His opportunity was, in effect, their adversity."[43]

Doerflinger has suggested that the major urban merchants and large landholders, who represented perhaps 10 percent of the white population, held as much as 65 percent of the personal wealth. Movement up the ladder was rapid, but conservative merchants could lose their wealth just as suddenly. Much more numerous was the colonial middle class, probably constituting about half of the white population, which accounted for about 20 percent of the personal wealth. That group included yeoman farmers, small storekeepers, master craftsmen, and a modest number of urban professionals such as doctors, lawyers, and ministers. Most of those individuals, for all intents and purposes, "were their own bosses," and gained in business and workplace independence whatever they lacked in pure capital. Recall, also, that for farmers and some craftsmen, children were viewed as net assets—not liabilities—and provided a substantial source of unpaid labor and uncounted capital.[44] Availability of land meant that no one had to accept his position for long, and indentures and apprenticeships were temporary conditions.[45]

Overall, however, the colonies on the eve of the Revolution were as wealthy—if not more so, per capita—than the mother country. Aggregate income for the colonies grew at an annual average of just over 3.4 percent, or about the same rate as population growth for the colonial period. But the early years of some of the colonies were so dismal that they substantially affected the growth rates overall: When incomes are examined for the 1700s, per capita incomes rose by perhaps one percent per year. Colonial per capita incomes have been estimated at $720, an amount that put the colonists of 200 years ago on a par with the privately held wealth of citizens of Mexico or Turkey in the late-twentieth century!

BUSINESS AND GOVERNMENT: EARLY RELATIONSHIPS

If large divisions in wealth existed in colonial America, and if mobility upward and downward resulted in a constant churning and frothing, virtually all groups at any given time understood one fundamental fact: They alone were responsible for the generation of wealth. Government had almost nothing to do with creating wealth, and little more to do with distributing it. Occasionally, merchants such as Hancock had to deal with British agents or customs officials; artisans, such as Paul Revere, only interacted with royal authorities if they needed to import or export specific items on the enumerated list of products required to be shipped to England for reshipment to other countries. Certain of the enumerated goods were subsidized, and others, bound for the colonies, were taxed. Other than those instances, most Americans never saw a representative of the Crown except at tax time. And excepting those items taxed or subsidized in the mercantilist system, from the 1650s to the 1750s, government erected few barriers to most enterprises, especially to small businesses.

Government did play a substantial role in the colonial economy of America, but the few edicts coming from London had little effect on average American enterprises. When taxes grew too onerous, as they did on tea, the colonists simply smuggled tea into the nation in huge quantities. More important, the government made no serious attempt to end the smuggling, giving its tacit approval.

The main instrument used by the government to regulate business was the charter, which in the eighteenth century implied monopoly powers to the group receiving it. Then, having handed a charter to a joint-stock company, the king looked to the company's English proprietors to administer the New World lands. Proprietors usually came from well-connected, landed families upon whom the king thought he could rely. William Penn, although a religious dissident and a rebellious son, inherited his father's estate and land in America (granted by Charles II in 1681). He intended to make a profit from the land, yet also to establish a safe haven for members of his faith, known as the Quakers (officially, the Society of Friends). Penn's grant, extended from New York to Maryland, represented an area larger than England and Wales combined and, unknown to Penn, "contained more valuable soil and minerals than any other province of English America."[46]

Penn, greatly resembling a modern real estate "wheeler-dealer," had to sell land and attract settlers to gain a profit from the grant. To that end, he offered parcels of up to 20,000 acres and advertised heavily in Europe and England. Like modern ads, Penn's promotions emphasized the benefits to the buyer's lifestyle. A 1683 advertisement for his colony boasted that "the air is sweet and clear, the heavens serene" in Pennsylvania. In writing about the city of Philadelphia in another advertisement, Penn enticed settlers with the promise of rising property values: "The improvement of the place is best measured by the advance of value upon every man's lot ... the worst lot in town, without any improvement upon it, is worth four times more than it was when it was laid out."[47] Although immigrants flocked to Pennsylvania, the colony never produced the profits Penn anticipated, in part because he never spent more than two consecutive years in America to manage his investment. His final days included a stint in an English debtors' prison before his death as a pauper in 1718.

Almost all colonists agreed that the proper role of government involved defense, especially protection from French and/or Indian attacks. Settlers on the Western frontiers wanted a permanent British presence—forts and soldiers—near the borders of Indian lands. Difficulties with the Indians, both from farmers wanting to expand westward and from new waves of traders filtering into the frontier, placed considerable pressure on the British to control the situation. In 1763, attempting to stem the flow of traders and farmers into Western lands, Britain established the Proclamation Line, prohibiting settlement west of the Appalachians. That appeared to favor the fur traders who benefited from government monopolies to operate in Indian territories. Land companies pressured the government to redraw the line in 1768, and in 1774 (following the Boston Tea Party) the Quebec Act reversed the decree yet again, extending the Quebec boundary to Ohio, and apparently handing fur traders a victory over settlers. Britain's inability to define its role as a "policeman" in the West, and its vacillations between courting the favor of land companies, on one hand, and fur trading companies, on the other, illustrated the difficulties a government faced when it ignored its basic responsibilities and sought to pick winners and losers in the economy.[48]

Government played its most successful role in business enterprise at sea, where, by the late 1680s, the Royal Navy had gained control over the oceans and thus ended or substantially reduced losses to pirates.

Control of the seas ensured safe trade lanes to Africa, South America, and the Far East, while denying the use of oceans to continental rivals, especially Spain. Access to the Far Eastern markets and raw materials thus constituted a powerful advantage for British and colonial merchants. Most important, however, the English government and its representatives in America maintained British property and contract law. In so doing, the government played its proper role of providing a secure foundation for business enterprise.

John Locke, considered by many historians to have had an intense influence on many of the American Revolutionary thinkers, had argued that to return to the "state of nature," man had to create a "civil state" that would ensure his liberty, and that the state would shrink as liberty grew. That sentiment, echoed by Jefferson as "the government that governs best, governs least," implied that in the state of nature there would be no government at all. Locke's view rested upon the proposition that government was not "natural"—that it was artificial and created by humans. Moreover, Locke's position stood in direct opposition to the classical positions of Plato, Aristotle, and Aquinas that politics constituted the most "natural" of human behaviors and had to fit with current religious doctrines—which in this context meant those in New England that spoke directly to economic matters.[49]

Misunderstandings over the doctrine of *laissez-faire* (so named by a group of French economic theorists called the Physiocrats) led many political economists to develop theories involving "perfect markets" in which no external forces, such as governments, affected supply, demand, or competition. Yet Adam Smith himself never envisioned a "perfect market," nor did he favor complete *laissez-faire*. Quite the opposite. The *Wealth of Nations* dealt at length with the proper role of government in the economy, not its absence from business affairs. Smith advocated, for example, maintenance of a large navy expressly for the purpose of protecting trade.

BUSINESS AS A REVOLUTIONARY FORCE

England had regulated trade within its empire through a series of laws known as the Navigation Acts (officially, the Acts of Trade and Navigation). Based on mercantilist principles of enlisting commercial activities in the interest of the state, the Navigation Acts created a set of colonial goods, including (of course) tobacco, sugar, molasses, and fur, that had to be shipped to England before transmission to other British colonies. Known as "enumerated" goods, the list gave England access to inexpensive raw materials while at the same time providing a market for colonial production. Other acts taxed or indirectly increased prices on goods shipped to the colonies (such as iron, fur hats, wool clothes, or finished products) or on sugar, tea, or rum imported from outside the empire.

As nettlesome as the Navigation Acts may have been to certain businesses, they hardly comprised a threat to political or economic freedom prior to 1763. The end of the Seven Years' War, however, and the subsequent new borders that resulted from the Treaty of Paris, saddled the British with seemingly endless wooded frontiers to patrol and fortify, and little revenue with which to pay for the task. A series of ministers and Chancellors of the Exchequer thus adopted a string of policies that transformed the Navigation Acts from regulatory nuisances to direct economic threats.

Such was the Stamp Act of 1765, a measure that required a government stamp be placed on every paper transaction, from marriages to the sale of property to divorces to dice. Of course, obtaining a stamp involved a tax, or fee. Citizens never before affected by Parliament's policies found themselves taxed at every turn in their daily commerce. The colonies responded immediately and resolutely, forming the first intercontinental congress, the Stamp Act Congress, to oppose the measure. Outraged delegates reiterated a principle stated earlier of "no taxation without representation." Having badly misread the colonists' response, Parliament repealed the Stamp Act in 1766. For the first time, however, merchants perceived that imperial regulations easily could be converted into weapons used to attack business. After new acts in 1767 further alienated the colonists, Samuel Adams (John's distant cousin), having flopped in private enterprise and having plodded through a string of government jobs, found his calling as a writer and organizer. Adams was no entrepreneur. Yet he had noteworthy skills when it came to assembling teams of writers, publishing their work, and circulating it to colonial state assemblies. He found support in the more than forty colonial newspapers that echoed his basic message, and while the merchant community provided the fuel for the American Revolution, newspapers generated the flame.

In 1773, British officials passed the Tea Act, which imposed a minor hike in the duties on tea, but opened the colonial tea trade to the East India Company, bypassing the English auctions. Conceived as a way to support the East India stockholders, the Tea Act was expected to gain a warm reception in America, where tea prices would fall somewhat. However, more than 750,000 pounds of tea entered the colonies through smuggling operations, and the crackdown on smuggling expected to accompany the Tea Act elicited a violent response from Americans. Rhetoricians such as Adams managed to make the illegal tea trade appear a legal "right"; many merchants, however, feared the ease with which the English government had imposed a law that could have destroyed American tea merchants.

The Tea Act shifted the debate from Britain's right to impose taxes to the process by which the government made decisions. Immediate colonial reaction came in the form of attacks on customs officials and, of course, the famous "Tea Party" of December 1773, when a number of merchants—including Paul Revere—dressed as Indians, boarded British ships bearing tea, and dumped forty-five tons into the waters at Boston Harbor. Merchants had emerged as the most unified voice against British policies, but in time they were joined by Virginia planters, Pennsylvania farmers, Connecticut woodsmen, and New England seafarers. First and foremost, however, the Boston Tea Party was a revolt against taxes—not only the burden of taxation, but arbitrary implementation of them. England ensured further resistance when it invoked the Intolerable Acts, closing Boston Harbor and requiring colonists to quarter British troops.

War broke out in 1775, whereupon the British attempted to establish a blockade. Colonial merchants such as George Cabot converted their fishing fleets into armed blockade runners, taking advantage of the demand for scarce American goods in Europe and for imported items. A related business involved privateering, which cost Great Britain 2,000 ships, 12,000 sailors, and $18 million.[50] American privateers made a significant contribution to the war effort by tying up the Royal Navy, destroying British supply lines, and providing colonial consumers with a variety of goods taken from captured vessels.

Nevertheless, there was no question that normal commercial routes were disrupted. Given the reality of the interruption of trade with Britain, American domestic production accelerated to meet the reduction in imports. Military demands alone accounted for an expansion in munitions, shoes, clothing, tents, and food, as well as the production associated with harnesses, wagons, and iron. Because of the entrepreneurial skill involved in organizing the production, collecting finished goods, and ensuring deliveries, "American merchants ... were both crucial to the success of the war effort and the principal material beneficiaries of armed conflict."[51]

THE COSTS AND BENEFITS
OF THE REVOLUTION

America's separation from England did not come cheaply. Thousands were killed or wounded; families were uprooted; property was destroyed; and relations between Canada and America soured for decades. Freedom from arbitrary control by a king or central government exacts a cost. In the case of the United States of America, trade routes temporarily deteriorated and foreign powers did not hesitate to demand tribute from American merchants that no longer had to contend with the superb Royal Navy.

For many years, economists hotly discussed the effects of the Navigation Acts as a cause of the American Revolution. If, for example, it could be proved that the Navigation Acts placed such a burden on the colonies that their economic life was at risk, then we could say with confidence that the Navigation Acts "caused" the American Revolution. But if their economic effect was minimal, then other explanations for the Revolution are needed.

Lawrence Harper, in 1942, was the first to attempt an economic analysis of the acts, measuring only the direct burdens on trade. But Robert Thomas, in his famous 1965 article, used a counterfactual model to assess what American economic life would have been like without the acts. Thomas calculated the burden on colonial commerce for exports, such as rice and tobacco, and examined the burdens on imports to arrive at a "gross trade burden" of $3.1 million in 1770, or about $1.24 per person. However, he acknowledged, the colonists gained from the imperial system as well, and the benefits of British trade preferences, bounties, and the protection of the English Navy came to $885,000, or about $0.40 per person. The net loss to the colonists of belonging to the imperial system was approximately $1 million, or less than one percent of income. Or, to say that "the British presence was not a serious financial hardship to the colonists," as Jeremy Atack and Peter Passell do in *A New Economic View of American History*, is an understatement. Thomas's was not the last word on the effects of the imperial system, of course. The most significant subsequent research came from Peter McClelland, who pursued a slightly different path to determine the burden of the Navigation Acts. McClelland computed the burden by analyzing the fraction of national income loss as a result of trade route distortions expressed as a fraction of GNP. He concluded that the upper-bound burden comprised about 3 percent of GNP, an amount, while slightly larger than that derived by Thomas, still represented a minor sum. Ultimately, the research suggests that, in this case at least, no one went to war for economic reasons alone.[52]

Neither the losses from remaining in the imperial system nor the small benefits it offered outweighed the perceived injustices to fundamental liberties. More than that, however, Americans took from their separation from England a deep-seated suspicion of government's power. Taxation, always a matter of concern, was targeted for special controls by placing it under the House of Representatives in the Constitution. States drafted bills of rights reiterating their commitment to property rights, personal liberty, the right to bear arms, religious toleration, and restricted government—all elements that finally became part of the U.S. Constitution. Whatever America's heritage of natural resources and land, it is unlikely that its entrepreneurs could have prospered quite as they did if they had been subject to British labor laws and the impositions of its social welfare programs of the late nineteenth century.

During and immediately after the Revolution, however, many of the advantages of being a part of the British Empire were obvious, while some of the benefits of independence were less so. Certainly one area in which the rebellious colonies, then states, suffered was in the lack of a stable money system. Fortunately, the young nation found an individual to meet the challenge.

ROBERT MORRIS, FINANCIER OF THE REVOLUTION

The effects of trade disruption rippled throughout the colonies after the outbreak of hostilities, producing rising prices and a shortage of money. All thirteen states and the Continental Congress printed their own paper money, but often without gold or silver backing. Consequently, the value of currency depended on consumer confidence that the value would remain constant or that the money had some redemption value (if, for example, it was receivable for taxes). Colonial presses of state governments and Congress produced generous sums of money. Congress produced more than $226 million worth of notes called "Continentals" within a five-year period. Accordingly, the value plummeted with each new issue, plunging to a ratio of 146 Continentals to a single silver ounce by 1781.

No one appreciated the dangers of inflation more than Philadelphia merchant Robert Morris, who had seen his own business severely damaged. At age 13, Morris had come to Maryland with his family, whereupon he soon accepted an apprenticeship with the commercial firm of Charles Willing. In 1757, he joined in a partnership with Willing and his son, Thomas. When war broke out, Morris—a signer of the Declaration of Independence and a member of the Continental Congress until 1778—continued his business activities during the war. His firm received $850,000 of the $2 million that Congress spent from 1775 to 1777, thanks in part to Morris's position on the Committee of Commerce. Rivals claimed Morris profited unfairly from his "insider" position, yet no criticism of the goods Morris's firm supplied, nor really of the prices it charged, arose at the time.

After the ratification of the Articles of Confederation in 1781, Congress beseeched Morris to remedy the young nation's financial problems. He assumed the position of Superintendent of Finance, proposing that the nation charter its first commercial bank, the Bank of North America, founded in Philadelphia in 1782. The bank acted as the fiscal agent for Congress, issued banknotes, and acted as a "national" bank. Its notes circulated as currency and retained their value because the bank redeemed the notes for gold or silver *specie*. Or, in the parlance of banking, the notes retained their *par* (face) value. To appreciate the significance of that fact, recall that the par value of a

Continental was $1, but its market value was 1/146 of a dollar! The bank made short-term loans to businesses, upon which it collected interest. It was no charity, either, paying stockholders a 14 percent return on their stock.

Morris's financial plans closely paralleled those of Alexander Hamilton, the nation's first Secretary of the Treasury ten years later. Morris insisted that the credit of the nation had to be maintained, regardless of whether it helped or hurt individual groups. The Bank of North America provided a case study for other banking institutions, such as the Bank of Massachusetts and the Bank of New York, which laid the financial groundwork for the new republic.[53] Those "merchants' banks" typically did not make consumer loans (to buy products) or even loans to farmers, but rather extended short-term credit to merchants to conduct trade. Consequently, several states issued paper money, which often struggled to maintain its par valuation. Merchants tended to blame the confederation's financial policies for any downturn in business. By 1786, however, most citizens agreed that the Articles of Confederation had a number of weaknesses that needed correction. To that end, a constitutional convention was called for in May 1787, a meeting at which American business leaders were prominently represented.

THE FOUNDATION OF BUSINESS: THE CONSTITUTION

A large number of issues related to business and the economy were addressed by the framers of the Constitution—so many that a vigorous historical debate has arisen over the extent to which the Founding Fathers simply institutionalized their own "class" advantages. The document itself includes clauses dealing with each of the following business or economic issues:

- Taxation

- Interstate Commerce

- Mails and the Post Office

- Patents and Copyrights

- Coinage of Money

- Internal Security

- Import and Export Tariffs

- Weights and Measures

- Armies and Navies

- Immigration

- Contract Enforcement

- Bankruptcy

- Self-Protection and Protection of One's Business Through the Right to Bear Arms

With the exception of slavery—the debate over which the founders postponed—the document created a political and legal climate conducive to economic risk taking. Inventors had property rights to their ideas. The security and safety of commerce, both internally and externally, was provided for under the clauses allowing the government to raise armies and to maintain domestic order. States and the federal government were prohibited from penalizing exports. The Constitution encouraged free transit of goods and labor, making the states a giant free-trade zone, since no state could levy internal tariffs. Reserving for itself the regulation of foreign and interstate commerce, the federal government ensured uniformity and consistency, two keys to successful business operations. Although it did not always occur in practice, the concept of providing a federal judiciary that would treat citizens of different states equally also promised to enhance commercial activity.

As important as the powers given to the federal government were, the powers reserved to the states—including licensing, inspection, and similar regulation of business activities—were equally important and greatly shaped business and the economy. Historians of the Second Amendment suggest that the clause prohibiting Congress from abridging the right to bear arms not only addressed concerns about national government power but also constituted a statement about self-protection against brigands. Protection of commerce abroad fell under the provisions that allowed Congress to raise armies and navies, an authority it exercised periodically. For example, President Thomas Jefferson dispatched the small U.S. Navy and its Marines to eliminate the threat to American trade in the Mediterranean by the Barbary pirates between 1804 and 1808.[54]

On the other hand, the framers avoided the key decision of the age by postponing any final judgment on whether slaves were people or property. The Constitution also left somewhat clouded the definition of money, since it used the term "coin" at a time when paper money was becoming increasingly popular. Nevertheless, the document proved remarkably flexible and resilient. For almost all areas affecting business, the Constitution reflected the understanding that political freedoms and freedom to innovate in the marketplace were inextricably linked, and that real riches came "from the power of production and supply, not bullion collected through a trade surplus."[55] Rather than seeking to place the state at the center of economic decision making, as had occurred under mercantilist regimes, the Constitution provided a framework of order, sanctity of contracts, and reliable measurements: The Founders assumed that the market could handle the rest.

The fact that the Constitution placed such a priority on property rights convinced some, such as Charles Beard, that the delegates had drawn up the document merely to protect their "vested interests." Beard's 1913 book, *An Economic Interpretation of the Constitution*, emerged from the author's Marxist perspective, in which all events are reflections of "class struggle."[56] Beard examined the background of the delegates, finding remarkable continuity in their economic status. But in 1958, Forrest McDonald's *We the People: The Economic Origins of the Constitution* challenged Beard's thesis by reexamining the delegates' occupations. McDonald contended that Beard applied a generic term "businessman" to a number of delegates who, in reality, were craftsmen and artisans. But, as we have seen in the discussions of colonial artisans, many were small-business owners or people who straddled both the world of labor and of capital.[57] A subsequent study, looking at voting behavior on specific issues at the Constitutional Convention, found significant patterns of voting for economic interests at the Convention but fused with what the study's authors defined as including "constituent interest."[58] Put another way, the delegates voted along certain lines that reflected the desires of their constituencies and communities. While doubtlessly different measures would have been adopted if the makeup of the Convention were different—either a heavy dose of backcountry farmers or former Tories might have made things interesting—"measures of ideology" remained the only consistent explanation for voting across all the issues.

The members of the Constitutional Convention were both men of substance and men of ideas; and the notion that they could not be the latter if they were the former is itself troubling. It would mean, among other things, that Beard himself must have been incapable of ideas independent of the influence of "class" or wealth, which is both demeaning and untrue of Beard. As for the document itself, its amazing durability and timeless truths suggest that the framers must have done something right.[59]

CHAPTER 3

Entrepreneurs in the New Nation: 1787–1840

It was apropos that Adam Smith's *Wealth of Nations* appeared in 1776, the same year as the Declaration of Independence. Both heralded the primacy of the individual over the state, marking a new stage in theories of political economy. Not until 1848, with the publication of the *Communist Manifesto* by Karl Marx and Friedrich Engels, did thinkers seriously attempt to restore the state to its pre-Smith position.

For entrepreneurs in America, most of whom had never heard of Adam Smith, business in the new republic simply reflected a commonsense approach to economics. After all, they assumed that they knew more about their abilities, talents, productivity, and markets than some members of the House of Burgesses or some representatives of the Continental Congress. During the war and the subsequent period under the Articles of Confederation—with virtually no assistance from government—entrepreneurs had opened entirely new markets. For a time, government involvement in the economy was minimal.

Trade routes, although damaged, were repaired quickly. New York merchants established new contacts with China while shipping ginseng root on the *Empress of China* from Canton in 1784. A burgeoning Far

East trade sprang up, and "soon wealthy Americans decorated their homes with directly imported Chinese rugs, wore fine silks, and sipped Chinese tea."[1] Primitive steam-powered vessels had already appeared, and within twenty years, fast American-built 1,000-ton "clipper ships" would sail to China, eclipsing the best vessels the British Empire had to offer.

GOVERNMENT AND BUSINESS IN THE EARLY REPUBLIC

Given the number of business activities that took place with no involvement from the national, state, or even local government, it is inaccurate to maintain that "most Americans felt that government at all levels was responsible for encouraging economic development and enterprise."[2] Few entrepreneurs of the late 1700s had known anything other than the mercantilist system, and therefore to portray them as "free marketers" is as equally inaccurate. Some businessmen wanted subsidies for their goods—as they had been conditioned to receive from the English—and groups battled over which stood to gain the most from the type of banking and financial system the government endorsed. At the same time, Americans had started to adopt the Lockean, or restrictive, view of government in things political. Individual liberties were set apart from authority granted to state or national governments. Gradually, Lockean interpretations of government's role in economic life replaced mercantilist assumptions. By the 1790s, therefore, Americans adopted a view of government as an impartial arbiter and enforcer of contracts. Such activities as road building—taken for granted today as a normal function of government—were carried out almost exclusively by private contractors who constructed turnpikes for a number of years.[3]

Nevertheless, both positions—that of government control and that of free markets—were represented in early American government in the persons of Alexander Hamilton and Thomas Jefferson, and therefore, it is worthwhile to devote some attention to their views, as they came to form the framework for business in America.

HAMILTON AND THE FOUNDATIONS
OF BUSINESS ENTERPRISE

Arguably, no American shaped the institutional structure of American business more than Alexander Hamilton, whom historians have characterized as one of the most eloquent defenders of state activism in the economy. Born an illegitimate son on the island of Nevis in the British West Indies in 1755, Hamilton was home educated and at age 13 took a job assisting a local merchant. Virtually penniless, he proved a capable and trustworthy employee, as well as a talented writer whose account of a hurricane in 1772 led a New Jersey minister to raise enough money to send him to New York for a formal education. He freely admitted that he wanted to advance financially: "I condemn the groveling condition of a clerk … to which my fortune, etc., condemns me, and would willingly risk my life, *though not my character*, to exalt my station" (emphasis ours). During the Revolution, Hamilton served time in Washington's army, often representing the general at conferences. The problems of supply, organization, and decentralized procurement in times of war convinced Hamilton that national strength demanded centralized authority. Ironically, then, through hard work, occasional good fortune, and little help from government, Hamilton had raised himself from the direst poverty, yet he came to favor a "planned" approach to economic growth with the government providing much of the planning.

Hamilton's predisposition to having a strong federal government direct certain aspects of the economy betrayed his essentially pessimistic view of human nature and his distrust of the actions of the masses.[4] Hamilton argued that it was in the best interests of the nation to align the "moneyed men" with the government by making them lenders.[5] However, he certainly appreciated the dangers of government meddling in the economy.[6]

For example, his fiscal plan for the nation, taken from the *Report on Public Credit* (1790), had four primary components, some of which would have reduced or limited the ability of government to intrude into the economy. The first component involved "assumption," wherein the federal government would assume the debts incurred by the thirteen states during the Revolution. The creditworthiness of the new nation was at risk if the government ignored the states' debts. While on the surface that appeared to expand the scope of the federal government's powers in the economy, Hamilton took for granted the nature of the Union as one whole—not fourteen separate entities. Since that single entity stood responsible for a mutually incurred debt, how best to pay it? Thus, he developed a two-pronged strategy: First, give the creditors a "menu" of choices of repayment, including trading old debt (with a 6 percent interest rate, but no stated federal commitment to repay) for new (at 4 percent, but guaranteed), or retaining their existing notes and their higher default rate. Second, subordinate old debt (the assumed state debts) to new debt, with the old debt retired through scheduled payments in a "sinking fund." The genius of Hamilton's plan was that it rewarded creditors for taking new issues at lower rates, but it also instilled discipline on government, which had to repay the old debt on schedule, whether or not it issued new debt.

The third component of Hamilton's fiscal plan, advanced in the *Report on a National Bank* (1790), involved the creation of a national bank. Hamilton reasoned that public monies needed to be retained somewhere, and that a bank paid the citizens' interest, while a government facility simply stored the money. He therefore chose to utilize the market to reduce costs to taxpayers, in essence "privatizing" the storage of public funds. The Bank of the United States (BUS), chartered in 1791, was owned four-fifths by private stockholders, but foreign stockholders had no voting rights.

But the monopoly charter of the BUS—being the only government bank—fit perfectly with the mercantilist view of using business in the service of government. In addition to its "special privilege," the BUS had other significant advantages in the market, even had there existed a number of strong private competitors (which at the time, there were not). Among its obvious advantages, 1) the BUS had a larger capital than any other bank at the time; 2) it had a huge pool of government funds on deposit; 3) its profitability increased, because it could make more and larger loans; and 4) it had the power of *interstate branch banking*, meaning that it could establish branches in any state it chose. Other banks, in subsequent years, were denied that authority.

Hamilton's position in his *Report on the Establishment of a Mint* (1791) supported the stability of markets by establishing standards and measurements. Hamilton's background with the English system of banking kept him from perceiving the economic benefits that privately produced money might offer, and thus he stopped well short of a free market position on money creation. But in other ways he limited the power of government over the money supply. He agreed with Jefferson's suggestion of a decimal currency and wanted the American currency at parity with the Spanish-milled dollar. Working together, Hamilton and Jefferson thus deprived Congress of the power to debase specie money, ensuring that business had a stable financial base—no small contribution! Hamilton's *Report on Manufactures* (1791) did lay the groundwork for "protective" tariffs for infant industries, especially iron and textiles, and scholars remain divided as to the necessity or value of those early tariffs. Economic historians Douglas Irwin and Peter Temin, for example, concluded that American textile products were sufficiently different from those of the British—our main competitors—and consequently, American textile manufacturers could have survived easily without the tariff.[7] Despite his bent for centralization and government activism, Alexander Hamilton nevertheless provided much of the free market framework for American enterprise. And despite his proclivity for government subsidies and tariffs, his more lasting contributions to American business were a sound financial system and a nation focused on keeping its debt low.

JEFFERSON'S LAND POLICIES

Ironically, the man who disagreed with Hamilton as much as anyone, Thomas Jefferson, had made his own contributions to a thriving base of enterprise.[8] More than any other person, Jefferson inspired the creation of a national market in land, influencing the Land Ordinance of 1785 that laid out the land in divisions of *townships*. A six-square-mile township was divided into thirty-six sections of one square mile each. A square mile contained 640 acres. Congress sold the land at $1 per acre, in minimum size lots of a section. This was far more land than a single family could farm in the late eighteenth century, so wealthy individuals and land companies formed by investors bought land and created subdivisions.[9] While the government sold land primarily for income, Jefferson thought individuals could make better choices than government. Perhaps more important, he "feared the potential abuse of power by the national government and wanted the land, whenever possible, removed from its grasp."[10] Jefferson determined the course of history not only by promoting private ownership, but by marking the landscape into neat squares that are today visible from the air, with streets that more often run in straight lines than meander.

Although the government-established price of land was low, Congress stipulated that the minimum auction purchase be 640 acres, meaning that in reality, land companies and speculators bought several of the sections. But since the government could not survey all the land immediately, a market developed for the unsurveyed land. Speculation thus allowed owners to adapt the true value of land to demand, revealing the futility of government's efforts to fix prices. Speculators provided land to tenants, and even provided credit with which tenants could purchase land. The role of the speculator was not as evil as has been frequently portrayed.

As equally important, a system quickly arose to settle the problem of unsurveyed lands, as when early courts recognized *preemption*, or "squatter's rights," wherein anyone who remained on a piece of land for seven years gained ownership of that parcel. In that way, large landholders could not buy land and "sit" on it: If they did not develop and inspect their land regularly, they stood to lose it. Squatters also found that if they could harvest and market crops before the owners discovered them, they could raise enough money to purchase the land they had squatted on.[11] Peruvian economist Hernando de Soto has argued that this key legal development, which permitted owners to acquire rapid legal title to their assets, marked the key distinction between successful and unsuccessful economies in the twentieth and twenty-first centuries.[12] As a further inducement to develop, rather than merely hoard land, the United States evolved a policy of land taxation that required landholders to pay taxes whether land was developed or not, which behooved them to develop their properties.

Jefferson anticipated that his land policies would create an agrarian republic—not a rural nation—with the key difference being that in Jefferson's vision, landowners would be more than self-sufficient small farmers.[13] Farmers routinely purchased more land than they needed precisely to sell some of it in difficult times, and most deliberately they purchased more than they needed to farm in order to sell some at future dates.[14] In that sense, the simplest farmer became a "speculator."[15]

A second law inspired by Jefferson, the Northwest Ordinance of 1787, permitted settlers to form a territorial government when the population reached 5,000 adult male inhabitants, then to apply for statehood when population exceeded 60,000 "free inhabitants." Jefferson wanted to ensure that no colonies developed on the American frontier, while business enterprises on the frontier never had to fear "taxation without representation," further solidifying the institutional setting for enterprise in new territories. Jefferson's contributions to the business climate of the nation were extensive, and while Jefferson was more geared to making America an "agrarian republic," he nevertheless displayed vision in critical areas. He did not hesitate to use the federal government's power to acquire land that American citizens could settle, as with the Louisiana Purchase. In 1802–03, he embraced free trade as France and England took a brief respite from their wars, and America's trade with Europe soared. Appalled at the practice of paying "tribute" (bribes) to the Barbary States, Jefferson dispatched the new American Navy on a series of punitive raids on Algiers, Tunis, and other pirate states. The naval action contributed to freer and cheaper Mediterranean trade. Exports tripled in value between 1793 and 1807, resulting in a business boom in large commercial cities. New York, Philadelphia, Baltimore, and other cities not only expanded, but increased their manufacturing base. In a rapidly changing world of commerce, a new generation of entrepreneurs appeared.

JOHN JACOB ASTOR: FURRIER, SHIPOWNER, SPECULATOR

Cutting and delivering meat hardly seemed the most likely starting point for "one of the preeminent businessmen of his day," but John Jacob Astor (1763–1848) learned the essentials of commerce at an early age working for his German father, a butcher.[16] Astor came to America in 1783, after spending four years in London with his brother. During the voyage, the vessel upon which Astor sailed became icebound in the Chesapeake Bay for two months, which gave Astor the opportunity to learn the fur trade in exquisite detail from agents of the Hudson Bay Company who were aboard. Astor promptly left for New York where he worked as a baker's apprentice, but had his vision fixed on the fur trade.

    Astor's break came when he took a job with a New York fur merchant, and by 1786 Astor had his own fur trading business—which at first did not make a profit, requiring Astor to make up the difference by selling musical instruments. But soon, the business achieved a sound footing. Astor's network extended up the Hudson, as far as Montreal, and he maintained business connections with London. Growth remained steady but slow until the unpopular John Jay Treaty with England in 1794. After that, Astor's furs could be shipped directly from the frontier and forests to New York, without making the previously mandated stop in London. As the fur trade grew, Astor's personal fortune exceeded $250,000.

On a visit to London, Astor acquired a license to trade in East India Company markets, particularly China. In 1801, his first ship returned from Canton, where Astor representatives had traded furs and pelts for silks, tea, spices, porcelain (shipped for ballast with the tea), and sugar. Astor repackaged many of the products for shipment immediately to England and Germany. A single voyage could yield up to $50,000, and Astor did not hesitate to purchase the best ships with ever-larger cargo holds. Although John Fitch's early steam-powered ship designs had proved a financial flop, already Robert Fulton had begun a search for profitable interior U.S. routes, and both steam and iron were in the not-distant future for overseas sailing trade. Thus, Astor kept his eye on the technology and on China, recognizing the new opportunities for the extension of this fur trading business when the Jefferson administration purchased the Louisiana Territory from France in 1803.

Despite the fact that the Mackinac Company, a Canadian enterprise, controlled the fur trade in the upper Mississippi Valley, Astor treated the region as though it were his own. He envisioned New York as the departure point westward for trading operations and eastward for sales operations. In 1808, Astor's American Fur Company received a charter from the New York legislature, but the establishment of actual trading posts came slowly. The company's central outpost, Astoria, founded in 1811 in the Pacific Northwest at the mouth of the Columbia River, fell to an Indian uprising. And Astor's main competitor was the U.S. government, which also operated a series of fur trading posts.

Using the Hudson Bay example, Astor established a managerial hierarchy within the fur trade. John and his son William directed the collecting and packaging of furs in New York; William Matthews outfitted trades and set them on their way from Montreal; and a pair of managers administered the Mackinac trading post, which itself soon became a business hub. A typical post featured office buildings, storehouses, sleeping quarters, a store, and facilities for smiths, artisans, and mechanics. An army of boatmen and interpreters annually went into the interiors from Montreal and Mackinac to a series of small stations on the frontier in Wisconsin, Illinois, and Michigan. At those posts, traders and trappers brought furs to exchange for goods transported by the boatmen. Since money was scarce, the furs themselves often circulated as currency.[17]

Despite his determination for success, Astor had more than a few undesirable character traits. He became so obsessed with saving pennies that it negatively affected other elements of his operations, while his notorious examination of the most minute items from each trading outfit's ledger books placed incredible pressure on the post supervisors to pay the lowest possible wages, even to the detriment of productivity. The lowest employees, the engages, received minimal wages and yet paid high prices at the early company stores established by Astor. His sophistication in forcing prices down in the urban areas pushed him toward uncivil treatment of his most necessary employees, another unwise business practice.

Astor finally forced the U.S. government out of the fur business, but eventually, of course, the market caught up with Astor, too. Competitors—independent traders—lured Astor's engages into more remunerative employment and obtained pelts from the Indians for higher prices. Over a period of fifteen years, his profits from the fur trade fell. New pioneer traders, such as Jim Bridger, opened the trans-Mississippi West to the Rocky Mountains, making their own connections and freezing out Astor, who sold his fur interests in 1834.[18]

Meanwhile, beginning with an investment of $80,000, Astor had developed a secondary business in Manhattan real estate. He purchased extensive chunks of New York real estate that was increasing at astounding rates: In 1813, Astor purchased $30,000 worth of Manhattan property, the value of which by 1819 surpassed $715,000. Among Astor's holdings was a tract of land called Greenwich Village. He sold the lots for $1,000 each, making a profit of 200 percent. In addition to being an astute fur trader, Astor was then revered as a "marvelous short-term speculator and real estate financier."[19] He further expanded into purchases of large sums of government bonds, often buying the bonds at large discounts. Then, in a dramatic burst of investment energy, he poured $1.25 million into Manhattan real estate between 1820 and 1848. Recognizing value, Astor purchased huge quantities of real estate that had plummeted in price during the Panic of 1837. He also realized that improving the lots and upgrading the property increased the value of his housing.

Thus, John Jacob Astor represented the new breed of entrepreneur who appeared on the scene in the early 1800s. He understood the necessity for and the role of management. Business dominated his life, as seen in his skimpy record of philanthropy. In stark contrast to the captains of industry who would appear after the Civil War—Andrew Carnegie, John D. Rockefeller, and others—Astor's few contributions totaled only a half-million dollars. But to say that he did not "give back" to the community would be wrong: Astor provided jobs for thousands and property for thousands more, virtually building Manhattan with his real estate ventures.

NEW COMMERCIAL VENTURES IN THE EARLY REPUBLIC

Astor's transition from managing a fur trading operation to real estate reflected the changing business specialties deemed important in the Jeffersonian era. Another one of those new areas was insurance, primarily fire and shipping insurance. Early insurance organizations were made famous by Edward Lloyd's London coffeehouse, which was a meeting place for merchants who pooled their funds to insure cargoes putting to sea. Insurance companies reached America with the creation of Benjamin Franklin's Philadelphia Contributorship for the Insurance of Houses from Loss by Fire (1752). By 1800, thirty-three insurance companies existed, including the Philadelphia-based Insurance Company of North America (INA, 1790), the Massachusetts Fire and Marine Company (1795), and the Insurance Company of New York (1796). Many, such as the INA, offered life insurance policies, although marine insurance remained the most significant source of revenue. Not until the 1840s did companies concentrate on selling life insurance, which farmers—still the majority of the nation's population—viewed as "downright useless and probably immoral, since it put a price on death."[20]

Both the appearance of insurance and Astor's real estate ventures reflected the impact of urbanization, allowing economies of scale to produce demand for new products and services, putting a premium on land. New York's population grew from 33,000 in 1790 to 313,000 in 1840, and Philadelphia's grew from 42,000 to 200,000 over the same period. The entire nation counted only 3.9 million souls in 1790, but by 1820, the South Atlantic region alone (as defined by the U.S. Census) exceeded 3 million.[21] But if the nation remained substantially rural, with thirteen of fourteen people living in rural areas as late as 1810, market influences generated by concentrations of people nevertheless expanded the "urban attitude."

Cities themselves reflected the staggering benefits already provided by early industrialization, with life spans increasing and health improving. One "weakness" constantly highlighted by critics of the Industrial Revolution—the crowded conditions of cities—in truth, illustrated one of its commanding victories: People who would have died in previous generations now lived, and they competed for the manufacturing jobs. Urban life also created new opportunities for manufacturers who, thanks to broader demand, pursued mass production of items previously made by artisans. That led to economies of scale, or the ability to maintain a profit by reducing per-unit cost of items through higher production. American entrepreneurs learned to take advantage of high-volume, low-cost sales. Urbanization also brought in close proximity numerous ancillary or support businesses to an individual's primary business. For instance, blacksmiths benefited from having a leatherworks close by because consumers with horses could attend to all their riding needs at once. Clothiers and furriers complemented each other. Most businesses used banks and many wanted insurance companies nearby. General merchants found that their businesses boomed from supplying other establishments.

Expanded production often required more than rising demand and additional funds: It demanded technological and organizational breakthroughs. Such was the case with textiles. Wool spinning factories had already appeared in New England in the 1790s, and by the early 1800s, spinning machines developed by Richard Arkwright had reached America in large numbers. At almost the same time, Henry Maudslay, a locksmith who had walked out of his London job, established his own workshop that soon took on the task of manufacturing wooden ships' blocks (from block-and-tackle devices) using a moving metal screw to carve the wood. Maudslay's lathe system used a series of belts and pulleys in a mass-production system, based on an idea given to him by Marc Brunel, a Frenchman who, it seems, had gone to England from America, where he had visited musket factories.[22]

Once again, Jefferson played a crucial role. As ambassador to France, he had seen the work of a French gunsmith who conceived of creating identical parts for his weapons, so Jefferson churned up support for the concept of "interchangeable parts." At the same time, a young inventor named Eli Whitney had brazenly bid for a government contract to make 12,000 muskets. On Jefferson's advice, Presidents Washington and Adams pushed through Congress a contract for Whitney in 1798. Whitney's ideas were hardly original: Two other gunmakers, John Hall and Simeon North, had started mass-producing guns by then. North, who had made farm equipment before switching to gun manufacture, had built the first standardized milling machine that ensured weapons parts built to preset specifications. But Whitney clearly adopted the threefold process of using standardized parts (borrowed from France), mass production (borrowed from Arkwright and Maudslay), and simple design (which Whitney may have arrived at on his own). Those elements formed the foundations of the "American system" of manufacturing. Working with gauges that standardized dyes, Whitney's system turned every worker or unskilled laborer into a craftsman. Power machinery took care of some aspects of mass production, while the standardization of the parts ensured interchangeability.[23]

Whitney had worked on his father's farm in Connecticut, spending a great deal of his time in the workshop. He produced metal instruments at the forge, earning a reputation as a blacksmith. After gaining a modest educational background, Whitney enrolled in Yale, from which he graduated in 1792. At Yale, Whitney met Phineas Miller, who managed properties in South Carolina for Catherine Greene. Miller managed to get Whitney a position as a tutor. Whitney—well familiar with farmwork—carefully watched the operations of the plantation, especially the difficulty with which slaves separated the seeds from cotton fibers. He devised a machine that featured a feeding bin, a short chute, and two rollers (one with teeth). The teeth strained the fiber through, leaving the seeds to fall below in a box; a second roller with brush-type teeth swept the cotton fiber from the first, at which point the worker cleaned the cotton off the roller for baling and shipping. Cleaning a single pound of upland cotton required a full day's work; but after Whitney's invention of the gin, a slave could process fifty times that much. From 1810 to 1860, production of cotton per slave rose from 119 pounds per day to 759 pounds per day.[24] Unfortunately, for Whitney, his machine, though patented, was so easy to copy that he never reaped the fortune he deserved from his invention. He joined Miller in a partnership, which allowed Whitney to return to New Haven to produce the gins while Miller, who proposed to conduct ginning activities, paid 60 percent of the profit to Whitney. After the copies of his gin proliferated, and after numerous fruitless suits, Whitney turned his attention to meeting a government contract for muskets, which is in fact what led him to the American system of manufacturing that is often, yet incorrectly, credited to him.[25] But regardless of the degree to which Whitney invented the American system, it is a fascinating point of history that he was, as much as any individual, personally responsible for the growing differences between North and South. His musket manufacturing embodied the new manufacturing systems that had started to dominate the North, while his cotton gin enabled the South to shift into a single-crop cotton economy and ensured the perpetuation of a profitable slave system. Indeed, it would be reasonable to argue that, aside from the first American presidents, no person was more responsible for creating the young United States as a stable world power than Mr. Whitney.

Some scholars, arguing for more government intervention in the marketplace, have claimed that the government, not Whitney and other entrepreneurs, sparked the key changes in the armories.[26] However, Donald Hoke's study of technology in early America concludes that "the American System is primarily and overwhelmingly a private sector phenomenon."[27]

But where the government expressed a desire for a product, enterprising individuals certainly sprang up to fill the demand. A case in point was Samuel Colt, perhaps the most famous gun manufacturer of all time. Like so many other early innovators, Colt hailed from Connecticut and had gone to sea while still a teenager. The story of the invention of the revolving pistol has several versions. In one telling of the story, Colt, on board a ship bound for India, carved a wooden pistol with a rotating cartridge cylinder that allowed for multiple shots without reloading.[28] After patenting his design in 1836 and hiring a highly paid gunsmith to make the weapons, Colt continuously waited for the demand of his product to rise. However, the orders did not come flooding in. Quite the contrary, Colt, employing hokum later associated with P. T. Barnum, traveled the nation as a chemical expert demonstrating laughing gas (nitrous oxide) for an admission fee of fifty cents per person. He finally obtained support from a cousin to start an arms manufacturing company, but his products did not impress the Army at a competition at West Point. By 1842, Colt's factory was deeply in debt and closed. Colt himself left for New York and took up the study of law for a time.

Actually, though, Colt's "first love" was even more remarkable than the revolver. Colt experimented with waterproof cartridges and antiship mines—what were characterized as "aquatic pyrotechnics."[29] He worked with concepts developed by Robert Fulton and Samuel Morse to connect underwater explosives with a telemagnetic cable, and in 1844 he blew up a 500-ton schooner sailing down the Potomac, much to the glee of an audience of thousands who gathered for the fireworks. Employing a theatrical touch, Colt even touched off two "decoy" or "dummy" mines first, deliberately misleading the crowd into thinking he had failed miserably!

After the Western frontier opened, however, settlers and ranchers suddenly realized after several encounters with the Plains Indians that they needed a portable weapon, one that did not require reloading after every shot, for use while on horseback. The popularity of the Colt five-shot revolver soared. In 1844, using revolvers purchased before Colt's factory closed, sixteen Texas Rangers fought a battle with Indians who outnumbered them five to one, yet emerged victorious. The Rangers sang the praises of Colt's weapon across Texas, ultimately making the Colt .45 caliber virtually synonymous with frontier self-defense. Although still in debt at the time of the Mexican War—at which point Colt tried, unsuccessfully, to enlist—the inventor received a contract for 1,000 revolvers. Lacking a factory, he subcontracted to Eli Whitney, Jr., who had his father's musket operations, and borrowed a small loan from Elisha Colt, Samuel's uncle. The Texas Rangers also put in a special order for a new, larger caliber handgun, which Colt produced as a six-shot .44 called the Walker, literally named for Colt's avid supporter—Walker, Texas Ranger. Overnight, orders for both weapons streamed in. To fill the orders, he opened a new armory at Hartford, placed under the management of Elisha Root, an expert in mechanical systems.

At the Hartford armory, Colt installed "over a thousand belt-driven machines that allowed him to produce a revolver that was 80 percent machine made."[30] Only then, after repeated failures, disappointments, part-time jobs, and utter poverty, did Colt become wealthy. After miscues, patent problems, and years of personal debt, Colt turned his first profit in 1849. He also became famous. Invited by the British to establish a factory in England, Colt set up an armory on the Thames. (Whitney had declined such an appeal.) Colt was far more attuned to salesmanship than Whitney and even "recognized the euphonic appeal and symbolic potential of his name. 'Sam Colt' has all the snap and crackle of the pop icon he became."[31] The British press referred to him as "Colonel Colt, a Thunderbolt," while Samuel himself adopted the powerful moniker of a stallion known as a "rampant" (i.e., a dominant colt) as his trademark. Even before Colt's arrival, though, the English manufacturers had started to recognize that American technology and manufacturing processes had outstripped their own. Those manufacturing techniques spilled over, diffusing into a spectrum of consumer products that further accelerated the rise of the mass market.

MANUFACTURING BUSINESSES: THE ORIGINAL "MANAGERIAL REVOLUTION"

Entrepreneurs broke new ground in product design and manufacture, but they also blazed new paths in managerial techniques and strategies. By 1800, mass-production techniques, powered by steam engines characteristic of the Industrial Revolution, spread throughout America. Several manufacturing industries already had incorporated the acquisition of raw materials, the production of a product, and the distribution of the finished good into a single system. Traditionally, historians have accepted the thesis, advanced in Alfred Chandler's *The Visible Hand*, that vertical integration of that type did not appear until the 1850s, when the "managerial revolution" started with the railroads. Subsequent work, however, has cast doubt on that claim. In at least two major areas, iron production and publishing, signs of vertical integration appeared long before the railroads used that strategy. In New York, for example, iron production thrived as merchants expanded their businesses to deal in iron and iron products and developed sophisticated systems of production, warehousing, transporting, and sales.[32] Some of the earliest colonial commercial ventures involved digging iron ore and smelting it, with Virginia shipping the ore to England as early as 1609. Blast furnaces appeared in the 1640s, and by 1776, iron ore furnaces existed in every colony except Georgia. The production of so-called pig iron took place at large forges, and then the iron was molded into bars at a smaller forge. From that point, the iron manufacturer sold the iron to blacksmiths or fabricators who made smaller iron parts. By the early 1800s, the iron firms already had incorporated integrated factories and sales of shares of ownership to stockholders, making the iron firms among the first to employ permanent managers separate from ownership. Nearly 200 iron merchants operated in New York City alone by 1800, segmenting into specializations such as makers of pots and kettles, anchor manufacturers, and "hand" or curling iron producers. Customers included blacksmiths, masons, cutlers, shipbuilders, and anyone else needing a variety of hardware goods.

Iron production benefited from new marketing strategies, which somewhat offset the industry's allegiance to charcoal instead of coal. The principal sources of bituminous coal, needed to make coke to purify the iron, were found west of the Appalachians. By the 1840s, however, metallurgists found a way to make anthracite coal productive, and iron productivity swiftly shot up to levels equal to those of textiles.[33] David Thomas (1794–1882), a Welsh ironmaster, blazed the trail in the use of anthracite coal to make iron, constructing a number of furnaces for the Lehigh Crane Iron Company.[34] He created Lehigh Fire Brick Works to supply bricks for his blast furnaces and, at the time of his retirement in 1879, paved the way for vertically integrating a company.[35]

While mill designs and production innovations in iron traveled from ironmaster to ironmaster by word of mouth, the need for detailed, precise plans increasingly characterized the industry. And while reputation and personal recommendations represented the most trusted form of advertising, a new industry that had only recently come on the scene contributed heavily to the success of the iron manufacturers in reproducing and circulating designs and aided merchants in selling their product through the printed page.

A critical part of the iron industry's sales strategy, published advertising, itself depended on a broadening literate class of consumers. The early 1800s witnessed a dramatic upsurge in American publishing. Whereas Revolutionary broadsides rolled off hand-cranked presses in the hundreds, by 1840, weekly circulations of large newspapers exceeded 100,000. A decade later, the weekly story paper, *The Ledger*, poured out of a single factory at the rate of 400,000 per week! Book titles only numbered in the hundreds as late as the 1830s, but by 1850 the number neared 80,000. As one scholar noted, "The same individual enterprise at work in building ... early textile industries operated as well in the world of literature. These publishers and writers, book-sellers, periodical dealers, wholesalers—everyone involved in producing the printed word—were speculators on the frontier of economic development."[36]

By the 1850s, book publishers adopted the innovations first used by the ironmasters, organizing integrated factory systems, diversifying their products, developing mass marketing and advertising campaigns, and gaining managerial control over the market. As early as 1825, the firm of John and Sidney Babcock deployed managers to handle a wide variety of supervisory tasks; two decades later, the large publishing houses of Harper and Brothers in New York and Frederick Gleason in Boston had "brought together in one plant all aspects of book production: editing, printing, binding, storage, shipping, retail and wholesale sales, and, in some cases, even authorship and type founding."[37] Thus, in a half-dozen different ways, the publishing industry (like the iron industry) predated the managerial revolution.[38] Only in a single area, that of separating ownership from management through the creation of a class of stockholders, did iron manufacturers and publishers fail to anticipate changes decades later. Indeed, the evolution of American enterprise suggests that those and other early businesses had initiated the change, and the railroads adopted it at a later date.

SAMUEL SLATER AND THE LOWELL MILLS

Ironically, the first manufacturing sector to expand hardly used any of the new managerial concepts at all. Textiles, however, took advantage of formidable new technologies that increased an individual laborer's output ten times over. Once again, an immigrant made the most revolutionary contributions to the business.

Samuel Slater, an apprentice in an English textile mill, gained a detailed knowledge of the operations of textile firms by 1789, when he arrived in the United States. Slater had worked on Arkwright's spinning machines, and he observed that the "perpetual card and spinning" process developed by the Englishman had not yet reached America. Taking a job in a small mill in New York, he learned of Moses Brown, a Providence, Rhode Island, manufacturer who had specialized in candles. Brown and his brothers had capital; Slater had expertise. Assisted by a family of Pawtucket artisans, Slater built a small mill using the Arkwright designs that he memorized while in England. In 1790, the Slater spindle, using water power, started to produce textiles, marking the first mechanical weaving process in the United States. Within twenty years, Slater or his associates controlled half the spinning mills operating in the United States, causing Brown to write to his children, "Our people had 'cotton mill fever.'"[39] At maturity in the 1830s, Slater's mills had over 9,500 spindles, and his business interests spanned several state lines. His companies diversified into wholesaling and marketing, although he carefully limited the variety of his products to a minimal number.

Slater, like Whitney, showed that the first entrepreneur to develop a process did not necessarily know how to run it most efficiently (although Slater accumulated a fortune by the standards of the 1800s). He frequently missed opportunities to install more up-to-date equipment; he remained extensively dependent on capital from his friends; and his outlook remained rooted in the traditional single-owner business structure, with Slater firmly—and totally—in control.

Consequently, it took another aspiring businessman, Francis Cabot Lowell, to introduce the kinds of inventory controls and distribution systems needed to take advantage of the prodigious output of Slater's mills. Lowell did share one trait with Slater that proved indispensable in gaining access to loom technology: a keen memory. Born into a merchant family, Lowell attended Harvard—which suspended him after he started a bonfire on the university's yard—and he moved into the family's trading business until Jefferson's 1807 trade embargo virtually ended all international trade. But that stimulus led Lowell and other American merchants to develop their own textile manufacturing. After a visit to England, where he absorbed the latest weaving technology, Lowell took advantage of the dearth of foreign products during the War of 1812 and united with a group of Boston merchants and formed the Boston Manufacturing Company in 1813, located at Waltham, Massachusetts. The operation—converted from a paper mill—had double the capitalization of Slater's mills ($300,000) and, more important, featured an integrated manufacturing process that incorporated then-separate processes for spinning, dying, and printing.

The Waltham mill used water to turn gears and pulleys, running a number of spinning processes at one time. It allowed the flow of production along an organized, steady series of steps. Production was simplified and standardized, as well as measured with a primitive accounting formula devised by Lowell. By 1822, five years after Lowell died, the investors searched for additional sites with abundant water and found a location on the Merrimack River. Incorporated as the Merrimack Manufacturing Company in 1822, the mill needed large numbers of new employees, whom the proprietors found as young women, most of them from rural areas where the meager production coming from inferior lands forced the women into domestic manufacturing. Already possessing some independence from the home because of their contributions in manufacture, the young women moved into a wider arena of social independence. The Waltham owners, recognizing they had to make the factories attractive places to work, created "a social environment in the mills that was both protective of young women and conducive to the development of intellectual independence from parental authority."[40] In addition to paying good wages and offering a reasonably clean working environment, the Lowell mill boarded the women in dormitory-type arrangements, from which Lowell and his investors anticipated the women would leave after a few years for marriage. The women (called the "Lowell girls") worked ten-hour days, and although the mills were relatively isolated, the women were under strict supervision to defuse any potential objection from farm families.

By 1845, the Merrimack Company's five cotton mills rolled out a quarter-million yards of cloth each week from its 1,300 looms. Its capital had risen to $5 million, making most of its original investors wealthy. More significantly, the Lowell mills showed that the new organizational gains made in iron and publishing and the technological gains made by Whitney could be translated to yet another industry—one on the precipice of explosive growth. The experiment with the "Lowell girls" proved less successful, and soon the mills resorted to hiring recent immigrants. Economists have yet to sort out the exact reasons the mills changed, but whatever the cause, the mills soon found themselves resembling the impoverished English towns Lowell was determined to avoid.

Of course, any industry begins and ends with the entrepreneur, whether Astor's fur trade or Lowell's textile mills. And virtually anything could be sold and marketed under the right conditions. Frederick Tudor, for example, did not exactly "sell ice to Eskimos," but he did sell ice, and lots of it! Tudor was one of those "rich kids" that everyone envies while growing up: His father was a lawyer, his brothers all went to Harvard, and his family had enough money that Tudor did not have to work in any but the most comfortable surroundings. Tudor, instead, left school at age 13 to take a job as an apprentice with a spice merchant, during which time he became acquainted with food preservation. In 1805, while at a party, Frederick and his brother discussed the potential for harvesting ice from New England ponds and shipping it south. They explored the demand with merchants in Martinique and other Caribbean islands.[41]

Supported with a small investment from his cousin, Tudor spent $10,000 to carve and ship 130 tons of ice to Martinique. Although he sold much of his stock, Tudor realized that people who had never used ice before would need an introduction to the use of ice in storage and food preparation. Thus, he had to educate as well as sell. His inventory melted, leaving him with a $4,000 loss at the time he sailed for Cuba to negotiate still more contracts. Twice he verged on bankruptcy, hiding on the family farm as the creditors pursued him. His business had virtually died, and most people would have given up, but not Tudor. After the War of 1812, with connections all but severed with many of his previous customers, Tudor redoubled his efforts to fashion new markets. He explored demand in the South, traveling through states to demonstrate the value of ice packs to doctors and staging side-by-side comparisons of iced drinks to warm drinks for bar patrons. Indeed, Tudor gleaned that iced drinks would become a national standard, and he envisioned ice as a central component of every saloon. He identified a prominent bar and provided the owner with ice for a year, free, as a way of promoting his product.

By the 1820s, Tudor annually shipped 2,000 tons of ice from the Boston area (two-thirds of the total) for about $0.10 per pound. Realizing that it was only a matter of time before a wave of competition caught up to him, he improved the harvesting, delivery, and storage of ice. Efficiencies and cost cutting, he reasoned, could enable him to store additional ice for shipment later. Testing his methods in Havana, Tudor built aboveground insulated sheds, experimenting with everything from wood shavings to sheepskins to maintain cold temperatures. At the same time, he met Nathaniel Wyeth, a hotel owner who wanted to sell ice in southern regions. Wyeth patented an ice cutter in 1825 that sawed deep trenches in pond ice, allowing manual laborers to finish the harvesting by making the last cuts and prying up the blocks. Tudor and Wyeth negotiated an agreement for Tudor to obtain the patent, giving Wyeth the position as manager of the ice company.

Tudor's markets extended as far as Calcutta by 1838, then areas in the Middle East. He not only constructed ice depots, but educated local residents in the manufacture of small refrigerators. By 1846, Tudor, who had started harvesting ice at Walden Pond, Massachusetts, accounted for much of the 65,000 tons of ice shipped from Boston each year. A number of middle-class Americans had iceboxes in their homes by the time of the Civil War, a development that was made possible only by the availability of ice. Frederick Tudor changed the very nature of American consumer culture by altering not only what people ate and drank, but when they could eat and drink.

MERCHANTS, FINANCE, AND COMMERCIAL BANKING

Already the capital demands of businesses such as the Merrimack Company or the Boston Manufacturing Company had started to exceed what friends and families could supply. Stock sales raised initial capital, but could not provide the daily working capital needed by any enterprise. Instead, merchants and early industrialists needed a way to allow the public to invest in their businesses without purchasing stock, in essence lending the entrepreneurs money without formal repayment times or schedules. They accomplished that by creating commercial banks.

As a rule, two types of banks emerged: private and publicly incorporated (or chartered) banks.[42] Private banks accepted deposits, made loans, and traded in foreign exchange. However, they usually did not issue their own notes—paper money—and did not have to obtain a charter from the state legislature. The absence of a charter did not necessarily constitute a disadvantage, because it also meant that the business did not have to submit to any kind of regulatory oversight. On the other hand, incorporated or chartered banks generally issued notes and had to undergo regular (usually annual) examinations and disclose their capital to state officials.[43] The term *private* referred to a bank's unchartered status, not ownership: Like "private" banks, all chartered banks were privately owned, except for a handful of banks chartered by states, such as the Bank of Tennessee.

One example of a private banking firm that emerged from primarily mercantile activities was Alexander Brown & Sons, founded in 1800 by a successful Irish auctioneer. Brown and his four sons, who ran the business after his death, carried on an extensive transatlantic trade with English cotton merchants, importing linen and exporting cotton, rice, or any other goods that were in demand. The oldest son, William, moved to England in 1809 to solidify the company's grip on the other side of the ocean. Gradually, the Browns came to emphasize finance over commerce and by the mid-1800s even moved their headquarters from Baltimore, where Alexander Brown had started, to New York City. Since the bank did not issue its own notes, it could establish offices, or branches, in a number of locations, including Boston, New Orleans, Philadelphia, and Liverpool, as well as, of course, Baltimore. According to historian Edwin Perkins, the Browns had a reputation as the preeminent banking house that financed Anglo-American trade.[44]

Other private bankers came from the ranks of shop owners and, later, railroaders or planters, such as William Johnston of South Carolina.[45] Less common in sheer numbers than the private banks, but better known to history, were the chartered banks. Using the Bank of North America as a model, several state legislatures chartered new institutions in the pre-1800 period, when more than thirty banks existed. Between 1790 and 1830, those businesses increased their capital stock from $3 million to $168 million as major institutions appeared in Boston, Baltimore, New York, and Philadelphia. The Bank of New York's charter was drafted by no one less qualified than Alexander Hamilton. Gradually, the banking boom (in which banks multiplied by a factor of twelve in the first two decades of the 1800s) centered on New England. There, growth rates exceeded 20 percent, and every town came to expect its own bank.[46]

Early chartered banks received their charter—their "license" to print money—from the state legislatures after drafting a petition in which the owners spelled out the details of their business. Charters still implied special privilege and, in many people's minds, monopoly powers; therefore the bank owners had to show that they were providing a public service, not merely making a profit or financing their own activities. Owners put up their own capital, in the form of gold or silver specie (coins), then issued notes, which they put into circulation through loans. The specie reserve stood as a guarantee that the notes would be honored, although no specific reserves were required in the charters. A legislature could refuse to grant a charter based on its perception that a bank's capital was inadequate, but once the bank received its charter, the legislature more or less lost control of its activities. Banks regulated their own functions based on the amount of specie they kept in their vaults as a reserve against the notes they issued. If a bank issued too many notes, its reserves plunged, creating the danger of failure; and if it did not issue enough, its reserves—and thus, unemployed capital—lingered in the vaults. The trick was to find exactly the proper balance between employed specie and note holders' demand. That constituted the essence of all modern commercial banking, *fractional reserve banking*, in which banks maintain only a small portion of funds on hand relative to the amount of deposits (or claims against the bank) outstanding at any given time. While charters did not specify the reserve level or reserve ratio, a bank's failure to redeem notes in specie could result in the legislature revoking the charter, and some states even allowed flogging the directors of a failed bank!

When many banks experienced "runs," or people lining up to redeem their notes, it was called a "panic" or "run." If it appeared that a panic had started, few banks maintained sufficient reserves to redeem all their outstanding notes (based on their practice of fractional reserve banking). Since banks could not pay out sufficient specie during a panic, they suspended specie payments, essentially telling customers, "We cannot give you gold and silver today, but maybe in a day or two we can." If an individual bank suspended specie payments alone, a panic could spread to solvent or nonsuspended banks. But if all the banks in a city or region suspended together, they could break the runs and end the panic. In such a case, the legislature seldom revoked the charters of all the banks, for then no one would have access to loans or notes. More important, although note holders—and the public in general—groused about most suspensions, they accepted them as one of the inconveniences of business, much like getting the wrong order at a modern drive-through restaurant. In large part, such an attitude developed because most suspensions were highly localized and/or temporary. But when a panic became national, and banks across the nation suspended, the public grew outraged.

STEPHEN GIRARD AND THE SECOND BANK OF THE UNITED STATES

A national panic occurred in 1814, when many banks labored under the credit-generation necessities related to the War of 1812. Americans blamed the chaos on the number of new banks created without restraint, issuing calls for some degree of control over the financial system. In 1811, Congress had allowed the charter of the First BUS to expire. Several factors contributed to the death of the country's first national bank, including concerns about the influence of foreign stockholders, the bank's privileged position, and a sweeping hostility to elites that started to surge through the young nation. After the war, those demanding that Congress charter a new national bank to restrain the issues of the state-chartered banks prevailed. In 1816, Congress obliged by chartering the Second BUS, again owned four-fifths by private stockholders. It had a capitalization three and a half times larger than the First BUS, but otherwise resembled the original in structure and special advantages, especially its interstate branching powers.

Stephen Girard of Philadelphia, a French immigrant orphaned at age 12, played a key role in persuading Congress to create the Second BUS.[47] Girard had made himself into an able captain and ship's pilot by age 24, whereupon he started to deliver cargoes from the West Indies to New York. During the Revolution, he docked in Philadelphia, where he turned his efforts to merchandising. By 1807, Girard had ships spread across the ocean and cargoes stretched across Europe. The situation with the Napoleonic Wars convinced Girard that he needed to get his merchandise and transports out of harm's way and repatriate his assets to the United States, either in government bonds or by purchasing shares in the First BUS.

The demise of the First BUS coincided with the high point of Girard's asset relocation, and by 1812 he had $1 million in cash that cried out for investment. He invested in the office of the defunct national bank, opening a bank under his sole ownership, supplied with a capitalization of $1.5 million. Within two years, the bank's capital doubled. Girard's reputation and influence grew to the point that, like Robert Morris before him and J. P. Morgan after him, he almost single-handedly bailed out the government from dire financial straits. Washington's sudden drop in tariff revenues left the government precariously close to bankruptcy, and Congress requested an $11 million loan, but subscriptions reached only $6 million. Girard and John Jacob Astor then rescued the Treasury by forming a syndicate to raise $10 million.

THE NEW YORK STOCK EXCHANGE AND THE SECURITIES MARKET

Financing manufacturing and commerce through pools of local capital proved adequate for new business and local companies. Entrepreneurs engaged in larger-scale enterprises needed to sell stock to a wider universe of investors. In 1792, a group of twenty-four New York City merchants and brokers forged an agreement to standardize their commission fees on the new federal government bonds issued to pay the debts left from the Revolution.[48] The brokers continued to deal in their securities on Wall Street, but the activity remained at a low level until after the War of 1812, when the number of securities issues started to expand. When the brokers formally organized the New York Stock Exchange (NYSE) in 1817, they adopted a constitution to establish trading and administration rules. Gaining membership in the NYSE required that the trader operate a brokerage business for a year and win a vote of the existing members, making the exchange a somewhat restrictive club. Members met twice daily to buy and sell securities in a "call market," a term taken from the practice of reading the name of each stock from the podium, at which time the brokers called out their bids to buy and shouted their orders to sell. When the president heard two brokers agree on a price, he announced the sale, which was then recorded by a secretary. When all the sales of that particular stock had terminated, the president moved to the next security.

Until the 1830s, most of the securities traded on the NYSE were federal, state, and municipal government bonds. That situation changed with the influx of new railroad, mining, and insurance companies in the 1830s; then, after the Civil War, the number of securities swelled to more than 300, mostly coming from railroad companies in need of capital. Of course, the securities of all companies were not traded on the NYSE. Instead, outside on the streets the curbstone brokers dealt in those stocks not traded inside. Those brokers formed the New York Curb Exchange, and later made up the American Stock Exchange.

FINANCE FOR OTHER BUSINESSES: THE ROLE OF MONEY AND NOTES

Agriculture and commerce were financed in a much different way, using short-term credit to get from planting time to harvest. Those short-term loans came in the form of paper signed to the borrower. Often, planters in the interior areas endorsed those notes to intermediaries in New Orleans, Mobile, Savannah, or other coastal cities. That allowed planters to purchase seed and implements in the cities, then return to the plantations to raise the crops. Merchants, on the other hand, frequently borrowed and were given notes redeemable in gold or silver at the bank. These notes or "IOUs" were used to pay for goods. Consequently, a blizzard of bank and personal notes circulated throughout the United States in the antebellum period.

It might appear that no one could transact business with such a diversity of money instruments. In fact, the system was relatively stable and fairly systematic. Bankers and large merchants maintained a book, published annually, called *Dillistin's Bank Note Reporter*, which provided up-to-date information about the value of most banknotes in existence. If a note arrived in Baltimore from a bank in New Orleans, the bank teller checked the note against the *Reporter*, which told the teller the discount. If a note had a one percent discount (considered high for all but the most distant notes), the bank knew that the money was not as valuable as one trading at a 0.5 percent discount. Distance counted: The further away the source of the note, the greater cost involved in redeeming it and thus the higher the discount.

TRADE REVISITED: THE SOURCE OF AMERICAN BUSINESS GROWTH

Once the financial structure expanded sufficiently to provide a variety of financial instruments to merchants, industrialists, small businessmen, and farmers, American enterprise increasingly found itself able to compete in the international markets. Trade with England and Europe, made possible by American business's unique set of comparative advantages, drove the expansion of the early 1800s in which exports grew at a level of 6 percent to 7 percent of the GNP. Trade centered on agricultural production or processed food, such as flour, with raw materials and grains comprising two-thirds of United States exports, while manufacturing—for all its revolutionary innovation—made up less than one-quarter. Cotton dominated all other exports and thus financed expansion in other sectors. For all its export growth, the United States did not have a favorable balance of trade from the 1820s to the 1870s, the period of greatest growth in the nineteenth century.

Nevertheless, a heated debate arose over the role of tariffs, especially protective tariffs. Of course, Hamilton proposed the tariff in his 1791 *Report on Manufactures*, arguing that "disparities" in the maturity of American industry relative to that of Britain required that the government "protect" U.S. manufacturing. Without protection, infant American companies might be overwhelmed by foreign competitors. It was an appeal that virtually all small or new producers have used ever since: Established companies (or countries) have advantages and reserves that allow them to lower prices and eliminate competitors.

No industry seemed to have a greater claim to protection than early textile manufacturing, which faced the most potent industrial power in the world, England. American cloth (of much lower quality than that made in Britain) sold for 10.17 cents a yard, while English competitors exported linen at 12.77 cents a yard, but had to pay a duty of 8.75 cents, making the final price 21.52 cents a yard. American manufacturers had a cushion of over 11 cents a yard. Taking advantage of the learning curve, domestic manufacturers should have achieved higher productivity and lower costs.

John Jacob Astor characterized a new type of entrepreneur who greeted a new era in American business. Gradually, market ideas had displaced mercantilist mentalities. The role of the government in the economy had been established—occasionally as a participant, but more often as an umpire—and most entrepreneurs thought in terms of market first, government favors second (if at all). Private sector advances in clock-making, gun manufacture, and textiles placed American business on a plane close to that of England, and in some cases, ahead of European rivals. New managerial innovations in iron production and publishing had initiated sweeping changes that made possible substantial efficiencies and extended business markets.

Entrepreneurs took the pro-growth land policies of Jefferson, combined with the stable financial structure founded by Hamilton, and applied American innovation. As a result, pioneers like Slater, Whitney, and Colt established the basis for manufacturing in the United States, while individuals like Stephen Girard and Alexander Brown provided the capital and commercial ties. Within the subsequent three decades, a revolution in transportation brought their efforts together in ways they scarcely could have imagined.

CHAPTER **4**

The Entrepreneurial Explosion:
1820–1850

Perhaps no age in American history—save the modern—has witnessed as explosive growth in business and entrepreneurship as the so-called "Middle Period," or the era from the Missouri Compromise to the end of the Mexican War. Private enterprise, especially small businesses, flourished. Fueled by waves of immigrants who came for the cheap land and for opportunity, businesses expanded to accommodate the new demand. Europeans flooded in, eager to acquire land in the "West" (Ohio and Kentucky). For a mere $160, a family could acquire 640 acres—a virtual estate in Europe—and by the 1820s, when land prices dropped below $2 an acre, the simplest European peasant could own his own farm. As millions of acres were transferred from the hands of the government to individuals, farming brought its own calls for better transportation networks to get crops to market.[1]

For the first time people could move from a radius of a few miles beyond the nearest town. As late as 1790, "most of the 3.9 million Americans ... still lived within a hundred miles or so of the Atlantic Coast."[2] More than 200,000 settlers populated Tennessee, Kentucky, and Western Virginia by John Adams's presidency, and by the Monroe administration at least 1.5 million had crossed the Appalachians to the

West. They faced high transportation costs on the one hand, or extremely limited localized markets on the other. Settlers, farmers, and merchants all knew that they needed cheaper ways to ship goods to the urbanized areas. The question was, how could the transportation costs be reduced, and who would do it?

GALLATIN'S PLAN

Jefferson's Secretary of the Treasury, Albert Gallatin, had an answer: "The General Government can alone remove these obstacles."[3] Gallatin delivered an extensive report to Congress in 1808 on the status of roads and canals in the United States. He outlined the benefits for the business world from a sophisticated system of internal transportation, and the challenges to developing such a network (citing, among other problems, interest rates). Gallatin then made an astonishing proposal, especially coming from one appointed by the proponent of small government, Jefferson: He recommended that Congress fund a ten-year, $20 million project in which the federal government would construct roads and canals itself or provide loans for private corporations to do so. Gallatin detailed $16 million worth of specific programs, including a canal to connect the Atlantic Coast and the Great Lakes, while he included a $3.4 million allocation for local improvements that enhanced the overall plan. By all comparisons, the plan dwarfed anything the government had ever proposed. The entire budget for the federal government in 1810 was only $10 million, and Gallatin's ambitious outlays were five times those of the government under Jefferson in 1808![4]

Jefferson had reservations about the government's role in the scheme and argued that a constitutional amendment might be needed to proceed legally. Ultimately, some elements of Gallatin's plan were enacted, such as the national road from Maryland to Wheeling, Virginia (completed in 1818). But the revenues for the plan had to come from tariffs, which had produced steadily lower returns after the troubles with Britain between 1807 and 1809. Much of the design of Gallatin's project did appear through the efforts of private entrepreneurs, not the government.

ROADS, TURNPIKES, AND ENTREPRENEURS

Early roads consisted of little more than narrow paths, well-worn Indian trails, or occasionally, logs laid crossways to traffic to form "corduroy" roads. Flat plank roads were an expensive luxury, and the cost of transportation reflected the difficulty of construction and the problems of maintenance of such roads. A trip from Boston to New York in 1820 cost $10, or two days' wages, while taking a coach to the Western frontier cities could run as high as $80.[5] Travel, under any circumstances, was tedious at best and dangerous at worst: A typical journey by coach involved the vehicle turning over at least once, and a man traveling from New York to Cincinnati in 1829 reported his coach had overturned nine times.[6] Coaches, which already clogged such European cities as Paris and London, now jammed up New York, Philadelphia, and Boston, filling them with an odor of manure from the thousands of horses and providing employment for scores of children who gathered up the defecation for pennies a bag. More substantial profits were to be made by the teamsters, who charged up to $5 to carry barrel-size cargoes ten miles over potholes and bogs, pushing road transport to $30 per ton-mile by 1815.

Reducing such costs demanded more, and much better, roads. Turnpikes, often built with the process developed by Englishman John McAdam and other English builders, consisted of solid rock or gravel foundations and flat surfaces of gravel. Flanked by drainage ditches, these roads must have looked like superhighways to early travelers. The Lancaster Turnpike Road, a sixty-two-mile artery linking Philadelphia and Lancaster, Pennsylvania, was the first attempt by private companies to provide better transportation. The company issued $300,000 worth of stock, started construction on the road in 1792, and completed it two years later at a cost of $465,000. Yet, even if the road produced strong toll traffic, it would have had to have carried a constant stream of travelers and freight to pay the $7,500-per-mile construction costs. Instead, the road only returned dividends of 2.5 percent to the stockholders. Entrepreneurs discovered that potential customers had developed a variety of toll-avoidance maneuvers, including taking side trails called "shunpikes"—short detours around tollhouses. One turnpike president estimated his company's revenue would have been 60 percent higher if not for such fraud. Perhaps at first, turnpikes may have held promise for substantial returns if the companies could police the routes and keep construction costs down. Certainly enough roads were built. Northern states witnessed a private construction boom, resulting in more than 400 road corporations chartered in the Northeast by the 1820s. Those companies raised capital through stock sales to the public, anticipating returns from the tolls. To that end, the private corporations pumped more than $6 million into New England alone, laying thousands of miles of highway—two-thirds of the nation's total by 1810. Similar levels of activity touched other northern states: Between 1812 and 1840, New York issued charters to more than 130 companies, constructing 1,500 miles of roads, while Pennsylvania chartered more than eighty turnpike corporations that invested nearly $40 million to build 2,000 miles of roads.[7]

When examining only the returns from travel on the roads, few businessmen could have justified their investments. The Salem Turnpike in Massachusetts, for example, only paid average annual dividends of 3.1 percent over sixty years, and it was considered one of the most successful of the road companies. However, measuring profits by such strict definitions of return may not provide an accurate understanding of the motivations for entrepreneurs to build roads and for stockholders to invest in them. Not surprisingly, most of the stock in turnpikes was owned in the towns through which the roads passed.[8] In Kingston, New York, for example, the local newspaper, the *Ulster Palladium*, which served as the medium for business groups to publicize their efforts, argued that bad roads "not only dampen the enterprising spirit of commerce, but would produce the same effect on agriculture and manufacture."[9] Another local paper agreed, suggesting that a turnpike would "add materially to the prosperity of the inhabitants of this village."[10] These inhabitants benefited from the fact that goods and customers could come to them, even if they never ventured onto the roads themselves. Everyone in the town benefited from the access to other areas. Those who benefit without paying are "free riders." It took the involvement of government to extract, in the form of taxes, some of these gains. On the other hand, the roads also held promise for the fledgling steam carriage industry that had started to blossom in England. But the combination of early railroads—which often received subsidies from state governments—and the horse carriage industry threw the weight of regulation toward canals and rails, and perhaps short-circuited an early steam automobile network.[11]

As a result, the purely private toll roads increasingly gave way to government-supported projects, although private roads certainly did not disappear.[12] Private road builders were clearly testing the ability of the market to pay for their endeavors, and the paltry profits returned by both public and private companies indicated that insufficient traffic existed to justify their existence yet. It remained far cheaper to ship by water. Early economic assessments of turnpikes examining comparative savings between waterborne traffic and roads—an admittedly strict form of cost analysis—reveal that fewer than 10 percent of New England's 200 turnpike businesses paid even average dividends.

Historians agree that the transportation revolution yielded economic benefits to society beyond the direct profits earned by the companies immediately involved, as when the turnpikes opened new markets, facilitated shipping, and encouraged settlement in more remote areas. Economists call those benefits "externalities," meaning that the business could not "internalize" all of the benefits to itself. However, those who celebrated the societal gains at the expense of individual turnpike entrepreneurs soon learned that externalities had a dark side, too. Companies also can shift costs to society as a whole, such as costs related to reducing or cleaning up pollution, the noxious smells, offensive sights, or blaring sounds imposed on neighbors of some businesses.

Ultimately, the issue boiled down to property rights. At what point did an entrepreneur wishing to build a road have to purchase all the land needed without resorting to eminent domain? Such pressures encouraged many otherwise independent businessmen to ally themselves with state and local governments, whereby they could acquire land in the name of "society." And transportation issues became even more clouded after 1812, when the federal government started to construct the National Road to extend from Cumberland, Maryland, to Columbus, Ohio. It represented the largest internal improvement ever undertaken by the government, justified by the need to move troops around the nation for purposes of defense. (Even this—the crown jewel of American highways—hardly qualified as a smooth, even highway in the modern sense since "contractors building the National Road ... were permitted to leave any tree stump less than eighteen inches tall in the roadway."[13]) Eventually, the National Road carried a steady stream of traffic, convincing states to lobby for federal assistance for their own road projects. Congress relented and, after 1803, required that 5 percent of the proceeds from the sale of federal land support road construction. Still later, the federal government provided surveys and mapping through the U.S. Army Corps of Engineers.[14]

PROPERTY AND LAW

Road building touched on the essence of capitalism, namely, the security of private property. The entire structure of antebellum property law evolved out of a debate over the conflict between so-called "pristine" property rights (i.e., untouched land) versus developmental rights and its associated "social return" or "social savings." James Willard Hurst's *Law and the Conditions of Freedom* analyzed that tension through numerous court cases in the early 1800s, especially focusing on cases known as the "Mill Acts."[15] Hurst concluded that American business law favored developmental rights over pristine property rights. A farmer who dammed a river to build a mill—thus flooding the farmers' lands above him and reducing the flow of water to those below him—provided a societal benefit greater than the harms caused the other individual farmers. Characterizing the prevailing legal approach as the "release of energy," Hurst noted that property rights were enforced as long as the property was productive, reiterating the same assumptions underlying the preemption laws and property taxes. In the early republic, these concepts were always tempered by the application of legal common sense, in which the damage done could be considered reasonable and could be addressed through some form of restitution. Such common sense was also used when cities, the states, or even the federal government invoked *eminent domain,* in which private land could be seized after a public process that involved paying "fair value" for land deemed necessary to the public use. In such cases, courts and juries tended to side with the state in instances of "holdouts," or individuals possessing, say, the last parcel of land on the entire route of a road and who were holding out for payments far in excess of "fair value."

Allowing for infrequent declarations of eminent domain, American courts supported property development, at the same time allowing redress for damage caused by road, canal, or rail companies to occur under liability and negligence laws. While courts tended to dismiss charges against railroads brought by farmers after sparks from a train's metal wheels burned crops, or refrained from citing slaughterhouses for the smell they produced, the courts nevertheless granted restitution for genuine harm that occurred when companies had a reasonable expectation of damage. The law emphasized intent and foreknowledge, and did not penalize businesses for accidents that the owner "should have known about" in an abstract or hypothetical sense. Rather, claimants had to show proof that the damage was due to more than bad luck and that claimants were not negligent or fellow workers contributory.

COMPETITION FOR THE ROADS: CANALS

Competition to roads from a new transportation system, canals, made it even more difficult for road builders to obtain scarce financing. By comparison, the costs involved in road construction paled next to those of canals, whose expenses reached the millions of dollars. As might be expected, entrepreneurs looked to use public money whenever possible and turned to the states to garner support for canal projects more than they had in the case of roads. One early canal company boasted the investment of George Washington. In 1794, the "Dismal Swamp Canal" was planned to improve access from tidewater Virginia to deep water ports. While the investment aspect failed, after twelve years, twenty-two miles of the canal was completed. Between 1817 and 1844 the "canal era" unfolded, bringing together more than ever before the efforts of business and government in what was called "mixed enterprise," and producing more than 4,000 miles of canals at a cost of more than $200 million.

Certainly private businesses built many of the early canals without government help. Projects such as the Middlesex Canal in Massachusetts and the Santee and Cooper Canal in South Carolina joined together existing trading areas. The returns from commerce and identifiable markets provided ample incentive for entrepreneurs to invest in short-route canals. But obtaining funds for longer canals, or for areas lacking mature markets, required other approaches. Those projects tended to link less-developed trading centers in the West with the Atlantic seaboard, or join up-country farming regions with port cities.

The success of the Erie Canal changed transportation financing in the United States. Built to connect the Hudson River and Lake Erie, the canal provided a route whereby produce from the Ohio Valley could reach the ocean without first traveling through Canada. Little population resided along the route, but the founders realized their anticipations quickly. Demand for such a route was so great that the state of New York—the builder of the canal—collected more than $1 million in tolls before the Erie was completed in 1825. Constructed over eight years, the Erie Canal regained its $9 million investment by 1836, with a net rate return of 8 percent. By that time, more than 3,000 boats had traversed the canal, bringing food and raw materials to New York City and returning with immigrants headed for the Old Northwest.[16]

An engineering feat, the Erie Canal was originally 30 feet wide, 4 feet deep, and 363 miles long. It required eighty-three locks that raised and lowered boats 565 feet, traversing rivers and streams using eighteen aqueducts bordered by towpaths for draft animals needed to pull nonsteam-powered vessels along the canal. As impressive as it was, the canal could not handle the volume of traffic that sought to use the route. New York enlarged the canal in the 1850s, so boats could pass each other and the Erie Canal finally reached its peak in tonnage in 1880.

No commissioner played a more important role in promoting and financing the "ditch" as De Witt Clinton (1769–1828), a New York lawyer and politician who served as mayor of New York City. The quintessential "career politician"—Clinton hardly held a job outside of politics until he was past forty—he was capable and talented. He also managed to drift between the major political parties of the time, serving as a Republican senator of New York and running for president as a Federalist. After successfully persuading the New York legislature to build the Erie Canal, he survived innumerable political wars to ensure its completion. Construction of the canal also benefited from economic disaster. When the Panic of 1819 put hundreds of farmers west of the Seneca River into bankruptcy, they went to work as construction laborers, at reduced wages, as the only way to keep their land away from creditors.[17] Clinton won reelection as governor of New York and then celebrated the opening of the Erie in 1825.

Increasingly, states and regions started to compete in efforts to gain federal expenditures for roads and harbor improvements. Internal improvements, such as the Maysville Road, became political cudgels used to bash enemies or precious jewels to reward partisan supporters. Every region could make a legitimate claim that it had projects that only the government could solve. The Chesapeake and Delaware Canal Company, for example, received substantial federal funds merely by pleading that it could provide strategic and military value for American armed forces. Rivers that traversed state boundaries fell under federal jurisdiction; therefore underwater obstructions such as trees and rocks that threatened vessels were federal problems. Between 1815 and 1850, of the 736 steamboats lost on the rivers, submerged obstacles accounted for 419 of them, and 20 percent of the total tonnage. Entrepreneurs could clear the snags (at about $4 per snag), but only by obtaining federal contracts.[18] Government hesitated to raise tolls to cover such costs, instead shunting them off on taxpayers, consumers, or importers. Nevertheless, the success of the Erie Canal convinced most voters that similar canal projects in their own states, funded by the state government, could vastly improve their lives. As a result, canal projects were able to attract financing for even the most outlandish ideas. Pennsylvania created its 394-mile-long Mainline Canal from Philadelphia to Pittsburgh that required 174 locks to cross a rise of mountains. Ohio and Indiana constructed elaborate networks of waterways to connect major cities and rivers. The canals certainly lowered freight rates over land transportation, with costs falling by an average of 15 cents a ton-mile on average. Cities along canal routes thrived, as did markets for raw materials in the American West.

For all of the obvious advantages of the canals, state financing for them came at a substantial cost. Typically, states issued bonds for construction projects or placed the full faith and credit of the government behind the enterprise. Unfortunately, when the canals failed, they flopped in colossal fashion. The heavy investment in bonds by state governments carried two fundamental dangers. First, they subjected states disproportionately to sudden economic changes that could have caused the value of bonds to plummet. During the Panic of 1837, the value of state-backed canal bonds collapsed, driving many states to the brink of financial collapse. Canal bonds bankrupted Indiana and Pennsylvania and eroded Ohio's credit, not to mention decimating dozens of banks across the United States. Private institutions, however, deserved their fate: They knowingly and deliberately—often enthusiastically—invested in canal bonds. Thus, the second deleterious effect fell on state taxpayers, who had to bear the brunt of debacles involving canals they never saw and could never use. When state-backed bonds went bad, the state had to indemnify the bondholders or repudiate the debt. Planters in upstate Louisiana and rural Mississippi paid costs for New Orleans canal bonds, just as backwoods South Carolina farmers later paid for failed railroads emanating from Charleston. More than 75 percent of canal investment came from public agencies in one form or another—although usually not through taxation—and often foreign investors, particularly British, bore the brunt of the losses when states or companies repudiated their bonds.

Such potential for losses that might be spread across the public as a whole or to foreigners seemed inconsequential to the commercial groups and politicians advocating canals between 1826 and 1840, who undertook exceptionally ambitious projects, usually with disappointing results. In 1828, the Chesapeake and Ohio Canal Company began work on a waterway to connect the District of Columbia to the Cumberland River, which it reached only in 1850, after significant cost overruns. A similar project, the James River and Kanawha Canal, never crossed the Appalachians. Ohio had produced a canal system that covered more than 800 miles at a cost of $16 million, but the toll revenue never repaid the investment. Indiana's Wabash and Erie Canal, which promised to join Lake Erie on the Ohio side to Evansville, Indiana, was the longest canal in the United States—and one of the worst investments. When investors lost fortunes, occasionally costing individuals their life savings, the public had some sympathy. But when foreigners were involved, no small amount of gloating took place. Many Americans remained oblivious to the damage done to state and local credit, a fact the Confederacy learned years later when it sought financial support abroad, only to be reminded that several of its member states had defaulted on loans in the past.[19]

Specific losses, however, did not diminish the genuine contributions of the canals to society and the economy. As Jeremy Atack and Peter Passell note, overall, canals drove down costs of shipping from 20 cents per ton-mile to two to three cents per ton-mile.[20] Ultimately, the authors concluded, even "a noted financial failure like the Ohio Canal yielded a respectable 10 percent social rate of return."[21]

STEAM POWER COMES TO SHIPS: FITCH, FULTON, AND VANDERBILT

During the early 1800s, shipping goods downriver was easier than sending them overland. But sailing upstream was extremely time-consuming and expensive, involving the use of keelboats propelled by men pushing long poles into the riverbed, or flatboats pulled by draft animals (mules or oxen) on towpaths constructed to the side. Either way was painfully slow, perhaps explaining why American river folklore evolved: Bored keel men or captains had to tell stories to stay awake. As for the use of flatboats, clearing a road for animals cost as much as making a primitive wagon road, defeating the purpose of the investment. Winter freezing also made some canals impassible for months.

John Fitch (1743–98) first addressed these issues in 1787, when he demonstrated a steam-powered, paddle-driven boat. It featured long oars, driven by gears from the top of the vessel, and waddled along at about four miles per hour.[22] But Fitch focused on the Delaware River, which had abundant alternative paths and was not particularly profitable for steam. The failure of his enterprise made this remarkable inventor the butt of jokes and led him to suicide by swallowing opium pills.

Robert Fulton, on the other hand, immediately perceived that the "right" river was the Hudson. In 1807 he unveiled his own steamship, the *Clermont*, and sailed from New York City to Albany. Fulton's technical accomplishment with the *Clermont* only accounted for part of his success; the remainder can be attributed to the fact that the "New York legislature gave Fulton the privilege of carrying *all* steamboat traffic in New York [State] for thirty years."[23] Along with his partner, Robert L. Livingston, Fulton created the Mississippi Steamboat Company in 1809 and constructed the *New Orleans*, a side-wheeler vessel for use on western routes. Unlike Fitch, Fulton understood that merely building the vessel was only half the challenge. Making money off the route was the other half. But as happened with Eli Whitney, Fulton's success merely demonstrated the feasibility of making steam-powered boats, and a host of imitators soon followed. Access to the business was easy, with basic vessels costing as little as $20,000, and returns accrued quickly at a rate of up to 24 percent, according to one study.[24] More than

700 steamboats plied the western rivers by 1850, constituting perhaps the single most important ingredient in the nation's internal trade.

Steam vessels played an even more important role on the Great Lakes, where ships occasionally exceeded 1,000 tons and, in the case of the *City of Buffalo*, displaced a whopping 2,200 tons. Operated by single entrepreneurs, partnerships, and corporations, the steam companies dominated transportation in the Great Lakes region: By mid-century, "the tonnage on the Mississippi River and on the Great Lakes exceeded that of all shipping from New York City by over 200 percent."[25]

With ease of access, relatively low technology costs, and open interstate waterways, it was to be expected that an industry as vibrant as steamboating would find itself at the center of constitutional questions. Steamboats, and a new star on the business horizon, Cornelius Vanderbilt, were involved in a key Supreme Court ruling on monopoly power of charters. Thomas Gibbons, a New Jersey steamboat owner, had hired a young entrepreneur named Cornelius Vanderbilt to challenge the Fulton passenger monopoly between Elizabeth, New Jersey, and New York City in 1817. Technically in violation of the law, and pursued by agents of the Fulton monopoly, Vanderbilt "defied capture as he raced passengers cheaply" between the two sites for sixty days, becoming a "popular figure on the Atlantic as he lowered the fares and eluded the law."[26] The rebellious captain even hoisted a flag over the mast of Gibbons's ship that read, "New Jersey must be free." Although the wheels of justice ground slowly, they finally provided a decision in 1824 in the case of *Gibbons v. Ogden*, in which the Supreme Court ruled that only the federal government, and not the states, could regulate interstate commerce. Citizens of New Jersey, cognizant that the Court had struck a blow for consumers, greeted Commodore Vanderbilt (as they called him) in New Brunswick with cannon salutes; New Yorkers launched steamships of their own—one named for John Marshall, the chief justice who had delivered the favorable ruling. Fares plummeted everywhere. The cost of a trip from New York City to Albany fell from $7 to $3 after Gibbons's (and Vanderbilt's) victory. Vanderbilt pioneered a concept that infused mass markets almost a century later called a *loss leader*, in which one product is sold cheaply (or even given away) as a means to attract customers, whereupon the business makes profits on related goods and services. A staple of the modern motion picture theater's business strategy, tickets to movies are disproportionately reduced in price while soft drinks and other concessions are sold at prices double or triple those of the products elsewhere. Vanderbilt understood the concept of loss leaders perfectly. When he moved his steamboat business to New York's Hudson River, he calculated that he could cut the fare to Albany from $3 to ten cents! Eventually, he charged no fare at all, estimating that if he could fill each boat with 100 passengers, he would make a profit if each person ate or drank up to $2 worth of food.

Vanderbilt's two-boat operation, called the People's Line, competed with the powerful Hudson River Association, which reluctantly admitted that it could not match his prices. The association concluded that it was cheaper to buy out Vanderbilt than to cut costs or increase efficiency, and it offered him a one-time payment of $100,000 plus $5,000 annually to leave the region—the 1800s version of the "golden parachute." Vanderbilt took the deal, and the Hudson River Association quickly boosted its rates back to around $3, but still slightly less than before the Commodore ever entered the fray. In the end, though, Vanderbilt not only made himself rich, but he managed to lower costs permanently for all travelers, because every entrepreneurial steamboater on the Hudson soon competed to carry passengers, with each promising a lower fare. All the association gained was a treasury that was $100,000 smaller.

Of course, Vanderbilt did not disappear. He watched the rise of another business, that of transatlantic shipping and passenger travel, especially after Congress started to pay shipper Edward K. Collins to deliver mail across the Atlantic for a subsidy payment of $3 million down and $385,000 per year. In return, Collins promised to outrace the British competition, the Cunard shipping line. Samuel Cunard himself had attained his dominance of the oceans through a subsidy from the British government to run a packet line from Liverpool to Boston. Congress, reacting to concerns over unfair competition, was certain no individual entrepreneur could defeat the English company without assistance. When the Cunard line added New York City to its destinations in 1848, competing directly with American companies, Collins saw an opportunity to convince Congress to subsidize an American competitor.[27]

The American sailing companies still clung to the beautiful, but suddenly obsolete, "clipper ships." With their numerous sails, clipper ships attained remarkable speed in their time, and they facilitated the China tea and porcelain trade. Eventually, though, as steam technology moved from the rivers to the oceans, the clippers found themselves outclassed. Cunard understood the exceptional advantages offered by steam, and when Collins made his first proposal for a subsidized line in 1847, the appearance of the Cunard line ensured that he received a warm reception. Collins formed the United States Mail Steamship Company, commonly called the Collins Line. He promised to build five steamships that would be the fastest in the world, and indeed his ships beat the English crossing the Atlantic by about a day. But his costs never fell. Using taxpayer money, Collins had no incentive to reduce costs at all; and his expenses doubled from 1847 to 1852! Instead of finding ways to improve his performance, and his ships' efficiencies, Collins lobbied in Congress for more money.[28]

Vanderbilt knew Collins's prices were too high, but the Commodore was not immune to the lure of government subsidies. Thus, when Vanderbilt first announced that he could deliver mail for less than Cunard and for half the price Collins received, his first goal was to obtain a federal subsidy for himself. He offered to run the Atlantic routes for $15,000 per trip (compared to $33,000 per trip for Collins). Congress, perhaps embarrassed by committing too much, too early to Collins, could not abandon him easily.

At that point, Vanderbilt took the battle directly to the market, slashing prices on both mail and passenger fares. He cut costs by eliminating insurance, and instead ploughed the money into sturdier ships and hiring excellent captains. His cheaper boats quickly attained greater economies than Collins's bloated fleet, but the Commodore still had to contend with the issue of subsidies. Even as he complained that it was "utterly impossible for a private individual to stand in competition with a line drawing nearly one million dollars per annum from the national treasury," Vanderbilt did just that.[29]

Rather than reduce his investment, the Commodore put more into the enterprise, spending $600,000 on a new steamship, the *Vanderbilt*, which beat Collins's ship in a race to England. Further embarrassment greeted Collins when two of his ships sank and the replacement vessel he constructed using government funds—a $1 million, 4,000-ton paddle wheeler called the *Adriatic*—was a phenomenal failure. Collins's ships featured the finest chefs and new rotating barber chairs, but they couldn't match the *Vanderbilt*'s reliability and efficiency. The most ironic twist of all came after Vanderbilt finally achieved victory over Collins, while simultaneously William Inman in England had driven out the subsidized Cunard line with his own version of Vanderbilt's unsubsidized fleet! Inman had revolutionized steamships by incorporating new screw propellers and iron hulls. By 1858, Vanderbilt and Inman had buried their subsidized competitors.[30]

Vanderbilt had one more lesson to teach on the superiority of market forces over government subsidies. This time, while struggling to gain a share of the burgeoning California mail, freight, and passenger business, he faced two competitors, each armed with annual $500,000 federal subsidies. Those lines charged a staggering $600 per passenger from New York to California, via Panama. Vanderbilt ignored Panama and constructed his own river route through Nicaragua, paying the Nicaraguan government $10,000 a year for canal privileges. He then slashed passenger fares to $400 and offered to carry the mail free. Within a year, New York to California fares dropped to $150. Typically, rather than compete with Vanderbilt, the established lines begged Congress for a higher subsidy; and when a Nicaraguan revolution resulted in Vanderbilt losing his canal rights, he simply moved to Panama and cut fares again, to $100. Unable to compete with the Commodore, the California companies finally bought him out, at a cost of $672,000, or 75 percent of their (increased) annual subsidy. As might be expected, the California steamers raised prices, to $300. Vanderbilt still gained, because he supplied many of the engines for the California-built riverboats that took passengers and freight from San Francisco inland to Sacramento.

Was Vanderbilt, who almost single-handedly made steamboat travel affordable for the average customer, lionized as a friend of the consumer? One could hardly tell it by some of the comments of the day. According to one court, Vanderbilt's price-cutting was "immoral and in restraint of trade," while the *New York Times* compared him to "those old German Barons who, from their eyries along the Rhine, swooped down upon the commerce of the noble river and wrung tribute from every passenger that floated by."[31] Polemics aside, it is difficult to see how a man who did not even charge fares "wrung tribute" from anyone. But even when he no longer competed directly, the Commodore's influence benefited travelers: The $300 fare charged by the California companies after they raised prices still represented a 50 percent reduction from the pre-Vanderbilt rates.

BIRTH OF THE RAIL AGE

Just as steam technology improved transport by water, it had a revolutionary effect on transportation on land, via a relatively new invention, the steam-powered locomotive. In 1825, George Stephenson developed effective locomotives, and in 1830 his *Rocket* made its debut in England, "speeding" down rails (at four miles per hour in its first runs, but eventually reaching fifteen), connecting Liverpool and Manchester. The American railroad industry was born when a hardware merchant and bank president named Phillip E. Thomas led a group of Baltimore businessmen to obtain a charter for the Baltimore and Ohio Railroad (B & O) in 1828 to compete directly with the Chesapeake and Ohio Canal. Hardly a technological wonder at first—the company depended on horse-drawn wagons that rode the rails—the B & O received its first steam locomotive that summer. At that time, a New York inventor named Peter Cooper brought his "Tom Thumb" to the line: It promptly lost a race against a horse and left investors to discount the value of steam-powered rail traffic. But steam-powered railroads did not go away. By 1831, several railroads demonstrated steam locomotives, and the B & O adopted steam as its sole means of rail power.

One of the first railroads to show that steam locomotives could be profitable was the South Carolina Canal and Railroad Company, which extended westward from Charleston. In 1830, its locomotive, *Best Friend of Charleston* (the first ever built for sale in the United States), lugged its 140 passengers on the first steam locomotive trip in American history. Within a few short years, railroad building reached levels contemporaries referred to as a "fever," a "frenzy," and a "mania." The explosion in railroad building benefited from associated gains in technology. English engineers created the wrought-iron "I" section of rail that could be mass-produced in fifteen-foot lengths, making track-laying efficient. Then the American, Robert L. Stevens, the president of the Camden and Amboy Railroad in New Jersey, created the T-rail, a remarkable advance that allowed the "I" and "T" rails to rest on large wooden ties laid across crushed stone roadbeds.[32] Matthias Baldwin of Philadelphia, a bookbinder searching for better ways to power his tools, emerged as one of the leading locomotive manufacturers in America. When his first attempt to deliver a locomotive resulted in his buyer attempting to cheat him out of his share of the $4,000 investment,

Baldwin swore to never build another; but working railroads soon heard of his invention and besieged him with orders.

In 1839 and 1840, Baldwin created his flexible-beam design that transmitted power to three axles, with the front two capable of pivoting. Armed with a winning design, Baldwin nevertheless found sales slow in the early 1840s, leading him to develop a new sales strategy in which he accepted half his payment in cash upon delivery and the remainder within six months.[33] Baldwin's factory actually consisted of three machine shops by 1850, supported by a boiler factory, a foundry, and a smith shop, each with its own foreman. As the biographer of the Baldwin business noted, the foremen "oversaw all work in their departments, ensuring that parts were made on time to the required dimensions and coordinating output among the shops. These considerable powers made the foremen the absolute masters of their own departments."[34] Inside the shops, a small army of skilled artisans worked sheet iron and copper, built boilers, made patterns and molds, improved and repaired machines, etched metal, painted, and built the necessary lumber scaffolds. In addition, the firm employed numerous unskilled carriers. Up to 400 men could work at one factory alone by 1840, with a force of just over 200 capable of turning out a locomotive in sixty days. By the time of his death in 1866, Baldwin had turned out more than 1,500 locomotives.

Thanks to productive firms like Baldwin's, by the 1840s American railroads already were having a profound effect on daily life. For example, service on the Erie Railway linked Orange County, New York's leading dairy supplier, to New York City, and in 1842 an agent for the railroad, Thomas Selleck, persuaded a local farmer to ship his fresh milk to the city, where it sold out instantly. Shortly, the price of fresh milk brought by rail was lower than that of "swill milk"—milk from cows kept by brewers and distillers in New York, which till then had been the only source of milk for most people. Swill milk was also the source of such diseases as tuberculosis and cholera, contributing to the city's high infant mortality rate. Swill milk was virtually eliminated, thanks to fresh milk supplied by the railroad.[35]

Most states had railroads by 1840, and states along the Atlantic seaboard held more than 60 percent of the total rail mileage in the nation. Nevertheless, by the 1840s, the golden age of railroading was at least a decade away. In part, the Panic of 1837, whose effects lasted in some states until 1842, bankrupted several railroads and dried up financing of others. As with the canals, foreign investors suffered heavily in the collapse, forcing American railroads to turn to the early capital markets in New York or to the states for financing.[36] The high capital demands of railroads distinguished them immediately from other business organizations, even other large-scale enterprises, such as canals. Their unusually large capital demands often required the sale of securities to raise funds, which required a corporate entity. Moreover, railroads crossed long stretches of land and several modern time zones, making geographical oversight by a sole proprietor difficult.

Around the same time that the rail age was emerging, a series of court rulings established a general model for large-scale business that allowed corporations to expand beyond their more limited charter form.[37] In *Dartmouth College v. Woodward*, Dartmouth College won a case in which the United States Supreme Court upheld the sanctity of contracts. Less than two decades later, in the *Charles River Bridge v. Warren Bridge* case (1837), the Court ruled that a charter did not guarantee monopoly power unless such power was expressly stated, thus establishing the presumption of competition in the marketplace. Yet another case, *Bank of Augusta v. Earle*, introduced the principle of "comity" between states, holding that corporations could conduct business across state lines through mutual good faith that the laws of one state would be respected by another unless expressly prohibited by the legislature of the other state.[38] Entrepreneurs, therefore, had clear rules by which to operate—rules that favored free agreements, open competition, and geographic flexibility.

What neither the government—nor the courts—sought to control actively was the medium of exchange. It was assumed that gold would provide a standard of value, and that individuals or firms could issue their own money (notes) that would be tied to that standard. By the 1830s, the banking population had exploded, with the number of banks almost doubling between 1834 and 1840. Moreover, private investors were solicited primarily to provide loans to the directors and other so-called "insiders." Banks tended to finance smaller-scale operations and provided merchants and farmers with working capital, leaving larger-scale projects, such as canals and, later, railroads, to larger banks called investment banks.

Periodic panics (1819 and 1837) led to attempts to make the banking system sounder while, at the same time, relieving the state legislatures of the burdens of issuing charters individually. Yet knowledgeable legislators and bankers alike differed over the best way to accomplish those ends. Part of the difficulty stemmed from the tumultuous history of the Second BUS, and the "Bank War" that resulted in its death.

NICHOLAS BIDDLE, ANDREW JACKSON, AND THE "WAR" ON THE BUS

After its recharter in 1816, the Second BUS was blamed (inaccurately) for the Panic of 1819, but struggled through to stability by 1823, when the directors brought in a new president, Nicholas Biddle. A Pennsylvania lawyer and former secretary to the U.S. ambassador to France, Biddle found himself managing his wife's estate outside of Philadelphia. He threw himself into farming, experimenting with crops and livestock to improve productivity and publishing some of his research.

Biddle's previous political connections gained him a seat on the board of directors of the Second BUS, and in 1823 Biddle took over the reins of the largest business institution in the nation. Capitalized at $35 million, the BUS dwarfed other enterprises. Biddle took his job seriously and scientifically, and "in many ways [was] the forerunner of the modern business executive."[39] He oversaw the operations of the bank, exerting control over managerial personnel in branches, maintained a steady flow of information from the branch managers, and instituted regular inspections by teams of cashiers sent from the central office to examine the accuracy of records.

Under Biddle, the BUS was credited with maintaining discipline among the state banks, over which the BUS had no direct control. But, according to some scholars, the BUS restrained the state banks from overissuing notes by posing the threat of "raids." The discipline imposed by the BUS worked when state banks issued notes backed by specie reserves. A bank's notes were exchanged at other banks for specie, whereupon the notes were returned to the source of origination. The BUS, which had branches scattered throughout the Union, acquired the notes of most banks at one point or another during its normal business. If BUS managers suspected that a bank was overissuing notes, they could stage a "raid" in which the BUS would collect large amounts of the suspected violator's notes and, in a surprise visit, present them for specie or BUS notes. That threat, in theory, required the state banks to keep on hand either large specie reserves or substantial reserves of BUS notes. In either case, the BUS, acting as an early central bank, instilled discipline on the entire commercial banking sector.[40]

Most historians accepted this interpretation of the powers of the Second BUS, and they proposed an explanation of the Bank War and the Panic of 1837 as deriving from Jackson's destruction of the bank. Briefly, according to the traditional interpretation of the events as expounded by Bray Hammond, Biddle blundered by attempting to get the Congress to recharter the BUS in 1832. This was an election year, and four years ahead of the charter's expiration, but Biddle reasoned that the politicians could not oppose the recharter of such a popular institution.[41] President Andrew Jackson judged that he could gain politically from vetoing the bill. Jackson framed the debate as pitting what he called the "moneyed interests" who supported the BUS against the "common man" oppressed by the large, monopoly institution. Although Congress passed the bill, it did not have the necessary two-thirds majority to override Jackson's veto. Jackson then withdrew the government's deposits from the BUS, placing them in state banks controlled by his political friends, giving the banks their nickname "pet banks." With its deposit base shrunken dramatically and a charter certain to expire, the BUS limped through the last years of its life.

Meanwhile, according to the traditional interpretation, the state banks, released from the discipline of the BUS, started to "inflate" the currency by issuing notes in greater quantities. These notes gravitated to the western regions, where settlers used them to pay for newly purchased land. Jackson attempted to stop the practice of paying for land with paper money by issuing the Specie Circular (1836), mandating that buyers use specie to pay for land out West. At roughly the same time, Jackson took the federal government surplus and returned it to the states, but not in proportions they had paid in tariffs. The disruption of the financial markets caused by the massive shifts of government and private funds in all directions, topped by the Specie Circular, sparked the Panic of 1837. According to the Hammond interpretation, Jackson was responsible both for the pre-panic inflation and for the policies that started the worst depression in American history up to that point.[42]

A number of scholars, however, started to question the traditional school as early as 1961, when Richard Timberlake published the first of several articles and books on antebellum banking, and then later, with the appearance of Peter Temin's *The Jacksonian Economy.*[43] Those works showed that 1) the demise of the BUS had no significant effect on the inflation of the period; 2) the inflation could be traced to silver flows from Mexico to the United States to China to England, which lowered interest rates on loans to companies and projects in the United States; and 3) the depression occurred when the Mexican silver dried up, raising the interest rates. Subsequent research showed that Jackson and the Democrats were not opposed to a national bank per se, but rather one controlled by their political enemies.[44] Put another way, it was all about who got credit—both literally and politically.

The demand for banks and capital continued unabated, leading to a number of reforms, including general incorporation laws (called free banking laws when applied to banks), primitive deposit guaranty or insurance funds, and clearinghouse arrangements. Free banking laws allowed any individual or company to establish a bank after it placed on deposit with the secretary of the state in question a predetermined dollar value of acceptable bonds. Frequently, entrepreneurs used state government bonds or railroad bonds. Some states had unmitigated disasters with free banking, leading to calls for greater government control over the banking system, but in almost all cases, these occurrences were the result of poorly written state laws. When modifications were made, free banking proved a stable and efficient alternative to chartered banking.[45]

The state of New York attempted to curtail bank losses by establishing a type of reserve fund, called the Safety Fund (1829). Like modern deposit insurance, each bank in New York City paid an assessment to provide an emergency fund to cover losses to depositors. Although the fund failed to prevent the runs during the Panic of 1837, that did not keep advocates of deposit insurance schemes from using it as a successful example for federal deposit insurance in the 1930s. Boston tried a different approach, creating a clearinghouse association in 1852, whereby member banks established a central location for clearing notes and currency.[46] Both the Safety Fund and the clearinghouse associations represented nongovernment, private attempts to organize and streamline antebellum banking based on the assumption that bankers and depositors would behave rationally if they had reliable information. Subsequent studies on financial panics and manias has suggested that indeed the weakest element in the banking system in the nineteenth century was the transmission of information, an advantage the BUS had possessed, as its enthusiasts pointed out.[47]

Banks and railroads started to see common needs by the 1850s. The capital demands of the railroads had grown enormous: Each of the fifty largest railroads in 1860 had a capitalization more than *ten times* that of the next largest manufacturing company, creating virtually a separate market for railroad securities. States could meet some of the demand through bond sales, issuing more than $90 million in bonds to finance railroad construction between 1845 and 1860. But private investors, and not governments, supplied most of the capital required by the railroads in the antebellum period. Securities dealers scoured markets in Europe, while in America, prominent bankers formed syndicates, or large groups of investors, to fund railroad building.

Among the most famous of the early investment bankers, George Peabody, a Massachusetts dry goods merchant, had aided the state of Maryland when it verged on bankruptcy in 1835. Peabody and his partner Elisha Riggs sold $8 million in state bonds, saving Maryland from disaster, after which he returned his $200,000 fee to the state. Peabody's career was typical of a new generational path among businessmen, literally inverting the previous patterns. Whereas New England merchants started banks to support their textile, iron, and other businesses, in the 1840s and 1850s bankers themselves started to look at railroads as a source of investment. Peabody, for example, incorporated the Eastern Railroad in 1836, then, convinced his American managers could run the operation, moved to London, where he intended to develop his investment firm to support the railroad.

Another prominent investment house of the era, Drexel & Company, originated in Philadelphia in 1837. Anthony Drexel studied under his banker father and became a full partner in his father's firm in 1847. Within a decade, he had a reputation as the guiding genius of the operation. Drexel concentrated on government bonds and railroad issues, eventually taking as a partner Junius Morgan, whose own career had centered on bonds and stocks.[48] Morgan worked as a partner in J. M. Beebe, Morgan & Co., a Boston dry goods wholesaler, and in the course of that work he went to London as the company's representative. There, he met Peabody, who by that time needed a younger man to run his business. Morgan joined the Peabody firm, employing Morgan's son, John Pierpont (J. P.), as a secretary in the counthouse.

Firms such as Peabody's, Drexel's, and dozens of others had turned on the financial faucets to domestic industries, especially railroads.

The lifeline between the banks and the railroads extended further into the economy, boosting the already-flourishing iron industry, consuming some 30 percent of American iron production by the 1840s.[49] As with textiles, the iron industry reacted to foreign competition by appealing to Congress for protective tariffs against British iron producers. In 1842, Congress responded by placing duties on imported iron. When the tariffs ended and protection was greatly reduced, iron production in America *increased.*[50] American iron producers seemed stimulated by the renewed competition, and by 1860 American mills had become fully competitive with the British, in part because the end of protection eliminated the old charcoal smelters and obsolete mills, leaving the newer anthracite smelters in a position to meet the demand for newer, nonrail products.[51]

Thus, by 1850, the transportation revolution had caught within its web aspects of the U.S. economy as diverse as banks and boiler manufacturers; canals and couplers; wheels and wheat. Interlacing each of those elements—welding it to the others—was a revolution in communication and information that made standardized manuals, bond prices, train schedules, and toll costs available to a large segment of the business community.

COMMUNICATION NETWORKS, NATIONAL MARKETS

With vast distances linked by an expanding national network of roads, canals, and railroad tracks, the flow of information accelerated faster than ever, lowering prices for producers and consumers alike. "Information costs," as economists call them, refer to the "costs, to both buyers and sellers, of obtaining accurate and timely information for sound business decisions."[52] Banks, for example, had to hope that their edition of *Dillistin's Bank Note Reporter* was the most recent, or that they had the most recent bond prices if they dealt in bonds. Merchants could gain or lose significant amounts of money if they did not have appropriate information about their markets—a fact not lost on Lewis Tappan and his Mercantile Agency, which began as an abolitionist-morality spy association. It dawned on Tappan that he could use that same network for business reporting and credit information. Often Tappan's informants, many of them attorneys, provided highly personal information about such vices as excessive drinking or the frequenting of houses of prostitution, but in an age where character still was king, that information was seen as an indicator of credit-worthiness.[53] A rival business, the Cincinnati-based Bradstreet Company, founded eight years after the Mercantile Agency, beat its competitor to the punch, publishing the first credit-rating reference book in 1857. Bradstreet's reports emphasized large cities. Tappan's Mercantile Agency, on the other hand, which concentrated on country businesses, issued its first credit-reporting volume in 1859, thus providing no shortage of credit evaluation and reporting instruments for the business community before the Civil War. Yet another source of information, the Chicago Board of Trade, provided timely reports for commodities buyers about produce, meat, and grains.[54]

Also tying business information together was the U.S. Post Office, which had 18,468 branches by 1850, representing one post office for every 1,300 people. The postal system reached across thousands of miles, touching almost every developed area of the United States.[55] Lacking a post office branch, correspondents had to ship letters with regular transportation companies such as shipping firms or stage-coaches, known as "common carriers." A system so vast, of course, wielded considerable political clout, so much that in the mid-1800s, the position of postmaster general was a political plum next to secretary of state. By 1831 the postal system controlled more than 8,700 postmaster jobs—more than three-fourths of the entire federal civilian workforce and larger than the army.[56] Routes themselves were highly politicized, based on who had clout in Washington, and many new routes did not bear more than *one percent* of their cost. Public mail played a key role in another political instrument: the newspaper. Most newspapers, or "broadsides" as the first papers were called, were barely profitable. That changed in the 1820s when the new Democratic Party began to set up newspapers as strictly party organs, for the sole purpose of electing candidates. Many bore the name boldly on their masthead: *The Arkansas Democrat* and, later, *The Richmond Whig*, for example. Subscriptions never covered costs—the excess was simply absorbed by the political parties—and the papers rarely carried "news," but instead proudly saw themselves as propaganda machines. Parties selected editors, and, as Francis P. Blair, the editor of the pro-Jackson paper, *The Globe*, pointed out, his paper's position on any given issue was "determined by Jackson's stand on them."[57] Both parties played the game, and by 1850, political bias so dominated the newspaper industry that the U.S. Census estimated that nearly 80 percent of American papers were partisan, while other estimates put the number of partisan papers at close to 100 percent! Once a party got in power, it rewarded loyal papers with stupefying largesse: Printing profits for one Democrat paper, Duff Green's *U.S. Telegraph* (whose masthead motto was "Power Is Always Stealing from the Many to the Few"), averaged 40 percent a year during one ten-year stretch, and an official paper could receive tremendous lithographing, printing, and engraving fees.[58]

Given that Congress could favor newspapers with legislation, the number of newspapers transmitted through the postal system rose between 1800 and 1840, from just under 2 million to almost 40 million, creating a national market for information long before a similar market for goods developed. Of course, this growth came at a price. If newspapers had to pay the same rate as other mail, their transmission costs would have been 700 *times* higher, and since books and magazines did not enjoy the same miniscule postal rates, publishers concentrated on the more profitable newspapers and less on books.[59] Whereas prior to the Revolution, America's educated elites had read books, especially political theory and history, increasingly a "learned man" was informed solely by newspapers.

WELLS FARGO DELIVERS THE MAIL

Shipping packages, however, was a much different story from delivering letters and newspapers. In the late 1830s, a steamboat agent in New York City had started a package express delivery service to Boston, where the receiving agent was a former shoemaker with a speech impediment, Henry Wells. For several years, Wells had run a chain of speech therapy schools in central and northern New York, which, despite moderate financial success, had failed to solve Wells's own speech problems. Almost immediately upon the opening of the New York–Boston route, Wells imagined a stage carrier line running westward to Chicago and beyond. He worked through a string of jobs over a ten-year period in which he moved closer to his dream of a transcontinental stage line, in the process associating with William George Fargo. An encounter in 1842 with a hotel operator who desperately wanted to feature oysters on his menu provided the motivation for Wells to undertake unusual and difficult deliveries. He realized that some people would pay handsomely for the fastest possible delivery (Wells charged $3 for shipment of 100 oysters, an unimaginable sum at the time), and in 1845 he founded a company with Fargo and Daniel Dunning that stretched westward to Cincinnati, Detroit, and Chicago.

Wells's company embodied all that customers expect from a mail or delivery service. He dispatched messengers with simple instructions in the worst weather: "You are expected to get there. That is all."[60] The firm's exceptional record, and lower prices than the government, soon opened it to attacks by the federal monopoly. The central offensive came against the company in upper New York, where federal agents arrested the express messengers daily. Citizens, who realized the value of the Wells service, posted bail immediately, and for a short time the company carried virtually all the mail that moved between Buffalo and Rochester. For his own part, Wells detested government involvement, arguing "Government should do [as] little as possible of that which the People can do."[61] Not until 1851, when Congress lowered the postage rates to three cents, did the U.S. Post Office compete with the rates charged by Wells, and he proudly responded to a popular nickname given him, the "People's Postmaster General."

But Wells had a few more tricks up his sleeve. After associating with John Butterfield, a former competitor, the two divided up the market in a pool. In 1850, Butterfield, Wells, Fargo, and their other business partners consolidated their delivery services into American Express, capitalized at $150,000. The alliance came apart within two years, as Wells and Fargo split with Butterfield over a proposed extension of the route to California, leading to the formation of the famous stage company, Wells Fargo. The company's directors formed a second firm, the Overland Mail Company, in 1858 to run stagecoaches along a southern route through Texas to California, with a northern route running from St. Louis to Salt Lake City, then across the Rockies. Briefly, the company ran the Pony Express mail service, and by 1866 Wells Fargo stagecoaches dominated land travel in the West.

TELEGRAPHS AND THE DAWN OF MODERN COMMUNICATIONS

Just as Vanderbilt had forced the steamboat monopolists to lower their prices, Wells forced down the price of mail. An important difference existed, however, between the competitive effects on Vanderbilt's private rivals and Wells's encounter with the government. The U.S. Post Office had to lower prices. Businesses, of course, welcomed the lower rates provided by Wells, Vanderbilt, the government, or anyone else. But over the long term, the decision to free the Post Office from having to pay its own costs of operations on an annual basis (in essence relieving the government of having to charge a market price for mail delivery) had far-reaching effects for consumers, businesses, and the body politic.

Without the competitive pressure to incorporate the latest technology or cut costs, for example, the Post Office missed the most significant technological achievement in communications up to that point: the advent of the telegraph by Samuel F. B. Morse. A part-time inventor and professional portrait artist who lived for long periods in England, Morse's artistic career seemingly had peaked when Congress turned down his proposal to paint a fresco in the Capitol rotunda in the 1830s. Although still able to sustain himself by painting common portraits, Morse turned his attention to inventing, and in 1832 he met Charles Jackson, who demonstrated electromagnetism to Morse. Applying Jackson's idea to the transmission of concepts, Morse finalized his design in 1837 and applied for a patent soon thereafter, leaving Jackson to complain that Morse stole his ideas. When Morse could not interest private businesses in the device, he turned to government and received a $30,000 appropriation in 1843 to build a short telegraph line. He forged a partnership with his colleague, Alfred Vail, and started work on the demonstration line connecting Baltimore and Washington, D.C. Morse "had no talent for business and no idea of how to construct a line," and needed further expertise in digging trenches in which to lay his wire.[62] Morse engaged the services of Ezra Cornell, who had a trench-digging machine. But the trenches proved too costly, and the group switched to overhead wires hung from poles. In May 1844, they connected Washington and Baltimore, quickly displaying the remarkable potential of the new technology.

By that time, the government had eliminated any further funding—ironically just as the technical marvel had started to unfold—and Morse and his associates used their remaining resources to connect New York City with Washington. Neither Morse nor his partners knew how to market the new technology, and they repeatedly sought government support. When that failed, they sold licenses to the telegraph machinery. Using the Morse licenses, other private competitors (including Henry Wells and his associates in Buffalo) entered and grew the market—from 40 miles of telegraph lines in 1846 to 23,000 by 1852! After understanding both the principle and the potential, other inventors wedged their way onto the scene with new designs or technologies, most notably Royal H. House, a Vermont inventor who patented a telegraph and printer in 1846.

At that point, the most unlikely figure changed the shape of telegraphy. Hiram Sibley, a drifter and handyman who had gained some measure of respect as a real estate agent, a banker, then a sheriff in New York, learned about the House patent. In 1849, Sibley and a partner organized a telegraph company to compete in Albany and Buffalo, then switched to the Morse systems, acquiring rights to new areas for relatively small amounts, including the Midwestern rights, which he bought for $50,000. After a struggle with Ezra Cornell, who held most of the remaining Morse patents in the West in 1855, Sibley merged his company with Cornell's in a new enterprise called Western Union Telegraph Company.

The telegraph began to change the partisan nature of newspapers, pushing them to be objective purely by the need for an economy of words. Businesses already had realized the great value offered by this faster information transmission. Regional stock exchanges closed when investors could obtain reports quickly from New York; railroad dispatchers changed schedules and routes to accommodate traffic; and news of all sorts moved at lightning speed. The members of the Chicago Board of Trade (CBOT) used the telegraph to report grades and prices to members, and soon the CBOT competed with Wall Street in trading securities—an accomplishment made possible only by the telegraph's capacity to offset New York's advantage as a coastal city.[63]

INTERLUDE: THE PONY EXPRESS

Extension of the telegraph and railroads virtually destroyed a much more romantic, but less efficient, mode of communication: overland mail via the Pony Express. The brief history of the Pony Express provides a classic case study for understanding job creation and destruction in a free market. Created in January 1860, the Pony Express was the brainchild of William Russell, who had taken advantage of the postmaster general's dissatisfaction with his existing mail service to organize a company based on traditions of Mongol riders in China.[64] He envisioned horsemen covering a 1,966-mile trail from St. Joseph, Missouri, to Sacramento, California, with 119 stations interspersed for riders to change horses. Every 100 miles, the carrier was allowed to rest, but not for long: Speed in mail delivery was the key. The company hired predominantly Mormon riders who had good relations with the Utah, Ute, and Shoshone Indians in the territories and had grown up under such severe conditions that a ride of 100 miles did not seem extraordinary to them.

Russell gave his managers a mere sixty-five days to procure horses, mules, and obtain space in St. Joseph, Carson City, Sacramento, and other locations. The Express attracted some of the most unusual characters in the American West, and the arrival of the first mail by Pony Express set off celebrations and parades. The final riders crossed in October 1861. At final count, the company's riders had made 300 runs each way, covering a total of 616,000 miles and carrying almost 35,000 pieces of mail. Then, suddenly, the telegraph wires linked the coasts and the Express was made obsolete instantaneously. Dozens of riders and station masters awoke to find themselves out of work. Yet outside the Pony Express, the total number of jobs in the economy created by the telegraph grew exponentially, as workers had to place poles, string wire, run the telegraph offices, lay track, design and build telegraphs and locomotives, and serve as engineers and conductors on the trains.

Here was a classic example of a business made obsolete by technology, and were it a modern company, the media would focus on the suddenly unemployed workforce rather than the large number of new jobs. In the case of the Pony Express, however, even that would be a mistake, because the riders seem to have done quite well after their dismissal.[65] Their stories are inspiring. Don Rising, for example, carried dispatches at the battlefield for the Union Army, gaining promotions to assistant wagon master. He eventually moved to New Mexico, where he started a mercantile and hotel business. Harry Roff became an insurance salesman who received promotion after promotion to become Pacific manager of the Home Insurance Company. William Page, Elijah Maxfield, "Happy Tom" Ranahan, Robert "Pony Bob" Haslam, and many others stayed in the general occupation of driving stages or scouting. Still others (including John Frye, who, along with Johnson Richardson, was one of the first riders to ride the circuit) found work in rodeos and circuses and on ranches. Still others, such as Martin Hogan, found themselves in demand by the railroads. Of the riders that Raymond and Mary Settle, in their history of the Pony Express, could find information on, virtually all of them found better jobs when they were "downsized." The death of the Pony Express represented the old story of "creative destruction," where new industries replace the old and virtually everyone benefits.

SMALL BUSINESS, ENTREPRENEURS, AND THE ANTEBELLUM EXPERIENCE

Emphasizing the rise of large-scale businesses, such as the railroads, canals, telegraph companies, and textile and iron manufacturers, captures the glamour of the era and the heights to which a single entrepreneur could rise. However, it obscures the vast number of small-scale entrepreneurs who made comparatively moderate gains that constituted significant advances for the individuals in question. While Morse struggled with his telegraph prototype, jewelers in Newark, New Jersey, opened their first independent shops using a wide variety of new, small machines, including circular saws and lathes.[66] At a time when Vanderbilt's efficient steamers were driving the subsidized Collins lines from the oceans, more than 9,600 retail merchants did business in New York City alone.[67] When the male riders of the famous Pony Express were being fired, between eighty and 200 female entrepreneurs in Albany, New York, had established businesses that were successful enough to be listed in the R. G. Dun records for up to twenty years![68]

Entrepreneurship came in all varieties. It emerged from the ranks of manual workers in Poughkeepsie, New York, where up to 20 percent of all the journeymen of various trades opened their own shops during the period 1850–70.[69] It swelled from mercantile establishments on the Western frontiers, where peddlers became general store owners, then bankers, then mining company owners. It evolved from the laboratories and workshops of inventors like Morse and Fulton, or from the shipping businesses of Fargo and Butterfield, or from the iron forges of Matthias Baldwin. Most of all, entrepreneurship constantly involved providing new products or services—filling a gap in the market.

One of the most important services needed in the mid-1800s, when buyers and sellers still had to overcome distance and time without the benefit of rapid transit, was that of a financial or goods intermediary, or a middleman. In the South, middlemen known as "factors" purchased cotton in the interior and sold it in the seacoast cities, in the process developing powerful financial businesses of their own. Factors charged, on average, a 2 percent or 3 percent commission, for which they developed expertise in foreign markets and in domestic cotton or other products. They maintained large accounts with the New Orleans, Savannah, and Mobile banks, from which they advanced money to planters and purchased supplies for planters throughout the year. Until banks reached the inland areas of Mississippi, Alabama, and South Carolina, factoring remained one of the most influential and remunerative of businesses. If weather destroyed a cotton crop, driving several planters into debt, the factors who had advanced them money stood liable for their bills. Nevertheless, factors themselves faced extinction as banks extended branches into the southwestern areas, and indeed the presence of factors may have delayed the extension of banking services into areas of the South.[70]

When no factors appeared to serve as an intermediary between planters and buyers, the task fell to general store owners, who as part of their normal business made purchases that the planters and farmers needed.[71] When necessary, the shop owner accepted payment in kind—that is, in produce, livestock, or some other nonmonetary compensation. The scarcity of paper money and coins so afflicted early Missouri, for example, that citizens paid taxes in "shaven deer skin at three pounds to one dollar," while in California, cowhides circulated so widely they acquired the name "California Bank Notes."[72] Local store owners also extended credit, leading many of them into related fields of banking. Once a year or more, the store owners would journey to a large city—New York, Philadelphia, or New Orleans—where they would order goods for the coming season.

A multitude of relatively unknown entrepreneurs walked the American stage from 1830 to 1850, providing people on a daily basis with products and services. Society as a whole felt the benefits of their actions, even if it could not correlate them with specific names. Some, however, achieved such business success or made such products of lasting importance that they became almost synonymous with the product they created or the service they founded. Gail Borden, for example, was for years synonymous with milk. But for most of his life, Borden had nothing to do with milk, although he was born on a New York farm.[73] In fact, Borden's career had touched on almost everything except milk, and he had reached the point in his life when modern Americans plan their retirement. At age 56, Borden had worked as a schoolteacher, surveyor, newspaper editor, real estate salesman, customs collector, and inventor—the job he liked best. Unfortunately, Borden, a kooky "idea man," came up with products or contraptions that hardly seemed practical. He invented a "Terrapin Wagon"—a completely amphibious vehicle with wheels and sails that plunged a group of observers into the Gulf of Mexico. Living in Galveston, Texas, at the time, Borden proposed moving the entire population of the city into a giant ether-cooled refrigerated building that he planned to construct. His flat dehydrated meat biscuit flopped (or bounced, depending on the humidity that day!), although the concept appealed to judges at the 1851 Crystal Palace Exhibition in London, who awarded him a gold medal.

Borden's return voyage to New York from London changed his life—and ours—as a result of a tragic event: Four children died from drinking contaminated milk taken from sick cows on the ship. Determined to improve the safety and quality of milk, Borden applied his experience with the meat biscuit to his extensive knowledge of refrigeration, experimenting with processes that would remove the water from milk to reduce the moisture content and thus enhance its freshness. While visiting a Shaker colony in New Lebanon, New York, Borden witnessed the use of a vacuum process to condense maple sugar, and he reasoned that he could place milk in vacuum-sealed pans, boil it, and reduce the moisture content with a low level of heat, avoiding a burnt taste. He received a patent in 1856 for a process that took out 75 percent of the water from milk and added sugar as a preservative. Opening a small Connecticut plant, Borden failed and was out of business in a year.

Borden, like many other great entrepreneurs who failed then tried again, this time with better financing (although still capitalized at a relatively low level of $100,000 in 1857). When the Civil War started, his infant business took off as the U.S. Army ordered 500 pounds of condensed milk. Six years after his second milk company was founded, he opened a facility in Brewster, New York, that turned out 20,000 quarts of condensed milk *a day*! Only then did Gail Borden retire; but even in retirement he continued to invent, delving into the mysteries of condensing fruit juices and creating instant coffee. By that time—and for generations thereafter—"Borden" meant milk.

In many ways, Gail Borden typified the entrepreneur of his age. Mobile and willing to work at different endeavors, he persisted with his true interest until he could achieve success. A northerner, he was inspired by the needs of the markets in the South and West. A failure, he triumphed. Structurally, the Borden story also reflects the antebellum age: While he needed investors, the business remained fundamentally his to oversee and direct. He epitomized the entrepreneur-oriented business that is run by the owner-founder. But the sheer size of the nation—its vast geographic expanse and its swelling population—made for mass markets that few individually run businesses could serve. The speed of transactions, made possible by the railroad, steamship, and telegraph, compounded the difficulties faced by a single owner attempting to manage a business. Finally, the financial demands of larger enterprises required investors, and as the shares of ownership passed into the hands of numbers of unrelated people, permanent managers were needed. Fortunately, the Bordens, Vanderbilts, Wellses, and other trailblazing entrepreneurs did not disappear in the new age. Rather, they took on somewhat different responsibilities and challenges, controlling new corporate structures with their thousands of employees and facilities stretched across several states. Now, however, ambition and vision alone were not enough. The times demanded new skills and approaches for what would become a revolution in American business.

CHAPTER 5

The Rise of Managers: 1850–1880

More than fifty anxious, perspiring brokers pressed around the fountain in the "Gold Room" on Broad Street, next to the New York Stock Exchange, as the caller marched to his position on September 24, 1869. The operator cleared his throat, then shouted "145 for 20,000," a code indicating that he had a bid for 20,000 ounces of gold at $145 an ounce. Instantly the price surged still higher, streaking up to $155 as "operators became reckless, buying or selling without thought of the morrow or consciousness of the present."[1]

The account, a description of Black Friday, climaxed a struggle called the "Gold Corner," in which Jim Fisk and Jay Gould, two of the most notorious of business speculators, attempted to corner the market on gold. Fisk and Gould, acting on "insider" information bought from Abel Corbin, the brother-in-law of President Ulysses S. Grant, had assurances that the government would not sell gold when the price started to rise. Along with other members of their plot, Fisk and Gould had acquired futures contracts for gold at $135. Under the terms of a futures contract, a person places an order to buy a certain quantity of goods in the future at a price fixed in the present, and the group was convinced that—absent a huge sell-off in government gold—their buy orders would stimulate gold prices and send them spiraling up well past their purchase price. Indeed, the price climbed to more than $160, sending speculators into a frenzy as they attempted to grab what they thought were bargain prices.

President Grant surprised them by keeping the gold in the nation's vaults for a brief time, but he finally ordered the Treasury to sell gold, sending the artificially high gold prices plummeting as speculators now sought to get out before prices fell below their purchase price. Although Gould escaped with millions of dollars in profits, it was a paltry amount compared to what he would have gained if the government had not acted. The remarkable scene reflected the growing influence of Wall Street and the speed of communications, which made the stakes of such speculations higher than ever by linking investors outside New York to the nation's money capital. And while gold was the object of speculation in this case, other scams of the time usually involved selling bonds for railroads never built.[2] Together, the narrow confines of Wall Street and the vast ribbons of iron rails reaching across America represented the twin poles of a new age—magnetic opposites that at times both attracted and repelled. But they shared a powerful, common link in that they used and institutionalized a new corporate form, generally described by historians as a "managerial hierarchy."

RAILROADS AND THE RISE OF MANAGERIAL HIERARCHIES

Three factors combined to create the virtually new business arrangement in the mid-1800s: the speed of transactions, communications, and travel; the size of companies (including both numbers of employees and capital demands); and the scope of operations, spanning across thousands of miles. Simply put, no single owner could any longer expect to maintain tight control over an enterprise that might span three time zones, conduct business in a dozen different states, employ thousands of people, and require millions of dollars of capital every year.

Small shops, employing artisans or family members, still existed and still thrived. Silversmiths, tailors, mercantile stores, and other small businesses of almost every conceivable type operated efficiently with owners performing basic management chores. But railroads, with their rapid speed and phenomenal capital demands, ushered in a new era of business structure in which owners—consisting of thousands of stockholders who did not even know each other—delegated responsibility for running the business to professional managers.

Railroads triumphed in short order over canals in moving freight and people, taking advantage of their overwhelming productivity advantages, if for no other reason than they could run year-round while canals had to shut down for up to five months a year due to winter weather. Even the Erie Canal, which reached its peak traffic loads in the mid-1850s, could not compete with railroads. Rails could extend into areas canals could not reach, providing branchlines that could straddle factories or stockyards. Speed differentials between steamboats and railroads widened, with rail travel moving three to four times faster than boats on canals. River travel still possessed elegance and romance, and a brief window for steam-powered carriages opened, then shut, with railroads emerging the clear winner of the transportation "race" by 1840. Introduction of the steel track, which could be easily manufactured in fifteen-foot lengths, meant rails could be mass-produced. By 1860, 30,000 miles of railroad track crossed the United States—an astounding increase of more than 20,000 miles in the decade of the 1850s alone—with the Old Northwest experiencing a construction boom unmatched in other regions. Ohio and Illinois ranked first and second in miles of railroad by the start of the Civil War, and almost a dozen roads stretched into Chicago, the dominant departure point for the West. Branchlines connected to larger trunks that wove a quilt of track across the North, while in the South, shorter railroads linked waterways to cities. As one economic historian commented, "By 1860, it was possible to travel from any of the great East Coast ports to Chicago or St. Louis and thence to New Orleans at speeds inconceivable only thirty years earlier."[3]

Linking the roads together proved a remarkable market success. Many roads had been built with different gauge track, making uninterrupted shipment nearly impossible, especially in the South. There, "by 1860 only one connected route carried passengers from the East Coast to the Mississippi by way of Richmond and Memphis."[4] The solution became obvious to industry insiders: If you want to ship more efficiently, in unbroken lines, adopt the same gauge track as other roads. Within a few years, railroads began to convert to a uniform track width—all without a single government regulation or oversight body.[5] Other problems existed, however, not the least of which was the high level of competition, which drove profits down, and the high cost of construction. Three individuals in particular had a dramatic impact on developing a framework for more efficient railroad operations.

THOMSON, McCALLUM, AND FINK

J. Edgar Thomson and Daniel McCallum stood out as organizational geniuses of the mid-1800s, while Albert Fink introduced modern accounting methods to business organization. Together, these men brought railroading to a new level of managerial efficiency. Thomson achieved fame with the Pennsylvania Central Railroad (the "Pennsy"), chartered in 1846 by a group of Philadelphians. The president of the Pennsy, Samuel Merrick, already was well known as a successful businessman in a half-dozen different ventures, ranging from insurance to ironworks. He lacked an understanding of railroads, and to gain such expertise he hired Thomson, a professional engineer from a family with a history of canal and railroad building.

Thomson traveled extensively in England to study the operations of railroads and to analyze English technology on a firsthand basis. He returned to a position with the Georgia Railroad and Banking Company—just one of the many combination bank–railroad businesses popular at the time—extending the line westward to Atlanta, and then he took up Merrick on his offer to run the Pennsy. Thomson quickly demonstrated the difference between the new professional manager and the more traditional foreman. Moreover, he directed the railroad without consulting the owners (or the board of directors, who represented them). Expansion of the Pennsylvania Central under Thomson occurred rapidly, as the railroad joined Philadelphia to Pittsburgh, then ran onward to Chicago. By 1852, the board had named Thomson chairman, symbolizing the complete dominance of the new professional manager over the functions once performed only by owners.[6]

In a ten-year span, Thomson took a railroad with less than 250 miles of track and revenues of under $2 million and turned it into a railroad system with 438 miles of track and $11 million in revenues. Such expansion would not have been possible without developing a *managerial hierarchy*—a pyramidal framework of managers with a top-down authority structure in which *strategic decisions* (long-range, "big picture" decisions) are made by the top levels of management. This top level included the chief operating and chief financial officers, while daily or *operational decisions* resided with mid- and low-level managers. The primary function of any manager, however, was the transmission of information, moving strategic information downward to the line workers and pushing sales and customer information upward to top management. In this capacity, managers were like conduits.

Thomson was not the first to use that structure, nor the most famous. Daniel C. McCallum, who started his early career with the New York and Erie Railroad, had emerged as the best-known proponent of managerial hierarchies, formulating both a philosophy by which to understand them and a series of rules by which to create and empower them. Henry Varnum Poor, editor of the *American Railroad Journal*, was so impressed with McCallum's distribution of work and authority that he lithographed McCallum's organizational chart and offered it for sale.[7] By the late 1850s, the Pennsylvania Railroad, borrowing heavily from McCallum's work, reflected an entirely new organizational structure, roughly defined by *line and staff positions* that depicted the flow of authority and the basic function of each element of management. At the top was a general superintendent who carried out the president's strategic decisions by managing the flow of resources to each division. Each division had a superintendent who transmitted to the employees the strategic decisions of the top management. Broadly speaking, each division had little need to know about anything other than its own operations, and therefore the managers played a critical role in the transmission of information, much like the days that human telephone operators literally used to plug in lines connecting parties across miles of telephone lines. As information transmitters, the managers sorted out those items of information that each division needed to know from those it did not, evaluating marginal information in between. The system provided remarkable direction at the bottom, because workers did as they were instructed, with little opportunity (given the still local emphasis on news) to see the larger picture. Even so, lower managers also played the role of information transmitters by sending up the chain of command local sales reports, consumer comments, and the status of the employees' work.

Before leaving the New York and Erie Railroad, McCallum's 1855 "Superintendent's Report" to the stockholders established several principles that the new business organizations adopted, including the division of responsibilities, prompt and reliable reporting, and confidentiality.[8] Within just a few years, McCallum's structure and principles had spread to the other major railroads, which already had started to separate management of operations and finance. The combined functions of those two areas had opened the door to substantial mischief by allowing railroad officials to "create a construction company separate from the railroad's operating company... retain[ing] all of the construction company's stock for themselves."[9]

Early railroaders—and many of the later, unscrupulous ones, such as Jim Fisk and Jay Gould—did not pay adequately for new capital expenditures, refurbishing of equipment, or purchases of new locomotives and rolling stock. Roads deteriorated and became unsafe. Thus, McCallum's structure addressed those problems directly by placing long-term financing under a separate division, while dividing operations and scheduling into their own departments. This creation of "line" and "staff" designations acted as a check on the excesses of any division and tended to reveal any abuses of funds.

A constant, reliable stream of information proved key to the efficient operation of the new bureaucracies, causing the demand for information to generate a revolution in accounting. Indeed, accounting truly emerged for the first time as a profession, replacing traditional double-entry bookkeeping.[10] J. Edgar Thomson and the Pennsylvania Railroad again were involved in pioneering the new accounting practices, which fell into three major categories: financial accounting, capital accounting, and cost accounting. Financial accounting recorded the financial transactions of the railroads and prepared reviews of the company's financial performance. It required far more sophistication than bookkeeping offered. Capital accounting involved finding ways to depreciate the equipment and thus plan for its replacement at future, usually higher, costs. Cost accounting appeared last, as a means to track the performance of individual divisions. The company had to know how much gross revenue it needed for each part of the road to meet operating costs.

Albert Fink, a civil engineer, excelled at applying this new form of cost accounting. Fink, who worked for the Louisville & Nashville as its general superintendent, derived a carrying cost for one ton per mile of each of his divisions, a feat that required him to determine what percentage of each part of his rolling stock was full at a given time. He also understood that his estimates had to come from actual data from each class of rolling stock—not mere averages—which led him to develop elaborate mathematical formulas that he applied to the data.[11]

Achieving profitability from such estimates required the manager to take advantage of *fixed costs*—those costs that remained constant, such as a mortgage on land or a payment on a factory building. Other costs, known as *variable costs*, changed depending on the number of items produced, and included labor costs, raw materials, and expenses related to providing power, light, heat, or water to a factory. By taking advantage of fixed costs through a high volume of production, an entrepreneur or manager could achieve *economies of scale*. But extracting profits based on economies of scale required a commitment to making the railroad pay for itself out of its own operations. To many railroaders, the frenetic competition threatened to make it impossible to run a sound business enterprise. As Alfred Chandler, author of *The Visible Hand: The Managerial Revolution in American Business*, observed, "Never before had a very small number of very large enterprises competed for the same business.... And never before had competitors been saddled with such high fixed costs."[12] However, many of the well-known railroaders of the mid-1800s had little intention of holding on to a railroad long enough to improve it, let alone see it achieve productivity gains. They bought and held railroads for only one reason: to make quick profits from stock fluctuations. No incidents better illustrated the differences in goals and methods than a series of confrontations between some of the most famous railroaders of the day in what became known as a "Chapter of Erie."

VANDERBILT AND HIS FOES

Predictably, some railroaders ignored genuine business improvements and efficiency gains, trying instead to gain riches through manipulating the political machinery. The "Erie Wars," a series of clashes between some of the most flamboyant railroaders of the mid-1800s over the Erie Railroad, epitomized the role of "political entrepreneurs," or those who sought to use government favors to achieve a business advantage.

In 1853, Erastus Corning, a Albany iron business owner, created the New York Central Railroad. Corning had obtained a law authorizing the consolidation of a group of railroads, including the Erie, the New York Central, and others, into a single, giant corporation capitalized at $23 million. Having obtained the incorporation, Corning quickly tapped the company treasury to sell the road $1.09 million worth of his company's iron products. Corning had obtained and sustained his position only with the help of Cornelius Vanderbilt. The Commodore had a simple philosophy for running a railroad: "One, buy your railroad; two, stop the stealing that went on under the other man; three, improve it in every practicable way within a reasonable expenditure; four, consolidate it with any other road that can be run with it economically; five, water the stock; six, make it pay a large dividend."[13] Modern students might be alarmed at item number five, "watering stock," a scandalous term used by writers such as Charles Francis Adams, Jr., that referred to increasing the number of shares outstanding without increasing the paid-in capital or reducing the par value. This practice seemed to cheat the stockholders by diluting their equity. But with Vanderbilt the term was inapplicable. He held large stock positions in the railroads he ran, and under his management the stock of his railroads rose rapidly, and without increasing the number of shares, the prices would have skyrocketed. It constituted a form of "stock splitting" before that concept was really invented. In essence, Vanderbilt paid stock dividends and gave his stockholders additional shares rather than cash.[14]

By that time, Vanderbilt's railroad career crossed that of another legendary Wall Street figure, Daniel Drew. Starting his career as a cattle drover, Drew had originated the term "watering stock" when he adopted the practice of stopping his herds just outside the point of sale, feeding them salt, then letting the cattle drink their fill of water to increase their sales weight.[15] By 1853, Drew held substantial stock in the Erie, and even held a seat on the board of directors. Drew had a reputation for pursuing speculation in the stock of railroads, relying on his political contacts to affect the value of the road while completely ignoring the company's operational interests. In that way, Drew fit the "political entrepreneur" mold, which brought him into direct conflict with a "market entrepreneur" like Vanderbilt. The two men clashed in a pair of separate incidents known as the "Harlem Corner" and the "Erie War."

Both Drew and Vanderbilt had interests in the Harlem Railroad in 1857, and in 1864 the railroad sought to extend its line beyond its original charter. Drew, sensing the stock profits associated with the extension, purchased still more shares of the railroad and used his influence with the New York City Common Council to get the extension approved. He then *sold short*. Selling short involves borrowing shares of stock (say, 100 shares at $1 per share) from a broker and selling it immediately (for $100) with the promise to repay the *shares of stock* at a future date for a price determined at the time of the transaction. Obviously, a short seller hopes that stock prices would fall before the repayment date. (In this example, assume that the price indeed falls to 50 cents per share by the time the speculator needs to repay the stock. He sells for $100, then, at a later date, repurchases the same number of shares for $50, repays the broker, and has a $50 profit.) Short selling can lead to large profits; but the impending delivery of the stock also means that if the price rises after the initial sale, the short seller is in trouble and must acquire stock to meet his future obligations (known, literally, as "covering his shorts").

In the case of the Harlem Railroad, Drew first convinced the Common Council to *reject* the extension, causing the price to plummet, then abruptly reconsider and approve the extension (but only after he sold short and made huge profits). Drew would have both his railroad extension and his profits, while the council members and the state legislators—whom Drew had enlisted to sell short along with him—would have nice bonuses. If all went according to plan, Drew and his insiders would borrow shares of Harlem stock and sell it. When news of the extension rejection reached the street, Harlem shares would plummet; Drew and his friends would buy back in, repay their debts, and keep the profits. At that point, the Common Council would reconsider, forcing prices back up and restoring Drew's original stock holdings to their value.

One of the primary losers in the scheme was Vanderbilt, who did not appreciate being the object of a manipulation. Nor did he approve of the legislators acting against his interests. After all, he had supported some of them quite well and on occasion had himself enlisted their allegiance. As one observer quipped, "being a man of honor, [Vanderbilt] expected the legislature, once paid for, to stay bought."[16] In fact, however, virtually all business owners had to support one party or the other or risk harassment by local officials at the behest of their superiors. Usually, rather than going to government for help, Vanderbilt handled his own challenges, as he did in this case: Along with an ally, John Tobin (who also had suffered stock losses due to Drew's escapade), the two concluded they would teach the speculators a lesson. Using aliases, Tobin and Vanderbilt's agents moved into the market and proceeded to buy thousands of shares with funds from a war chest of more than $5 million. Just four days after the prices collapsed, they reversed again, rising to $125, then, after a week, to $137. Within a week, Vanderbilt's money pushed prices past $175, then to $224, as panicked short sellers themselves had joined in bidding for the scarce shares. Begging for mercy, brokers representing Drew and the legislators asked Vanderbilt what he would do. "Put it to a thousand," he replied. But he was counseled that such a move would spread to other, stable businesses, affecting all of Wall Street. He had, after all, taught a sublime lesson. Vanderbilt agreed to let the legislature off the hook at a price of $285, not only making millions of dollars for himself but "taking those millions out of the hides of people whose misfortunes were entirely self-inflicted."[17] Indeed, Vanderbilt had used the market to discipline a corrupt legislature and to reaffirm one of Wall Street's cardinal truisms: "Bulls make money and bears make money, but pigs never make money."

Drew, though temporarily defeated, hungered for revenge. He owed Vanderbilt and his associates more than $1.5 million, and after pleading for mercy—which the Commodore did not show—Drew became defiant, but then he quickly realized his predicament and apologetically approached the Commodore with a promise that he would support Vanderbilt's interests in the New York Central and would cease his attempts to drive down the stock prices of the Erie Railroad. In return for his mea culpa, Drew was allowed to remain on the Erie board.

Among the other members appointed to the Erie board in 1867 were Jay Gould and James Fisk, Jr.[18] Fisk had spent time as an animal keeper in a circus before joining a Boston mercantile firm. He had the great insight to set up an office in Washington, D.C., immediately after the first shots on Fort Sumter, wining and dining congressmen to generate a sea tide of federal contracts. Later, he ran the Union blockade of the Confederacy, and at the end of the war, the prosperous Fisk headed to Wall Street, where he met Jay Gould. Born on the same day as Vanderbilt—May 27—Gould worked as a child on his parents' dairy farm. He found a job as a surveyor, rendering maps of New York, Ohio, and Michigan in a delicate and artistic style. In his spare time he wrote a history of Delaware County, a 426-page manuscript that burned in a fire at the publishing house. Gould merely started again and reproduced the book from memory. He purchased stock in a small railroad, expanded his equity, and in 1867 found himself on the board of the Erie with Fisk, Drew, and a pair of Vanderbilt's agents.[19]

Individually, the Commodore could control any of them. Together, they made a formidable set of opponents, especially when lodged on the board of the Erie. Vanderbilt wanted the Erie to work with the New York Central and the Pennsylvania railroads to form a pool, and he was not interested in momentary stock speculation. Concluding that he could not control the Erie with surrogates, Vanderbilt set out to purchase the railroad outright, a feat of some undertaking, given the road's $17 million market value and considering that the Commodore had his money tied up in the Harlem Railroad, the Hudson Railroad, and the New York Central.

Making matters worse, Drew advanced the Erie Railroad $3.4 million, in return for 58,000 phantom shares. Breaking his vow never to go to court to fix a problem, Vanderbilt pursued legal remedies, and a court enjoined the Erie from accepting Drew's offer of a cash-for-shares exchange. Drew merely ignored the court's order, adding to the chaos. Increasingly, the entire market hung on a word: "Erie!"

Not to be left out, Jim Fisk weighed in with Drew, personally overseeing the printing of 50,000 new phantom shares of Erie stock, trying to make it impossible for Vanderbilt to buy control. Nevertheless, Vanderbilt and his allies held nearly 200,000 shares—and Drew, Fisk, and Gould had more than $7 million of Vanderbilt's money. But no sooner had they started to celebrate than the court gave the Commodore the breakthrough order he needed, dispatching sheriffs to bring in the trio for contempt. Unceremoniously, Drew grabbed the first ferry to New Jersey, although Fisk and Gould remained in New York, where they dined blatantly at Delmonico's Restaurant (protected by lookouts), before themselves retiring across the Hudson River with Vanderbilt's cash. From New Jersey, they not only defied the Commodore but also Judge George Barnard, who promised to have them arrested if they came into his jurisdiction. To ensure that no one took them back to New York against their will, the triumvirate turned the Taylor Hotel into "Fort Taylor," replete with armed guards and three twelve-pound cannons! They also attempted to convert the Erie Railroad into a New Jersey corporation, dragging the state assemblies of New York and New Jersey into the fray.

Realizing they could not win, Fisk and Gould negotiated with Vanderbilt, paying him for his shares and agreeing to remove Drew from the Erie board. Although the Commodore may have taken a small loss, he emerged from the battle essentially unscathed. However, after the settlement he paused to warn friends, "The Erie is going down."[20] It was a prophecy and not a threat, reflecting Vanderbilt's understanding of the approach to railroading held by Gould and Fisk.

Hardly had the ink on the agreement dried than Gould and Fisk made good on Vanderbilt's prediction. In 1868, Drew stepped down and Jay Gould took his place as president of the Erie, with Fisk his chief operating officer. The duo promptly drove down the price of the railroad's stock by 35 percent. The Erie had revenues of just over $14 million, but had expenses barely under that, leaving it with net revenue of $22,000. While the Erie lurched on, Vanderbilt's New York Central epitomized the new efficiency of the professionally run railroad. Between 1867 and 1868, the company's revenues rose only 2.9 percent, but Vanderbilt chopped 13.3 percent from expenses, increasing profits by almost 55 percent, or almost 200 *times* that of the Gould-Fisk-run Erie. Even more important, while the Erie had accidents that killed twenty-six and injured seventy-two, all of Vanderbilt's roads *combined* had zero fatalities and only eleven injuries. Accident rates on the Erie led reformers such as Charles Francis Adams, Jr., and his brother Henry Adams—great-grandsons of the second president of the United States and the grandsons of the sixth president, John Quincy Adams—to publish an expose called *Chapters of Erie*, which argued for public regulation of railroads.[21]

Partly due to the Erie Wars, Wall Street took it upon itself to reform the sales of securities internally. In November 1868, some sixty-five years before the creation of a Securities and Exchange Commission, the NYSE passed a resolution to require public registration of securities traded on the exchange, making it impossible to secretly water stock. After the resolution passed, only the Erie and three other similar companies had not complied. Within a year, even Jay Gould had to adhere to the registration requirement. As John Steele Gordon noted, "Effective self-regulation of the New York stock market would increase greatly in the next few years [and it would be] self-regulation rather than government that would successfully guide Wall Street for the next two generations, as it eclipsed London and grew into the largest financial market on earth."[22] Of course, the NYSE was not perfect in self-regulating, in no small part because each new evolution in financial instruments brought different challenges that the exchange could not anticipate. But there is little reason to suspect that the government could have done better—it completely missed the junk bond revolution in the 1970s, was flummoxed by the appearance of the currency futures market in the 1980s, and did not anticipate any problems with the proliferating number of mortgage-backed securities in the early 2000s. Indeed, shortly before the collapse of Fannie Mae and Freddie Mac, Congressman Barney Frank and Senator Chris Dodd proclaimed the institutions completely solvent and stable.

The Erie Wars marked Vanderbilt's final epoch. Though appreciating the essential necessity of having new management professionals focused on efficiency gains, Vanderbilt remained a man of an earlier business era. He was the owner who ran his businesses, the individualist who could see strategic issues and attend to minute details, the entrepreneur/speculator who could manage stock fluctuations and yet still understand the underlying basis of value in rolling stock and track quality.

Nor were Fisk and Gould, for all their notoriety, representative of the new wave of business leaders. Obsessed with making quick profits from stock manipulations or the rapid resale of roads, they had little interest in achieving productivity gains within the railroads themselves. More than Vanderbilt, however, Fisk and Gould characterized the attitude among most of the railroaders of the day in their quest to eliminate competitors, either by driving them out of business or through forming cooperative oligopolies. As early as the 1850s, most railroaders wearied of rate wars and sought stability and security within their established routes. To that end, railroad companies met at large conventions to set "official" rates that every company would comply with, thus standardizing the classifications of weight and making rates uniform. Senior railroad executives met in 1854 to agree, in J. Edgar Thomson's words, "upon general principles which should govern railroad companies competing for the same trade, and preventing ruinous competition."[23] They accepted basic principles of charging on the basis of value of the transported product, and arrived at a cooperative rate base. Still, individual railroaders occasionally evaded the agreements by secretly offering rebates, or refunds for heavy railroad use, and lowered their prices in public when they could.[24] For a time, the roads managed to maintain discipline, with brief exceptions during the Panics of 1857 and 1873, until a new era of competition dawned in the 1880s.

Rate-setting, however, generally did not prove as useful in maintaining market share as the tactic of dividing territory into spheres of influence. In 1870, three major railroads that ran the Chicago to Omaha route agreed to split traffic evenly. The "Iowa Pool" was copied elsewhere until the 1880s, when many of the informal arrangements collapsed. Most pools operated as follows: The railroads set prices and contributed a percentage of revenue to a pool. The pool then paid the difference when the traffic could not justify the preset rate, and the railroad shipped the freight at the below-rate cost. In addition to rate-setting and pooling, railroads tried yet another means of controlling their competition, whereby they purchased large blocks of the shares of competing roads. Owning substantial sums of stock allowed the railroads to put their own directors on a competitor's board, a tactic called *interlocking directorates*. Having the same people on both boards decreased the likelihood of competition. In the case of the New York Central and the Hudson River railroads, for example, Dean Richmond of the Central served on the board of the Hudson River, and while Vanderbilt was not personally on the Central's board, his handpicked agents were.

GOVERNMENT AND RAILROADS: THE PRELIMINARY PHASE

Competition ironically was reduced in another way: by the involvement of state governments and, eventually, the federal government. With the sole exception of James J. Hill and his Great Northern, most of the major railroads sought assistance from the states or Uncle Sam at one time or another. But the notion that the government had to step in because private entrepreneurs would not meet public demand for railroads has been challenged.[25] By 1860, the public had contributed more than $250 million to railroads—one-quarter of the railroads' total expenditures. Government aid for railroads usually came in the form of loans or bond guarantees from the states. By 1838, states had amassed a total railroad-related debt of more than $40 million, with the state of Missouri alone granting nearly $25 million to several rail companies. When not investing directly, states guaranteed the bonds of the railroads, pledging their "full faith and credit" should the roads collapse. States also granted generous charter conditions, including monopoly rights, to railroads, in no small part because they learned that even with the riskiest of railroad ventures, the effects of railroad construction on property values generated enough growth in property taxes to almost offset losses in worst-case scenarios and to give the state and communities a windfall in taxation in the event of successful railroad operations.[26]

Prior to the Civil War, the federal government did not involve itself in railroad grants, with the important exception of land given to a group that wanted to build a railroad to the Pacific that would cross the Nebraska Territory. The politics required to obtain land for that road were largely directed by Illinois Senator Stephen A. Douglas. But in the attempt to provide land for the railroad through the creation and settlement of two new territories, Kansas and Nebraska, Douglas set in motion the political events that led to the Civil War.

Both pro-slave and "free soil" settlers (those who opposed slavery) moved into Kansas in the mid-1850s, leading to violent clashes. Most observers thought that in time, free-soilers would outnumber the pro-slave immigrants, and the free-soilers would vote (under Douglas's concept of popular sovereignty) to make Kansas and Nebraska free states. In 1857, however, the United States Supreme Court issued a ruling in the *Dred Scott v. Sanford* case that said neither Congress nor popular votes could prohibit slavery from a territory. The decision sparked an upheaval in the financial markets as the securities of railroad companies with lines running west suddenly crashed (significantly, none of the roads that ran north and south were affected). Uncertainty over the future market conditions caused a panic that quickly spread to the New York financial markets in general, where the large banks held significant sums of railroad bonds. In the resulting Panic of 1857, the maturation of new mechanisms of transmitting financial and economic information, which had been occurring for a decade, suddenly became visible to many people for the first time. Anxious to prove their ideological points, spokesmen for the North and South both used the panic to argue for the superiority of their respective regions. The economic theorists of the South, for example, concluded that the Southern economy had surpassed that of the North, because few Southern banks even suspended operations, let alone failed, while the North experienced a crisis that nearly equaled the Panic of 1837.[27] Northerners, on the other hand, used the same information to suggest that slavery insulated the South from severe market reactions, and therefore market incentives could not prod slave owners toward emancipation.

Southern polemicists missed important factors that had protected the South in the panic. First, the South had very few roads that touched the West, and therefore had only a small number of companies that were affected by the developments in Kansas. Second, the banking system in the South—far more than the Northern banking system—had adopted branch banking, making the transmission of financial information much quicker and more reliable. That proved crucial in preventing a panic mentality from developing. The North resisted any tendencies toward the creation of larger banking institutions, so its banking structure retained inefficient unit banks, which only resulted in confusion and chaos during financial distress. A third, and final, factor contributing to the panic involved sudden changes in wheat prices in the North, related to the end of the Crimean War. Once again, the South read the wrong message. With an economy dominated by cotton, Southerners felt no reverberations from the war.[28] They also failed to realize that a cotton monoculture would itself be highly vulnerable in the future to its own enemies, such as the boll weevil.

Despite the immediate effects of the Panic of 1857, federal intervention in railroad construction expanded dramatically during and after the Civil War, especially in the form of providing land grants. Typically, the government granted land to a railroad in a checkerboard pattern along the right-of-way, giving the company only half the land fronting its railroad. Remaining land stayed in the hands of the government for other uses. The Illinois Central, for example, received several million acres of federal land in 1850, which it sold to settlers to establish farms near the railroad; the Northern Pacific—a transcontinental route—received 42 million acres. Land grants carried twin benefits: The land sales brought revenue, which railroads applied to track and rolling stock, while also establishing a built-in consumer base for the finished railroad, consisting of farmers who needed the railroad to ship products east and bring finished goods from urban centers. Accordingly, the land adjacent to railroads was the most highly prized and brought far higher prices than land further away.

Railroads earned nearly $500 million from land sales. Land-grant railroads transported government freight and mail at reduced rates, which saved the government millions of dollars over the years, exceeding the amount spent on the land grants by the taxpayers. But those savings, and the high social rates of return, came at the expense of private stockholders and bondholders by encouraging redundant, ill-planned, and speculative building. It also required taking large portions of Indian land (for which, in many cases, the U.S. government had to pay reparations decades later). Homesteaders did acquire land that was extremely valuable because of its proximity to the railroads. But did settlement occur artificially? Were many areas settled only due to the presence of the railroad line? It is difficult to measure the benefits of the transcontinentals when such considerations are taken into account.

Eager to sing the praises of the railroads (and, indirectly, the efficacy of government assistance), some historians have contended that the subsidies made completion of a nationwide rail network sooner than it might otherwise have occurred, linking the nation with a ribbon of iron rail. Clearly, many businessmen curried favor with the government for grants and prospered as a result—an exercise in political entrepreneurship but not market success. Measurable benefits indeed resulted, but they incurred not only the cost of the grants themselves, but also the subsequent cost of reorganizing or rescuing numerous poorly constructed or ineptly managed roads, factors that rarely play a part in the equations of economic historians examining the era. More important, however, grants created incentives to build without concern for efficiency or reliability. Subsidies thus only encouraged the activities of people like Fisk and Gould, perhaps discouraging other builders less interested in getting the land than they were in establishing efficient railroad networks. Clearly, the government, for its own reasons (many of them involving the war) aligned itself with some business interests. It is entirely possible that without the land grants there would have been fewer, but better, railroad systems at roughly the same time. Evidence for this exists in the accomplishments of James J. Hill, America's greatest railroader.

JAMES J. HILL'S GREAT NORTHERN

James J. Hill, born in Canada, supported his widowed mother by working in a grocery store for $4 a month. An accident deprived him of his right eye. Handicapped and poor, Hill hardly seemed destined for wealth and success. Yet after working for a shipping company, Hill learned the transportation business. He wove his expertise with a vision that included the North American plains filled with farms and cities. Hill completed his entrepreneurial persona with that final essential ingredient—faith. In 1878, he and a group of Canadian investors bought a bankrupt road in St. Paul, Minnesota. That railroad had received federal subsidies and had experienced stock manipulation and deplorable management, and its record was so pitiful that critics dubbed it "Hill's Folly" when Hill announced his intention to complete the route. It not only ran profitably upon completion, but the road's success inspired Hill to keep building, turning the enterprise into the Great Northern Railroad.

Extending his railroad across the Northwest, Hill built more slowly than those building the subsidized roads, knowing he had to pay the cost himself. He therefore chose routes for durability, safety, and efficiency, not scenery. "We want," he observed, "the best possible line, shortest distance, lowest grades, and least curvature."[29] Hill had no land from subsidies, which other roads sold to settlers; instead, Hill had to *pay* settlers to go West, offering $10 to each settler who would farm near his railroad. To ensure that the settlers prospered, Hill imported 7,000 cattle from England and distributed them at no cost to the pioneers along his line. He established his own experimental farms to develop new seeds and livestock and farming techniques for the arid, sparse soils of the northern Great Plains states.[30]

Not only did he expand the market for his service, but he understood that lasting profits came from lower operations and maintenance costs. That, coupled with his penchant for shorter routes and lower grades, allowed Hill to catch up to his subsidized rivals in the time it took his company to lay rail, and eventually outrun them. Although moving more slowly at first, due to the constant insistence on quality over speed, Hill built better roads that required fewer repairs that ate up construction time and effort. Whereas Hill's competitor, Henry Villard, who received more than 42 million acres of free government land, lavishly laid his tracks along areas of beautiful scenery, Hill chose the safest and most efficient paths. To be fair, Villard catered to tourists and to an extent had to place his routes through scenic territories, while Hill built for permanent settlers. Apart from their target market, however, Hill showed superior planning. Inevitably, his shorter routes and lower repair costs saved his road money on every trip. While Hill got his coal from Iowa, Villard had to ship his from Indiana at a cost of $2 a ton more than Hill.

Typically, Villard responded by attempting to use government—not the market—to battle Hill. Congress, which had granted Villard his land in the first place, frequently delayed permits to the Northern Pacific to cross Indian land, even though its rates remained lower than Villard's. Of course, Hill paid for his rights-of-way. Even with all their supposed advantages, Villard and the other transcontinental owners found themselves in dire straits during the Depression of 1893. Only Hill, who had received no money from the public treasury, avoided bankruptcy. The Union Pacific, the Northern Pacific, and the Santa Fe all had to be reorganized.

In retrospect, the subsidies themselves accounted for much of the mismanagement of the roads, in that subsidies were given based on miles completed, but not the quality of miles completed or the effectiveness of the road. The incentives of subsidies encouraged overbuilding and construction of circuitous routes aimed at laying as many miles of track as possible. With no concern for terrain, the subsidized roads ran up steep gradients that increased fuel cost, and along weak shoulders that contributed to accidents. Villard, for example, built his railroads well ahead of demand, often in rough, empty areas. Everywhere, the subsidies encouraged higher repairs and operating costs, while at the same time fostering a contemptuous attitude toward settlers: After all, the farmers needed the roads, not vice versa. Hill, in contrast, simply could not afford either the costs or the attitudes of the government-backed roads, and as a result he had lower fixed costs than all his competitors and an appreciation for the settlers he needed to make his railroad profitable.

Perhaps more important, the subsidies contributed to competition for federal favors instead of railroad customers, ushering in an era of corruption unmatched in American history. During the 1860s, a construction company for the Union Pacific (one of the subsidized transcontinental roads) called Credit Mobilier sold $150 million in bonds, a sum far beyond what the railroad needed for its construction. In 1867, Congress considered an investigation of the company, prompting Credit Mobilier to pay bribes to members of Congress and Vice President Schuyler Colfax in the form of selling them stock well below market price. Five years later, the scandal became public, tainting the already-damaged administration of Ulysses S. Grant and characterizing the period as the Era of Good Stealings.

Nevertheless, Credit Mobilier is viewed as a case that illustrates the weakness of "federal institutions to regulate such a crucial business event as the completion of the nation's first transcontinental railroad."[31] One business historian cited "this sort of behavior [as] just one cause for the widespread hostility toward railroads…. Protests arose over unfair freight rates, overcapitalization, sloppy or dangerous operating procedures, and monopoly or oligopoly control."[32] Yet neither appraisal is accurate or appropriate. The Union Pacific did not encounter difficulties because it was inadequately regulated, but because subsidies provided the road and its builders with the wrong incentives. To obtain government land, the Union Pacific built on ice, encroached on Indian lands, while both it and the Central Pacific tried to slow each other's progress by blowing up each other's tracks. And the subsidies had repercussions with consumers, whose complaints may have been directed at "unfair freight rates" or "monopoly control," but for whom the underlying issue involved the sense on the part of taxpayers that they had paid for the railroads and thus were entitled to certain considerations.

Meanwhile, the two subsidized roads worked from opposite directions to meet in the middle. One road, the Union Pacific, stretched from Nebraska westward. General Grenville Dodge, the chief engineer, supervised nearly 10,000 men laying track at a breakneck speed. With each new mile laid, the Union Pacific qualified for more land and loans, meaning that "the haste with which the road was built inevitably produced sloppy workmanship…."[33] From the Pacific Coast, the Central Pacific line labored to overcome the more difficult of the two routes, crossing the Sierra Nevada Mountains and other ranges. Four of the most powerful individuals in California history, Leland Stanford, Collis P. Huntington, Charles Crocker, and Mark Hopkins, controlled the Central Pacific, which imported most of its labor. Chinese workers were prominent among the Central Pacific's labor force and were given the most difficult and dangerous work.[34] A contemporary saying— "there is a Chinese buried under every tie"—sadly comes close to accuracy, and yet in the famous photograph of the joining of the tracks, a lone Chinese rail worker is visible. The Central Pacific shipped its tools, supplies, and the rails themselves by sea before bringing them overland to the railheads, and by early 1869 both it and the Union

Pacific had rails in proximity. They did not wish to connect, however, because their funding would have ended; instead, they surveyed land and built parallel roads. Finally, even Congress had enough, forcing them to join rails.

On May 10, 1869, a simple message was dispatched across the telegraph wires: "Done." Celebrations broke out across America when the United States learned that work crews of the Union Pacific and the Central Pacific had driven the famous golden spike at Promontory Point north of Ogden, Utah, completing the first transcontinental railroad. (Of course, that original spike wasn't left behind—looters would have stolen it and the gold it was made of would not have sustained the beating produced by trains; rather, the spike was put on display in California.) Another transcontinental, the Northern Pacific, soon appeared, followed by the Southern Pacific, which resulted from a political negotiation that allowed Rutherford B. Hayes to become president in the Compromise of 1877.[35]

Thus, five transcontinental railroads hauled freight and passengers across the United States, with total track mileage in the nation exceeding 193,000. Nevertheless, a depression in 1893, brought on by attempts to force the U.S. government to buy silver at above-market prices, resulted in the bankruptcy of three of the five transcontinental roads.[36] When the other railroads were in forced reorganization, Hill's Great Northern cut costs by 13 percent. Ironically, the government may have discovered that its policies had gone awry. In 1874, Congress passed the Thurman Law requiring the Union Pacific to pay 25 percent of its earnings to the government in return for its $28 million debt. Yet much of that debt stemmed from overblown construction costs, corruption, and poor planning that related directly to the subsidies and government funding.

Perhaps more troublesome to consumers, especially farmers, was the fact that the Union Pacific and the Northern Pacific both charged higher rates than did the Great Northern. In the past, railroads attempted to divide territory geographically with agreements not to compete in each other's region, or else to form pools. But the Great Northern offered different challenges to the rate structure. The transcontinental railroads already had a degree of geographic monopoly, and Hill would not participate in a pool. Concerned that they were losing business to their unsubsidized competitor, the roads (although certainly not all of them) lobbied for rate regulation, which Congress supplied in 1887 with the Interstate Commerce Act.[37] The act made it illegal to give discounts to shippers who dealt in large volumes or mass quantities, essentially outlawing the volume discount for railroads. Rather than reducing prices for the smaller shippers—as was the intent—the law required that prices be consistent, so shippers merely raised prices for the shipment of long-haul goods. In addition, the act created a new federal bureaucracy to determine the "fairness" of rates, with the authority to investigate the records of the nation's railroads.

Some have argued that many railroaders wanted federal regulation as a way to formalize their internal price-fixing arrangements. Others have contended that the railroaders hoped to avoid formal rate regulation and instead wanted the government to validate their informal pooling arrangements.[38] Only when the Interstate Commerce Act outlawed pooling did railroaders turn to the market by investigating profitable consolidation of existing roads—something for which Hill had argued.[39] Determining exactly what the railroad managers thought at a given time presents a host of problems, as does establishing a person's motivation for choosing any particular strategy. No doubt some wanted government help, and others believed they could work matters out among themselves. Regardless, while they may have differed over the strategy, the major railroad magnates did not hesitate to seek federal help in enforcing prices or in validating the pooling arrangements that they could not maintain through market forces alone.

Competition from the unsubsidized roads continued to drive prices down. During a thirty-year period after the Civil War, the rate for carrying wheat fell by 70 percent (at a time that general prices only dropped 14 percent), and individual roads sliced their fares. The Santa Fe cut its prices 42 percent; the Chicago, Burlington, and Quincy reduced rates by 50 percent; and the Northern Pacific by 46 percent. New advances in railroad technology, especially the sleeping and dining car developed by George Pullman and the air brake invented by George Westinghouse, also increased passenger traffic and forced prices down. Westinghouse, who was only twenty-two years old when he invented the compressed air brake, spent two years attempting to convince railroad officials that his invention would save lives. (Westinghouse made a fortune on the air brake, but did not quit inventing. He later worked on alternating current, or AC, electricity.) But whether due to technology or market pressures, the pooling agreements had failed to work, bringing an end to horizontal combinations.

Salaried, professional managers assumed active direction of the major roads, turning them into efficient vertical combinations. The railroads had, through convulsion and confusion, ushered in the managerial revolution in business.

Simply establishing line and staff organizations did not complete the transition from owner-operated businesses to the new form of business enterprise. That required another step in which firms vertically *integrated*—that is, they moved backward in their original product's supply chain to obtain control over raw materials or forward to absorb sales and distribution networks. With control established over raw materials, transportation of their product, wholesaling, and retail outlets (as well as, later, marketing and research and development), firms held their fate in their own hands. They did not have to rely on outside teamsters or railroaders for shipping—they had their own transportation networks. Companies established their own warehouses. Thus, at no point did outside businesses threaten to disrupt the flow of goods, and therefore the managers could plan for every aspect of the business. Increasingly, the focus shifted from eliminating competitors to stabilizing the flow of production. And, as Andrew Carnegie learned in steel, controlling costs was everything. Firms did not respond to price cuts by competitors as much as they constantly sought productivity gains within themselves. Managers, under whose authority the productivity increases rested, not only justified their existence, but were elevated to the pinnacles of business. At that point, when business evolved into vertically integrated, manager-dominated firms, American companies became "big business."

ALFRED CHANDLER'S VISIBLE HAND

The appearance of "big business," first with the railroads, then expanding to other areas of production, was the most obvious development in American enterprise between 1850 and 1890. A century later, in 1977, Alfred D. Chandler, Jr., produced a capstone work analyzing that evolution. *The Visible Hand* embodied major themes that Chandler had studied for years and presented in segments in several other books.[40] Chandler outlined eight general propositions that traced the appearance and dominance of what he called the visible hand of management (in contrast to Adam Smith's "invisible" hand of competition), which was itself the essence of the managerial revolution of the 1800s. The propositions were:

1. Modern business enterprise replaced small traditional enterprise when administrative coordination permitted greater productivity, lower costs, or higher profits than did the market.

2. The advantages of internalizing cost-saving activities required the appearance of a "managerial hierarchy," which Chandler argued was "a defining characteristic of the modern business enterprise."[41]

3. Modern business enterprise first appeared in history when the volume of economic activities made administrative coordination more efficient or profitable than market coordination.

4. Once the managerial hierarchy was formed, it became permanent and powerful within a business.

5. The managers became increasingly technical and professional.

6. As business grew in size and complexity, the management of enterprise became separated from ownership.

7. The professional managers favored policies that enhanced long-term stability rather than those that maximized profit.

8. Large enterprise, dominated by managerial hierarchies, expanded from railroads into other major sectors of the economy, thereby altering the structure of those sectors as well.

Cumulatively, the eight propositions described a business culture in which the most important enterprises, or "big business" in the Chandler definition, spread from railroads to most other large firms. In doing so, the structure of business enterprise was changed fundamentally, from a market-directed culture to a manager-directed one. More broadly, the new managerial firms de-emphasized competition and stressed internal controls for the purpose of increasing efficiency. While Chandler saw capitalism as maturing with the managerial revolution, his theory championed planning and nonmarket forces, fitting well with those (such as John Kenneth Galbraith) who sang the praises of government-business "cooperation." In Chandler's world, at least in its most modern manifestations, there was little room for entrepreneurs who built the businesses. Instead, the key parts were played by nonentrepreneurial managers, and the rise of big business signaled the death of the entrepreneur.

Of course, some of the managers exhibited entrepreneurial tendencies, as illustrated by J. Edgar Thomson and, later, Charles Schwab of Bethlehem Steel, Lee Iacocca at Ford Motor, and Citibank's Walter Wriston. Usually, however, when managers acted like entrepreneurs, they were entrepreneurs, owning large blocks of stock and having a substantial and immediate financial stake in the companies they ran. However, the confusion regarding the roles of the managers have led many business historians, perhaps in resignation, to treat managers as entrepreneurs, even to the point of defining them as such.[42] But to the extent that most managers did not use their own money, they were not, by definition, entrepreneurs. Thus, Chandler's theory seemed to suggest that the days of entrepreneurs had ended, displaced by a professional managerial class.

MEDICINES, MUSIC-MAKERS, AND MANUFACTURERS

At the very time that the managerial hierarchies started to reshape business enterprise, attracting the bulk of public attention with high-profile deals, ever-expanding production, and swelling ranks of labor, another sector of business quietly thrived. Entrepreneurs had not disappeared when railroads made professional managers a permanent feature of the business landscape, although occasionally their activities could appear less important due to the small size of most entrepreneurial firms. Indeed, some entrepreneurs just got lost in the shuffle; but others would stand out in any crowd.

Lydia E. Pinkham, one of twelve children, had received a solid education and held a job as a schoolteacher when she married Isaac Pinkham. Isaac readily took any job, yet never prospered. When the Panic of 1873 slowed the economy, the Pinkhams and their five children drifted into abject poverty. Partly out of desperation, in 1875 Lydia

Pinkham started selling her special vegetable compound for "female complaints" (a nebulous term that referred to any discomfort or injury related to the female anatomy). Giving away the "remedy" at first, Pinkham and her sons found that the compound was extremely popular. They manufactured the remedy as "Lydia E. Pinkham's Vegetable Compound" in their basement. Lydia oversaw actual production, while sons Daniel and William used wages they earned at other jobs to market the compound and procure supplies. Isaac, then in a wheelchair, folded pamphlets. Daniel distributed more than 20,000 "Guide for Women" pamphlets in ten days, whereupon a leading pharmacist started to sell the product. While in Boston, Daniel used $60 to place a front-page ad in the *Boston Herald*, and sales went up. Grasping the value of advertising, the Pinkhams dedicated more of their budget to newspaper promotions, even mortgaging their house to buy additional advertisements.[43]

At age 60, Lydia put her portrait on the remedy, giving it a recognizable trademark. The ad campaign reached billboards, bottles, newspapers, magazines, and streetcar signs, turning Pinkham into a household name. Offered $100,000 for the company, the family declined. In 1881, annual sales surpassed $200,000. After both of her sons contracted tuberculosis and died, Lydia gave up control over the business to other family members, who maintained the business until the 1980s. The firm increasingly came under attack from public health officials and the medical profession as ungrounded in any medical science. It was ultimately the product itself, and not the entrepreneurial form of the company, that ended Pinkham's business.

Lydia Pinkham started late in life, but never considered herself too old to succeed. And if age proved incapable of stifling the entrepreneurial instinct, so did bad luck. Heinrich Steinweg, for example, was as unlucky as one person could get. At age 11, Heinrich's mother and many of his siblings in Germany died fleeing from the advancing troops of Napoleon. Years later, Heinrich, along with his father and remaining three brothers, took shelter during a thunderstorm in a small hut but lightning struck the building, killing everyone but Heinrich. Left an orphan, Heinrich Steinweg joined the army, where he learned to make musical instruments, including pianos, in his spare time.[44]

Steinweg married and had five sons who joined him to construct pianos in Germany. When business dropped during the revolution of 1848, Steinweg and his family decided to move to the United States.

When they arrived in New York in 1850, they realized that the pianos that sold in Germany might not appeal to Americans. Consequently, all of the Steinwegs took jobs with different New York piano factories to learn American tastes and technology. Confident they had absorbed all that American piano manufacturers had to offer, the family started the House of Steinway & Sons in 1853, producing a single piano each week. Within twenty years, Steinway pianos had received some of the world's top prizes for musical instruments, bolstering the company's reputation and battling imitators who used similar-sounding names, such as "Steinmay" or "Shumway." Despite the look-alikes, the demand for Steinways reached such proportions that in 1872 the family built Steinway Village in Long Island—a model housing project for employees that included a library, school, and free bathhouse. The family retained control until 1972, and the name stood for quality for many more years.

Another piano manufacturer, Jonas Chickering, born in New Hampshire, began in cabinetmaking but quickly apprenticed with a leading American piano maker. By 1830 he had a partnership making musical instruments, and after his partner died at sea in 1841, Chickering managed the business by himself. Even after a fire destroyed his Boston factory, Chickering built the business all over, in the process gathering patents for new piano frames and revolutionizing piano construction.

Steinway and Chickering seemed to find their specialty early in life. Elisha Otis, on the other hand, took twenty years of repeated business failures to find his calling. Born in 1811 in Vermont, Otis had a building business in Troy, New York. Later, he started, operated, and closed a gristmill in Vermont; built fine carriages for seven years until that enterprise dried up; and then labored in Yonkers, New York, as a master mechanic at the Yonkers Bedstead Company. His inveterate tinkerer's spirit led him to invent a machine for automatically turning parts of bedsteads much faster than could be done manually, and Otis then contracted that and other labor-saving machines.[45] Seeing an opportunity to create his own business, Otis attempted to manufacture machinery of various types until his water supply was appropriated by the city of Albany. At age 40, Otis was again in debt and out of work. However, his former Yonkers employer hired him to supervise the construction of a new factory. Otis had considered going to California to search for gold. Unexpectedly, success got in the way.

While studying a problem with the new factory, Otis had to move heavy woodworking equipment to the second floor of the building. He constructed a platform hoist, but unlike other elevators of the day, it had a safety device—a ratchet and spring that engaged when the main cable broke, stopping the elevator instantly. As he made plans to leave New York, the burly mechanic was contacted by a furniture business that had experienced an elevator accident and wanted to ensure that it never happened again. Encouraged by the demand for his product, Otis formed the E. G. Otis Company in 1853. That ended his intentions to strike it rich in the mountains and streams of California—although he no doubt wondered if he made this decision perhaps too quickly, because his early torrent of orders soon turned to a trickle. Freight elevators were common in New York, but no landlord wanted to risk human passengers in one of the contraptions, and thus the largest market in the city remained closed to Otis's elevators. A true entrepreneur, Otis displayed the faith and vision that had characterized the Pinkhams, the Vanderbilts, the Astors, and others. Otis did what few other entrepreneurs seldom did: He put his own life at risk based on his faith in his product. He demonstrated his lift at the 1854 American Institute Fair at the Crystal Palace in New York. Standing on the platform (with some boxes and barrels for added weight), Otis was elevated far above the thousands of people watching when he ordered an assistant to chop the cable. The lift plunged instantly, but the safety catches brought it to a sudden stop. Otis bowed deeply and stated loudly, "All safe, gentlemen, all safe."[46]

Having obtained free publicity that would otherwise have cost him thousands of dollars in advertising, Otis expected a new surge in orders. He was mistaken. The next year he sold only fifteen elevators, and the year after that, twenty-seven, all freight lifts. Not until 1857 did Otis make his first passenger elevator sale, to a five-story Manhattan china store—an elevator that still carried passengers in 1984. Otis did not live to see the business he started reach maturity. He died in 1861, leaving his two sons to run the $5,000 company. Like the Steinwegs, the Otis family not only continued the business but improved and expanded it. Charles and Norton Otis invented more than fifty patented technical refinements for elevators, including air brakes (1864) and the introduction of the electrical elevator (1869). Elevators as a product, however, differed substantially from home-remedy medicine and pianos in that they required a sales force with technical expertise to instruct buyers and a qualified repair and support staff. The Otis Company provided both. By training sales personnel to understand the technical basis of the elevators, Otis's company further accelerated the professionalization of business management brought on by the railroads, continuing and spreading the managerial revolution still further.

For residents of multistory buildings, however, elevators were nothing less than blessings. The elevator also made more convenient some of the most famous tourist attractions in the world: Otis elevators carried people to the top of the Washington Monument (1888) and the Eiffel Tower (1899) and returned them safely. When combined with the architectural advances of William Jenney, who in 1885 had perfected a method that used an iron frame to support a building's weight, the Otis elevators made possible true skyscrapers.

John Deere had a much less difficult life than Pinkham or Steinweg, and unlike Otis had an immediate demand for his product. He received an education in Middlebury, Vermont, schools. He took a position as an apprentice to a local blacksmith, where he quickly learned the trade. Deere's quality work earned him a reputation with the state's farmers for producing the finest shovels, hoes, and pitchforks. In 1836, anxious over the depressed condition of Vermont's economy, Deere joined other Vermonters relocating to Grand Detour, Illinois. There he established a new forge and held the respected position of village smithy, when he learned that farmers had difficulty tilling the heavier western soil with their eastern plows. Deere, "working with a discarded sawmill blade," built a prototype of a new plow with a curved shape made of highly polished steel.[47] The new plow immediately gained popularity with the local farmers, and by 1846, Deere contracted a Pittsburgh steel company to supply steel, allowing him to mass-produce the plows. Within a year, Deere moved his facilities to a better location, near the Mississippi River. At his new factory in Moline, Illinois, sales reached 10,000 by 1857.

Deere continued to refine his plows and make other implements. He changed his marketing strategy, growing more sophisticated. Once he loaded a wagon with plows and visited farms until he had sold them all. Later he developed a network of local dealers who sold the plows on commission. Deere watched his dealers carefully, recording in a book his observations about their personal honesty. Charles Deere, John's son, joined the company in 1858, and as the business grew, John and Charles looked for still further improvements in tilling the soil. In 1874, they devised the first two-wheeled riding plow, in essence heralding the advent of the high-volume farm implements of the late 1800s, during which time the Deere Company also employed a technically skilled sales and repair force to join the managerial revolution.

When it came to advances in farm equipment, no entrepreneur had a greater impact than Cyrus McCormick, who revolutionized wheat harvesting. Born in Virginia, Cyrus had watched as his father worked unsuccessfully on their Shenandoah farm to develop a mechanical harvester, a design that Cyrus built in modified form in 1831, using a saw-toothed blade to cut the stalks pulled into the cutter by a reel device. By 1834, he had a patentable reaper, but then he inexplicably turned his attention to other matters for half a decade, flirting with an iron business that failed. It wasn't until 1840 that McCormick improved the design further and made his first sale. He quickly beat back competition from a rival, then relocated to Chicago in 1848, becoming "one of the first American industrialists to face the necessity of making a major move in order to be closer to his markets."[48]

McCormick's reaper could harvest fifteen acres of wheat in a day, and while effective on its own, generated extensive productivity gains when combined with other mechanical devices just starting to appear, including binders, steam threshers, and other powered machinery.[49] Even when the reaper did not "pay for itself" initially, farmers often purchased the device with the intention of expanding their wheat crops, now that the harvest of more acres could occur before the wheat turned from ripe to spoiled. The reaper, in essence, changed the way farmers thought about their business.[50]

Not only did McCormick usher in agribusiness, he continued the trend toward vertically integrated companies through his business practices. His factory had the capacity to turn out forty reapers a day, and in 1856 the McCormick Company produced 4,000 machines. But the new equipment differed substantially from other mass-produced items of the day in that no one had seen a reaper before—making it an alien piece of technology—and it bore a hefty price tag ($115 in 1850 dollars, or the equivalent of well over $100,000 in today's money). Farmers pooled their resources to purchase reapers jointly, and professional reaper and thresher companies passed through the farmlands regularly with the large machines and the team of up to twelve horses required to pull them.[51] Nevertheless, to overcome the "purchase anxiety" of his potential customers for the reapers, McCormick enlisted salesmen who learned the operation of the product and could demonstrate it. He offered credit to make it easier to purchase the expensive reapers, requiring only $35 in a down payment. By instituting the use of credit, McCormick placed an additional demand upon the dealers, requiring them to judge the creditworthiness of buyers or, when necessary, to collect on past-due accounts.[52] The dealers, assisted by heavy doses of company advertising from the Chicago office, not only sold the reapers, but they had to provide efficient service for the equipment, again supported by the Chicago administration that ensured delivery of spare parts.

After the Civil War, a new challenger, the "individual combine," eclipsed the McCormick reaper, but Cyrus McCormick, admitting he was bested in one area, applied himself to the production of wire binders, an associated technology invented by Charles Withington in 1877. McCormick's entry into the market put him into competition with John Deere's Deering Plow Company. The two titans, both born of farmer-entrepreneurs, merged into a single business, the McCormick-Deering International Harvester Company, in 1903.[53]

Thanks to McCormick and Deere, rapid advances in agricultural technology generated an abundance of crops that flowed from American farms at levels previously unimagined. The combined effects of mechanization in wheat production, provided by devices such as the reaper, and the westward movement of farmers resulted in, by one estimate, an astronomical 377 percent increase in labor productivity between 1840 and 1910.[54] Associated with such astounding productivity, Northern farms returned profits at an average rate of more than 12 percent on every dollar invested.[55] Although the full impact of the mechanical advances and comprehensive settlement of the American West was not as clear in the mid- to late-1850s as it would be decades later, many observers at the time already pointed to vastly different—and, to them, mutually incompatible—economies and business cultures between the North and the South that they traced almost exclusively to slavery. Both the North and South used the economic events of the 1850s to justify their business and labor systems, initiating a debate that touched the very essence of free market systems.

SECTIONAL DIFFERENCES: "FREE LABOR," BUSINESS, AND ECONOMIC GROWTH

The sectional split had festered since the signing of the Constitution in 1787, which received support from Southern delegates only on the grounds that it would contain no prohibitions against slavery. Delegates at the Constitutional Convention had their most heated debates over those sections of the Constitution involving representation and taxation because they realized that the outcome would affect the direction the nation would take toward slavery. Following a series of compromises, the Convention agreed to permit slaves to count as three-fifths of a person for purposes of representation and taxation, and to place a twenty-year moratorium on any legislation related to the slave trade. Otherwise, slavery went untouched.

In 1808, Congress banned the importation of slaves, but that merely added to the value of slaves already within the United States. By that time, plantation slavery had been thoroughly rooted, making it impossible for minor legislative tinkering to redress the problem. Slavery spread to every Southern state, as well as Delaware, Maryland, the District of Columbia, Kentucky, and eventually Missouri, but the economic impact of slavery was suppressed until Eli Whitney invented his cotton gin in 1793. When the cotton gin solved the problem of cleaning the short-staple cotton that grew easily in the rich soil and the temperate climate of the South, production increased across the entire lower tier of American states, especially in the land along the Mississippi River Valley. Pulled westward by steadily higher yields, the momentum of "King Cotton" showed no evidence of slowing. That, in turn, placed increasing stresses on the American political party system that had been designed to avoid a confrontation between the sections. After the Missouri Compromise of 1820, each new territorial expansion raised the specter of war, and yet each new expansion, so desperately sought by Southerners, increasingly illuminated the political weakness of the South.[56]

When the Republican Party appeared in the 1850s, its opponents labeled it an antislavery party, but some of its major spokesmen, such as Abraham Lincoln, only wanted to limit the extension of slavery into the territories, not prohibiting it outright. Lincoln espoused a position known as the "natural limits" of slavery, which held that slavery only could function in cash-crop plantation settings. This view held that cotton- and rice-producing areas that existed in the South were, through processes of land expiration, moving steadily to the southern and western regions, and therefore if trapped within its "natural limits" and lacking new territories to prolong its life, slavery would vanish.[57] Unfortunately for Lincoln and subsequent proponents of the natural limits theory, the relentless expansion of the cotton frontier and the introduction of slaves as urban and industrial labor suggest that slavery would not have disappeared on its own. Indeed, research by James Huston confirms that slave capital in the South exceeded the North's investment in railroads and heavy industry *put together*![58]

BUSINESS, "FREE SOIL," AND "FREE LABOR"

Perhaps of more immediate concern to businesses in the 1840s and 1850s were the new arguments made in favor of, and against, slavery from the perspective of labor. Slavery became thoroughly intertwined in the minds of both slavery advocates and proponents of "free labor" (a term used to describe work for wages) with other issues such as the tariff and "free soil" (a term for territory without slaves). Lincoln assumed a prominent role in the debates, as did leaders of the business and industrial communities, and in many ways they touched on the understanding of entrepreneurship in the 1850s.

The term *free soil* referred most often to territories in the West that were threatened by the expansion of slavery. Slaves had traveled with their masters as far as Utah and California—although not in great numbers—and the potential for slavery in the territories dominated the politics of the era. Many thought the issue solved when Henry Clay had drafted the Missouri Compromise in 1820, which prohibited slavery north of latitude line 36 degrees 30 minutes, but which allowed new territories admitted to the Union as states *below* that line to choose to be free or slave states. New controversies arose with the admission of Texas and the subsequent Mexican War, which made California a state. In 1854, the Kansas-Nebraska Act formed two new territories that sought statehood on the basis of a new doctrine introduced by Senator Stephen Douglas of Illinois: popular sovereignty.

Each new controversy heightened the tension over slavery. Northern political economists argued that the extension of slavery directly attacked the foundation of free labor—of workers free to select their employment and bargain for their pay. The basis of individual advancement came through hard work, which produced high wages. Many Northerners feared that the competition from slave labor would drive down wages paid to free workers. Settlement on free soil offered an attractive solution. Nevertheless, many writers in the North supported high tariffs and free soil as a primary means of maintaining wages for free labor.[59] Some argued purely from the perspective of wages, contending that land would draw away "excess laborers" and thus raise wages.[60] For many advocates of free soil, the issue transcended wages. Available land promised any individual the opportunity to improve his lot in life, and slavery threatened that opportunity. Some theorists, including Lincoln, saw industrial work as a passing phase to farm ownership and running a small business, the ultimate expressions of entrepreneurship. Free soil, then, embodied the essence of entrepreneurship, even if it was closely linked in the minds of its advocates with wage labor and tariffs.

Free labor meant wage labor in the North: the ability to work for the employer of one's own choosing at a wage mutually agreed upon.[61] But at least one well-known Southern critic of the industrial system, George Fitzhugh, attacked free labor as slave labor, arguing that the wages paid in the North provided a living standard worse than that of plantation slaves. A Virginian and an unabashed socialist, Fitzhugh's controversial book *Cannibals All!* revealed exactly how far slavery was from free markets. He contended that the only true freedom came when a person's needs were met, and that only slaves enjoyed such a healthy situation. Northern factory owners "enslaved" their workers with inadequate wages; but plantation owners cared for their slaves' needs conscientiously. Thus, in one of the classic inversions of capitalism, Fitzhugh maintained that free labor (i.e., wage labor) in reality meant slave labor, while slave labor really constituted free labor! He called for a socialist government that would care for all people, run by a few masters who were enslaved by their obligations. No one was truly free, he contended: We are all "slaves without masters."[62]

Many critics in both the North and South had suggested just the opposite, namely that the South lagged behind the industrial North in providing material well-being for its employees because the system of slave labor was not as productive as free labor. As Nathaniel Banks argued in 1857 before audiences in Boston and New York, slavery was "the foe of all industrial progress and of the highest material prosperity."[63] Likewise, Frank Blair, of the influential family of Missouri and Maryland antislave activists, wrote that "no one from a slave state could pass through 'the splendid farms of Sangamon and Morgan, without permitting an envious sigh to escape him at the evident superiority of free labor.'"[64] But were such assertions true?

Plantation agriculture had entrenched itself in the life and culture of the South since the 1600s. Buoyed by primogeniture, mixed with the chronic labor shortage and the economics of cash-crop production of cotton, rice, or tobacco, the financial logic of using slaves was unchallenged by all but a few Southern theorists. Writers such as Hinton Helper urged non-slaveholders to resist the political programs of the slave owners, but for every Helper there were more influential pro-slave voices, such as John C. Calhoun, or more idiosyncratic ones.[65] Of course, almost half of all Southerners had no slaves, and most of the slaves were held by 12 percent of all slave owners.[66]

The economics of slavery were relatively simple. The number of slaves in the United States had risen from 894,000 in 1800 to 3.95 million in 1860, with most of the slaves employed in agriculture. A prime field hand cost $1,800 in 1860, and prices rose steadily because new slaves could not be regularly imported. Regardless of its immediate profitability, slavery was viable, meaning that the costs of raising slaves—food, shelter, medical care, and even interest—were less than the prices at which they could be sold, with the differential widening between 1815 and 1860. *Profitability* was a different concept, relating to whether slaves produced more than it cost to purchase them and care for them. For a few decades, some debate existed about the profitability of slavery. Some economists and historians, relying on the manuscript plantation records of owners as evidence of income and expenses, concluded that slavery was not very profitable.[67] Owners tended to overstate their expenses or difficulties—particularly in correspondence to family members or friends—and thereby underestimated their returns. Others erroneously counted items as expenses that really belonged to other investment categories. Kenneth Stampp found that slaveholding returned 8.4 percent on investment, not counting the increasing value of slaves for resale purposes.[68] In 1958, Alfred Conrad and John Meyer applied modern accounting techniques to plantation records and found slavery was profitable in almost all cases, and in the more fertile western lands, returns ran as high as 13 percent.[69]

Subsequent studies have sustained and refined the conclusions of Conrad and Meyer. It was hard *not* to make money with slave labor. Slavery, as a business practice protected by state laws, provided unfair advantages against those employers not using slaves, and thus the economic incentives supported and sustained slavery within its sealed environment. Most important of all, the incredible grip on the South of slaves as property meant that Southerners could never accept any infringement on the definition of slaves as chattel. That meant, over time, that those property rights would have to be accepted even in the North, and that sooner or later, the logic of slavery was that Northerners would have to allow slavery back into their societies. Businesses did have substantial incentives to make a transition into manufacturing. One study found, for example, that by 1860 the *lowest* rates of return on industrial capital in Southern manufacturing exceeded 22 percent (and the highest, 45 percent).[70] The researchers also found that large-scale manufacturing in the South and West in the pre–Civil War decade greatly resembled the pattern set in the Northeast.[71] However, many Southerners knew cotton cultivation well; it held few surprises and produced regular profits. It would have required exceptionally daring farmer-entrepreneurs to abandon cotton for the unfamiliar enterprise of manufacturing and industry, although clearly many did make exactly that transition. But it also required that individuals resist the social and cultural milieu that encouraged slave-based agriculture, and for many the pressures exceeded returns of even 22 percent.[72]

Successful plantations achieved steady profits on the basis of an organizational system for slaves called the "factory in the fields." That term described gang-based slave labor in which a handful of managers—slave drivers and overseers—could control hundreds of slaves picking cotton. Although the rate of exploitation (or *expropriation*—a term meaning the difference between the amount produced by the slave and the amount consumed by the slave) was a relatively low 12 percent when measured over the entire lifetime of the slave, the exploitation rate during a field hand's prime years reached as high as 65 percent.[73] That exploitation constituted the essential difference between free farmers and slaves. Slaves worked longer hours as well, making it difficult for even the worst planter/businessman to lose money with a slave workforce.[74] In their controversial 1974 work, *Time on the Cross*, Robert Fogel and Stanley Engerman concluded that

Southern agriculture was 35 percent more productive than Northern farms, and slave plantations produced even higher efficiencies, and in his later solo work, *Without Consent or Contract*, Fogel reiterated that the "technical efficiency of the slave farms, particularly the intermediate and large plantations, accounted for about 90 percent of the Southern advantage [over farms in the North in the antebellum period]."[75]

If Southern industrialization was retarded by slavery, other elements of the South's economy actually had surpassed in sophistication their counterparts in the North, including aspects of its banking system. The South had high rates of patent registration and other evidence of technological innovation, although over time the South appeared to drift behind the industrialized North in the ratio of patent registrations.[76] And clearly the South as a region was neither poor nor insulated from market factors. Its manufacturing base, however, trailed the United States per capita value-added average in 1860 by a substantial $7, and pockets of deep rural poverty existed.[77] The government support of slavery in the South insulated slavery from market forces and meant that it would be extremely difficult for the market alone to overthrow the slave regime.

CHAPTER 6

Entrepreneurs in the Age of
Upheaval: 1850–1880

David Kennedy arrived in Fink, Tennessee, in 1842 to start a dry goods store. Within a few years, his reputation for solid business practices led to his election to the board of directors of the Fink branch of the powerful Bank of Tennessee, and he eventually resigned to form his own bank, the Bank of Northern Tennessee. He continued to run a prosperous but uneventful business until April 11, 1861. On that day, the South Carolina "fire-eater" Edmund Ruffin touched off a cannon fuse that opened bombardment on Fort Sumter, igniting at the same time the bloodiest conflict in American history. For the next four years, while war raged, Kennedy's banking business experienced swings as the Confederacy attempted to persuade Kennedy to support the new nation with his bank's gold (he would not) and then as Union troops took Clarksville. As federal troops drew near, Kennedy loaded whatever gold he could carry on his horse and made his way through Mississippi to a point that he could catch a steamer to New Orleans. There, he transferred the bank's assets to safety in an account in England. After the war, he withdrew the assets and shipped the specie from England to Tennessee, where he reopened the bank, one of the few in the entire South to survive the war.

Kennedy's difficulties during the Civil War, first in resisting confiscation of the bank's assets by one government and removing them from the grasp of another, underscores the tremendous difficulty in conducting most businesses during time of war. While certainly some businesses can prosper during wars, especially arms manufacturers, as a rule, businesses dread the disruption of their markets and the human toll that war takes. Companies involved in interregional or international trade suffer particularly extreme hardships in time of war.

THE CIVIL WAR AS A BUSINESS STIMULANT

The American Civil War exacted such a cost on business. During the conflict, the Republican Congress granted extensive lands to the railroads, enacted the Homestead Act, passed protective tariffs, and established a system of national banks—all seen by many historians in past generations as supportive of business, though increasingly challenged by more modern writers.[1] The Civil War left more than half a million men dead and inflicted long-lasting wounds on the Southern economy. But for the North (and, on average, the nation as a whole), historians have debated the long-term effects. Some have contended, beginning with influential early works by Charles Beard and Louis Hacker, that the war was a positive development and a turning point for American economic and business growth.[2]

The Beard–Hacker thesis held that the shift of political power to Northern business interests from the Southern "slavocracy" ended agrarian resistance to capitalist industrialism. By destroying slavery, the war ended a feudal or precapitalist labor system. Finally, the wartime demand for goods and services in the North accelerated the nation's economy, despite the costs of the conflict. Beard went so far as to tout the war as the "Second American Revolution," opening the floodgates for corporate expansion and social equality.

This turning point concept offered an attractive interpretation of the Civil War, except it wasn't true. According to the comprehensive analysis of recent research on the effects of the Civil War, Jeremy Atack and Peter Passell conclude that "it is very difficult to identify the Civil War as the turning point in economic growth or industrialization from the historical data."[3] The U.S. economy grew more slowly in the decade after the Civil War than in the decade before it; the manufacturing sector especially slowed down, falling by 1.8 percent per year. During the 1860s, however—precisely the time that wartime economic expansion should have been at its peak—commodity output fell by 2.6 percent.[4]

Clearly, however, national averages would include the ravaged South. What would happen if the analysis could be limited to the winner—the North? Here, growth tests make a somewhat better case for the Beard–Hacker thesis, although not much. From 1840 to 1860, per capita income in the North rose at an annual rate of 1.3 percent, while from 1860 to 1879, the rate was 1.7 percent—an increase, though hardly a revolution. A central question remains, however: To what extent did the period 1860 to 1879 merely ride on the coattails of efficiency gains already put in place before 1860? The railroad, the reaper, the steam engine, the telegraph, and dozens of other critical technologies had just moved into the market. Would not that alone have accounted for substantial post-1860 growth?

Indeed, some shocking anomalies exist for the proponents of the Beard–Hacker thesis, not the least of which is the intriguing fact that boot production fell by 13 million pairs from 1855 to 1865! Considering that boots were a staple of any army, shoe and boot manufacturing should have skyrocketed during the war. Wool production rose substantially because of the shift away from cotton, which the South had embargoed as a strategic measure, and which failed miserably.

On the other hand, the Civil War inflicted huge economic costs, the most important of which were the 600,000 Americans killed and 500,000 wounded. In purely sterile terms, such as those used by insurance companies' actuarial tables, economists have put a value on those lives of approximately $2 billion.[5] Static approximations, however, offer no way of guessing how many Andrew Carnegies, Cornelius Vanderbilts, or, for that matter, Abraham Lincolns were among the dead. In other words, averages provide at best a still photograph of a situation, but they can in no way capture the dynamics of people who may have been in the infant stage of making a fantastic discovery, embarking on a nation-shaping political career, or founding an extraordinary business when the war cut short their lives.

Nor when the cost of the destruction of physical property (exclusive of slaves) is calculated—which was on the order of $1.1 billion to

$1.4 billion—can it be estimated how many new factories on the verge of exceptional production gains or new firms on the threshold of gaining remarkable management efficiencies were abruptly ended. Of course, some factories were in the process of decline, or other businesses were failing—but the point is that no average or measurement can predict the appearance of an individual genius or business superstar. Predicting what gains might have been made is an impossible task, but the record leaves hints. For example, the banking system in some Southern states had achieved a degree of sophistication unseen in the North through widespread branch banking. Tennessee, North and South Carolina, Georgia, and Virginia all had thriving branch banking systems that virtually evaporated with the Confederate defeat. In turn, that contribution could have been substantial. Had such systems survived intact and perhaps spread to other, newer Southwestern states, such as Oklahoma, Colorado, or even into the Midwest, to Kansas and Nebraska, it is possible that much of the banking collapse of the 1920s and 1930s might have been averted. And, to ignore the "elephant in the room," the instant legal conversion of billions of dollars' worth of slaves from property into people was one of the most important economic events in all of Western civilization.

CIVIL WAR LEGISLATION AND BUSINESS GROWTH

Several measures passed by the Republicans during the war did benefit certain sectors of the economy and specific businesses. Tariffs raised revenues and fulfilled the promises that Republicans made before the war to Northern interests. The Homestead Act (1863) sold western government land at the minimum price of $1.25 per acre or at a maximum price determined at an auction. With vast new acreages opening up, and the advent of mechanical devices like the reaper, the man-hours of labor per acre of wheat dropped from thirty-five to twenty between 1840 and 1880; for corn, the numbers dropped from sixty-nine to forty-six. The number of farms rose from 2.6 million in 1870 to 4.5 million by 1890, and continued to rise well into the twentieth century.[6] Farm acreage shot up to 623 million by 1890, from 407 million two decades earlier. While certainly many farmers would have moved west even without the Homestead Act, it nevertheless contributed to the settlement of the Plains states and the extension of the farm belt.

Equally important—and perhaps more so—Congress passed a series of bills from 1862 through 1865 collectively known as the National Bank and Currency Acts. To finance the war, Secretary of the Treasury Salmon P. Chase had chosen to avoid taxation as much as possible, relying instead on bond sales. The National Bank Act provided the mechanism for selling those bonds by establishing a new system of chartering national banks that had to purchase U.S. government securities with a portion of the charter's capital. In return, banks received National Bank notes (i.e., money) for up to 90 percent of the face value of the bonds. Banks then emitted the banknotes through loans or in exchange for specie. Each national bank had its name inscribed on the notes it received—an extremely valuable source of advertising.

Bank purchases of bonds proved critical to financing the war, but the national banks found themselves in competition with state-chartered banks, and the restrictions placed on national banks, including lending restrictions on real estate and higher capital requirements, made the federal charters less attractive than those offered by individual states. Consequently, Congress passed a 10 percent tax on all state banknotes that drove out of circulation most state and private note issues. Without their note advantages, state banks could no longer compete with the national banks, and the numbers of national banks grew rapidly. As state banknotes disappeared from circulation, the United States found itself with a uniform currency for the first time in its history. Until the national banknotes appeared, greenbacks constituted the primary currency for the first few years of the conflict. Issued by the Treasury, the government declared them legal tender, meaning that citizens and merchants had to accept them for payment of debts. With specie payments on banknotes suspended during the war, the greenbacks made up much of the circulating medium in the North until the appearance of the national banknotes, and tended to fluctuate in their gold value based on users' assessment of Union war prospects.[7] Greenbacks were not redeemable in specie immediately after the war, but the government, true to its promise, redeemed them in 1879.

As commercial and savings banks opened in the American West, they became ingrained in the romantic images of the wild and woolly frontier, usually in the context of a bank robbery. Unfortunately for Hollywood, there were no Western bank robberies to speak of in the horse-and-buggy era. Bank buildings were located in the middle of town (so robbers couldn't arrive unnoticed), usually with other buildings adjacent. They were, in fact, constructed not only with security in mind, but also with an eye toward image. It was critical, for example, for a bank to look prosperous. Banks featured the finest cabinetry, ornamentation, and metalwork, and they were likely to be the first to use masonry construction. In short, banks gained the trust of customers because they appeared solid and safe. The remarkable security of bank buildings constituted half of the visible symbols of safety that bank customers evaluated when they decided to place their savings in a bank, with the other being the status and reputation of the banker. Before a merchant could think about entering banking, typically he had to prove himself with years of successful business experience, usually in a mercantile firm. Bankers had to have personal wealth, most likely as a sign that they could be trusted with the cash of others. And to start a bank, an individual had to provide most of the capital himself, signifying a long-term commitment to the community.[8]

For local economies, the unregulated banking system worked remarkably well. Few banks failed in normal times, and even fewer unscrupulous characters bilked customers. Instead, bankers reinvested their earnings into mines, railroads, ranches, civic projects, and local charities. An even more important financial sector, investment banking, had grown during the Civil War, and it brought to the fore a remarkable salesman, Jay Cooke.

JAY COOKE'S BOND SALES

Born in Sandusky, Ohio, Jay Cooke grew up in a political family. His father practiced law, winning several terms in the Ohio legislature before going on to the U.S. House of Representatives. Cooke attended local schools, then Adams Academy, gaining enough skills to clerk in local stores and keep their books. Eventually, he migrated to Philadelphia, where he worked for his brother-in-law, William G. Morehead, the president of a prominent transportation company.

Cooke learned to craft eye-catching newspaper advertisements, well out of the normal style of such ads in major papers. But only a year after he joined the Washington Packet & Transportation Company, it failed (just as had a previous business). Rather than become depressed or consigned to lifelong failure, Cooke instead took stock of his talents and searched for another job to pay the bills until he found his career interest. While bookkeeping in one occupation, he came to the attention of an exchange broker, E. W. Clark, who had a Philadelphia banking house. Within two years, Cooke's skill at balancing accounts and reconciling overdrafts of up to $100,000 gained him the opportunity to write business columns for the *Philadelphia Daily Chronicle*. More important, his tasks at Clark's bank familiarized him with sales of federal securities for the Mexican War, as well as municipal and state securities issues.

Yet fate was not finished with Cooke. Clark's numerous banking houses could not withstand the Panic of 1857, and the company dissolved into several smaller units owned by the remaining investors. Cooke, out of a job again, at least had a substantial "nest egg" from his employment, but he also had several mouths to feed, being married with five living children (three others had died in infancy). Again, Cooke demonstrated his character, settling his obligations stemming from the panic "so conscientiously that his father and his brother Pitt reprimanded him for extreme generosity."[9] He spent approximately four years working with railroad reorganizations, where he learned to price railroad securities and to evaluate the companies' books. Then, using money he saved from Clark, and just months before Abraham Lincoln was inaugurated, he ventured out on his own. Jay Cooke & Company opened at the most inauspicious of times, as the nation drifted toward war, markets soured, and the federal debt soared.

Cooke saw a silver lining around the cloud. Remembering the Mexican War experience, Cooke's company snatched up all the U.S. government bonds it could acquire at a time when other banks refused them. As cannon shells hit Fort Sumter, Cooke's firm obtained $200,000 worth of government securities for resale. Using his newspaper advertising experience, Cooke reasoned that he could market bonds to the general public with a patriotic sales pitch. His first chance came with a bond issue in Philadelphia, where he distributed handbills across the state urging the public to come to the aid of the Commonwealth in its "hour of trial," and reminding patriotic investors of the bonds' 6 percent interest rate! Cooke sold every bond he had, not to mention some he did not have. The loan was oversubscribed, requiring Cooke to purchase still other bonds from the state.

In 1862, Cooke opened a partnership in Washington, D.C., that provided entry into the Treasury circles. The Union government struggled to sell its 6 percent, $500 million bond issue, and Treasury Secretary Salmon Chase turned to Cooke, naming Cooke's banking house as its special agent for the marketing of securities in 1862. Although he was not the "exclusive agent," Cooke alone aggressively pushed the bonds, engaging 2,500 agents to one issue. Employing posters and handbills to great effect, Cooke also used his staple advertising medium, newspapers, which he enjoined to run favorable stories about the bonds in return for advertising business. He pressed his own writing skills into the service of the Republic, as when he wrote a pamphlet entitled "How to Organize a National Bank Under Secretary Chase's Bill" to promote the National Bank Act of 1863.

Although the national banking system pushed bond sales to new heights, it was Cooke's strategy of involving average American families in bond sales that changed the nature of the market, as more than a million citizens held the securities by 1863. Cooke's firm made little profit on all this activity—an astonishingly low one-sixteenth of a percent! Yet politicians and those newspapers in which he did not advertise carried stories of outlandish returns to the company. His personal commission totaled $300,000, but his contributions to the Union victory could not be measured. When Chase's successor, William Fessenden, tried to eliminate Cooke (and his commission), the Treasury's agents sold only $133 million worth of a new issue of bonds, whereupon he contritely begged Cooke to reassume his old duties. In less than six months, Cooke sold $600 million, most of that after Appomattox. By 1865, the Philadelphia house had earned profits of $1.13 million, of which Cooke sent 10 percent to charities. Memorials appropriately remembered the efforts of gallant soldiers who fell in combat, but the man who ensured that they had adequate boots and bullets went largely ignored. No coins celebrated his accomplishments; no statues marked the deeds of the financier of Union victory. Nevertheless, in only three years, Jay Cooke had revolutionized the sales of securities to the American middle class.

BUSINESS AND THE STATE IN THE UNION AND CONFEDERACY: "YANKEE LEVIATHAN"

The activities of the federal government during the Civil War and the ostensible states' rights emphasis of the Confederacy have led many scholars to assume that the Union succeeded in part because it had better planning and federal direction of the war effort. Certainly, the land grants to railroads, the National Bank and Currency Acts, tariffs, income taxes, and the Homestead Act all reflected an activist government role, and one not seen prior to 1860.

At the outset of war, the Union had substantial military, material, and economic advantages over the Confederacy. Yet the federal government managed to allow the market to provide the necessary war materiel with a minimum of statist controls. A remarkable study by Richard Bensel comparing Union and Confederate wartime mobilization concluded that "the Northern war effort left the industrial and agricultural sectors almost untouched by central state controls and only skimmed the surface of Northern labor pools...."[10] Union officials informed businessmen and factory owners of their needs, provided a means to pay, and then allowed the business sector to meet the demand. Northern inventors churned out a torrent of new military devices, including the Sharp's breech-loading rifle, the Spencer repeating rifle, and Dr. Richard Gatling's rapid repeating "Gatling gun." Not only did Northern enterprise rise to the occasion, but the response left the federal armies with few shortages.[11] Rounding out the Union effort, a mature railroad system, which was in place prior to Fort Sumter, contributed mightily to the comprehensive economic mobilization in the North and its ability to provide military supply.[12]

But the surprising fact of the Civil War was not that the Union did not use statist policies to direct the business community as a whole, but that the Confederacy did. In the Confederacy, "the all-encompassing economic and social controls ... were in fact so extensive that they call into question standard interpretations of Southern opposition to the expansion of federal power in both the antebellum and post-Reconstruction periods."[13] If, however, as has been argued here, the South was not so much a capitalist region as precapitalist, with pockets of market sophistication, then the concept does not appear quite as novel. In fact, a commonsense understanding of the situation puts Civil War mobilization in perspective. When a society has the necessary open-market mechanisms for supplying the military with wartime materials and for financing that expansion, government can simply skim the surface of private enterprise and its productivity. However, when a society lacks an abundance of industrial resources, as did the Confederacy, the state must force production in necessary areas.[14]

Constant deficiencies of resources afflicted the South throughout the war. The planters' concern with maintaining their postwar cotton monopoly led them to retain all their slaves in the production of cotton. But cotton was not exported due to the Confederate embargo, denying the South either the income from cotton or the slave labor that could have been used for war-related tasks such as repairing railroads, building forts, or otherwise doing tasks that kept white soldiers from the front. Worse, the Confederacy "simply took away the corn, mules, food it needed…. It was easiest, if harsh, to take corn and mules from the small farms," run by the wives of soldiers on the battlefields.[15]

The absence of a widespread, thriving industrial sector on the same scale as in the North handicapped the Confederacy, and even as it created arsenals, foundries, and munitions works, Southern production of small arms was "woefully deficient," as Secretary of War Judah P. Benjamin noted.[16] Southern businesses did contribute to the war effort in substantial ways—Georgia entrepreneurs Louis and Elias Haiman manufactured swords, then branched out into sidearm production, while private production of salt in Florida occurred despite constant federal raids—but the South lacked a strong manufacturing base, and when the war created a sudden demand by the government, interference from bureaucrats effectively squelched any early burst of capitalism.[17] Moreover, the industrial expansion that did occur relied exclusively on demand provided by government.[18] Perhaps the Confederacy's greatest success came in its improvement of an internal railroad system. Although construction and renovation was uneven and incomplete, the resulting network of routes cultivated by the Confederacy may have been the rebellion's most lasting geographical and physical legacy.[19]

EMANCIPATION AND ENTERPRISE

Lincoln's Emancipation Proclamation, the symbolic expression of Union victory, constituted perhaps the single most significant business-related event of the war. While having no immediate effect—it freed not one slave in the Confederacy, and it did not affect slavery in the border states or territories—the long-term impact of this executive order changed forever Southern enterprise. Some Lincoln critics continue to invoke the "needless war" arguments to contend that slavery would have disappeared due to market forces, and that the growth of government in the North over the long term "enslaved free men."[20] Slavery was certainly not on the verge of extinction, and the suggestion that Lincoln provoked the South has been laid to rest by a generation of historians.[21] Ultimately, the only defense of the so-called states' rights position relies on Calhounian interpretation of the Constitution as a compact of states, not people, which, of all the founders, perhaps only George Mason really accepted. Moreover, the promises to protect life, liberty, and the pursuit of happiness demanded that no individuals could be denied their constitutional rights. Lincoln, therefore, prioritized the protections of liberty inherent in both the Declaration of Independence and the Constitution, applying the protections to all. His actions had three dramatic consequences, two of which are well discussed and a third, which is important to business history, that has not been quite so deeply examined.

First, when emancipation became the war aim, no longer would any debate exist over the personhood of slaves. In essence, the Proclamation symbolically extended the "free labor" umbrella to all workers and made the South itself free soil. Second, the ex-slaves not only constituted a change in the labor force—a point beaten to death by historians and economists—but also embodied a huge addition to the nation's consumers, for in the technical sense the slaves had not been consumers in that they had no choice about their consumption. The addition of 3 million consumers to the nation would have demanded remarkable changes; but when they were contained almost exclusively in the South, it represented a revolutionary transformation. Third, free slaves, both men and women, often became entrepreneurs themselves, and among the 3 million souls able to use their skills, talents, and ideas for their own purposes, thousands of self-employed business owners would emerge.[22]

Most, of course, began as farmers or sharecroppers, and based on evidence from North Carolina, at least, a surprising number of blacks owned their own land by 1870.[23] Sharecropping arose out of the unique situation in the South after the war in which, previously, "labor was wealth and wealth chiefly labor."[24] It entailed the sharecropper "paying" up to one-third of the cotton grown on the land to the landowner. That arrangement worked well for a society in which blacks had no land or capital but had labor, and whites had no labor supply but still retained their land. It offered a sense of independence and entrepreneurship in that the freedmen could gain personally by increasing production. However, it had a drawback in that, without ownership, the freedmen had little incentive to invest in long-term improvements on the land (digging ditches, building fences, and so on), and without the full profits from the crop, and with tenants who often had few alternatives, the owners usually did not improve the land.

By 1880, blacks owned a small percentage of the land in the cotton South and tenanted approximately 30 percent, sharecropping two-thirds. At the turn of the century, blacks owned 27 percent of the land they worked and rented 36 percent.[25] Freedmen acquired land, although it was a slow process. Still, as Robert Kenzer's study of North Carolina showed, in five counties black ownership of town lots rose from 11 percent in 1875 to almost 19 percent by 1890, despite the fact that cultural attitudes, legal codes, and racism all presented barriers.[26] Free blacks before the war, especially mulattoes, had distinct advantages over the freedmen. Nevertheless, by 1880, in an economy in which whites owned most available land already and dominated the political structure, blacks already owned 8 percent of the total land in the South. Farming paid well enough that some wage laborers could choose to farm rather than work for wages, and whites comprised the majority of sharecroppers (60 percent by 1900).[27]

Alabamian Nate Shaw, an illiterate tenant farmer who grew up in a society of ex-slaves, moved from farm to farm, expanding his share and using his mules to haul lumber or do other odd jobs on the side. Despite the fact that he faced competition from an influx of poor whites, unscrupulous landlords who repeatedly attempted to defraud him of his crops, and merchants unwilling to extend credit, Shaw became self-sufficient and eventually became a leader in the Sharecroppers Union.

Hauling lumber paid well, but Shaw was determined to become completely independent of others. Even after he joined the Sharecroppers Union and went to prison in a protest against land seizures by sheriff's deputies in the 1930s, the land he had worked to secure remained in the hands of his family.[28]

Andrew Jackson Beard, a slave born in Jefferson County, Alabama, owned a farm near Birmingham. Once he tried to sell apples in Montgomery using a team of oxen to pull his wagon, but after the trip took three weeks, he quit farming and constructed a flour mill in Hardwick, Alabama. Experimenting with plow designs, Beard patented a plow in 1881, and then sold it in 1884 for $4,000—a fantastic sum at the time. He continued to refine plow designs, then, with his total savings—approximately $30,000—Beard entered the real estate market. Still, he continued to invent, creating a remarkable rotary steam engine patented in 1892. Early work in railroad yards provided Beard with a firsthand exposure to the hazards of hooking railroad cars together. The process was done entirely by hand, requiring a worker to stand between cars and place a metal pin in the coupling devices at the very instant that the cars came together. Fingers, hands, and arms all fell prey to accidents with the metal couplers, and Beard suffered the loss of a leg in a coupler accident, focusing him on a solution. In 1897, he received a patent for the famous "Jenny" coupler, in which the coupling devices secured themselves when bumped together, like in a handshake. An improved version of the Jenny remains the foundation for the modern automatic coupler, and Beard saved untold hundreds of railroad employees from severe personal injury.[29]

Even before the Civil War, a few slaves had established an entrepreneurial legacy. "Free Frank," the slave of George McWhorter, managed his owner's estate and received permission to hire himself out for the purposes of buying his own freedom. After securing his own emancipation in 1819, along with that of his wife, he engaged in a wide range of business enterprises in Pulaski County, Kentucky. Migrating to Illinois, Frank acquired hundreds of acres of land that he improved, then sold, and founded the town of New Philadelphia, selling lots in the town and continuing to purchase slave children to free them.[30]

Of course, not all the new entrepreneurs in the black community were either freedmen or self-manumitted former slaves. Elijah McCoy, born in Canada where his parents had fled to escape slavery from Kentucky in 1837, had benefited from his father's successful lumber business by going to Scotland for training in mechanical engineering. After becoming a master mechanic and engineer in Edinburgh, McCoy returned to the United States after the Civil War and settled in Ypsilanti, Michigan, where he worked for the Michigan Central Railroad. His skills and technical training qualified him for a position as a fireman— no lowly position but a prestigious job "somewhat equivalent to the copilot of an airplane" today.[31] McCoy surpassed the requirements of his job, using his technical skills to address problems with the locomotives, especially their tendency to overheat. The locomotives needed regular engine oil, but if they stopped frequently, the delays cost the company time and money. McCoy invented a device that lubricated the engine parts while the train was in motion, securing a patent in 1872 and making constant improvements to the design. White workers degraded the devices, at first, but then "they listened carefully when the oilers were installed and he gave instructions on their use."[32] Imitators attempted to sell their own lubricating cups, but McCoy maintained a standard of quality so high that people referred to his parts as "the real McCoy." At age 77, he patented an improved air brake lubricator, and that same year (1920) he founded the Elijah McCoy Manufacturing Company in Detroit, although he owned little stock, having sold rights to the patents for cash to develop still other inventions.[33]

Overall, black entrepreneurs comprised a substantial portion of the business community in the South. No comprehensive study is available, but snapshots tell a great deal. For example, from 1865 to 1879, R. G. Dun & Co.'s credit records for the state of Virginia contained credit information on up to 1,000 enterprises, of which more than 220 were operated by blacks (based on notations made in the record books). Despite the fact that Southern whites wrote the credit reports sent to Dun, many of the personal evaluations testified to the high character of black entrepreneurs. Although black businesses were usually located in towns of higher-than-average black population, the advertising from the businesses indicated that black entrepreneurs had white customers and seldom appealed to strictly black customers. Most of the Virginia black businessmen in one study were in either a mercantile business or a skilled trade, and almost 80 percent were single-owner firms. The owners apparently gained experience in business, because over time the ratio of new firms to failed firms dropped after 1869, and many businesses were considered failed simply because the proprietor died.[34]

In fact, the Virginia data showed virtually no difference in failure rates between black merchants and white merchants from 1870 to 1875 (which included the panic years): Of black merchants in business in 1870, 71.2 percent survived through 1875, compared to 71 percent of the white merchants.[35]

OLD SOUTH, NEW SOUTH

Many whites, like the freedmen and the yeoman farmers of the antebellum period, remained on the land and struggled to create a New South. Cotton prices, though falling in the Reconstruction period, remained higher than other commodities, making it attractive to farm.[36] Manufacturing, however, marked the New South far more than it had the old: In 1860, the South had approximately 30,000 manufacturing establishments; by 1870, it had 50,000, then, by 1890 the number rose to 60,000.[37]

Southern entrepreneurs established themselves in traditional industrial enterprises, beginning with railroads, creating a construction boom.[38] In the 1880s alone, railroad mileage in the South increased by 108.6 percent, with more than $150 million invested between 1879 and 1881 alone. Birmingham, Alabama, emerged as the center of the new iron business that served the railroads. Milton Hannibal Smith, who headed the Louisville and Nashville (L & N) for half a century, helped direct more than $30 million of railroad money to furnaces and iron ore production. But just as the iron mills depended on the railroads as their primary consumers, the railroads benefited from shipping iron. In 1888, the L & N carried more tonnage in pig iron and minerals than the annual average weight of the entire cotton crop of the nation for the previous fifteen years. Henry DeBardeleben, the son-in-law of the powerful New Englander, Daniel Pratt, mobilized a coal and iron empire that included seven blast furnaces, seven coal mines, and 900 coke ovens, as well as quarries and railroads. After once bragging that he "wanted to eat up all the crawfish [he] could," DeBardeleben "was himself soon gobbled up in a series of buyouts."[39]

Another road to success in New South businesses came from textiles, where Henry Hammett, George Gray, and Daniel Tompkins rose to the top ranks of enterprise in the late 1800s. Hammett, a North Carolinian, had been born of a yeoman family and worked in a cotton broker's office in his youth. He learned the trade, gaining promotion to business manager, and after a brief fling with railroads, he founded the Piedmont Manufacturing Company at the peak of the Panic of 1873. By 1890, he had three mills that made better grades of cloth; "his buildings and villages became models for other mills, while his plants served as training schools for future owners and managers."[40]

George Gray swept factories in twelve-hour shifts for ten cents a day when he was eight years old. Later, he applied a natural mechanical ability to mill machinery, attracting the attention of his supervisors. His expertise gained him repeated promotions until he became mill superintendent; then, in 1888, he founded the Gastonia Cotton Manufacturing Company at Gastonia, North Carolina. Within twenty years, he had a dozen plants that featured the most recent technology and hydroelectric power.

Daniel Tompkins, on the other hand, was born into affluence. His family's plantation survived the war, and Tompkins went to the University of South Carolina and Rensselaer Polytechnic Institute. Over a nine-year period, he worked at Bethlehem Iron Company, gaining experience in the iron business. He moved to Charlotte, North Carolina, where he eventually established mills and newspapers that emphasized industrialization.

While Hammett, Gray, Tompkins, and other New South entrepreneurs moved into the industrial vacuum created by the Civil War, a broader trend encompassed business enterprise in all regions as the managerial revolution accelerated. By the postbellum period, the managerial hierarchies that had originated in the railroads spread to firms in four areas: 1) users of continuous process technology; 2) processors of perishable products; 3) machinery makers who required specialized marketing services; and 4) manufacturers of large-scale, specialized machinery. Starting in the 1880s, mass production met mass distribution in each of those areas as managers embarked on the strategy of vertical integration. For a brief period, production capacity surged ahead of distribution networks; but quickly businesses shifted their focus to sales, marking a traditional ebb and flow of business management strategy. Each of the four areas of focus can be closely identified with one or two well-known entrepreneurs.

CONTINUOUS PROCESS TECHNOLOGY AND THE FATHER OF "BIG TOBACCO": JAMES B. DUKE

High-volume production machinery permitted managerial change in the first area: that of continuous process technology. When automation technology appeared, as in the adoption of the Bonsack cigarette machine or mechanized canning and jarring processes for food, hand production virtually overnight transformed to mass production. James B. Duke's American Tobacco Company illustrates not only the rapidity of change, but the scope of dominance one company could have. Washington Duke, a former Confederate soldier who had returned to his Durham, North Carolina, farm to find it looted by scavengers, took advantage of the only resource untouched by the vandals—a store of tobacco. With his two sons, James Buchanan and Benjamin, Washington Duke cured and prepared tobacco for sale in packages under the brand name "Pro Bono Publico."[41] Within a decade, Duke's backyard operation became W. Duke, Sons & Co., which competed directly with the major chewing and leaf tobacco manufacturer Blackwell & Carr and its "Bull Durham" brand. By that time, James Duke, who directed the operations, chose to target another product, rolled tobacco, assisted by a cigarette roller he had helped develop in 1878. The Bonsack machine made packaged cigarettes possible, for a single Bonsack could produce 120,000 cigarettes a day. Since the major markets were in the North, the company established an operation in New York City in 1884, where it advertised heavily. Production soared, well above the capacity of his existing network to sell or distribute the cigarettes, leaving Duke with warehouses of unsold product.

Duke embarked on a program of developing an extensive sales organization, complete with marketing agreements with wholesalers around the world. He established advertising campaigns, purchased storage and curing facilities, and systematized the flow of cigarettes, to the point that Duke's company grew to be the largest manufacturer in the industry. By 1889, Duke's machines produced more than 830 million cigarettes with sales of excess of $4.5 million. When competitors attempted to compete with Duke on his own grounds of high production and marketing, Duke's advertising costs soared—as did their own. Although competitors hoped to buy out Duke's business, instead he offered a consolidation: In 1890, the four major cigarette manufacturers merged into the American Tobacco Company, with Duke as president. American Tobacco controlled 90 percent of the market, with products ranging from smoking tobacco and chewing tobacco to cigarettes and tobacco retailing. Duke abhorred inefficiency and constantly emphasized cutting waste. Like other successful entrepreneurs of his day, he left a vast fortune—$100 million—to charities, much of which went to Duke University, which created a famous medical school known today for its research into lung cancer.

Similar mechanization and processing changes took place in businesses engaged in producing canned and bottled goods. Heinz pickles and Campbell's soups were introduced after the Civil War to also serve the soon-to-emerge consumer market. Henry Heinz was surrounded by bricks as a child. He worked in his father's brickyard and even purchased an interest in this family business from the proceeds of his "other" business, selling a horseradish he bottled. Although he had a knack for business, Heinz at a young age learned the harsh realities of the market when he and his partners drove their pickle company into bankruptcy. When he was only twenty-five years old, Henry Heinz was arrested twice for fraud related to the bankruptcy—although he was cleared both times—and his reputation was all but destroyed. At that point, most people would have retired to the safe confines of the family brickyard, but not Heinz.

With $3,000 he borrowed from relatives, he again entered the food business. More conservative with his cash this time, he audaciously marketed his name, emphasizing brand names for bottled and canned goods. He used one of his best-known products—pickles—as a marketing tool. His remote location at the 1893 Columbian Exposition Chicago World's Fair made it easy for fairgoers to ignore Heinz's booth. He quickly assessed the problem and had a local printer make thousands of small white cards that offered a free pickle to anyone presenting the card at the Heinz booth. Located on the second floor, the booth suddenly attracted such large crowds that fair officials had to strengthen the supports of the gallery floor. By the time the Chicago World's Fair ended, Heinz had given away one million pickles, but had also gained advertising that would have cost far more if he had paid for it directly. Newspapers and magazines further publicized the stunt, so that schoolchildren soon begged for a "Heinz pickle" lapel pin.

Heinz had turned the corner. He also had a "hook"—something with which to grab the public's attention. In the 1890s, Heinz had seen an ad for a local shoe company that promoted "21 styles of shoes." The idea of identifying the product with a number led Heinz to create the slogan "57 Varieties," even though he already had more than sixty different kinds of pickles alone. Before long, "Heinz 57 Varieties" graced billboards and railroad cars, making the Heinz products a household name without naming a particular product. Heinz, too, had a new name: the pickle king. He increased his efforts to improve his product and expand advertising. The company built a huge industrial complex in Pittsburgh, a building designed so well that it won architectural awards, and he offered guided tours of the plant. In 1900, Heinz erected a huge billboard that was among the first to use electric lights, costing the then-astronomical price of $90 a night to illuminate.[42]

Heinz's pickle company and Campbell Soup both made use of new technology. There were thousands of years of history behind preserving food in containers. For canned food, until the Civil War increased demand, each can was made by hand. Glass jars, too, changed, with molded glass making containers cheaper and consistently strong. Heinz and others developed canning and jarring production lines to turn out millions of items a year. Joseph Campbell, who founded Campbell Preserve Company, packed products under several private labels, including Crescent and Joseph Campbell & Company. Not until the 1890s, however, did the company produce its trademark soup. Dr. John Dorrance, a nephew of Arthur Dorrance, who had run the company after Campbell's retirement in 1893, discovered that for all the products Campbell's offered, it did not make soup. Dorrance, a chemist, devised a process to condense soup so that its ingredients did not separate after canning. Even so, the public "had to be educated to eat soups."[43] Cookbooks omitted soups entirely (since, for a typical soup, the recipe would have been to "take any food you have and add water to make it seem like more food"). Franco-American and Hutchins both represented strong competitors, too. But Dorrance had created a high-quality product that the company produced more cheaply than its rivals. With Dorrance's intense advertising campaign, including clear instructions on how to prepare the condensed soup, Campbell's soon stood alone at the top, selling more than 16 million cans of soup by 1904.

Concern for efficiency constituted a dominant theme with all producers using continuous processing. As a result, the use of waste products gave birth to entire new industries that themselves used continuous processing, such as soap and candles made from animal fat obtained from slaughterhouses. One of the most famous soap manufacturers, Procter & Gamble, was created from a partnership between a candle maker and a soap maker from the pork production capital of the nation, Cincinnati.[44] British-born soap maker William C. Procter and his brother-in-law, James Gamble, began processing and selling lard, candles, and soap in 1837. The Civil War brought new contracts for candles and soap for the Union Army and made "P & G" a nationally known company. Procter & Gamble used mechanical processes to mix and crush the products used for bar soap, turning out 200,000 cakes of its Ivory Soap daily by 1880.

Gamble conceived of the new soap in 1878, charging his chemists to achieve the fineness of luxury soap without using expensive olive oil that constituted the major ingredient of fine soaps. While working on the new product, an employee ran a mixing machine too long, puffing the soap mixture more than usual so that it floated. That gave Gamble the advertising hook he needed: It Floats! The company's analysis of the composition of Ivory showed it contained only 0.56 percent useless impurities, allowing the company to declare the product was "99 and 44/100 percent pure."[45] P & G placed itself at the vanguard of the new marketing wave, spending $400,000 on advertising by 1905. But the company went beyond marketing, and in 1886, P & G built its Cincinnati plant, introducing labor programs that others considered radical, including giving workers Saturday afternoons off with pay and, in 1887, instituting one of the first profit-sharing plans in the nation.

SEMI-PERISHABLE PACKAGED PRODUCTS AND GUSTAVUS SWIFT

The second category of industry in which managerial hierarchies reshaped consumer habits was in the production of semi-perishable packaged products. In the case of meat, the movement of those products over short distances had relied on ice cakes cut from lakes that were used to cool crude refrigerator cars. For shipping over longer distances, however, live animals had to be transported in cars for local slaughter and processing. In the 1870s, Gustavus Swift implemented a more efficient approach. Born in Sandwich, Massachusetts, into a family of twelve, Swift worked at his brother's butcher shop. There, he "perceived the simplicity of the business" that allowed a butcher to purchase an animal, slaughter it, and carve it into cuts and then sell the parts for more than the cost of the whole animal.[46] He soon had his own shops, purchasing local cattle and extending his sales operations to Albany and Buffalo, New York.

Swift recognized that most beef came from the West and was shipped live to markets in the eastern United States—a process that embodied substantial waste and inefficiency. Almost two-thirds of an animal was inedible, yet the whole cow was transported thousands of miles. If the cattle could be slaughtered in Chicago, with only the processed meat shipped east, lower freight costs alone would make beef cheaper. Chicago butchers had already experimented with shipping meat in refrigerated cars, so Swift moved to Chicago in 1875, where he purchased a local slaughterhouse and used the strategy of shipping meat hung in cars, relying on cold winter air to keep the meat fresh. But Swift sought a better alternative. In 1877, he hired a refrigeration engineer named Andrew Chase to develop a completely insulated refrigeration car that had ice packed into the roof. The car required Swift to acquire a secure source of ice along the route and to sell the meat immediately once it arrived, or again refrigerate it quickly.[47] Using his own shops and storage houses, Swift employed local sales forces to move the dressed meat in refrigerator cars to nearby locations. His shops placed a few select cuts of meat on display—usually the slower-moving cuts—in glass cases. After early resistance, competitors soon followed Swift by building comparable networks of branch houses, including Chicagoan Philip Armour and the Cudahy brothers in Omaha.[48]

Obsessed with efficiency and eliminating waste, Swift introduced overhead conveyors to transport the animal carcass to each processing station within the slaughterhouse. His focus kept returning to Chicago's Bubbly Creek, which ran behind one of his yards and into which the effluent from his slaughterhouses ran. Swift continuously examined the water for its fat content, and was convinced that any fat in the water meant that too much of the animal carcass was discarded. Thus, for economic, and not environmental, motivations, Swift cleaned up the water by finding ways to use virtually all parts of beef and pig carcasses. He developed a series of by-products that included glue, soap, fertilizers, beef extract, and bone products, joining the many uses for other parts of the animals—leather shoes, gloves, baseball covers, even red paint made from animal blood—already in place. A century

later, the process that Swift started reached almost 100 percent efficiency, but even during his time Swift accurately could boast that "we
use all of the hog but the grunt."[49]

MACHINERY MAKERS:
ISAAC SINGER'S SEWING MACHINES

Manufacturers started to bypass wholesalers in another area, that of
new machines produced in high volume that nevertheless were not
especially simple to operate. Such machines not only required a skilled
sales force capable of explaining and demonstrating complex products,
but also demanded mechanical expertise to service and repair the
devices. One example of a device that required special sales training
and a qualified repair staff was the sewing machine.

By the 1850s, the sewing machine industry had given birth to several competitors, each with a staff of sales agents and marketing organizations. Agents operated on a small salary and a commission, but
lacked any means of extending credit to buyers and often personally
had little understanding of the machine itself. Isaac M. Singer, an actor
in a onetime theatrical troupe in Fredericksburg, Ohio, was the individual who revolutionized the industry. Out of work and nearly broke,
Singer found employment at a printer's type factory. There, he invented a type carver that he hoped to sell to New York and Boston publishers. During his unsuccessful sales trip, he observed a sewing machine
in a Boston shop and immediately saw opportunities to improve the
design. Indeed, "Singer's changes constituted a new invention" that
formed the basis of his company, which he founded in 1851.[50] A New
York lawyer named Edward Clark acquired an interest in the business
to manufacture the Singer products. Singer, however, was soon served
with a lawsuit by Elias Howe claiming Singer had replicated his patented needle and lockstitch. Clark fought the suit on behalf of the company for years, until the court ruled that Singer had to pay Howe a $25 per
machine royalty. Undaunted, Singer mass-produced the machines with
a heavy reliance on hand-finishing.

One area where Singer had modernized, however, was in copying
the tactics of a rival to establish branch sales offices, each with a

female demonstrator, a sales staff, and a full-time mechanic. Offices provided credit to purchasers, endowing Singer with important advantages over enterprises relying on commission agents. Although he was not the industry leader at the time, Singer nevertheless dominated the market: Singer and two other competitors controlled three-fourths of the industry's output by 1860, with Wheeler & Wilson manufacturing 85,000 sewing machines a year and Singer coming in second at 55,000.

After 1860, Singer began to establish branch stores supervised by full-time sales agents.[51] Clark had convinced Singer of the shortcomings of a commission-oriented staff, which failed to manage inventories, waiting too long before ordering new machines, then telegraphing large orders. Singer turned the business over to Clark in 1863, whereupon Clark expanded and reorganized marketing and extended overseas operations.[52] Singer Sewing Machines built factories around the world, including the largest ever constructed, in 1871, in Elizabethport, New Jersey. The Kilbowie, Scotland, plant had the capacity to manufacture 10,000 machines a week, whereas less than a decade earlier it had taken thirty-one boys and men in a Glasgow factory to produce thirty units. To prevent delays or other interruptions in work, the company had its own timberlands, iron mill, and railroads.

Other businesses imitated the organizational structures of the sewing machine industry. Cyrus McCormick's reaper company began to employ full-time sales staff and territorial agents who provided repair services and credit. John Deere & Company used its expertise in plows to market other, less complex farm implements through its sales organization. Each company constantly looked for opportunities to expand beyond its original product, but into machinery that required similar expertise or production skills.

E. Remington & Sons, for example, had become famous for manufacturing the modern breech-loading rifle. Although the company was quite familiar with mass-production manufacturing, producing an astounding 350 barrels a day at each of four furnaces at the hands of only four men, Remington also made use of the contractor system.[53] After the Civil War, the company searched for nonmilitary customers, investigating products to fabricate in its metal-manufacturing facilities. When the company moved into farm implements, it did not employ the McCormick-type sales force—and failed. Likewise, when approached by a former Singer executive to develop a new sewing machine,

Remington, despite having a technically superior sewing machine, failed to create the necessary sales force, and failed again. At that point, many people would have, literally, stuck to their guns. Not the Remingtons. An inventor named Christopher Sholes visited the Remingtons in 1873 with his new device, the typewriter. Moving conservatively this time, the Remingtons worked with a firm that had existing networks and finally established a solid business. Unfortunately, when Remington attempted to sell the typewriter overseas, the company approached Singer, which had the best foreign network. When Singer refused to market the typewriter, E. Remington & Sons was forced to establish its own, expensive organization. That, and the recession in the firearms industry, pushed Remington into bankruptcy in 1886, at which time the typewriter division was sold off as Remington Typewriter.

HEAVY SPECIALIZED EQUIPMENT AND GEORGE WESTINGHOUSE

Just as Andrew Jackson Beard had saved countless railroad workers' limbs and fingers with his Jenny coupler, George Westinghouse saved untold numbers of lives and injuries with his compressed air brake. Westinghouse was only twenty-two years old when he approached a group of railroad executives to demonstrate his invention in 1868. During the test, a horse would unseat its rider onto the rails in the path of an oncoming train. Westinghouse and the railroad executives were standing off to the side. To stop a train, it typically took a large crew of burly brakemen to manipulate the heavy brake shoes then in use, but during this demonstration, a single engineer activated the Westinghouse brake and the onrushing train ground to a halt only four feet from the hapless horseman. At the end of the test, no executive needed any further convincing. Within a year, Westinghouse Air Brake Co. began filling orders for the air brake from its Pittsburgh factory, and by 1873, Westinghouse air brakes appeared on more than 10,000 locomotives and cars.

Not yet thirty years old and a millionaire, Westinghouse went to work every day as if he was a brakeman himself, and he never stopped inventing. During the 1880s, he started work on alternating current (AC) electrical systems, a superior alternative to the direct current (DC) systems then in use. Whereas AC could travel over longer distances, its high voltage made it more difficult to control. Westinghouse founded Westinghouse Electric Company in 1886 to build the equipment needed to control AC, developing a system of transformers and generators. He proved the reliability and safety of the AC equipment, but found himself in competition with the legendary Thomas Edison whose devices used DC. Edison's company enthusiastically publicized accidents from AC voltage, to the point of conducting experiments in which cats were electrocuted to show its dangers. Newspapers cooperated with stories whose headlines read "Electric Wire Slaughter" and "Another Lineman Roasted to Death."[54] After the state of New York adopted electrocution (using AC) as its means of capital punishment, Edison officials referred to it as "Westinghousing" the condemned.

Most people who worked with electricity knew better. In 1892, Westinghouse won the contract to provide lighting for the Chicago Columbian Exposition, proving to the world the safety and efficiency of AC power. Over a six-month period, the fair was illuminated nightly with safe AC electricity without a single accident. That was the breakthrough Westinghouse needed, and contracts to provide electricity to homes and businesses flooded Westinghouse Electric. In his mid-sixties, Westinghouse retired, confined to a wheelchair. His relentless inventor's spirit still propelled him to create, however, and he spent his last year working on an electric wheelchair.

Large machinery of types other than electric dynamos also demanded specialized sales and technical service, requiring well-trained and skilled technicians. Elisha G. Otis understood that assuaging the public's fears of elevators depended in no small part on his reputation for installing and servicing his elevators, and after his death his sons centralized the administration of the business and oversaw the vertical integration of the company. The family-owned Otis Company was, by the late 1890s, a "big business," yet because it did not separate ownership from management, it did not fit the Chandler definition of a modern business organization. But the neat, clean separation of management and ownership did not always occur in the emerging corporate giants, as seen in the case studies of Frederick Weyerhaeuser's lumber business.

FREDERICK WEYERHAEUSER, ENVIRONMENTALIST AND LUMBERMAN

Driven from Germany at a young age by revolution, Frederick Weyerhaeuser found employment as a day laborer on construction crews, a lumber grader, and a bookkeeper. In 1857, the Illinois lumberyard he managed went bankrupt, putting Weyerhaeuser on the street and out of work. He managed to raise the necessary funds to purchase the bankrupt lumberyard, then, using the wood to barter, Weyerhaeuser worked a number of trades with local farmers. Leasing an idle sawmill in Rock Island, Illinois, he purchased logs and hired a miller to saw them, then used the cut wood to construct houses and other buildings.

Already, Weyerhaeuser had vertically integrated, obtaining raw lumber, owning the processing facility, and selling the final, finished product. Although never a woodcutter himself, Weyerhaeuser filled almost every other position in the company at one time or another, overseeing the production, accounting, sales, and financing. Earnings were solid, but not spectacular—$8,000 for the first year and nine months. When the Civil War brought new demand, Weyerhaeuser joined with his brother-in-law to expand further, taking advantage of the relative dearth of lumberyards and abundant timber in the Midwest.

Weyerhaeuser employed a firm called the Beef Slough Company to collect logs, float them down the Mississippi, and sort them for cutting. But he realized that at any time his supply could be interrupted by management decisions at Beef Slough or by natural impediments to shipping. He therefore started to purchase his own timberland of yellow pine in Wisconsin. Along with other loggers, he formed his own river transportation company. By 1885, the firm processed more than 500 million board feet of lumber.[55] The phenomenal amount of timber that passed through Weyerhaeuser's mills only convinced him further of the need to maintain his own supplies of raw timber, leading him to embark on an ambitious land acquisition program. He held more than 300,000 acres by 1879, but already focused on the newly developing western territories. In 1891, he moved to St. Paul, Minnesota, residing next door to James J. Hill, whose Great Northern had become a major purchaser of Weyerhaeuser's timber for railroad ties.

Hill already understood the value of having consumers next to his road, and Weyerhaeuser appreciated his largest customer. By the 1890s, the Great Northern Railroad had sold some of its own timberlands to Weyerhaeuser, including 900,000 acres in 1900. The sale required $5.4 million, forcing Weyerhaeuser to put together a large syndicate under the name Weyerhaeuser Timber Company. When he sent inspectors to the lands, however, Weyerhaeuser learned that they were not as rich in virgin timber as he had believed. At about that time—perhaps because of that sudden awareness—Weyerhaeuser started to devote considerable resources to reforestation, soil erosion, and fire prevention.

Then, as today, more net forest lands are lost due to fires (most of them natural, caused by lightning) than are lost due to harvesting. Stephen Pyne's magisterial book on fire, for example, records that in the period from 1940 to 1965, lightning ignited more than 228,000 fires in the United States.[56] The very remoteness of such fires has made it difficult, if not impossible, to fight them, which made the fires phenomenally destructive, often burning more than one million acres of forest![57] Weyerhaeuser recognized the threat nature posed to his empire and fully realized that without trees, he had no business. Certainly he could not contribute to deforestation. Thus he embraced conservation, which as a movement was in its infancy.

The strategy of replacing forests had started in the timber business, including measures far more aggressive than just "not cutting." Already all the major users of lumber and paper products had adopted reforestation measures. International Paper, which owned land since 1898, established its own nurseries, by the 1990s turning out 190 million seedlings a year. As of 1924, International Paper controlled 20 million cords, or 4 million more than it consumed, and added 800,000 new cords of wood every year through forestry methods already in place.[58] (By the 1990s, International Paper alone planted more than 48 million trees a year—five times more than it harvested—and donated or sold the rest for additional reforestation.) Another producer of paper products, Kimberly-Clark, in 1902 embarked on the first long-term woodlands management program that employed hundreds of professional foresters.[59]

In one sense, Frederick Weyerhaeuser and other lumber producers faced unique problems from other entrepreneurs in that they dealt with a resource that, unless replenished by humans, could have been depleted entirely, especially given the time lag between planting a tree and harvesting it. Cotton growers or textile manufacturers did not face the same resource problem. From another perspective, though, Weyerhaeuser typified several of the major entrepreneurs of the day, for even amid the managerial revolution, he maintained control and ownership over his organization. Adopting the structure of managerial hierarchies, he retained the substance of entrepreneurship.

In farming and food sales, entrepreneurs also sought ways to adopt new management methods to family-owned firms. Innovators in agriculture perceived that the days of the small acreage, limited crop farm had ended. Successful food-oriented businesses, even if families retained control, had to incorporate elements of the new management structures and extend their markets. A. P. Seabrook, for example, had farmed a relatively small acreage in Bridgeton, New Jersey, in the 1880s—an unlikely prospect for evolving into the world's largest farm.[60] Seabrook specialized in peas, beans, limas, and spinach of such quality that others contacted him about furnishing seed. His vegetables, packed in ice and shipped by rail, reached Philadelphia, New York, and Baltimore. After learning of a Danish process for growing cauliflower using overhanging pipes that sprayed water, the family installed the system and realized a profit of $25,000 on the operation. By the early 1900s, the Seabrook family started to can its own foods and mechanize its farming.

Weyerhaeuser in lumbering, A&P in grocery stores, Seabrook farms, Jack Daniel with his whiskey, and Dr. Welch's juice company—all demonstrate how family businesses had started to make the transition to modern corporations. None of them, however, better bridged the gap between the traditional structure of an owner-controlled business and the new organizations relying on professional managers than the greatest nineteenth-century entrepreneur of them all: Andrew Carnegie.

ANDREW CARNEGIE AND AMERICAN STEEL

Enough chroniclers have told Carnegie's story that all the details need not be repeated here.[61] A Scottish immigrant raised in poverty, Carnegie rose to the pinnacle of American business, becoming the greatest steelmaker in history. Carnegie left Scotland when he was thirteen. With little formal education, he and his family located in Pittsburgh, where he worked a number of jobs, including one as a bobbin boy. He toiled twelve hours a day for $1.20 a week, and by 1849 he had a better position at the O'Reilly Telegraph Company, where his keen memory and ability to translate Morse code without writing it down first made him a valuable employee.

By age 16, Carnegie earned more than his father, but his career had only started to develop. His telegraph talents had caught the eye of Thomas Scott, district superintendent of the Pennsylvania Railroad, who hired Carnegie as his personal secretary. In a few years, Carnegie had gained precious experience in two booming industries: steel and railroads. Scott even educated Carnegie on the stock market and loaned him money to purchase stock in Adams Express Company. Several transactions followed, with Carnegie making a small fortune in each. With his available cash, Carnegie invested in Keystone Bridge Company, where he became a partner. That investment served as the "parent of all the other works" and proved a brilliant choice. Railroads had started to stretch across the nation, and at each valley or river they required a bridge. Thus, as one Carnegie biographer observed, "Carnegie's decision to found a company to build iron bridges put him into the middle of one of the most rapidly changing technologies of the day and at the same time opened spectacular opportunities for achievement."[62]

The short jump from bridge construction to steel manufacturing seemed natural to Carnegie, who had invested in iron forges in 1861 and had organized the Cyclops Iron Company in 1864. Whether in bridge construction or iron production, Carnegie energetically devoted himself to controlling costs. When it came to manufacturing iron, he learned that few of the experienced iron manufacturers even knew their costs, with owners providing tons of raw materials to mills daily without an accurate accounting of the supplies delivered. His accounting systems detailed the expenses of every department, at which point Carnegie reduced costs. But his most significant efforts to control costs involved backward and forward integration. The Cyclops and Union mills supplied iron plates and beams to Keystone Bridge, and in 1870 he ordered construction of the Lucy blast furnace to provide pig iron to the mills. That furnace turned out record tonnage of iron—642 tons in one week, compared to an industrial average of 350, and 100 tons in a day—and Carnegie's blast furnaces worked so hard that he had to reline the interiors every three years.

Still, American technology lagged behind that of the British, especially after the introduction of a new process designed by Henry Bessemer, who discovered that he could purify hot pig iron of its carbon with a blast of cold air. Bessemer's converter looked like a large, open-topped egg, with air blasted into the molten iron through vents in the bottom. The infusion of oxygen cleared the iron of silicon, and it was not long before steel masters were able to control the exact content of carbon in the steel through the Bessemer process. Alexander L. Holley of Connecticut, who studied Bessemer's plants in Sheffield, England, returned to America to create his own Bessemer furnace in Troy, New York, in 1864.

Carnegie recognized the technology as the wave of the future and entered into Bessemer steel production in 1866, using imported British equipment. Attracting other investors, Carnegie maintained the controlling interest in a new company, Carnegie, McCandless & Company, with the goal of producing rail steel with the Bessemer process. Always aware of the contributions of experienced and talented employees, Carnegie hired many of the best iron and steel men in the industry, and more than a few came to him because of his reputation. One of the best, "Captain" Bill Jones, proved a superior plant manager. Others, such as Julian Kennedy, constantly improved Carnegie's plant technology, contributing more than 100 patents (of which more than fifty found their way into Carnegie's plants during Kennedy's lifetime). Carnegie did not hesitate to employ any technology—homegrown or otherwise, regardless of cost. He hired Alexander Holley to build a mill near Pittsburgh, naming it the J. Edgar Thomson Steel Works—ever with an eye to his chief customer, the railroads.

Carnegie attracted most of his senior managers with shares of ownership. Only Bill Jones declined such an offer and instead demanded "one hell of a big raise," which Carnegie paid ($25,000, then a fantastic sum). The Carnegie companies were partnerships, with Andrew Carnegie the majority partner. In an age when ownership and management of corporations were separated, Carnegie merged the two as never before. All new partners came into the firm under the "Iron Clad Oath," in which they agreed to offer their shares for sale back to the other partners before putting them on the open market. In that way, Carnegie constantly built up his ownership position when partners left or, in some cases, were forced out. Giving the top managers a share of ownership produced unmatched gains in output, although, again, Jones was the exception. After he received his big raise, he promised Carnegie that his mills would outproduce the Cambria Iron Works, and they did, turning out 8,000 more tons of steel in 1881 than Cambria. The partnership business form that Carnegie took allowed him to finance virtually everything internally, providing a constant circle of profits back into the business, to the consternation of some stockholders. Carnegie virtually never paid dividends, and while the stock value soared, the partners received little cash flow other than their salaries. Internal financing gave Carnegie the enviable advantage of having money when no one else did. In depressions, such as the Panic of 1873, he bought when others sold at bargain-basement prices. He eagerly scooped up new mills and equipment from overextended competitors, often obtaining state-of-the-art machinery at a bargain. And in all of his dealings, Carnegie stayed focused on the bottom line of cutting costs in order to reinvest and expand. Hardheaded at times, Carnegie could be persuaded when confronted with evidence, especially if it showed lower costs.

Those traits made him a ruthless competitor—even more so because "his competitors were considered enemies, not gentlemanly rivals."[63] There was none of the collusion that had befallen the railroads with Carnegie, who sought to bury his challengers, not praise them. When he acquired the Homestead Steel Works, he offered the owners cash or the equivalent stock value in his own company; they foolishly took cash. The only investor who took stock saw his $50,000 stake grow to $8 million in a fifteen-year period. To the dynamic Carnegie, the key was action: The Scotsman "bought in depressions, rebuilt in depressions, restaffed in depressions, and then undercut his competitors when business was good."[64] In so doing, Carnegie performed an extraordinary public service, as he forced prices for steel downward until it became a basic metal. He, of course, did not refuse government help when he got it, supporting the steel tariffs of the 1870s, although he contended that "even if the tariff were off entirely, you [British] couldn't [sell] steel rails west of us."[65]

A conspicuous exception to his obsession with lowering prices involved hiring and retaining expensive labor. Carnegie reasoned that the most expensive labor in a free market was also the most valuable due to its productivity. In this, he was persuaded by Jones, who argued on behalf of an eight-hour day because "it was entirely out of the question to expect human flesh and blood to labor incessantly for twelve hours."[66] Others, particularly union leaders, often failed to understand Carnegie or, conversely, understood precisely that his relationships with labor required thoughtful workers willing to bargain individually. That was anathema to union organizers, who fought Carnegie repeatedly over collective bargaining. Carnegie did not mind paying higher wages, as long as individuals negotiated them. Indeed, nowhere in the American labor movement does the fundamental philosophical difference appear starker between those who believed that individuals were helpless and those who thought that all power emanated from the individual than in the clashes between Carnegie's company and the unions.

By the time the issue came to a head, however, Carnegie had left for Scotland, leaving a man of less lofty ideals, Henry Clay Frick, to preside over one of the worst strikes in American history. Frick was not without his own success story to tell, starting as a clerk in a department store. By age 22, Frick had his own firm, having founded the Henry C. Frick Coke Company in 1871, forging it into one of the most powerful businesses in America, and bringing him into Carnegie's orbit. In 1882, to ensure a steady supply of coke for his steel mills, Carnegie had purchased half of Frick's interests, making Frick a Carnegie partner. At that time, Frick, age 33, wielded control over 1,200 coke ovens. A few years later, Carnegie made Frick president of the Carnegie companies, reorganized yet again in 1891 as Carnegie Steel Co.

Carnegie already had crossed swords with the Amalgamated Association of Iron and Steel Workers when it won a strike at Homestead in 1889. The new contract came up for renewal in 1892, by which time Carnegie had left the tactical details to Frick, although advising his president to shut down the plants and let the workers decide to come back. Instead, Frick provoked a fight, turning Homestead into a fortress with armed guards. When the entire workforce went on strike, Frick tried to break it by hiring Pinkerton guards who were little more than otherwise unemployed riffraff. The Pinkertons, supposing to take the mill under the cover of darkness, arrived from the river to avoid the picket lines; but they were spotted, and a miniature war broke out on the riverbank. After the Pinkertons surrendered, they walked through the town that had felt the brunt of the labor policies. A crowd turned into a mob, killing several Pinkertons and beating most of them. After that, the union's advisory committee, in full control of Homestead, "ran the town with a heavy hand reminiscent of Robespierre's Committee of Public Safety."[67] The governor called in the state militia to restore order, and then Frick reopened the plant with nonunion workers—although union workers were invited back on a prestrike basis, and after the strikers realized they had lost, they, too, returned to work. Homestead operated as a nonunion plant, with each worker signing an individual agreement with the company. In a statement to the Pennsylvania grand jury related to the case, Chief Justice Edward Paxon of the Pennsylvania Supreme Court reiterated the fundamental rule of free markets: "The relation of employer and employee is one of contract merely. Neither party has a right to coerce the other into the making of a contract to which the mind does not assent."[68]

Ironically, both Carnegie and the union emerged as villains, while Frick survived just short of a hero—at least, temporarily. Frick's status derived from an unsuccessful assassination attempt on him during the strike by an anarchist. Alexander Berkman burst into the president's office, shot Frick twice in the neck, then attempted to commit suicide and blow up the room by biting down on a capsule of fulminate of mercury. After the maniac was subdued, Frick sat in his chair while a doctor removed the bullets without anesthesia. Not only did Frick remain at his job that day, but he wrote his mother a letter in which he scarcely mentioned the incident. Meanwhile, editors and labor leaders heaped scorn on Carnegie, who, they argued, could have prevented the episode at Homestead with a word. (Carnegie, of course, had no more control over Frick than did the union.) The Amalgamated suffered a fatal blow to its prestige from the ease with which modern production methods replaced the skilled craftsmen, who learned that mechanization had made the craft unions obsolete. Even Frick, though, ultimately had to pay for his role in Homestead, finding himself pushed to the periphery of Carnegie's business. Frick still owned his Frick stock, resulting in a bloody battle with Carnegie to exact full payment for his shares. After a suit, Carnegie paid Frick $31 million, then did not speak to him again, except once, in old age, when the Scotsman offered to reconcile. Frick told the intermediary, "Tell Mr. Carnegie I'll meet him in hell."

Carnegie turned his company over to a young genius, Charles Schwab, who had started as a stake driver at the Edgar Thomson plant, rising to the top of the corporate world as the president of Carnegie Steel at age 35. Schwab knew how to persuade Carnegie, barraging him with data on savings until he achieved his goal. Schwab continued the

Carnegie evolution of integrating the company entirely. Although Carnegie Steel owned its own sources of coke and limestone, it still had to purchase iron ore. That weakness became all too apparent when John D. Rockefeller purchased control over the rich Mesabi, Minnesota, iron ore range, making Carnegie dependent on him for his raw materials. Carnegie moved quickly, working out a lease arrangement with Rockefeller for the land. He built his own railroad to haul ore from Lake Erie to Pittsburgh, saving the company $1.5 million annually. Next, he acquired a fleet of ore boats that saved an additional $2 million, all the while increasing his capital investment in his main business, steel.

Those improvements, and Carnegie's good sense in attracting talent, made Carnegie Steel the most efficient steel manufacturer in the world. Between 1888 and 1898, the company's capital rose from $20 million to $45 million while its production tripled, rising to 2 million tons of pig iron a year and 6,000 tons of steel a day. By 1900, Carnegie accounted for one-third of all the steel produced in the United States and had surpassed the British in efficiency.

Called a "robber baron," Carnegie astutely summed up the entrepreneurial realities: Two pounds of iron shipped to Pittsburgh, two pounds of coal (turned into a quarter pound of coke), a half pound of limestone from the Alleghenies, and a small amount of Virginia manganese ore yielded one pound of steel that sold for a cent—"that's all that need be said about the steel business," he adroitly noted.[69] But that was not all that needed to be said about Carnegie. He once admitted that his life's goal was to give away $300 million, but he did not do it: He gave away more! His Carnegie Institute of Technology received $27 million, and his retirement fund for teachers netted $10 million. By 1904 alone—about the time he started giving away money full-time—he already had donated more than $180 million to charities.

Most of that money came from the sale of Carnegie Steel in 1900. For some time, J. P. Morgan had listened to Schwab explain the advantages of streamlining the steel industry. Morgan had reorganized railroads and thought structure could be brought to steel, too. Morgan was aware that Carnegie had considered selling the company, flirting briefly with a syndicate involving John W. "Bet-a-Million" Gates of Chicago. Gates, who had founded a thriving barbed-wire business, was known for his outlandish bets, yet the key sale of his life—of barbed wire to a group of San Antonio ranchers—was hardly a gamble. Gates had challenged the ranchers to bring their steers to town to test a fence made of his wire. Suspecting that no rancher would risk his own cattle, Gates had his own wild-looking (but actually docile) steers run into town, where, promptly, they stopped at the wire and ensured his sale.[70] But the sale of Carnegie Steel to the Gates group fell through, and Morgan talked further with Schwab. The banker asked Schwab to serve as the courier and asked Carnegie to fix a price. Dutifully, Schwab, the president of one of the largest companies on earth but reduced to the capacity of a courier, transmitted Morgan's request to Carnegie on the golf course. Schwab and Carnegie made a few calculations, then Carnegie scratched a figure—$480 million—on a small piece of paper. When Morgan saw it, he said, "I'll take it." The titans finalized the deal aboard Morgan's yacht, the *Corsair*, with Morgan extending his hand to Carnegie, saying, "I congratulate you on becoming the richest man in the world."

Although Carnegie's role in his steel company ended, Morgan, true to his vision, reorganized Carnegie Steel into U.S. Steel Corporation, which included Federal Steel, National Tube, American Steel and Wire, American Steel Hoop, American Tin Plate, American Sheet Steel, American Bridge, Shelby Steel, and many other holdings. The final business, capitalized at $1.4 billion, constituted the world's largest corporation. Under Schwab's leadership, the company maintained unprecedented production levels. But under Morgan, Schwab managed a much different steel business than he had under Carnegie. Unlike the Scotsman, Morgan wanted stability instead of innovation, and he failed to see the elegant simplicity of cost-cutting to obtain market share. Soon, Schwab was gone.

The young executive had not abandoned Carnegie's concepts, however, and at his own private company, Bethlehem Steel, Schwab quickly repeated, and even surpassed, his performance at Carnegie. He selected fifteen young men "right out of the mill and made them my partner," Schwab recalled.[71] Within ten years, the *New York Times* called Bethlehem "possibly the most efficient, profitable, self-contained steel plant in the country."[72] The workforce at Bethlehem doubled every five years; U.S. Steel's workforce shrank.

Schwab proved that it was not the size of the company that mattered, nor even its heritage. No company was better grounded to capture the American steel market entirely than U.S. Steel after Morgan finished his consolidation. Instead, U.S. Steel abandoned the vision and faith that had created it. Morgan should have known better: As a banker, he broke new ground constantly, taking unimaginable risks. But as a manager of a steel empire, he lost sight of the soul that gave life to Carnegie's structure, namely, the willingness to sacrifice existing plants and systems for the potentially better and cheaper processes. All Morgan had to do was to heed Carnegie's words: "Watch the costs and the profits will take care of themselves."

BIG BUSINESS, BANKING, AND J. P. MORGAN

It was fitting that Morgan took over for Carnegie, much the way only a Joe DiMaggio could wear the Yankee pinstripes made legendary by Babe Ruth. Morgan also personally represented the fusion of the sole-proprietor entrepreneur with the managerial approach of the new integrated industries. He attacked problems aggressively and individually, relying on the help of syndicates but never becoming beholden to them. More than any person, Morgan reorganized businesses with managerial hierarchies, introducing them to stability and conservatism. Yet Morgan's deals themselves epitomized entrepreneurship and risk taking—the exact opposite characteristics embodied in the managerial revolution.

Raised in a home as luxurious as Carnegie's was bleak, Morgan increasingly focused his career on rescuing distressed railroads. As the price for his support, Morgan insisted on managerial changes. He merged unprofitable lines with sound railroads, underwrote securities to equip roads that lacked internal funding, and corrected abuses in chronically overextended roads such as the B & O. During the process of selling securities for the New York Central, Morgan obtained a seat on the board of directors. From an inside position, Morgan demanded management changes, setting a pattern for Morgan's future dealings. While reorganizing the Reading Railroad, he perfected the voting trust, giving bankers control over a company until the company met prescribed performance objectives. Not surprisingly, by the late 1800s, railroads came to look like banks with their professional management structures. Morgan's more important accomplishments, however, involved his contributions to investment banking and, indirectly, the structure of the American banking system itself.

By the late 1800s, national and state banks provided the commercial funds and circulation needed for daily economic life. Large investment banks, such as Morgan's, handled the issue of securities for new firms or to recapitalize old ones. When necessary, the syndicates formed by the investment banks could supply even the U.S. government with cash. Thus, while historians have referred to the "dual banking system" of state and national banks, really there were two sets of systems, one involving regulatory oversight and control and the other dealing with the types of services and funds provided. Both, however, suffered in the event of a depression or panic.

In 1873, the failure of Jay Cooke's bank triggered runs and a panic. The system lumbered along for two more decades, struggling to provide enough cash in flush times or to contract the money supply in tight periods. With the amount of national banknotes tied to the amount of bonds that the banks had on deposit with the government, expanding the money supply rapidly proved difficult. Moreover, the seasonal nature of a still-strong agricultural sector placed particular demands on certain areas of the country that were not shared by the large industrial centers. Political shenanigans with silver (the Bland-Allison Act of 1878 and the Sherman Silver Purchase Act of 1890) tended to exacerbate the institutional problems with the money supply, ultimately contributing to the Panic of 1893. The overvaluation of silver caused money to flow out of the nation at unprecedented rates, threatening the financial structure of the United States itself.

Into the breach stepped J. P. Morgan. He formed a syndicate with August Belmont & Company and the European bankers, the Rothschild family, to deliver to the Treasury 3.5 million ounces of gold—certainly the largest private "bailout" of the government in history. "For a private banker to stem the gold outflow of the United States was a breathtaking feat," but to some, Morgan's assistance represented the worst of the American business system and the weaknesses of the banking system that still required the efforts of one man to set it right.[73] Many saw it as a sign that the nation needed a central bank capable of doing what Morgan did, supplying money in recessionary times. Several monetary reform movements were spawned during the late 1800s, most of them somehow tied to the creation of the American Bankers Association in 1876. The association initially focused on making uniform state banking laws, but at its Baltimore convention in 1894, Alonzo B. Hepburn and Charles C. Homer put into motion a plan that ultimately served as the basis for the Federal Reserve Act, reforming the financial system.

Indeed, no term better captured the thrust of the new business-government relations than reform. Americans came to view big business increasingly as bad business. Labor unions, social activists, politicians, editors, and others complained about monopolies, the profits earned by "robber barons," and inordinate power of large corporations over American politics and life. An entire political movement, the Progressive wing of the Republican Party (then later, the Progressive Party itself), stood for reform of all aspects of society, including several aspects of business and the economy.

In some ways, then, Morgan's actions in 1893 marked the temporary end of a relatively brief period in the nation's business history when a small minority of talented individuals completely dominated the scene, improving the lives of everyone in quantum terms. Thomas Edison not only provided light, he changed American nightlife and the landscape of the cities. Carnegie not only produced cheap steel, he made buildings, railroads, and ships safer than ever before. Swift did not just find a more efficient way to produce beef and pork, he improved the dietary habits and health of generations.

Perhaps it was the very fact that not everyone could accomplish those great feats—that a chasm stood between the vital few and the average American. Yet countless numbers of average Americans suffered setbacks and financial failures before developing products and services that changed all our lives for the better. But the convergence of large-scale industry, combined with a national market and the elements of mass production and marketing, allowed anyone of exceptional talent to rise to unprecedented levels of success. Right behind them, however, marched an army of professional managers, more conservative by nature, who could not replicate the feats of the captains of industry. The appearance of the professional managers fit nicely with the new Progressive movement, which reveled in constant, evolutionary reform toward an ill-defined notion of perfection. Progressives not only viewed human control over commerce as superior to that of the market, but also assumed that their own intellect was superior to the collective wisdom of the market.

CHAPTER 7

The Big Business Backlash: 1870–1920

An 1889 cartoon by J. Keppler, called "The Bosses of the Senate," showed diminutive senators sitting in their chamber while behind them stood a line of obese figures in top hats with the names "Steel Beam Trust," "Copper Trust," and "Sugar Trust" emblazoned on their vests. By the turn of the century, many Americans shared the cartoonist's view that huge business combinations controlled their lives—or, at least, their economic lives. Politicians tapped into such fears and hostility and turned it into votes for reform and regulation. The attempts by some individuals to monopolize, the constant search for government favors, and the hostile attitudes toward labor all contributed to the Janus-faced image of businessmen in the late 1800s. On one hand, they looked forward, standing for achievement and progress, personally embodying the American dream of rags to riches. Few people rejected material wealth in the name of greater spiritual or ideological values at the time, and fewer still did not somewhat envy the successful individuals who had attained prosperity, especially if they had earned it rather than received it through inheritance.

On the other hand, business looked backward to the mercantilist era when it received monopoly power through government favors, or even to feudal times when owners treated labor as expendable. Those attitudes led many people to suspect that the "robber barons" had come by their riches unethically or simply illegally, and virtually always at someone else's expense, whether the laborer, the farmer, the consumer, or other small businesses. Certainly, many people compared the vast wealth and earnings of a Carnegie with common wage earners who toiled for only a fraction of the value of their products. While the public admitted that perhaps some business leaders indeed had gone from rags to riches, the perception developed that an even greater proportion had received inordinate advantages from government or other members of their social class, inheriting or stealing wealth rather than producing or creating it.

THE MYTH OF HORATIO ALGER'S "RAGS TO RICHES" STORIES

Such attitudes were reinforced by a best-selling author of the day, Horatio Alger, whose message over the years has been distorted and misunderstood. Modern Americans associate Alger's name with the phrase "rags to riches," which implies that investment, business talent, and perseverance can take an average soul to a life of abundance. But a self-made man such as Carnegie would never have recognized the career patterns of the Alger characters. According to popular misconceptions, Alger's heroes represented the downtrodden rising to wealth through hard work and personal achievement through business enterprise. But Alger, the son of a Unitarian minister and recipient of a quality education, disliked capitalists, and, indeed, the most frequent villain in his stories was a mill owner. While Alger emphasized good morals, good luck was the central element in the success of most of his heroes. Alger associated with the Newsboys' Lodging House in New York, where he picked up stories of young boys who had gotten out of poverty. Ironically, Alger accepted "hereditary determinism," or the belief that genetic history would foretell someone's future, and the paupers who climbed to wealth in his stories often had wealthy or noble ancestors.

Usually, Alger's stories involved a young boy who made the (fortunate) acquaintance of a wealthy patron, then, through charm, virtue, and some industry, received a legacy from his guardian. *Ragged Dick*, Alger's first book (1868), proved enormously popular, and soon his *Luck and Pluck* (1869), *Tattered Tom* (1871), and other volumes dominated the 1800s version of the best-seller lists. But in Alger stories, seldom did hard work result in riches; usually characters achieved middle-class status; and heroes seldom advanced through traditional capitalist enterprise but rather through luck and connections. Thus, while criticized as perpetuating the rags-to-riches myth of American business, Horatio Alger's message was the opposite of the values later associated with him: achievement through capitalism, effort, and working one's way up the ladder. At best, Alger fashioned a formula for modern capitalism that "could be used by a diverse class of audiences to make sense of, participate in, and even protest against and rectify abuses of modern capitalism."[1] Only after securing his place in literary circles with his novels did Alger write biographies of self-made statesmen, such as Lincoln, but he still eschewed stories of entrepreneurs. Producing more than 110 books—writing as rapidly as one book every two weeks—Alger spent virtually every cent he got. As a result, his own life turned out just the opposite of his stories, for he went from riches to rags and died poor.[2]

Alger made good reading, but most of his contemporaries did not believe that serendipity would transform their lives, any more than today's modern, bored housewives think that reading a "bodice ripper" reflects the likelihood that Brad Pitt will appear at their door in plumber's attire ready for romance. Instead, many Americans saw large business combinations threatening their traditional labor patterns and blocking their route to personal economic growth. The rise of the factory system and the appearance of managerial hierarchies only made more impersonal the already-frightening factory work that claimed the labor of so many workers. At the same time, the scope of industrialization translated relatively small per-unit profits into vast sums of wealth for ownership. Astute investors, such as Cornelius Vanderbilt, Andrew Carnegie, and John D. Rockefeller, who created an oil empire at that time, gained millions of dollars by risking capital to own substantial shares of (what turned out to be) successful businesses. Understandably, average American workers seldom saw or even considered the risk and investment that originated the businesses, or the fact that the returns per unit were tiny, only that the final tally was more wealth than most of them ever could hope to own. From the perspective of publicity, the highest echelons of the business class made matters worse by flaunting their money in the most unimaginable ways.

LIFESTYLES OF THE RICH AND FAMOUS, 1800s-STYLE

The tycoons and social elites (although they often were not synonymous) had gained notoriety in the late 1800s for their often blatant and outlandish displays of wealth. Their exploits received widespread attention in the press because the wealthy sought and craved public attention at a certain level and the public often secretly envied them, desperately hoping for a peek at how the other half lived. Social columns in urban newspapers reveled in recording the latest balls at immense mansions. Surreal stories emanated from the elites' abodes at Newport, Rhode Island. There were tales of partygoers who lit cigars with $100 bills—at a time when most wage earners never received a *weekly* wage of that magnitude—and threw parties where favors included diamond bracelets and pearl necklaces. Delmonico's Restaurant in New York, often the scene of similar shenanigans, hosted a dinner for a pet dog: The owner presented the pooch with a diamond necklace worth $15,000, while one millionaire reputedly had holes drilled into his teeth to insert rows of diamonds so that he could flash his "million-dollar smile."[3] Such behavior seemed obscenely wasteful, affronting and insulting wage laborers, farmers, and small-business owners.

The sheer gap in wealth far transcended that seen in modern America (perhaps with the exception of Bill Gates), with the top groups holding 300 to 400 *times* the capital owned by ordinary working people. For many people, however, the houses built by the rich, and in particular, Newport's mansions—"a froth of castles" erected by wealthy business leaders—struck many Americans as beyond the pale.[4] There, servants' quarters contained more square footage than the typical middle-class house, while the mansions themselves had more rooms than some hotels. Biltmore, one of the Vanderbilt family's estates, in Asheville, North Carolina, had four acres under its roof, including forty master bedrooms and a dining room with three fire-places abreast.[5] Yet many people, while envious, were not surprised at the extravagance: Quite the contrary, they understood it and would have done the same, had they such wealth.

A number of critics sought "sumptuary legislation" against the rich, to restrict the amount that could be spent on housing or other displays of vanity. Social—and socialist—reformers found themselves aligned with some members of the older business elites, to whom the appearance of the new magnates whose wealth came from industry or finance represented a departure from traditional avenues of economic improvement, such as commerce and agriculture. Witnesses testifying before the U.S. Senate in 1885 complained that a farmer worth $1,500 was considered well-off, but Carnegie's sale of his steel company gave him the *daily* income of $40,000![6] The fact that the number of millionaires in the nation rose from a handful to more than 4,000 between 1865 and 1892 was often cited as a negative statistic rather than as a sign of America's immense opportunity.

BUSINESS'S IMAGE

Outlandish displays of wealth only composed one of the reasons that business leaders suffered attacks on their image in the post–Civil War era. Another set of criticisms arose from the perceived declining position of that traditional source of economic independence, the family farm, and the conclusion that the plight of the farmers somehow was inversely related to the wealth of the industrialists. The most oft-used target of scorn and blame for farmers was the banker, especially the "big city" bankers who, many people were convinced, pulled the strings that manipulated the political system as well as the economy.

Farmers' complaints tended to address two major issues. First, farm prices had fallen sharply in the decade after Appomattox. Using an index base of 100, prices plunged from an index high of 161 in 1864 to less than half that in 1878. Declining prices reflected the general deflation that had occurred in the late 1800s due to international conditions, but most critics focused their rhetoric on federal policies, dwelling on the government's refusal to monetize silver or issue new paper currency. Lower prices for all goods, even those farmers purchased, did not alleviate agrarian distress, they argued, because farmers had signed long-term mortgages on their land whose rates did not change with other falling prices. Thus, farmers saw themselves drifting further behind other enterprises, with the only solution being an inflated money supply that would boost overall prices.[7]

Second, farmers depended heavily, and in some cases almost exclusively, on railroads and grain elevators that stored their grains until the trains arrived. In some cases, a relative monopoly existed, insofar as most areas only had one grain elevator or were close to one railroad. Even when others existed, farmers complained, they were so far away as to make real competition nonexistent. Railroads and the elevators, farmers alleged, then took advantage of their position to levy exorbitant rates.

Often, perceptions *are* reality, of course, and certainly the cost of farming had climbed regularly in the late-nineteenth century due to the rising real price of land and to the high cost of new farm machinery. Steel plows, reapers, and other new equipment created economies of scale: Farms with more acres planted could lower their cost per bushel. Farmers occasionally defrayed the cost of buying machinery by forming cooperatives, and the most expensive machinery was owned by people who would bring the equipment through farm regions at the time it was needed. Mortgages, however, constituted a different problem. Most mortgages were short term—often three years or less—with large balloon payments required at the end of the mortgage period. Despite complaints that the monopoly power of the local banks permitted them to charge exorbitant interest rates, evidence suggests that the mortgage industry in the western regions was immensely competitive.[8] Other evidence contradicts the notion that farmers' mortgages made them susceptible to falling price levels: Interest rates on the short-term mortgages were readjusted every renewal. One study showed the typical life of a Kansas or Nebraska mortgage was 3.6 to 3.7 years.[9] Mortgage rates did not reflect a permanent condition. Moreover, farmers knew better than to borrow at levels their crop production could not support, as seen in foreclosure evidence that showed the "risk of individual foreclosure was quite small," as low as 0.61 percent in Illinois in 1880 and 1.55 percent in Minnesota in 1891.[10] Robert Fogel and Jack Rutner found that from 1849 to 1899, the average real income of farmers increased in every decade.[11]

As for the existence of monopoly profits of railroaders, few lines even managed to maintain their rates, let alone increase them: Freight rates fell along with crop prices, and even dropped faster than other prices after 1890.[12] Critics retorted that the issue was less about an actual monopoly than arbitrary discrimination, where shippers were charged different rates. The criticism might have had more validity if farmers had no options, although some monopolies existed for brief times in some areas. Regions in the far West, for example, frequently had only one railroad, so rate discrimination against local shippers was possible. In the Midwest, however, where the clamor against the railroads reached its acme, few such monopolies survived. Jeffrey Williamson's study of railroad rates in Kansas found little to suggest farmers labored under excessive freight rates.[13] Closer to the Atlantic Coast, rates fell by two-thirds between 1870 and 1900. Overall, as one survey of the literature concludes, "it is difficult to make a strong case for widespread victimization of the farmers."[14]

Still, it would be a mistake to dismiss the agrarian discontent as simply irrational. Enough farmers joined organizations like the National Grange and expressed their frustrations at the ballot box to conclude that many of them truly were struggling. But it would be equally erroneous to assume that farmers universally opposed corporations or other large business firms. Most of them did not hate business or want to socialize America, nor did organizations such as the Grange want to eliminate corporations, only reduce their power. Early groups such as the Southern Alliance hoped to substitute fraternal support systems for the intrusive grip of industry.[15] Even the grand master of the National Grange told the Chicago Conference on Trusts in 1899 that the Grange hoped to frame legislation that would not interfere with legitimate enterprises or the development of the resources of the nation.[16] In that vein, the philosophy behind many of the "Granger Laws" regulating railroad rates rested on the premise that unequal or discriminatory rates violated freedom of enterprise and thus denied individual farmers, lumbermen, and merchants opportunities to engage in business activity due to an uneven playing field.[17]

The farmers' discontent stemmed from the fact that they themselves were the problem. While farm prices fell about 25 percent between the Civil War and 1900, output of farm products increased. This occurred because the acreage expanded, new hybrid crops increased yield per acre, and amazing changes occurred in machinery.

This massive increase in the production was not matched by increased demand; in fact, population growth was slowing. Many farmers of the era were structurally unemployed—that is, there weren't enough jobs as farmers, and the unemployed (or underemployed) were not able to fill the opening jobs in industry because they didn't have the skills, were just too far from the available jobs, or found it difficult to give up an ancient way of life based on soil.

While the number of farms decreased, the acreage farmed more than doubled from 1870 to 1910.[18] The steel plow made it easy for one person with a mule to break the tough sod of the prairies, and soon huge threshers and reapers with teams of a dozen (or more) animals were available to rent. Hand harvesting limited the amount of crop planted, because when the crops were ready to harvest, leaving them in the field risked destruction by mold or hail and other weather conditions.

Output per acre also increased in the late 1800s as scientists developed more productive corn and wheat hybrids. This abundance of food came as the birthrate declined, population growth slowed, and retaliatory tariffs kept U.S. agricultural products from export to the rest of the world. And even farming succumbed to the changes in business that demanded accounting and organizational structure, providing the impetus in part behind the Morrill Act that sought "to make agriculture a scientific endeavor practiced by educated professionals."[19]

Agrarian protests constituted the first of two major sources of impetus for regulation of business in the late 1800s (with the other being the Progressive movement), culminating in the rise of the Populist Party. Organizations of farmers had originated as early as 1867, when Oliver Kelley, a government appointee sent to the South to investigate agricultural conditions, created the secret fraternal society called the National Grange of the Order of Patrons of Husbandry. The Grange swelled to more than 850,000 members by 1875, and was soon followed by similar groups, including the Farmers' Alliance in the 1880s. However, the most important of the farm protest organizations, the Populists, broadened their base by attracting miners and wage earners through their calls for an expanded money supply to alleviate farm credit problems.

SILVER AND CREDIT

The discovery of new silver veins had led to increased production of silver, shifting the ratio of the value of silver to gold from 16:1 to 17:1, presenting an opportunity to inflate the money supply by requiring the government to buy and mint silver coins at the higher (artificial) price. When Congress passed the Coinage Act of 1873 (in the 1890s called "the Crime of '73"), it discontinued the silver dollar, essentially recognizing that the nation had adopted a monometallic standard based on gold. Bimetallism, it has been argued, might have benefited the nation by reversing the general deflation.[20] As silver production rose and prices fell, silver producers pressed for new legislation to mint silver, including the Bland-Allison Act (1878), which required the government to buy large quantities of silver, but at market prices, not fixed inflationary prices. Legislation finally passed in the form of the Sherman Silver Purchase Act (1890), in which the government would purchase and mint ("freely") the metal at an increased ratio of 16½:1, a premium price that also would produce more money and the inflation desired by farmers. The economic dislocations that followed were solved ultimately only by repeal of the Sherman Act and through a massive loan of gold to the U.S. government by banker J. P. Morgan. Populist power reached its zenith in the election of 1896, when the Democratic Party nominated Williams Jennings Bryan of Nebraska for the presidency, whose speech at the convention—the famous "Cross of Gold" speech—tied the Democrats to the "free silver" movement. Republicans nominated William McKinley, who ran on the gold standard as his primary platform plank.

McKinley won the election in what political scientists term one of many "watershed" elections in American history, insofar as it solidified the Republican base for the next thirty years. More important for farmers, McKinley's victory destroyed the Populists as a political movement. Their longest-lasting contribution was an unwitting one: Populism served as the basis for the classic story, *The Wonderful Wizard of Oz*, a remarkable tale on several levels, written by L. Frank Baum, a remarkable businessman.

THE WIZARD OF OZ AS A
PARABLE OF POPULISM

Frank Baum, born into a wealthy New York family, had watched his father skim crude oil off the river that flowed through the fields. Benjamin Baum, Frank's father, established himself as a moving force in the Syracuse region, but young Frank had little interest in the oil business, preferring instead the entertainment and consumption side of capitalism.

As a teenager, Baum loved the theater, writing and producing plays, and acting. In the midst of his acting "career," he fastened on merchandising, turning his focus to sales of an axle grease made of crude oil under the name Baum's Castorine Company. His wife toured with him, and her family planted themselves in Aberdeen, South Dakota. By the late 1880s, Baum had established a retail store, Baum's Bazaar, along the lines of the F. W. Woolworth chain he had seen in Utica, New York. Baum honed his already-substantial marketing skills in his new business, employing a steady stream of newspaper ads to sell Chinese lanterns, candy, cigarettes, ice cream, and other products. A depression that struck the region destroyed the economy, putting Baum's store out of business. While certainly not broke, Baum, out of work, turned his attention to a newspaper he acquired, writing almost everything in the paper.

That, too, proved short-lived, failing in 1891 due to the continued business blight. This time, Baum was broke, nearly losing all of his property. He moved again, to Chicago, arriving there in the midst of the building and sales boom accompanying the Columbian Exhibition. Having failed twice, Frank Baum stood on the threshold of his greatest success. After a brief stint with a newspaper, Baum took a position with a leading crockery and glass wholesaler, and before long he was on the road again. He thrived in the new business, emerging as one of the best salesmen in the company, regaining much of his fortune. Then, tired of the road, Baum hit upon a crucial change in merchandising.

Aware of a strong need on the part of Chicago retailers for show windows, Baum "had a plan, a method, a new display strategy that would show merchants how to move their goods and increase profits."[21] Modern retailers, he surmised, required a new treatment of goods based on new display techniques that could produce drawing power.

The window offered the best sales tool of all, and Baum was particularly suited to decorating and presenting merchandise. Baum began publication of *The Show Window*, a monthly, heavily illustrated journal replete with drawings and photographs and full of advertising. The journal instructed merchandisers in the use of lighting, display arrangement, mechanical devices, and virtually anything to get consumers to look at the window. He also founded the National Association of Window Trimmers in 1898, which soon claimed 200 members. But Baum's reputation rested in large part on his journal, called by some "the Bible" of merchandise advertising.

Baum's writing skills extended well beyond advertising into children's books with the publication of *The Wonderful Wizard of Oz* in 1900. It reflected his South Dakota years and demonstrated his writing skill. Baum deftly weaved a simple story on the surface with a powerful Populist message buried underneath, yet retaining its entertaining quality for both children and adults.[22] In the story, Dorothy, living in Kansas—a hotbed of Populism—is lifted up and transported to the Land of Oz in a tornado. After all, the Populists thought of themselves as a whirlwind, disrupting "politics as usual" in Washington. Dorothy lands on the Wicked Witch of the East—an allusion to East Coast capitalists—and is instructed by the Good Witch of the North to take the shoes off the deceased hag. Unlike the movie version, which had ruby-red slippers (in Technicolor), Baum originally described the shoes in the story as being silver.

Told to visit the Wizard of Oz to find out how she can get home to Kansas, Dorothy starts on her journey, where she encounters several characters symbolic of different elements in society. Dorothy first encounters the Scarecrow, who has admirable character traits but needs a brain. The Scarecrow symbolizes farmers. The Tin Woodsman had been a human lumberjack before the axe flew off and amputated a limb. With a metal ("bionic") arm, the Woodsman worked even faster, and subsequent accidents left him completely made out of metal but extremely efficient, illustrating that the more industrial workers adapted to mechanization, the more efficient, but less human, they became. The Woodsman, therefore, only wants a heart. Finally, the party meets the Cowardly Lion, a caricature of all politicians, but most likely William Jennings Bryan, who needed courage, as the Populists thought Bryan weak on several issues. As the group travels the "yellow brick road," the image of Dorothy's silver shoes landing on gold bricks paints a clear portrait of the Populist goal of bimetallism. Moreover, the motley group marching on Washington looked remarkably like Coxey's Army, a protest march on Washington led by Jacob Coxey in 1894.

When Dorothy and her companies arrive at the Emerald City (ostensibly Washington, which virtually ran on greenbacks), they meet the Wizard individually. To each character the Wizard appears in a different form—just as politicians tend to say different things in front of different groups of voters. Each character must perform a task on a journey west, after which each will be granted his or her desire. Along the way, the party encounters the Wicked Witch of the West, whom Dorothy defeats by dousing with water: After all, the American West's most pressing need was water, and water solves all the region's woes. Upon returning to the Wizard, the Woodsman learns he had a heart the entire time (he is the only one to cry!). The Scarecrow finds he had a brain all along (he can devise a strategy for every emergency), and the Lion had courage in several incidents. The Wizard stands revealed as a little man, impotent and insignificant. Stripped of his office and regalia, he is like anyone else. But he has no way to return Dorothy to Kansas. She only returns home when the Good Witch of the North instructs her to click her heels together three times and say, "There's no place like home," symbolizing the expansion of the money supply by multiplying the silver on top of the gold.

The Wonderful Wizard of Oz saw print after the Populist movement itself was all but defunct. Politically, many of the agrarians in the Populists had moved into the Democratic Party, while many of those concerned with reforming business drifted to the Progressive wing of the Republican Party. Ironically, both the children's book Baum penned and the design concepts he advanced survived much longer than the ideas of the Populist Party about which he wrote.

CORPORATIONS UNDER ASSAULT

Prodigal lifestyles by business leaders and complaints by agrarians about railroads, banks, and elevators all contributed to the declining image of business in the late 1800s. Critics of business found yet another ally from a most unexpected source—business itself. Business enterprises had contributed to their own bad press coverage through the excesses of Fisk and Gould and the other "robber barons." Small-business owners continually blamed their problems on large corporations, and big business repeatedly sought protection or other special favors from government in the form of tariffs, land grants, or informal support of private collusive activities that injured smaller firms.

Increasingly, concerns over the power and wealth of the industrial sector smoldered, then ignited under new reformers known as Progressives. At the same time, an urbanized counterpart of the farmers' distress appeared among the new masses of factory workers. Factories, unlike the small owner-operated firms, relied on mass production that fostered impersonal relationships between managers and laborers. Many capitalists viewed workers as another cog in the machinery of industry—a standardized part to be used until worn out. The fact that they paid laborers steadily higher wages did not mollify their anxieties. After all, real wages, which measure purchasing power, rose between 1860 and 1900. Real wages for manufacturing in 1865 hovered at just under $1 a day, and then nearly doubled by 1890.[23] With a brief downturn between 1870 and 1880, real nonfarm earnings rose by more than 60 percent from 1870 to 1900. Real wages for adult males in most regions of the country rose at over one percent per year, then after the Civil War increased "somewhat more rapidly after 1860 than before," at approximately 1.4 percent annually.[24] But whereas factory work may once have represented only a brief phase in a laborer's career, preceding self-employment or farming or even homemakers' duties, by the turn of the century, factory work increasingly became a permanent position, and no one can question the difficulty of a monotonous, and occasionally dangerous, factory job.

Yet factory work paid well, as we have seen. What, then, constituted upward mobility? Was it the ability to acquire a more prestigious job, or did rising wages alone prove satisfactory? The entire question of whether upward mobility still existed in America thus seemed appropriate. A sociologist, C. Wright Mills, proclaimed the end of opportunity for individuals to advance as early as 1840, and in 1893, historian Frederick Jackson Turner, with his announcement that the frontier was "closed," indicated the possibility that farm ownership had forever disappeared.[25] Even education did not provide security, with stories abounding of college graduates unable to find advancement.[26] Stories of "class dominance" circulated well into the 1930s, when a study concluded that "about 10 percent of the population produced 70 percent of the contemporary business leaders."[27] Another study, however, done in Scranton, Pennsylvania, found that out of forty founders and developers in 1880, "only nine of [them] had even one son, son-in-law, or grandson who forty years later was an officer of even one corporation in Scranton."[28]

Among prominent American families, one could point to successful offspring who followed in the founder's footsteps, such as William Vanderbilt, who emerged as a renowned railroader in his own right. Vanderbilt understood railroads and invested in them accordingly. But none of Cornelius's other children did as well as William. In contrast to William Vanderbilt, Conrad Matthiessen, the son of a wealthy sugar-producing family, inherited management of the Glucose Sugar Refining Company, which he mismanaged by paying out high dividends instead of reinvesting in the manufacturing plants. But even Matthiessen had worked his way into management of the business, starting as a production worker at $1.50 a day, then going to college. More examples could be found of children who either struggled in the family business or accepted a quiet buyout.

Some of the industrial giants, such as Carnegie, left no heirs to the business while for others, such as J. P. Morgan, the family line of exceptional bankers disappeared after his son, J. P. "Jack" Morgan, died. The Rockefellers became more interested in politics than business after a generation. Banking—considered the epitome of the capitalist elite class—proved a remarkably mobile profession. Into the middle of the twentieth century, bankers almost universally came from the ranks of merchants, peddlers, farmers, or shipping agents, not from banking families.[29] The railroads, on the other hand, for a brief time permitted nepotism because a relative could hide in the bureaucracy, protected by layers of professional managers. As managerial hierarchies spread throughout industry, sons of the early magnates often had a lifetime job. Seldom did they run a company; less seldom still did they run it well; and rarely, if ever, did they exceed the growth curve established by the founder. A survey of the railroad managers or owners in the *Encyclopedia of American Business History and Biography* revealed that in the nineteenth and twentieth centuries combined, there were 171 men who achieved the level of manager or above, with 106 listed as heirs. Only sixty-one of the sons achieved the same level or above as their father or grandfather. This is, however, only a stark statistical assessment. More telling might be the number of sons who matched their father's or grandfather's *influence* on the company or the industry, based on the people viewed as worthy of inclusion by the *Encyclopedia*'s editors. Based on that criteria, in the nineteenth-century volume, only in two of thirty-four cases did sons of famous railroaders achieve a position of such influence that they rated a biography in the volume on their own merits, and both were Vanderbilts! The Commodore's son, William, and grandson, Cornelius II, both held official positions, but of all the heirs, only William came anywhere close to replicating what his father accomplished.

Nor were railroads unique. In the same *Encyclopedia* series, the volume on nineteenth-century iron and steel listed 184 men who attained the level of manager or above. Of the 127 listed heirs, only sixty-four of the sons achieved the same level as their father or grandfather, and only one had a son or grandson in management before 1900. For every James B. Duke who improved upon his father's enterprise, there were dozens of Remingtons who presided over decline.[30] Of sixteen industry leaders found in the *Encyclopedia* for an even more modern industry—airlines—none had a son or grandson who had reached a level of prominence in the industry.[31] Children of the wealthy business classes had an initial advantage, as illustrated by the number of sons of railroaders who worked in management, but those advantages fizzled out in a professional sense fairly quickly, so that by the third generation, few benefited from their grandfathers' positions.

Moreover, the specialization of the new managerial hierarchies made a rapid rise to riches through the corporate ladder difficult without the benefit of technical and/or professional training and education. Carnegie's promotion of Bill Jones stood out as unique. Usually, the new managerial class consisted of professionals who had training in mechanical engineering, accounting, banking, or other specialized credentials. They attempted to separate and segregate themselves further through the establishment of professional journals and societies. It became rarer to find laborers who, through hard work within the corporation, ended up in the boardroom. Instead, those of meager backgrounds who successfully stormed the corporate gates did so through new ideas that allowed them to form their own firms, in essence sidestepping the corporate ladder in favor of the elevator.

Several studies have sought to dispute the rags-to-riches story in American business. Most of those studies, using examples of business leaders or CEOs of large corporations, found few of them coming from lower-class families or from the ranks of unskilled workers. William Miller, for example, examining more than 200 leaders of early twentieth-century corporations, found fewer than 3 percent of them started as immigrants or American farm boys.[32] C. Wright Mills, who used biographical entries from the *Dictionary of American Biography*, concluded that business elites virtually always came from money, with fewer than 3 percent coming from working-class families.[33] Herbert Gutman, however, conducted a case study of Paterson, New Jersey, wherein he found that while it was true that people who had started life as workers seldom headed major *existing* corporations, they started their own businesses in droves. Gutman, recording fantastic upward mobility, concluded that "so many successful manufacturers who had begun as workers walked the streets of the city [between 1830 and 1880] that it is not hard to believe that others less successful or just starting out on the lower rungs ... could be convinced by personal knowledge that 'hard work' resulted in spectacular material and social improvement."[34] While Carnegie's ascent is remembered by most students of business, forgotten were the dozens of other partners—many of them engineers, including Andrew Kloman (who provided Carnegie's first foundry) and Julian Kennedy, Carnegie's talented chief engineer. Indeed, the managerial revolution had brought a new emphasis on education and technical expertise, but often the most stellar career histories frequently belonged to men (and, by the latter part of the nineteenth century, women) of limited education and formal training.

Without question, though, the *perception* was that upward mobility had slowed by the late nineteenth century. Ironically, the rise of a class of middle managers, whose success depended less on entrepreneurship and risk and more on "book learnin'" and practice, reinforced this position when it proved the exact opposite. Factory laborers did not see their counterparts who moved on to start new businesses; instead, they saw professional managers directing their activities based on credentials that most of the laborers never hoped to attain. Factory conditions exacerbated the concerns of laborers. Often unsafe, factory work was more often numbing in its mechanization. An early 1900 volume called *Work in America*, prepared by a task force working for the

Department of Health, Education, and Welfare, found that "significant numbers of Americans are dissatisfied with the quality of their working lives. Dull, repetitive, seemingly meaningless tasks are causing discontent among workers at all occupational levels."[35]

More than the nature of work had changed. The composition of the labor force itself added to workers' insecurity and perceived career stagnation of the new industrial system. A growing number of immigrant workers arrived at Ellis Island with "irregular" work habits. Some of those work habits were so "irregular" that "Great Lakes dockworkers believed that a vessel could not be unloaded unless they had from four to five kegs of beer."[36] Social historian Herbert Gutman reported the practice of starting the "real" workweek on Tuesday was widespread.[37] These attitudes set the stage for the great labor-management clashes of the late 1800s, with efficiency-obsessed managers seeking to squeeze out higher productivity, and independent, artisan-oriented laborers seeking to reacquire a bygone era in the Europe they had left.

Overall, the immigrant workers understood the opportunities that free enterprise offered, and despite their hesitations about the factory system, they flocked to American shores. From 1891 to 1910, immigrants from Italy, Austria-Hungary, and Russia alone exceeded 7 million; and Chinese, especially, came to the United States in large numbers until, in 1882, the government enacted restrictions on them.

Intellectual critics of capitalism pounced on the unease they saw among the "working masses." Henry George's *Progress and Poverty* (1879) used such an approach to argue for a "single tax" on revenue derived from land. Sales of *Progress and Poverty* topped 2 million copies, bringing George substantial royalties.[38] In 1888, Edward Bellamy's *Looking Backward* was published, in which the hero falls asleep in 1887 and awakes more than a hundred years later to a utopian society in which the government owned all factories and businesses, although Bellamy cloaked the tale in softer language and a general appeal to nationalism. Henry Lloyd's *Wealth Against Commonwealth* (1894) epitomized the more straightforward hostile attacks and was described as a "prolonged diatribe against the Standard Oil Company and a call for nationalization of the trusts."[39] As the financial editor for the *Chicago Tribune*, Lloyd had ample opportunity to express his anti–Standard Oil views, and in an article for the *Atlantic Monthly*, he described the company as "the greatest, wisest, and meanest monopoly known to history."[40] Ida Tarbell, whose "History of Standard Oil Company" was serialized in *McClure's* (1902), remains a monument to the new journalism called "muckraking," and her work later became a book in its own right. Tarbell concealed the fact that her father was a disgruntled Pennsylvania oil producer and competitor of Rockefeller.[41] Without question, muckraking sold, and magazines such as *Life*, *Harper's*, and *Collier's* all joined the chorus of Standard Oil critics while racking up profits.

Matthew Josephson synthesized the individual attacks on all the large corporations into a single, convenient volume, *The Robber Barons* (1934).[42] While offering no new charges, the book offered an across-the-board attack on virtually all sectors of business, epitomizing the view that the few had gained at the expense of the many, and it remained a standard work on the era until demolished by Burton Folsom's powerful little book, *The Myth of the Robber Barons* (1993). Josephson's book did not reach middle-class Americans the way a more graphic novel, *The Jungle* (1906), by Upton Sinclair, did.[43] Sinclair described the experiences of Jurgis, a Lithuanian immigrant who arrived in Chicago with the dream of working hard in order to own a home. Soon, however, the entire family finds itself laboring twelve hours a day in horrid conditions, including shoveling manure until covered with it from head to toe. The most grotesque scenes involved the meatpacking plants, where sausage was dyed to conceal rot and disease, and where workers routinely fell into meat-cutting machinery without so much as a stop in the line. With that story, Sinclair hoped to provoke a socialist revolution in the United States. Instead, *The Jungle* stirred Americans to demand government quality control for food and drugs, resulting in passage of the Pure Food and Drug Act (1906) and the creation of the Food and Drug Administration.

Nor did tales of the dangers or working conditions in factories dissuade millions of immigrants from pouring into the United States. Where Sinclair and George saw only oppression and evil, people around the world saw opportunity, freedom, and hope. While Tarbell and Lloyd railed against the shackles of capitalism, immigrants all but beat down the doors to get into America. While to most social critics, American business constituted an impediment to "real" progress, to millions of people around the world, just getting to America was real progress.

IMMIGRANT ENTREPRENEURS

An Eastern European immigrant couple, Hyman and Rebecca Cohen, came to the United States seeking that progress in the 1860s. Hyman Cohen made hats and expected to send all of his nine sons to college. One son, Joshua Lionel, enrolled in Peter Cooper Institute and then proceeded to ignore his studies—with the exception of a technical shop class. As a teenager, he developed an electric doorbell, but dropped the idea (probably the first such doorbell) when a teacher convinced him it had no practical value. He next set to create what he called an "electric flowerpot," which was a tube with a battery at one end and a light bulb at the other, designed for illuminating potted plants. Conceived as a decorative device, the flowerpot flopped, although Cohen sold the rights to a restaurateur, Conrad Hubert, who then took out the flowers and sold only the handheld light as the Ever Ready Flashlight. Hubert and Cohen became millionaires from the project.

Cohen continued to invent, creating a mine detonator for the U.S. Navy and earning a respectable $12,000. At only twenty-three years of age, Cohen and a friend founded the Lionel Manufacturing Co., working on their first product, a small fan-driven wooden railroad car and strip of track for use in display windows. Glass display windows had only started to enjoy widespread use as a sales tool, and the circular wooden train seemed a natural to attract attention. Indeed it did. The first day, the store owner returned to Cohen's office to request six more trains to sell! Only then did Joshua Lionel Cohen realize that he had in his "Lionel Train" a children's toy and not a window display item. He quickly added metal tracks, miniature suspension bridges, and electric-powered cars, advertising his toys through a catalogue that, by the 1950s, was the third most widely distributed catalog, behind those of Sears and Montgomery Ward.

By then, Cohen had Americanized his name as Cowen and manufactured not just trains but a childhood rite of passage: Every young boy had to have a Lionel Train. His ads focused on father–son relationships and spurred model railroad building as a hobby for adults. Ultimately, the end of the railroad era and the arrival of the jazzier space age caused the decline of the toy train business, until, in 1958, Cowen sold his interest in the company and retired.

It is misleading to suggest, however, that only the downtrodden, politically oppressed, or poor saw opportunity in America. People of almost any means or background could succeed. A shining example of this was Adolphus Busch, a salesman with a St. Louis brewery who came from a wealthy family.[44] His father had a brewer's supply company in Germany, making it possible for Adolphus to attend the most prestigious schools in Europe. The large Busch family (Adolphus was the youngest of twenty-one children) was neither poor nor oppressed, but Adolphus concluded that his opportunities, even with access to a family business, were better in America. In the depression year of 1857, Busch arrived in St. Louis and started at the bottom of the ladder, working as a clerk with a wholesale firm. Busch's father died in 1859, leaving him an inheritance, which allowed Adolphus to go into business selling supplies to local breweries. At that point he met Eberhard Anheuser, who had been the principal creditor to the Bavarian Brewery in St. Louis. Anheuser had struggled, lacking knowledge of the brewing business and taking as a receiver the assets of a company that scarcely stood out among dozens of German beer makers in the city. When Busch married Anheuser's daughter, he acquired an interest in the brewery and improved the beer's sales.

Busch proved a spectacular salesman, developing a trademark jackknife with the company's logo with a peephole at one end, which revealed a picture of Busch himself. He also procured beautiful delivery wagons that he drove through the streets with teams of show horses. Flash and glitter, however, only took the mediocre beer so far. Busch had to have a higher-quality product for the business to grow. In 1876, a friend brought back a recipe for a new beer that he had tasted in the German village of Budweis. That beer had a natural carbonation brought on through a European brewing process called Kraeusening, providing not only an unusually smooth texture but also preserving the flavor over long periods, even after bottling. Employing the sales techniques that had served him well with an inferior product, Busch attacked the market with his high-quality "Budweiser" beer, hosting parties for customers to introduce his new beer. Trays and posters bearing the Budweiser logo were given out freely, and even a hundred years later, the Clydesdale horses pulling the beer wagons are familiar symbols of a quality alcoholic beverage.

While already making a fine beer, Busch endeavored to develop a higher-quality drink that would appeal to elites—a beer that liquor drinkers might consider in lieu of brandies or wines. He produced a draft-only beer called Michelob in 1896. Since the beer was only sold in draft, Busch had to provide an infrastructure to support it, establishing a railroad distribution system that used refrigerated railroad cars and a string of icehouses along rail routes. With products like Budweiser and Michelob, Anheuser-Busch surpassed the national leader, Pabst, in 1901 as the largest beer producer in the United States, with sales of one million barrels annually.

BOOTLEGGERS AND TEETOTALERS: FAMILY BUSINESSES IN THE CORPORATE AGE

Beer production, like other items requiring processing in volume, reached ever-increasing levels of efficiency in the late 1900s. Ultimately, successful entrepreneurs had to find ways to mass-produce and sell even specialized products such as Budweiser. Nevertheless, amid a growing number of manager-dominated companies, family firms still survived and thrived. Two such businesses involved competitors, of a sort, to Anheuser-Busch. At age 7, Jack Newton Daniel had started to learn the secrets of distilling fine whiskey from sour mash, and the source of his knowledge, of all people, was a Lutheran minister.[45] When the minister's congregation forced him to abandon his hobby, he offered the business to Jack, who by then was only thirteen years old. Jack Daniel shipped his product from Lincoln County, Tennessee, to Huntsville, Alabama, during the Civil War, selling first to the Confederates then to the Union occupiers. After the war, he moved his still to Lynchburg, Tennessee, where he found a location with particularly sterile water that Daniel then purified again through a filter of charcoal. Unlike Busch, Daniel had no extensive sales network, but his product, "Old No. 7" whiskey, achieved widespread fame by word of mouth. By 1890, he was the largest sour mash maker in Tennessee, and a wealthy man. But he never created a management structure to distribute or sell his product; only after he passed his company on to his nephew, Lemeul Motlow, did the business take on the form of a modern corporation.

Jack Daniel had a great deal in common with another entrepreneur, Dr. Thomas Welch. Both were extremely devout and religious men—

Daniel a Baptist and Welch a Methodist. Obviously, however, Daniel read the passages in the Bible admonishing men to not be drunk with wine as to allow room for other spirits! Welch, on the other hand, so detested alcoholic beverages that he "cringed at the thought" of using an intoxicant such as wine in church communion service.[46] As a dentist, Welch often accepted fruit in lieu of cash for his services, providing him the raw material he needed to search for an alternative beverage. Nightly he experimented with treating grapes so that they would not ferment, which he accomplished by putting the grape juice in pots of boiling water, destroying the yeast particles in the fruit. Having successfully produced a nonalcoholic grape juice, Welch discovered that churches wanted no part of it. Traditional, fermented wine remained a staple of communion. Welch's son, Charles, envisioned the grape juice as a commercial product. Using a $5,000 loan from his father, Welch created a production facility, coined the name "Welch's Grape Juice," and, like the "Pickle King," Henry Heinz, gave out free samples at a booth he rented at the Columbian Exposition. More important, he gained entrance into broader sectors of society through ads in national magazines, devising clever puzzles and gimmicks for the promotions. Welch never lost touch with his father's original goal, promoting temperance, and one of his ads featured a young woman with a glass of grape juice and the caption, "The lips that touch Welch's are all that touch mine." When Prohibition was enacted, the company spent $575,000 a year on advertising that emphasized its nonalcoholic quality, at which time Welch's started to develop the managerial hierarchies similar to those in place at other food-processing firms.

Another food was developed by Charles Post, who probably thought his life could not get any worse than it was in 1890. That year, at age 37, Post was nearly broke. He had invested in a land development scheme and textile mill in Texas, and his health failed. Stomach disorders and nervous problems, with which he had struggled most of his life, grew worse after his financial collapse. Perhaps naturally, he also suffered from severe depression. Only on the advice of his relatives did he agree to move his family to Battle Creek, Michigan, in 1891.[47]

Battle Creek was home to the idiosyncratic doctor, John Harvey Kellogg, who practiced restorative treatments at the Seventh-Day Adventist Sanitarium. Kellogg, true to the Adventist faith, was a vegetarian and an advocate of "biologic living," or what might today be called holistic treatment. Along with his brother, Will Kellogg, John Harvey endorsed hot tub baths, exercise, inspirational talks, and a diet of "natural foods," especially molasses, fruit, and bran. When Post arrived at the sanitarium, he had virtually no money, even to the point that he had to trade in blankets from his bankrupt mill as a down payment on the medical costs. Unfortunately for both Post and Kellogg, Post's health deteriorated further. His wife, in desperation, withdrew Post and placed him in a Christian Scientist's home for treatment. There, remarkably, he recovered.

By that time, Post was nearly forty and still without a means of employment. He did, however, have something of a reputation as the man who came back from the (nearly) dead. Post used that "hook"— his recovery—as a basis to start his own health sanitarium, La Vita Inn. Meals at La Vita stressed grains and bran, as well as a coffee substitute made of New Orleans molasses, bran, and wheat berries. In 1895, he marketed his coffee substitute to retail grocery stores under the brand name Postum. Did things change for Post? Not hardly. He lost $800 on the product in the first year, and he was still lacking money needed for advertising.

Post's breakthrough came when he persuaded a Chicago advertising firm to lend him money for ads in *Scribner's*, *Harper's Weekly*, and other publications. He had considerable writing skills, which he focused on the dangers of coffee drinking, successfully frightening thousands of consumers into trying his product. Post accused caffeine of causing rheumatism, heart disease, blindness, cowardice, sloth, and stupidity! His ads challenged consumers with questions such as, "Is your yellow streak the coffee habit? Does it reduce your working force, kill your energy, push you into the big crowd of mongrels?"[48] Post's tactics worked. Sales of Postum reached $3,000 a month by 1893, but already he had started work on his next product, a cereal of yeast, whole wheat, and malted barley flour called Grape-Nuts. The cereal was not made from grapes or nuts, but its texture was nutty and the baking process turned the starches into a sugar that tasted like grapes. Post sold cereal, became a millionaire in a few short years, and founded a cereal empire. He nevertheless probably would have been chagrined to learn that the company that bears his name today markets such unhealthful products as Oreo O's and Cocoa Pebbles.

MASS PRODUCTION AND
THE QUEST FOR EFFICIENCY

Although some companies, like Jack Daniel's and Thomas Welch's, lagged behind the trend toward managerial hierarchies, many large companies were now achieving higher levels of production and more efficient distribution by changing their control structures to that of a managerial hierarchy. In turn, managerial hierarchies had imposed vertical combinations on most industries. For such operations, labor had to perform different tasks—in different ways, and at a different pace—than ever before in the past. The relaxed, careful artistry of skilled craftsmen in Whitney's musket shop or Baldwin's locomotive works had long since given way to a frenetic, often dehumanizing, pace of laborers assembling machinery, slaughtering animals, pouring chemicals, or shoveling piles of fertilizer. Factory work, even when demanding highly skilled labor, such as the manufacture of steel, still tended to be repetitious, noisy, and, above all, dangerous. Carnegie's best manager, "Captain" Bill Jones, had died in a furnace explosion—a fate that claimed hundreds of steelworkers a year with less publicity. Coal mines caved in; catwalks collapsed over moving machinery; and fingers, hands, arms, and legs disappeared daily in a blizzard of moving gears and slashing blades.

Labor grudgingly adjusted, and with acceptance came a certain competence bringing improvement in safety as well as demands that factory owners improve conditions. The most serious complaint for workers was neither hours nor pay, but loss of job autonomy to the bosses. That was epitomized by the shift in practice from each worker bringing his own tools to the appearance of furnished workstations. Individuality vanished even more when managers started to examine the laborers' physical movements to identify wasteful motion and energy.

From management's viewpoint, coordination and control over the activities of its labor force involved more than squeezing out marginal efficiency gains. By 1900, the sheer size of a factory workforce could dwarf the employees at what would have been considered a "big" business fifty years earlier. Plants employed thousands, as in the case of the McCormick factory in Chicago with its 4,000 workers in 1900 and 15,000 employees in 1916.[49] Other plants, such as Ford's Highland Park, Michigan, facility, counted more than 33,000 workers. Management, by then obsessed with efficiency gains as a means of providing stability for their companies, saw the direction of labor as crucial to achieving the rule of the "visible hand."

Directing the productivity of labor on such a scale demanded structures and tactics unheard of by Jack Daniel, who emphasized personal sales of whiskey, or Lydia Pinkham, who produced and sold her "vegetable compound for women" with the assistance only of her family. Factory management relied upon discipline, organization, and a steady stream of seamless effort from workers. Yet managers realized that not every employee could produce with the same efficiency or equality of talent. That led a metal manufacturer named Frederick W. Halsey to create a rudimentary piecework system. Another metalworks manager, Henry Towne, presided over the introduction of a system in 1884 that used a contract with the workforce to share any per-unit savings with all employees. Up to 40 percent of the savings that the company received from increased productivity went to line workers, while foremen received smaller shares.[50] By the 1880s, most managers had investigated a number of ways to improve the productivity of labor, and certainly many of them were a far cry from the Simon Legree image of a black-clad, mustachioed overseer brandishing a whip on the backs of helpless wage laborers. On the other hand, managers tended to view workers as pieces of machinery to be fine-tuned, not human creations to be encouraged and nurtured to attain greater accomplishments. A Midvale Steel Company manager named Frederick W. Taylor came to be associated with this latter view. Taylor's fame emerged from a process he called "scientific management," the details of which first appeared in a journal called *Shop Management* in 1903. Then, in 1915, his famous book, *The Principles of Scientific Management*, called the "most influential work on management ever published," expanded these principles.[51] Taylor's scientific management typified the Progressive-era reliance on statistics to evaluate and science to govern a wide range of human activities, from criminal justice to municipal planning. He emphasized, for example, time-and-motion studies, in which he used a stopwatch to determine a standard time in which each task in the factory could be performed. Based on that standard time, workers either received higher or lower pay according to their output. Contrary to the fears of the workers, Taylor never favored increasing production without a systematic and equal increase in wages. Indeed, the greatest difficulty Taylor faced was in convincing management (which had to be scientifically reorganized as well) that the sum total of productivity improvements would generate more than enough revenue to pay higher wages.[52]

Monitoring the work of the line laborers, Taylor proposed an elaborate system of administration that relied on eight layers of clerks and bosses, including a "shop disciplinarian" who reviewed the workers' "virtues and defects" and assisted them in making corrections.[53] An earlier attempt by Taylor to supervise a system of controls using slips filled out by the foremen and workers had proved unworkable, as no one wanted to spend the time to fill out the papers properly. Even under his new, scientific system, Taylor's approach tended to lack a clear chain of command, focusing, as one critic of the day said, on the specifics of individual tasks rather than on the production processes of the entire organization. But it still constituted an improvement over most other management systems, and Taylor rapidly became known as a guru whose advice enabled ordinary managers to extract extraordinary production out of their labor forces. Consequently, other businesses quickly copied Taylor's methods: Remington's typewriter factory created its own "department of productive efficiency," charged with studying all manufacturing methods and labor activities.

Taylor had intense opposition, of course. Unions attempted to block imposition of piecework at every turn. Taylor found management even more difficult than labor, with managers consistently failing to follow the principles he laid out. Congress went so far as to outlaw time study and incentives in 1915 at the crest of the Progressive tide. It was a losing battle. After World War II, U.S. experts introduced Taylorism into Japanese factories, where, without the union and government opposition that existed in America, they took root.

The role of managers took on added importance after 1890, when new waves of unskilled immigrants reached American shores. Managers assumed that they needed to monitor the workforce more closely, but labor and management alike realized that the new highly technical processing machinery required more than reorganization of the workplace itself. Accountants in the organizations appreciated the waste and inefficiency of ill- or under-trained labor. Clearly, in an era when Gustavus Swift was dipping his finger in the streams behind his slaughterhouses to determine the amount of fat and therefore the degree of waste emanating from his plants, the potential productivity gains from an educated and skilled workforce did not escape the efficiency-obsessed managers of the late nineteenth century. Thus, business participated in the widespread efforts to improve education, whether within public schools or at the new trade schools. Resources devoted to education in the United States doubled between 1860 and 1900, with businesses seeing an opportunity to enlist the contributions of taxpayers into their drive to improve labor efficiency. From that perspective, it certainly worked, because expenditure for public education rapidly outpaced expenditure for private-sector education. Business also realized—as many critics of American capitalism were quick to point out—that public education provided a convenient introduction to factory-style organization with its structure and its management of tasks according to the clock. Critics rightly maintained that education socialized recent immigrants for the purposes of patriotism and introduced some of them to structured organizational settings. Certainly education served to "Americanize" the foreign-born. English language classes, reading, writing, and basic arithmetic all enhanced the value of an immigrant child as a future worker.

THE UNION RESPONSE

Despite the influx of relatively unskilled labor, it appears that wages rose in close proximity to productivity increases (or about 1.3 percent to 1.5 percent annually). Perhaps equally important, however, workers enjoyed greater amounts of leisure time, reducing both the workweek and the individual workday. Contrary to Sinclair's depiction of poor Jurgis toiling away for more than fourteen hours a day, the number of hours worked by the average laborer had *declined steadily* since 1860. A typical workweek consisted of sixty hours as early as the 1880s, and by 1914 had dropped to just over fifty-five hours.[54] And the workweek continued to shrink, in part due to the electrification of factories. As work hours were reduced, however, business expected increased attendance and attention from its labor force. Gates on factories were introduced in combination with time clocks to regulate when workers could arrive, leave, or take lunch breaks; companies levied fines or dismissed employees who were chronically absent; and talking or wandering around the workplace without direction could bring disciplinary action.

Labor reacted to the increased mechanization and control over workers' lives with dismay. One response—the formation of unions—has received considerable attention and evoked romantic portrayals of labor's pioneer leaders, but prior to 1900, the movement itself remained small and highly concentrated in a few industries. As of 1900, less than 3 percent of the workforce was unionized, and, indeed, until the 1842 Massachusetts court decision, *Commonwealth v. Hunt*, government treated labor unions as "conspiracies," and the general rising wage levels had made it difficult to organize large segments of labor. After the Civil War, however, labor organizations found new life as mass production lumped workers into categories. Large numbers of workers were suddenly bound together by the factory whistle and, soon, Taylor's stopwatch, providing them with a common experience.

Terence V. Powderly's Knights of Labor, while not the first national union, was the first to claim such a title. Hoping to attract workers of all types—skilled and unskilled—the Knights enlisted more than 700,000 laborers by 1886, but because it even allowed farmers as members, it proved far too ill-defined and became unwieldy and unfocused. An incident in 1886 at Chicago's Haymarket Square doomed the Knights of Labor when a protest against the McCormick Reaper Works turned into a riot as a bomb exploded in the crowd, killing ten people and injuring dozens. Although anarchists loosely associated with the Knights had called the meeting for their own purposes, a jury nevertheless convicted eight Knights members of murder. The episode ended the Knights as a force and provided a lesson that unions had to screen their members carefully—especially in light of the fact that government at that time was clearly not in their corner—and stay focused on economic issues.[55]

In labor history, it would be hard to overstate the role of Samuel Gompers in improving the life of American skilled laborers. Gompers, an immigrant like so many other wage earners, arrived in the United States from England less than a month after Pickett's ill-fated charge at Gettysburg. When Gompers had disembarked onto the streets of New York City, the looting that had accompanied the draft riots had only recently subsided. In England, Gompers had worked as a cigar maker, a trade wherein one of the workers usually served as a "reader," providing an oral summary of the important newspapers and magazines of the day to other workers in the quiet shop. A natural organizer, Gompers had read Marx, but apparently adopted only a bit of rhetoric needed for his own purposes.[56] Nevertheless, Gompers rejected radicalism in the union and excluded from any role in union policy any intellectuals who were not genuine laborers. He appreciated the crucial role that coordinated effort played in the success of a union, and he intended to eliminate "wildcat" (unauthorized) strikes in his trade union, even if it meant allying with management in the process.

Despite his European background, he did not fear industrialization's effects on labor in the way some radicals did. On the contrary, he wanted laborers to control and master the change, not be controlled by it. By insisting that the unions make good on contracts—even those that left their members at a disadvantage—Gompers ensured that he would gain public support when management reneged on some of its contracts. Gompers appreciated the weaknesses of Powderly's Knights of Labor scheme, especially in its goal of uniting skilled and unskilled workers. In a sense, he secured the labor unions for labor, eliminating the rancorous radicals that alienated the public or the pompous intellectuals who had little in common with the rank and file. By focusing his efforts on skilled labor only, he gave the union a weapon to fight with, namely, the skills of its members. Basing his efforts on an earlier organization called the Federation of Trades, Gompers created a new union to replace the Knights called the American Federation of Labor (AFL), organized in 1886. The AFL was ingenious in its "federation" design because all members were not required to strike for the demands of a single, small union. All could go on "sympathy strikes," but tanners did not have to walk out simply because the electricians did. That brought a flexibility sorely missing among the Knights of Labor. Gompers did not avoid conflict with management when necessary, but otherwise stressed policies that brought labor into the very middle class that previously had distrusted it.[57] The AFL stuck to the bread-and-butter issues of wage increases and shorter workweeks, and sided with the middle class on policy matters such as literacy tests for immigrants. Moreover, Gompers had the philosophy of preparing the union for strikes and using the strike only as a last resort, preferring to wait for victory instead of rushing to defeat. Thanks in large part to Gompers's strategic vision, by 1893 the AFL had over a quarter of a million members.

The union's general compliance with the law also gave it a much stronger base of support with the public than the Knights or other rival unions enjoyed. Gompers realized that until the labor movement convinced businesses and voters that it posed no threat to social harmony or economic growth, it would face opposition from each, manifested in frequent applications of state power against labor. In 1877, President Rutherford B. Hayes had used federal troops to break the railroad strike; in 1892, state troops ended the Homestead Strike that had resulted in the defeat of the Pinkerton detectives; and in 1894, President Grover Cleveland used federal soldiers to end the Pullman Strike.

More damaging to the labor movement on a daily basis were the various tools that industry used to resist unions, including the "yellow dog" contract (in which a prospective employee had to agree not to join a union as a condition of work), the blacklist (a list of organizers that was circulated to all local employers), the injunction (a court order restricting strike activity), and highly effective harassment techniques available to public officials at all levels, from sheriffs to tax collectors. Progressive legislation figured prominently in changing the face of the workplace, though not always for the most admirable reasons.[58] But shorter workweeks also stood squarely in the middle of Gompers's approach toward identifying achievable, tangible results as opposed to the lofty, often illusory goals of radicals and socialists. Shorter workweeks enhanced the worker's independence and reduced his actual working time. Organized labor, led by Gompers, joined business in supporting restrictions on immigration and on child labor.[59] Such measures—whatever their motivation—reflected the gradually increasing influence of labor (although union membership still did not exceed 10 percent prior to World War I) and, more important, the willingness of Americans to use the government to redress perceived inequalities in business. Nevertheless, despite the contributions of Gompers and the gains of organized labor, the modest shifts in labor law paled in comparison to the broader and more substantial uses of government power against corporations in the arena of antitrust law, which accelerated under the Progressive movement.

REGULATING INDUSTRY: FROM "SUNSHINE" TO SHERMAN

State and federal regulation brought together the separate streams of protest in the agrarian sector and within industrial labor, merging the conceptual rapids of high idealism from socialists like Bellamy and

George with the calmer waters of pragmatism represented by reformers like Charles Francis Adams. While people quickly identified the names of Sinclair, Lloyd, Tarbell, and George, it was Adams who played the more critical role in changing the face of regulation.[60] The public knew Adams from the numerous articles he wrote for *North American Review*, including one 1869 piece called "Chapter of Erie." Viewing railroads as having acquired an identity and character unique among all businesses, Adams contended that a lag had occurred between the evolution of the railroad industry and the institutions developed by the public to respond to it. Adams argued for creation of a permanent, apolitical body to regulate large industries such as railroads. Far from resisting the drift toward monopolies in railroads, Adams contended, society should accelerate the tendency, because only when a railroad could handle the largest possible volume could the community obtain the lowest possible price. But Adams recognized that Americans called for more competition, not less, and argued for creation of a permanent commission to investigate more than regulate.

As a result of that publication, Adams won an appointment to the Massachusetts Board of Railroad Commissioners—not the first regulatory agency in America, but the most important. It represented the first incarnation of regulatory bodies. The commission's primary purpose was to disclose, and publish, important railroad data on safety, rates, and schedules. Once the public had information, Adams maintained, it would regulate industries through the market—hence the concept of a "sunshine commission" that shed light on a business. Sunshine laws, such as those requiring publication of bank balance sheets or the memberships of boards of directors, took an elevated view of the consumer, assuming that if the public knew relevant information concerning a bank or railroad, consumers could make their own decisions.

Sunshine commissions did not satisfy the more rabid critics of industry, especially critics of the railroads. In the 1870s, largely in response to increasing complaints about discrimination against individual shippers and localities from Midwestern states, the federal government was petitioned regularly for national regulation and control of railroads. Although a review of aggregate rates has shown no such discrimination, individual cases of discrimination had led to a widespread fear that railroads wielded monopolistic power. The so-called "Granger Laws," enacted between 1871 and 1874 in Illinois, Iowa, Minnesota, and Wisconsin, reflected the concern over rate discrimination. The laws used independent regulatory commissions with powers well beyond those of the sunshine commissions, including the authority to set rates. Small businesses, seeing an opportunity to lower their own rates, also joined the Grangers in their cases, the most famous of which, *Munn v. Illinois*, involved an elevator operator from Chicago charged with violations of interstate trade. In 1877, the Supreme Court, which had heard eight Granger cases in total, ruled that the states could regulate a business in the public interest.

Nine years later, the Supreme Court further expanded regulatory power over business, although denying it to the states, in the case of *Wabash, St. Louis, and Pacific Railway Company v. Illinois*. The case was significant for two reasons. First, it involved an appeal regarding a state ruling that had prohibited a shipper from charging more for a short haul than a slightly longer haul. Of course, modern air travelers know that longer routes frequently cost less to operate than shorter routes, in part due to the fuel costs involved in taking off, but also in the expense entailed in stopping to load or unload passengers. Second, not only did the Court rule against the railroads, it also ruled against the states, finding differential rates to be evidence that states could not regulate railroads effectively. Even though no express federal laws on the regulation of interstate commerce existed, the Court held, states did not have the power to regulate interstate commerce.

A new regulatory wave ensued, evolving from sunshine (exposing industry operations and rates to public scrutiny) to actual control. In 1887, Congress acted against rate discrimination by passing the Interstate Commerce Act, prohibiting pooling, outlawing different rates for short hauls and long hauls, and prohibiting discrimination between persons, commodities, or localities. The act established a five-member commission to enforce the law, "not to usurp the actual rate-making function, but to [relieve] individuals from the indifference, incompetence, and malice which in the real world frequently impede the smooth workings of economic theory."[61] Railroad historian Albro Martin concluded that the failure of Progressive regulation came when the railroads "were deprived of the freedom to follow *their* own self-interest in a society in which all others retained that right."[62] By the 1880s, however, the menace of railroad power seemed to grow inordinately through its alliance with other large-scale enterprises, especially steel and another new industry, petroleum. The potential for malicious behavior, critics thought, reached its zenith with the combination of railroads and oil, especially under the control of John D. Rockefeller.

JOHN D. ROCKEFELLER SAVES THE WHALES

Described as a "brooding, cautious, secretive man" who founded the "wisest and meanest monopoly known to history," John D. Rockefeller made plenty of enemies in his lifetime.[63] At the time of Rockefeller's death, one observer quipped that "Hell must now be half full." Forever associated with the concept of the oil industry, Rockefeller was hardly a founder of Greenpeace. Nevertheless, he may have done as much to save the whales as any animal rights activist who ever lived.

Americans had relied on a number of different fuel sources for their light and power. The advent of steam engines made coal a valuable resource, but people still heated their stoves and fireplaces in many parts of the nation with wood, candles, or whale oil. Demand for the latter, of course, gave rise to a large American whaling industry.[64] Although people knew of the existence of crude oil, which some people bottled as medicine, most farmers disliked the black film, plowing around it on their land. A Yale chemistry professor, Benjamin Silliman, Jr., had experimented with the oil, in 1855 purifying it into a product called kerosene, which he found provided an even better illuminant than whale oil. The oil did not seem a practical energy source, however, because Silliman and his fellow investors would have had to transport small deposits of the crude oil from northwest Pennsylvania to the larger urban markets. Silliman's Pennsylvania Rock Oil Company of Connecticut dispatched an unemployed railroad engineer, "Colonel" Edwin Drake, to Titusville, Pennsylvania, to undertake a drilling operation based on principles learned from salt-well drillers who encountered oil as a by-product. Silliman thought that oil could be pumped out of the ground just as water could; and in 1859, Drake had constructed a thirty-foot-tall derrick that burrowed seventy feet into the earth. In the face of rampant skepticism, Drake struck oil.[65] The low cost to enter the oil business—as little as $1,000 purchased the drilling equipment (substantially more than a McCormick reaper, but infinitesimal compared to the cost of starting even a small railroad), and a refinery could be built for as little as $200—combined with the availability of oil land to open the business to almost anyone. Within a year of Drake's demonstration, speculators streamed into the region. Even then, perceptive observers could see the inevitable impact of the new fuel source: "Good news for whales," wrote one reporter.[66] So many producers appeared that no one could make a profit. Drake himself died in poverty, earning little from his breakthrough. Crude oil prices plummeted from $4 to $0.35 a barrel (forty-two gallons) in 1862 alone. Yet when the Civil War started, the Union Army's demand drove prices up again, to a whopping $13.75 a barrel. According to one report, a blacksmith purchased $200 worth of drilling equipment to drill a well worth $100,000, while yet others lost fortunes just as quickly.[67] Within a decade, oil production rose to 5 million barrels, much of it in the form of kerosene for homes, where it displaced whale oil, but soon oil was also providing new factory fuel and finding a wide variety of by-product uses, including in tars for paving, as lubricating oil, and as paraffin for candles.[68]

John D. Rockefeller ended his oil career as the wealthiest man in American history, but he had a childhood of anxious want as the son of an often-absent peddler and a straitlaced mother.[69] He recalled at an early age being trained to work, save, and give. He attended a Cleveland high school, and upon graduation, immediately started work as an assistant bookkeeper at fifty cents a day. Like Carnegie, Rockefeller began the road to riches with a low-wage job. All the time he did the books, Rockefeller studied the business for which he worked, absorbing the intricacies of enterprise. Bookkeeping suited him in a sense, because he had a penchant for exacting detail and justice. A business partner noted, "If there was a cent due us, he wanted it. If there was a cent due a customer, he wanted the customer to have it."[70] A devout Baptist, Rockefeller made certain that the Lord had His, too, tithing his entire life. Fittingly, and perhaps on the biblical principle of "give and it shall be given unto you," Rockefeller met Samuel Andrews at church, where Andrews related to Rockefeller a new, exciting venture he had invested in, oil drilling. In 1865, Rockefeller joined Andrews in speculative ventures, building a refinery.

Fascinated with oil and kerosene, Rockefeller nevertheless directed most of his energy and talent into an agricultural wholesale products firm, where he worked until 1867. Along with Henry Flagler and Andrews, Rockefeller started a new partnership to drill oil and refine the petroleum, although he quickly emphasized refining over drilling. Employing the same pursuit of efficiency that had characterized James Hill in railroads and Gustavus Swift in meat production, Rockefeller set out to reduce the excessive waste he saw in petroleum refining. He examined by-product uses; avoided paying for insurance on refineries by building them to last; and hired his own plumber and purchased his own timber. Rockefeller saved more than $1.50 per barrel by having his own kilns to dry the wood and wagons to haul it. The Rockefeller, Andrews, and Flagler barrel production business alone constituted a remarkable demonstration of cost-cutting and mass production. The business soon grew to one of the largest in Cleveland, at which point Rockefeller reorganized, bringing in his brother William and naming the firm Standard Oil Company.

One of the first results of Rockefeller's quest to eliminate waste was that prices fell so low on kerosene that not only did it drive out fuels such as whale oil and coal oil, but for a while it kept electricity at bay. Standard Oil hired chemists to find still other uses for oil by-products, eventually producing more than 300 different products from a single barrel of oil. But Rockefeller did not ignore increasing production and eliminating waste from the refining process itself, pushing prices still lower. Between 1865 and 1870, kerosene prices dropped by 50 percent, though Rockefeller still made a profit. By that time, other refiners failed in droves, but consumers cheered each new drop in the price of the fuel—as did the whales, no doubt.

Standard Oil embarked on a program of ambitious expansion, interrupted by a brief attempt to form a pool in 1872. Tom Scott of the Pennsylvania Railroad had suggested an alliance between the large refiners and the railroads in which they would agree to fix prices. Rockefeller stood to gain from the stable prices and rebates, but in the process he antagonized the public—his consumers—with the resulting outcry leading the Pennsylvania legislature to revoke the charter of the price-fixing company Scott designed, which never shipped any oil. Rockefeller abandoned attempts to form pools with others, admitting it was a mistake, and turned his attention to forming the world's most efficient oil company.

Like Carnegie, Rockefeller acquired other companies in his industry for a pittance, usually buying in depressions. As he purchased or absorbed other businesses, he welcomed their officers and employees, placing several individuals from merged firms in positions of power within the Standard Oil hierarchy. When possible, however, he exchanged Standard Oil shares instead of money—again, like Carnegie, reinvesting the cash in the company. The tactic worked: Dozens of other refiners joined him or sold directly to Standard, giving the company 80 percent of the kerosene market by the 1880s. With size came special clout with the railroads. Since Standard shipped far more oil than anyone else, the company could obtain "rebates," or discounts, from the railroads, which were caught in their own price wars. The rebate became the symbol of unfairness and monopoly control; but in reality it constituted a commonsense response to the fact that some customers used the service so much that the railroad gave them a "volume discount." Virtually any modern American shopper who has purchased an item at a small, boutique grocery store in an urban area, and then priced the same product at a large "mega-supermarket," understands that all businesses grant, and seek, volume discounts. Rockefeller himself saw the rebates as benefiting the railroads more than Standard Oil.[71] No market justification existed, then or now, for criticizing rebates. Companies as disparate as submarine sandwich shops and video stores offer frequent-user cards that are punched and then redeemed for a free sandwich or video rental after all the squares have been punched. Businesses from auto dealers to children's shoe stores provide rebates in the form of cash back or free products. Not surprisingly, consumers do not complain about rebates they receive.

Yet to some members of the public then, and to many of Rockefeller's competitors on the losing end, the rebates represented an unholy alliance of the large railroads and Standard Oil. Phrases such as "ruthless price cutting," "unfair pricing," and "unfair competition" afflicted the major magazines and ingrained themselves into the American vocabulary. Yet at the very time Standard reached 90 percent of the market, prices had fallen from twenty-six cents a gallon for kerosene to eight cents, completely in contradiction to traditional scenarios of monopoly pricing. Meanwhile, the tonnage of imported whale products had started a precipitous decline as their prices rose dramatically relative to oil.[72] But at no time did Rockefeller have in mind driving all the competitors from the field: Rockefeller's partner, Charles Pratt, stated, "Competitors we must have, we must have. If we absorb them, be sure it will bring up another."[73]

It is also clear that Rockefeller had far more on his mind than money. In his 1909 memoirs, Rockefeller wrote: "I know of nothing more despicable and pathetic than a man who devotes all the waking hours of the day to making money for money's sake."[74] It is worth noting again that he contributed 10 percent of his income *throughout his life* to his church and his religious beliefs. He gave away, proportionally, more money than most modern charitable organizations can raise in a healthy year—hardly suggesting a money-driven miser who wanted to count his pennies at the end of every night. Instead, Rockefeller wrote in 1885, "Let the good work go on. We must ever remember we are refining oil for the poor man and he must have it cheap and good."[75] He told a partner, "Hope we can continue to hold out with the best illuminator in the world at the lowest price."[76]

Standard Oil had organized itself vertically, acquiring supplies of crude oil from Standard-owned fields, building its own tanker fleets, constructing pipelines, and then, integrating forward, establishing systems of licensed dealers and even overseas subsidiaries. Typically, however, one of the most significant gambles required Rockefeller to risk his own capital. In 1885, drillers had found oil in the Lima, Ohio, area, but the oil had a sulfur base that caused it to smell like rotten eggs, which made drilling for it totally impractical. Producers and customers alike shrank from the Lima oil field—all except for Rockefeller, who purchased leases representing more than 40 million barrels of the sulfurous, and useless, oil. Rockefeller was convinced that it could be made fully practical, however, and he hired chemists to purify the oil. By that time, even his directors recoiled in horror at the thought of spending another dime in the stink-oil fields. Rockefeller voluntarily offered to personally underwrite whatever was necessary to make the project work, at which point the board concluded that hope must exist for the chairman to exude such confidence. The project ate still more money—by the millions—until finally "one of our German chemists cried 'Eureka! We ... at last found ourselves able to clarify the oil.'"[77]

At that time, whales no longer were at risk; rather, the entire American oil industry was. Russians had drilled for oil in Baku, staking out the finest oil lands in the world and determined to dominate the world's oil markets. Within six years of the Russian oil discoveries, America's share of world production of refined oil fell from 85 percent of the total to 53 percent. The U.S. oil industry found itself on the endangered species list, with Standard Oil at the top. In every way, the Russians had significant advantages over Standard Oil, including a more centralized location, more productive wells (280 barrels per well daily for Baku, compared to 4.5 barrels for American wells), a better quality natural oil, and a closer location to European and Asian markets. European competitors made matters worse by offering low-grade oil that they labeled "Standard Oil Company," tarring the name of Rockefeller's quality product. Undaunted, Rockefeller built a large fleet of tanker ships, unleashed his chemists to squeeze yet more product out of a barrel of oil through the "cracking" process, and further chopped costs, using less iron in the barrel hoops and removing the waste from coal heaps to fire his refineries. In the penultimate demonstration of efficiency, Rockefeller made fuel out of leftovers, junk, and waste. Despite those gains, Standard had to sell higher-quality oil for a lower price (just over five cents a gallon) than the Russians to regain Standard's reputation. In the decade 1882–91, Standard grabbed more than 60 percent of the world market in oil, prying much of it from Russian hands.

Yet as chairman of one of the richest, most powerful companies in American history, Rockefeller still found time to visit the fields, loading barrels with workers, or carrying shavings at the barrel works in wheelbarrows, or praising employees. Other oilmen considered Rockefeller the equal of Carnegie in hiring and retaining the highest-quality employees and managers. Throughout it all, he put God first, praying daily and attending church regularly. Perhaps for that reason, Rockefeller said of himself, "I was not what might be called a diligent business man," because his work came third, after faith and family.[78] Folsom thus asks a legitimate question about Rockefeller: "How could someone put his career third and wind up with $900 million?"[79] As Rockefeller himself said, "Mere money-getting has never been my goal. I had an ambition to build."[80] But Rockefeller even outdid Carnegie when it came to giving. His tithes increased from $100,000 per year at age 45 to $1 million annually by age 53. Rockefeller gave away $138 million when he was eighty, with his lifetime philanthropies exceeding $550 million, mostly for schools and churches.

RISE OF THE TRUST

Rockefeller's personal philanthropy accounted for little in the minds of those who thought he and his corporate "robber baron" friends wanted to end all competition. And Rockefeller gave them plenty of ammunition! Convinced that pools would not work (he called them "ropes of sand"), Rockefeller devised a new form of corporate organization called a trust. The creation of S.C.T. Dodd, one of Rockefeller's lawyers, the trust had a legal history as a fiduciary device used to manage property or savings of another. Dodd suggested using the mechanism to trade stock in a voting trust, "a technical form of business organization," wherein the former owners received trust certificates in exchange for the shares of stock in their own companies.[81] Or, in essence, the smaller businesses turned over control of all of their businesses for a part ownership in the trust. Standard Oil formed its trust in 1879 in Ohio, and three years later some forty oil companies exchanged their shares for Standard Oil trust shares. Sugar, whiskey, cottonseed oil, linseed oil, tobacco, lead smelting, and other industries all witnessed the formation of trusts by the major producers by the 1880s. However, they soon aroused more hostility than pools or other forms of combinations ever had.

The trust also had a serious flaw: It was a matter of public record.[82] Suits flooded state courts, arguing that the combinations restrained trade, and in 1892 the Ohio Supreme Court began the final unraveling of the Standard Oil trust. But even before that, the trusts had come under sharp attack at the national level. When Senator John Sherman introduced his antitrust bill in 1890, Congress thought public sentiment against trusts so clear that the combined Senate/House vote was 294 to one in favor of the Sherman Antitrust Act. But did that mean that the public despised all the large combinations? Were they all viewed as evil? Perhaps no such sentiments lay behind the Sherman Antitrust Act at all. It was so broadly worded as to be absolutely unenforceable—symbol without substance—and business itself "regarded the Act as impractical, unenforceable, and hence innocuous."[83] Monopoly and monopolistic power, in the form of the trusts, offered an easy target for politicians and a symbol, similar to the BUS in Andrew Jackson's time. The antitrust act allowed Congress to pass a public resolution, and to take credit for farsighted legislation. Meanwhile, it had "punted" the difficult issues of sorting out which combinations were monopolies to the courts and to future administrations.

Aware that neither state governments nor the federal government would allow trusts to proceed without challenge, many of the corporations turned to yet another form of organization: the holding company. Most states only allowed holding companies, wherein one company could hold, own, or control the stock of another, by special chartering legislation. In 1889, New Jersey liberalized its general incorporation laws to permit holding companies, even if the "held" companies were in other states. Within a decade, several companies had established themselves in New Jersey, abandoning their trust framework for that of the holding company. Standard Oil, recapitalized in 1899 to $110 million, was one of them. As with many other businesses, Standard changed little but the names on the stock shares: Its officers and directors from the "old" Standard continued to administer Standard Oil of New Jersey.

The most publicized holding company was the creation of J. P. Morgan and James J. Hill, called the Northern Securities Company. Hill had battled another railroader, Edward H. Harriman of the Southern Pacific Railroad, over the Chicago, Burlington, and Quincy Railroad, which represented a crucial rail link to Chicago. Hill had acquired the Burlington, extending his line from Chicago to the Pacific, essentially shutting Harriman's Northern Pacific out of the route. In 1901, when Harriman tried to acquire a majority share in Hill's Northern Pacific (something Hill had no intention of letting him do), a bidding war for Northern Pacific stock erupted, sending the price of shares up to $1,000 each.

To prevent the railroad stock war from affecting Wall Street, Morgan stepped in to form a holding company that would incorporate both Hill's and Harriman's interests. The Northern Securities Company—again incorporated in New Jersey—was capitalized at $400 million and brought under one umbrella the stock of the Northern Pacific, the Great Northern, and the Burlington. The new president, Theodore Roosevelt, who had succeeded the assassinated William McKinley, was a Progressive who supported federal restraint on the power of business. Roosevelt instructed his attorney general to file a suit against Northern Securities on the grounds that it violated the Sherman Act. In 1904, the Supreme Court ruled against the Northern Securities Company, contending that it constituted a threat to the freedom of commerce, even though it had not engaged in any behavior that threatened commerce. The Court had taken antitrust legislation to a new level in which existence alone posed a threat to commerce. Ultimately, the Supreme Court's action did not restore competition to the Midwestern lines, but only eliminated an efficient and sensible consolidation of rail properties, forcing Hill and Harriman to do informally what they would have preferred to do publicly.

Thanks to the Northern Securities case, Teddy Roosevelt acquired the moniker "trustbuster." And although Roosevelt started a case against Standard Oil's trust, it was the administration of his successor, and self-admitted Progressive, William Howard Taft, who pursued it. Thus, the best-known antitrust case of the early 1900s came before the Supreme Court in 1911, at which time the chief justice, Edward White, required Standard Oil to be broken up into more than thirty subsidiaries separated from the parent company, with some of the companies developing into long surviving companies like Exxon and Chevron. At the same time, however, the Court inserted the "rule of reason" into antitrust jurisprudence—a sure invitation to mischief, for "reason" varies among "reasonable" men and women! Only combinations that "unreasonably" restrained trade were unlawful, the Court said, opening further the door to business consolidation. Teddy Roosevelt himself, three months later, grudgingly recognized "the inevitableness and the necessity of combinations in business."[84] Ultimately, antitrust law became a morass: "Neither the presidents, the regulatory agencies, nor the courts put forward an effective measure of concentration that could be understood by potential offenders and used as the lynchpin of antitrust policy."[85] They did not state what to some may have been obvious—that no such measure could be devised.

THE MERGER WAVE

Indeed, the antitrust legislation Congress enacted had the exact opposite of what the lawmakers intended, in that it helped spark the largest merger wave in American history. After all, the intent was to increase competition and reduce the control large firms had over the marketplace. Between 1895 and 1904, however, the most frenzied period of business combination ever witnessed up to that point swept across the American corporate scene. Business had reached the stage at which it became more efficient to have fewer producers rather than more. Companies were absorbed in droves, with more than 2,500 taken over from 1898 to 1902 alone. The ability of the large investment banks to marshal significant amounts of money on short notice meant that they could market securities by, in essence, guaranteeing the success of a stock offering with some of their own funds. This merger wave probably resulted from the confluence of a unique set of historical events, including the maturation of mass production, the unparalleled growth of capital-intensive industries, and the business recovery after the

Panic of 1893. Mass production, which also required capital in the form of machinery, had economies of scale; as the number of units produced increased, the cost of manufacturing each unit decreased. The electrical power, telegraph, and telephone industries certainly experienced this phenomenon. Once wires were strung to an area, adding extra users added little to cost. Railroads were another example: Once the road was laid and the engines were pulling cars, more frequent trips or longer trains were not costly.

The merger wave could be interpreted as a preliminary to the "Roaring Twenties," interrupted by World War I, yet historians often overlook one of the most important elements in such a growth spurt—namely, business and consumer confidence. If the Panic of 1893 represented a financial reaction to Congress's ill-advised experiment with the silver standard, then by 1900, the nation had witnessed a period of almost unbroken growth. Productivity particularly rose at a rapid clip, but the value added in manufacturing came disproportionately from companies that had achieved high concentration ratios. Thus, it may well be that the merger wave merely *reflected* optimism that the economy would continue to expand. Ironically then, many Americans may have railed against large combinations while at the same time they provided the very psychological safety net and optimistic encouragement needed to make them successful. And while enacting laws designed to limit the power of business consolidations, the government actually fostered the formation and stability of the most productive and efficient of those combinations.

CHAPTER 8

The Emergence of a
Consumer Market: 1880–1920

As the twentieth century dawned, fundamental changes occurred in the production and marketing of food, soap, clothing, and other consumer goods. By the 1920s, transportation had changed from dependence on animals to autos, while food was now packaged and sold in supermarkets. Whereas housewives once almost exclusively made dresses and clothing articles for children, now they purchased them through catalogs or at one of the new department stores. The home garden was enhanced by the exotic seeds of Burpee; home-brewed beverages gave way to Coca-Cola; homemade soap was replaced by Lux. The neighborhood barber gave way to Gillette's razor, and the carriage was replaced by Henry Ford's car.

Given the extent of this change, it is unlikely that the career of any individual entrepreneur captured the full range of the transition affecting business as a whole in the first decades of the 1900s. After all, individuals in history rarely span the entire spectrum of change in any area of human endeavor. Still, on occasion an individual's career crosses through momentous transitions and reflects them. Such was the case with Henry Leland.

HENRY LELAND AND THE
DAWN OF THE AUTO AGE

It is odd to think of Detroit, the "Motor City," as a place hostile to unions. But at the turn of the century, one of Detroit's great attractions to entrepreneurs involved the antiunion attitudes in many of the machine shops. That reputation, among other natural advantages, drew Henry Leland to Detroit in the early 1890s. Leland came from a farm family that had gone broke, forcing Henry to take a shoe factory job when he was eleven. Like John D. Rockefeller and John Harvey Kellogg, Leland had strong religious roots (in his case, Seventh-Day Adventist), and like virtually all entrepreneurs, he had a penchant for hard work. Through his church, he found a position as a mechanic on textile machinery, providing him the experience that shaped the remainder of his career.

During the Civil War, Leland went from repairing and maintaining machinery to designing it, making lathes for production of musket stocks. In 1865, however, Leland was fired. That merely inconvenienced a person with Leland's skills and talents, but none of the jobs Leland subsequently held, including police work, satisfied him. Eventually, he found an opportunity at the Brown & Sharpe Armory in Providence, Rhode Island, a company known for its cutting-edge technology in machine tooling. Leland absorbed everything Joseph Brown could teach him, especially the production of interchangeable parts. Leland worked on everything from screws to sewing machines and, ultimately, was put in charge of the sewing machine division. When not involved in designing new machines, Leland "would conduct Bible readings during lunch time and lecture the workers on theology and morality."[1]

Leland's designs included more than factory machines. He created a horse clipper that proved so adaptable that barbers adopted it: By the 1880s, Brown & Sharpe turned out more than 300 Leland clippers a day. In 1889, however, Leland took perhaps the biggest risk of his life. Convinced by a traveling salesman that the Detroit area offered exceptional opportunities for machine shops, Leland left Brown & Sharpe to form his own company, Leland, Faulconer & Norton, in 1890. Leland had impressed his former employers so much that they loaned him more than half of his share of the investment in the business. The company quickly achieved success by manufacturing everything from pencil sharpeners to bicycle gears, becoming one of Detroit's leading industrial firms.

At that point, mass-production technology that had dominated industry in the nineteenth century met the automobile, the innovation that dominated much of the twentieth century. An automaker named Ransom E. Olds had a demand for three times as many engines as his factory could produce. Olds placed an order with Leland for 2,000 engines, even though Olds had only sold 200 cars up to that point! Leland responded with new tweaks on the Olds design, to the point that the Leland redesign was so superior to the Olds engine that Olds had "to retard the L & F engine so it would idle as roughly as his own."[2] Olds, who had done much to pioneer automobiles in America, let his stubbornness stand in the way of greater success. When Leland offered a newly designed, 10-horsepower engine that was better than the Olds power plant, the automaker rejected it.

Leland found a new buyer, William Murphy, a Detroit lumberman who had an auto design and needed an engine. The new motorcar, named after the French founder of Detroit, was the Cadillac. Although expensive ($750 for the cheaper "A" version and $900 for the "B"), the Cadillac became the nation's best-selling automobile, gaining a reputation for the highest quality in the industry. In 1907, three Cadillacs were completely disassembled at a London racetrack with the parts painted red, yellow, and blue, after which a team of judges selected parts at random that were reassembled. Each of the three randomly assembled cars then was driven 500 miles![3]

Leland's authority within the company continued to expand, and he eventually managed the entire auto production process. By 1906, Cadillac sold more than 4,000 cars, only to see the Panic of 1907 almost drive the company out of business. In 1909, Leland and Murphy sold Cadillac to William C. Durant, who was the founder of General Motors. Leland then organized a new auto company of his own, the Lincoln Motor Company, for which he built "Liberty" engines.

Ironically, Leland, who may have best embodied the new generation of auto entrepreneurs, failed at his next venture, in part because he refused to take advantage of the First World War to make a profit on the Lincoln. Only a few years after the end of World War I, America's two best automobiles, the Cadillac and the Lincoln, both existed due to the efforts of Henry Leland. But the short postwar depression all but killed sales of the Lincoln, and Leland offered the company to a rising star in the automotive world, Henry Ford. Although the sale called for

Leland to have a managerial position in Ford's company, he soon excused himself, unable to tolerate the imperious Ford. The appearance of primitive motorcars at the turn of the century heralded a new age in manufacturing for those who perceived it.

NEW BUSINESS STRATEGIES FOR A NEW AGE

Henry Leland reflected the difficulty nineteenth-century entrepreneurs would have adapting to the twentieth century. Large-scale manufacturing could bring vast profits, but sudden shifts in the market could also mean huge, often insurmountable, losses. The federal government, once all but invisible on the shop floor, had become a presence with labor and antitrust legislation. Perhaps more relevant for many businesses, Uncle Sam also could be a substantial customer. As rails, roads, and telegraphs linked the country, the sheer size of the American economy connected even local and regional firms to other businesses around the nation. Depressions in one sector often spread to others, while the boom and bust cycles in manufacturing industries affected a growing number of suppliers, including many entrepreneurial or smaller firms.

As a response to the new environment, large corporations had internalized the need for planning. More important, the managers who made up the top levels of decision makers in corporations had come to believe in the concept of planning, which they saw as a necessity, not an option. The strategic view of managers whose business philosophy emphasized steady—if smaller—profits in return for greater stability tended to make corporations more risk-averse and less entrepreneurial. Increasingly, businesses wanted government to enhance economic stability, whether through tariff adjustments or the financial structure, so that their own strategic plans would not be disrupted. Perhaps grudgingly, but often willingly, business accepted regulation as a fair trade-off for government's contributions.

Progressives enjoyed the broad support of the public for most of their legislation. It was easy to show outlandish examples and genuine suffering, even if it represented a fraction of the business or product under scrutiny, while the tiny erosion of each consumer's welfare was all but impossible to publicize. A clear case involved the federal government's expanding powers over food products. Respectable journal-ists and less-upstanding muckrakers had energized the public to demand health standards for the meat and drug industry. Just as *The Jungle* had outraged the meat-buying public, so, too, did a series of scathing articles in *Collier's* in December 1905 aimed at the pharmaceu-tical industry. The two businesses seemed naturally to fall under a sim-ilar regulatory rubric in which the federal government needed to pro-vide basic inspections and maintain health and safety standards in food production and food handling. In 1906, passage of the Pure Food and Drug Act and subsequent Meat Inspection Acts of 1906 and 1907 gave the federal government the authority to inspect meat and ban the sale of tainted, or rotted, meat (providing the famous "USDA Approved" stamp). Likewise, products such as Lydia Pinkham's Vegetable Compound had to acknowledge their drug content—in Pinkham's case, the company had to state that the elixir contained almost 20 percent alcohol, explaining its remarkable ability to ease pain!

PROGRESSIVE FERVOR AND "THE REAL THING"

Ironically, one of the products that many people assume was affected and changed by the Pure Food and Drug Act, Coca-Cola, had already eliminated cocaine from its recipe two years before passage of the law. Coca-Cola originated with an Atlanta pharmacist named "Doc" John Pemberton and his partner, an advertiser named Frank Robinson. Pemberton had the inspiration to create a competitor drink to hot cof-fee or tea, a drink that in the South could be poured over ice or served cold. In 1886, he mixed kola seeds (which had only been made avail-able commercially a few years before) with sugar, caffeine, caramel, citric acid, and a fluid extract of coca leaves, otherwise known as cocaine. Although modern researchers into Coke's past have difficulty establishing the level of cocaine in early mixtures, it had four times as much caffeine as modern Coca-Cola, as well as sugar and the coca extract. Certainly, Pemberton had created a drink that promised excite-ment! Pemberton himself, however, soon fell ill—one biographer sug-gesting that he had developed a cocaine addiction—and Robinson took over merchandising the product with a remarkable ad campaign, including hundreds of posters, 500 streetcar signs, and materials for almost every soda fountain operator in the major cities of the South. But as Pemberton's health continued to fade, Robinson found himself with nothing to sell. The partner entrusted with manufacturing the beverage simply had not done his job.[4]

Robinson soon met another local druggist, Asa Griggs Candler, who suffered from frequent headaches. Robinson had touted Coca-Cola to Candler for almost a year before Candler found that the drink alleviated his pain and even helped his indigestion. He took over manufacturing of the product and, with Robinson, started to look for ways to reduce the cocaine content. By that time, cocaine (which only a few years earlier had been hailed as the wonder drug for all sorts of health woes) had come under a low-level but growing attack. The company still had not taken off, and in 1892 a stock offering fizzled. Candler responded with one of the earliest Coke "taste tests," sending letters to people all around the country with tickets to redeem for a free taste of Coca-Cola. In no time, the company had redeemed $50,000 worth of tickets. Pharmaceutical tests showed that the amount of cocaine in the drink at that time was one-thirtieth of a grain of cocaine, meaning that after many drinks, an extremely sensitive person might feel some effects.

Candler was on the horns of a dilemma. The growing clamor for the regulation of drugs could damage his product, but for honesty in advertising and security of his patent and trade name, he thought he needed a slight by-product of the coca leaf in the syrup. After several evolutions, Candler arrived at a "secret formula" that so diluted the cocaine that "it seemed unlikely that cocaine (or anything else for that matter) could survive." Coke had eliminated coke, although Candler fought a twenty-year war with the Food and Drug Administration to prove it. The final twist came in 1909–10, when the government, no longer able to claim that Coke had cocaine in it, initiated a series of charges against the company over the process it used to dilute the cocaine out. The leader of the government's case, Dr. Harvey Wiley, not only was a prominent nutritional reformer but, as one might expect, a leading Progressive.[5]

Most companies willingly changed their advertising, regardless of personal testimonies or claims, rather than invoke the wrath of the federal government. For the most part, the public supported the government, suspecting that unscrupulous hucksters or murderous meatpackers would afflict helpless consumers whenever possible. And certainly, neither the fraudulent snake-oil salesmen nor the vile packinghouses described by Upton Sinclair were fictions. From the 1890s to the 1960s, however, the government settled into a role of establishing standards for meat, fixing acceptable levels of foreign objects that an efficient and careful manufacturing process would allow, and separating fraud from advertisers' embellishments. Contrary to the Coke experience, the federal agencies concerned themselves less with product claims and more with the presence of harmful contents in ingredients.

Businesses had incorporated statisticians and accountants in the railroad age, and even by Carnegie's time many of the corporate leaders came from the ranks of bankers instead of production men. Not surprisingly, then, business and government gradually started to share a worldview—not in all things, of course, but in enough that government bureaucracies and business managerial hierarchies looked similar. In the event of a crisis, their interests could merge rapidly, as occurred during World War I. The fusion of business and government in wartime, however, was made possible only by one last set of Progressive reforms that gave the federal government unprecedented control over the nation's capital: the income tax and a central banking structure.

PROGRESSIVES AT HIGH TIDE: INCOME TAXES AND THE FEDERAL RESERVE

Although Prohibition would be their last and most fatally flawed program, the Progressives advanced key elements of their economic worldview by enacting new banking legislation and gaining passage of an income tax amendment, both in 1913. Those "reforms" represented the cumulative efforts of the Roosevelt, Taft, and Wilson administrations, all of which considered themselves "Progressive" in one or another sense of the term. The income tax and the creation of the Federal Reserve System contributed heavily to the economic upheavals of the subsequent sixteen years, with income taxes accounting for stagnating U.S. Treasury revenues and contributing to the rising postwar debt, as well as the 1920–21 recession, and the Federal Reserve System seriously constricting the banking system at key times in 1929–30.

An income tax of 3 percent on all incomes above $800 had been enacted in the Civil War and the rates increased twice thereafter. Then, in 1894, Congress passed a 2 percent tax on all incomes of more than $4,000. The following year, the Supreme Court ruled income taxes unconstitutional. During the Progressive era, calls for income taxes had led to the imposition of a corporate tax of one percent on the net income above $5,000 of every corporation.[6]

Income taxes had some appeal in that they could replace the then-central method of raising government revenue, the tariff system. At the time, the government was small and federal budgets did not exceed $1 billion, making it possible for tariffs and land sales to provide all the money the government needed. But tariffs, it was argued, unfairly targeted certain regions, and the population paid for tariffs through higher prices on other goods, while businesses benefited from the reduced competition. Perhaps more important, as economic historian Stanley Lebergott has stated, the substitution of income taxes over tariffs "efficiently conserved legislative energies: Life became simpler for Congress [because] the battle against tariffs had always involved direct, urgent, and threatening lobbies," whereas the income tax "affected only a small group of widely censured individuals...."[7] At the same time, as the historian of American tax policy, Elliot Brownlee, observed, passage of the income tax amendment involved a cession of power from the legislative to the administrative/executive, and shifted the control of taxation from the local to the national.[8]

Thus, the most important advantage of the income tax that supporters could point to was that it promised to "equalize tax burdens borne by the various classes ... [and] paid by the wealthier classes."[9] Many Progressives sought an income tax solely as a way to redistribute wealth, which had been the basis for many of the radical writers' tracts in the late 1800s. The income tax had little to do with revenue and everything to do with reform.

But since income taxes were unconstitutional, proponents had to secure a Constitutional amendment, the Sixteenth Amendment, ratified in 1913, to enable Congress to tax incomes. Once again, reformers only could gain support for their program by making it appear to afflict only "the rich." The subsequent tax code featured low rates and generous exemptions. Anyone earning less than $3,000 (and married couples earning less than $4,000) paid no tax, while those earning $20,000 to $50,000 paid only 2 percent. The top rate was 7 percent on incomes over $500,000, leaving most Americans paying no taxes at all or a mere one percent, with the entire tax form contained on a single page. Carried away with the prospects of an egalitarian utopia made possible by the income tax, one Missouri congressman beamed that passage of the income tax marked "the dawn of a brighter day, with more of sunshine, more of the songs of the birds, more of that sweetest music, the laughter of children well fed, well clothed, well housed ... good, even-handed, wholesome Democracy shall be triumphant."[10] Just over seven decades later, Stanley Lebergott's conclusion stands as a monumental understatement: "The net contribution of the income tax to inducing equality is not obvious."[11]

The combination of higher wages, the agricultural depression brought on by renewed European output, and the suddenly expanded labor pool of returning veterans all contributed to the 1920–21 recession. Still, high taxes played an important role in choking off investment and expansion, as well as sending a clear signal about incentives to achievement. Even Wilson, a professed Progressive, knew that the government was taking too much: He admitted that "in peace times high rates of income and profits taxes discourage energy ... and produce industrial stagnation," and more than one historian has found strong links between Andrew Mellon's tax cuts and Wilson's positions.[12] Nevertheless, Wilson's successor, James Cox, ran in 1920 on a platform of continuing the high tax rates.

An equally momentous change occurred in the nation's banking system when two decades of reform efforts resulted in the Federal Reserve Act. By 1900, the financial structure of the United States operated with commercial and investment banks allocating commercial credit. They circulated national banknotes and government-issued money that was backed by a gold standard. By 1913, the banking system had started to display problems, beginning with the so-called "dual banking system" of national and state banks.

In the farm states, mostly in the North and Midwest, that prohibited branch banking, hundreds of small one-office "unit banks" appeared. As a result, the banking system was not as integrated as it could have been, making it difficult to withstand financial crises, especially in the Northeast commercial centers where the economic upheavals often struck. Bank panics were common. A bank would fail, and then people worried about their deposits at other banks. "Runs" would ensue. Since the banks had loaned out most of the money deposited, other banks failed, too. These situations demanded coordinated responses. By their very nature, panics are irrational and usually required little more than the appearance of stability. In unit-bank systems, however, getting hundreds of banks in rural states such as Kansas to act in concert, especially in an age before telephones and computers, was impossible. Fearful depositors, panicked by the latest rumor, could close a perfectly healthy bank before the system could mount a response. Moreover, the tendency of unit banks to reflect the health of local economic conditions made them highly susceptible to sudden downturns in a particular crop or an unusually cold winter. On the other hand, local problems could taint larger regions, since small banks often had deposits at banks in larger cities, creating a pyramid that peaked in New York City.

In the years 1900 to 1912, the international gold standard functioned well, trade deficits at any given time were low, and nations either could adjust their prices, employment, and output or fix their imbalance by adjusting the value of their currency against gold. Like a teeter-totter with two people of approximately equal weight on opposite ends, the system tended to balance in the middle with mild economic swings. However, it behooved any nation that acquired gold through trade surpluses to expand its money supply, while those countries with deficits worried about running out of gold to pay their deficits. Only in that way could a nation's prices rise and the trade cycle balance out—only in that way could the teeter-totter swing back. If a nation constrained the growth of its money supply, it could have serious international repercussions because other nations could not climb out of their own recessions and, ultimately, would cease to consume products made by the nation having the surpluses. Conversely, the system also punished any nation *not* abandoning the gold standard if all others started to leave. Imagine a group of people holding a huge cement block, and then one by one individuals start pulling out on their own—at some point, the last person under the block will be crushed![13]

ENDING NEW YORK'S "MONEY POWER"

A final problem afflicted the American financial system—one of perceptions and image. As New York replaced Philadelphia as the money center of the nation, other regions started to fear the financial might located in New York City, especially among the largest banks. People used phrases such as the "House of Morgan" or the "Money Power" to characterize New York's growing financial presence, frequently with the assertion that a "conspiracy" to control the nation's money was directed from within the boardrooms of the banks. Each new panic resulted in a search for scapegoats. The fact that individuals such as Morgan actually saved the U.S. Treasury on occasion only tended to exaggerate the fears of a New York money conspiracy, especially during the Populist era. Consequently, when designing any new system, the banking reformers of the late nineteenth century inevitably sought to reduce New York's influence. That concern—along with the efforts to address elasticity, provide a lender of last resort for the nation's banks (in place of Morgan), and centralize some of the banking functions in the United States—played a key role in shaping the eventual legislation that became the Federal Reserve Act.

In November 1910, in a setting that could well have been viewed as itself "conspiratorial," five men met in secret on Jekyll Island, Georgia, to design a new financial system for the nation. Frank Vanderlip (of National City Bank), Paul Warburg (a powerful partner in Kuhn, Loeb & Co.), Senator Nelson Aldrich of Rhode Island, Henry Davison (a Morgan partner), and Harvard professor A. Piatt Andrew created a plan that provided the skeleton for the Federal Reserve System. After they presented their plan to Congress, it drifted listlessly, in part because the concept was too centralized, and in part because it failed to address the problem of diminishing the power of New York. It became even clearer in 1912 that any plan had to deal with the issue of New York influence.[14]

If anyone needed any evidence that the "money conspiracy" theorists were correct, the Pujo Committee sought to provide it. In 1912, Louisiana congressman Arsene P. Pujo, using the House Committee on Banking and Currency to investigate the "Money Trust," called witnesses (including Morgan) and gathered more than 30,000 documents on the concentration of financial power among the nation's largest banks.[15] The committee revealed that through directorships, stock ownership, and holding companies, the concentration of wealth in the country was worse than critics had alleged. George F. Baker, the chairman of First National Bank of New York, for example, held 58 directorships in 1912. But the committee's investigation, spearheaded by Samuel Untermeyer, described as "a wealthy New York corporate lawyer who had become increasingly anti-big-business," tried to redefine "trust" as cooperation by bankers instead of formal consolidation.[16] Untermeyer's questioning of Morgan produced testimony that frustrated critics of the "big banks" and, indeed, of the entire business system. Untermeyer asked Morgan if he favored cooperation over competition. Morgan replied he liked combination, but "I do not object to competition, either. I like a little competition...."[17] At that point Untermeyer, thinking he had Morgan, asked, "Is not commercial credit based primarily upon money or property?" To which the banker responded, "No, sir, the first thing is character.... Before money or anything else. Money cannot buy it."[18]

The irony of the Pujo hearings was lost on most of the reformers. Through the clearinghouse systems the nation's banks had taken important steps to reduce the likelihood and severity of financial disruptions, but the most crucial tool in defusing panics was the cooperation and collaboration of the major banks. In essence, Untermeyer attacked the bankers for *strengthening the system and protecting depositors*! More ironic still, in the 1930s, Ferdinand Pecora, as counsel for the Senate Committee on Banking and Currency, "by contrast, effectively blamed the *competitiveness* of the securities industry for the 'evils' that beset the market during the late 1920s."[19]

The Fed's role of "lender of last resort" was obvious: It provided a central pool of reserves for emergencies and could shift funds (if necessary) from one district to another, and the Fed could lend money to member banks using their assets as collateral for the loans. That allowed a basically solvent bank—but one with liquid assets, such as property or business loans—to borrow against that collateral by "rediscounting" them at the Fed. If a bank held a note from a business worth $50,000, it could "sell" that note to the Fed. As a "banker's bank," the Fed provided a psychological as well as monetary stability to the system. The Fed also introduced new paper money, Federal Reserve Notes, that replaced the National Bank Notes, further federalizing the money supply.

Great controversy surrounds the strategies of the Fed between 1913 and 1930. Some historians, including Elliott Brownlee, complain that the Fed exercised too little control over credit and "contributed strongly to the [post-WWI] inflation."[20] Others, including economists Milton Friedman and Anna Schwartz, have argued that the Fed's actions later in the 1920s triggered the Great Depression.[21] Still others, emphasizing the role played by the international gold standard, maintain that the Fed failed to understand or control the effects on the U.S. financial system of the gold standard.[22] Critics of the Fed from the Left, including Gerald Epstein and Thomas Ferguson, have sought to show that the Fed erred because it sought to protect bank earnings, while others, such as David Wheelock, have shown that the Fed's policy remained *too* traditional from its World War I experience and therefore did not permit the board of governors to protect bank earnings or take other necessary actions. In fact, most of the views can be squared with the observation that the government consistently failed to enact the appropriate policies.[23]

"OVER THERE" SHAPES "OVER HERE"

The Civil War had provided a dry run for the mobilization that would occur in World War I, although the federal government had gained vast new powers since 1865. Unlike the Civil War, however, America's mobilization for the world war did not occur when the first shots were fired. European powers drifted into war in the fall of 1914, at which time the United States declared strict neutrality and stated its intention to trade with all belligerents based on international rules of freedom of the seas. Of course, the U.S. Navy at the time was too small to enforce true neutrality, being unable to prevent the British from stopping and boarding American ships or to protect merchant ships from German U-boats.

President Woodrow Wilson had hoped to keep the United States neutral in its other dealings as well, but that, too, proved impossible. Britain, as America's largest trading partner, also held millions of dollars in U.S. investments. Exports almost doubled (from 6.1 percent in 1914 to 11.5 percent in 1916), and did not fall to the pre-1915 levels until 1918.[24] As the Allies purchased supplies, they converted pound sterling and francs into dollars, making the United States a net creditor and shifting the center of international banking from London to New York. Even if the American public could have remained neutral in emotions—an impossibility given the Anglo heritage of a majority of Americans—the economic health of the United States increasingly demanded that the business community support the Allies. Moreover, the prospect of a Europe united under an Imperial Germany did not bode well in the long run for American freedoms.

English and French demands for American supplies soon out-stripped the credit arrangements the Wilson administration had made. By 1915, Britain and France needed to borrow directly from the American public, or the domestic markets could be plunged into depression. J. P. Morgan's son, "Jack" Morgan, who had taken over the famous firm upon his father's death in 1913, had maintained his bank's connections with England. When Wilson permitted the Allies to sell bonds, J. P. Morgan & Company sold $500 million to U.S. investors through a network of 2,200 banks—over the staunch opposition of Irish and German-American groups. Over the course of the war, Americans purchased nearly $1 billion in Allied bonds, while the Morgan firm handled Allied orders for more than $3 billion worth of supplies from the Allies and earned commissions of $30 million.[25] After America joined the war, Morgan even loaned the Coast Guard his father's yacht, the *Corsair*, for use as a submarine chaser.

German U-boat attacks on merchant ships and on the *Lusitania* passenger ship in 1915 signaled that the United States could not remain neutral for long, generating an entirely new set of problems. The last American war, the Spanish-American War in 1898, had revealed serious military (and logistical) deficiencies and, at the same time, powerful advantages. Admiral George Dewey's ships far outclassed the obsolete Spanish tubs in firepower, armor, and speed. On land it was a different story. American soldiers faced Spanish adversaries armed with smoke-less powder and still used the thirty-year-old Gatling gun as the staple automatic weapon. The Spanish-American War also had highlighted a growing need in the economy to maintain specialized weapons manu-facturers. Armor plate for battleships, for example, had only one cus-tomer, the U.S. Navy. Producing specialized armor diverted resources from steel that a company could sell to private consumers, and as a result prices for armor plate ran as high as $545 per ton. Most armor plate was produced by Morgan's U.S. Steel, allowing it to charge high prices. The Morgan network expanded further in 1915 when the com-pany acquired Midvale Steel and Remington Arms Company, creating a military "mega-manufacturer."[26]

Merely getting material across the Atlantic also involved great risk. As the British dedicated their fleet to more direct military purposes, American shippers raised rates accordingly. The prospect of having one's ships blown up by U-boats caused transportation companies to charge substantially to sail through war zones (virtually everywhere) and, of course, generated accusations by the Secretary of the Treasury,

William Gibbs McAdoo, that the rates were "absurdly high" and representative of an "orgy of profiteering."[27] McAdoo's solution, a state-owned shipping business, overcame stiff opposition from numerous groups besides the expected shipping lobby. The Emergency Fleet Corporation was created in 1917, and within a year, the government had absolute control of merchant shipping that in any way related to the American war effort. It marked the initial, but not the last, creeping intrusion of government into enterprise that previously was the domain of private capitalists.

Anticipating the need to mobilize, in 1916 the Army Appropriations Act created the Council for National Defense charged with organizing civilian advisory boards to plan for mobilization. Based on the Civil War experience, planners concluded that it would use existing private companies, and not government plants, to supply munitions and arms. The private sector already had responded to the needs of the Allies: The Allied Purchasing Commission (a Morgan-originated bank) purchased $10 million in war materiel every day by private individuals for use by the Allies, making Morgan the single largest consumer in history.[28] Physical production also soared after 1914. Henry Ford had introduced a four-wheel trailer designed to be pulled by a Model T in 1915, making it possible to use trucks in transport. By 1917, "truck convoys from Detroit to Baltimore proved that long-distance truck transportation could be feasible." Moreover, already an American had contributed unknowingly to the technological breakthrough that would defeat the trench. Henry Holt, whose caterpillar-style tractor was seen moving equipment around behind the lines, gave British Colonel Ernest Swinton the idea for the first tank in 1915.

Directing and allocating the increased production to more effectively prepare for war proved difficult. Government enlisted the aid of hundreds of business and industrial leaders, who served as advisers for a token salary of one dollar. Known as "Dollar-a-Year Men," the business leaders brought expertise, but they soon found that the more than 5,000 agencies of the Wilson administration diluted their influence. Boards and bureaus overlapped each other, fought over control, and had ill-defined responsibilities, resulting in "economic havoc as the army spent over $14 billion in three years through its inefficient supply system."[29]

When the government put one individual in charge of an operation, as occurred when Bethlehem Steel's Charles Schwab was named the head of the Emergency Fleet Corporation, it got better results. Schwab replaced the "cost-plus" system at the shipyards, where shipyards received a set profit over the cost of building a ship, with a "fixed-price" system in which the builders received a flat fee and had to achieve cost-effectiveness to make a profit. When shipbuilders exceeded production, Schwab paid them bonuses, if necessary, out of his own pocket.[30] Visiting the shipyards and giving pep talks to the laborers, Schwab even won applause from the radical Industrial Workers of the World. He coaxed Rear Admiral Frank Fletcher into awarding medals and flags to overachieving plants. It worked. Under Schwab's direction, within a few months ships were being completed ahead of schedule, representing, in Carnegie's words, "a record of accomplishment that has never been equaled."[31]

For the most part, however, the system did not run smoothly. Not until 1918 did Wilson turn coordination of the war industry over to the War Industries Board (WIB), led by Wall Street investor Bernard Baruch. The WIB mediated between the powerful and conflicting bureaus, moving arms and supplies along to their proper destinations. As Baruch explained, the WIB addressed complex questions: "Should locomotives [be sent] to [General] Pershing to carry his army to the front ... or to Chile to haul nitrates needed to make ammunition...? Should precedence be given to destroyers needed to fight the U-boats or to merchant ships ... being decimated by the German subs?" Although the WIB had powers never before granted to a government agency, including the authority to seize and operate plants, Baruch hesitated to use a hammer when he could use a key, choosing instead to unlock resistance through conciliation and persuasion. Business often proved pliable because many business leaders themselves had pursued a more rational system, and government planning fit well with the managerial revolution and its emphasis on stability and statistical controls.[32]

Ultimately, the war effort succeeded, not because the bureaucrats demonstrated any great omniscience or special talent—although many were quite capable—but because American consumers sacrificed conveniences, workers went without pay hikes, and owners dedicated themselves to ensuring that American troops had all they needed. Certainly, the armed forces gave their all: The government drafted 2.8 million men, of which 2 million served in France under General John "Blackjack" Pershing, and of which 116,500 were killed. Americans at home willingly gave up freedoms to guarantee victory. Laws punishing espionage and sabotage, and censorship over printed matter, illustrated the personal freedoms that Americans generously sacrificed. No less important, however, infringements on economic and consumer freedoms touched everyone directly or indirectly. The Food Administration promoted "wheatless" and "meatless" meals; the U.S. Grain Corporation "effectively fixed the price of wheat"; the Sugar Equalization Board set prices on sugar; and the Food Administration established a price for hogs.[33] Conserving fuel for military needs, the Fuel Administration diverted gasoline and coal from civilian uses to the war.

A more difficult problem developed with the railroads. Over the years, the Interstate Commerce Commission (ICC) had refused railroads' requests for rate hikes, but by the winter of 1916–17, the railroad unions, demanding higher wages that the railroads could not pay, had threatened a strike. Regulation and labor union demands had starved the railroads of capital to modernize, and thus when the war placed its demand on the obsolete system, it collapsed, throwing the distribution networks on the East Coast into chaos. At the suggestion of McAdoo, in December 1917, President Wilson took control of the railroads, directing them through the newly created U.S. Railroad Commission under McAdoo's control. Historian David Kennedy called the takeover "the most drastic mobilization measure of the war," and it had fulfilled the dreams of the Populists.[34] Virtually the entire American railroad industry was operated as a single unit. Imposing both wage hikes for the railroad brotherhoods and smaller rate increases (that the ICC had denied the railroads while in private hands), the government ensured that the dominant industry of the nineteenth century subsequently would depend on government subsidies. Not only had the transfer guaranteed that the taxpayers would support the railroads, but it severely handicapped the railroads' ability to respond to the penultimate postwar threat to its viability—the automobile. Even after 1920, when the government returned control of railroads to private managers, most never regained their flexibility or independence from federal assistance.

World War I accelerated many of the larger trends evident in American business history. The war had four especially noticeable effects on enterprise in America. First, it brought corporate management and government officials into close, often daily contact with each other. Not only did that familiarize each group with the practices and problems of the other, it opened opportunities for mobility between the two sectors. Managers in business, some of them for the first time, appreciated the security available in government service, while frustrated bureaucrats saw the freedom offered by private enterprise.

Second, the war increased the government's expansion into the private sector dramatically. While many of the wartime controls receded after 1918, government power never returned to its previous level, validating the "ratcheting effect" of crises documented by economist Robert Higgs.[35] From the perspective of 1918, the intrusiveness of government by 1920 had diminished significantly; but from the levels it had stood in 1913, the scope of federal authority and the expansion of the bureaucracy had grown a great deal.

Third, the infusion of so many businessmen into wartime programs—the Dollar-a-Year Men—impressed on them the need for long-term planning on a macro scale and further solidified the position of professional accountants, economists, and other academics in the business sector. After the war, business leaders who had an "entrepreneurial mentality" as opposed to a "managerial mentality," but who had served on the government boards or in federal agencies, came away with a greater affinity for planning and its benefits. No Carnegies were transformed into faceless bureaucrats overnight, but overall the introduction of businessmen into government strengthened the appeal of "scientifically" predicting and planning for business change, then controlling it. As Charles Whiting Baker, in his review of government–business relations during the war, wrote in 1921: "Doctrines that were deemed ultra-radical thirty years ago … are accepted today without question by railway presidents, financiers, and captains of industry."[36]

Finally, to many, World War I seemed to validate the premises of the Progressive movement, successfully using the income tax, effectively mobilizing the capital markets through the Federal Reserve System, and revitalizing farming through the wartime farm programs. Wartime controls had subdued labor with the carrot-and-stick approach of controls and increased wages, while mollifying corporations by legalizing price-fixing in certain circumstances.

IS THERE AN ENTREPRENEUR IN THE HOUSE?

By 1920, the activities of government and the collective effort of the war had obscured the impact of entrepreneurs. Carnegie and Morgan had died, leaving behind capable and even entrepreneurial successors in Charles Schwab and Jack Morgan. But in firm after firm, the expansion-oriented risk taker tended to be replaced with conservative risk avoiders—men bent on sustaining a slow momentum of growth without realizing that all momentum slows on its own.

Entrepreneurs hardly disappeared from the mix, however. As the crest of the wave of new consumer products started in the previous century, the decades from 1900 to 1930 produced some of the most famous American businessmen and women in history. Most successful entrepreneurs of the era accepted, rather than resisted, the changes wrought by Progressivism. Recognizing the new social attitudes, the new entrepreneurs tapped into them, or rechanneled the energies of the time into a new wave of individualistic expression (as did Henry Ford). A scant few actually internalized the Progressive doctrines or embraced the collectivist principles that had undergirded the writings of Ignatius Donnelly, Upton Sinclair, Jack London, or Edward Bellamy. But one did, and his contributions continue to affect the daily habits of millions of Americans.

KING GILLETTE'S CLOSE SHAVE

Usually, any entrepreneur who, as his main objective, focuses on making broad improvements in society will fail, while the person who attempts to improve society one product at a time will succeed. This generalization, however, did not apply to King Gillette, who not only changed the look of society but its daily routines.[37]

Gillette intended to become a writer, like Sinclair or London. He published a critique of society and the economy in 1894, *The Human Drift*, that attacked the competitiveness and greed in American business. Calling for a "world corporation," Gillette envisioned a society in which everyone would work, all would be cared for, and cooperation would reign. In Gillette's utopia, all people would have to work five years for the cooperative before they could work for themselves. Fortunately for Gillette, no one paid any attention to his book, forcing him to improve people's lives in a more direct fashion. Gillette had made a living as a salesman, representing, among others, the manufacturer of a disposable bottle stopper. The idea of using a product once, then throwing it away, appealed to Gillette, who focused on a disposable razor blade. Introduction of such a product, however, required altering the entire grooming culture.

Shaving was a time-consuming activity in the late 1800s. From lather to steam towel, the process could consume half an hour. Using a straight razor to shave beards required painful practice that could only be inflicted on oneself, and maintenance of the razor itself demanded some attention. Foisting the entire activity off on a paid barber explained the popularity of barbershops in the late 1900s, but when tastes shifted and beards went out of style, daily visits to a barbershop became impractical.

Gillette's remedy was a small, sharpened blade that could be clamped into a handle, with enough of the blade extended to cut the hairs, but not so much as to slice flesh. He approached the disposable blade methodically, examining all available products in the field. Experimenting with the designs, and achieving the fine tolerances necessary in the razor's manufacture, required more money than Gillette could earn as a salesman. Obtaining $5,000 from friends to form the Gillette Safety Razor Company, he nearly went bankrupt, and survived only when a second group of investors poured $60,000 into the enterprise. Not until 1903 did Gillette produce his first razor for sale. With blades cheap enough so that customers could throw them away rather than sharpen the blades when they dulled, Gillette had his market. By 1904, the renamed American Safety Razor Company sold more than 12 million blades and 90,000 razors, aided by a memorable color ad showing a lathered baby shaving himself, to demonstrate the safety of Gillette's device. Downplaying the product's disposability, Gillette emphasized its safety. Gradually, even the most loyal straight-razor customers switched to the convenient disposables, but not before a rift between King Gillette and his primary investor, John Joyce, led to Gillette's sale of his interest in 1910.[38]

Government, however, provided the company's ultimate customer. During World War I, soldiers needed portable shaving products, opening the door for the sale of millions of Gillette razors and ensuring a loyal customer base after 1918. Gillette had improved the lives of almost every adult American male, yet he continued to see himself as a social reformer and writer. His books flopped miserably, even after he had his portrait placed on every blade box in an effort to promote his books. All Gillette accomplished was to permanently associate his own clean-shaven (but mustachioed) image with that of the Gillette razor.

RETAIL RULES! STEWART, BURPEE, SEARS, AND WARD

King Gillette appreciated the extent to which the mass American consumer market had grown since the late 1800s. His advertising showed that he also knew how to tap it. Certainly he was not the first businessman with that revelation. Alexander H. Stewart was one of the first large-scale merchants, and one of the few entrepreneurs who inherited his "start-up" capital. In 1823 he opened a small shop on Broadway, close to another soon-to-be retail giant, Lord & Taylor. Stewart anticipated Carnegie's later practice of expanding during depressed times. In the Panic of 1837, he acquired $50,000 worth of silk and sold it for a profit of $20,000.[39] He promptly planned to reinvest his earnings into a risky venture, a huge shopping emporium in New York.

Although most contemporaries, including John Wanamaker, thought Stewart foolishly chose the wrong location, the store soon emerged as the locus of Manhattan's retail district. *The New York Herald* called Stewart's store the "Marble Palace," and carriages lined up for the grand opening in 1846.[40] More than 1,000 visitors an hour strolled through the magnificent structure, examining the $600,000 worth of merchandise—a virtual cornucopia of products. Stewart's New York department store soon evolved into a large-scale retailing enterprise that used the latest in marketing methods to move huge quantities of merchandise to distributors. By 1870 alone, Stewart distributed $42 million in goods and employed 2,000 people.[41] Stewart extended short-term retail credit, divided his organization into specialized departments, and actively recruited the most talented staff. At one time, Stewart was the nation's largest importer and one of the world's leading retail dry goods merchants.[42] It became common for retailers in other cities to compare themselves personally with Stewart: Potter Palmer of Chicago was known as the "A. T. Stewart of the West," and John Shillito was called the "A. T. Stewart of Cincinnati."

Like Gillette, Stewart concocted grandiose plans for a utopian community, located at Garden City, New York. But in other ways, Stewart looked nothing like the other business icons of the nineteenth century. When he died, he left nothing to charity; he collected valuable artworks, but gave nothing to public museums. To modern thinking, he did not "give back to society"—an astonishing contention considering the products he made available for the first time to thousands of ordinary customers, the breakthroughs he attained in sales and marketing that made millions of people's lives more comfortable, and the employment and wages he paid to thousands of employees over the years. It could be argued that Stewart's customers and employees were his charities. The business quickly disintegrated after Stewart's death: He left no heir, and in a bizarre incident, grave robbers dug up his body and held it for ransom (itself an act of questionable mental capacity, given that he had no heirs!).[43] Reports at the time had Stewart's body popping up as frequently as Elvis sightings in the modern day.

One of Stewart's contemporaries, John Wanamaker, opened his fabulous Philadelphia palace in 1911. Standing twelve stories tall (with three more belowground), Wanamaker's store featured a center court with a 150-foot-high dome resting on exquisite marble arches. Bays opened to the court on seven stories, and from them could be seen the largest organ in the world—one of three in the colossus—allowing Wanamaker to quip, "Surely we are well organized."[44]

John Wanamaker started his business life selling clothes in Philadelphia, dedicating most of his off-hours to the First Independent Church of Philadelphia. Applying his business acumen to religious enterprises, in February 1858 he opened the Bethany Mission in South Philadelphia, bringing to it "the same evangelical drive and conviction that would characterize his retail career."[45] Wanamaker had maintained a sales operation and, with a partner, opened a new clothing store just as the Civil War broke out, which resulted in a burst of orders. Embodying the essence of capitalism—which is service—Wanamaker insisted that merchants had to serve the public. He personally delivered the uniforms that he sold to the military armory nearby, transporting the ordered goods in a wheelbarrow.[46] Wanamaker put every extra income into advertising, using billboards and flyers passed out on the streets, and he kept his prices 10 percent lower than any competitor, if the customer paid cash.[47]

In 1869, Wanamaker opened a New York store, bringing him in direct competition with Stewart. Searching for the finest men's clothing items, Wanamaker traveled to England in 1871, where he realized the potential of a new type of store, a true department store that went beyond even what Stewart offered. He needed a building, though, which he found at the abandoned freight depot of the Pennsylvania

Railroad. That gigantic facility offered the space he needed. After donating the building to revival meetings for a year ("the Lord's business first," Wanamaker stated), a mass of workmen descended on the site, turning it into an American version of the Bon Marché in Paris. Opening in 1876, with clothing for men and boys manufactured on the premises, the Grand Depot store covered two acres. In a year it was so large that Wanamaker provided a guidebook to give directions and explain policies of the emporium. With more than 120 counters and 2,000 clerks on a ground floor that covered three acres, Wanamaker's easily was the most impressive retail store in the nation. Departments, eventually including ladies' clothing and all other "dry goods," rippled out in concentric circles, adding to the visual image of energy and enterprise.[48]

Wanamaker eventually acquired Stewart's company after his death and "resurrection," and although he remained with the Philadelphia store, he dispatched a trusted subordinate to operate the New York business. Fittingly, Wanamaker's acquisition of Stewart's store united the companies that had introduced the department store to America.

Department stores such as Stewart's and Wanamaker's expanded through branches that stretched from the major urban areas to smaller cities, laying the foundation for twentieth-century chain stores such as Wal-Mart.[49] But a second market existed outside the major cities, where rural areas depended almost exclusively on local merchants and general stores. Those businesses served critical daily needs, but they could not offer much choice and seldom carried the latest products. Satisfying that market depended on a newly maturing business, that of the mail-order house. One mail-order pioneer, Washington Atlee Burpee, originated his famous seed empire out of his parents' home. Except Burpee did not start with seeds—he sold purebred birds, including chickens, geese, and pigeons.

As a high school student, Burpee already had established himself as an expert on the breeding of fowl, writing articles for poultry trade journals. Then Burpee's father, a physician, insisted that his son go to medical school, and he complied, attending the University of Pennsylvania for a year after convincing a wealthy Philadelphian to invest in a poultry business. The firm, W. Atlee Burpee & Company, intended to sell mail-order birds, but a significant factor in maintaining the health of the birds was proper food, leading Burpee to offer several varieties of farm seed in his catalog. Orders rolled in, but not for birds. Everyone wanted the Burpee seeds. In 1880, Burpee shifted the emphasis of his company to seeds, advertising cucumbers, tomatoes, turnips, and other garden foods and a one-time-only price of 25 cents (normally a $1 value). He also offered a free sewing machine to anyone wanting to become a Burpee dealer and who sold 300 packages. The response was overwhelming, with each promotional sale bringing more than 400 orders a day to the company. Although Burpee maintained livestock in his catalog, the seeds dominated the advertising, and the Burpee catalog itself, filled with humorous anecdotes and farm stories, soon became a popular reading item on its own. Not content with the success his business already had achieved, Washington Atlee Burpee scoured Europe for new types of vegetables, fruits, or flowers that he could bring to American homes and farms. He "discovered" for American consumers Burpee's Iceberg Lettuce, Golden Bantam Corn, and Bush Lima Beans. After Washington Atlee Burpee's death in 1915, his son David took over the business with great success, even mounting a national campaign to have the American marigold declared the national flower in 1959.[50]

Other pioneers in the infant mail-order catalog business had intentions of providing a wider variety of products than seeds. Aaron Montgomery Ward, a former barrel maker, had switched to retailing at a local general store at age 19. That started a career in retailing, in which he gained experience as a traveling salesman before starting his catalog business in 1872 specifically to reach the farm communities through the mail. The proliferation of railroads, the rise of express companies, and the appearance of telegraphs and improved postal systems made a mail-order business much more feasible after the Civil War than it had been before. Ward, who had worked for the Marshall Field department store, produced a single-page catalog that featured low prices and an emphasis on customer satisfaction. In 1873, Ward received a contract from the National Grange, opening a massive new market. Aware of the opportunity the Grange contract presented, Ward gave Grange members a ten-day grace period on payments and advertised the fact that his was "The Original Grange Supply House." As important as the Grange business was, however, Ward benefited from his own guaranty policy that made it clear that the company would accept any returned goods. Over a twenty-year period, Montgomery Ward's business thrived, and he expanded his catalog to feature more than 24,000 items in 500-plus pages. Marking Ward's success, the Ward tower rose on the Chicago skyline at the turn of the century, and by 1913 the company had annual sales of $40 million.[51]

Such success naturally caught the attention of competitors, including Richard Sears and Alvah Roebuck, two watch salesmen. Roebuck had gone to work for the Sears Watch Company in 1887, which had a watch and jewelry catalog sales business. After a brief retirement and "unretirement" by Sears, he returned with a larger stake in the company than he had before. The partners quickly expanded their merchandise to appeal to Ward's customers. Although they still emphasized watches, chains, and jewelry, they also added soap, firearms, and sewing machines. A. C. Roebuck & Company was founded in 1893, and less than fifteen years later it had an annual business of $38 million, due in large part to the contributions of Julius Rosenwald as head of the firm in 1895. The company (renamed "Sears, Roebuck") divided the business into departments that specialized in certain goods, with a separate catalog division charged with marketing the products. Individual warehouse managers handled the inventories at their businesses and placed new orders.[52]

Both the Sears and Ward firms relied on rural consumers and competed primarily with local merchants—the mom-and-pop stores associated with small towns, which energetically resisted the encroachment of foreigners into their markets. Consumers loved the concept of mail order, however, lobbying Congress in 1912 to expand postal service specifically to make it easier to obtain the mail-order catalogs.[53]

The challenge for the mail-order and catalog firms, however, was the demographic shift in America. Since the Civil War, families had left the farms in increasing numbers, flocking to urban areas. World War I accelerated that pace with its promise of employment, and Sears found itself with skyrocketing inventory levels after the 1920 recession. In 1924, Julius Rosenwald, who by that time managed the company and had put up $20 million of his own money to keep the business afloat during the depression, hired a former army quartermaster and participant in the construction of the Panama Canal, Robert E. Wood, to stop the hemorrhaging. Wood urged Rosenwald to de-emphasize the catalog portion of the business and to enter retailing in the larger urban areas. Rosenwald authorized Wood to proceed with his plan, and after four years, 324 Sears, Roebuck stores (with the name eventually shortened to "Sears") appeared in major urban centers. Wood stressed sales of large electrical appliances, such as stoves and refrigerators, that were quickly becoming necessities in 1920s households. The company maintained the catalog sales, but increasingly carried catalog items in the stores, where customers could purchase them in person.

Even with the services provided by Montgomery Ward and Sears, Roebuck, a gap remained in the retail market. Large urban areas had the major stores and rural areas had catalog sales, but small cities were not really touched by either source. A new form of retailer, geared toward smaller towns or suburbs, emerged in the form of James Cash (J. C.) Penney. Originating in Kemmerer, Wyoming, at the end of fifteen years the J. C. Penney Company had seventy-one outlets with sales of more than $3.5 million. While Sears management still pondered whether to establish its own chain of stores, J. C. Penney had opened more than 500 stores, with the number rising to more than 1,400 stores by the mid-1930s.[54] The company relied on high volume, coordinated and centralized merchandise purchases, centralized accounting, and an obsession with placing stores in prime locations.[55]

RISE OF THE SUPERMARKETS

The economies of scale offered by centralized purchasing played a key role in the expansion of chain grocery stores, which represented the earliest supermarkets. In 1859, a New York company, exclusively focused on selling tea, evolved into the earliest of the supermarket chains. George Gilman and George Hartford had purchased tea in large quantities directly from ships, cutting costs and lowering prices. Within a decade, the Great Atlantic and Pacific Tea Company had several stores, and by 1880 it had more than 100 locations stretching from St. Paul, Minnesota, to Norfolk, Virginia. Known increasingly as A&P, the company handled a variety of beverage and baking products, including coffee, sugar, cocoa, and other traditional grocery items.

A&P hardly resembled a modern grocery store, though, despite its wide variety of products and its policy of allowing customers to "run a tab." John Hartford, George's son, concluded that a practical cash-only business might be more profitable, and the company allowed him to open such a store under the A&P name in 1912. The cash business proved so profitable that A&P created a separate division that established stores at the rate of fifty per week. By 1925, A&P had 14,000 outlets, virtually all of them small operations run by the owner. Consequently, A&P reconsidered its entire approach and eliminated more than 10,000 of its outlets in favor of fewer, but larger, supermarkets. No longer flush with the volume profits provided by the additional 10,000 stores, A&P integrated backward, starting its own food brands, including baked goods, sugars, and coffee, as well as creating salmon canneries, a cheese warehouse, and laundry service.

Other companies rose to powerful market positions in other regions, such as Kroger and Safeway. Kroger was the creation of Bernard Kroger, a failed Cincinnati farmer and subsequently, tea peddler.[56] Safeway had become a powerful competitor by the 1920s, thanks to the efforts of Wall Street securities broker Charles E. Merrill, who had pioneered a new marketing approach to stock sales and had invested heavily in Safeway. Well after the turn of the century, grocery stores still had the old-fashioned touch, using stock clerks to take items from the shelves for the customer and box the purchases. Even that tradition faded when a Memphis grocer named Clarence Saunders applied assembly-line techniques to grocery store shopping in 1916 at his Piggly Wiggly store. All items were marked with a price and displayed on shelves. The customer walked down the store aisles with a basket and pulled products off the shelf for checkout with a clerk in the front of the store.

Saunders's strategy only worked when products came in packages that consumers could identify clearly. Packaging already had become an integral part of selling a number of products, especially foods, of which "there has probably never been a product that sold its package more aggressively than Uneeda [biscuits]."[57] Rather than emphasizing the crackers in the box, Nabisco's Uneeda advertising campaign, introduced in 1898, stressed Nabisco's patented "In-Er-Seal" package that kept crackers fresh. Before the appearance of packaged products, grocery stores kept goods in bins, filling the customer's request for, say, a pound of flour from an open bin. Unfortunately, any number of foreign objects, including codfish, kerosene, salt, floor sweepings, or even lost earrings, could fall into the bins, then into the customer's package. Of course, Nabisco was not the only food processor to use packages. Heinz's vegetables and sauces, Campbell's soups, and many other products were sold in packages by 1900. That practice allowed grocery owners like Saunders to rearrange their stores to feature shelved items instead of large bins.

Taken together, the change in packaging, combined with the appearance of supermarkets, chain stores, department stores, and mail-order businesses, brought products much closer to the consumer than ever before. That, in turn, severely reduced what once had been a thriving layer in the economy—the middlemen. Between 1879 and 1929, the ratio of goods that reached retailers through traditional wholesale networks and those purchased directly from manufacturers fell from 2.4:1 to 1.5:1. Urbanization accounted for some of the transformation, but other factors contributed mightily. Transportation had improved enough that people could shop in different locations to compare prices, even to the point of traveling to different towns in the same weekend. Electricity made possible better displays in stores, making products more attractive, and at the same time allowed stores to lower their prices by reducing the energy component of mass production. Wonders such as the telephone and radio caused a revolution in communications, making it difficult for even rural areas to remain too isolated. Consumer tastes changed as well, symbolized by the acceptance of Gillette's razor, and consumer attitudes were shaped by (although not controlled by) new marketing techniques among advertisers. For the first time, advertising became an industry unto itself.

HUCKSTERISM BECOMES RESPECTABLE

P. T. Barnum's great strength and great weakness was his constant self-promotion. Until the late 1800s, in many quarters it was considered poor taste for businesses to promote themselves. Aside from the posting of a bank's ownership and hours in a newspaper, for example, early bank advertisements refrained from making any claims about service or even (usually) safety. And while gradually firms and individuals published a simple notice of their existence in newspapers, few companies actively advertised any aspects of their products other than the brand name.

Although change did not occur evenly, after the Civil War entrepreneurs began to advertise in the modern sense. The notion that publicizing the benefits of one's products was mere "hucksterism" slowly faded as companies experimented with different ways to attract the public's attention. The free sample—made famous by Heinz at the Chicago World's Fair—worked well enough, but many items were too large or expensive to be given away or tried out before purchase. Using a familiar brand name, such as Burpee's seeds or Campbell's soup, also succeeded, but it hardly helped the person with a new product or the business trying to sell in a new section of the country. Moreover, after the advent of "Sunshine Laws," the government required businesses to prepare and make public some information. Why not accentuate the positive elements of that data for the consumers, such as the capital for a bank or the number of departures for a train? Accordingly, advertising "developed from a modest $10 million business in 1865 to a hefty $95 million industry by 1900."[58]

The rise of mass-circulation nineteenth-century newspapers was a direct result of the need by political parties to get their message to the pubic, and the value of turning news into free advertising was not lost on hucksters such as Barnum, of course. But by the late 1800s, the audience had become national. With the proliferation of magazines, such as *Harper's Weekly* or the *Atlantic Monthly*, companies could reach every region of the country with their advertising. A sudden burst of women's magazines in the 1870s and 1880s, including *McCall's*, *Woman's Home Companion*, *Good Housekeeping*, and *Cosmopolitan*, further expanded the advertising base. None, however, surpassed the *Ladies' Home Journal*, founded in 1883, which reached a circulation of one million by 1900. So-called "block" ads touted everything from books to violin bows, with the emphasis on brand names.

Advertising expanded beyond the scope that businesses themselves, or even the journals, could manage on a regular basis. Instead, specialists were needed who could place ads in national magazines and newspapers, write effective ads, and track the appearance of the advertising. Early advertising middlemen acted much in the same way as land speculators had. They purchased blocks of newspaper space, then resold the space in smaller parcels to the advertiser at whatever price the parties could negotiate. Writing the ad, arranging artwork, and editorial matters remained only the concern of the buyers of the ad parcels. N. W. Ayer & Son, a Philadelphia business founded in 1869, marked a departure from the "speculator" model. Francis Wayland Ayer (the firm was named after his father) and his son Frederick worked for a fixed commission, turning the advertising specialist into a professional. Within twenty years, the company had a full-time copywriter and had lined up accounts from numerous national businesses, including National Biscuit Company (later Nabisco), Procter & Gamble, Burpee Seeds, and Montgomery Ward.

The professionalization of advertising, replete with editors, artists, writers, and typeset designers, fit into the Progressive preference for having specialists, especially academics, directing society's activities wherever possible. Agencies soon incorporated psychologists to analyze consumers' desires and the impact of pictures or copy on potential customers. But the most prevalent type of advertising remained either publicizing a brand name (hence, quality) or the increasingly popular "reason why" copy, in which the written portion of the ad explained to the consumer why purchasing a particular product would be beneficial. As a historian of advertising explained, "Not charming or amusing or even necessarily pleasing to the eye, a good ad was a rational, unadorned instrument of selling...."[59] Far from trying to appeal to the customer's base instincts, "reason why" copy appealed to the intellect, all the while seeking to "predigest" the content for the consumer. Only later did companies stress the romantic benefits of products, and then in subtle fashion.[60]

J. Walter Thompson, a New Yorker who worked in advertising most of his life, set the stage for much of the "reason why" copy. Thompson was employed in the 1860s by a small Manhattan agency, and over time, so many advertising firms had their headquarters in New York on Madison Avenue that the street itself symbolized the profession. He mustered sufficient cash to purchase the business in 1878, changing the target of his advertising strategy to magazines, correctly observing that women spent much of family disposable income and they tended to read magazines more than newspapers. In 1896, Thompson incorporated his business as the J. Walter Thompson Company, known in the business simply as JWT. But while the firm became the largest advertising agency in the world by 1916, Thompson himself was spent. He sold the company for $500,000 to a group that included one of his most talented writers, Stanley Resor.

After a short stint with Procter & Gamble's ad agency, Resor worked his way up within the Thompson agency. He perfected "reason why" advertising and started to look for ways to expand the appeal of the ads. Along with his capable coworker and wife, Helen Landsdown, Resor sought to incorporate romantic images with the written copy. Their most famous collaboration—but primarily Helen's concept—became the most famous print ad in history. Developed for Woodbury's Facial Soap, the ad used an Alonzo Kimball painting that showed a man in a tuxedo and a woman in an evening gown embracing, highlighted with the phrase, "A Skin You Love to Touch." A small amount of traditional "reason why" copy was placed at the bottom of the picture, but the emphasis was no longer solely on intellectual appeal. The Woodbury ad led many to credit Helen Resor with the first use of sex appeal in marketing.

In fact, Helen Resor relied on a keen sense of psychology to introduce another advertising technique that soon was an industry standard. She thought that people could be persuaded to purchase products based on the recommendations of others, especially celebrities, giving rise to the testimonial, in which well-known people related their own positive experience with a product. Testimonials worked particularly well, she thought, if the person providing the testimony was in a higher social class than most consumers. To that end, by 1926, Resor had lined up socialites and royalty, doctors and clergy, to hawk different products. In addition to the queens of Romania and Spain, Helen and Stanley Resor ultimately ran ads with philosopher John Dewey, writer George Bernard Shaw, and actresses Joan Crawford and Janet Gaynor. Even today, the testimonial remains an important tool for advertisers.

JWT, in particular, secured inexpensive testimonials from dozens of movie stars at a time when Hollywood had suddenly started to capture the public's attention. The firm's Hollywood representative, Danny Danker, provided a free crate of Lux soap to then-unknown actresses in exchange for their promise to endorse the soap if they became stars, allowing JWT to gain the services of Crawford, Gaynor, and Clara Bow for pennies.[61]

Stanley Resor had proved his own worth to the firm in a much less obvious way. Shortly after he took over, Resor eliminated two-thirds of the company's accounts, retaining only the largest and most profitable. He hired exceptionally talented professionals, including John Watson, who introduced the first "blind" taste tests in advertising. Shielding the brand name, Watson asked subjects to taste or use a product, finding that they seldom could tell the difference between their favorite and a competitor's brand. Unfortunately, Watson's research was misinterpreted to suggest that, in the most simplistic sense, consumers were merely sheep who could be "programmed" to purchase a particular brand. Such tests missed the point that brand names often achieved their appeal less on the basis of a particular single experience but rather on consistent quality or service.

Still, no doubt existed as to the value of effective advertising and no one worked harder on a product than a competitor of the JWT agency, Lord & Thomas, with its premier executive, Albert Lasker. Lord

& Thomas was a Chicago firm founded by Daniel Lord and Ambrose Thomas, a pair of New Englanders who had started their company in 1881 to place advertising for Christian periodicals. Lasker, on the other hand, came from Texas, the son of a reporter. He gained entry into the business through his newspaper knowledge, expecting to stay in Chicago only a short time before moving on to New York to work as a reporter. At Lord & Thomas, he found himself in the unceremonious position of sweeping floors and emptying cuspidors. Worse, he acquired a $500 gambling debt, which he repaid with a loan from Thomas, thus requiring that he remain on his job. Before long, Lasker was on the road as a salesman, where he demonstrated an uncanny ability to reel in large accounts.

Most advertisers wrote their own copy and the agency merely placed the ads. Lasker, however, convinced a company to let him write the ad for a slightly higher fee. His strategy proved so successful that by 1902, Lasker hauled in $10,000 annually, and then, within a few years, $50,000 a year. To Lasker, the only measure of an ad's effectiveness was the number of products it sold, and to that end he originated a department solely focused on evaluating the results of Lord & Thomas's ads. Lasker bought part of the Lord & Thomas Agency, and soon became its director. His ability to focus on the bottom line led him to hire unusual employees, such as George Washington Hill of the American Tobacco Company. Hill was a relentless chain-smoker with a four-pack-a-day habit who headed the Lucky Strike cigarette account. As Lasker said of Hill, "I would not call him a rounded man. The only purpose in life to him was to wake up, to eat, and sleep so that he'd have strength to sell more Lucky Strikes."[62] The monomaniacal Hill massaged the Lucky Strike account into $12.3 million in billings in 1929—just under one-third of Lord & Thomas's total billings and the driving force behind the company once again becoming one of the top ad firms in the United States. Just as Helen Resor specifically targeted females as consumers, Lasker and his adman Hill sought to make women into smokers. They recruited actress Helen Hayes to direct ads at women with the campaign phrase, "Reach for a Lucky instead of a sweet." Not only did Hill's campaign set off a war with the candy industry, but it introduced women to men's vices, with female alcohol use rising in the 1920s along with increased smoking by women.

Lux soap and Lucky Strike cigarettes showed that a single campaign could make or break an agency, and likewise, companies found products saved from mediocrity by effective campaigns. Lambert

Pharmaceutical Company, for example, produced a mouthwash called Listerine that lumbered along with slow sales until two Chicago copywriters found an obscure medical term for bad breath called "halitosis." An ad campaign that treated smelly breath as a disease—and not simply a failure to brush one's teeth or eat correct food—suddenly gave Listerine the respect of a medicinal product. Using the tagline, "Even your closest friends won't tell you," the campaign propelled Listerine sales from $100,000 a year to more than $4 million.[63]

Not all advertisers took such an amoral approach to the use of truth in advertising. Bruce Barton, who edited a series of magazines and wrote ads on the side, during World War I used his writing talents for the United War Work Campaign that benefited the Salvation Army, the YMCA, and the YWCA. While in the process of planning those sessions he met Alex Osborn, a Buffalo adman, whose acquaintance translated into an offer to join with Osborn and Roy Durstine in a new agency, Barton, Durstine & Osborn. Like Wanamaker, Bruce Barton planted his business and advertising philosophy on his Christian faith and his knowledge of the Bible. From one passage he concluded that new generations will not remember the things of the old, and that products must be constantly resold to the present generation. The agency located in New York and quickly became the hot agency in town. Sharing the same building with another firm, that of George Batten, the two businesses merged in 1928 to form Batten, Barton, Durstine & Osborn, known as BBD&O.

Even as the work piled up—"We are creating, creating, creating all the time," Barton observed—he reserved time for a major book he had in mind.[64] In 1923, Barton started a revisionist presentation of Jesus Christ, presenting a masculine savior of great compassion but also great humor. Barton stressed that Jesus had all the traits of an advertising executive: persuasiveness, combined with the ability to recruit followers and touch each individual with a different message about the same product, topped off with management skills. When *The Man Nobody Knows* appeared in 1925, it sold 250,000 copies in just over a year.[65] Barton wanted to do more than place Jesus in a contemporary context, however. He sought to elevate all types of work to the level of a religious calling and to suggest that capitalism was a moral system as much as an efficient economic system.

By that time, Bruce Barton had become one of the gurus of advertising. Still phrasing marketing slogans in the imagery of religion, Barton argued that "if advertising speaks to a thousand in order to influence one, so does the church." Rejecting the notion that advertising "created" demand, Barton said to a friend in 1926, "We spend our vast advertising appropriations trying to steal each other's customers here in the home market."[66] He also noted that advertising needed to move in a different direction, away from "reason why," observing: "Today there is no more need of advertising the details of automobiles to the American public than there is for advertising the multiplication table."[67]

Barton hoped to aspire to people's better qualities, and no doubt would have been chagrined to see that his predictions about the industry were all too accurate. Over time, the use of subliminal advertising and sex appeal increased, neither of which Bruce Barton would have approved. Nor did Barton share the view that advertising, per se, could sell products people really did not want, and over time a number of marketing studies proved him right.[68] He was not alone in his view that consumers had an inherent sense of value and dignity. Other entrepreneurs, in fields as diverse as autos, communications, electricity, and securities, had recently come to much the same conclusion, most notably Henry Ford.

HENRY FORD AND THE "PEOPLE'S CAR"

If, as some historians claim, the railroads had an unprecedented effect on American economic growth, the arrival of the automobile matched and, in most respects, surpassed the contributions of the railroads. Autos fundamentally changed transportation from a collective undertaking, whether in boats or railcars, to a principally individual experience. Cars represented independence, not only freeing people from the confines of the city but from restrictions imposed by a particular geographic region. Over time, the automobile released people from the tyranny of chronic poor weather, the injustice of local prejudices, and the inequality of restrictive labor markets, opening doors to business opportunity and social mobility. Almost overnight, the automobile made real the promise of a truly national market for goods and services.

Charles Duryea had demonstrated a primitive car that used a gasoline-powered engine in 1893 and drove the vehicle from Cleveland to New York in a road test four years later. Others, of course, already also had built cars: Chicago's Columbian Exposition of 1893 (otherwise known as the Chicago World's Fair) displayed six different cars. Still, the auto industry remained small and segmented. By 1900, for example, just over 4,100 cars were sold in America—a tiny fraction of the more than 450,000 cars registered in the United States only a decade later.

As business historians Keith Bryant and Henry C. Dethloff observed, "The automobile industry developed under ideal circumstances."[69] Americans had a high (and rising) per capita income; steel and petroleum, two key ingredients in the success of motorcars, had achieved a level of maturity. The concept was novel enough that autos were virtually unregulated. America possessed both a large, skilled workforce and individual inventors familiar with mass-production and factory processes that could be adapted to operations. The auto manufacturers came from the ranks of mechanics and bicycle makers, but a significant percentage (more than one-third) had lived or worked on farms. A study of the automotive industry by Burton Klein revealed that of twenty-five well-known pioneers, seven had fathers who were farmers and five others worked in machine shops or manufacturing.[70] That background, a heritage of a "nation of tinkerers," as the United States once was described, enabled sons to learn the basics of technology from fathers. Moreover, the majority of the industry's pathbreakers investigated by Klein had only a public school education, but knew enough to observe the factory system in operation. And while Duryea had started in Massachusetts, Detroit, Michigan, quickly emerged as the auto center of the nation because of its proximity to water, copper, iron ore, and other natural resources, as well as its reputation as a carriage and bicycle manufacturing center.

Henry Ford was illustrative of all those characteristics. He grew up on a Michigan farm, showing a keen mechanical talent. At a job with Westinghouse, Ford worked with steam engines, then, in 1891, he moved to Detroit where he joined the Edison Electric Company, giving him the opportunity to work with Thomas Edison. According to some, Ford decided on making a car rather quickly. While at Edison Electric, the story goes, Ford read an article in *The American Machinist* in 1896 that detailed the new horseless carriage. It was enough to convince the thirty-three-year-old Ford that he personally could build one. In fact, however, Ford had intermittently labored over automotive concepts for years and was convinced that horseless carriages would be powered by steam. While at Eagle Iron Works in Detroit, he repaired an internal combustion engine. Then, in 1893, assisted by his wife, Clara, he assembled a one-cylinder internal combustion engine in his kitchen, and he continued to assemble a car ever since that time. In 1896, after assembling a four-cycle engine and mounting it on a carriage frame, Ford had his car. The vehicle resembled a large, modern baby stroller without the covering, with the lightweight chassis resting on four bicycle-type wire wheels. Unfortunately, he had constructed the entire vehicle in his woodshed with no consideration for its width. Unable to get it out any other way, he took an axe to the walls of the shed.

Lacking any formal engineering education, Ford's ideas advanced by trial and error. Adaptation, not invention, typified Ford's best work. He recruited other talented mechanics to help him, contracting out ironwork and buying available parts from existing firms. Yet Ford also had developed the engine and wheels himself, and he always seemed to have the needed mechanical concept when others did not.

Retaining his job at Edison, Ford tested his automobile for three years. Then he made his leap of faith. With several reputable Detroit investors, Ford formed the Detroit Automobile Company, only to have it collapse in 1900. He started another company, and in 1901 it, too, failed. Demonstrating the tenacity typical of successful entrepreneurs, Ford started another company in 1903, the Ford Motor Company, with the intention of building every auto exactly alike. But the notion that Ford invented universality in mass production has its skeptics. One associate of Ford, Charles Sorensen, contended that "Henry Ford had no ideas on mass production. He wanted to build a lot of autos … [and just] grew into it, like the rest of us."[71] Some took that to mean that Ford did not deserve credit for the Model T, or that he had a mechanic's view of the world rather than an entrepreneur's. Some of the impressions of Ford resulted from his own view that there was a virtue in productivity itself.[72] On the contrary, Sorensen insisted, Ford, unable to read blueprints, contributed most of the major ideas, including the use of vanadium steel, the design of the transmission's planetary gears, and the decision to use a detachable head for the block, even though no one knew how to build a head gasket strong enough to withstand the pressure.[73] Moreover, he had the key entrepreneurial characteristics of understanding his consumer at the time and the faith and vision that his product would meet the needs of others.

Prior to the Model T, Ford built eight models (driving his shareholders to distraction), including the Model N, which he introduced in 1907. The Model N had orders for 100 cars a day. Losing money on heavier cars, such as the Model K (a "regular limousine," according to Jonathan Hughes), Ford redirected his efforts to simpler, cheaper autos.[74] Speed was not required—the city of Detroit had a speed limit of eight miles an hour around city hall, and speeders paid fines of up to $100, or two months' wages—but shedding the weight in the heavier lines was. Throughout 1908 and 1909, Ford attempted to eliminate larger cars while concentrating on a new design that would change history: the Model T. Ford placed all his faith in the new car and instructed his company that he would sell no other model. Furthermore, the Model T would be painted only one color, black. Unveiling the "Tin Lizzie" to the public, Ford advertised with a statement of his vision: "I will build a motorcar for the great multitude…. It will be so low in price that no man making a good salary will be unable to own one…."[75] Indeed, Ford sold more than 12,000 Model T cars, at a price of $850, in twelve months. With each new innovation and product improvement, Ford lowered his price, and with each price drop, Ford sold more cars. By the 1920s, he boasted that every time he dropped his price by a dollar he sold 1,000 additional cars.

In 1913, Ford introduced the moving assembly line at the Highland Park facility, perhaps the single most dramatic innovation associated with his career. When the plant reached full capacity in 1916, the continuous line process had reduced the chassis assembly process from twelve hours to less than two. Giving credit to Ford for the assembly line has proved controversial. Eli Whitney and others had used mass production and standardized parts a century earlier, and Henry Leland had pioneered the technology that improved the ability to manufacture with fine mechanical tolerances. When one of Ford's superintendents arrived at the company from International Harvester, he commented that he found little he hadn't seen at the Deere/McCormack companies. Perhaps so. But more than the other visionaries that revolutionized manufacturing, Ford appreciated the complete interchangeability of parts. His Model T contained 5,000 parts, all standardized. On the other hand, one of Ford's subordinates probably suggested the revolutionary step of moving the assembly line to the worker. Even so, if Ford has received credit where he did not entirely deserve it, his dogged pursuit of turning out cars in the most efficient way possible permitted the constant refinement of the moving assembly line between 1912 and 1914.

All was not harmonious. Ford had perfected a system that brought materials to the workers, which from a management perspective was more efficient. From a labor perspective, especially one steeped in the skilled trades of the late 1800s, it was degrading. Worse, managers could speed up the line, placing pressure squarely on the shoulders of workers. At Ford, laborers quit in droves. The turnover reached almost 400 percent, prompting Henry Ford to offer higher pay. Contrary to the image Ford promulgated, he did not raise wages out of love for his workers, but because he ran out of options to retain them. He also planned to introduce three eight-hour shifts and had put out a call for new workers, which brought in so many unemployed that violence broke out at the company's gates. The message that others wanted the jobs held by Ford employees came through loud and clear inside the factory, however. But it is doubtful that anxiety over jobs caused the soaring production that ensued after the wage hike.

Whatever his motivation, in 1914, Ford introduced the $5-a-day wage, an amount that represented a truly stratospheric salary to ordinary workers. Only after the wage rate went up did Ford appreciate the fact that one of his employees could purchase a Ford automobile on less than a year's salary (and as prices fell and wages continued to rise, on as little as a month's salary). At that point it became apparent that he was ensuring his own sales through his wages. And, to see that workers did not squander their wages on unnecessary products (presumably, cars from rivals!), the company created a "sociology department" that policed the lives of employees. Company inspectors visited workers in their homes and interviewed neighbors.

In 1916, Ford lowered the Model T price to $345, causing sales to soar to more than 734,000 units, an amount that comprised almost half of all the cars sold in the United States. The price cut—the single greatest leap of faith that Ford had to take—produced an inevitable feedback loop. Falling prices allowed more people to buy Fords, then, as more people bought Fords, the company could lower its profit margin per unit and still make money, with the result being still lower prices for the customer. Yet cost never drove Ford's strategy. His principles of operation stressed the primacy of service over profit. Certainly, he admitted, a "well-conducted business enterprise cannot fail to return a profit," but that profit, he noted, "must and inevitably will come as a reward for good service."[76]

Ford certainly had his human failings, some of them severe. A bigoted anti-Semite, he referred to Bernard Baruch as a "Jew of super power," and disgracefully published the *Dearborn Independent*, a weekly newspaper that initiated a campaign against American Jews in 1920, running such editorials as "The International Jew, the World's Problem." A 1922 *New York Times* article describing Adolf Hitler's headquarters in Munich reported that pictures of Ford and a translation of Ford's book were found on the premises. Ford's ignorance of world affairs and pigheaded refusal to see any event in less than the most simplistic terms was renowned, although occasionally misrepresented. "History is bunk," Ford was quoted as saying, although as David Kyvig and Myron Marty have shown, he in fact spent millions of dollars collecting and preserving historical artifacts and thought "nearby history" was indeed important.[77] In other circumstances, Ford's "do-good" internationalism led him to finance a "peace ship" in 1915 to take himself and other peace cranks to Europe to instruct the Kaiser to call off the war, oblivious to the boiling cauldron of issues that had caused World War I. Bamboozled into making a speech to the inmates at Sing Sing prison, Ford inserted his foot firmly in his mouth: "Boys, I'm glad to see you here."[78]

Whatever his lack of vision in international affairs or limited understanding of even American politics—he could not even name the causes of the Revolutionary War when he ran for the U.S. Senate—Ford knew cars and car buyers. Early in his career, especially, he had a fundamental appreciation for what a mobile America needed, and he supplied it. Only later, after other automobile manufacturers had caught up with and then passed Ford, did he lose touch with consumers. As with many entrepreneurs, Ford failed to know when to change, sticking to his original vision long after its time had gone. Eventually, Ford's family had to force him out to save the company he built.

DURANT, SLOAN, AND GENERAL MOTORS

As with any business enterprise, when Ford Motor stopped meeting the needs of Americans, its dominance of the market tailed off. A new company, built out of the Buick Motor Company, had emerged under the leadership of William Durant. A mass-produced car for ordinary citizens was a necessity for a successful automaker in the early 1900s. But Durant, a Flint carriage maker, recognized that sooner or later people would tire of a single model in a single color. He sought instead to tap into the varieties offered by several companies, bringing them together in a single corporate entity that could sell different models to meet different tastes and price ranges.

Durant brought together Buick, Cadillac, Oldsmobile, Oakland, and six other auto companies, plus truck makers and parts manufacturers, to form General Motors (GM) in 1908. Expansion was both Durant's lasting contribution and his fatal corporate flaw: The company's growth lacked direction and strategy. No sooner had he created his empire than sales for automobiles dipped, nearly driving the new company into bankruptcy. Only Durant's ability to convince Wall Street bankers to lend him $13 million saved GM, but the bankers wanted control. They immediately liquidated unprofitable parts of Durant's conglomeration and named a team of managers that included Charles Nash, the head of Buick. Nash's replacement at Buick, Walter Chrysler, eventually left GM to rejuvenate the Maxwell Motor Company, renaming it Chrysler in the 1920s. Although the bankers and the management team continued to increase auto production, they fell behind the prodigious output at rival Ford. GM's market share was halved.

Meanwhile, Durant had approached Louis Chevrolet, a race car driver, to develop an independent company and a new, inexpensive car line to compete with the Model T. Chevrolet became disaffected, quitting the firm in 1913. Thus, Chevrolet and Buick had found key elements in the future GM line, yet had disassociated themselves from the largest automaker in history. Durant, on the other hand, used his stake in Chevrolet and the profits it produced to acquire shares of GM stock until, in 1916, he gained back control of GM and handed the bankers their walking papers. A key ally in Durant's revival, Pierre S. du Pont, came from the famous chemical family that produced explosives, dyes, and paints. The Du Pont family had received huge profits from wartime production, but recognized that peacetime might bring a substantial reduction in business, which led them to look for other investment opportunities. By the end of the war, the family held almost 30 percent of GM. Nevertheless, Pierre du Pont managed his family's chemical business, leaving the auto company to Durant. Characteristically, Durant pursued growth at GM.

He laid the groundwork for his new corporate structure in 1916 by converting the General Motors Company (chartered in New Jersey) into General Motors Corporation (with a Delaware charter). Then, between 1918 and 1920, Durant added Chevrolet to GM, as well as

Fisher Body, Delco, and other parts accessories firms. Again, however, Durant's great weakness surfaced. His inability to plan, structure, or rationalize the corporation's growth meant that each division produced and invested without consideration of the whole. Buick might invest in new plants when the greatest need was at Chevrolet. Divisions independently ordered inventory, which the shocked head office had to pay for—often without approving the orders in the first place. And when divisions had cash, they did not necessarily turn it over to Durant's office, meaning that although "General Motors" as a whole was solvent, parts of GM were flush while others struggled. Durant's inability to control the divisions led to another near disaster: In 1920, GM had to borrow $83 million from the banks. In desperation, Durant personally had borrowed $30 million that he used to buy GM stock to maintain the price. Forced out a second and final time, Durant turned control of the company over to Pierre du Pont, who resigned from his family's business and assumed GM's presidency.

Du Pont relied on Alfred P. Sloan, Jr., an MIT graduate, an "engineering and managerial genius," and the president of Hyatt Roller Bearing at the time it had merged with Durant's GM. Sloan understood the deficiencies of Durant's helter-skelter system. As a remedy, he prepared a study of the organization that he submitted to Durant, who shelved it. After Pierre du Pont took over, the study was revived and its proposals adopted in 1920. Over the next four years, GM management restructured the company along a rational division system that reported to the head office. Management clearly delineated the distinctions between the different divisions' products, making certain that each division had its own market niche and price. Moreover, the divisions were autonomous to the extent that each contained its own general manager, engineering, production, and marketing, yet all were supervised by group vice presidents who headed one of four related groups of products: accessories, affiliated businesses, export products, and the centerpiece of GM, the car and truck division.

Top management divided authority between the executive and finance committees, strengthened by modern statistical controls. The central office received production reports from the divisions and sales reports from the dealers, which then were assessed to establish a statistical estimate of return on investment. GM's new "decentralized" management structure, which resembled that of the Du Pont Company, featured a reliance on economists and statistical specialists. In many ways, the reorganization of General Motors marked the high tide of the managerial revolution started more than sixty years earlier. Though not all large corporations switched to the decentralized managerial hierarchies, most accepted the need for professional managers to run the companies, even if they did not decentralize management. As a symbol of the entrepreneur with the ability to manage a large company, only Henry Ford seemed to emerge unscathed. But even he would ride a roller-coaster in the next twenty years as entrepreneurs went from the victors of World War I to once again being the villains.

CHAPTER 9

Deliverance and Despair: 1920–1939

Hurricane Katrina, which struck the American Gulf Coast in August 2005, demonstrated nature's destructive power. For the businesses of New Orleans, it also demonstrated how disruptive natural forces can be. Massive federal and state aid poured into New Orleans (and the rest of the Gulf Coast), but years later, the region still struggled. Natural disasters can also reveal the incredible resourcefulness of entrepreneurs, none more amazing than Amadeo Peter Giannini, founder of the Bank of Italy. In April 1906, an intense earthquake rocked San Francisco, ripping up train rails and splitting water lines. Fires ignited everywhere as buildings collapsed.[1]

Giannini, who in the previous two years had built a thriving business by serving the North Beach Italian community with his Bank of Italy, walked seventeen miles to the city. Along the way, he noted, "I had seen so much panic on the faces of the people … I didn't have much hope for the bank."[2]

Upon arriving at the bank, Giannini found his vault intact, but the fire was spreading in his direction, fast. With the help of family and bank officials, he loaded the contents of the vault into two wagons, then, concerned with looters, camouflaged the contents with boxes of oranges. With the rest of the banks in San Francisco having their money trapped inside safe—but superheated—vaults, Bank of Italy was the only institution capable of making loans. Two days later, Giannini did just that, setting up a desk on the Washington Street wharf, even though the governor had proclaimed a "bank holiday," making Bank of Italy's actions illegal. No matter, people responded in overwhelming numbers, and in the midst of tragedy, Giannini did through heroism and initiative what no government agency could ever do: Inspire the people.

Over the course of the next two decades, Bank of Italy would become a powerhouse in California, developing one of the best state branching systems in the nation.[3] Giannini would personify the peaks and valleys of business in the 1920s and 1930s, losing control of his by-then renamed "Bank of America" system, then regaining it. Bank of America not only survived the Great Depression, but provided important support for business in California during that trying decade. It reflected America's transition from a purely industrial and agricultural power into the world's top financial center.

And the center of American finance was not San Francisco, but Wall Street. New York's money nexus would finance the great boom known as the Roaring Twenties. Virtually every one of the high-growth businesses in America during the decade, including automotives, electric utilities, radio communications, and consumer goods, sought to enlist the capital of investors through the investment banks in New York, and they responded.

English historian Paul Johnson, analyzing the history of the modern world from distant shores, has stated flatly, "The view that the 1920s was a drunken spree destructive of civilized values can be substantiated only by the systematic distortion or denial of the historical record."[4] Some distortion has been pure ideology. Some has derived from guilt, as there is no shortage of moralistic commentators who assume that all pleasure must be accompanied by pain. Parties, after all, must be "paid for," a view made popular by economist John Kenneth Galbraith in his famous book, *The Great Crash*.[5]

Occasionally, however, the misperceptions have resulted from the tendency to approach the 1920s as a unified whole, essentially treating it as the decade that created vital technology of our modern era, rather than vice versa. Instead, the 1920s prosperity was fueled by the simultaneous maturation of a number of technologies, capitalized by innovative and aggressive capitalization efforts from Wall Street, energized by the tax cuts proposed by Secretary of the Treasury Andrew Mellon, and incubated in the warm, supportive attitudes of the Coolidge administration. Stretching over the decade like an umbrella, the optimism of average Americans galvanized the market.

None of the technologies that would dominate the 1920s were actually invented in that decade; rather, numerous industries, businesses, and technologies matured together in a coalescing not seen since the Industrial Revolution. By reinforcing each other's expansion, they accelerated the business boom. And although it requires the investigation to go back a few decades into the nineteenth century, perhaps the best place to begin is with Alexander Graham Bell, who inaugurated a communications revolution with the telephone.

LISTEN TO ME

Western Union's telegraph lines covered America, transmitting messages over thousands of miles and intertwining every sector of the economy. The telegraph had replaced the infinitely slower—and, in its time, equally revolutionary—Pony Express, and by 1879, "Western Union had insinuated itself into the very fabric of American enterprise and seemed destined for years of triumph."[6] The company should have suspected that new technology would allow others to challenge its position, but Western Union's management did not have the historical evidence that future generations of businessmen would have—namely, that the established leader in an area is usually unlikely to pioneer the next major breakthrough. Telegraph communication did not develop out of the steamship packet mail business, or out of the newspapers. Communication changed dramatically in 1876, however, when Alexander Graham Bell, a Boston teacher of the deaf, invented the first telephone, or "harmonic telegraph," as he called it. Bell's device had company, for on the same day as Bell filed his patent, Elisha Gray challenged the patent, claiming to have invented a telephonic transmitter himself. But Bell had the support of Gardner Hubbard, a lawyer with extensive investments and a man familiar with the telegraph. Hubbard immediately saw the potential for revolutionizing the telegraph business. The two men, along with Thomas Sanders, a Haverhill leather merchant, and Bell's lab partner, Thomas Watson, organized the Bell Telephone Company in 1877.[7]

Bell was always more the inventor than the businessman, and he kept to his laboratory while Hubbard handled marketing. Hubbard's first commercial foray involved leasing telephones. Early telephones lacked exchanges and consisted of little more than two-way connections, much like a walkie-talkie. Understanding the voices required all but an interpreter to filter out the oppressive crackling sounds, unless, of course, one had the voice of an operatic tenor.[8] The phones themselves were heavy wooden boxes that sent human speech over a grounded iron telegraph wire through the use of electrical impulses. The partners needed a company that had established lines, and that meant dealing with Western Union. While the new technology might seem natural to the telegraph giant, Western Union's president, William Orton, called the phone a "toy" and rejected Bell's offer to purchase the rights to the telephone for $100,000. With that dismissal of the telephone, Western Union once again demonstrated how difficult it is for the leading company in a field to appreciate and embrace radical new technology.

Even Bell's own people did not fully understand the potential of the new technology, touting it as an improved telegraph. Bell himself envisioned telephone offices where people would go to place calls, much like a brokerage house. The first customer, a Boston banker, reported satisfaction, and within a year the company had leased more than 5,000 of its devices at a rate of $40 a year for businesses and $20 a year for residential leases. Commercial leases brought in more than $50,000 in six months. Hubbard, tapping his former railroad connections, recruited a small army of licensing agents who controlled specific geographic areas and who leased the phones, installed the hardware, strung wires from customer to customer, and collected rentals. Early agents included wealthy investors or merchants who themselves had well-established community roots. All of this rested, however, on a somewhat remarkable and flimsy foundation: the Bell patent. The technology itself was so basic that any knowledgeable electrician could have copied it, which is precisely what Bell hoped to use to his advantage. After all, he reasoned, no one could copy the telephone without violating the Bell patents, in theory giving the Bell Company a monopoly over telephones for years.

Bell's nightmare, that Western Union would realize the threat to its market, became a reality in 1878 when Western Union dusted off one of

Elisha Gray's old patents. In essence, Western Union had been sitting on a telephone of its own for over a year. Terrified of an all-out competitive battle with the industry leader, Bell desperately sought a negotiated settlement with Western Union, hoping to split the market. Again, Western Union rebuffed Bell's offers. The telegraph company had offices in all the major towns, a sprawling system of wires, and a network of potential agents, all of which could be mobilized rapidly to create a long-distance telephone system. A technological breakthrough in 1878 brought such a system closer to reality when a Connecticut Bell licensee created a switchboard, allowing any one subscriber to contact any other subscriber in the system without a direct wire connection between them. By that time, Bell was telling investors that "it was now possible to envision a telecommunications system in which 'cables of telephone wires could be laid underground or suspended overhead communicating by branch wires with private dwellings, country houses, shops ...'" and opening the possibility of worldwide voice communication.[9]

By the late 1870s, both the ill-capitalized Bell and the well-endowed Western Union had improved their respective technologies with new transmitters. Although both businesses had expanded their systems, Western Union alone had gained the key cities of Chicago and New York. Bell instituted patent infringement suits against Western Union, which hardly slowed the telegraph company but which served to persuade Bell licensees to remain loyal. Bell's offensive netted more than 30,000 new phone licensees within a year. Still, Western Union would win over the long haul unless Bell developed a new strategy.

When Hubbard united Bell and New England Telephone in 1879 to form National Bell Telephone, he brought in an extraordinary manager, Theodore N. Vail, whose experience in management (like most others') came from the railroads. Hubbard then turned the presidency over to William H. Forbes, one of the new investors in the $850,000 company. With Hubbard's departure, essentially both of the original Bell founders had been pushed out of the telephone business. Invention and entrepreneurship had given way to professional managers. Although Vail and Forbes engaged in a thorough restructuring of the company, creating a foundation of telephone manufacturers, solidifying their control over the licensees, and aggressively expanding the company's patent claims, Bell still toiled away at a considerable disadvantage to Western Union.

At that point, two events changed the shape of the telecommunications industry forever. First, the patent attorneys advising Western Union concluded that Alexander Graham Bell's claim to be the inventor of the telephone was indeed valid. At minimum, Western Union looked at paying perhaps millions of dollars in back licensing fees. The second event, however, involved railroad magnate Jay Gould's American Union Telegraph Company, which was the main competitor to Western Union. Gould had failed once before to mount a challenge to Western Union's power, but the possibility of combining his own lines and offices with the Bell phones suddenly made Gould a significant threat. Overnight, Western Union reconsidered the Bell offers to settle or consolidate. In 1879, the resulting compromise had Western Union "sell its 56,000 telephones in twenty-six cities to Bell and grant [Bell] control over the competing telephone patents until 1894, in return for 20 percent of Bell's licensing fees."[10] Furthermore, this new National Bell Telephone Company would provide telephone service only—which was local in nature—while Western Union would retain rights to long-distance communications. That limited the Bell exchanges to a fifteen-mile radius of any central office and constricted communications to personal calls only: Business communications, stock market quotations, and sale messages were to be the domain of Western Union.

Some observers thought Vail had inherited all the problems of the local exchanges with none of the benefits of the long-distance service. Western Union, on the other hand, mistakenly thought the new market would involve primarily business communications. Moreover, the prevailing opinion was that the telephone technology was limited. It could not handle prolonged conversations; it could not replace business mail; and the transmitters were too weak to permit voices from being sent more than a few miles. But even as the ink dried on the agreement, improvements made it possible to send voice messages over distances of more than forty miles. Vail, meanwhile, seeing the potential to link the exchanges without violating the letter of the long-distance agreement, won a key point in the final negotiations to develop telephone business between exchanges, virtually opening up long-distance transmission in fifteen-mile segments. Vail completed his coup by reorganizing and recapitalizing the company as American Bell Telephone in 1882 and acquiring Western Electric, Western Union's equipment manufacturer. Then, in 1885, at a point when Western Union was no longer powerful enough to resist, the newly formed subsidiary of American Bell, American Telephone and Telegraph (AT&T), opened the door for the company to move into long-distance communication.

Although it might not have been clear to all observers at the time, Bell had achieved utter domination over Western Union and claimed the bulk of the communications market. The episode once again demonstrated how market dominance imposes blinders on the potential for new technology. Companies achieve a certain corporate comfort level—a competence with their technology or product—and almost any breakthrough presents (on the surface) far more problems than solutions. Pressing into unknown waters requires resources that must be diverted from the company's existing area of expertise. Vail, meanwhile, came into conflict with the Boston investors, and in 1887, he resigned. At the same time, the Bell patents expired and a swarm of independents entered the market, encouraged by public perceptions that the Bell system had profited unreasonably from its monopoly. Once again, Bell needed cash to reorganize, leading to its acquisition by a J. P. Morgan–led syndicate. Morgan wanted Vail back as the president.

With Morgan's money and Vail's talent, AT&T gradually bought out the independents, improved its own service, and lowered rates. Vail also acquired 30 percent of Western Union in 1909, an acquisition that only evoked howls of protest from the trustbusters. Company officials held talks with the Wilson administration, resulting in a deal that left AT&T in a position of overwhelming dominance in the telephone business. The AT&T empire linked the nation as the telegraph never had. Already by 1912, there were more than 9 million phones in the nation, with more than 3.5 million supplied by non-AT&T providers.[11] AT&T represented possibly the best-operated quasimonopoly in American history.

After 1910, telephones were destined to increase in popularity, regardless of the skills of the telephone companies to market or improve them. Moreover, telephones symbolized the new thirst for physical and spatial independence put in motion by the automobile. Sheer numbers revealed the telephone's popularity. In 1920, there were sixty-one telephones per 1,000 city dwellers, and by 1928, there were ninety-two per 1,000, as the telephone became a standard feature in middle-class urban housing. The telephone contributed to the growing economy of the 1920s by making it easier for investors to place orders with brokers, to maintain contact with businesses and markets, and to conduct enterprise over an ever-expanding area. Telephones combined with another item commonly found in typical houses, the radio, and further enhanced communication.

Guglielmo Marconi had conducted radio broadcasts across the Atlantic in 1901, and the introduction of a functional vacuum tube in 1906 made feasible the broadcasting of words, not merely signals, to the general public on a practical basis.[12] After the *Titanic* disaster, where a nearby ship could have saved hundreds of passengers had it had a listener for its radio, ships soon employed full-time radio crews. Marconi Wireless received a contract to handle maritime radio service for American ships in 1916. Then after, a group of telegraph and telephone companies, including AT&T, Westinghouse, and General Electric, formed a consortium to assume the assets of American Marconi. The new company, Radio Corporation of America (RCA), had as its first chairman Owen Young, but the most important influence on the actual management of the business was David Sarnoff, who had advanced to the position of general manager of American Marconi.[13] Years earlier, Sarnoff had begun his career in 1900 at the age of nine, when his family struggled after emigrating from Minsk, Russia, to New York. His first job, selling newspapers, allowed him to learn to read English, and he was able to attend school for a short time. By fifteen, however, as a full-time office worker at American Marconi, he began learning about wireless communication. After working in several remote wireless stations, including in the Arctic, he took the job at the Wanamaker department store, where he became famous for rebroadcasting the *Titanic* news he picked up on his transmitter. Although Sarnoff exaggerated his own importance in the *Titanic* incident, he would become one of the most famous names in broadcasting.[14]

A Westinghouse scientist had discovered broadcasting, which sent signals out over airwaves for whoever wanted to pick them up (as opposed to two-way wireless communication). For a small sum, a consumer could purchase a radio and potentially have access to a wide variety of music or information going out over the airwaves. Thus, the initial impetus for supporting radio broadcasting stations came from the indirect profits gained by RCA through the manufacture of radio sets and broadcast equipment. Westinghouse applied for the first license to operate a radio station in 1920—KDKA in Pittsburgh. KDKA's first broadcast, to an estimated 500 listeners on November 2, was the election returns showing that Warren G. Harding had won the presidency.[15] A year later, WJZ in Newark, New Jersey, broadcast the World Series (actually, reannounced it, by relay, from the Polo Grounds), gaining as much attention as KDKA had.

By 1922, more than 200 stations had licenses (distributed by the Department of Commerce) to broadcast over the airwaves. Radio equipment manufacturers supported the expansion of radio broadcasting, endowing it permanently with its indirect funding character. As the price of radios fell, and as more and more homes acquired radios, broadcasters ran paid commercial advertisements. By 1922, radio advertising sales topped $60 million, and two years later exceeded $350 million. In 1926, AT&T rented wire connections that linked several stations, forming the first radio networks, but the creation of radio station groups under both RCA and AT&T produced concern about a "radio trust." Rather than fight that battle, AT&T sold its systems to RCA, which reformed the enterprise under the leadership of David Sarnoff as the National Broadcasting Company (NBC).[16]

Sarnoff always saw opportunities to tie in related technologies to his radio company, although he was not always successful in obtaining them. After Warner Brothers released *The Jazz Singer* in 1927 as the world's first motion picture with sound, Sarnoff purchased patents to the technology from General Electric and forayed into film production with Joseph Kennedy. A year later, RCA had a stake in the Radio-Keith-Orpheum (RKO) theater chain, which used RCA sound equipment. With Westinghouse and General Electric, RCA obtained the Victor phonograph company, renaming it RCA Victor, pushing RCA into phonograph sales and recordings. Shortly after the Great Depression had started, the government filed an antitrust suit against RCA, General Electric, Westinghouse, and other members of the so-called radio trust, prompting the major investors in RCA to divest their holdings in the company, making RCA completely independent for the first time. By that time, the government had created a Federal Radio Commission to assign frequencies to stations, ensure a better geographical distribution of broadcasting stations, and to limit power output. Until 1929, however, the future of radio looked bright, especially as the number of radios in the hands of consumers soared from 60,000 in 1922 to more than 7.5 million in 1928. The radio's popularity coincided with Madison Avenue's growing influence, and with advertisers' quest to wield every tool they could to sell products. Advertisers quickly learned also that another burgeoning industry could assist in selling products: movies.

MOTION PICTURES AND MADISON AVENUE

Another form of mass communication, the rapidly growing motion picture business, joined radios and telephones in tying the nation together. What had started as moving pictures for small nickelodeons in the early 1900s had become an entirely independent industry by the 1920s. A group of inventors, led by Thomas Edison, formed the Motion Picture Patents Company in 1908 to collect royalties from anyone using the moving picture process. In 1917, the Supreme Court, responding to the complaints of independent producers who claimed that process did not constitute content, ruled against the patents company and opened movies to anyone capable of making them. Paramount Pictures, which contained a powerful distribution company, started to produce its own movies, signing the famous Cecil B. DeMille as a director. Paramount soon found itself in competition with another production and distribution firm, Metro-Goldwyn-Mayer, headed by Louis B. Mayer and using the extensive chain of theaters belonging to a partner, Marcus Loew. The new business included the Goldwyn Picture Corporation, started by the famous Samuel Goldwyn, who then left to start an independent production company. Other powerful competitors included the Warner brothers (Harry, Jack, Sam, and Albert) and Columbia. Those giants battled over control of distribution, whereby they could produce, distribute, and exhibit their own films.

Ensuring distribution to theaters required presales, which in turn demanded that the companies turn out formula movies. To that end, motion picture companies hired directors, actors, and actresses on long-term, exclusive contracts, under the likes of which aspiring young actors like John Wayne would make dozens of highly forgettable pictures on their way to film immortality.[17] Resisting the star system, Mary Pickford, Douglas Fairbanks, Charlie Chaplin, and director D. W. Griffith founded a company called United Artists to ensure that movie artists retained control over their products. Unlike other full-scale integrated companies, however, United Artists only produced films, relying on other companies to distribute and market them. Typical movies had soared in cost, with *Birth of a Nation* (1915) costing $100,000 and *Ben Hur*, a decade later, $6 million.

Still, the industry remained relatively small ($5 million in assets) until Warner Bros. worked with Western Electric and AT&T to create a

talking motion picture, *The Jazz Singer*, which completely revolutionized the industry. Al Jolson's lines—"Wait a minute, wait a minute ...
You ain't heard nothin'"—became literally prophetic. Overnight, leading men with less-than-appealing voices and leading ladies who fum-
bled their lines found themselves replaced by actors and actresses who
could speak as well as emote. And, overnight, the industry's popularity
soared. The number of recording machines in Hollywood increased by
100 in one year. By 1927, the year *The Jazz Singer* was released, the
industry was producing 400 to 500 feature films a year, plus a variety of
short subjects, and by 1929, the motion picture companies held net
assets of more than $160 million.[18] Construction of theaters, therefore,
played an important role in the business: Palaces such as the Capitol
Theatre in New York seated 5,300, while the renowned Grauman's
Chinese Theatre in Hollywood captured the architectural style of the
Orient. Huge Wurlitzer's organs provided a musical background before
the advent of the talkies, while Willis Carrier's new air-conditioning systems were first used on a large scale in New York movie theaters in the
1920s.[19] Carrier himself had the concept for air-conditioning after working on processes for drying lumber and coffee, then finally created his
system while working on a solution to humidity in a lithograph plant in
Brooklyn.

Oddly enough, the Great Depression cemented the position of the
movie industry because it remained one of the few cheap modes of
escape remaining to people, although most of the eight major studios
lost money during the early 1930s. As in other businesses, though, the
New Deal attitudes and impediments to entrepreneurship resulted in
the major studios securing more of the market: By 1939, the eight major
studios controlled 76 percent of the feature films.[20] Weekly attendance
fell from 80 million in 1930 to 50 million by 1932. By that time, the
movie stars themselves had been enlisted to sell products such as soap
and cigarettes for Madison Avenue, commercials that in turn went out
over the radio waves. Movies also provided a gentle incentive for consumption, showing people in all parts of the nation the latest and most
luxurious goods, creating a demand for products yet unseen in other
parts of the nation. But they also reinforced the public perception that
business was somehow responsible for the Great Depression, especially in the gangster film genre. An exception to that pessimistic view
came from an unknown cartoonist, Walt Disney, who introduced the
world to a whistling mouse in *Steamboat Willie* (1928).[21]

During the 1920s, both motion pictures and radio became industries unto themselves and intertwined thoroughly with Madison Avenue. Whereas radio sold products directly, motion pictures advertised a higher standard of living, generating a generic demand that Madison Avenue filled through specific radio ads, but there the similarity stopped. Unlike movies, the real-time effect of radio made it a part of daily business. Radio reports increasingly relayed critical economic information to investors and traveling salesmen. The radio and the telephone enlarged the information network geometrically, and as radios and phones became common items, the ability to transact business over long distances, and even from one's home, accelerated another trend that began later in the 1920s—a rising stock market that seemed to grow perpetually higher.

RUNNING WITH THE BULLS

Some of the purchases (though certainly not the majority) were facilitated through the growing use of *margin buying*, wherein brokers accepted a down payment of 10 percent to 15 percent and loaned a customer the balance to purchase stock. If, for example, someone wanted to buy a $100 stock and had a solid relationship with the broker, $10 would acquire the stock and the rest would be advanced "on margin." If the stock dropped in value, the stock owner had to put up more cash so that the ratio between the stock price and the loan was constant. When this happened, it was referred to as a margin call. Why did brokers act so generously? The answer was simple: The market had not gone down for years. It was, in gambling terminology, "a lock." Margin loans rose from $1 billion in 1920 to $8 billion in 1929, leading one wag to quip that people were borrowing not only on the future but also on the hereafter.[22]

Margin buying acted as a lubricant, not a stimulant. People bought stocks because they represented profitable investments, not because credit was available. Led by utilities and industrials, productivity growth brought higher profits and stock prices throughout the 1920s. Using an index of common stock prices for the year 1900 amounting to 100, the index topped 130 in 1922; 140 in 1924; and 320 in 1928. At the time of the crash in 1929, stock prices hit their then-record high of 423 on the index.[23] Individual corporate stock prices reflected the general trends, with the purchase of a few thousand dollars' worth of the right stock netting hundreds of thousands of dollars in half a decade. Stocks refused to go down. RCA, for example, which never paid a dividend, went from $85 a share to $289 in 1928 alone, while General Motors common stock, worth $25,000 in 1921, was valued at $1 million in 1929. Again, however, substance backed up the stock values. Total assets of the largest 200 enterprises doubled, while individual companies, such as RCA, experienced phenomenal success. General Motors hummed along in 1929, producing profits of $200 million a year. A line worker at GM could own part of the auto giant for which he toiled. For a few dollars a month, an insurance salesman could become a partner with the Morgans.

The criticism, of course, was that average Americans did not hold stock, only the wealthy. Statistical analysis suggests a different picture, though. Two major changes in the makeup of the investment community indeed had occurred: There were more people holding and trading in stocks, and they constituted more of a social and economic cross-section than ever before. In 1900, extrapolating from a study of stockholder lists of railroads, economic historian Stanley Lebergott estimated that 15 percent of American families owned stock. Most of those families, based on the availability of stock and its share costs, were in the upper class. By 1929, 28 percent of American families held securities, indicating that, obviously, groups other than the wealthy purchased securities. Some analysts expressed skepticism that ownership was spread to a substantially wider segment of the public. Evidence of specific issues, however, confirms that it was. For example, one analysis of those "buying fifty shares or more in one of the largest utility stock issues of the 1920s shows that the largest groups were (in order): housekeepers, clerks, factory workers, merchants, chauffeurs and drivers, electricians, mechanics and foremen."[24] Metalworkers held more stock than doctors, and machinists more than lawyers. Dressmakers, on a six-to-one ratio, held more stock than bankers. And people did not, in fact, borrow excessively to speculate in the stock market.

Another indicator that common people could, and did, purchase stocks appeared in the subtle shift in advertising and marketing securities that occurred in the decade. No individual did more than Charles E. Merrill to convince middle-class investors to pick up their phone and place an order to purchase the stock of capital-hungry companies.

CHARLES MERRILL:
SELLING STOCK IN AMERICA

College may provide many people with the training they need in their careers, but dropping out of Amherst College in 1906 opened doors for Charles E. Merrill to occupations he had never considered. He went to work as an editor of a Florida newspaper, gaining a keen insight into the motivations of the public. He played minor league baseball, which emphasized teamwork and dedication to a goal. At a textile plant, he obtained "the equivalent of a university course ... in credit, finance, cost accounting, and administration."[25] Moreover, the textile job put Merrill in contact with Edward Lynch, a soda equipment salesman. In 1909, Merrill got a job with a brokerage house on Wall Street, where in time he headed a newly created bond department. In 1911, Merrill wrote an article for *Leslie's Illustrated Weekly* called "Mr. Average Investor," in which he emphasized a close personal relationship between the investor and securities adviser. He also perceived that profits could be made by meeting the securities needs of thousands of small investors as well as with a handful of rich ones.

Merrill brought in Lynch in 1915, and the two fashioned a plan to sell bonds through direct-mail solicitations that consisted of informative circulars instead of the advertisements of the securities day that bordered on fraud. Gradually, Merrill had invented a new type of securities market oriented to the ordinary person of limited means. That same year, as World War I escalated, Merrill formed his own company.

Merrill Lynch, as the firm became known, underwrote securities for several chain stores, including McCrory and Kresge, gaining a reputation on Wall Street for specializing in chain-store offerings. War interrupted Merrill's business career. He served with the Army Air Corps as a flight instructor. The war also taught Merrill an important lesson about investment. He watched Americans purchase U.S. War Bonds on a regular basis, suggesting that the basis existed for selling securities to a broad panoply of middle-class investors.

After the war, Merrill Lynch continued to underwrite chain stores, acquiring in the process controlling interest in Safeway Stores. Assuming a management role in Safeway, Merrill forged a merger between that company and another chain his firm had dealt with, MacMarr Stores. The resulting Safeway had 4,000 outlets and was the third largest in the United States. Although he did not serve as chief executive officer, Merrill held enough shares that he could decide who held that position, and he played a key role in developing advertising campaigns for the chain.

Management of Safeway further reinforced Merrill's interest in mass-marketed, high-volume business. Yet he never abandoned his most fundamental principle, namely, that investors deserved the truth. Anticipating the great crash, Merrill Lynch sent a letter to all the firm's clients in March 1928 urging them to quietly liquidate their securities and get out of debt. Nevertheless, the straightforward approach of Merrill Lynch did not keep the firm from being tarred with the broad brush that colored other brokerage houses after 1929. Merrill rebuilt the firm's image and emerged from the Great Depression and World War II with a renewed commitment to reestablish the securities markets as a place for sound investment by the growing middle class.

A REASSESSMENT OF THE 1920s

Charles Merrill helped extend investment opportunities, which previously only the wealthy and connected had enjoyed, to people of all income groups. Yet while he may have broadened the investment boom, he did not create it. Americans could see for themselves the prosperity and optimism that surrounded them. In retrospect, a few economic Jeremiahs invoked biblical images of destruction after the Great Crash, falsely reasoning that the growth of the 1920s produced a speculative fervor. Edmund Wilson likened the decade to a "drunken fiesta," while F. Scott Fitzgerald sneered that Americans had engaged in the "greatest, gaudiest spree in history."[26] Even conservative writers have argued that the new investment mechanisms and margin buying "provided additional superstructure of almost pure speculation."[27] Reality was much different, and most people knew it. The stock market boom was an indicator of genuine expansion, but it also was a critical lubricant, bringing together the funds of millions of investors to fuel the production of automobiles, plate glass, gasoline, ironing machines, vacuum cleaners, radios, telephones, and other goods.

Referring to the "consumer-durables revolution" of the 1920s, Stuart Bruchey has recorded estimates that showed that by 1928, 27 million American homes had 15 million irons, 6.8 million vacuum cleaners, 5 million washing machines, 4.5 million toasters, and 750,000 electric refrigerators.[28] Auto registration rose from 9.3 million to 23 million between 1921 and 1929 alone, while auto production soared 255 percent during the decade. Cars were important because they facilitated production of—and purchases of—a vast multitude of other products. Tires, glass, paint, metal, cement, lumber, steel, cotton, and leather were all needed to make the finished automobile or the factories that produced it. Thus, automobile production generated a boom in rubber and cotton production, construction, gasoline refining, and other industries directly tied to serving the auto industry. Car owners needed roads and other peripherals, including good tires, gasoline, and spare parts. A highway construction frenzy began, with initial private highways appearing first. Soon, however, politicians raced to fill the public's demand for cheap roads by sending a flurry of state bond financing that went through Wall Street. As more people drove cars, the stocks of the automakers rose in value to new heights, prompting still more interest in auto securities. The automakers used the cash that flooded in to further electrify their operations, expand facilities, and thus gain greater economies of scale that lowered prices. Lower prices enticed more people to buy cars, and the cycle started again.

It should start to become obvious, now, how the telephone and stock market facilitated the rapid expansion of the automobile, and how the phenomenal boom in electrical power generation (almost 300 percent between 1899 and 1929) in turn acted as a multiplier for mass production, as well as for providing a direct source of energy for the refrigerators, radios, fans, heaters, and dozens of other consumer appliances that appeared in American homes. Once electricity was available, anyone could use a radio to obtain the latest news and, based on that news, make certain financial decisions, some of which might require the instantaneous communication offered by the telephone. Electricity, however, actually played a much more expansive role than was reflected in the sheer number of new electrical items, for the *efficiency* of electric power generation rose at unprecedented rates. In 1899, electrical motors accounted for 5 percent of the installed horsepower in the United States, but by 1929, electricity generated 80 percent of the installed horsepower. More important, whereas steambelt-driven machines only transferred a small fraction of the horsepower they produced, electric motors increased the amount of deliverable horsepower by as much as 60 percent.

But the effects also ran in reverse: Anyone could see that electricity was a growth industry. Electric utilities stocks thus emerged as among the most prized of Wall Street securities. With each new offering, utilities companies could open new plants and generate more power, causing prices to fall. With each fall in prices, more homes and businesses could afford electricity, leading to increased profits at the utilities company and, completing the circle, causing utilities stocks to rise even higher.

At each point, investment in a growing industry, even state-originated investment through bond issues, further contributed to the efficiencies and expansion of the financial sector. In 1918, state expenditures on highway construction reached $70 million, but by the time the stock prices had finished falling in 1930, state highway construction expenditures had grown to $750 million. More often than not, commercial banks as well as investment banks prospered. Finance companies started to provide direct installment credit for smaller items, and installment loans more than doubled, from $1.3 billion to $3 billion between 1925 and 1929. The finance companies had to do something with their swelling deposits. Likewise, the correspondent banks around America (except for those in depressed agricultural areas) had excess reserves that they dumped in big-city banking institutions, providing yet another pool of capital. Unlike a snowball rolling in a single direction, however, the growth of the 1920s more resembled a huge pond ripple, spreading wealth in a geometric progression in almost all directions simultaneously.

SMALL BUSINESS AND ENTREPRENEURS IN THE ROARING TWENTIES

Because the expansion involved fitting together large, previously unrelated sectors, growth tended to occur predominantly through existing businesses. At least one study suggests that failure rates among small-business manufacturers were "notoriously high," and another specific study of Minnesota cities reported more than 62 percent of the firms in the study closed between 1926 and 1930.[29] Yet the same study of manufacturers found that the total number of business firms in the United

States rose from 1.7 million in 1919 to 3.02 million in 1929. Small business had taken advantage of new service industries, as well as new openings in radio broadcasting and in motion pictures, to move away from manufacturing.

While the number of large corporations rose by more than 150,000 over that same period, few memorable entrepreneurs outside the areas of advertising, motion pictures, and radio during the 1920s readily come to mind as compared to other decades in the nation's business history, although some exceptions existed. Hallmark Cards, which grew from Joyce Hall's little door-to-door postcard sales operation into a string of card stores that ran from Missouri to New York and employed 120 people in the manufacture of greeting cards, had established itself by the 1920s. Hallmark recovered from a near-fatal factory fire in 1915, at which time Hall rebuilt the company.

Firms such as Hallmark demonstrated the hypothesis of Harold Vatter that the 1920s was "a poor decade for new, small manufacturing enterprises, but a decade of expansion in the size of both small and other-sized established manufacturing firms."[30] Total plant numbers did not increase as rapidly as one might expect in such a boom; but the number of corporate manufacturing firms rose from 67,000 to 92,000 during the decade, and the output per establishment rose by more than one-third between 1919 and 1929. But the evidence that noncorporate enterprises "must have suffered a high mortality rate" is not as obvious as some argue, because the new technologies and products entailed new levels of service, and service businesses were not counted among manufacturing firms.[31] Nevertheless, it well may be that the Roaring Twenties did not represent a high tide of entrepreneurial new businesses as much as a vast expansion of already established small and mid-level businesses. Whatever the source, a wide expanse of the American public achieved improved levels of living as never before in history.

Home construction, for example, soared. Starting in 1920, the United States embarked on its longest building boom in history, with more than 11 million families acquiring homes by mid-decade.[32] (Again, the role of the automobile cannot be overstated in allowing homeowners to live farther from their place of employment). More than three-fourths of all urban and nonfarm households had electric service by 1930, contributing to the boom in household appliances. Not only did homes reflect the new affluence, but the entire way of American life.

Such affluence, across such a wide spectrum of the population, could only have been possible if the income growth of most Americans actually improved, and indeed it did. Using a 1933–38 economic indicator index of 100, the nation had gone from 58 in 1921 to 110 in 1929, marking an increase in real per capita income from $522 to $716. The rising tide of affluence allowed people to save and invest as never before, acquiring life insurance—policies passed the 100 million mark in 1920—savings accounts, and securities. Moreover, indices of such growth actually understated the improvement in the average worker's condition, because tax rates fell from 1920 to 1928, allowing people to retain even more of their earnings. In addition to John Maynard Keynes, economists such as John Kenneth Galbraith and Peter Temin have argued that "under-consumption" caused the Great Depression. But the evidence hardly suggested that consumers lacked either incomes or the desire to purchase goods. In 1921, the consumers' shares of the GNP was $54 billion, and only a decade later it had risen to $73 billion, representing an increase of an additional 5 percent of GNP, even while prices on consumer goods fell by 14 base points during the 1920s. While in no way causing the boom, government set the tone for the decade, in essence telling people that their efforts mattered and that their wealth was their own. Uncle Sam then proved it by allowing them to keep more of the fruits of their labor. One can see the statistical results, but perhaps more important were the hidden benefits of government's attitudes. Businesses no longer were treated as outlaws or renegades to be brought to justice.

Warren Harding (R-OH) began the transformation in 1920 by insisting that the nation return to normality, and he campaigned on the promise to return the United States to its prewar tax rates. By giving Harding 60 percent of the vote (the largest majority recorded to that point since Washington) and by handing the Republicans control of the Senate and House, the nation expected the president to make good on his promise. He quickly announced his cabinet, made up of "a cross-section of successful America: a car manufacturer, two bankers, a hotel director, a farm-journal editor, an international lawyer, a rancher, an engineer, and only two professional politicians."[33] The most important of his appointees, insofar as it affected American entrepreneurs and working families, was Andrew Mellon, a sixty-five-year-old millionaire of so few words he might make "Silent Cal" Coolidge appear verbose.

Mellon had taken the train to meet Harding at his home in Marion, Ohio, only to encounter a line of local job seekers. Waiting his turn, despite the fact that the president-elect had requested the meeting, Mellon finally shook hands with Harding and proceeded to explain why he should not be appointed the secretary of the treasury. Harding had exactly what he wanted: A man with enough wealth that he was not for sale, and a person who did not want the job. For Mellon, heading the Treasury Department required him to leave his safe corporate position at the head of a banking and oil empire to test his theory that the rich had avoided an increasing amount of taxes as tax rates steadily had risen. It represented the first official test of what later came to be called "supply-side economics."

ANDREW MELLON SLASHES THE NATIONAL DEBT (AND HELPS THE TAXPAYER!)

Upon assuming office, Mellon suspected that for years the rising tax rates had made it consistently more advantageous for the wealthy to shelter their income rather than invest it and pay taxes on profits. In 1921, he started to analyze the tax rates and resulting revenues systematically. He found that between 1917 and 1921, the number of returns filed by people earning more than $300,000 had plummeted fourfold. Net income of those earning above $300,000 likewise had fallen from $731 million in 1917 to $153 million in 1921. Yet anyone could see that there were more rich people in America than ever before. What was happening?

Mellon surmised that wealthy investors had shifted their money into tax-exempt bonds issued by cities and states. At some point, municipal bonds paying a low interest rate returned a higher net amount because of the tax savings. According to Mellon's estimates, by 1923, Americans held $12 billion in tax-exempt bonds, representing an amount equal to half the national debt. Cities built baseball stadiums, recreation centers, and parks while American businesses suffered from capital anemia. Moreover, Mellon, thanks to his family background as an oil driller, knew how risky many corporate investments were. Government bonds, on the other hand, presented safe places for capital. Mellon thought the wealthy should pay their fair share of taxes, and the best way to get them to do so was by cutting the tax rates.

The trick, he realized, lay in making industrial investment profitable, which required tax cuts. He found opposition. Groups of all ideological stripes were against tax cutting: Progressives had long favored a growing government and rising tax rates as a way of promoting economic equality, while conservative budget-balancers worried that lower tax rates would produce less government revenue and, hence, a larger national debt. Both groups were wrong about the effect of lower taxes. Mellon intuitively understood a phenomenon that would be called, fifty years later, the "Laffer curve," a proposition so simple and unshakable that most critics do not attempt to debate its merits, rather its effective rate. According to the creator of the Laffer curve, Arthur Laffer, there are two tax rates any government can impose that will produce no revenue at all. If there is a tax rate of zero, the government collects no taxes. If, however, the tax rate is 100 percent, the government will not collect taxes there either, because no one will work to pay his entire income in taxes. Human nature dictated that when government confiscates too much of one's earnings, a person will find ways around the tax code legally or, ultimately, refuse to abide by the law. Laffer's simple premise was that at some point, a government can generate greater revenues by lowering rates. He did not establish at what point that transpired, but argued that the effect looked like a curve, with tax revenues rising and with tax rate increasing to a certain point, then declining after that point. So a tax rate of 95 percent might bring in far less revenue than a rate of half, or even one-third, that rate.

In 1921, of course, Mellon could not know of the Laffer curve, since it wasn't proposed until the 1970s. But Mellon understood human nature, and he predicted that at rates above 25 percent, rich people put their investments in nontaxable shelters or even consumed more rather than pay taxes.[34] Although it took repeated convincing of Harding—but less so of his successor, Calvin Coolidge, who was easily the most favorable president for entrepreneurs in the nation's history—Mellon proposed his plan to Congress. It consisted of four points and marked a policy stance as momentous as that taken 140 years earlier by Alexander Hamilton. First, Mellon urged that Congress cut the top income tax rate from 73 percent to 25 percent. Second, he insisted that taxes on lower incomes had to be chopped as well. People making more than $4,000 per year paid 8 percent, and those making under

$4,000 paid 4 percent. Mellon wanted to cut those rates to 6 percent and 3 percent, with an eye toward lowering the rates still further at a later date. Related to the lower-class rate reductions, he sought a tax credit of 25 percent on earned income so as to further reduce the burden on working-class taxpayers. Progressives, perhaps showing their true colors, resisted any rate reduction on any groups: Robert La Follette, the leader of the Progressives in Congress, wanted taxes to start at incomes of $1,000, and as governor of Wisconsin, he had supported a state tax on those making as little as $800. Mellon's third proposal was a reduction in the federal estate tax. Not only did he see estate taxes as properly the domain of the states, but, again, high estate taxes merely encouraged the creation of tax shelters. Finally, Mellon pressed for efficiencies in government, cutting staff in the Treasury Department at the pace of one a day, every day, in the 1920s.[35]

Reductions did not come easy. In 1921, 1922, and 1923, Mellon battled the Progressives on taxes, gaining a substantial reduction in large income rates (to 46 percent) but losing on corporation taxes (raised by one percent). Although the Progressives agreed to the politically popular measure to decrease rates for those making less than $8,000, Mellon ultimately found himself running in mud. Then Harding died, leaving Coolidge as the president, whereupon the new chief executive concurred completely with Mellon's plan to lower top rates in order to ease the burden on lower groups.[36] Throughout it all, Mellon anticipated that some of the new revenue growth that he expected as a result of the lower rates would be targeted toward the national debt.

By the time the final incremental reductions fell into place, the top bracket of taxpayers paid almost 50 percent more than before the cut, while those in the lowest brackets paid between 40 percent and 70 percent less. A study by Gene Smiley and Richard H. Keehn concluded that the lower rates ended tax avoidance by a considerable extent.[37] Just as important, Mellon increased revenues to the U.S. Treasury so much that the United States paid off one-third of its national debt—not deficit, but total debt—in less than eight years![38] Given the huge and almost constantly rising size of the national debt after World War II, certainly any modern politician who equaled Mellon's feat would be celebrated as a deficit-cutting hero.

The falling national debt did not cause the prosperity, but rather reflected it. Keeping more of their earnings than at any time since 1916, entrepreneurs launched new firms at a frenzied pace, soaking up the labor pool, until in 1926 the unemployment rate reached an astonishing one percent—perhaps the only such achievement in the history of the American peacetime economy. The index of manufacturing production rose from 15 percent in 1920 to 23 percent by 1929, yet the annual earnings of employees rose by one-third and the number of hours worked in manufacturing fell by 5 percent. With little to complain about, workers ignored the unions: The AFL's membership dropped from 4 million in 1920 to 2.7 million in 1929, and overall union membership shrank slightly faster.[39] Union leaders complained that the affluence and luxury produced by the economy had made their role superfluous.

Government's role in the boom consisted of more than cutting taxes and providing rhetorical encouragement. The Harding and Coolidge administrations also avoided any foreign entanglements, not always a desirable policy when the fascist state of Italy was giving rise to a new type of totalitarianism. The administrations' business policies were not perfect, and Coolidge and Mellon in particular tended to support tariffs—and ultimately one tariff, the Hawley-Smoot, contributed heavily to the Great Depression. Nevertheless, when Coolidge left office the United States stood as the world's economic power. As a share of world production in 1929, America held 34.4 percent, compared to Britain and Germany, each with a little over 10 percent.

Coolidge had good reason to say that "no Congress … ever assembled, on surveying the state of the Union, has met with a more pleasing prospect…. The country can regard the present with satisfaction and anticipate the future with optimism."[40] Authorities as varied as historian Charles Beard and writer Walter Lippmann echoed these views: *The Nation* published a three-month series on the permanent state of prosperity, with discussions of the pockets of people not yet enjoying its benefits. Ironically, the opening article coincided with the sharpest drop in stock prices in the history of the New York Stock Exchange. Coolidge, it appears, anticipated a recession, and he intuitively appreciated the fact that despite his austere approach to federal spending, which remained virtually flat during his tenure, the government's growth had placed undue pressures on the economy. He despised his successor, a "forgotten Progressive" Republican named Herbert Hoover, who had wielded federal power as head of the Food Administration during World War I, then as secretary of commerce in the Harding-Coolidge administrations.[41] Steeped in his wartime experience with crisis, Hoover employed the government willingly to solve the nation's problems, especially in the agricultural sector, where he personally stepped in to craft the 1929 Agricultural Marketing Act. Far from being a *laissez-faire* capitalist, Hoover more closely resembled the corporatists that had gained power in Europe, envisioning a mutual cooperation between business, labor, and the government. He rejected fascism and overt statism, seeing himself as a free society's alternative to Italy's Benito Mussolini. Most important, Hoover embodied the managerial revolution's maxim that efficiency could be attained through planning, and that a scientific and rational approach to the economy would yield beneficial results. As Hoover quickly found out, planning proved a thoroughly inadequate shield against irrational panic, and nor did planning help when it relied on constructs that put into motion some of the problems management was expected to solve. Indeed, planners had struggled for a decade with solutions to the recession in the farming sector, with little to show for it.

WEAK SPOTS IN THE 1920s BOOM: THE FARM FIASCO

Farmers had produced at record levels during World War I. Slogans such as "Plow to the Fence for National Defense!" and "If You Can't Fight, Farm" reiterated the critical role food played in the conflict, as trench warfare ranged over Europe's farmlands. Government guarantees gave farmers profit levels usually associated with the greedy railroad monopolists. Well into the war effort, the Wilson administration had guaranteed farm prices and, as late as June 1920, the price of land reflected the new incentives. Whereas land values rose less than 5 percent a year from 1870 to 1915, suddenly, over the next five years, values gained over 11 percent a year. Seeing an opportunity to make unprecedented profits, farmers borrowed as never before on land. American wheat farmers had the price of their product pegged by Congress at $2.26 a bushel, when Australian farmers received only 98 cents a bushel. As might be expected, the United States "was sitting on a mountain of surplus wheat."[42]

Then, reality hit agriculture like a twister. As European and Australian farmers returned home and restored the fields, prices plummeted, but the balance on the mortgages held fast. Yet even at their peak in 1927, the bankruptcy rate for farmers (1.8 per 100) was still below that of all businesses. Large corporations had suffered from the speculation of the agricultural boom and bust, too. National City Bank, speculating on the high sugar prices, had opened sixteen branches in Cuba in 1919, and then paid for it heavily when world sugar prices plunged.[43] By most statistical measures, farm values remained high; farm income had risen, making the 1920s moderately prosperous for agriculture.[44] But by comparing farm to nonfarm income, using a formula developed by the USDA's Bureau of Agricultural Economics called parity (which set minimum prices on farm products to maintain a constant ratio between farm products and other goods), farm lobbyists argued that farmers were falling behind. Like all other businesses, farmers, through the National Grange and the Populist movement, had sought special favors for agriculture from the government. By the 1920s, farmers possessed one of the most powerful lobbies in Washington (as they did in Germany, where Adolf Hitler would tap them), and after World War I they supported import tariffs with increasing enthusiasm.

Beginning in the 1920s, farmers opened a new campaign to gain federal export subsidies. The McNary-Haugen Bill, named after Senator Charles McNary of Oregon and Representative Gilbert Haugen of Iowa, attempted to boost farm income. McNary-Haugen contained the contributions of George N. Peek, a former John Deere executive and head of Moline Plow Company who worked under Bernard Baruch in the war. Peek and his associate, Hugh Johnson, sought to fix domestic prices for farm products based on a parity relationship between farm and industrial goods using a price structure indexed to 1909–13 prices. It encouraged "dumping" the surplus—which it did nothing to alleviate—at world market prices. Sensibly, Coolidge vetoed the measure, twice, acting on the advice of his Secretary of Commerce Herbert Hoover. Hoover understood "a serious, probably fatal flaw in the McNary-Haugen proposals: the omission of production controls, specifically the production that farmers could achieve."[45] When it came to agriculture, though, even the pro-market Coolidge abandoned his better judgment, arguing that government "must encourage orderly and centralized marketing," and supported federal funding of marketing co-ops.[46] The real dilemma for farmers, and the one they refused to confront, was simple.

On the one hand, there were still too many farms, producing too much, to be profitable, especially when considering the strong increase in Canadian and Russian grain exports. Limiting the analysis to the United States alone, it took only half the nation's farmers to produce 90 percent of the agricultural output. The remainder constituted self-sufficient family organizations more than actors in a capitalist market, especially in pockets of Appalachia and northern Wisconsin. On the other hand, there were too few farmers to force through pro-farm legislation with veto-proof majorities. Ultimately, farmers never mustered a great deal of support from the large urban areas because, ultimately, "Americans were reasonably well-fed."[47] The public used its surplus to buy luxuries, such as cars, and not more food.

Automobiles, of course, had helped improve farm productivity by greatly expanding market points and permitting greater mobility on the farms themselves. Farm productivity rose from a 1909 index of 100 to a 1929 index of 110, with the labor hours per unit of virtually every farm product falling from 1915 to 1930. Much of that productivity growth occurred due to the mechanization of agriculture. Farmers purchased more than a million tractors in the 1920s. The Fordson, a small, gasoline-powered tractor introduced in 1917, had started the application of automotives technology to the farm, followed by the International Harvester row-crop tractor, with its width-adjustable rear wheels that allowed a farmer to plant, cultivate, and harvest row crops. Allis-Chalmers introduced a rubber-tire tractor in 1929 that permitted farm vehicles to move on public roads for the first time, while the rubber tires gave the machine improved traction. The Model T engine was a power source for many farm tools even where the farmer couldn't justify a tractor. But these advances produced surpluses, resulting in a surge in supply that forced prices down 25 percent from the wartime high. The value of farmland and buildings plummeted by more than 50 percent in a six-year span.[48]

Adding to the woes in the prairies and mountain areas, the unpredictable weather slammed different regions, each in their turn. Wyoming, for example, had record cold winters in the mid-1920s, destroying cattle herds and making business operations difficult (it was so cold in some cases the ledger books froze shut).[49] The crash in wool prices all but destroyed the sheep industry in Nevada, and yet, ironically, a rise in cotton prices had sparked a surge in cotton production in the South that contributed to a worldwide cotton glut, eventually causing that sector to collapse. Cotton swung wildly from a high of $0.42 per pound to $0.09. Droughts in the Great Plains served only as harbingers to much worse conditions in the 1930s. A boll weevil invasion further helped to destroy Southern cotton production.

Yet agricultural policy damaged the farm recovery more seriously than the weather. The government began new programs that emphasized cutting production, urging farmers in the South to destroy every third row of cotton. (Farm politicians sarcastically suggested a better strategy would be to destroy every third member of the Farm Board.[50]) By subsidizing crops through federal irrigation projects, the government only lowered prices. Potatoes produced on federal irrigation projects cost potato farmers overall $15 million, reducing the price four cents per spud. Preaching to farmers to limit production, the federal government gobbled up wheat at eighteen to twenty cents above world prices, sending a clear signal to grow more.

The fantastic productivity achieved by farmers—to their detriment—was repeated in a number of farm-related businesses, again with reverberations to the farm itself. Cheese, for example, had constituted a relatively small part of Americans' use of dairy products until the early 1900s, when James Lewis Kraft, a grocery clerk, reasoned that he could sell more of the product if it were less perishable.[51] Typically, stores kept a huge wheel of cheddar cheese on a counter protected by a large glass jar, with the grocer slicing off a wedge at a time (and in the process leaving the exposed part open to spoilage). Worse, in hot temperatures, the cheese separated into butterfat and solids that reeked with an unmistakable odor. Kraft concluded that the product would maintain its freshness if he packed it in smaller glass jars or tinfoil packages. In 1916, he patented a blending and pasteurizing process that extended the shelf life. The U.S. Army, needing lightweight packaged foods that troops could carry into battle, purchased 6 million pounds from Kraft in 1917.

Further experimentation yielded the tinfoil-wrapped five-pound cheese brick that then went into a wooden box for sale. Within a month after developing the foil wrap, Kraft's factory processed 15,000 blocks of cheese daily. By 1923, Kraft saw sales reach $22 million, and in 1928, Kraft merged with a rival, Phoenix Cheese Co., acquiring its famous trademarked product, Philadelphia Cream Cheese (which was always produced in New York City!). At the time of the stock market crash, Kraft produced 40 percent of the cheese consumed in America. James Kraft, like Jack Daniel and Thomas Welch, was a religious man, serving as a Baptist deacon and supporting the Northern Baptist Theological

Seminary. As Kraft became a household name, his contributions to extending the shelf life of dairy products allowed Americans to waste less cheese than ever before, bringing prices down despite higher overall cheese consumption.

In general, crop prices remained low because production remained too high. Government plans, such as McNary-Haugenism and Hoover's schemes, attempted to control production voluntarily, and modern critics have faulted President Hoover for failing to impose a statist solution of production controls on farmers.[52] Yet even pro-agrarian voices admit that opportunities for improvement outside of farming existed if farmers wanted to move, and an unwillingness to abandon agriculture—for whatever reasons—led many to remain on the land far longer than was economically feasible. One of the most damaging developments for farmers was the deflation of the early 1930s, which made farm mortgages vastly more expensive in real dollars, adding to the desperation in the Farm Belt. Still, had agriculture remained an isolated depressed part of the economy, the problems may have straightened themselves out after enough farmers left the business to make the occupation profitable again. Instead, as the agricultural swamp deepened, it started to drag into it another victim: the banking sector.

BANKS IN CRISIS

Banks in agricultural states suffered horrendous losses even in the prosperous 1920s. Farm problems themselves decreased bank portfolio balances, needless to say. Yet structurally, the banking systems of almost all of the farm states had adopted a particularly weak method of attempting to ensure stability: deposit insurance. Later heralded as the savior of the banks in the New Deal, deposit insurance in fact promulgated widespread instability in states that adopted it.[53] Studies by Charles Calomiris, for example, revealed that states with mandatory deposit insurance were more likely to fail than those with only voluntary deposit insurance or those with no deposit insurance. States with branch banking proved the most stable and solvent of all. Meanwhile, anecdotal evidence from legitimate bankers and unscrupulous swindlers suggests that the notion that the depositors were protected by the government tended to encourage more reckless use of bank investments.[54]

No structure, or system, no matter how well designed, could mitigate some of the more severe problems of banking in the agriculture sector. South Carolina, for example, averaged a suspension rate for banks double the national average in 1920 and 1936, and the bottom five states in bank suspensions featured only one nonagricultural state (Michigan). South Carolina's case was especially interesting and, by all measures, unusual, because of all the states that experienced high failure rates in the 1920s, only South Carolina allowed branch banking, but even branching could not save that state's banks from the decline in the agricultural sector. Banks in agricultural states could run, but they could not hide. With that exception, however, the other disasters afflicting banks during the 1920s almost exclusively struck states that prohibited branching, even if they allowed chain banking, in which a single owner held several banks but the assets and operations of each remained independent. One chain bank, therefore, could not help out another easily.

The most notorious chain bank failure, in Nevada, again resulted from falling farm-sector prices—this time the plummeting wool price. George Wingfield had built a banking empire in Nevada by financing sheep and mines. The cantankerous banker, determined to beef up security in his chain of banks, instructed all banks to keep a shotgun handy, "for instant use in the bank," and distributed weapons and shells to every office in his system, for which he later billed the cashiers![55] Wingfield operated a chain of banks, which meant that although he owned a majority of stock in many banks, the institutions could not shuffle or commingle their funds. Even intrastate branch banking might not have saved Wingfield's chain because it was heavily committed to the state's sheep growers. Yet contrary to the images of evil bankers anxious to throw helpless farmers off their lands, Wingfield continued to carry the sheep ranchers long after it was commercially prudent. When finally his chain had to be closed, Wingfield still had not abandoned the ranchers.[56]

Banks in other states suffered from completely unrelated, and often unpredictable, shifts not entirely related in any general sense to the health of the economy. In Florida, for example, a bust followed a boom in the early 1920s because tourist attitudes abruptly changed, plunging Florida's banks into a depression.[57] Whether with sheep or sunbathers, trouble in a variety of unrelated business sectors steadily chiseled away against the banking industry, awaiting only a sudden shock to crack the edifice permanently.

THE CRASH AND THE GREAT DEPRESSION

On October 15, 1929, stock prices, which had fluctuated for a month, turned down for good. The serious losses began on October 24, "Black Thursday," and by the following week, on "Black Tuesday," October 29, 16 million shares traded hands as stock prices plummeted. Even the blue-chip industrials saw their values tumble, with General Electric, U.S. Steel, and AT&T prices dropping anywhere from 17 to 47 points in a day. Volume overwhelmed the technology, causing the stock tickers to run more than an hour and a half behind, further inflaming the panic. In less than a month—by November 13—the stock index stood at 224, down from 452 only weeks before. The bad news was that it had just started: By 1932, the index bottomed out at 58! U.S. Steel shares, once selling for more than $260, could be acquired for $22, and mighty General Motors, which had boasted profits in the hundreds of millions just months earlier, had its stock collapse to $8.

What caused the Great Crash? Most economic historians subscribe to the view that multiple factors coalesced to drive down confidence, including falling industrial production and a restrictive Federal Reserve policy that began in 1928 but had just started to affect business by mid-1929.[58] To those factors, others have added irrational panic and the aforementioned speculative bubble.[59] While those explanations might adequately describe some of the contributing factors, none of them provides a useful clock by which to determine the timing of the crash. One explanation does, and while it receives some attention by economic historians, on a broader scale it suffers from neglect because it has not been produced by one of the academic fraternity, but rather by a private-sector economist.

Jude Wanniski has made a convincing case that the trigger for the Great Crash involved the Hawley-Smoot Tariff of 1930. An attentive reader immediately should ask, "How could an event in 1930 affect the crash of 1929?" In American politics, key decisions often do not involve final passage of legislation; instead, with the committee process in Congress, interested parties can often know the eventual outcome of a bill based on its fate in certain committees. The Hawley-Smoot Tariff threatened to raise tariffs on most imported goods by as much as 34 percent. Manufacturers who needed raw materials or finished technology from abroad stood to have their costs rise by at least that percentage, as well as having higher interest rates, if the tariff bill passed. A close correlation of the status of the bill in committees and stock movements in October reveals that when the tariff fluctuated, stock prices did the same. The Hawley-Smoot legislation cleared its final committee hurdle, ensuring its passage before the whole House and Senate, just before the October crash. On the day President Herbert Hoover agreed to sign the bill, the market collapsed further. The inevitability of massive new manufacturing and import costs sent the market into a panic. More important, businesses realized that not only did Hawley-Smoot presage hard times domestically (requiring them to sell securities to gain liquidity, thus driving prices down further), but tariff barriers raised in the United States promised to elicit retaliation abroad. It would be significantly more difficult to sell products overseas after Hawley-Smoot, investors realized.

When combined with other factors, such as monetary policy mistakes, the tariff bill easily could have plunged the economy into chaos. In September 1929, the Bank of England had raised its interest rates, making it more difficult to sell American goods in England. Then, the Federal Reserve Bank, which already had raised interest rates trying to rein in the stock market, suggested it might hike rates a second time. Economists still debate the relative importance of a variety of factors contributing to the avalanche, but the economy slid rapidly in the fall of 1929. The *New York Times* Index of September 1929 was at 216, more than twice what it had been in July 1928. However, September 3 was the last "good" day, and by November 13, it was down to 113, and it continued decreasing. By 1930, problems spread to every sector of the economy and bank failures accelerated. Panic set in. As monetary contraction contributed to the panic, continued decreases in the money available for spending turned panic into depression. Bank customers cashed out their deposits and buried their coins and currency in coffee cans in the backyard. As people pulled their money out of banks, banks grew weaker, leading more people to pull out their deposits as well. Whatever started the cycle, the Fed proved unable or unwilling to break it.[60] Instead, private bankers' clearinghouses responded remarkably well, and in some cases might have prevailed if the monetary authorities had provided more strategic liquidity assistance as, for example, in Chicago.[61] But the Fed did not act, and the destruction of money rippled throughout the system with the money supply declining by one-third. As banks lost deposits, they stopped lending. Without loans, businesses could not acquire inventory and had to lay off employees. The December 1930 failure of the private bank, Bank of the United States, frightened even foreign depositors. The money supply plummeted. Leading economists Milton Friedman and Anna Schwartz measured the drop in the money supply at 30 percent, leading to their labeling this period "the Great Contraction."[62]

' By 1930, a recession was in full swing. President Hoover, a Progressive with a proclivity to bureaucratic solutions, had no qualms about using the government to attack the problems America faced. He slashed immigration, thus reducing the flow of free labor and entrepreneurship. European immigration plummeted 90 percent, just as the totalitarian dictators grasped power and drove the best and the brightest from their borders. Hoover's subsidies to shipbuilding produced a glut at the same time his tariffs choked off trade in the products those ships might carry. His solution to the difficulties, the Reconstruction Finance Corporation (RFC), offered taxpayer-financed loans to struggling banks and businesses. As with many government programs, however, the cure only made the disease worse. Recipients of RFC loans had to be listed in newspapers, which made people doubt further the solvency of any business listed as an RFC borrower.

Hoover also tried a tax cut—not the supply-side cut that would have encouraged businesses to invest, but a 1929 consumption-oriented, across-the-board one percent cut that disappeared instantly and increased deficits. Surprisingly to many, Hoover also tried spending money on public work projects. This resulted in running larger deficits to the GNP than later happened under Franklin D. Roosevelt. Never fully convinced of the benefits of tax cuts, and faced with an embarrassing level of deficit, Hoover abruptly reversed course and imposed a huge tax hike—the worst in peacetime history—sending the top rates to 63 percent in 1932. Nothing seemed to work. By late 1932, the gross domestic product (GDP) was down 45 percent and consumer purchasing power had dropped 26 percent from 1929.[63] The nation thought Roosevelt could do better, and certainly business thought he could hardly be worse than Hoover. A study of business expectations from 1929 to 1939 shows that, based on orders, anticipated employment, and other indicators, business prepared itself for a strong recovery after 1932.[64] (That was strongly adhering to the unceasing torrent of comments by business leaders that the economy was sound, or that recovery was "just around the corner.") Roosevelt had his opportunity. He had already promised a "new deal for the American people" in his 1932 nomination acceptance speech. Unknown to the voters, at a time when the nation needed confidence in the economic system more than anything else, FDR, for political advantage, had deliberately refused to announce any support of Hoover's programs, even when he agreed with them entirely. Thus, before he initiated a single policy to save the United States from the Great Depression, Roosevelt already had ensured its extension.

In his last months in office, Hoover presided over a nation in turmoil and, worse, an international economic debacle that in many ways needed a healthy American economy as a stabilizer. The United States had unemployment rates of 25 percent and, in some states, the rate was nearly double that. Both the agricultural and financial sectors had collapsed, with more than 9,000 banks failing since 1928 and farmers, unable to obtain prices for their goods that offset costs of getting them to market, allowing entire wheat, apple, and other crops to rot rather than harvesting them.

Traditionally, a lower interest rate would stimulate investment. But by 1932, even interest rates of as low as one percent did not spur borrowing, as a shroud of pessimism hung over the nation. More than a million people wandered about, representing the nation's first truly homeless group. Railroads, counting transients that they eventually had to kick off their trains, tallied more than 186,000 trespassers in 1931 who spent at least one night riding the rails. Soup kitchens and "Hoovervilles" marred the urban landscapes, while an army of unemployed veterans who camped in Washington seeking early bonus payments were driven out at gunpoint by soldiers. The Soviet Union, sensing a huge propaganda victory, advertised for 6,000 skilled workers and received applications from 100,000.[65]

The auto industry, of course, collapsed as people attempted to stretch the lives of their existing cars. Production plummeted from 4.3 million cars in 1929 to 1.5 million in 1933. Over half the assembly-line workers in Detroit were idle, and without incomes, they ceased to pay taxes, causing Midwestern cities' finances to nosedive into the red.[66] Indeed, the whole economy resembled a car, but a V-8 running on two or three cylinders because the ignition wires to the others had been pulled out. Fundamentally, nothing was wrong with the car, but reality said that supply and demand within the economy were not making contact. Monetarists added that, since the money supply fell so drastically, people could not make the connections: The money just did not exist.

"DO NOT PASS GO": CHARLES DARROW INVENTS MONOPOLY

One of the millions of unemployed in 1933, a heating equipment salesman from Germantown, Pennsylvania, had taken odd jobs where he could find them. In between, Charles Darrow invented such useless items as a new bridge scorepad and a contraption that combined a ball and bat. All the time, Darrow thought about success, wealth, and property. If he could not have the real thing, at least he could pretend with his little game, "Monopoly."[67]

Darrow used his memories from Atlantic City, New Jersey, where he and his wife had visited on vacations. His game consisted of a board, dice, and most important of all, "property" that the players could acquire. The deeds carried the names of Atlantic City streets (Boardwalk and Park Place being the most expensive) and the railroads—the Pennsylvania, the B&O, and the Reading—that were American legends. Unlike other board games, however, where players attempted to gain an objective, in Monopoly they just went around the board, collecting property, paying rent, until finally one player had everything and the others were broke. The game encouraged trades, purchases, improvement of one's property, and even included elements of fortune with cards called "Chance" and "Community Chest."

Meanwhile, game makers George and Charles Parker, known as "Parker Bros." (with "brothers" never spelled out) had, like other game manufacturers, languished since 1929. Although it still had one popular game, Mahjongg, Parker Bros. struggled, and the opportunity to sell a new game like Monopoly seemed natural. Instead, when Darrow met with company executives, hoping to sell them the rights to the game, they found it too complicated and unstructured for their customers. Darrow had to sell the product on his own, placing games store by store. The game caught on in Philadelphia, where Wanamaker's department store placed an order for 5,000 sets. Darrow did not have the capacity to make 5,000 Monopoly games, and this time Parker Bros. stepped in. In 1935, Darrow sold the rights to Monopoly to Parker Bros., which was suddenly swamped with orders. Within a few months, the company produced 20,000 games a week and still had orders for more. By 1936, orders topped 800,000.

Aside from a few isolated businesses (such as Parker Bros., some of the movie studios, and the radio industry), hope for getting out of the crisis was dim. If life was like Monopoly, then Hoover seemed the cruel landlord. It is ironic, then, to realize that he had started more public works, including the Hoover Dam and the San Francisco Bay Bridge, than any administration in history. His RFC threw loans at the sinking economy to the tune of $1.6 billion in cash and $2.3 billion in credits in 1932 alone, and, true to his big-government tendencies, his 1932 Revenue Act saddled Americans with the largest peacetime tax increase in history. Some pockets of enterprise endured. Movies and the more unsavory segments of the entertainment industry, such as striptease shows, continued to draw. (James Thurber reported that strippers were making as much as $475 a week in 1932![68]) But Americans wanted a change, and it came in the person of Franklin D. Roosevelt and his "New Deal."

THE NEW DEAL

Roosevelt realized that he had a short time to convince the country that things could change. He first tackled the banking crisis, closing the banks in March 1933 by presidential order. The bank holiday shut down the banks, pending federal investigations and a certification that they were healthy. With the Banking Act of 1933, the Federal Deposit Insurance Corporation (FDIC) was created to restore confidence in the banks, and in the process generated a myth that it saved the banking system. Business historian Joseph Pusateri wrote, for example, that "no single legislative step did more to restore, calm, and reduce the likelihood of further panics."[69] However, other evidence is extremely strong that it did no such thing. Economic historians have isolated Roosevelt's order taking the United States off the gold standard as perhaps the single most important act contributing to the end of the banking crisis. Once the gold reserves of the Fed were off-limits to foreigners, runs on the dollar abroad ended, allowing the banking system's liquidity to build up again.[70] But the rising asset value of banks due to other, unrelated factors also enhanced their resurrection.

To revive the manufacturing sector and stabilize production and employment, FDR employed a different tactic, seeking to enlist big business in his program. As previously seen, business was receptive, although uneasy, when FDR introduced the National Industrial Recovery Act of 1933. That act established the National Recovery Administration (NRA) to regulate, under the auspices of a government–business partnership, prices, competition, output, wages, and virtually all other functions of a free economy. The NRA, headed by Hugh S. Johnson (from the War Industries Board in World War I), drafted codes of fair competition, in essence cartelizing existing firms and closing out newly forming businesses. Of course, most businesses did not mind that aspect of the NRA. Another element, though, guaranteeing labor's right to collective bargaining, antagonized big business as well as small.[71]

To revive the agricultural sector, the New Deal provided the Commodity Credit Corporation (CCC) in 1933 to offer loans to farmers who participated in acreage limitations, as enacted by the Agricultural Adjustment Administration. Yet farmers could limit acreage on one type of crop, receive a federal payment, and produce another crop for which they had not signed a rental agreement with the government. Other market distortions rapidly surfaced: Farmers learned to plant more on their allowable acreage; landlords who received government checks purchased tractors and evicted sharecroppers. Food prices rose, but the distortions in the market more than offset any gains. Prices never got high enough to keep many farmers solvent, and consumers—already struggling—paid more for food. The federal deficit got worse, and what few taxpayers there were shouldered still a greater burden. Although the Supreme Court declared the Agricultural Adjustment Act (AAA) unconstitutional in 1936, Congress finessed the ruling by passing the Soil Conservation Act (1936) and a second AAA (1938) that survived court challenges. In 1935, the administration admitted that the farm recovery program "had ironically created many victims of its own" when it created the Resettlement Administration to resettle dispossessed farmers and displaced tenants.[72]

Efforts to create jobs included the Civilian Conservation Corps and the Public Works Administration (PWA), as well as the Works Progress Administration and the National Youth Administration. Depending on how one interprets the statistics, the unemployment rate fell from 25 percent nationally in 1932 to 15 percent in 1936, before rising again in 1938.[73] If the classical economic models are correct, the economy would have returned to the "natural" level of employment without the distortion of the New Deal anyway.[74]

THE NEW DEAL: A FIFTY-YEAR VIEW

Roosevelt's program of reform along quasi-socialist lines represented an approach to recovery, but it was only one path. Another was not tried—a radical political program directed at free market, pro-enterprise reforms, elimination of tariffs, reduction of taxes, and curbing the power of the Fed to affect financial markets. Distinctions between Hoover and FDR are unwarranted, as both were enemies to entrepreneurship. Furthermore, the economic debate, by nature of the evidence, has tended to focus on what Roosevelt accomplished in the recovery from 1933 and seldom assesses the impact of the New Deal *forward* to look at its impact on post–World War II business.

A recent survey of American history, *A Patriot's History of the United States*, contains a three-page chart of New Deal programs with their intended goals and their unintended consequences.[75] The authors conclude, "The political and economic policies of the New Deal almost without exception created long-term unintended effects that severely damaged the nation.... In almost every case, the temporary fix offered by the New Deal program resulted in substantial long-term disruptions of labor markets and financial structures and reduced American competitiveness."[76] Another analysis, by economist Gene Smiley, summarizing the economic literature, concluded that "though the analytical work necessary to provide quantitative estimates of the retarding effects of the entire New Deal on the recovery ... has not been undertaken ... it seems likely that this retardation was substantial."[77] Many elements of long-term structural damage done by the New Deal did not start to affect the American economy seriously until the 1970s, and by the 1990s, virtually every New Deal initiative had produced a disaster or a time bomb. Farm subsidies had seriously damaged American agriculture, idling as much as 78 million acres of farmland in 1988, until finally, in 1995, the Republican-led Congress ended most of the New Deal agricultural policies—too late for millions of consumers who had paid higher prices at the store for sixty years or the thousands of farmers who were routinely priced out of world markets for sixty years.[78] As tends to happen, slowly, many of these policies had crept back into the system by 2007. Social Security, enacted solely as a retirement supplement, had grown in such perverse ways that no respected official or private analysis of the program posits any hope for the system to survive the baby boom retirements without complete restructuring. New Deal banking legislation restricted the growth of American commercial banking.[79] With very few exceptions, the scholarly literature has concluded that minimum wages and the stifling effects of tax policy have had a negative effect on employment, especially on youth and minority employment—and yet in the name of "compassion," Congress routinely hikes the minimum wage, even as more businesses voluntarily pay above minimum wage. Minimum wage increases prolonged the Great Depression. Taking the long-term view of the costs of the programs, the New Deal was nothing short of a deadweight on the enterprise of America—an "I.V. drip," dispensing a dulling, but temporarily soothing narcotic. The damage it caused haunts us still in the emphasis on government "solutions" not only to problems of the economy but to economic problems of individuals.[80]

CHAPTER 10

Business in War and Postwar America: 1940–1960

Frequently, foreign observers understand America better than Americans. Certainly the young French aristocrat, Alexis de Tocqueville, proved uncanny with his predictions and unerring in his analysis of American culture and politics. In the case of World War II, historians have long maintained that the exceptional skill of American fighting men won the war, only to be challenged by Europeanists who claim that the overwhelming might of the Soviet infantry was the decisive factor. Still another group suggests that the superior technology of the United States—culminating in the atomic bomb—made the difference.

British historian Paul Johnson offers a much more straightforward assessment: "The real engine of Allied victory was the American economy."[1] After only a year of hostilities, industrial productivity in the United States exceeded that of Germany, Japan, and Italy combined. Johnson concluded that the "astonishing acceleration was made possible by the essential dynamism and flexibility of the American system, wedded to a national purpose which served the same galvanizing role as the optimism of the Twenties."[2] The war, he observed, "acted as a boom market, encouraging American entrepreneurial skills to fling her seemingly limitless resources of material and manpower into a bottomless pool of consumption."[3]

American entrepreneurs proved as adept at fueling the engine of democracy as they had in building railroads and starting banks. From the traditional entrepreneurs like Henry Kaiser to eccentric innovators like Howard Hughes, from boatbuilders like Andrew Jackson Higgins to dreamers like Preston Tucker, business leaders in the United States, looking forward from the systematic harassment of the New Deal, did not shrug. They picked up the globe and carried it, emerging from the war with two-thirds of the world's economic production and markets. Not only did they win the war, American businessmen then turned around and rebuilt the devastated economies of their former enemies, ensuring that the defeated nations soon would become their chief competitors.

WAR, TOTAL WAR, AND THE LESSONS OF WORLD WAR I

Despite its title as the Great War, World War I was not a total war effort for the United States. No American cities suffered attack, and at no time was the entire population mobilized to the point that everyone served either at the front or in a factory. Yet the First World War represented a new departure in productivity of military goods and in their lethality. Casualties in a single day exceeded one million at the Battle of the Somme in 1916. By the 1940s, when war again broke out in Europe, the explosives delivered on Nazi Germany alone dwarfed the amount used in previous wars. The Second World War, coming after the New Deal, already had many elements of centralized economic planning in place.

Total war, as World War II would be, demanded cooperation between government and industry to maintain production of war supplies adequate for the country's needs. The nation looked to its World War I experience as a partial guide for the new conflict. After all, while the nation had relied on private contractors for most of its war production, the government had introduced centralized ship designs and built large shipyards that operated alongside private shipbuilders Electric Boat and Newport News.

Government management during World War I, in the form of the War Industries Board (WIB), dramatically expanded the scope of federal control over daily economic life, affecting clothing items as well as food and fuel. Entrepreneurs chafed at the intrusion into their businesses, with U.S. Steel's chairman, Elbert Gary, suggesting that the government, through the WIB, had attempted to nationalize steel during the war.[4] During wartime, central planning was essential; but it also required the full cooperation and commitment of business and entrepreneurs, as well as consumer sacrifices by a willing public. World War I implied that, if left to their own devices, business could manufacture the weapons of war as efficiently and cost-effectively as any government-owned plant if provided production goals by the government. Therefore, in the interwar years, the government adopted a policy of identifying industries, and even specific companies, that it might need in a military emergency.

WINGS! THE AIRPLANE AGE OF JUAN TRIPPE AND HOWARD HUGHES

In the case of the aircraft industry, from 1919 to 1929, the peacetime uses of airplanes (predominantly through the airlines) did not produce sufficient profits to maintain several aircraft suppliers. American aircraft companies had produced 14,000 planes in 1918 to fill $365 million in contracts, but profit margins were small, and government dictated the number and type of aircraft built, making it difficult, if not impossible, for aircraft firms to look ahead to peacetime. In 1920, the entire industry had only $5 million in capital and received no direct support from the government, surviving instead on actual orders. Several mergers swallowed up weaker companies, leaving only four major airframe builders and two engine companies by 1939.[5]

To the extent that the aircraft industry received any help from government, it came from mail contracts, with some of the largest going to Pan American Airlines at the behest of the U.S. Navy.[6] Juan Trippe, who created Pan Am in the 1920s and pioneered the use of flying boats, provided the government with detailed maps and identified areas that might become new landing fields. Trippe's Boeing-built China Clipper flying boats scheduled flights between San Francisco and Hong Kong, and they even flew directly to England by 1938.[7] Well into the 1960s, Trippe's airline profited from government connections, keeping abreast of Air Force contracts with Boeing and Pratt & Whitney to make decisions about upgrading his fleet. But it also proved Pan Am's eventual undoing, because its reliance on the government left the airline uncompetitive in a deregulated world and often reduced incentives to invest in new technology. Mail contracts subsidized some elements of operations, but they hardly provided the necessary capital for radical and innovative new designs. As one observer commented, "Trippe's company had lived by the state and died by the state."[8] Indeed, while the government had, to mix metaphors, kept the aircraft manufacturers afloat from 1919 to 1941, the mail subsidies came with a high price: The U.S. Postal Service got to dictate routes and the postmaster general even meddled in engine and other technology selection.[9]

While the government fretted about the proper engine for its subsidized "babies," new aircraft innovations had started to appear, transforming the industry. In the mid-1930s, Donald Douglas, who had a small manufacturing company in Santa Monica, California, met with TWA vice president Jack Frye to finalize specifications for a new twin-engine aircraft, called the DC-3, that provided unprecedented passenger comfort with improved operating capabilities. According to C. R. Smith, president of American Airlines, the DC-3 was "the first airplane in the world that could make money just by hauling passengers."[10] The advances in aircraft design usually came from barnstorming pilots, backyard mechanics, and wealthy eccentrics such as Juan Trippe's *bête noire*, Howard Hughes.

Hughes already had made a movie about flying in the late 1920s called *Hell's Angels*. Having inherited his father's tool business (which was founded on the unique Hughes drill bit), Howard Hughes spent half a million dollars to create a private air force consisting of vintage World War I–era airplanes for the movie. Flight became a passion for Hughes, and he began designing aircraft. The Depression grounded Hughes Tool Company, and Howard did his share to siphon off funds with his extravagant playboy lifestyle, leaving Noah Dietrich to represent him at the company. Yet when confronted with the desperate plight of the company, Hughes had Dietrich restructure his debt, sell some of the company's stock, and renegotiate the contracts of the talented top executives to ensure their services for several years by giving them raises. He then dispatched his top executive to Houston to oversee the operations, expanded the research staff, and started, for the first time in his life, to study the reports sent to him from Texas.[11]

Hughes continued flying, working undercover as a baggage handler to get into American Airlines' pilot-in-training program, where, after handling luggage for eight hours a day, he plopped into the copilot's seat for his flying lessons. Ultimately, someone recognized him as Howard Hughes, and his secret life as an airline pilot ended. By that time, flying had captured the American imagination: In 1927, Charles Lindbergh crossed the Atlantic, returning to a fantastic ticker-tape parade in New York City. Hughes studied flight and practiced ceaselessly, learning to fly "almost every type of aircraft in existence, from oceangoing amphibian seaplanes to the roaring Fokkers."[12] In 1932, he assembled a team to build the fastest airplane in the world. Fabricated in secret and shrouded by a canvas cover, the H-1 *Silver Bullet*, built at a cost of $120,000 and tested in wind tunnels at Caltech, launched Hughes Aircraft when it was unveiled in 1935. Hughes posted a world speed record of 351 miles per hour, smashing the existing record held by a French pilot. Then, typically for Hughes, the engine lost power and the plane nearly crashed. Hughes climbed out, unhurt, into a beet field, to announce he could get the aircraft to 365 miles per hour.

With each flight, Hughes added to the technological base of the American aircraft industry. Although still viewed as an amateur by some, Hughes continued to plow his fortune into developing better, faster, and more fuel-efficient aircraft, setting a world record by flying a Lockheed Lodestar around the globe in three days, nineteen hours, and seventeen minutes. Lost in the public celebration was the fact that Hughes and his chief adviser had resurrected the Hughes Tool Company, which had made possible the funding of Hughes's exploits. The company posted profits of $6 million in 1935, $9 million in 1936, and $13 million in 1937, with new bits coming in a steady stream from the expanded research and development team Hughes had empowered. He also had assembled a team of aviation specialists in a 1,300-acre facility in Culver City, where, anticipating the demands of the coming war, they experimented with inexpensive wooden airplanes.

In 1939, William John "Jack" Frye, a former stunt pilot who was the director of operations for TWA (at the time T&WA), approached Hughes with a proposal for Hughes to finance thirty-three Constellation aircrafts. Hughes bought nearly 80 percent of the shares of TWA. Assuming hands-on management and applying his aviation secrets and practical experience, he developed a strategic plan for the airline that doubled TWA's income in 1940. Passengers rose 57 percent from 1939 to 1941, but Hughes had an even grander plan to create a fleet of superliners capable of carrying sixty or more passengers. He asked Lockheed to submit a bid to build the planes. The resulting airplane, the Constellation, set an industry standard for size, comfort, and range.

The war did not bring the prosperity to Hughes Aircraft that its founder had anticipated. Hughes aircraft and tool plants manufactured machine-gun chute feeders for B-17 bombers (which, ironically, used ball turrets produced by another maverick entrepreneur, Preston Tucker), as well as wing panels for trainer aircraft. Hughes Tool Company also provided manufactured parts for bombers and gun barrels for the U.S. Army. But Hughes hoped to develop unique wooden transport planes for the military, without any interest from the government. He poured millions of his own money into prototypes, including a spy plane, the XF-11, but he did not land a major aircraft contract until he signed a cooperative deal with Henry Kaiser to build a flying boat for the U.S. Navy in 1942.

The concept was simple: Defeat the U-boat threat by simply flying troops and materiel over it. The task, in reality, was gargantuan: No one ever had constructed a 200-ton airplane, let alone an aircraft that size built out of wood! His designers intended to bond skin and structural parts together in layers of wood and waterproof glues. The project proved beyond the capabilities of the Hughes–Kaiser companies within the time allocated (and, we should note, of any company since). The Hercules (derided as the "Spruce Goose") was not complete when the government canceled its contract. Infuriated, Hughes undertook an ill-advised test flight of the XF-11, which he flew longer than the test plan allowed. The XF-11 malfunctioned, then plummeted down, giving Hughes enough time to steer the plane over the Los Angeles Country Club, landing on the ninth hole in a blazing end-over-end crash. Nearly dead, Hughes was rescued, and after a desperate hospital stay, he cheated death. And, again, he flew.

The U.S. Senate had launched an investigation into Hughes and other "war profiteers" and required the eccentric Hughes, who reviled contact with strangers, to testify in person. Outraged, Hughes took advantage of a recess in the hearings to return to California for one last attempt to prove that the government had not wasted its money. With the "Spruce Goose" finally assembled, in October 1947, Hughes climbed into the pilot's seat. After taxiing around the bay, he opened the throttles of all eight engines—much to the surprise of his copilot—and the Hercules lifted off, flying for about a mile. Hughes had proved that the largest airplane ever built—and entirely of wood—could fly.[13]

Although the cumulative effects of the crashes and possible drug addiction accentuated Hughes's eccentricities, turning him into a virtual hermit and ending his personal contributions to the aircraft industry, Howard Hughes had shown that entrepreneurial progress came in all forms. His contributions to aviation, most clearly seen in the continued operations of TWA, affected the entire aircraft industry and helped give the United States its dominant lead in combat aviation by the end of World War II. On the other hand, Hughes lacked the same focus as other, more successful entrepreneurs, such as Henry Kaiser. In fact, he never fulfilled a single aircraft contract over which he had direct control. Years later, when Hughes Aircraft had a stellar reputation for building satellites and missiles, the company met its obligations and delivered hardware primarily because Hughes left it alone.

The fact that Hughes, along with Preston Tucker and Andrew Jackson Higgins, came under investigation after the war for profiteering or other alleged infractions indicated the morass that even the most capable entrepreneur found himself in when dealing with military contracts. And Hughes's nemesis, Juan Trippe? He merely introduced the first regular international jet airplane service with Pan Am, force-feeding jet engines into the aircraft market and democratizing travel.

HENRY KAISER AND ANDREW JACKSON HIGGINS BUILD SHIPS

Called by historian Paul Johnson the epitome of the American "capitalist folk hero," Henry J. Kaiser had participated in large-scale projects before the war, including (with John McCone and Henry Morrison) the Hoover, Bonneville, Grand Coulee, and Shasta dams, as well as San Francisco's Golden Gate Bridge. He had created the first integrated steel mill in the American West as well as a huge cement plant for his projects.[14]

Roosevelt placed Kaiser in charge of shipyards in California and the Pacific Northwest, instructing him to turn out ships, regardless of cost. Before he could do that, Kaiser surmised that he needed a larger workforce than California and the Northwest could provide. He placed ads in large papers around the nation, luring workers westward. When they arrived, knowing they needed housing, Kaiser embarked on the largest prefabricated home construction projects ever undertaken. With a workforce in place, Kaiser started to build Liberty ships, cutting construction time, at first, from 355 days to 108 days. In some cases, he directly changed ship welding or construction techniques, while in others he expanded the workforce or found ways to allow laborers to work smarter. Eventually, the mass-production methods reached a zenith when the Liberty ship *Robert E. Peary* was fabricated in less than five days! Kaiser yards turned out everything from cargo ships to aircraft carriers, with the final tally of the yards more than 1,400 warships and thousands of transport ships.

The government had learned during World War I that it needed experienced private managerial teams to run its contracts. That, in turn, meant giving additional resources to those who produced, such as Kaiser—an ironic twist in that New Deal bureaucrats, like Harold Ickes, had "systematically harassed" Kaiser in the 1930s.[15] Of course, this was serious, now. This was war.

Criticism of Kaiser developed after the war as well. Complaining that Kaiser was not a model of free enterprise, one historian argued that the government "supplied [Kaiser's] capital, furnished his market, and guaranteed his solvency on the cost-plus formula—and so spared him the need for cost efficiency ... and came close to guaranteeing his profits."[16] Historian Bruce Catton echoed similar sentiments in his *War Lords of Washington* (1948).[17] Those charges ignored a few obvious facts, the most glaring of which was that Kaiser was successful where others, receiving far more government support, failed. German, Italian, and Japanese businessmen, bound by socialistic governments and anticapitalist ideologies, were thoroughly outperformed, while Soviet manufacturers (lacking any free enterprise at all) were essentially driven by the lash and subsidized extensively through aid by people such as Kaiser![18] Critics also overlook the fact that after the war, Kaiser, when his profits were not guaranteed, did not hesitate to risk his fortune on an entirely new enterprise—automobiles. He bought aluminum plants in

Washington, Louisiana, and West Virginia, and his steel mill in California stood its ground with companies on the East Coast. Not only had he created the first prefabricated housing, but he introduced employee health care facilities, "the forerunner of modern health maintenance organization systems."[19] After the war, he moved to Hawaii, credited by his biographer, Mark Foster, as the "*malihini*, or newcomer, who exerted the greatest force in changing [Hawaii's tourist industry]."[20]

Henry Kaiser, a true "market entrepreneur," played the game under whatever rules existed. During the years 1941 to 1945, Uncle Sam wanted weapons and wanted them fast. Kaiser merely satisfied his customer, as did another capitalist pioneer of the age, Andrew Jackson Higgins. Born in landlocked Nebraska, Higgins had a lackluster high school career, then worked in the lumber business in Alabama, then settled in New Orleans, where he graduated from the slower sailing craft to speedboats.[21] Like Howard Hughes, Higgins loved speed, building racing boats that set records for the New Orleans–St. Louis course, before branching into pleasure craft in the early 1930s, expanding his business in the teeth of the Great Depression. Neither speedboats nor pleasure craft made Higgins so valuable to the war effort, however. Instead, responding to a demand for shallow drought fishing vessels for the bayous and narrow channels of south Louisiana, Higgins developed the "Spoonbill" bow that enabled his boats to run full speed onto sandbars or riverbanks.

Prior to World War II, the U.S. Marine Corps had shown an interest in the Higgins boats as amphibious warfare vessels. Higgins added a ramp that dropped forward onto a beach, allowing troops to charge off in rapid order. The LCPs (landing crafts, personnel) and LCMs (landing crafts, medium) gave the U.S. Navy and Marines exactly what they needed for amphibious operations. In 1941, Higgins Industries had $10 million in sales and $3 million in profits, placing Higgins on a plane equal to that of Kaiser. It had not come without personal hardship. One Higgins biographer described the situation as follows: "Twice bankrupt and once forced to sell his wife's jewelry, Higgins, who owned nearly 70 percent [of the stock,] could boast of being one of the wealthiest men living in the Deep South."[22] Seeing himself as an underdog, locked in competition with huge shipbuilders, such as Ingalls and Newport News, Higgins never wallowed in pity. He once said that he did not "wait for opportunity to knock. I sent out a welcoming committee to drag the old harlot in."[23]

Higgins's "welcoming committee" went out to find postwar business well before the conflict ended. Envisioning a peacetime market for pleasure craft and prefabricated wooden houses, Higgins encountered a raft of problems after 1945, including labor troubles. He closed Higgins Industries in 1945 rather than give in to union power. Opening a new corporation, he next ran into the Securities and Exchange Commission, which charged him with stock manipulation, much as fellow entrepreneur and ball-turret manufacturer, Preston Tucker, was charged and later cleared. The business floundered and, facing bankruptcy, was sold to a New York shipbuilding firm in 1959.

Detractors lamented that Kaiser, Higgins, and other large-scale producers received contracts at the expense of smaller companies. One study, for example, found that between 1940 and 1944, half of all contracts went to the top thirty-three corporations, and profits for smaller businesses fell from 26 percent to 19 percent between 1939 and 1944.[24] Numbers such as those obscure rather than enlighten. Small business, by nature, depended heavily on one individual or a handful of partners. Military service claimed thousands of such small-business owners, who gladly put on their country's uniform to fight, in the process condemning their business to a temporary state of suspended animation or, in the case of their own death, final extinction. Even in a partnership, the loss of an active partner to enlistment or the draft ended hundreds of small enterprises. Large corporations would neither die with the loss of an officer, nor were they likely to suffer if even a large percentage of the male employees went off to war. Instead, they hired women, and more than 8 million "Rosie the Riveters" joined the labor force.[25]

A second fact of life for new entrepreneurs and small businesses— high taxes—served as a death knell. The Revenue Act of 1942 raised the excess profits tax from 60 percent to 90 percent, making it virtually impossible for rapid growth through reinvested profits. Although high taxation partly accomplished one of its objectives—lessening the postwar debt by financing 40 percent of federal revenue from 1940 to mid-1944—tax rates on individuals rose to intolerable levels (94 percent on "the rich") and exemptions fell. More onerous, the Internal Revenue Service, beginning in 1943 (again with the cover of the war to insulate it from criticism) enacted a pay-as-you-go system, today known as withholding, to replace the one-time payment. By making taxes convenient and hidden, the government ensured that it could raise them with much less opposition in the future.[26] But perhaps the most crushing blow for entrepreneurs came when the government hiked the bottom tax bracket from 4.4 percent in 1940 to 23 percent in 1945, an increase of more than 400 percent! Under such burdens, only the largest and most secure businesses could survive.[27]

AMERICAN WARTIME PRODUCTION IN RETROSPECT

The absolute dominance of the American economy during the war had two additional results. First, it seriously damaged the notion that the New Deal had "rescued" or "saved" private enterprise from the excesses of capitalism. War had motivated business to productive levels not theretofore imagined. Why, then, had the New Deal not energized entrepreneurs? Perhaps, some thought, the business system had not needed saving after all. Such considerations played a key role in allowing the United States to return to a less-regulated and nonsocialized environment after 1945, in sharp contrast to Britain and the European nations.

Second, America's economic power translated directly into increasingly deadly technology—culminating, of course, with the atomic bomb—that the enemy could not match. That was true of Japan as early as 1942, when General Douglas MacArthur's troops in Guadalcanal achieved a 16:1 casualty ratio. At Kwajalein, that ratio reached nearly twice that, or 32:1. On the tactical level, such overwhelming productivity as American industry could provide led to almost comical matches. During the Normandy invasion, the Allies put 11,000 planes in the skies over the English Channel; Germany responded with two. Hitler, of course, ignored reality long before the Red Army arrived at his bunker. By then, even *der Führer*, in his madness, knew that Allied aircraft could vaporize entire cities, as they did in Hamburg in 1943, when almost 40 percent of the population died. He also knew, based on the failed attempts of German scientists to produce an atomic bomb, that the Allies could not be far from success.

Although Britain led the United States in early design work for the atomic bomb, once again the American drive to produce the weapon, regardless of cost, soon superseded the effort in England. Dubbed the

Manhattan Project, the ultrasecret research married European physics theory to Yankee resources and "entrepreneurial adventurism."[28] Roosevelt ultimately authorized $5 billion for the project, which he placed under General Leslie Groves, who in turn enlisted the best scientists, then ruled them with a mixture of threats and encouragement. Groves acquired any resource the Manhattan Project required, and, in the course of work, the team created the first fully automated factory, the first plant operated by remote control, and the first sterile industrial process (which laid the foundation for all subsequent work in computer chip manufacturing). Estimates have put the compression factor—that is, the time under normal peacetime circumstances needed to accomplish the same work—at seven. The Manhattan Project developed the bomb in four years, while it should have taken thirty.

A final explanation for why the war experience allowed the recovery of industry, when the New Deal did not, lies in the attitude of government toward entrepreneurs. In the case of war, the nation knew it needed its business leaders, and so it restored to them the power and prestige that had been stripped away by Ickes, Tugwell, and other New Dealers. By renewing business confidence in private property rights, the war accomplished what FDR could not. Regardless, World War II demonstrated once again that when it came to the American military, the "arsenal of democracy" could provide the nation's soldiers and sailors with unprecedented firepower and cutting-edge technology.[29]

GOVERNMENT AND MANAGEMENT OF BUSINESS

Aware of the need to squeeze the most out of the private sector that he had assaulted for almost a decade, Roosevelt realized he had to provide incentives to business. The government permitted accelerated amortization of plant expansion, for example, and frequently used the more profitable "cost-plus" contracts. Antitrust prosecutions abruptly ended. To the extent that he could, though, FDR remained a central planner, and he sought to manage the wartime buildup through a jungle of bureaus and panels. Prewar planning had been "mismanaged, confused, and marked by political expediency."[30] One FDR-appointed board, charged with preparing a mobilization plan, failed miserably when Roosevelt refused to appoint a chairman, causing the public to refer to the commission members as the "Headless Horsemen."[31]

Ultimately, the RFC under Jesse Jones emerged as the most powerful of the prewar bodies. Jones himself later admitted that the RFC wielded "perhaps the broadest powers ever conferred upon a single government agency."[32] Jones's vast powers still proved inadequate to organize all the wartime agencies into a coherent force, and in 1942 yet another body was created, the War Production Board (WPB), headed by Donald Nelson, a Sears and Roebuck executive. The WPB entirely ended production of some consumer goods, such as autos, but it lacked the power granted the WIB during the First World War. Instead, Roosevelt created even *another* layer of management, the Office of War Mobilization (renamed the Office of War Mobilization and Reconversion in 1944), under the "assistant president" James F. "Jimmy" Burns. The resulting maze of bureaucratic structures, dominated by a struggle for succession to the presidency, meant that "the Roosevelt administration ... did a poor job in coordinating the economic side of the war effort...."[33] Fortunately, the offices only supervised the production of the Higginses and Kaisers, with occasional suggestions as to what they should build. Some have credited the government with eliminating the risk for entrepreneurs, for example, by owning most of the plant capacity for manufacturing of weapons and large-scale tools. Those facilities were virtually unwanted after the war, testifying to their uselessness in building peacetime, consumer goods. Auto dreamer Preston Tucker acquired the largest aircraft plant in the world for almost nothing from the government, so he had more space than an automaker twice his size could use to manufacture his revolutionary "Tucker Torpedoes." Nor was he an exception: Many facilities were given away for a song. Far from providing business with state-of-the-art factories, the government had thrown up the structure for a wonderfully efficient war machine, but one totally unrelated to peacetime needs. War's last blessing for business was that it gave the National Association of Manufacturers (NAM) a break from New Deal legislation long enough for the "voice" of manufacturers to transform and reshape its public relations and labor policies. As a result, NAM regained influence that it had lost during the Depression, achieving at least equal footing with labor.[34]

World War II did not vindicate Keynesianism, and it was not government spending per se that stirred American business out of the Great Depression.[35] Robert Higgs has shown that if one examines personal consumption expenditures, when properly deflated for the effects of price controls, real consumption fell after 1941 and did not recover until 1945, not significantly growing until the postwar period.[36] It was not a simple equation, "government money in, production up," but rather a crisis situation that prompted American entrepreneurs to plunge themselves and their resources ruthlessly into the cause of defeating the totalitarian powers. It also spurred millions of Americans to sacrifice, both in consumption and to commit themselves to extended work hours, to defeat Hitler, Tojo, and Mussolini. (Of course, it goes without saying that vast numbers of soldiers, sailors, and airmen made the ultimate sacrifice.) As Higgs concludes, "It is difficult to understand how working harder, longer, more inconveniently and dangerously in return for a diminished flow of consumer goods comports with the description that 'economically speaking, Americans never had it so good.'"[37] The Nazi threat, not the Keynesian promise, spurred the most astounding military buildup in history. While huge amounts of resources were employed in defeating the Axis powers, as the authors of a study on unemployment in this period concluded, "the World War II era is less of an economic success story than is often portrayed."[38] They calculated the growth rate during the war years at a good but not exceptional 4 percent, but cautioned that the price deflators were subject to dispute. Furthermore, they argued that if more realistic deflators are used, real wages may have even *fallen* during the "Keynesian expansion."

Instead of producing a recovery through government demand, the war endowed American business with a level of credibility that collapsed on Black Thursday, restoring the nation's entrepreneurs in the public esteem that disappeared during the Depression. The pent-up consumer demand that had been interrupted by the Great Depression and the war returned stronger than ever after Japan's surrender. Wartime production was the best public relations campaign the American business sector could have mounted, creating a momentum that swept it into the preeminent position in the world after the conflict.

AMERICAN BUSINESS
DOMINATES THE WORLD

Once the ink on the surrender documents dried, the war officially ended. But a serious conflict remained: The Soviet Union was a power-ful enemy, the governments of many European countries teetered on the brink of collapse, and the communist parties in almost every nation saw in the wartime destruction potential for radical political change. The United States had to ensure that the victory gained on the battle-fields and in the factories was not lost at the ballot box.

At that point, American business again stepped in to flex the sinews of democracy. The U.S. GNP in 1950 reached $284 billion, almost triple the level of 1940 ($100 billion). More important, the U.S. share of world industrial production reached almost 45 percent in 1953, and the U.S. share of world trade steadied at more than 15 percent. European nations and Japan had few factories capable of producing domestic goods such as automobiles or radios. That gave American business a market of captive consumers. Moreover, the United States entered the postwar period with the most efficient industrial machine in the world, making it the world's leading supplier. Business saw the potential of that situation readily.

Trade with Europe and Japan required that foreign countries have money and, ultimately, some productive capacity to generate their own wealth. The Marshall Plan (1947) offered $12.5 billion in direct aid to more than a dozen democratic nations in Europe, specifically to short-circuit communist disaffection with the governments there. American banks generously supplied loans, bought European government and industrial bonds, and otherwise facilitated an economic revival. Historians have referred to the results as either a "European Miracle" or written of the "European Lazarus."[39] Japan was occupied for seven years after the war ended while America restructured the Japanese government, legal system, and business procedures. By 1968, Japan had developed into a world economic power and trading partner.[40]

Loans provided a way for foreigners to obtain dollars to buy American products until such time as they could sell their own goods for dollars. But foreigners also "bought American" when possible, and U.S. businesses responded by producing high-quality goods that were superior to those made in other places in the world. "American made" constituted a trademark of excellence. Whether in automobiles, electronics, or clothes, American dominance was clearly visible. U.S. auto manufacturers made 9 million cars in 1955, more than four times as many as Germany, France, Italy, and Canada put together![41] The car culture not only affected Americans, who owned more autos than the rest of the world put together, but it placed a final ironic epitaph on the Nazi gravestone, mocking Hitler's promise that the Germans would have a "people's car," with the resulting U.S. freeway system dwarfing the vaunted autobahn. Despised by intellectuals as the epitome of crass consumerism, cars offered independence that the Europeans envied, proving even effective weapons in the Cold War. When John Ford's movie *The Grapes of Wrath* was shown in the Soviet Union in hopes of depicting the plight of American migrant laborers, Soviet authorities were dismayed to find that Russian viewers "were impressed by a country where even some of the most abject of poor people wore shoes and owned cars."[42] Ford and GM especially competed to satiate the foreign demand for American cars; but the car companies were hardly alone. Increased overseas trade and investment pushed U.S. firms into the international arena as never before. Foreign investment by American entrepreneurs dated back to the nineteenth century, with the construction of a railroad in the Panama Canal region. Vanderbilt and others, of course, had established facilities in Central America, and I. M. Singer's sewing machine plant in Glasgow, Scotland, constituted one of the first "offshore" production facilities owned by Americans. Singer's sales abroad made up half of all the company's sales by 1874. Western Electric followed, building a manufacturing plant in Belgium in 1882, while Edison, Standard Oil, Eastman Kodak, and American Tobacco all established American-owned foreign sources of distribution.[43]

For almost a century, America had been a debtor nation. Indeed, the periods of its most rapid growth—in the 1830s and 1850s, for example—were characterized by extremely high foreign investment, mostly British. World War I changed the situation, making New York the world's money center and the United States a creditor nation. Paradoxically, some managers sought to invest abroad out of fear. They had accepted the view, somewhat inherent in the managerial hierarchies, that domestic markets were exhausted and that Americans could buy no more appliances, steel, or clothes. That message, preached early in the century by communist dictator Vladimir Lenin in his *Imperialism: The Highest Stage of Capitalism*, reached sympathetic ears in the United States, where the depressions of the 1890s and 1907 intensified the belief that American markets were saturated. Quite the contrary, there may have been a glut of "bads," as George Gilder calls them, but there was no glut of "goods." Incredible new technologies had just been invented, including the automobile and the radio and even household devices like the electric washer and electric iron, awaiting only the infusion of new capital and the maturation of related technologies to bring them to consumers.

After World War II, interest in foreign markets revived. As the Europeans and Japanese became genuine competitors, American business moved to establish a permanent presence abroad.[44] Often, the multinational corporation, which had joint ownership by Americans and foreign investors, or which was a corporation with producing branches or subsidiaries in more than one country, proved the only acceptable solution as many nations resisted penetration by U.S. firms. Beginning in the 1950s, led by the petroleum companies' investments in the Middle East and Asia, multinational expansion accelerated. Then, in the period 1960–80, multinationals exploded, with the value of American direct investment overseas rising from $32 billion to $227 billion (and surging to almost $2 trillion by the late 1980s).[45] Of course, business welcomed and benefited from government assistance: The Agency for International Development, for example, subsidized loans to firms investing in foreign countries; the United States Import-Export Bank facilitated transfers of funds; and both the International Bank for Reconstruction and Development and the Inter-American Development Bank provided incentives for multinational expansion.

BUSINESS, BUILDING, AND BABIES

War's capital demands required that the government restrain consumer spending from 1942 to 1945. Price controls eased just as waves of servicemen returned home to marry and start families. With bulging bank accounts and new children on the way, the postwar families needed new housing, and they purchased homes at an unprecedented pace. Banks used loans from the Veterans Administration (VA) and the Federal Housing Administration (FHA) programs, which the federal government insured, to accommodate millions of new and first-time homeowners. In 1948, approximately 18 million Americans owned their homes, and within five years 25 million were homeowners. The situation stood in stark contrast to the dark days of the Depression and "Hoovervilles."

Housing contractors benefited from two shifts that took place almost simultaneously. First, in most cities, middle-class families started to move to the "suburbs"—outlying residential communities developed out of farmland. Suburbs sprang up as mass-production techniques, such as those used by Henry Kaiser, were adapted to the postwar housing shortage. Suburban living also benefited from the other "big-ticket" item purchased by most families after the war: the automobile. Auto sales soared after 1946, giving unprecedented mobility to families and allowing them to live farther from the workplace.

At that point, great bankers joined with dynamic builders, and the countryside bloomed with structures. The most famous suburb, Levittown, New York, on Long Island, was adding a new home every fifteen minutes by the year 1950 when house builder William Levitt appeared on the cover of *Time* magazine.[46] But the real crucible where builders and bankers forged an alliance that had implications for the entire nation was in the West, particularly California and Arizona. California home building had advanced as the Bank of America, under A. P. Giannini's son, Mario, used the FHA/VA loans at record levels, providing builder Paul Trousdale enough money to construct two houses a day, seven days a week. During one stretch, Trousdale had 300 houses under construction each day. By 1948 alone, the Bank of America had $600 million in housing loans outstanding, and during the 1950s the bank supplied San Francisco builder Henry Doelger, who began with a credit line of $110,000 in 1936, with more than $75 million to put up tracts in Los Angeles.[47]

As early as 1951, California was linked to 23 percent of all FHA/VA mortgage loans bought nationally and, per capita, perhaps exceeded only by Valley National Bank in Arizona.[48] Even a tiny insurance agency, the A. B. Robbs Agencies, got in on the action by originating FHA/VA loans, using insurance money from the Northeast. Between 1947 and 1950, the small company acquired the accounts of nine East Coast investors, who purchased more than $12 million in FHA/VA mortgages. By 1953, the company had twenty Eastern investors and $30 million worth of home mortgages, supporting the phenomenal growth of Phoenix, which by 1958 ranked eleventh among the nation's top cities in new home construction.[49]

The growth of cities such as Phoenix, Los Angeles, Albuquerque, El Paso, San Diego, Tampa, Orlando, Dallas, and Houston characterized a geographical relocation from the Rust Belt to the Sun Belt. It had started during the war as contractors and military personnel relocated to the open areas for security purposes. As an increasing number of people were exposed to the natural beauty and generally pleasant climate, they returned after the war or when they retired, sparking yet more opportunity for entrepreneurs to provide goods and services. Open spaces around most of the Sun Belt cities offered room for expansion, and in the West in particular, the uninhabited areas provided essential space to develop and test military weapons, aircraft, and cars. The dry climates of Southern California, Arizona, and parts of Texas and New Mexico soon attracted electronics manufacturers and, later, computer chip makers.

Quickly, a major demographic shift occurred in which the American population moved from North to South and from East to West, bringing with it the relocations of major enterprises—or at least, the establishment of large, regional subsidiaries. State governments contributed to the new, hospitable climate for business through a number of specific policies, including lower taxes, construction of state-of-the-art airports, and "right-to-work" laws that eliminated union pressure and lowered wage costs to businesses. Yet labor did not suffer, because the cost of living was cheaper and taxes were lower than in the unionized Rust Belt states. Over a thirty-year period, Lockheed, Motorola, Delta Air Lines, Disney, Martin Marietta, McDonnell Douglas, Boeing, Hewlett-Packard, Garrett, Dole Foods, Rockwell, and many others either expanded or relocated to the Sun Belt, and they needed housing for their employees. These new homes had to be furnished, landscaped, then "improved." Homeowners would find there was no end to the list of these home improvements.

EMMETT J. CULLIGAN: "HEY, CULLIGAN MAN"

At age 28, a landowner with property valued at more than $200,000, Emmett Culligan was on top of the world. He had a reputation as a shrewd business negotiator, farmer, and land developer. Then a recession struck, knocking the price of Culligan's land to almost nothing. Bankrupt, Culligan had to leave California, where he had just settled in 1919, and return to frozen St. Paul, Minnesota, to live with his mother.

Unwilling to wallow in pity or despair, Culligan happened upon an old friend who sold a water filter device that removed hard minerals from water by using a natural greensand called zeolite. Culligan borrowed a bag of the sand, experimented with it in a coffee can he had perforated, and used tap water to wash diapers. Immediately he determined that his future was in water treatment.

Culligan began by selling products for his friend's company, then started his own firm in St. Paul in 1924. Difficulties still battered Culligan, with a nasty patent suit costing him more than $40,000. Although he won the battle—the case, in this instance—he lost the war: With little money left, his company died during the Great Crash. Gold Dust Culligan Company overnight became dustbin Culligan. Twelve years had ensued since his last fortune disappeared, and again, Culligan was broke. He moved again, this time to Illinois to take a job with a minerals company. He continued to ponder the main problem of his now-defunct business, however—namely, how to bring down the cost of the $200 to $400 water softener.

The difficulty was in selling the product. What if he could lease it, selling, in essence, a water treatment service? Basing his business on the telephone company's practices, Culligan would install the machines at no charge for a monthly user's fee. He then launched his new enterprise at a time most experts would deem disastrous, in 1936, during the peak of the Great Depression. He had only $50 and a small bank loan, taking out a lease on space in a Northbrook, Illinois, blacksmith shop. He made conditioning machines out of spare parts and used water tanks from junkyards; he saved on electricity by using a converted auto engine to run his machinery. When he started to market his product, he stressed that the customer could cancel the service at any time with no further obligation. He had over half a million subscribers on the eve of World War II.

But consumers of the 1950s were different from those of the 1930s. In the past, Culligan had hired salesmen to go into homes to demonstrate the products, much like the famous vacuum-cleaner salesmen and the "Fuller Brush Men." The door-to-door salesman was viewed as a nuisance in the new suburban environment, however, and Culligan struggled to find a way to get inside people's homes for the critical demonstrations. In 1959, a Los Angeles ad company came up with a new advertising campaign with a woman yelling, "Hey, Culligan Man." The promotions worked, reviving at-home sales and providing the water-softener company with a well-known image. By the early 1960s, Culligan sales had doubled, and Emmett Culligan retired—for once, not forced out by unpleasant circumstances.[50]

A NEW WORLD FOR MOMS

The population shift not only meant more builders and developers appeared in the West and South than ever before, but it signaled a fundamental transformation of American business. Electronics, computers, biomedical instruments, financial services, and defense-related businesses all started to boom. With important exceptions in Massachusetts and parts of New York, most of the new growth occurred in the West and South, although these structural changes remained hidden because autos, steel, coal, and the traditional chemical industries still commanded much of the world market. But it was readily apparent in the growth of the banking systems of states like California, North Carolina, Georgia, Arizona, and, to a lesser extent, Texas and Oklahoma, where the financial sector outpaced banking growth in the Midwest and North. Whereas in previous eras, large manufacturing businesses may have had to obtain credit from New York or Chicago, by the late 1950s and early 1960s they could get loans from the Bank of America, Texas Commerce, Security Pacific, or powerful regional giants.[51]

New houses reflected the need for more family space as well as simple mobility to new locations, because families themselves were growing. In 1947, a record 3.8 million babies were born—hence the famous baby boom generation—and the rising birth levels continued until 1964. Between 1950 and 1960, the U.S. population, including immigrants, rose from 150 million to 179 million. By 1958, kids fifteen years and under made up almost one-third of the population; toy sales that year exceeded $1 billion; and diaper services swelled into a $50 million business. Children were not only the objects of parental love but of parental consumption, and they, themselves, consumed. Frank Gerber's baby food company took off during the boom years under the leadership of his son, Dan. Running a small canning company with his father, Dan had a firsthand encounter with straining baby food in the 1920s when he had to delay a social engagement to prepare peas. They had first introduced canned baby food in the late 1920s, offering their products for free to mothers and their children who would test them. Achieving national sales with an ad in *Good Housekeeping*, the company gained stability in the 1930s, but it wasn't until the late 1940s that it took off. In 1948, the company sold 2 million cans of baby food a day, marketing its product with a label that featured a charcoal sketch of a baby's head. Capturing the look of innocence, the "Gerber baby" has since found its way into most American households. The company introduced chemical additives to its product to make the taste more appealing and to preserve it on grocery shelves, and by the end of the 1950s, store-bought baby food was associated with a single name, Gerber.[52]

War also introduced thousands of new women to the workforce, and while the postwar baby boom sent most women home to raise their children, as the kids got older, mothers looked for part-time jobs to help fill the days. Russell Kelly had the perfect position for them. Kelly, who had served as a fiscal management analyst in the Army Quartermaster Corps, had created a centralized system to speed up typing, duplicating, and addressing business correspondence among Detroit firms. He brought the work to his office, until an emergency call in 1946 from an accountant looking for a typist gave Kelly a new idea: hiring skilled, temporary workers to businesses from a central location. He recruited at churches and PTAs, training older women who were discriminated against because of their age. The employees were known as "Kelly Girls" for decades. By the 1970s, Kelly Services had grown into the largest provider of temporary services in the United States.[53]

In 1945, Earl Tupper founded the Tupper Plastics Company with a patent bought from the U.S. government for an airtight bowl to store food that closed with a "burp." In 1948, his innovative product was sold by Stanley Home Products through its "Hostess Group Demonstration

Plan," a combined social gathering and sales event. Tupper's product became so successful that a new company was formed just to sell it. Representing the fact that the product was marketed to women, the new company appointed a divorced mother, Brownie Wise, as general sales manager in 1951. Another woman joined the company management in 1953. The "hostesses" were all independent contractors, working for products or other commissions. In July 1958, Earl Tupper sold the product to the Rexall Drug and Chemical Company for $16 million, bought an island in Central America, and retired.[54]

UNPRECEDENTED TRAVEL OPPORTUNITIES SPAWN NEW BUSINESSES

Faced with a postwar slump (temporarily alleviated by the Korean War military orders), the aviation industry aimed at new business from family and corporate travelers. Airline companies, such as Eastern, American, and TWA, offered "coach class" tickets to compete with railroads. Passengers could fly most anywhere in the country for a few hundred dollars—still a substantial sum, but significantly cheaper than ever before. Pan Am's Juan Trippe observed that for the first time, ordinary people could afford air travel, and airplanes opened up the same vistas in the late 1950s that trains had a century earlier. Boardings doubled between 1951 and 1958, to 38 million, and on a single day in 1954 New York City played host to the first air traffic jam when 300 airliners stacked up in holding patterns above the Big Apple, delaying 45,000 passengers.[55]

Flights became faster and routes expanded to new locations. In 1953, TWA offered the first nonstop air service from New York to California. TWA and Pan Am raced to offer the first nonstop Atlantic flights, with Pan Am the victor. Trippe's company introduced the first true transatlantic airliner, built by Douglas Aircraft (the DC-7) in 1957, surpassing the Lockheed-built Lodestar as the most advanced passenger aircraft. Thanks to the DC-7, Pan Am could compete with TWA, which had provided transatlantic flights with only a single refueling stop since the early 1950s, introducing travelers to a new physical and mental malady called "jet lag."

When people could not fly, at least they could travel in their cars. Approximately 40 million cars transited the nation's 1.6 million miles of surfaced highways by 1950. Some 60 percent of the households owned at least one car, and the "Big Three" (Ford, General Motors, and Chrysler) dominated this market. A handful of smaller competitors struggled to stay in business, including Nash, Hudson, Studebaker, and Willys-Overland, and a new entrant, Kaiser-Frazer, experienced strong sales growth. Nevertheless, Ford and GM posted healthy profits: Both automakers produced their 50 millionth vehicle in the 1950s, and GM controlled more than 50 percent of the market. Chevrolet alone offered forty-six models, thirty-two different engines, and more than 400 accessories by 1960. Chrysler, meanwhile, lagged behind Ford and GM because it had the most substantial reconversion to do after the war. Ford made trucks during the war—and still did—but Chrysler had made tanks, which had no postwar demand. Yet Chrysler retained a position well above the smaller competitors, making it appear on the surface that the Big Three were impenetrable.

Henry Kaiser's attempt to crack into the auto market illustrated that even the extreme concentration in the industry by the late 1940s could not keep out new entrants. Founded in 1945 by Kaiser and partner Joseph Frazer, the Kaiser-Frazer Company consistently lost money despite increasing sales. It had a good product, but as Kaiser later admitted, his company was terribly undercapitalized from the start. Initial stock offerings received a warm welcome on Wall Street, raising $16 million, but all things are relative. Kaiser needed $320 million to make a dent in the market. Within five years, despite consistently rising sales, the company recorded a $34 million loss. The end came in 1950 when Kaiser-Frazer introduced the "Henry J," a compact car priced at $2,000, aimed at the frugal middle-class buyer. Instead, American customers chose a new European product, Germany's Volkswagen, and Kaiser ended production of the Henry J in 1954. Kaiser-Frazer ceased all auto production in the United States in 1955, by all accounts having entered the business more than $2 billion short of the necessary ante.[56] On the other hand, Kaiser had proved that, sufficiently capitalized, a new auto company could have a future, and that contrary to the depiction in the Francis Ford Coppola film *Tucker: The Man and His Dream*, no "Detroit conspiracy" kept entrepreneurs out of the industry. Quite the contrary, Kaiser showed that managerial talent made up for a myriad of other weaknesses, suggesting that Tucker was more dreamer than businessman.

AMERICANS, AUTOS, AND THE SEARCH FOR FAMILIARITY

Contrary to most textbook coverage of the 1950s, which portrays the decade as one of drab sameness, near-robotized daily life, and tranquility, the 1950s represented a period of great angst about the atomic bomb, race relations, and new mobility.[57] For the first time, large numbers of Americans could, and did, travel extensively. Yet this newfound freedom of movement for pleasure as well as business also contained a search for the familiar, whether in food, hotels, or music. Some of the most familiar American businesses identified these trends and developed products or services to address them.

Kemmons Wilson, a Tennessee architect-builder, frequently, like other travelers, stayed with his family in one of the numerous motels across the nation. He always had the same complaints. Rooms were dirty, there was not enough space for kids, and children were charged the same as adults. Wilson decided to open his own motel chain, but not before he had in mind the ideal dimensions, conveniences, and facilities he wanted for himself in a motel. After traveling cross-country with his wife and family, staying every night in a different room, Wilson had his composite motel firmly in mind. He designed the optimal room for a family of four and decided that kids would stay free at his motel. In 1954, Wilson opened the first Holiday Inn. Common sense dictated that each motel would have the same features, but did not have to be identical. So while the 400 green-and-gold inns with more than 30,000 rooms that were scattered across thirty-five states by 1962 all conformed to Wilson's original design specifications, each also maintained certain idiosyncratic touches that made it special. The Alexandria, Minnesota, Holiday Inn featured a bar shaped like a Viking ship and a pool area enclosed under the trademarked "Holidome" that allowed residents to swim in any weather—an especially useful characteristic of a motel in the frozen North. At Las Cruces, New Mexico, the Holiday Inn featured a restaurant area designed as an enclosed miniature city skyline of old Mesilla (the original Mexican pueblo where Las Cruces now stands). Wilson, appearing on a television talk show in the 1970s dedicated to self-made men, pointed out that he never sought to get rich. All he wanted was to provide Americans a place where a family could get a "good night's sleep" at no extra cost for children.[58]

Camping was a popular way to avoid even the modest cost of a Holiday Inn. The national parks offered campsites for free. Families loaded the car with a canvas tent, a camp stove, and sleeping bags and could take the family on vacation for practically no cost. Those who wanted more comfort could buy a tiny travel trailer to pull behind the car. John Crean went to work making those trailers in 1946, but had trouble keeping a job because of his drinking problem. In 1949, he began tinkering around in his father-in-law's garage to improve upon the venetian blinds that were de rigueur window treatments in the trailers of the postwar period. By 1950, married with two children and still living with his in-laws, Crean quit drinking and founded a company that evolved into Fleetwood, a Fortune 500 manufacturer of motor homes and manufactured housing.[59]

The widespread availability of car and airplane travel, placed within the budget of ordinary people, not only opened up the vast new motel business, but improved transportation of all manufactured products and made delivery of everything from mail to mussels and peas to porcelain more rapid and hence cheaper. Detroit automakers and hotel magnates across the country celebrated when Congress passed the National Highway Act in 1956 to construct vast new four-lane interstate highways across the United States. Just as the railroad subsidies had accelerated the dominance of trains, so did the Highway Act ensure the triumph of passenger cars and freight trucking, completing the victory already under way in the auto industry. Already, however, the increased—and increasingly rapid—highway travel, along with the appearance of suburbs, had facilitated the phenomenal rise of one of the best-known chains in American business history.[60]

Just as Americans looked for places to stay that were familiar, the mobility of the automobile brought a new premium to restaurants that could provide consistent, reliable meals. A fifty-two-year-old paper cup salesman seems an unlikely candidate to start the largest fast-food empire in the world. Perhaps more surprising, Ray Kroc had just quit his sales job to focus on a new device, a multiple-milkshake mixer, throwing aside any security he had built in his former position. But paper cups had led him to the milkshake mixer, and the mixer took him from Chicago to the McDonald brothers' store in San Bernardino, California.

Kroc had heard of Mac and Dick McDonald's drive-in that assembled fries, hamburgers, and beverages on a mass-production basis, and in 1954 he traveled to California to observe the operation in person. He later said, in his autobiography *Grinding It Out*, that "I felt like some latter-day Newton who'd just had an Idaho potato caromed off his skull."[61] Kroc admired the simplicity of the procedures that allowed the McDonald brothers to concentrate on quality. He "was carried away by the thought of McDonald's drive-ins proliferating like rabbits, with eight Multi mixers in each one."[62] Working out a franchise agreement with the brothers, Kroc envisioned a network of drive-in restaurants, with each building like the original (including the famous Golden Arches) and the name, McDonald's, on all of them. It took a year to open his first locations in Des Plaines, Illinois, which Kroc perceptively saw as a prototype of many other stores; therefore, he repeatedly refined the design to eliminate problems. During that time, Kroc continued to sell multiple-milkshake mixers, working, in essence, two full-time jobs. The key, as he saw it, was to maintain the quality he had witnessed in California, and he paid strict attention to the tiniest details, whether cleaning up the litter in the parking lot or turning on the sign at exactly dusk. As Kroc said, "Perfection is very difficult to achieve, and perfection was what I wanted in McDonald's. Everything else was secondary for me."[63]

Ray Kroc carefully tailored a family image. But above all, he didn't want people hanging around to eat. There were no jukeboxes, no pay phones, no vending machines, and the chairs were somewhat uncomfortable. After more than a year, the first location started to operate as Kroc hoped. He then expanded with three franchises into California, where he could show potential lessees and landlords the successful San Bernardino drive-in still run by the McDonald brothers. By 1956, Kroc opened eight stores in eight months, moving back to the Midwest with some of his new locations. After five years, McDonald's had 200 restaurants; by 1963, it opened more than 100 per year. Kroc established a training facility, called "Hamburger University," that put employees through the rigors of making every product served at McDonald's. Hamburger U., though, soon took on the task of training McDonald's owners and primary operators.

Meanwhile, McDonald's had purchased millions of potatoes, which it stored to achieve the special McDonald's flavor. That storage cost a great deal of money and was inefficient. One major supplier, J. R. Simplot of Idaho, had sold potatoes to the original McDonald brothers, and while Kroc took over the business and made it grow, Simplot experimented with an easier way of storing spuds. He had managed to freeze-dry both onions and potatoes, and suggested the concept to Kroc, who agreed to try frozen french fries at a few stores. On the basis of a handshake, Simplot invested in a facility capable of producing 39,000 pounds of fries an hour. By 1960, Simplot produced 170 million pounds of frozen french fries, and sold approximately 40 percent of them to McDonald's.[64]

Simplot's breakthroughs in freezing potatoes reflected similar advances in other frozen foods that were once considered a luxury, but by the 1950s were now a staple of suburban homes. The rapidly expanding supermarket chains, including Safeway, Kroger, and A&P, had added massive freezer sections. Manufacturers such as Birds Eye, Libby, and Minute Maid also acquired new refrigerated trucks to safely haul their products. Once again, standardized products were desirable to consumers in an era of fragmentation and growing mobility.[65]

If McDonald's represented the postwar approach to fast food for the average citizen, rock 'n' roll and rhythm and blues captured the new musical tastes as music became big business. At the same time, the burgeoning entertainment industry offered opportunities in areas that had scarcely been exploited in the past. Two of the most original entertainment companies launched in the 1950s, Motown Records and the Disneyland theme park, in odd ways reflected the continued impact of the automobile. They also illustrated the entrepreneurial opportunities that waited in the field of entertainment that made allowances for mobility and travel.

Detroit assembly-line worker Berry Gordy, Jr., aspired to write songs. He had even opened a jazz-oriented record store in 1955—an enterprise that failed, but provided Gordy with experience in record retailing. Along with his sister and a friend, Gordy wrote a song recorded by Jackie Wilson, who soon returned to the autoworker for another ditty. Gordy penned "Lonely Teardrops," and his connection to Wilson led him to an up-and-coming group called Smokey Robinson and the Miracles. Gordy virtually stole them from under the nose of another studio, paid for their recording costs, and leased their record to nationally distributed labels.

Under a number of different labels and organizations, Gordy continued to record, produce, and publish songs by a variety of black Detroit and northern Indiana acts. Using $800 that he borrowed from his family, in 1959 he formed Tamla Records, which recorded the

Temptations and Mary Wells, along with his current bands, such as the Miracles. Although some of the acts never achieved notoriety, many of the Motown songs—often written by Gordy—became classics: "Do You Love Me? (Now That I Can Dance)" and "Money," for example. They all featured a common sound, with the drums brought to the fore on as strong a plane as the vocals, driving the beat like a Detroit diesel. Gordy reorganized Tamla in 1960 as Motown Records, taking his name from the auto industry that he had worked in for so long. The sound seemed to fit the city.[66]

With U.S. record sales reaching $600 million in 1960, Gordy had entered the market at the right time. Motown had some of the hottest groups in the nation, and, despite the fact that all the Motown acts were black in a nation where many stations refused to play black artists, Motown dominated the charts. Early Motown stars included the Supremes ("Where Did Our Love Go?" and "You Keep Me Hangin' On"), the Four Tops ("I Can't Help Myself" and "Baby, I Need Your Loving"), and the Jackson 5 ("ABC," "I'll Be There," "Never Can Say Goodbye"). The Motown sound became such an integral part of American culture; even today, dozens of television and radio commercials continue to use the familiar tunes with new variations of lyrics to sell products. Almost without thinking, people sang along to the catchy melodies.

Gordy developed a formula that did for music what Ray Kroc had done for hamburgers, applying an assembly-line approach to record production. All groups had access to staff songwriters, choreographers, and etiquette coaches. He knew that although he had to keep the core black audience, real growth only could occur if he tapped into the other 88 percent of the listening and record-buying market. Groups had to look good and dance even better; they were instructed on public speaking for interviews, ditching black inner-city dialect in favor of proper English, and they had to maintain, at least in public, proper manners. Most of all, they had to stick to the formula. That meant that Gordy did not want groups writing their own material—an issue that finally drove Michael Jackson and the Jackson 5 to a new record label. Finally, Gordy realized the facts of recording industry profits—namely, that while the popularity went to the performers, the profits went to the producers and owners of the songs.

By 1972, *Black Enterprise* magazine recognized Motown as the top black-owned business in America. Although Motown eventually lost most of its top artists over the control issues that drove Jackson away, it set the example for black and other minority-owned businesses. Appealing to whites, Gordy proved that business is not a "race thing," but a "money thing." Moreover, except for A&M Records, no other company has survived as Motown did simply by expanding from a string of hits.

As unlikely as an auto assembly-line worker was to develop a major record company, it was perhaps even more unlikely that a cartoon artist whose claim to fame was a stick-figure mouse would establish the standard for interactive entertainment, theme park operations, and crowd control. Walt Disney (1901–1966) had gained a reputation as a cartoon genius for his *Steamboat Willie* talking cartoon in 1928. He moved from cartoon shorts to animated full-length features with *Snow White and the Seven Dwarfs* in 1934, defying the naysayers who claimed no one would pay for a full-length cartoon, especially at the height of the Great Depression! Instead, with the success of *Snow White,* Disney added 750 employees to his studios.

"Walt," as everyone referred to Walter Elias Disney, always considered himself a child trapped in an adult's body. He loved amusement parks, yet found most of them dirty, disorganized, and with rides frequently broken. After spending one uncomfortable day at an amusement with his two daughters, Disney nurtured a vision of an amusement park that would be immaculately clean, with well-mannered staff, and a source of optimism, patriotism, and good, clean family fun. Unable to convince his brother, Roy, who handled the studio's finances, to support the project, Walt cashed in his life insurance policy in 1952 and created WED Enterprises to fund his dream: Disneyland. Walt's "Disneyland" would be free of litter, hustlers, unsuitably dressed workers or guests, and any other sights not meant for children. He located the theme park in an orange grove near Anaheim, California. Although studies he commissioned had estimated the costs at $11 million, Disney had to pour $17 million into the park before it opened. In an incredible act of faith, Disney had staked his last penny on Disneyland.

Construction began on the 160-acre park behind twenty-five-foot-high embankments to shield it from public view. During construction, Disney convinced the American Broadcasting Company (ABC) to air a weekly show from the park for which ABC paid $500,000 and guaranteed $4.5 million more. In addition, ABC purchased one-third of Disneyland stock (kept separate from WED, which owned one-third, while Disney personally owned 17 percent).

On July 17, 1955, Disneyland opened with national television coverage. The cameras recorded a steady stream of disasters. Water fountains were in short supply on the hot day due to a plumbers strike. Twice as many people showed up than were expected. Fess Parker, the star of Disney's television show *Davy Crockett*, rode in on horseback just in time for the sprinkler system to malfunction and drench him. The full-scale replica riverboat *Mark Twain* nearly capsized because of the overcrowding, and the lagoons dried up in the boiling sun. "A nightmare," one called the opening, "a giant cash register, clicking and clanging."[67] For Walt, the setbacks comprised only minor irritants. He had created a new environment. The compulsive perfection of the environment was new also. Disney did not want a family's day together to be disturbed by the least negative thought. The turn-of-the-century town on Main Street, Frontierland, Fantasyland, Tomorrowland, and even Adventureland were all sanitized. Main Street was paved, and if a real horse left a real calling card in Frontierland, it was instantly removed by a suitably costumed host with a specially designed device. Tomorrowland was without the scary visions of science fiction. Adventureland limited overexcitement by putting the Jungle Boats on underwater rails. At the end of ten years, almost 50 million people had passed through Sleeping Beauty's Castle, including Soviet Premier Nikita Khrushchev.[68] Walt Disney's ideas became the industry standard at SeaWorld, Six Flags, Universal Studios, and any number of other theme parks oriented toward the mass public. Even Las Vegas has morphed into a city of theme hotels that surpass Disney's wildest dreams. As at Disneyland, a monorail links the lands of Paris, Venice, Rome, and Egypt.

But despite Disneyland's success, Walt had become frustrated with the location in Orange County. He failed to control the surrounding commercial properties, which spawned a raft of seedy, cheap motels and restaurants not owned by Disney or controlled by the company. Walt thus secretly started to buy Florida property in the Orlando area for a new project—Walt Disney World. Opened in 1971, after Walt's death, Walt Disney World was built with an eye toward correcting all the problems of Disneyland. It was larger (and had much more room to expand), with the park itself sitting on a tiny section of the surrounding 28,000 acres Walt had secured for other parks, hotels, campsites, and shopping centers. In 1982, Epcot Center opened on some of the adjacent acreage in the Orlando property, while Tokyo Disneyland took the Disney touch abroad. France's Euro Disneyland followed in 1992, although with much less success than the other parks. Invading Universal Studios movie-studio theme park monopoly, Disney opened the Disney-MGM Park in Orlando, all the while updating and improving each of the existing facilities with new attractions.

After Walt's death, the company languished until a new management team, headed by Michael Eisner, revitalized it. Eisner put life back into the Disney animated full-length cartoons with megahits like *The Little Mermaid, Beauty and the Beast, The Lion King,* and *Aladdin,* but then the studio, lacking another major hit, turned out a series of average animated works. But Eisner had more success with the theme parks, realizing that modern teenagers, who had significant chunks of cash to spend, would no longer be interested in cartoon mice and ducks. If Disney characters did not translate into rides, Eisner reasoned, he would have to "Disneyfy" existing non-Disney characters. With special marketing arrangements, George Lucas was retained to design and construct a simulator ride called "Star Tours" based on his colossal hit *Star Wars.* Later, Lucas and director Steven Spielberg collaborated on the design of the "Indiana Jones" ride. Disney obtained rights to the highly popular "Muppets" from the company founded by master puppeteer Jim Henson.

But it was Walt Disney, not George Lucas, who showed what could happen when a vision of fantasy was joined to mechanical reality. Walt did not live to see most of the robotics and simulator rides available to later engineers, but he certainly would have been the first to say, "That's great. But where can we go from here?"

BIRTH OF THE "ELECTRONIC BABYSITTER"

Both Berry Gordy's Motown and Walt Disney's theme parks owed much of their success to electronic media—Motown, obviously, because the proliferation of radios and cheaper phonographs made possible widespread access to the music, and Disneyland because the key to its advertising was its contract with ABC television. In different ways, radio and television, the new electronic media giants, dominated American culture in the 1950s.

Radio had blossomed after the war, after a hiatus during the conflict when the government prohibited new construction of radio broadcasting stations. Once the Federal Communications Commission (FCC) permitted new applications, the number of stations rose from just over 900 in 1945 to more than 3,000 by 1948. Two-thirds of the stations were traditional AM broadcasters, which were joined by a thousand FM stations. The National Broadcasting Company (NBC) and the Columbia Broadcasting System (CBS) dominated the airwaves in the early 1940s, with 160 and 107 affiliates, respectively. Programming had expanded to include children's shows, musicals, comedies, mysteries, adventures, news, and the traditional soap opera (so named because of the soap companies that advertised on the programs).[69] The two major broadcasters battled for advertisers and listeners, with CBS making itself into a powerful competitor to David Sarnoff's NBC, thanks to the efforts of William S. Paley.

Paley, fresh out of college, had worked at his father's cigar company until he noticed the exceptional response that a radio ad for the company's cigars had elicited. On the eve of the Great Crash, Paley mustered $450,000 to invest in the Columbia Phonograph Broadcasting System, renaming it CBS and taking over as its president. He expanded it in the teeth of the Great Depression, multiplying the number of affiliates by a factor of six and, equally important, keeping the business profitable.

CBS grew in popularity because Paley attracted a stable of radio personalities, stealing them, if necessary, from NBC. He signed Bing Crosby, Jack Benny, Kate Smith, and newsman Edward R. Murrow. As the CBS personalities became famous, Paley pressured the affiliates to provide them with permanent time slots, gaining control over programming, which in turn allowed him to market the slots to advertisers. His strategy also shifted power from independent producers and affiliates to the national broadcaster, creating a "master–slave" relationship wherein the "locals" (as the affiliates were called) meekly received what the national source sent out.

Radio, which had gained great credibility as the only instantaneous source of news during the war, found itself atop the mass communications market, peering down smugly at the newspapers that it had displaced. The industry scarcely noticed the determined, fledgling technology that was climbing that mountain from the back side—television.

A television transmission had taken place in 1927, but then, unlike radio, television suffered during the Depression years. War needs limited the availability of electronic parts, further stifling development, although RCA opened a studio in 1944. By 1946, more than a million TV sets received signals in some twenty cities generated by more than thirty broadcasting stations. Modern television programming began in 1947, with *The Howdy Doody Show*, *Kraft Television Theatre*, and *Texaco Star Theater*.[70] NBC, again, dominated the early activity, with stations in New York, Philadelphia, and Washington linked by a cable. The drawback was capital, because it required hundreds of thousands of dollars to set up a citywide broadcast network. Yet the potential was so enormous, investors willingly put up the phenomenal capital requirements to develop the technology and the networks, confident they could recoup their costs from advertisers. Evidence rolled in rather quickly: In 1952, Hasbro Toys, perceptive to the large number of children watching television, ran the first TV ad for a toy, Mr. Potato Head. A few years later, Ruth Handler, a vice president at Mattel Toy Company, would launch a new doll—Barbie—marketed directly to kids through television. Belatedly, radio realized that it had a genuine competitor.

Television use spread like wildfire, with more than half of all American homes sporting a television set in the mid-1950s. The tiny black-and-white circular tubes of the early years had by then given way to larger screens, with a Sears Silvertone television selling for less than $150 in 1950. When the first color TV sets went on sale in 1954, they cost between $900 and $1,300, or almost five times the cost of a black-and-white unit and one-fourth a typical household's annual income. Television at first drew families together as they tuned in together. An entire generation grew up with Milton Berle, Lucille Ball, Red Skelton, the Lone Ranger, Superman, and, late in the 1950s, a host of cookie-cutter Westerns that taught clear moral lessons. In virtually all cases, however, the values emphasized were positive: honesty, loyalty, religious faith, family, and, for the most part, industry and enterprise. Seldom were businesses portrayed as the villains—unless, on occasion, a land grabber in a Western had to be dispatched by James Arness in *Gunsmoke*. Quite the contrary. Television reinforced the message, already internalized by most Americans, that the economic freedoms that had been defended during the war had made the United States the most powerful nation on earth.

AMERICAN BUSINESS AT HIGH TIDE

Children of a later generation would learn about the 1950s through yet another television show. The 1970s situation comedy *Happy Days* presented the weekly theme that the 1950s were, well, happy days. After Korea, the United States was not involved in a shooting war for almost a decade. The economy was steady and occasionally spectacular, and new products continued to pour onto the shelves of American stores at an unprecedented rate.

The businessmen—mostly men—had regained their pre-Depression position as heroes, and if books hinted that they achieved out of obedience to a mindless routine (as in William Whyte's *The Organization Man*) or accused advertisers of selling the public products they really "didn't want" (as in Vance Packard's *The Hidden Persuaders*), for the most part American business would have agreed that the 1950s were indeed happy days.[71]

American enterprise reached something of a high tide in 1959. U.S.-made autos and steel dominated the world, and the entertainment sector had come of age with a vibrant motion picture industry and a fledgling technology for broadcasting color television. Less visible, but in the long run just as important, a new recording revolution had started, thanks to Elvis Presley, a white boy out of Tupelo, Mississippi, who sang black music. Within fifteen years, his songs, and those of hundreds of other American artists, black and white, would constitute the most copied and emulated music in history.

Unseen by many business leaders, however, were a number of warning signs those new trends carried with them. Steel and automobiles, safely insulated from foreign competition, lulled other industries into complacency. Meanwhile, the appearance of mass media television outlets gave rise to a new generation of Progressives, as members of the new reform elites proved as active as their predecessors of the late 1800s. They created the first consumer movement, gave birth to environmentalism, and used the legal system to generate the first substantial class-action lawsuits in history. Although it was not readily apparent to anyone involved in free enterprise, the 1960s and 1970s would be far less hospitable to business than were the happy days of the 1950s.

Business's Winter of Discontent: 1960–1982

When the congenial, silver-haired man in the baseball cap took the makeshift stage at one of the hundreds of Wal-Mart discount stores around the country, he hardly looked like a billionaire. "Whooooooooo," he yelled. "Whooooooooo," the crowd—all Wal-Mart employees—shouted back. "Pig. Sooey. Razorbacks!" he concluded with a whoop. What was the ruckus? It was just Sam Walton, founder of the largest retail chain store in the nation, talking to his employees. "Just a little chat between him and the 'associates,'" as he called them.

Sam Walton was one of the "rich who got richer" in the 1980s. He did so by expanding his chain from 200 stores to 1,600. He did so by creating 212,000 new jobs in the 1980s alone. And he did so by lowering prices for consumers on a panoply of retail goods.[1] Hardly a miser counting his money by candlelight, Sam Walton started in retailing in the 1950s. In the 1960s, he started a chain of discount retail stores and began providing incentives to his managers. In 1966, he had twenty stores and was doing very well. The inflation of the 1970s would make buyers more price conscious. They looked at new ways of buying goods that saved them money. They were willing to drive out of town, buy in bulk, and put up with less service, less selection, and more spartan surroundings. Sam Walton gave them the lower prices they wanted.

He focused on cutting costs any way possible and opening stores as fast as he could. By 1985, he was the richest person in the United States.[2] He made it by improving the lives of millions of people, hiring elderly or handicapped "greeters" to do little more than say hello at the front door. Yet many in the media and academia concentrated only on the perception that Wal-Mart destroyed downtown areas or "mom-and-pop stores." He was not the only one to change retailing in the 1970s. Kmart, Target, and Costco originated in that inflationary decade. For other retailers, it was change or die.

Obsession with improvement, efficiency, and cost control had driven Walton the same way it drove Andrew Carnegie and John D. Rockefeller a century earlier. But in a sense, Walton was a throwback to this earlier era. A new quality-obsessed entrepreneur was on the rise after World War II. These inventors and innovators focused on new products that filled key niches in the American economy, and while cost mattered, it now took a backseat to the special appeal of brand name and quality. No one exemplified the new entrepreneur more than Mary Kay Ash, not the least because she was a woman in a businessman's world. Divorced, with three children, lacking any job training and possessing only a high school education, Ash would have been an ideal character for a movie. She supported her family selling cleaning supplies, making in-home demonstrations. By the late 1950s, working for another firm, a direct sales organization, Ash had attained a more-than-respectable position and salary of $25,000 a year. She was ambitious, which proved a temporary curse when the company grew concerned about her internal power base, leading to a clash and her resignation.

Mary Kay Ash took with her a decade's worth of experience and knowledge of the direct sales industry and, in 1963, decided to launch her own company, Beauty by Mary Kay, in Dallas. Joined by her son, Richard Rogers, Ash targeted a part of the market that the largest competitor, Avon, had ignored: skin care. Simple door-to-door sales no longer worked, however, so Ash used the concept of a "party"—a two-hour, in-home beauty show in the residences of women who agreed to act as hostesses. The Mary Kay representatives provided a clinic on makeup, and then performed personalized makeup lessons on the participants. Ash realized that the key to successful sales of any good product is the sales force, causing her to explore new and unconventional motivational techniques. She handed out bonuses and monetary prizes and made certain that talented people moved up the organizational chain. Within three years, the company had sales of $800,000; then, by 1972, volume totaled $18 million.

Suddenly the growth stopped and reversed. The company could have continued on a path to collapse had Ash not analyzed the problem correctly. She and Rogers found that the cash bonuses had fallen well behind inflation, and that a sales director in real dollars earned no more in the late 1970s than almost a decade earlier. In addition to the cash bonuses, Ash added special incentives, awarding pink Buick Regals to salespersons (mostly women) who met a certain volume, and then kicking in an extra $300-a-month bonus to the commissions. Shortly, the sales directors' salary had almost doubled in real terms. Soon, Ash increased the incentives by upgrading from pink Buicks to pink Cadillacs. Recruiting her sales consultants from the ranks of suburban housewives, Mary Kay Cosmetics had more than 120,000 employees in the late 1980s, all of whom could compete for mink coats, diamonds, resort vacations, and other luxuries. The pink Cadillac became much more than a song by Bruce Springsteen—it became, literally, a "cosmetic" symbol of success.[3]

MANAGERIAL HIERARCHIES GONE WRONG

Ash was an entrepreneur who maintained control over her business, which allowed her to make changes quickly when conditions in the economy changed, making her the exception to the rule of new managerial hierarchies. By the 1960s, those organizational structures, which had once given U.S. business its international advantage, now started to become a drag on innovation and flexibility.

Just two weeks after John F. Kennedy defeated Richard Nixon for the presidency of the United States, Ford Motor Company announced the end of its ill-fated model, the Edsel. The automaker lost $350 million on the car, named after Edsel Ford, Henry's son, who died in 1943. During Edsel's life, Henry had berated and humiliated the boy endlessly. Perhaps, then, it was fitting that the car that bore Edsel's name returned to haunt the company.

A much more dangerous ghost patrolled the halls at Ford. Robert Strange McNamara, a vice president of the car and truck division who had been with the company since 1946, was appointed the new Ford president in 1960. He brought with him a reputation as a "numbers man" who was clever with statistics but did not understand production or manufacturing. Although he had opposed the Edsel, he had developed and encouraged the economic models that prompted the company to develop it. No matter: McNamara's significance to business lay in his personal embodiment of a powerful new trend that swept American business in the late 1960s, in which the "finance men" and the "numbers men" finally achieved superiority within the corporations over "production guys."

Managerial hierarchies had become the final evolution of the gray-suited corporate executive of the 1950s. Nowhere was this more evident than in the American auto industry.[4] Automobile companies enthusiastically embraced and went further than other industries in allowing division chiefs outside of manufacturing to have access and control of the businesses. McNamara's ascension at Ford, though short-lived, heralded the promotion of the finance divisions in many American corporations. For the most part, the new leaders from finance or accounting had little appreciation for cars—what made them work, why customers liked them, and, most important, why people bought them. Worse, by 1960, many of the accountants and finance gurus had inverted the original intent of having finance and accounting departments in the first place.

Early railroads embraced planning because of their exceedingly high capital demands, and because they had to prepare for the obsolescence of track and rolling stock. In the nineteenth century, finance and accounting executives came from entrepreneurial backgrounds. Many worked on the railroads, or in the steel business, and they appreciated the role of planning to facilitate growth and investment, not to impede it. Railroads viewed the finance divisions as the place from which to manage investments, and Andrew Carnegie aggressively used what is now called cost accounting.

Professionalizing management in the late 1800s produced an unintended consequence in the early twentieth century, however. As managers became educated specifically for investments and accounting, they no longer had time—nor, usually, the desire—to work their way up through the business. Many of them disdained physical labor and manufacturing. As David Halberstam pointed out in *The Reckoning* (1986), his comprehensive study of Ford and Nissan, the separation from production and manufacturing alienated the other divisions, which came to view the front office as opposing necessary innovation and investment.[5] Buffeted by ever-increasing directives from Detroit, managers soon learned that since the only thing that mattered to headquarters was numbers, they needed to produce numbers. They "learned to cheat Detroit as best they could in order to preserve the integrity of their own operation," Halberstam recorded, and they "did this with admirable cunning." For example, they manipulated test instruments to yield appropriate results, losing the essential quality that the test was to measure. They increased production—in a devious way that the union failed to detect—by narrowing the space on the conveyor belt by three inches, thus moving more items down the belt, but then simply stored the additional production "for a rainy day when Detroit came down with some impossible production quota that they otherwise could not handle." Managers quietly referred to the reserves as "the kitty." And when the front office expressed its displeasure with plants reporting leftover parts (which, in theory, could not happen due to the planning and statistical controls by executives such as McNamara), the managers "dumped thousands and thousands of useless parts into the nearby Delaware River," making the numbers match what was demanded by the front office.[6]

Detroit's lack of innovation—a characteristic certainly not confined to Ford—took its most visible form in the styles of the automobiles it made. Cars consistently got longer, heavier, and more expensive. Meanwhile, an increasing number of Americans were looking for economy. Even in 1970 only a small percentage of cars on U.S. streets were foreign brands; however, baby boomers were learning to drive, commuters often had longer drives, and even homemakers wanted a car to get to local shopping. Only in Europe and Japan were automakers producing small and fuel-efficient cars. The Volkswagen Beetle became dominant in the parking lots at colleges in the late 1960s. American manufacturers tried, very unsuccessfully, to displace them with the Chevy Corvair, the Ford Falcon, and the Studebaker Lark. The Pinto, introduced in 1970 to specifically address the economy market, ranked third in a 2007 "Hunk of Junk Hall of Fame" (Chevrolet's Vega was number five).[7]

In 1965, Lee Iacocca, then Ford's president, introduced the immensely popular Mustang. Its sporty look and feel made it an instant success. A decade later, it had grown by several inches and more than 1,000 pounds, in the process losing all semblance of a sporty auto. That trend would not have been quite so damaging if Japanese automakers had not captured the compact car market in the United States with fuel-efficient and stylish cars like the 1969 Datsun 240Z.

The accession of the finance and accounting divisions had a second influence on management at the major automakers. Publicly owned corporations had an obligation to their stockholders to make a profit and pay dividends on a somewhat regular basis. Increasingly, the pressure to maintain stock prices, some critics argued, prodded management to adopt short-term profit horizons over longer-term interests. Other observers suggested just the opposite: that the pressures on stocks forced the major corporations to perform, and made them accountable to a broad segment of the market beyond the sales during a particular model year.

Chandler's managerial hierarchies featured a balance between the divisions in the first eighty or so years following the managerial revolution. By the 1960s, that balance no longer existed. Halberstam, among others, argued that the finance divisions gained control at precisely the same time that securities markets demanded short-term performance, thus locking the auto industry into a downward spiral of shortsightedness and lack of quality.

CONSUMERS, ENVIRONMENTALISTS, AND ACTIVISTS

In 1964, a Harvard-educated lawyer named Ralph Nader signed a $2,000 contract with a publisher to produce a book on auto safety, which he delivered a year later under the title, *Unsafe at Any Speed.*[8] A friend later described Nader as having "the classic zealot's worldview, paranoid and humorless, and his vision of the ideal society—regulations for all contingencies of life, warning labels on every french fry, and a citizenry on hair-trigger alert for violations of its personal space."[9] Nader had taken on Ford's main competitor, General Motors, arguing that its Corvair model tended to roll easily. At the time, few bothered to read Nader's book, and virtually no one bothered to check his facts; instead, GM executives panicked and launched a personal investigation into Nader that backfired, and the company had to pay $425,000 in damages to the then-unknown writer.

Years later, independent tests of the Corvair showed that it behaved no worse than any other similar-size car on the road, but by then Nader had gone on to other crusades and the U.S. automotive industry had the reputation of sacrificing safety for profits.[10] Meanwhile, business found itself confronted by a burgeoning health and safety lobby, with no immediately apparent effect. The 1960s became the first decade in American history where traffic fatalities per 100 million miles driven failed to decrease. Fatalities per 10,000 registered vehicles actually increased.[11] Ironically, at a time when more Americans lived longer than they had at any time in history, a tide of graduates poured off college campuses full of reformist zeal. As Michael Fumento noted in *Science Under Siege*, a new phenomenon soon characterized the environmentalist and consumer movement, in which people who had suffered an accident or disabling disease identified a product or industry that seemed to have a relationship as the "cause" of the problem or injury. Thus, he observed, the "victim as expert" pointed media attention to a source of harm that had yet to be tested scientifically, let alone proven dangerous.[12]

To its discredit, businesses frequently attacked the critics personally rather than providing the public with new, and better, research for its own claims. Some of the activists made important points—Rachel Carson's *Silent Spring* addressed the dangers of DDT transmission into the food chain, for example—but by the time the intentions evolved into law, they had serious consequences for business and industry that many did not expect or want. By 1979, for example, total costs to U.S. business of regulation exceeded $100 billion a year. A cornucopia of environmental, health, and consumer laws imposed mountains of paperwork on businesses, attended by armies of regulators and met on the field of battle by industry's own hired guns, lawyers. An entirely new division of the managerial hierarchy took its place with a standing equal to the finance and accounting groups, as legal divisions appeared in most major companies. Whereas common sense, not to mention the costs of retaining expensive attorneys, had limited the number of lawsuits, the appearance of Nader's "class-action" suits not only told people they were "victims" but provided a way to pay for their litigation at virtually no personal cost. The resulting explosion in the legal field—both defending and prosecuting corporations—made law a growth industry itself. By 1980, America had four times as many lawyers per capita as West Germany and twenty times as many as

Japan. The boom in litigation and regulation was reflected in (or caused by, depending on the analyst) ballooning federal staffs. Both the House and Senate staffs increased 55 percent during the 1970s; committee staffs exploded by 165 percent, and congressional research rose by 15 percent. Meanwhile, the numbers of regulations churned out by federal bureaucracies, and the often trivial use of the court system to settle any product liability problem or consumer complaint, produced an explosion of paperwork and court cases.

Frequently, various regulations had contradictory requirements. The National Traffic Motor Vehicle Safety Act (1966) established a new agency that imposed safety standards on automakers, such as seat belts, impact-absorbing steering columns, dual brake systems, and padded dashboards. In 1975, Congress passed the Energy Policy and Conservation Act, mandating that car companies achieve an average fuel efficiency of 27.5 miles per gallon by 1985. Little note was made of the fact that the physical weight added by the requirements of the 1966 Act—however small—detracted from gains made in the second! Perhaps the most paradoxical outcome of the entire era was the decline of the niche "muscle cars," such as Pontiac GTOs, Dodge Chargers, and Chevrolet Chevelles, which critics took to mean that America had moved to less individualistic tastes in automobiles. Some even hoped that it signaled the advent of greater popularity for mass production. Instead, twenty-five years later, virtually all of the "tricks" that the "muscle car" racers had used to improve performance and lighten their cars for competition had moved into the mainstream consumer autos, including fuel injection, turbo- and superchargers, ultra-lightweight plastic bodies, and advanced suspensions.

It would be erroneous, however, to blame federal regulations or the consumer movement for Detroit's ills, which instead were largely self-inflicted. From 1968 until the early 1980s, management at the Big Three ignored possible responses to the consumer and environmental movements that might have assuaged some as to business's intent; instead, the automakers provoked even more scrutiny from Washington. Rather than undertaking substantial design changes and rethinking the traditional V-8, front-wheel-drive engines, Detroit sought temporary solutions or pursued paths of least resistance. The Big Three chose to use a catalytic converter to reduce emissions, which brought a switch to unleaded gasoline, which, in turn, reduced engine performance. Car companies made no significant headway improving gas mileage until the oil crisis of 1973, and well into the 1970s automakers struggled with poor designs, including the Ford Pinto (which provided late-night comedians with an endless stream of gags about its fuel tanks, which were susceptible to explosions when struck from the rear), the Chevrolet Vega (whose aluminum engine heads warped after a year of use), and the ungainly American Motors Gremlin (an aptly named auto, to say the least).

Catalytic converters did reduce air pollution in the short run, which certainly was no longer an option after passage of a string of antipollution laws. In 1965, the Motor Vehicle Air Pollution Act, followed by the Clean Air Act (1970), made national standards in line with those already in place in California, where "smog" (smoke and fog) constituted a significant health threat. Antipollution legislation virtually wiped out emissions from new autos, and by the 1980s, most vehicle air pollution came from older cars lacking smog-control equipment. However, improved safety and pollution controls came at a significant cost to consumers and the industry. According to one study, environmental regulations enacted before 1990, not even counting the Clean Air Act, have reduced the national product by 2.6 percent, or about $150 billion. Other researchers think that the 2.6 percent estimate is at least half too low, a claim that, if true, would yield $300 billion, or "about half of the combined federal, state, and local expenditures on education."[13]

Environmental laws remained popular with the public, mostly because the benefits were visible to the naked eye while the cost of regulations remained largely hidden, although passed on to consumers in higher prices, unemployment, and lower productivity.[14] In 1975 alone, 177 proposed "new rules appeared, as did 2,865 proposed amendments to existing rules, 309 new final rules, and 7,305 final rule amendments, for a total of 10,656 new and proposed rules and amendments, most of which applied to nearly all firms."[15] Attempts to inject market forces into areas such as pollution control have proved difficult, because, as one study concluded, "there is strong resistance to considering alternative and sometimes truly innovative approaches" because of the risk-averse, rigid, and inflexible bureaucracy.[16]

As a result of environmental regulations, consumer safety requirements, and its own shortcomings, U.S. industry started to sag in the late 1960s, although profits remained high. Productivity, however, the compass point of good management, started to reflect the oppressive burdens. The American economy, particularly industrial production, slipped into a virtual coma by 1980, with scant life signs. Especially after the effective date of the new regulations, manufacturing productivity slowed, growing by only 27 percent in the period from 1967 to 1977, compared to 70 percent for Germany and 107 percent for Japan. If, however, we start the trend line from 1975, when the most burdensome of the new social regulations went into effect, manufacturing in the United States actually declined. Of course, the capital gains tax laws and the unrelenting inflation after 1968 played a role, but even without the pernicious effects of poor tax policies and rising prices, it has been estimated that the regulations placed a burden of 1.4 percent per annum on growth across all industries.

JAPAN, INC.

Despite clear evidence that Detroit's problems lay within the car companies themselves and, to a lesser extent, Washington, many within the auto industry, from labor to management, saw a different culprit: foreign competition, specifically Japan. By the early 1970s, Nissan, Toyota, and Honda had made substantial inroads into the U.S. automobile market. Nissan captured the small pickup market in the mid-1960s, while the Honda Civic, introduced in 1973, held its own against American compacts. By 1980, Japan produced 11 million cars, or almost twice as many units as the United States auto companies manufactured, sending many of them to American shores as exports. That represented a drastic change from the situation twenty years earlier, when Japan made only half a million vehicles, and an almost complete inversion of 1950, at which time U.S. auto producers commanded 80 percent of the world market.

Lobbyists in the auto industry, as well as steel, textiles, electronics, and other businesses, claimed that the Japanese had an "unfair advantage" because their Ministry of International Trade and Industry (MITI) subsidized many Japanese corporations. Yankee manufacturers, it was argued, needed protection from that unfair competition, and sectors of American industry, appropriately selected by the government, should receive subsidies. MITI, however, had unsuccessfully attempted to force its own automakers to combine, inadvertently giving them their competitive ferociousness; and MITI did everything in its power to discourage a new motorcycle manufacturer and former lawn mower designer, Soichiro Honda, from entering the auto business at all. Such realities did not diminish the myth of MITI, to the point that by the 1980s, many analysts of the American economy spoke in hushed, reverential tones when describing Japanese industrial policy or reverently discussed planned economies.

At the time, however, auto executives and labor leaders were more interested in complaining about Japanese advantages than in learning from their productive policies. "Japan, Inc.," the bogeyman frequently used by industry to explain its own shortcomings, had little to do with Detroit's problems. Instead, the auto industry only had to look at its own executives, designers, and labor leaders to find its weaknesses.

THE STEEL INDUSTRY FOLLOWS DETROIT'S LEAD

Had only the auto industry fallen prey to shortsighted management and gluttonous wage hikes, the overall impact on the economy might not have been significant. Automotives, however, had always maintained a symbiotic relationship with steel (much as had the railroads), and the management practices tended to mirror each other. Just as American automakers had total domination of the domestic market and virtual control of much of the world market after World War II, American steel companies claimed 60 percent of the world output of crude steel.

Even more rapidly than with autos, however, the U.S. steel industry saw its international power whittled away, dropping to 20 percent by the late 1970s. Reducing plant capacity in a nonrecessionary period for the first time since Carnegie, United States Steel, the successor to Carnegie's old company, had struggled with competitors such as Bethlehem Steel, as well as Republic and National, all of whom had expanded aggressively. Prior to the Great Depression, U.S. Steel had entered into an era of "benign restraint" under Elbert H. Gary; then the company found it difficult to convert from heavy iron and rail products to new items, such as sheet steel and strip steel, that were then in demand.[17] After the war, a new merger movement allowed Jones and Laughlin and Inland Steel to expand their markets. Smaller producers fell by the wayside, with the resulting mergers leaving the industry in a position to be more competitive.[18]

Unfortunately for steel, both the nature of the market and the resolve and ability of international competitors had changed. Across the board, steelmakers failed to adapt to rigorous Japanese competition, despite a substantial infusion of revenue into American plants in the 1950s. Improvements were evolutionary, not revolutionary: Only one new plant was built between 1950 and 1970, a Bethlehem Steel facility in Indiana. Nowhere did one see the creative destruction practiced by Carnegie; instead, the changes eliminated problems of flow within the mills without making substantial capital investments. While productivity rose temporarily, increasing by 50 percent by 1960, overall output of American steel barely changed between 1948 and 1982. Leading steelmen, like Armco's William Verity, sought to diversify their companies out of steel.[19] Meanwhile, foreign competitors increased their production by 700 million net tons, reflecting the missing long-term transformation to new technology. And, in addition to foreign products, steel had to compete with aluminum, fiberglass, plastics, ceramics, and concrete as these products improved and offered lower prices. Steel's descent also related directly to the hard times in the auto industry and, by the 1970s, to the new federal fuel-efficiency regulations requiring cars to be lighter, thus encouraging the automakers to use less steel. Labor unions contributed to the decline, forcing the cost of labor to more than six times that of comparable foreign workers.

By the mid-1960s, spiraling wages, a shifting demand for steel products, poor management vision, and sharply lower profits led to the expected calls from unions and industry alike for protection from ("unfair?") foreign competition. In 1968, government obliged with the Voluntary Restraint Agreements to reduce steel imports; but that only whetted the industry's appetite for protective measures, and in the mid-1970s, while the Japanese were attaining labor costs that were only 70 percent that of the Americans, U.S. companies raised charges of dumping by foreign competitors.[20] Appealing to government for relief on the grounds that the "unfairness" came from Japan's subsidies to its steel industry had excellent lobbying value on Capitol Hill, but little basis in fact.

During the time that American steel producers drifted into an oligarchy, Japan gave birth to more than fifty-three integrated steel firms, many of them ultramodern and staffed by managers newly trained in American and European methods. Japanese steel was not merely cheap, it was good. Japan had fourteen of the world's largest modern blast furnaces by 1978, while the United States had none, and the seaport location of Japanese plants made it cheap for them to burn low-cost coal and have iron ore, often from the United States, delivered to their door by ever-larger freighters. That year, Japan exported 40 million metric tons of steel—7.5 million tons to America—whereas U.S. firms exported only 3 million metric tons.[21] Japanese assets in steel plants increased 23 percent from 1966 to 1972, compared to a meager 4 percent increase among the American producers, in part because U.S. executives continued to return almost twice as much to investors. Meanwhile, the voluntary restraints failed to deter U.S. consumers of foreign steel products, and Washington, to its credit, refused to go any further. Ultimately, the message to American steel was very Carnegie-like: "Modernize, get competitive, or die."

American firms also labored under a union system that Japan had avoided. With each new contract, shortsighted unions and management agreed to skyrocketing benefits packages that would only come due in the "out-years"—future dates when both the union leaders and the executives would be enjoying their retirements. Yet those benefit packages soon made it impossible for American labor to stay competitive with foreign labor, and by 2007, companies such as USX were paying more for the health care packages of their employees than they were for iron ore and other raw materials.

THE "MILITARY-INDUSTRIAL COMPLEX"

President Dwight Eisenhower, the first general since Ulysses Grant to win the presidency, probably never thought that one of the most memorable phrases of his presidency would come from his 1961 farewell address. Yet in that speech, after urging the nation to provide for a permanent defense industry, he warned about the power and influence of a "military-industrial complex."[22] As quotable as Ike's phrase was, it misrepresented the facts concerning the relationship he identified. For more than a century, defense contractors had lobbied the federal government for arms contracts. The fundamental change in the relationship between government and industry occurred after World War I, at which time the technology of weapons advanced so significantly that new and large items, such as ships, required long lead times to produce.

During World War II, when cost was no issue, American manufacturing was capable of truly phenomenal feats. But the production of a tank in five hours or an aircraft carrier in fifteen months was achieved at peak production levels, with all the learning skills and machinery in place. No nation could keep that type of production effort in peacetime, nor survive the drain on the private-sector economy, as the Soviet Union eventually discovered. Consequently, a postwar industry demobilized at the same time that the level of sophistication of weapons increased the lead time between the date the government placed an order for an item and the day the contractor delivered it.

Three trends, then, tended to define the "military-industrial complex." First, the government realized that in the event of a modern war, it could not expect instantaneous production of weapons. Most strategists expected that a sudden Soviet offensive would conquer Europe in a matter of weeks, and that the conflict would be over before the United States could produce or deliver a single weapon. Thus, America was committed to maintaining a full-time production capacity of the most necessary weapons and the rapid start-up capability for new items.

As a result, the U.S. government frequently found itself asking if a particular contractor needed to be supported in order to maintain national security. On occasion, some manufacturers gambled on their government contracts and, in turn, came to the point that they totally depended on Uncle Sam for survival. Grumman Aircraft, for example, arrived at this point in the 1980s, when the government's decision not to renew the famous "Top Gun" F-14 Tomcat fighter virtually put the aircraft operation out of business. Other companies, such as Lockheed and McDonnell Douglas, struggled to maintain a strong component of civilian sales to offset the vicissitudes of government contracting. Lockheed still almost went bankrupt in 1971 after it lost $200 million on the C-5A transport and failed to sell the L-1011 TriStar in sufficient numbers to the airlines. The government concluded that it needed Lockheed, which had produced the exceptional F-104 aircraft, and bailed out the contractor with loan guarantees.

A second trend involved a high level of concentration among defense contractors. Douglas merged with McDonnell Aircraft, and numerous missile and electronics manufacturers were absorbed by larger corporations. When not combining directly with other defense contractors, companies sought to diversify or merge into nondefense businesses. North American Aircraft merged with Rockwell-Standard, a machine manufacturer; Martin Aircraft merged with Marietta Corporation, a cement producer. The trend toward consolidation in aircraft and shipping illustrated the falling number of units ordered by the government. Purchases of military aircraft fell from more than 5,000 units in 1956 to 2,700 units in 1969.[23]

Those factors contributed to a third trend, in which the declining numbers of weapons had the corollary of requiring that the weapons that the nation did buy had to be as advanced technologically and as capable as possible. "More bang for the buck" became the slogan in the halls of Congress, driving the military to high-tech weaponry that had the perverse feedback-loop effect of making each unit still more expensive. Attempts to break the cycle failed.

Jacques Gansler, in an insightful article called "How the Pentagon Buys Fruitcake," traced the circuitous methods by which the Pentagon awarded contracts and procured products. In the case of fruitcake, government regulations stipulated the exact number of cherries and weight of nuts in a single slice![24]

To restate the central point, business's winter of discontent started in the 1960s, in spite of superficial economic growth, and the problems involved falling productivity, government regulation, and inflation. And that inflation had its origins less in the "military-industrial complex" than in the federal deficits mostly driven by domestic spending. The idea that defense spending caused falling productivity or inflation has no grounds in the data: Defense spending, except for a brief period during the Vietnam War, had fallen consistently since the Korean conflict. In 1960, for example, federal spending on defense as a percentage of GNP stood at 9.5 percent. By 1970, it had dropped to 8.3 percent, and by 1980 it had been cut almost in half, to 5 percent. In the mid-1950s, however, federal deficits started to appear, and after Eisenhower achieved a near-balanced budget in 1960, a condition of almost permanent deficits took root. Meanwhile, government expenditures as a share of GNP started to rise in the 1950s, growing from about 20 percent of GNP in 1950 to almost 35 percent of GNP in 1975.[25]

OIL TAKES CENTER STAGE

From 1953 to 1969, oil prices fell in relative terms; then, from 1963 to 1969, oil prices dropped in absolute terms. Government policies often kept domestic prices lower than world prices, erecting disincentives to drill in the United States and creating incentives to import. By 1960, America had become a net importer of oil, despite having its own rich domestic fields. Middle East oil, up to that point, had remained under the control of seven large firms, often called the "Seven Sisters": Jersey Standard (Exxon), Socony (Mobil), Standard Oil of California (Chevron), Texaco, Gulf Oil, British Petroleum (BP), and Royal Dutch/Shell (Shell). Britain had emerged from World War II with the premier position in the region, producing 80 percent of the oil, while the major American presence came through a joint venture between Standard Oil of California and Texaco called ARAMCO (Arabian-American Oil Company). Then, in 1960, the Arab states and other non-Arab oil producers, including Iran and Venezuela, met to wrest control of their natural resource from foreigners. Representatives established the Organization of Petroleum Exporting Countries (OPEC). Eventually numbering thirteen nations, OPEC bargained for higher royalties in the 1960s, finally gaining enough clout to obtain higher profits through the threat of withholding oil. The largest producer, Saudi Arabia, led by Sheikh Ahmed Yamani, had used the West's growing dependence on oil to force the oil companies to relinquish a share of ownership. After the Arab-Israeli War in 1973, the Arab countries started to view OPEC as a diplomatic weapon to be wielded against Israel's allies, especially the United States. Urged on by the radical members, especially Libya and Iraq, OPEC not only announced a price increase of 70 percent but curtailed exports to America by 80 percent.

Normally, demand would fall as prices soared. But the U.S. government, concerned that the American oil companies might gain "windfall profits," placed ceilings on prices that companies could charge. The ceilings ensured that oil would be artificially cheap, with predictable results. Filling stations ran out of gas; motorists drove for miles (burning scarce fuel) to top off their tanks; cars stacked up around gas stations, curving completely around city blocks; and fistfights (and worse) developed as people tried to cut in line. Gas rationing was imposed in many areas. Even with the price ceilings, gas cost more than it had, prompting consumers to charge that "Big Oil," and not the Arabs, had used the crisis to squeeze profits from oppressed consumers. Some thought that the oil companies got rich from the episode.[26] If that was the case, however, the oil producers were not the American companies but the Arab states that retained the profits, and in any event, U.S. consumers paid far less than they would have if the government had not established the ceilings. On the other hand, the distribution would have been far more efficient and the lines nonexistent had the price of oil reflected conditions accurately. The real tragedy did not involve American motorists paying a slightly higher price at the pump, but the fantastic damage done to developing economies that relied on oil for their tractors and factories. Thousands, perhaps millions, starved as a result of OPEC's "oil weapon," as Third World incomes plummeted, dropping below their 1970 level—the first such reversal of the modern era.

Domestic oil production soared with a number of successive strikes in the post-Rockefeller years. The most significant of the early strikes occurred in Beaumont, Texas (at a place called Spindletop), in 1901.[27] As oil gushed out of Spindletop, Texas far surpassed any production ever seen in Pennsylvania. Anthony Lucas, who brought in the Spindletop gusher, gathered a cadre of backers from the Mellon Bank in Pittsburgh and formed Gulf Oil. Soon a second syndicate's drilling operations appeared in the area. Texas Company (Texaco) and Gulf presented new challengers to the traditional oil companies, spurred on by the automobile craze, and in their efforts to outproduce each other, crude oil prices dropped to ten cents a barrel. Oil-producing states, seeing their tax revenues plummet, sought to ration or otherwise restrict output, even begging the federal government for help. FDR's New Deal administration, of course, did not hesitate to impose controls on oil shipments across state lines. Restrictions effectively threw up barriers to domestic production and, not surprisingly, foreign imports increased. By the time of the 1973 oil crisis, with its $50-a-barrel prices, the nation suddenly searched frantically for the domestic producers earlier administrations had regulated and harassed. Oil's impact on domestic inflation—already ratcheting upward—threatened to push it into double digits. Nor were the oil shocks over. In 1979, Shiite Muslims backing the Ayatollah Khomeini in Iran overthrew the Shah's government there, sparking a second round of steep price hikes. Led by the Muslim clerics, Iran joined the OPEC hard-liners of Iraq, Libya, and Algeria to reduce production and boost prices as punishment to the "pro-Zionist" West. While it is true that per-barrel profits for the oil companies rose as the price of a barrel of crude went up, overall consumption of imports fell. It was hardly a windfall for the oil companies: Estimates put the net income of Exxon, Gulf, Mobil, Chevron, and Texaco at $3.6 billion in 1970 and $14.5 billion in 1980, but that ignores the high inflation of those years. Politicians demanded that domestic producers find new sources of oil in the United States, then pay steep taxes for the privilege of drilling, then suffer attacks from environmentalists and pay millions in lawsuits for destroying habitats. Small wonder that companies only drilled when assured of substantial enough profits to offset all those disadvantages.

COMPUTERS AND THE BIRTH OF THE MICROCOSM

Beset by rising energy expenses, inflation, government regulation, and soaring labor costs, business productivity dropped. Investment in research and development (R & D), which had risen more than 64 percent from 1960 to 1970, fell to an increase of only 12 percent during the next decade. Worse, basic research, which had grown an astounding 120 percent in the 1960s, crashed, dropping to barely 7 percent, despite an increase in the federal government's share of research.

Amid all the troubles facing American business in the 1960s and 1970s, a quiet revolution had occurred, offering more promise of transforming society than the automobile and the airplane put together. The computer generated what industry analyst George Gilder called a "quantum revolution," geometrically expanding the dimensions of enterprise and productivity. Of course, it did not occur instantly. The concept for a computer had existed since 1900, when Charles Babbage designed a steam-powered card-punch machine. World War II brought renewed investment in the technology, resulting in ENIAC (Electronic Numerical Integrator and Computer), which used vacuum tube technology. The Bureau of the Census saw the potential in an ENIAC-type machine for working the census numbers and contacted J. Presper Eckert and John Mauchly, the two men who had built ENIAC. After World War II, Mauchly and Eckert designed a new computer called UNIVAC (Universal Automatic Computer) for the government, only to discover that the production cost far more than they could afford. Remington Rand Corporation, an office equipment manufacturer, stepped in to purchase the company and produce the UNIVAC for the Census Bureau, delivering the first in 1951. Despite its apparent dominant position in the field, Remington Rand soon found itself in stiff competition with Thomas Watson's International Business Machines (IBM). Watson had emerged as a top executive at National Cash Register (NCR), then under the direction of John Patterson, who had pioneered a strategy of giving salesmen specific territories within which to sell the company's products and rewarding them with performance bonuses.[28]

After World War II, Watson prepared his son, Tom Watson, Jr., to run IBM, and in 1952 the elder Watson passed the baton to a new generation. The younger Watson saw computing equipment as the wave of the future, leading IBM to deliver its own large computer (called the mainframe) that year. IBM surged to first place in the market, controlling more than 60 percent of the computer business in the mid-1960s, even though its product was never better than the products of its competitors. Rather, IBM emphasized sales and marketing, practicing the time-tested methods that had served Singer Sewing Machines, International Harvester, and Otis Elevators well.[29]

Even by the late 1950s, however, it was becoming clear that the vacuum tubes represented a major hurdle in reducing the size and thus the cost of computers. Switches were the key—they were, as George Gilder explains, "the substance of the artificial mind."[30] Thus, the invention of the transistor not only was the first step in the creation of the new technology, it was the origin of an entire revolution as deep as the commercial revolution that swept Europe centuries ago. On July 1, 1948, William Shockley announced that his employer, Bell Laboratories, had sponsored the successful achievement. Shockley had provided the crucial cost-effective switch that computers required.

Bell Labs found that its transistors did not work well in high heat, which made the discovery relatively useless for military purposes. Consequently, while the most important technology of the twentieth century unfolded, the Department of Defense unimaginatively funneled huge amounts of money into vacuum tubes. In that context, if the Pentagon illustrated America's "industrial policy," it can be stated that the United States succeeded in spite of its national industrial policy, not because of one. Still, to make the transistor truly effective required peripheral and supporting technological discoveries. At that point, in 1952—just as IBM's large mainframe machine was working out its bugs—a small electronics firm in Dallas called Texas Instruments (TI) made the next breakthrough. TI engineers reasoned that by using silicon, with its ability to sustain temperatures of 1,200 degrees Celsius, they could eliminate heat as a problem for the transistor. After more than a thousand attempts to manufacture a silicon transistor, the TI researchers succeeded.

As often happens in such discoveries, the TI researchers had tried only to solve a specific, narrow problem, but when the company actually started manufacturing silicon semiconductors, it found that silicon dioxide was "both electrically and chemically inert and thus could both protect and insulate the devices of near-micron dimensions that would appear in the next two decades."[31] TI prepared to produce en masse silicon transistors in 1954. Bolstered by the instantaneous success of silicon transistors, TI's revenues rose from $24 million in that year to $232 million six years later, growing at a rate of 200 percent a year. Even so, a more significant leap still lay ahead, when silicon transistors could be packed tightly together on a single chip, insulated by their own oxide. When that occurred, in 1971, not TI but another small company, Intel Corp., managed to put an entire computer on a single silicon chip called a microprocessor. Another irony associated with the microprocessor was that Intel's first customer, Busicom (which made calculators), did not foresee the potential for the microprocessor, so the entrepreneurs at Intel decided to give the customer more than it asked for and then bought back the rights to the chip. A heated competition to pack more, and faster, microprocessors together ensued, giving birth to the next era of computers, dominated by the personal computer or PC.

Once the industry had the capability to compress several miniature computers, in the form of microprocessors, on a single chip, an exponential growth in computational power followed. In sharp contrast to almost all other industries, the technology of computers held that power was gained as the chips got smaller. That represented a fundamental change in the way progress had taken place over history: Virtually every other machine only got more powerful by getting larger, as symbolized, ironically, by the internal combustion engines powering the "muscle cars" at the very time the PC was invented.

Intel also created the first usable PC. A California company formed in 1968 by Gordon Moore and Carver Mead, Intel had produced its computer on a chip in only three years. That proved a watershed event because the basic raw material of the silicon was sand, which no one could claim was in short supply. But if Intel pioneered the chip and the PC, it took yet another small start-up company to make PCs popular.

At that point, one might have expected the leader in the computing field, IBM, to have brought personal computers to the vast market of consumers. But IBM continued to focus on larger machines, completely missing the real revolution. Instead, a pair of California college dropouts, Steve Jobs and Steve Wozniak, ushered in the PC age.[32] They had assembled a small computer called the Apple in Jobs's garage in 1976, which they introduced and sold without a monitor or keyboard for the price of $666.[33] In part, the product's success relied on the fact that it offered on-board read-only memory (ROM), and orders quickly reached into the hundreds. The Apple, and its more popular successor machine, the Apple II, generated tremendous publicity, bringing Jobs and Wozniak considerable financial support in the newly ascending section of northern California now called Silicon Valley. Bank of America provided a loan to further capitalize Apple. In 1977, Jobs and Wozniak launched Apple Computer, Inc., and within two years, the company had a stratospheric sales total of more than $118 million, turning Jobs and Wozniak into computer gurus, gaining them reputations as wizards of technology. Apple joined the ranks of Fortune 500 companies in less time than any other company in history by making computers easy to use.[34] The third-generation computer, called the Macintosh, introduced the computer "mouse" and desktop "icons." But the company also had significant marketing problems, not the least of which originated in the scheme to reap profits from peripheral product sales that would surpass that of the computer itself. In the long run, that encouraged the company to try to retain its technology rather than share it so as to make it an industry standard.

Nevertheless, Jobs and Wozniak had taken a technology of government and big business—perhaps the ultimate in depersonalized machinery—and humanized it, putting power in the hands of the people in the most immediate sense of the term. The revolution over which they presided was nothing short of spectacular. In 1960, the United States had about 10,000 computers in operation, but thirty years later, there was one computer for every 2.6 people. Still, one last ingredient was necessary to link the technology to most average people. Computers were still machines—and, in some sense, extremely complex machines. They required a highly specialized language to operate—a secret code that nonspecialists had to learn to communicate commands to the electronic "brains."

A Seattleite attending Harvard, Bill Gates had read about a personal computer in a 1974 issue of *Popular Mechanics*. Gates's personal background differed sharply from that of many other entrepreneurs. He lived a comfortable life as the son of a well-to-do attorney and obviously had access to a top-flight education. He and former high school classmate, Paul Allen, had become absorbed with computers at the time that other teenagers were dating or playing sports. While still a junior, Gates started a business that made computer data analysis devices for the metal boxes on highways that recorded the traffic. They made $20,000 before the federal government started to offer traffic analysis free of charge. At Harvard, Gates developed legendary work habits, putting in thirty-six straight hours before taking a short nap, then returning to work. He also played computer games such as "Space Wars," which allowed him to better learn the processes of computers.[35]

When he and Allen discovered that the computer in the magazine still had problems with the programming language, they immediately contacted the company to suggest that they could solve the problem. In 1975, they boarded a plane to Albuquerque, where they went to a small office in a strip mall with their software program, which was a refinement of the popular BASIC language. To everyone's surprise, the software responded the first time it received a command. Gates and Allen moved to Albuquerque, working as software engineers, but they quickly formed their own company, Microsoft, developing software that tailored BASIC to specific computers.

Inherent in the new technology and software was a partial rejection of the "hacker ethic" that encouraged a free flow of information to fellow hackers—with the emphasis on free. For Gates, the obvious problem was, "How do you get your money back after investing it?"[36] Instead, software development was aided by a series of court decisions that upheld intellectual property rights. At first, however, piracy of the BASIC language actually benefited Gates by incorporating the Microsoft product into thousands of machines—some of it purchased, some of it stolen. The net effect was to expand consumption of the overall product (similar to how bootleg records helped to spread rock 'n' roll throughout the Soviet Union) and, in the case of Gates, to align users with Microsoft software to the extent that it became the industry standard.

Eventually, Gates and Allen focused on the "Windows" interface language, a mouse-controlled, icon-oriented program that pushed Microsoft's revenues over the $1 billion mark. Windows came to be the standard software for every personal computer. Even Apple had to make its computers compatible with Microsoft. Only fifteen years after he started his company, Bill Gates, then in his mid-thirties, became the youngest billionaire in American history (reaching a wealth level in real dollars equal to that of Andrew Carnegie).

AIRLINES: FROM DESPAIR TO DEREGULATION

Computers and rising fuel prices had simultaneous and polar opposite effects on the growing airline industry in the 1970s. The introduction of transistors meant better radios, which in turn meant improved air-to-air and air-to-ground communications. That translated into better safety and rising traveler confidence. Defense spending had spin-off effects, providing the private sector with better radars, aircraft design, avionics, and, as military pilots became civilians, more capable pilots. Over the long run, quality improvements brought lower costs, but those often were difficult to see as fuel costs rose early in the decade.

Airlines were involved indirectly in another, unplanned deregulation of the market. In the early 1960s, a Yale junior named Fred Smith wrote a term paper on the deficiencies of the mail system, particularly problems related to long-distance air freight.[37] He deplored the lack of control or accountability for packages, handled almost exclusively by Flying Tiger or Emery Air Freight, both of which had solidified their oligopoly positions under government regulation. Smith had a love of flying, and after serving two tours of duty in Vietnam, he used money from a small stake he had in a restaurant his father had sold to purchase an interest in Arkansas Aviation Sales, which Smith turned into a used lot for airplanes. He netted a profit of a quarter of a million dollars in a few years. Smith still toyed with the idea of competing in the air freight business, though. Although he realized that his two largest competitors each had revenues of $100 million, he suspected there was a high level of dissatisfaction with their service.

Commissioning two consulting firms to conduct surveys of the incumbent carriers' clients, Smith learned what he already knew. Deliveries were erratic, packages got lost, and overall satisfaction was low. Moreover, more than three-quarters of the shipments originated outside the largest twenty-five markets, especially new research and manufacturing complexes located in more remote industrial parks. Smith observed that since most commercial airlines were not flying between 10:00 p.m. and 8:00 a.m., a window of airport operations was open in which he could conduct takeoffs and landings without concern about air traffic.

It took almost all the capital he and his family had (nearly $8 million) in start-up costs, but Smith gained the confidence of investors, who contributed another $40 million, then he brought on board a few banks, bringing the total capital to $90 million. At the time, that represented the "largest single venture capital start-up in American business history."[38] Federal Express, incorporated in 1971, purchased thirty-three French Dassault executive jets that were the largest aircraft Smith could get without meeting CAB requirements for freight haulers. Smith had investigated United Parcel Service (UPS), which itself had intruded into the monopoly of the U.S. Post Office, and observed that the seventy-five-pound limit standardized package sizes and eased loading and unloading. More important, Smith developed a hub-and-spoke operation that sent all packages to a central location in Memphis, then moved them to their final destinations from there, keeping close track of them at all times. Federal Express saw itself as a freight service with 500 mph delivery trucks, catering to electronics, medical, and computer firms that needed rapid service. The company's jets featured bright orange and purple paint, and even more important, the company offered a rock-solid guarantee of delivering any package to the areas it serviced in twenty-four hours.

The early years posed a challenge, causing Smith to have to sell his own personal jet to meet a payroll and to use winnings from a blackjack game to pay bills. Employees helped, too, leaving personal jewelry as deposit for company gas and hiding the jets when sheriffs came to repossess them. But at that point, the good fortune of the other airlines—now in the process of deregulating—rubbed off on Smith. With so many new passengers flying, the major airlines lacked sufficient aircraft. They willingly sacrificed their parcel service, which Federal Express gobbled up. In 1974, UPS had a strike that took it out of the market for a time, and rival REA Express went out of business. Although Federal Express continued in the red throughout 1975, in 1976 it reported net income of $8 million on revenues of $109 million. After deregulation, Federal Express acquired larger aircraft. It also by that time had shipped, under the guise of FedEx Letters, mail that in previous years would have been shipped by the U.S. Post Office. Although technically in violation of legislative intent, Federal Express had the market on its side. The U.S. Post Office had a reputation for losing mail, slow delivery, and inefficiency. Federal Express, or FedEx, finally pushed the U.S. Postal Service to compete with its own forty-eight-hour delivery promise. Once again, however, the market had outperformed government-sanctioned monopolies.

Fred Smith revolutionized delivering packages quickly. A trucker, Malcom McLean, revolutionized a slower system. Transporting goods by sea had always been the cheapest way to send goods long distances. McLean and his siblings started a trucking company with one truck and Malcom as the driver. In North Carolina, the company first transported tobacco barrels, until it grew to own 1,770 vehicles. The trucking company was sold in 1955 for $25 million, which allowed Malcom to buy a shipping company (which federal regulation prohibited while he was still a trucker). Regulation had also supported the way longshoremen loaded ships: taking each package off railcars or trucks and using cranes on the ship to lower the packages into the ship's hold where experienced hands planned to make the best use of the space available. McLean wanted to implement his vision: The railcar or the trailer of the truck would travel on the ship, without ever being opened. This would save labor and prevent theft of the contents. Initially, he used tanker ships, carrying liquid as well as trailers, but by 1960 he had perfected the "Sea-Land" system. Containers could be attached and detached from truck or rail bases so that just a metal box was loaded on the ship. Since the crane needed to do the loading was located on the dock, dockworkers resisted the changes, slowing growth. McLean, running short of cash for expansion, sold the company to R. J. Reynolds, making $160 million personally. Sea-Land Corporation was spun off from RJR in 1977 and eventually became part of Maersk and Horizon shipping companies. McLean bought and grew two more shipping companies, USL (which failed) and Trailer Bridge, Inc. (still operational today).[39]

SLOW THAW

One of the most important components of success that American business had lacked for a decade was faith—the faith that its investments would not be taxed away or eaten by inflation, and the faith that federal regulations would not discourage invention, innovation, and risk taking. Without faith on the part of business, capital for new projects had stayed in tax-free bonds, while the wealth of the rich went to purchase private art collections or to hold gold as a hedge against inflation. Even middle-class entrepreneurs struggled to protect themselves by trading houses, taking advantage of federal home mortgage loans and the spiraling inflation that pushed home prices up, neglecting critical investment in small businesses. It was increasingly clear that capitalists would not take risks in an atmosphere that punished them for doing so.

In the 1970s, economists were baffled by the economy. Unemployment climbed steadily starting in the late 1960s, reaching nearly 10 percent by 1979. But Keynes policies were no help. John Maynard Keynes would have recommended increasing government spending to halt recession. Spending was already high—high enough to be causing the most serious inflation of the century. Nixon had stifled it for a while with price controls, but the resulting shortages were even more painful. Americans coped by buying real estate, art, antiques, and even autos to protect themselves from losing everything. Blame was placed. It was hard to find jobs for returning Vietnam vets and the baby boomer women entering the labor force. Welfare programs supposedly had created "hard-core poor" who had never worked and never would. General Motors pioneered a program to give new employees alarm clocks—and teach their use.

The situation, termed "stagflation" for its combination of inflation and unemployment, worsened in 1979. It did not help when the president of the United States, Jimmy Carter, said that Americans had to get used to the situation. The press referred to it as Carter's "malaise" speech. The National Chamber of Commerce recognized the dire straits into which the nation's enterprise had fallen with its 1980 slogan, "Let's Rebuild America," indicating American business had fallen into disrepair.[40]

The public, it seems, had never lost faith in business. Public opinion polls from 1966 to 1980 reveal that while confidence in business leaders fluctuated, with very few exceptions business leaders were always held in higher regard than the government that regulated them or the leaders of organized labor.[41] This faith was about to be challenged.

When Ronald Reagan was elected president in 1980, he wanted to destroy communism. Not only did this goal seem hopeless, it seemed irrelevant. The stagflation of the 1970s was getting worse. Inflation was above 13 percent and rising.[42] Unemployment jumped from 5.8 percent to 7.1 percent in less than a year.[43] The economic problems were turning to disasters and malaise was turning to depression. Industries began to fail, starting with the savings and loan associations.

DECLINE AND FALL OF THE S&L INDUSTRY

Savings and loan associations (S&Ls) had existed as the "junior partner" of the banking industry for generations. Formed to pool capital for home mortgage lending, S&Ls attracted savings accounts at one rate and loaned long-term at a higher rate. During the New Deal, the Glass-Steagall Act separated S&Ls from other banks, prohibited them from providing checking accounts for businesses (demand deposits), but required them to keep 75 percent of their loans in real estate, primarily home mortgages, and to pay one-quarter to one-half percent higher interest rates on deposits than could banks. S&Ls sometimes found that they experienced short periods in which falling home prices led to foreclosures and even failures, but in general the S&L industry found that making money could almost be taken for granted.

The inflation of the 1970s put the S&Ls in a serious position, however. As interest rates rose in the economy and the rate they could pay on deposits remained at the low rates fixed by Congress, customers took their deposits and invested in other assets. Stockbrokers began to offer mutual funds consisting of short maturity assets to attract this money, and savings accounts flowed from the banks to these "money market mutual funds." Brokers invested the money into government bonds and loaned it directly to corporations. This "disintermediation" effect threatened to erode the capital base of the S&Ls. They had to raise cash, and fast. The interest paid on traditional deposits, however, remained unchanged until the Depository Institutions Deregulatory and Monetary Control Act (DIDMCA) of 1980. DIDMCA allowed S&Ls to set the interest they paid on deposits. This action did not stop the S&L failure, so in 1982, another law allowed S&Ls to engage in activities such as offering consumer loans, credit cards, and checking accounts and to go even farther outside their traditional business. S&Ls became partners in real estate developments, restaurants, hotels, airlines, and other businesses where they had no experience. Locked into mortgage loans that stretched over a fifteen- to thirty-year period, the S&Ls had to find new loans that were repaid over a much shorter time. Even these higher-risk activities could not overturn a ten-year decline in the industry's profitability. In a single year, from 1981 to 1982, S&Ls lost $12 billion.

Another component of the S&L problems stemmed from the presence of deposit insurance. S&L owners had increasingly growing pressures to find profitable outlets. The more profitable, of course, the riskier the investment, but even conscientious S&L executives could rationalize that drastic measures were needed, and that, after all, the depositors were "covered" by the Federal Savings and Loan Insurance Corporation (FSLIC), after DIDMCA, up to $100,000 per account. Economists call this phenomena "moral hazard," in which compensation for a loss, such as fire insurance, creates incentives to have more losses, even through illegal activities such as arson. Some critics argued that owners and managers invested wildly in junk bonds, but portfolio analysis showed that the weaknesses of the S&Ls had more to do with property investment than with junk bonds.

By the mid-1990s, the industry had collapsed. From 1980 to 1994, 1,617 banks failed. Texas alone lost 599 banks with 43 percent of its bank assets.[44] Congress ended up paying $150 billion to ensure that depositors would not lose their funds.[45]

Deregulation of airlines and trucking had benefited the vast number of consumers, and even with the S&Ls—whose "deregulation" masked far deeper distortions of the industry by government earlier via the "moral hazard" of deposit insurance—the legacy of deregulation was unmistakable: Natural gas prices fell almost 40 percent in the first two years after its deregulation, and had dropped by almost 60 percent after ten years. Even as deregulation lowered prices in multiple industries, larger macroeconomic pressures overwhelmed producers and consumers alike, beginning with the inflationary burst that started in the 1970s. High interest rates soared to record levels by 1979, with home mortgage rates reaching 10 percent. The most creditworthy firms found it difficult to get loans; construction almost stopped, taking down with it the lumber and cement business and the appliance market. Auto sales plummeted, leaving most of the postwar showrooms abandoned. As it turned out, though, the drop in money supply growth would end the excessive inflation and lower the high unemployment rates. The year 1982 marked the end of the cold winter and the emergence of new industries.

During the long winter of discontent endured by American business, the arrival of the computer marked a bud of spring—a turning point, symbolizing the transition from a world of steel and material resources to the universe of ideas and exponential growth. A new version of an industrial revolution was under way, often miscategorized as an "information revolution." The true impact of computer technology, which even by the 1990s had not really been experienced, was to multiply productivity and enhance individual power, turning upside down the tyranny of the physical over the mental and the material over the spiritual. That revolution, paradoxically, had its first impact in the very industries it soon would replace: steel and autos.

CHAPTER 12

Business in Renaissance: 1982–1989

In 2005, Craig McCaw, although uncomfortable in the public eye, stood by as his wife, Susan, was sworn in as the U.S. Ambassador to Austria by the George W. Bush administration. Susan was a Stanford and Harvard grad, a former investment banker, and model-beautiful, too. But as Craig squirmed under the glare of cameras and attention, someone probably quipped, "Does anyone have a cell phone?" Because without the invention of the cell phone, the McCaws might not have been there.

Second son of a flamboyant Seattle cable TV and radio promoter named Elroy McCaw, Craig grew up in comfort, attending the same private school as Bill Gates. McCaw was known to be extremely bright, but he was never very comfortable in social situations. Elroy died of a stroke when Craig was a nineteen-year-old sophomore at Stanford. While the lifestyle had been extravagant, the debts were huge. McCaw and his three brothers were left only with a modest cable business in Centralia, Washington, prompting Craig to start running the business from his dorm room. Delegating power to his employees, McCaw learned the business and focused on strategy. By the early 1970s, the company was worth $200 million. He moved into pager services, and at a trade association meeting of radio common carriers (RCC), he heard about a new technology called cellular communication.[1]

As a child, Craig had heard his father tell stories of how others made money when they received TV broadcasting rights. After studying up on AT&T and monopoly rights, he decided that he would focus on gaining a license from the FCC to provide a new service. His experience with pagers, combined with his own roving habits, made him sure that people would love the freedom of cell phones.[2]

Gaining the radio spectrum necessary to provide cell phone service would prove challenging. The AT&T monopoly on telephone services dated back to 1913. The Bell System gave AT&T a monopoly on providing telephone service, and it was an end-to-end monopoly, which meant that AT&T had full control of any equipment that hooked into the telephone system. For consumers, that meant every phone had to be purchased from "the phone company" and the company had to install it. Phones were hardwired to a particular spot. Until the 1970s, there were one or two styles available and both were black. For companies, the "switchboard," approved and installed by AT&T, connected phones on desks. "Getting to a phone" was a panic situation exploited in movie plots.

By 1972, AT&T was having trouble defending its monopoly. Customers were clearly unhappy. To appease them, the company introduced beige instruments and "Princess phones" as more stylish instruments that came in pink, blue, and white. Teenagers demanded this upgrade, but business telephone users groaned and started using pagers and closed, radio-based systems originally developed for combat. MCI was already offering microwave transmissions in some areas for private communication systems.[3]

Ronald Reagan's election changed all that. His assistant attorney general, William Baxter, "looked upon the Bell System as a government-protected monopoly," and he did not approve of their rights. He promised to prosecute AT&T "to the eyeballs." AT&T's president, Charlie Brown, bowed to the inevitable. In 1982, AT&T kept the monopoly on long-distance service and granted local monopolies to other companies (the "Baby Bells") for local service.

By 1982, the FCC had acknowledged that competition in the telephone industry might be useful, but it moved cautiously, allowing only two licenses to provide service in each geographic area—and one of those licenses would go to the existing (wired) phone monopoly company in the area.[4] While the wired phone companies got their licenses immediately, other applicants had to submit detailed proposals verifying their technical competence.

Applications arrived by the thousands. One applicant brought the paperwork in a semitrailer. MCI sent thirty employees on a six-block walk, each carrying a box of paperwork. McCaw teamed up with a handful of other paging companies to apply for licenses in the Pacific Northwest cities of Portland and Seattle. Realizing that reviewing these applications was an impossible task, the FCC urged applicants to combine, to create fewer applications, and then began granting licenses on a lottery system. Everyone scrambled to enter. One winner was the first lady of Arkansas, Hillary Clinton. She and her partners promptly sold their license to McCaw.[5] He was ready to change the world.

The Baby Bells, which had their licenses first, weren't idle. Sam Ginn at Pacific Telesis (later just Pac Tel) knew his company was a horribly inadequate phone service provider in California. Caught between state regulators' refusal to increase the rates the company could charge and AT&T's reluctance to provide more capital without rate increases, the situation seemed hopeless until a court ruled that the local companies could diversify. Ginn decided that offering cellular phone service would be the company's salvation, and he vowed to introduce the service at the 1984 Los Angeles Olympics. As the runner carrying the flame trotted through Dallas, Texas, the mayor of Los Angeles, Tom Bradley, was calling the runner from his car. Another car, stationed in Dallas, received the mayor's call and handed the phone to the runner, creating a photo op of a runner talking on the phone while still carrying the torch. At the Games, Ginn staged another marketing opportunity. When Carl Lewis won the 100-meter dash, Ginn dialed his cell phone to communicate the results. People in nearby seats quickly took advantage of his offer to let them call their relatives and friends, thereby inaugurating the soon-to-be-ubiquitous phrase, "You'll never guess where I am!"[6]

The phones used at the 1984 Olympics were developed by Motorola. They were the size and weight of a brick, which gave them their nickname, and they cost $3,500. Motorola began developing the phone in 1977 to demonstrate the company's expertise and to win support for an experimental cellular system for Washington, D.C. In spite of the phone's and the cellular system's limitations, Pac Tel began receiving orders after the Olympics even faster than expected. In two months 7,000 customers a day were signing up. Pac Tel decided to expand.

McCaw had already been buying other licenses, recalling, "We just started vacuuming up the country, as much and as fast as our little hearts and wallets could allow." He didn't worry about the Baby Bells, trusting that their big company mentality would make them easy targets. But when Pac Tel tried to buy the license from GTE for San Francisco, McCaw's team went to war. He asked the FCC to block the acquisition to prevent the reformation of monopoly power. McCaw lost the first skirmish of the "Great War" in the cellular communications industry, but Pac Tel paid $11.50 a POP (potential customer) for the acquisition.[7]

McCaw bought MCI in 1986 for $122 million, raising the money with junk bonds sold through Michael Milken, who was financing many of the newer high-tech industries. The number of cellular customers in the United States reached 682,000 that year. As McCaw's company grew, he formed alliances with other companies he could not buy, even forming a partnership with Pac Tel as part of the settlement of his lawsuit over the purchase of GTE. The industry seemed to have no limits. McCaw decided to take an even bigger risk. He sold all his other assets to concentrate on wireless. In 1987, he took his company public, raising $2.39 billion.[8] He sold one-third of the company to AT&T in 1992, for $3.8 billion.[9]

In spite of all the growth in the cell phone business, even up to the early 1990s, almost all the phones were actually car phones that sold for about $1,000. Truly portable phones had not yet dropped in price to attract a mass market, nor had they achieved anything close to service reliability. These problems would be solved with the release of more wavelengths, particularly those formerly used for shortwave communications, new digital technology, and ongoing miniaturization, creating phones that were smaller with more efficient power usage. The last major boost to the industry came with the full deregulation of communications in 1996 and a resulting surge of innovation in products.

EMERGING FROM "MALAISES"

Cell phones were one—but only one—of the hundreds of new products that were revolutionizing daily life. From Sam Walton's discount megastores to Ken Iverson's Nucor Steel and its "mini-mills," American business entered a renaissance. Predictably, the entrepreneurs behind the economy and the boom itself went unreported. News stories covering the economy actually diminished as the economy improved throughout the 1980s, leading economist Warren Brookes to describe the decade's growth as the "Silent Boom."[10] Indeed, never in history has such a period of economic growth gone so uncelebrated in the popular media.

In part, however, the untold story reflected the nature of the growth itself: Millions of individual entrepreneurs, and thousands of small businesses, fueled the explosion. The most vibrant new sector, information technology (comprised of computers, software, telephones, fax machines, and the like), only stood out in a few large companies such as Xerox and IBM. Yet it was exactly in that sector that individual entrepreneurs drove the revolution, inventing and developing new technologies. Start-up companies, unburdened with the trappings of managerial hierarchies under which the large corporations staggered, revived several industries, while executives in the traditional big business sector "downsized" and eliminated layers of management and bureaucracy. And no industry more sharply contrasted the old-style, managerial hierarchies in distress with the new wave of thin management layers than steel, where a revival had occurred.

Continuing a trend that had appeared in the 1960s, "Big Steel"—that is, the largest steel corporations—continued to lose market share into the mid-1980s. U.S. Steel led the way, but deep problems beset all American steel companies. Steelmakers had fallen behind their foreign rivals in technology and paid far more for labor. From 1974 to 1986, steelmaking jobs fell by more than 337,000, and between 1982 and 1987, the industry eliminated 50 million tons annually—more than 30 percent—of its raw steelmaking capacity.[11] One-fourth of the industry went bankrupt, and 75 percent of all steelworkers in America lost their jobs in the crash.

Numerous problems afflicted the steel companies, not the least of which was a worldwide shift in demand. Auto manufacturers, especially, had ceased to use steel in many parts of the manufacturing process, substituting newer, lighter plastics and composites. Consequently, all the major steelmaking nations lost output—not just the United States—with total output of Western nations dropping from 494 million metric tons in 1974 to 368 million tons in 1986. What was once an American steel industry quickly became a *world* steel industry, but the Americans were slow to recognize the new competition.[12]

Friend and foe of business all agree on this point: The management of the largest steel companies—the same types of people who had sent Detroit into a free fall—failed utterly to invest in the future. Just as the finance men resisted the production managers at Ford who wanted to install modernized but expensive paint ovens large enough for vans, the steel managers resisted radical modernization. The one thing the steel managers never understood "was how to invest money shrewdly in manufacturing technology, and ... they were never able to inspire the hot metal to do much of anything except to go out on strike."[13] Many managers who were business-school graduates never even walked the mills, or appreciated the process of turning molten iron ore into steel. Unions played a role, too, repeatedly crippling the industry with strikes and outrageous demands. Unionized steelworkers received $20 an hour (plus benefits) in the United States, while their competitors worked for $3 an hour in Korea. Government policies took its toll on profits as inflation and regulation placed a further drag on productivity.

Ultimately, however, management had to assume most of the blame. Consequently, even when Big Steel turned the corner in 1987, a year in which the six largest domestic producers earned $1 billion and managed to increase prices, the major companies still had to scramble to regain the technological momentum. That year, the steel production of the United States was exceeded only by the Soviet Union and Japan as individual nations, although the United States remained behind the total production of the European Community. By 1993, however, American steel trailed only the Japanese and comprised over 11 percent of the world market (97 million tons, out of 814 million tons produced in the world).

A clear example of how far the large American steel companies had come—and how far they still had to go—could be seen in the case of U.S. Steel. The company founded by Andrew Carnegie as Carnegie Steel and incorporated by J. P. Morgan as U.S. Steel adopted a new name in 1986, USX Corporation, with the "X" referring to the NYSE symbol for the company. USX, symptomatic of other struggling manufacturing companies, had tried to solve its problems through diversification into nonsteel businesses, acquiring Marathon Oil in 1982 and Texas Oil & Gas in 1986. What once was U.S. Steel by that time was more than two-thirds nonsteel business. Much of the revival of USX could be credited to Thomas Graham, the president, who saved U.S. Steel from bankruptcy in 1983. "We tore three layers of management out of this company after I became president," he proudly noted.[14] A restructured USX accounted for approximately 11 percent of the total amount of steel produced in America by the 1990s, when it was the leading U.S. steelmaker in volume and total earnings. Even in its successful retrenchment, however, instead of recapturing the glory of the Carnegie years, USX tried to insulate itself from failure in the steel business through diversification out of steel. But fear of failure never stopped Carnegie, and "creative destruction" was a way of life at the early Carnegie mills. Modern corporations avoided risk, however, especially when it meant radical new technology such as the electric minimill.

In 1965, a small multiproduct manufacturing company called Nuclear Corporation of America (later known as Nucor) came to a similar point in its history as had USX in 1983. One of the company's chief subsidiaries, Vulcraft Corporation, made roof joists of steel bar for shopping center roofs, but it also had an air-conditioning duct business. Its stock dropped to 11 cents a share, and the company had invested in several long-shot technologies. The board of directors needed to take drastic action, and it brought in a division chief, Ken Iverson, as the new president. Iverson concluded that Nucor needed to get into the steelmaking business to supply Vulcraft with its own steel. However, Iverson's vision went beyond filling a niche, as he already had started thinking of competing with foreign steel companies.[15] Nucor could not afford to build its own blast furnace for smelting iron ore (at a cost of $200 million), pushing Iverson to an alternative steelmaking process that used an electric arc furnace. For raw material, Nucor melted junk metal, which was abundant in America. Iverson wanted to leapfrog the American steel industry, not just catch up.

In 1969, Nucor melted its first heap of steel at a minimill in Darlington, South Carolina, using an entirely nonunion workforce. By 1980, Iverson had opened Nucor's fourth minimill, and at the same time took over much of the joist business that the major steelmakers were leaving in force. Nucor's earnings reached $42 million by 1980. Iverson increasingly resembled Carnegie: Convinced that the Darlington mill, built only nine years earlier, was decrepit, he had it torn apart and rebuilt. "Big Steel" looked on the electric arc process with skepticism. Experts from the traditional companies thought it impossible to make steel profitably the way Nucor did. But other new competitors thought otherwise, so much so that by 1980 a dozen minimill competitors pressured Nucor. Hurricane Industries, Border Steel, Bayou Steel, Florida Steel, and many others hunted Nucor the way Nucor had hunted USX. In the process, the minimills fulfilled Iverson's vision by killing the importation of foreign bar steel into the United States. Iverson had hit the target.

Companies such as Nucor paid wages equal to the unionized steelworkers' pay, but with a major difference. In the minimills, bonuses for production played a far more important part in the total wage—more than half in the case of Nucor. All Iverson had to do to keep unions away from Nucor was to tell employees the harsh statistics: There were once 450,000 steelworkers in the United States and in the 1980s there were only 130,000, and that massive unemployment occurred at the height of union power. Like many of the minimills, Nucor gave its employees stock at regular intervals. With one exception, Nucor never laid off any employees, and in that one event, the Nucor front office overruled a manager who had fired forty employees, then fired the manager himself. As for bureaucracy, Nucor operated out of a rented office the size of a group dental practice, and as of 1988, it had twenty-two manufacturing plants, with a ratio of 0.8 corporate front-office people per factory!

By 1988, Nucor stock hit $40 a share and the company produced 2 million tons of steel from junk melted with electricity. At a net profit of a penny a pound, Nucor earned $50 million a year net profits. Yet Iverson continually looked for new technology. He opened a new plant in Crawfordsville, Indiana, in 1989 that featured the world's first continuous steelmaking machine, the Compact Strip Production Facility—a machine 1,177 feet long that would produce hot band steel used in truck frames and water tanks and then "cold-roll" some of the same steel into paper-thin sheets for computer parts, filing cabinets, and auto fenders. The company specifically located the plant in the Rust Belt because, as Iverson reasoned, the Rust Belt had scrap. Crawfordsville represented a desktop steel mill, capable of unimagined labor efficiency gains. Whereas the most efficient traditional steel facilities, such as USX's plant in Gary, Indiana, required three to four man-hours to manufacture a ton of hot-band (not finished) steel, the Crawfordsville facility used only 0.6 man-hours to produce a ton of virtually finished steel. That represented a level of efficiency approximately five times better than the best Japanese plants. Success with the Crawfordsville design allowed Nucor to open a similar plant in Hickman, Arkansas, in 1993. That year, Nucor stock passed the $50-a-share mark, and Nucor stood in fourth place among all U.S. steel companies.[16]

As the chief consumer of steel, the auto industry had struggled as well. Its inability to make small, fuel-efficient cars in the 1970s had allowed imports to enter the U.S. market successfully. Imports as a share of the American auto market rose, surging above 25 percent by the end of the 1970s.

Lee Iacocca moved to chaotic Chrysler from Ford in 1978. Undertaking a massive top-to-bottom purge of the executive structure—firing thirty-three of thirty-five vice presidents—Iacocca insisted that the company focus on quality to compete with the Japanese.[17] His greatest feat, however, was the successful acquisition of federal loan guarantees of $1.5 billion in 1980 and the negotiation of "voluntary" restrictions on Japanese imports.[18]

Nevertheless, Chrysler made good. As profits of all the U.S. auto manufacturers rose, Iacocca showily repaid the loan and produced a new line of restyled front-wheel-drive cars, recapturing some of its American market share. Convinced that he could sell the product better than an actor, Iacocca went before the cameras to film a series of highly successful commercials. Overnight, Iacocca went from auto executive to media personality. Iacocca restored the public's trust in Chrysler. After a setback, in which the company was indicted for resetting the odometers on cars that had been driven by Chrysler executives and then selling them as new, Iacocca filmed a commercial in which he asked, "Did we screw up? You bet we did…. [Chrysler's actions] went beyond dumb and reached all the way out to stupid."[19] By the time he published his autobiography in 1984, Iacocca was held in greater esteem by the public than any business figure since the 1920s.[20]

REGULATIONS AND BUSINESS

Businesses were subjected to a blizzard of federal regulations that one author called a "legacy to nightclub comics." Among the rulings handed down by federal agencies or lawsuits heard before courts, and other extreme examples of regulatory "overkill," are the following:

■ Simply "annoying" a kangaroo rat could result in a fine of as much as $100,000 and a sentence of one year in jail. Shining a flashlight on the animal was considered annoying.

■ The Food and Drug Administration (FDA) demanded that a small herring smokehouse install $75,000 worth of new equipment, despite its excellent record over a twenty-year period of having produced 54 million fillets without a single case of reported food poisoning. The business closed instead.

■ A striptease bar in Los Angeles, the Odd Ball Cabaret, had to install a wheelchair ramp into the shower stall used in shows because the lack of a ramp discriminated against strippers who needed a wheelchair.

■ Burger King was sued by a deaf woman who claimed that the drive-through windows discriminated against deaf people.

■ Obesity, alcoholism, and drug addiction were designated "protected" disabilities by the Equal Employment Opportunity Commission. Likewise, businesses found they faced federal investigation when they attempted to fire employees who had serious mental problems and were violently dangerous to other employees and customers.

Businesses found such rulings distressing and costly. By 1995, federal agencies alone added 200 pages of new rulings and regulations per day in the Federal Register. The cost to businesses reached billions of dollars per year, passed on to consumers in higher prices and lower productivity by American firms.[21] Regulatory costs ate up as much as 10 percent of the GDP per year in the 1990s, much of it comprised of paperwork. Individuals seldom noticed the hidden cost of regulations, but by 1996 federal regulatory mandates alone cost each American household $6,083.[22]

Many Americans freely ladled new regulations on business because the media had fostered strong antibusiness sympathies for almost two decades. One analysis by Stanley Rothman and Robert Lichter studied 240 journalists regarded as America's most influential media institutions, such as *The New York Times*, *The Washington Post*, *The Wall Street Journal*, *Time*, and *Newsweek*; their study also included the major television networks and 216 executives in management of major corporations. Rothman and Lichter concluded that the media elite "grew up at some distance from the social and cultural traditions of small-town 'middle America,'" and that on attitudinal questions they were strongly antibusiness. Almost one-half of those in the media elite thought the government should guarantee a job to everyone who wanted to work. Perhaps most tellingly, when asked "Who should rule?" the media elites chose themselves![23] The divisions were deep between the media and the business community: When presented with hypothetical scenarios, media elites much more frequently than business elites interpreted situations in such a way as to suggest hostility to authority and economic success.

Not only did the media resent business, but a second group looked disparagingly at America's new entrepreneurs. Displaced upper classes—the "patrician rich" of yesteryear, or what George Gilder called "the declining rich"—saw the surging business class as a threat to its once-secure social position.[24] Like Sam Walton, many of the members of the new entrepreneurial wave came from distinctly nonelite areas such as Bentonville, Arkansas; Boise, Idaho; Phoenix, Arizona; or Charlotte, North Carolina. Unlike the wealthy political families, such as the Rockefellers and Kennedys, the new rich, like Ken Iverson, were accessible by a single telephone call, working in a nondescript office with one secretary. They frequented Burger King and the Waffle House on Main Street as often as they did Spago in Beverly Hills or the Four Seasons in New York City. They were as likely to drive pickups and Chevy Camaros as Mercedes and Ferraris; and they vacationed at Disney World or Las Vegas instead of the Hamptons or Europe.

As they rose, through video rental businesses like Blockbuster, software companies like Microsoft, or hamburger chains like McDonald's, the new entrepreneurs embraced risks—which the "declining rich" avoided. Instead, the declining rich chose to work in law, politics, universities, or the nonprofit sector as they struggled to maintain their families' declining fortunes. Consider the Kennedys, whose wealth for decades was cemented by Joseph P. Kennedy's willingness to plunge into the stock market at its lowest point, but whose siblings and grandchildren have abdicated the business sector in favor of law and politics, eschewing the difficult path to re-create the patriarch's financial success. In 1995, the family sold one of the last vestiges of its privileged position—the Palm Beach mansion—and even the Rockefellers, unable to sustain their manorial estates, turned some of them over to the National Trust for Historic Preservation.

SMALL BUSINESSES, GROWING BUSINESSES

If most entrepreneurs did not come from the "established classes," where did they come from? Obviously, they had not disappeared. Indeed, the quickest way to wealth in America remained business. Even more important, entrepreneurship remained virtually the only path to riches open to ordinary citizens who were minorities. The 1996 Forbes 400, for example, featured twenty-three immigrants and sixty women, with women falling off the list rapidly as the "old wealth" disappeared (such as Mary Malone, an inheritor of the Campbell Soup fortune) and new, truly entrepreneurial females with their own wealth replaced them, such as Oprah Winfrey.[25] But while many entrepreneurs saw their efforts result in phenomenal growth, as with Bill Gates or Sam Walton, most business start-ups remained small.

The revival of small business, declared dead as an independent force by John Kenneth Galbraith in his 1971 book *The New Industrial State*, more than offset the decline in employment by the large corporations. Between 1974 and 1984, for example, employment in *Fortune's* 500 largest companies fell by 1.5 million while net employment in small business, under a variety of definitions, rose. In the 1980s, the phenomena of small-business employment growth accelerated, as the United States created 20 million new jobs, with over three-fifths of them generated by independent small businesses with under 500 employees. A record number of start-ups, which had accelerated during the 1980s, allowed 9.5 percent of the workforce to be their own bosses. As early as 1981, then Governor Richard Lamm of Colorado announced that "there is a tidal wave behind me. Its name is small business. Any politician who does not look over his shoulder at that wave will be a politician out of a job."[26]

Even the statistics, however, presented an inaccurate picture of the extent of small business's influence on the economy. As one authority on small business pointed out, "hundreds [of the 3,000 largest corporations] are in reality large small businesses still run by their founders or family heirs."[27] Consider our earlier example of Sam Walton and his family business: Is Wal-Mart a "big business" run as a "small business," or vice versa? More to the point, the goal of small business is to grow, and if successful, any small business will grow into a big business. Those lamenting the demise of "mom-and-pop" stores in downtown areas miss the essential dynamism at work in which mom and pop became Wal-Mart through growth and talent.

As small firms grow, they become attractive targets for acquisition by larger companies. During the 1970s, for example, 2,000 to 5,000 publicly announced mergers with a value of more than $500,000 occurred, of which 95 percent involved small companies.[28] Growth among small firms also led to an explosion of incorporations. Small business drove a corporate expansion of 20 percent a year, totaling more than 650,000 new incorporations since the mid-1980s. Although all of those were not true businesses—some were simply tax dodges or were created for other legal purposes—the corporate and noncorporate start-ups represented $70 billion in new business investments per year. At the same time, businesses also failed, and 400,000 corporations ended their operations every year, although most terminations represent the retirement of the principal owner.

Static assessments of the American economy failed to capture the revolution in productivity that small business had sparked. Between 1974 and 1984, the U.S. economy grew by 20 million net new jobs, and at the same time accepted 12 million immigrants. Meanwhile, the European Economic Community (EEC) generated *zero* net new jobs—none whatsoever—during the decade. The U.S. rate also exceeded Japan's new job growth by a factor of three. American manufacturing held firm at 48 percent of all existing jobs, but Europe lost 10 percent of its manufacturing jobs. Since most of that job growth in America came from small business, which counted large numbers of immigrants, the numbers were skewed further as Taiwanese, Koreans, Vietnamese, Mexicans, Cubans, and people from scores of other nations surged into the United States creating restaurants, laundries, computer stores, video outlets, software businesses, and grocery stores. Usually, they capitalized their stores with savings and the labor of their families, much of which went unreported in the national wealth and income statistics, but nevertheless was real. In the flight from the Castro regime in the 1960s, more than 200,000 Cubans arrived in Florida in less than two years. Doctors, architects, and lawyers escaped to work as busboys or dishwashers in America, while less educated laborers took what they could get. By 1987, those busboys and waitresses had created more than 25,000 Cuban-owned businesses in Dade County alone. A typical entrepreneur, Jose Pinero, peddled secondhand records until he could afford to refurbish a small shop. His record store, called Ultra, catered to Latin customers with the most recent imports. Soon he had expanded his Ultra stores into new shopping malls, and he built a warehouse that imported from throughout the Caribbean and Latin America.[29]

But the Cuban, Vietnamese, and West Indian immigration that generated the new boom was nothing new in American history. Consider Nathan Handwerker and Ida Greenwald, two Polish immigrants who came to America during the immigrant wave of the early twentieth century and worked in Coney Island restaurants. A pair of singing waiters named Jimmy Durante and Eddie Cantor suggested that the couple— who wed in 1913—start their own frankfurter stand. Drawing on their $300 life savings, Nathan and Ida established Nathan's in 1916 using a secret spice recipe to fashion a tasty hot dog that became the company's trademark. Seventy-five years later, Nathan's Famous, Inc., was one of the best-known hot dog businesses in the United States.

Nathan's story illustrated the first reality of almost every new business: It did not originate with a bank loan. Most new businesses receive neither bank funds nor government support. And, like most other businesses, Nathan's embodied two other significant realities. First, small business requires labor, but since family labor is not recognized in official ways (such as Social Security, FICA, and so on), the wealth those businesses generate often goes unreported or underreported. Nevertheless, of those statistics we do have, since World War II, families with zero assets based on traditional accounting measurements generated billions of dollars in net value when measured in other ways. Consider entrepreneurs such as Michael Zabian, a Lebanese businessman from Lee, Massachusetts, who toiled to bring produce from the nearby farm areas of Massachusetts and Connecticut to his town, eventually parlaying that labor-intensive business into a network of clothing, office, and retail stores, or Jerry Colangelo, an Italian from the Chicago streets who ran a sports clothing business until he got an opportunity to work with the Chicago Bulls, only to work his way into the position of general manager, then owner, of the Phoenix Suns basketball team and Arizona Diamondbacks baseball team. Both men typified the process of rising from virtually nothing to the heights of achievement.[30]

Many entrepreneurs, and some of their family members, have been labeled "workaholics." Lebanese businesses were open, on average, sixteen to eighteen hours a day, while a study of Koreans in Atlanta showed that they worked an average of sixty hours a week in their stores.[31] The owner's personal presence on the scene ensured quality control and business relations that half a dozen hired employees might not provide. More important, hard work is absolutely critical to economic improvement. Studies from the Institute for Research on Poverty, based on work effort levels outside the home, have concluded that to improve in one's economic class, a person must work harder than those already in it. By the 1980s, the poor in America—by the same index—worked fewer hours a week, even after correcting the data for age, education, and other credentials, than previous groups in poverty.[32] Indeed, the National Bureau of Economic Research (NBER) found that the presence of programs such as Aid to Families with Dependent Children (AFDC, frequently generalized as "welfare") drove down labor force participation. One NBER study found that labor participation would increase forty-seven hours a month for husbands and thirty-two hours a month for wives without such programs. The unfortunate conclusion of the government's own study was that welfare recipients "cannot find entry-level employment that pays much better than the government subsidies to nonemployment" after considering the effect of taxes and work-related expenses.[33]

A second reality of new or growing businesses, also involving families, stood in sharp contrast to common perceptions. It is still widely believed that the only route to business success comes through inheriting assets. As seen in our numerous case studies throughout this book—with Nathan's as but one example—virtually none of the truly successful entrepreneurs received any substantial inheritance. Studies of male supermillionaires (women are excluded because they often are recipients of inherited wealth) revealed that by 1978, only one-third inherited a significant portion of their money; and in the second tier ($2 million net worth, in 1979 dollars), 71 percent reported no inherited assets at all. Moreover, in 1996, one in nine members of the *Forbes* 400 were new to the list, and since 1990, 238 new members had displaced an equal number of others. As *Forbes* itself commented, "Forget old money. Forget silver spoons. Great fortunes are being created almost monthly in the U.S. today by young entrepreneurs who hadn't a dime when we created this list fourteen years ago."[34]

An extensive study of more than 1,100 millionaires in the early 1990s by Thomas Stanley and William Danko, fittingly called *The Millionaire Next Door*, found that *"80 percent of America's million-*

aires are first-generation rich" (emphasis in original).[35] More impressive, more than half of America's millionaires never received a penny in inheritance, while fewer than 20 percent inherited even 10 percent of their wealth and lived, in disproportionate numbers to less wealthy earners, below their means. Most millionaires never paid more than $30,000 for an automobile (and nearly one-third were driving cars two years old or older), or they never bought a suit of clothes that cost more than $300! Such frugality allowed them to plow more capital back into their businesses.

Starting with no inheritance, using money borrowed from family or friends, and working extensive hours—all these factors made for a difficult life for most entrepreneurs, at least in the beginning of their enterprise. Sacrifices were made, and perhaps such sacrifices should guarantee success. But they never have: Two-thirds of all new businesses in America fail within five years. Many entrepreneurs, who failed once, or even twice, never quit. Thomas Edison tried more than 2,000 experiments before he got his lightbulb to work, and writer Louis L'Amour, author of more than a hundred Western novels, with 200 million copies in print, received 350 rejections before his first publication. Radio personality/entrepreneur Rush Limbaugh declared bankruptcy and was fired several times before becoming the highest paid radio host of the most popular radio talk show in history. Indeed, failure and destitution often provide the crucial prod to motivate an individual to success. Actor Sylvester Stallone, with the screenplay for *Rocky* in his hands, lived in an apartment without electricity until he could sell his story with himself as the lead. Forest Mars, after one bankruptcy, failed in two other ventures. He then entered the candy market, making a fortune in the process. That stubborn refusal to quit marked the careers of some of the most famous success stories in America, business or otherwise: Elvis Presley was fired from the Grand Ole Opry after one performance, and Lucille Ball was told by the instructor of her drama school, "Try any other profession. Any other."

To an entrepreneur, failure is never final, but risk taking is essential. Jerry Jones worked in his parents' Little Rock, Arkansas, grocery store, went to the University of Arkansas on a football scholarship, and sold anything and everything—at one time buying student football game tickets for $1 and reselling them for $20. After college, he started working in the oil fields, investing in drilling operations, taking chances no one else would take. He focused on areas where others had failed, hitting on thirty-three of thirty-four wells. In 1989, he purchased the Dallas Cowboys for $140 million, when experts said the franchise was only worth $120 million. By 1998, as the most valuable sports franchise in the world, the Cowboys were valued at more than $200 million. Through it all, he worked hard, maintaining twenty-hour days on occasion, but he could relax from time to time by looking at the three Super Bowl trophies Dallas had collected under his ownership.[36]

Business, and particularly small business, not only represented the major avenue to achievement by business owners, but it has constituted a source of employment for millions of workers and become the single most significant employer of minorities. Four-fifths of minorities by 1980 held jobs in small companies. Because small firms tended to be more labor-intensive and experienced more rapid net increases in capital value than the giants, they hired workers in ever-expanding numbers. Most important, however, small businesses often gave workers their first jobs, providing crucial training in "real life" employment that teaches employees—usually young people—how to be well groomed, arrive on time, and take on tasks that are not immediately pointed out to them. Often derided as "minimum wage, dead-end" jobs, small-business positions, in fact, ensure success in more long-term, career-oriented jobs. Nor were critics correct in arguing that there was any particular surge in part-time jobs, especially by those who had other options. A 1994 study showed that "there has not been a huge increase in part-time employment throughout the 1980s and early 1990s and that involuntary part-time workers (i.e., those forced into part-time labor due to hard economic conditions) actually fell between 1982 and 1992."[37]

Fast-food franchises, which in the strict sense are part of big business, but to the franchisee owners are the epitome of small business, play a particularly vital role in job training. McDonald's, astoundingly, has given employment to one out of fifteen first-time job seekers in recent years! Approximately 75 percent of McDonald's restaurant owners are franchisees, but virtually all of them can look not only to company founder Ray Kroc, but to other employees who made good. Michael Quinlan, onetime president and CEO of McDonald's, began as a mailroom clerk with the company; Fred Turner, chairman of the board in 1989, was a door-to-door salesman who started as a "burger flipper" at age 23; Ed Rensi, former president of McDonald's USA, dropped out of Ohio State to hustle fries; and more than 50 percent of the store managers started behind the counter.[38] Women made up half of the store managers nationally (at an average salary of $28,000), and McDonald's was the largest employer of black youth in the United States.

As significant as the creation of new businesses and jobs was—jobs in restaurants, laundries, auto shops, landscaping, artistic design, and a host of other businesses—it paled by comparison to the dynamic entrepreneurial upheaval of the 1980s in the computer industry, where many more small businesses were creating a new way of life. By the mid-1980s, the personal computer (PC) reached a watershed point when some 100 PCs, wired together, beat a Cray supercomputer in a game of chess. That demonstration heralded the arrival of PCs that contained all the computing capabilities of machines once available only to the Pentagon and the largest corporations in America. It also reflected the fact that the computer would have the most wide-ranging effects on all business operations and productivity of any device since the steam engine.

COMPUTERS, FIBER OPTICS, AND JUNK BONDS

A remarkable symbiotic relationship developed in the 1980s between the telephone and computer industries. Devices called modems allowed personal computers to be connected, through phone lines, to other computers and databases. For all practical purposes, an individual with a modem (invented at Bell Labs in 1958) and enough expertise could gain access to any database in the world. This development opened immense prospects for individuals who wanted liberation from the workplace—allowing workers to literally "phone in" certain types of work from their homes or off-site offices. But that just scratched the surface of the real revolution. A more complete understanding of the phenomenal, truly revolutionary changes that overtook American business in the 1980s and 1990s requires a historical foundation in several industries. Perhaps the best place to start is with telephones.

When the Justice Department brought an antitrust suit against AT&T in 1974, the main challenge came from MCI Communications, a microwave-based communications firm under the leadership of William McGowan, who was constantly prompting the Justice Department to end the Bell monopoly.[39] The assistant attorney general wanted a divestiture that indeed produced unsubsidized competition; he wanted the unregulated portions of AT&T's business separated from the regulated, protected elements. In 1982,[40] under the new agreement, a division of territory occurred in which the Baby Bells could provide local service but had to stay out of long-distance telephone operations. More important, perhaps, the Baby Bells were prohibited from requiring the use of their own telephone equipment. A new creation, AT&T Network Systems, took the place of Western Electric supplying equipment. AT&T also created other subsidiary systems to handle new high-technology markets.[41]

Breaking up Ma Bell involved many of the same arguments used against the railroads. Important rate differences existed between long-distance service and local phone service, with the former subsidizing the latter. After the breakup, costs had to be recovered from the service offered.[42] That forced AT&T to regain its competitiveness: The company had become "bovine: the great all-American cash cow to be milked and massaged," dispensing a reliable flow of dividends in its protected environment.[43] Despite the fact that both the transistor and the laser had been invented at Bell Labs, under AT&T, the company had not invested aggressively or embraced new technology. That was especially true in the case of fiber optics, to which Bell Labs also had contributed. FCC rules added to AT&T's lethargy, making the company depreciate telephone equipment over periods as long as fifty years. Moreover, AT&T made use of a system in which wires were cheap and switches were expensive. Consequently, the system composed a top-down pyramid in which wires ran from every household to switches at a central office that served up to 15,000 phones. Where operators once plugged patch cords into switchboards at central offices, they were replaced by faster, magnetically controlled switches, but switches had now been replaced by computers.

Most obviously, plummeting prices of silicon chips made computers themselves simultaneously more powerful yet less expensive. The most important economic fact of life was that the price of computer chips had fallen from $7 in 1956 to one ten-thousandth of a cent in the 1980s, pulling prices of PCs down and resulting in the installation of 50 million PCs (half the world's total) in American homes and worksites.

Prices fell so fast that within seven years, any computer function would expand in power by a factor of ten, while costs would fall by more than ten times. That reordering of the communications world made the old Bell system of many wires and few switches obsolete. Suddenly, it made more sense to have fewer wires and more switches, because simultaneously the fiber-optic revolution made it possible for wires to carry quantum higher volumes of information than copper wire. In such a structure, the "intelligence" of the system would move from large, centralized locations to homes and offices (the customer's premises) through switching systems in the phones and computer faxes.

Fiber-optic, silicon-glass wire became available by 1978. Glass proved immune to corrosion and lightning and had all the reliability and durability of copper. But AT&T expressed reluctance to move to glass wire, with good reason. As the industry leader, it had a global base of copper wire and microwave-based systems. It took a new company, with everything to gain and little to lose, to embrace the new technology. The opportunity came from the antitrust consent decree that had opened the door for MCI to move into the market. William McGowan, MCI's president, recognized the possibilities for fiber-optic telecommunications, especially since his company used microwave technology. The network of fiber-optic wires would cost upwards of $3 billion, well above what MCI, with its $230 million in revenues, could raise. But as for Craig McGowan, the savior of the American telecommunications industry had arrived in the form of an unorthodox bond broker from Drexel Burnham Lambert: Michael Milken.

During the 1970s, Milken had refined—although everyone agrees he did not invent—the high-yield, high-risk securities called "junk bonds." Traditional Wall Street investment banks had ranked, or graded, the bonds of businesses, with AAA being the best. Milken made an "end run" around the system, offering new, ungraded securities for companies unable to obtain investment support from the traditional investment banks. Junk bonds are a loan to a company and convey no rights to control. This was an advantage to high-tech start-ups with owners who did not want to give up control or the huge profit they expected. Junk bonds paid high but fixed interest—if the company survived. Investors bought them in a variety of young companies, knowing that some would pay as promised and others would not. (The notion that junk bonds were inherently bad was, in the words of management

guru Tom Peters, "baloney…. [J]unk bond financed companies are creating jobs at four times the average rate for the economy as a whole …
[and] have a third greater productivity, 50 percent greater growth in
sales, and about three times faster growth in capital spending."[44]
Michael Jensen correctly noted that junk bonds meant the "eclipse" of
the public corporation because they took capital out of the hands of
Wall Street elites and democratized it, while Glenn Yago credited junk
bonds with nothing short of restructuring corporate America.[45]

Milken saw junk bonds as the currency of fast-rising companies
whose bond ratings had not caught up to them. In MCI, Milken perceived that new companies had an ocean of "uncapitalized capital" and
concluded that McGowan could make a public offering of $1 billion for
his new fiber-optic system—at the time, the largest public offering in
history. When Milken had completed the bond issue, he raised $2 bil-
lion for MCI, which ordered more than 62,000 miles of Corning glass
fiber wire. Corning, for its part, thus cemented its worldwide lead in
technology it had pursued for almost two decades. But the story still
was not complete. It required expansion in two other technological
areas to reach full potential.

CABLE TELEVISION AND CELLULAR PHONES

Phone companies, of course, were not the only businesses to employ
glass wire. Cable television companies had originated in "community
antenna television" in 1949, when enterprising small-town businessmen
would erect large antennae atop nearby mountains or tall buildings to
receive signals sent from distant cities and pass them on to home televisions of system subscribers who paid for the service. During the
1960s, cable television moved into many of the country's major cities,
but it did not achieve any real profits until the 1970s. The turning point
came in 1975, when a subsidiary of Time, Inc., initiated the first national, satellite-delivered programming service. Local cable system operators promised subscribers a channel of commercial-free, recent motion
pictures and other entertainment features under the name Home Box
Office (HBO). When more "premium" channels replicated HBO's innovation, cable television offered an attractive alternative to convention-

al network programming fare. By the mid-1980s, more than 40 percent of American television homes received cable; by the 1990s, almost 2 million new homes were wired with cable every year.

Cable television, plus the appearance of a fourth major broadcast network, Fox, in 1986, accelerated the decline of network television. Whereas the three national networks (NBC, CBS, and ABC) once controlled 90 percent of the share of viewers in the evening prime-time hours, in the mid-1980s that number dropped to roughly 70 percent. The appearance of unfiltered coverage of Congress by C-SPAN, the introduction of TV-based retail sales through the Home Shopping Network, and hundreds of niche programs, including religious, sports, history, and science shows, suggested that the decline in the share of television programming commanded by the major networks would continue, if not accelerate.[46]

With the arrival of highly intelligent home-based PCs, however, television technology suddenly had the potential to manipulate video signals, replaying them, zooming in or out, storing, and even editing pictures, essentially bypassing the VCR. Data for such a system had to be digital, bypassing the airwaves in favor of delivery over cable. Digital signals had the advantage over the traditional television analog signals in that they could be stored and manipulated without degradation. When combined with the carrying capacity of fiber-optic wires, the basics existed to transmit television directly to PCs. More important, the technology completely reversed the "top-down, master-slave" model of delivering TV programming to the home and instead transformed into a system with the brains now residing at the bottom—in the home PC—and the programming sent through telephone lines.

The final component of the telecosm—the television/computer nexus—involved the appearance of cellular phones, which did not use wires at all, but, like television and radio, used the airwaves to carry transmissions. Ironically, then, "while television service is moving increasingly from air to wire, telephone service is shifting increasingly from wire to the air."[47] (It is therefore erroneous to argue, as does Peter Temin, that the technology shift represented some sort of temporary opportunity: While he correctly points to the emphasis on fiber-optic cables, he mistakenly assumes that the product carried by those cables will remain the same, rather than, as Gilder argues, "flip-flopping" with the traditional television product.[48])

AMERICAN COMPUTERS
DOMINATE THE MARKET

Driving the entire revolution, the computer was, and remains, essentially American. The U.S. computer industry held a worldwide market share of 70 percent in 1995, and more important, American entrepreneurs formed a widespread network of innovation, invention, and capital. More than 20,000 computer firms conducted business in the United States, including 14,000 software companies, 800 digital processing companies, and 1,000 companies in the field of multimedia programming.

Junk bonds were responsible for the rapid growth of the computer industry, thanks to the limitations of traditional financial markets. Between 1986 and 1990, junk bonds financed 80 percent of the industry's expansion, and the share financed by junk bonds could only continue to grow as long as advances in chip technology moved faster than the staid Wall Street investment firms could assess their positions and give their seal of approval. Small firms such as Microchip Technology, of Chandler, Arizona, had their chip sales skyrocket in the 1990s. Microchip's stock went from $18 per share to $38 per share, splitting three-for-two, starting again in the low $20s, then rising again to $41 per share by 1995. Microchip, which invested $75 million in new production facilities, was not even listed on the New York Stock Exchange, nor were thousands of other high-tech firms that generated the bulk of the nation's growth in the 1980s and 1990s. Although American chip manufacturers outproduced the Japanese by almost $6 billion (when adjusted for exchange rate fluctuations), perhaps most telling was the commanding lead that the United States enjoyed in software. In 1987 America accounted for $23.6 billion worth of software sales, an amount that represented more than half of the world's software market and a ratio of market share that was increasing.

The role of entrepreneurial companies in the computer industry should not obscure the resurgence of the industry giant, IBM. Whereas some saw "Big Blue" as a looming, threatening figure on the American computer scene, the company had struggled to stay competitive. From 1990 to 1993, IBM took an $8 billion loss on hardware sales. Its total revenue fell below $64 billion in 1993, and its research and development budget dropped by half over a four-year period. But IBM had a reputation as a cutthroat company, and the CEO, Louis Gerstner, was known for starting meetings with his managers by flashing a photo of Microsoft's Bill Gates on the wall and announcing, "This man wakes up hating you!"[49] Gerstner knew IBM was in trouble from newer, more agile companies like Microsoft, which had a $5.2 billion business in personal computer software—a marketplace in which IBM barely ranked. Although Gerstner sliced his workforce by some 25 percent, by 1994 IBM still had not reached its profit levels of 1990. When IBM did start to recover, however, it was precisely because of the competition from Bill Gates, Steven Jobs, and other entrepreneurs. To make inroads into the PC software market, in the summer of 1995 IBM launched a $3.5 billion hostile takeover bid for Cambridge, Massachusetts-based Lotus Development Corporation, the third-largest software maker in the world.

Meanwhile, industry dynamos such as Intel rattled out a string of chips that increased processing power by *1,000 percent in less than seven years*. Indeed, by the 1990s, even the optimists had underestimated the growth of the American computer industry. Industry estimates placed the increase in the number of PCs at 33 percent. New software and chips made quantum leaps in processing power, with the Intel Pentium chip alone featured in 60 percent of new systems; by 1996, more than 80 percent of systems sold contained the Pentium chip, significantly upgrading their capabilities, even as new chips came on line that ran at 1,000 megahertz (MHz), or *quadruple* the speed of the (up to that point) newest Pentium. Domestic penetration of PCs grew at a rate of 40 percent a year, while the price of a bit of semiconductor memory over a thirty-year period had plummeted 68 percent a year![50] Meanwhile, the Japanese were nowhere to be found in the forecast of growth in the computer market. Andrew Grove, CEO of Intel, acknowledged: "In the mid-1980s, people like me were fearing that Japanese companies would take over the U.S. personal computer market.... Today, I find them a surprisingly inefficient force."[51]

REVOLUTION IN THE AIR

American success stories soon appeared even in industries long associated with Japanese domination. Radios and televisions, once the proud domain of RCA and GE, Philco and Magnavox, had yielded their markets to the Japanese invasion in the 1960s. Yet many aspects of the radio and television business illustrated the axiom that it is not the saddle that carries the rider, but the horse.

The advent of stereo-sound-enhanced FM radio transmission in the 1960s led to a gradual shift away from popular AM radio. Traditionally, AM stations played "top forty" songs of no more than two and a half minutes in length (program executives thought that was the attention span of teenagers, the largest listener group the AM stations had). By the late 1960s, however, FM stations started to embody the "counterculture," playing music of styles and lengths that AM programmers would not. Groups unable to get their music on mainstream radio, including Janis Joplin, Jimi Hendrix, Cream, Grateful Dead, and, later, Pink Floyd, Alan Parsons, and Yes, prospered on the FM wavelength. At the peak of student unrest and discontent over the Vietnam War, FM stations were viewed by many radicals as the "voice of the people." (Contrary to popular myth, however, the rock music industry lagged well behind the radical movement in opposing the war. In fact, the recording industry did not produce, nor did stations play, any significant number of antiwar songs until long after the popular tide turned. By then, the war no longer was as well supported by the general public as it was from 1964 to 1966, when the number one song was "The Ballad of the Green Berets."[52])

Television continued as the dominant entertainment medium in the United States. The most significant development in television technology in the 1960s to 1980s, the arrival of the videocassette recorder (VCR), contained significant lessons for small entrepreneurs and large companies, as well as implications for "industrial policy." The triumph of the VCR and, ultimately, of one format of VCR, was not a foregone conclusion. Like other inventions, it had to establish itself against strong competition. Videotape had existed since 1956, when a group of American engineers at Ampex succeeded in putting images and sound to magnetic tape. At the end of their two-minute demonstration, the group of observers "suddenly leaped to their feet and started shouting and hand clapping."[53] Ampex led the field for a short time, but failed to advance the technology from the seven-inch reels of half-inch tape that could record an hour's worth of programming. Early bulky, heavy versions of the videotape machine required an operator to wind the tape through the reel to start the process. And even though American producers experienced stiff competition from Sony and other Japanese companies, early models introduced in 1966 sold for more than $1,000, finding markets mostly in schools or other educational settings.

Enterprising entrepreneurs started to notice that newly released videocassette-format movies did not have any prohibitions against rentals. Stores renting the Hollywood-made videos sprang up, with dealers going through a process of learning which titles rented well and which did not. Moreover, dealers themselves heard from customers which were the good movies, regardless of the reviews, and acquired films accordingly. Not surprisingly, some of the most popular films were those difficult to obtain—old "classics" and pornography. When larger video-rental chains appeared, such as Blockbuster, they concluded that the family audience was more profitable and abolished X-rated movies from their shelves.

Ultimately, no industry fared better from the development of the VCR than the motion picture industry, which had rigorously resisted taping machines due to its concerns about the loss of intellectual property. Consumers soon realized that the networks still only offered a limited number of programs at set times; that the movies that did appear on television were old; and that programs were interrupted with commercials and/or edited, which detracted from the original product. Consequently, an entire movie sales business appeared, with companies such as SunCoast Video providing hundreds of videocassette movies that had recently appeared in theaters, as well as classics, rock videos, documentaries, and exercise tapes. The expansion of VCRs had created an unforeseen demand (certainly unforeseen in the movie industry) for movies—not to be viewed in theaters, but in homes. By the 1990s the phrase, "I'll watch that when it comes out on video" represented a common market judgment on movies, as well as a testament to the real product of the development of the VCR. And, contrary to the dire predictions of the motion picture industry, theater admissions were up. After a brief dip in the mid-1980s, admissions soared to all-time highs in the early 1990s, while theater grosses hit a record $5.1 billion in 1993. Astoundingly, in 1998, the blockbuster motion picture *Titanic* portended to become the first billion-dollar movie, having eclipsed the $530 million mark before even getting to video. So much for the VCR killing the movie theater.

Wayne Huizenga saw the potential for renting movies. In 1987, he found a small company that was doing just that and bought it for $7 million. That company later became Blockbuster Video. In 1994, Huizenga sold the company for $8.4 billion. By then there were 3,700 stores in eleven countries renting movies on videotape for a day at a time. The first person to start three *Fortune* 500 businesses in the United States, who had a net worth of $1.8 billion in 2001, Huizenga had started his career collecting garbage.[54] After working for another company for two years, he bought his own truck. He collected trash from 2:30 a.m. to noon, and then spent the rest of the afternoon getting new accounts. When he had forty trucks, he merged with another company. Waste Management Inc. was the biggest garbage collector in the country when Huizenga entered the movie rental business. A typical serial entrepreneur, Huizenga started another company after selling Blockbuster. His next company, AutoNation, became the first nation-wide auto dealer. As it grew, he started a hotel chain.[55] He also had his "hobbies." As owner of the NFL Miami Dolphins, the NHL Florida Panthers, and for a while, the MLB Florida Marlins, he enhanced the fame and fortunes of his home state's sports activities.

Nor did the "revolution in the air" end. New surprises were in store in the 1980s, for radio especially. Television and newspapers had dom-inated news coverage by the 1980s, but increasingly Americans told pollsters that they believed less and less of what the major media news-casters said and wrote. People simply no longer trusted the major media outlets as sources for news; worse, they often thought that politicians did not listen to their constituents at home. At that point, AM radio made a remarkable U-turn to overtake FM radio by tuning in to the listeners—embarking on "talk radio" formats that encouraged listeners to call in and discuss issues with hosts. Usually, the talk was political, and the dominant voice in the industry was a former low-level marketing employee of the Kansas City Royals who had been fired eleven times from deejay positions. Rush Limbaugh decided his fate rested in his own hands, creating a talk-show format that eschewed guests and used callers as a way to set up Limbaugh's discussions of issues of interest to him. Those issues happened to be of interest to lis-teners as well. Starting in a local station in Sacramento, California, Limbaugh moved to New York where he produced the first three-hour political talk show in history for a national audience. In no time, Limbaugh's program ran on 660 stations (out of 1,130 total by 1995 that had a talk format), generating $30 million for his syndication.[56] The real revolution, though, involved Limbaugh's impact on traditional newspa-pers and television news, whose readership and viewers dropped after talk radio expanded. Indeed, the "Big Three" television news broad-casts steadily lost market share with the revival of AM radio. For a medium considered dead by its more "hip" competitor, FM, and by its other media foes, especially television, AM radio had come back from the grave, stronger than ever.

AMERICANS AND THEIR ENTERTAINMENT

With computers dominating every other aspect of modern life, it is hardly surprising that they have become a staple of games. By 1995, the home-electronic game industry (not counting PCs upon which people who are "working" play solitaire or "minesweeper") had grown into a $6 billion industry in America. Once again, it proved ironic that the Japanese were most closely identified with an industry dominated by Americans.

Nintendo of Japan transformed itself into one of the world's most powerful companies, surpassing automaker Toyota in profitability, stock performance, and market penetration. The game manufacturer paid higher dividends than almost any other company traded on the Tokyo Stock Exchange between 1988 and 1992.[57] Video games easily outsold movies (by $400 million in 1993), and Nintendo seemed to be at the top of the industry. Before it could get complacent, however, another Japanese company, SEGA, vaulted ahead of it with newer tech-nology and the wildly popular—and violent—"Mortal Kombat" game. A seesaw battle erupted between Nintendo, which introduced its Nintendo Entertainment System in 1985, and SEGA, which followed with the faster and more vivid Genesis video game system, to which Nintendo responded with the Super Nintendo Entertainment System in 1991. In May 1995, SEGA upped the ante again with the Saturn game console and was joined by Sony's PlayStation. Then, in late 1996, Nintendo introduced the "Nintendo 64," pushing the boundaries toward three-dimensional gaming.

Protectionists and doomsayers predicted that the Japanese would control the market. Yet at the very time the Japanese companies pro-ducing the game machines dominated the market, American computer firms were increasingly developing the games played on them.

Moreover, American firms were creating computer simulations in the movies upon which many games were based. Silicon Graphics, a $1 billion California-based company, used state-of-the-art computers to create the digitized special-effects dinosaurs in *Jurassic Park* and the incredible melting T-1000 cyborg in *Terminator 2*, while other American companies provided the astounding special effects for *Titanic*. Silicon Graphics signed a deal with Nintendo in 1994 to provide a 64-bit microprocessor, considered imperative for the game giant to stay even with its competition.

Competition among the major game manufacturers put more than 30 million game machines in the hands of American consumers, with SEGA and Nintendo roughly splitting the $6 billion market. In the 1990s, however, Panasonic and Atari entered the 64-bit fray with their 3DO and Jaguar systems, respectively. The Japanese quickly realized that Americans had vastly different tastes than did Japanese consumers. For example, Americans wanted sports games that focused on basketball and, especially, football. SEGA and Nintendo quickly located American design and production teams, then opened development offices in the United States. American arcade designers, including the popular Midway group out of Chicago, emerged as powerful design forces. Although the Japanese controlled 90 percent of the game console market, the pattern that first appeared in computers resurfaced as American software and development companies, developing the software at lower cost, soon captured more than 50 percent of the market and by 1995 controlled as much as 60 percent.[58] Moreover, as digitization merged with motion pictures and video games, American film stars, such as Dennis Hopper and Tia Carrere, started to appear in compact-disc games, while big-name Hollywood producers, such as George Lucas, assisted in producing games, such as the "Star Wars" series, promising even further domination of the game/software market by American companies and entertainers.[59] And none of those developments touched on the entirely separate game industry developed for PCs, a market almost as large as the SEGA/Nintendo business—virtually all of it developed domestically.

The connection between games, computers, and money was even more pronounced in gambling. Las Vegas, Reno, and Lake Tahoe, the traditional bastions of the gaming industry, were challenged by several newcomers. Atlantic City legalized casino gambling in 1976 amid promises of prosperity for the city (that failed to materialize) and a host of casinos sprouted up on Indian reservations (legalized in 1987 by the Supreme Court). Cities and states also got into the act. In April 1989, Iowa passed a bill allowing gambling on casino boats traveling the Mississippi; Chicago planned a $2 billion gambling zone; and by 1993, Minnesota had more casinos than New Jersey, including Atlantic City. Computers and slot machines seemed to have a great deal in common, but gambling had its own psychology and economics that differed from the computer game mentality.

A better approach to uniting innocent games and the higher-stakes gambling products appeared in Steve Wynn's hotels in Las Vegas, the Mirage and Treasure Island, which featured Disney-style rides, attractions, and family shows. Within five years, the Excalibur, the Luxor, and the MGM Grand Hotel all copied the Wynn concept with a family orientation. The Luxor even sported a kids-oriented state-of-the-art arcade with rows of "virtual racers," dozens of arcade machines, and even two full-size flight simulators, while the MGM and the Circus Circus Hotel and Casino featured their own indoor amusement parks.[60] A merger of Disney and Nintendo, if not the actual companies, then the conceptual essence, promised "virtual vacations" in the future.

Entertainment had become a substantial industry. By 1993, motion picture industry gross admissions passed the $5 billion mark, while employment in the movie industry exceeded 400,000 that year. Hollywood—which by the 1990s included small motion picture companies located far from California—released 431 new pictures in 1993, or fourteen more than the previous year. Music, too, had become "big business," with more than 900 million units sold, including compact discs, cassettes, and music videos. Since 1982, sales had risen more than 50 percent. Whether minority filmmakers, who have produced well-regarded and profitable movies on minuscule budgets, or rock 'n' roll millionaires, many of whom lived in abject poverty while "making it," entrepreneurial opportunity in entertainment was stronger than ever.

The strength of the American entertainment industry had important implications for the computer business as well. Increasingly, the most valuable element in a computer system is the information it holds; and increasingly in the 1990s entertainment products (including games and music) had moved to the compact disc (CD) format for the computer. American entertainers have long dominated foreign movie and music markets, spanning the careers of Jerry Lewis to Huey Lewis and Madonna to Merle Haggard. Thus the trend reinforced America's lead in the value-added element of computer technology, because American-created entertainment dominated creative content.

THE SERVICE ECONOMY OR THE "SERVICEABLE" ECONOMY

As the 1980s ended, the perception existed that America had become a "service" economy. Typically, that implied lower wages and brought to mind images of McDonald's employees stacking fries and flipping burgers. Of course, service jobs included accountants, nurses, lawyers, doctors, financial analysts, top executives, middle managers, professors, and hundreds of other job classifications that were light-years removed from flipping burgers in terms of skills or education needed. Contrary to popular belief—and the claims of labor unions—service jobs on average paid well above the average annual salary in the United States, approaching $26,000 by the late 1980s and an amount far beyond the minimum-wage jobs usually associated with services. But because services are viewed as "personal," many economists and sociologists have contended that they cannot be made productive. As a result, the United States, with its "service economy," was doomed, in their view, to become a second-class country to the manufacturing nations.[61] Ironically, one of the books making this argument, called *Manufacturing Matters*, is a superb example that allows us to conclude that manufacturing does not matter as much as is argued. As George Gilder points out, the manufacturing costs of a $30 book are, at most, $2. Most of the value—and cost—in the book come from services, including writing, editing, layout, art, and marketing. Or consider a compact disc, which costs pennies to manufacture. Most of the value lies in whatever is on the disc, whether information or music or a $60 video game.

Only recently have American service businesses seriously grappled with productivity. Taco Bell and Burger King have cash registers that either spell out or show a picture (an icon) of the item ordered, so that employees can hit a single button and put the order up on a screen immediately over the food-preparation area. The single-button system also keeps track of inventory (Wal-Mart and Toys "R" Us use scanners with the same function) and reduces communication errors. Smaller inventories meant storage costs were reduced and also permitted a better understanding of what consumers wanted. However, such advances also contained the potential seeds of destruction: Single-button cash registers reflect the negative fact that most managers no longer think their employees can handle the simple math needed to make change or ring up the proper charge; and to that extent they have perpetuated the "dumbing down" of industry by lowering standards. Moreover, the icon systems discouraged traditional business skills—serving the public with custom orders or personal attention, delivering more than required, or simply keeping an agile mathematical mind. To a certain degree, then, the icon-based systems have lowered productivity, even though they offer the potential for important productivity increases in areas of ordering and inventory.

THE USUAL SUSPECTS

Entering the 1990s, American business witnessed a remarkable renaissance. Several factors coalesced, including the arrival of numerous complementary technologies, the deregulation of a wide range of key industries in transportation, communications, and finance, and a national optimism that shook entrepreneurs out of a decade of doldrums. Major industries, such as automotives and steel, staged unexpected comebacks, while entirely new markets had appeared. The information explosion, largely due to advances in telecommunications and computers, had the dual effect of pressing decision making within organizations downward, reducing the efficiency of—and necessity for—many mid-level management positions, while at the same time it heralded an unprecedented expansion in the potential productivity of the individual, who was unshackled from the burdens of geography and time.

Nevertheless, when assessing the business advances of the 1980s, it is easy to ascribe too much credit to technology itself and not enough to the usual suspects, the entrepreneurs who had the vision and faith to develop and use that technology. Although history suggests that eventually "someone would come up with the idea or product" had a specific individual not done so, it is hard to fathom the appearance of cellular phones and fiber-optic networks without the financial genius of Michael Milken or the relentless attacks of MCI's McGowan; or the revolution in retail sales without the discipline Sam Walton imposed; or the direct sales or the breakthroughs in steel manufacturing brought by Ken Iverson; or most of the modern personal computer market without the contributions of Steve Jobs, Steve Wozniak, Michael Dell, Andrew Grove, and Bill Gates. If the charges were "inciting a business revolution," it would not take a police lineup to spot the perpetrators!

CHAPTER 13

The New Economy:
The 1990s

Jeff Bezos was looking for a business—any business—in which he could take advantage of a vast new marketplace that he saw offered by the Internet. In 1995, Bezos hit upon books. His selection was odd, because Bezos was hardly a bibliophile, and not even what one would call an avid reader. He did, however, perceive that books presented an excellent product for Internet sales: They were relatively easy to ship, which meant a minimal labor force was needed, and they were perfect to advertise online. Bezos had identified a market in what would be called the New Economy, defined as being based on "intangible assets, such as people, knowledge, relationships, intellectual property, patents, and prophecies."[1] Value was no longer just based in things and money, but in buyer relationships, organizational assets, and ideas that could be converted into money.

Bezos appreciated the radical nature of what he was attempting to do—make an "end run" around traditional brick-and-mortar bookstores, including giants such as Barnes & Noble. While he ultimately sold books, initially he intended to sell trust: faith in the product support his network would provide. Bezos understood the blinding speed at which the Internet would grow. The number of American households with personal computers had risen from 7 percent in 1984 to 25 percent a decade later.[2] It was a gamble, but a well-reasoned one, to expect that online sales would only grow. But how could Bezos have guessed that from 1994 to 1998 alone, online households would increase fivefold?[3] Or that 15 percent of households would be purchasing online by 1999?

Instead, Bezos focused on attaining dominant market share, whatever the eventual numbers were. Achieving a dominant market position might entail losses for several years, but once in place, the infrastructure of such a business would easily lend itself to such products as videos, music, and even toys. His business model required attaining a level of consumer loyalty rarely seen in the late 1990s, and to achieve that loyalty Bezos constructed a unique consumer profile for each customer. New products specifically tailored to that buyer were flashed on the welcome page; book selections designed around the consumer's previous purchases would be displayed; and every effort was made to obtain rare, out-of-print books. He also intended to build on the breakthroughs in transportation and rapid mail delivery put in place by companies such as Federal Express some two decades earlier.

It took the new company, Amazon.com, eight years to show a profit. By that time, Amazon dominated online book sales, challenged only by the late-arriving Barnes & Noble online subsidiary, and had expanded from books to all types of products. Amazon emerged as a model for the new online merchant, and was known for superlative customer service, including no-cost, easy returns. Indeed, by 2000, Amazon threatened European e-commerce, as it, and LandsEnd.com, a clothing retailer, were sued by the Germans for providing an unconditional product guarantee to consumers. The Germans feared such a guarantee would put undo pressure on their domestic companies. Bezos's success reflected both the promise and the pitfalls of the new Internet economy, where it was essential to have a clear sales model in mind before entering the market.

A PRODUCTIVITY REVOLUTION

Information technologies, often referred to in shorthand as the "computer revolution," began to change American business on a broad scale in the 1980s. Companies started to employ computer tracking codes to manage inventories, place orders, and identify sales patterns. Manufacturers such as General Motors had already embarked on a robotics revolution, itself largely based on information technologies. Across the board, productivity increases accompanied the introduction of computing and information systems—but refinement was important, because until those technologies reached the point that they were cost-effective, they remained luxuries to many firms.

By the mid-1990s, the cost of computers and chips had plummeted, while processing power had skyrocketed. Digital storage ability alone had seen an increase of 50,000 times in half a decade, an unprecedented surge in the history for any technology.[4] The United States increasingly shipped actual manufacturing of computers and some parts abroad, retaining the more lucrative, value-added functions at home. Those value-added capabilities included microchip and software design, programming, and new product conception. The diversity of processes and systems that could be improved by computing power seemed endless. What George Gilder called the "microcosm" bound together American information and entertainment systems. Just as relentlessly, the entrepreneurial affairs of individuals and the financial/political affairs of nations were bound together in neural networks of fiber optics, faxes, and computers.[5] Gilder rightly recognized that the silicon revolution, based on the ubiquitous element of sand, was the first in human history to yield a product—the computer chip—that got more powerful the smaller it got, and ran faster the hotter it got! Individuals had unparalleled levels of creativity and capability at their fingertips. That did not mean, necessarily, that every company or firm applied computers well—or even used them at all. Instead, it suggested that entrepreneurs had more of an opportunity than ever before to reach untapped markets.

The advent of the personal computer in the 1970s sparked the demand for a corollary function that would improve the computer's usefulness, a means of linking together PCs in different locations so that they could communicate to each other. In 1977, the first "e-mail" application appeared, and in 1980, Tim Berners-Lee devised the communications protocols for the "World Wide Web," making it easier to travel around the new Internet. By 1982, any server could access any other server, and in the early 1990s, Marc Andreessen developed "Mosaic," a web browser that eventually became Netscape and that offered a user-friendly means to "surf" the Web.

At the same time, another revolution was occurring in telecommunications. Early telephone modems (developed by Bell Labs in the 1950s) blessed the user with a connection for sharing data, but these early modems were accompanied by the curse of incredibly slow response and data transfer speeds. For there to be a truly useful Internet, the technology had to geometrically increase the amount of information that one computer could transfer to another. Corning Glass chipped into the revolution by providing a fiber-optic telephone wire that allowed faster digital transmission rates when the computers' modems "dialed up" the Internet. Broadband connectivity improved from a twelve-second delay in 1997 to a three-second delay in 2001, while Internet traffic soared with a 5,000-fold increase between 1994 and 2001.[6] Part of the increase in speed occurred over new digital phone lines, but the rest came from cables laid primarily to provide television service.

WIRED FOR THE NEW ECONOMY

Some 39 million miles of fiber-optic cable was laid by 2001, far more than was needed. Less than 3 percent of its capacity was in use. Companies such as Qwest poured money into laying new cable as part of a long-term endeavor to bring new television services, not Internet connectivity, to family living rooms. Here was a case of the Internet "piggybacking" on the existing demand for television access. Once the cables were laid, however, with their vast unused capacity, it wasn't long before television providers began investigating delivery of data services through their cables as well. It took only seven years for the Internet to spread to one-quarter of the U.S. population, marking the shortest time in human history a revolutionary technology had made it into the hands of the people. The personal computer itself had taken sixteen years to become a mainstream product; the telephone, thirty-five; and the automobile, fifty-five years.[7] An early breakthrough came from America Online (AOL), which had created a program for using the Internet for communicating and playing online games. One of the pioneer Internet service providers, AOL offered many Americans their first ever Internet account. AOL went public in 1992 and quickly raised $23 million, but like all things in the rapidly changing field of computers, the once-hot company soon found it was outperformed by dozens of smaller Internet service providers and was acquired by Time Warner.

Some firms found remarkable new ways to adapt their strengths to the Internet. A Dayton, Ohio, company called TransWave developed an electrostatic signature system to remotely monitor the protective coating inside a buried pipeline carrying petroleum. After running a pilot program with Dayton Power and Light, TransWave could examine pipelines around the globe without requiring soil samples from near the pipeline itself. Upon signing a deal, TransWave would place microprocessors inside the pipeline, then receive the signals back in Dayton and constantly monitor the lines for damage.[8]

In a 1998 lecture at the University of California at Berkeley, Federal Reserve Chairman Alan Greenspan labeled the United States as entering a "New Economy." He said:

> The question posed for this lecture of whether there is a new economy reaches beyond the obvious: Our economy, of course, is changing every day, and in that sense it is always "new." The deeper question is whether there has been a profound and fundamental alteration in the way our economy works that creates discontinuity from the past and promises a significantly higher path of growth than we have experienced in recent decades.
>
> The question has arisen because the economic performance of the United States in the past five years has in certain respects been unprecedented. Contrary to conventional wisdom and the detailed historic economic modeling on which it is based, it is most unusual for inflation to be falling this far into a business expansion.
>
> Many of the imbalances observed during the few times in the past that a business expansion has lasted more than seven years are largely absent today. To be sure, labor markets are unusually tight, and we should remain concerned that pressures in these markets could spill over to costs and prices. But, to date, they have not.

Greenspan attributed the improved flexibility of the American economy to several factors. One was the increase in productivity due to increased international trade. With trade, more can be produced with the world's existing resources. The second reason for the improved economy, he noted, was a financial system that could provide funds when equipment or goods were needed, which allowed improvements in the equipment to occur when new technology became available.

Finally, he noted that "there were important technological changes ... that are altering, in ways with few precedents, the manner in which we organize production, trade across countries, and deliver value."[9]

This New Economy was further described in a 1999 policy report as having characteristics that "include an increase in knowledge-based jobs, higher levels of entrepreneurial dynamism and competition, reduced delays between design and production, faster times to market, increased product and service diversity, constant technological innovation, the advent of the Internet and the information technology revolution, globalization, the replacement of hierarchical organizational structures with networked learning organizations, and relentless economic churning. These are more than economic fads or passing trends; they go to the heart of how the New Economy works."[10]

The hottest trend in entrepreneurship was Internet business. By the mid-1990s, every business needed a web page. It was like placing an ad in the telephone book, the standard procedure for companies from the 1950s to the 1990s, only this time with the company placing basic information such as its address and phone numbers on the Internet, with maybe some artistic embellishments. New start-up companies emerged that would create these web pages for other companies for a modest price. These new companies usually made their money by "hosting" the web page: keeping it on a computer linked to the Internet so that others could view it.

More sophisticated were interactive web pages that allow customers to place orders via their computers. Soon, virtually anyone could start a business, theoretically, that existed only in "cyberspace," without needing a physical building or storefront ("bricks and mortar"). That's how Amazon started: The only "bricks and mortar" was a Seattle warehouse Bezos rented to store inventory.

Typically, a new 1990s Internet business went through four stages: start-up, marketing, ramp-up, and maturity. Under the start-up phase, an entrepreneur with a new idea would establish an Internet presence, preferably the first business of its type. Such firms started with funding from family and friends or, often, credit cards. Occasionally, these new firms could obtain seed capital from an "angel"—an investor who sees a large-scale return from the product or service. As start-ups became common, contests developed between these angels to find the best ideas for firms. To attract the angels, potential entrepreneurs developed two-minute "elevator pitches" that hopefully would draw attention to the idea they had. Once the entrepreneurs had the attention of investors, they had to develop a business plan explaining the details of how the company would work and outlining the "exit strategy" whereby the investors would get their money out.

Once start-up money was obtained, it was important to establish the web presence before another group got the same idea. Then the company had to grow as fast as possible in terms of the number of people ("eyeballs") visiting the website. Each website had a highly visible counter, reminiscent of McDonald's old billboard declaring "300 million hamburgers sold." This ramp-up period perhaps constituted the most important period of a new web-based firm's growth, because if the number of visitors was not high enough, the company was quickly replaced by a competitor. For faster growth, the company would make strategic alliances with complementary companies, advertising their products as the other company returned the favor, and even allowing "click through" so that by clicking on the other company's ad, the web user could visit the other company's website without laboriously typing in the web address. As the company edged ahead of its competition, it could obtain venture capital, available to new but up-and-running companies. It is crucial to understand that the Internet companies did not focus on profits at this early stage, and that they expected to struggle as they acquired market share—fully in line with the Bezos/Amazon model.

During the maturity stage, a company could begin to allow outside investors with an initial public offering (IPO). A classic example of this model is Yahoo!, which was founded in 1994 by Stanford graduate students Jerry Yang and David Filo in Sunnyvale, California. Yahoo!, like its competitors Lycos and Excite, provided a web search engine, software that scans websites for phrases and images. Within a year, it had already had one million hits. When it went public in April 1996, Yahoo! shares nearly tripled in price on the first day of trading. Recognizing the jewel they had, Yang and Filo launched an IPO that brought $33.8 million.[11]

THE END OF THE VISIBLE HAND?

Much of whatever "anxiety" existed in the 1990s stemmed from radical transformations that had begun in the 1980s. While large corporations appear to wield great power and control substantial numbers of jobs, it is entirely possible that they are dinosaurs in the twenty-first-century economy—huge, lumbering beasts incapable of adapting to their environment, losing the life struggle to smaller, quicker creatures. As they seek to survive, one of the major casualties appears to be the managerial hierarchies that gave them their strength for so long.

It is therefore ironic that the "visible hand" theory of Alfred Chandler gained widespread acceptance at the very time that the computer started to render the managerial hierarchies Chandler described less efficient, and occasionally downright out of date.[12] In the nineteenth century, when communications were slow, expert and educated managers sorted and transmitted relevant information that individual on-site employees could not obtain or lacked the education to understand. Managers had, for want of a better term, the "big picture" because of their access to information. By the 1980s, however, computers transmitted information far faster than humans could, with workplaces wired for electronic mail, providing instantaneous communication with employees. While managers still had much of the authority for making the decisions as to which information was important, they could not begin to function quickly enough to process it. They became bottlenecks for information, rather than sources of information transmissions. The result often was a blizzard of "net" messages spewed out to everyone's computers or, worse, a torrent of paper memos.

Equally paradoxical, just as Chandler's thoughts started to dominate the academy, American industries, from automotives and steel to aircraft and electronics, had come under sharp competition from more efficient foreign rivals. U.S. business found that it had become bloated with the very bureaucracies Chandler celebrated, and it no longer could adapt quickly to meet emerging markets or rapid shifts in demand. Instead, American business hesitated, then launched into a remarkable downsizing, relying on automation and computers to improve efficiency. Companies literally shrank into profitability. At the same time, business searched for new and different ways to manage, discarding the traditional managerial hierarchies in favor of unconventional structures, as touted by highly sought-after consultants like Tom Peters or popular economic writers like Peter Drucker.

Inside corporations, the very nature of computer usage was changing as well. While computers still handled accounting, calculations, and design, by 1990 they had also replaced typewriters. The computer's speed, the ability to copy files, the functions of editing and saving information—all made traditional "advanced" electronic typewriters obsolete. Word processing software, pioneered by Apple (ClarisWorks), Borland (WordPerfect), or later Microsoft (Word), offered indentation and centering, pagination, line and font changes, footnote/endnote creation, and editing at the touch of an "F key." Overnight, paid typists, who had serviced legions of college students, were out of work as students now typed their own papers, including doctoral theses, thanks to the ease and precision of these writing programs. Even executives began typing their own memos. Specialized programs for tax preparation, screenwriting, spreadsheet analysis, and accounting popped up, further enabling an exodus from trained professionals to "do-it-yourself" activities.

One upshot of this transformation was U.S. productivity increases, which steadily outpaced Europe and matched that of Asia. Another result was an incredible investment boom in the 1990s that was spearheaded by soaring expenditures for computers. Stacey Tevlin and Karl Whelan found that this boom was vastly underestimated at the time, largely because economists failed to understand the pace at which firms replaced depreciated capital and the cost of the capital improvements themselves.[13]

A 1999 advertisement featured suit-clad executives outdoors, sitting on a rock and apparently deeply engrossed in discussion with a pipe-smoking guy in a sweater. A small black rocket ship was poised in their midst. The ad conveyed that location would soon no longer be relevant in business. It introduced a wireless handheld device called the "BlackBerry" that could text message, send Internet fax, and browse the Web, and, of course, provide voice communications, too, as well as serve as a "personal data assistant" with address book, calendar, and "to-do" lists. Designed for a business professional, the BlackBerry had a built-in keyboard tailored for "thumbing," or letting users type with their thumb while holding the device in one hand. By 2007, some 8 million BlackBerry devices were in use.

Meanwhile, cell phones incorporated some of the BlackBerry features, then, adding still more capacity and processing power, began to offer video services. Newer phones, attached with an earpiece, offered "hands-free" operation. Nowadays, the men or women you see walking around talking to themselves, who you once thought were candidates for a mental ward, are, rather, successful businesspeople, or at least people with lots of friends. Worldwide cell phone use topped 2 billion in 2007, meaning that many parts of the world had more cell phones than users.[14] And, with unpredictability that is predictable, customers often used cell phones for reasons largely unrelated to their original purpose: The built-in clock in most cell phones has replaced the wristwatch.

SILICON SUPER-SUCCESS

American leadership in computers, chips, and software accounted for the overwhelming advances in cell phones, satellite communications, and other technology advantages that characterized the economy in the 1990s. Bill Gates's Microsoft led the way in sustained return on investment during that period, but not without considerable controversy. Microsoft typically bought up other companies with innovative ideas, replicating the strategy of John D. Rockefeller or Andrew Carnegie a century earlier. "If you can't beat 'em, join 'em" changed to, "If you can't beat 'em, buy 'em out." And Silicon Valley, home to thousands of small software and technology firms, was a breeding ground for get-rich-quick entrepreneurs who could turn a single idea into a buyout opportunity. By 1992, for example, 47 start-ups reported $100 million in revenues. Attempts by individual states, as in the case of Massachusetts with its subsidized Route 128, failed to generate even half as many $100 million companies.[15]

Silicon Valley was home to more than a third of the high-tech firms created since 1965. A typical example of such a company is Cisco Systems. In the mid-1980s, Sandy Lerner and her husband, Len Bosack, two computer administrators at Stanford University, found that their respective departments could not exchange e-mail or swap software because the computer networks could not "talk" to each other. Bosack designed a system that linked the computer networks to share databases and software, and when he and Lerner could not interest an existing company in their product, they quit their jobs to start Cisco Systems in their garage.

They received a good reception for their product, but suffered constantly from a cash shortage, living on credit cards and taking a second mortgage on their house. With each new order that rolled in, so did a stack of bills. In 1990, after selling stock to raise cash, they lost control of Cisco, in the process selling their stock for $200 million. The company went on to be valued by Wall Street at $5 billion.

Standing above all these exceptional men and women was the geeky Bill Gates, whose Microsoft had reached a level of dominance akin to that of General Motors in its heyday. As such, Microsoft had lost its luster as a "revolutionary" company and instead assumed the role of industry villain. Although they looked nothing alike, critics kept seeing the image of John D. Rockefeller when they looked at Gates. Competitors complained about Microsoft's tactics, while suppliers carped (as they soon would with Wal-Mart) about the domineering attitude coming out of Microsoft. The company was generally apolitical and gave little to either party, which also deprived it of political allies.

Thus, Microsoft found itself in the crosshairs of the Clinton Justice Department for antitrust violations. In 1998, Microsoft was formally charged with violating Internet integration by "bundling web browser, Internet Explorer, with Windows operating system." Most experts agreed that Microsoft had an inferior web browser, deficient in detecting and removing "spam" (unwanted e-mails) and in blocking "pop-ups" (advertisements that would automatically pop up on a screen when a browser linked to a new site). Unable to compete, it claimed, with Microsoft's bundling advantages, Netscape released the code for its Communicator browser under an open source license. While Netscape's move was cheered as a victory for open markets, it also was viewed as a concession to the dominance of Microsoft. Using the Netscape code, Mozilla began to develop its own browser, released in 2002, which is generally considered to be far superior to Internet Explorer.

Silicon Valley entrepreneurs fancied themselves as swashbuckling mercenaries who owed little allegiance to any company and jumped ship at the best offer. Whatever was lost in maintaining experience inside the firm, however, was more than offset by the creativity and energy of so many ideas moving about so freely. One man's start-up was another man's acquisition; one company's weakness was another's opportunity. Silicon Valley's close proximity to the University of California and Stanford didn't hurt, either. Perfectly situated, the industry seemed impervious to traditional business cycles.

MERGERS AND RAIDERS

The New Economy had another characteristic that changed the way America did business. The Internet evolved from a consumer-oriented toy to a corporate tool. Bar codes and scanners could track inventory, computer models could calculate when to reorder, online ordering replaced paper purchase orders, and fast delivery services put inventory in hand in a day or two. People, in other words, were being replaced by computers. New technology was not just replacing factory workers, it was replacing managers.

During the 1980s, a new wave of acquisition had occurred, capped by 1985, when the total value of the fifty largest mergers and acquisitions reached $94.6 billion. That year, Philip Morris acquired General Foods for $5.7 billion and General Motors bought Hughes Aircraft for $4.7 billion. The previous year, Chevron purchased Gulf Oil for $13.2 billion, and in 1986 General Electric absorbed RCA, USX (U.S. Steel) acquired Texas Oil & Gas, and Burroughs merged with Sperry. In part, the relaxed regulatory environment encouraged mergers, and several of the mergers, such as USX's and GM's acquisitions, represented attempts to diversify and thus stabilize the companies against market fluctuations. Raiders performed a valuable function. They enforced stricter accountability on management by stockholders, who frequently had little impact on how companies directed their affairs. Usually, the raiders sought to cut bloated layers of management, the residue of Alfred Chandler's "managerial revolution." It was not true that they stripped physical plants or cut back on productive capacity: In one study, one-quarter of the firms (including Ford, ITT, DuPont, and Goodyear) during the 1970s and 1980s invested more in physical plants and R & D than traditional margins demanded.[16] Rather, the "internal systems for profit planning and capital budgeting tended to work against attempts to invest in the organizational capabilities needed for long-run survival."[17] Put another way, the managerial revolution in the 1800s spawned a financial and budgeting system that in the twentieth century did not account for managerial talent very well because those organizational capabilities were not easily quantifiable in the cash flow financial systems.

The most serious criticism of the "merger mania" that hit the United States in the 1980s and 1990s involved the charge that companies assumed more debt with each new takeover attempt. Warnings that the American corporate structure was "overloaded with debt" completely missed the point: By 1990, the worth of corporate equity in the United States exceeded its debt by $1 trillion! The level of equity increased during the so-called "decade of debt," rising by $160 billion since 1980.

Increasingly in the 1990s, what companies were "overloaded" with was managers. And the new CEOs at acquired companies began slashing their workforces. For the first time, the media sympathized with white-collar executives as thousands received "pink slips." *Newsweek* even ran a cover story in 1996 with the faces of CEOs Robert Palmer of Digital Equipment Corp., Albert Dunlap of Scott Paper, Robert Allen of AT&T, and Louis Gerstner of IBM, along with the numbers of jobs they had eliminated, under the bold title, "Corporate Killers!"[18] Obligingly, a week later the *New York Times* ran a series of seven articles on "The Downsizing of America," in which it referred to the "battlefields of business" and "millions of casualties." The *Times* writers went so far as to show a headline from another paper, "Sears Kills Catalog," conjuring images of a crazed CEO bursting into the catalog division at Sears with an AK-47 and a bandolier.[19] *Newsweek* and the *Times* did not point out that such ebb and flow of jobs, with unproductive functions fading out and new, revolutionary work appearing, was common to all capitalist economies and was a healthy sign. For example, in 1900, there were more than 100,000 carriage and harness workers in the United States, and some 74,000 boilermakers, yet both those jobs had entirely disappeared by 2007. Meanwhile, in 1900, there were no professional athletes, optometrists, television or radio announcers, medical technicians, or airline workers. But by 1993, there were almost 2 million of these jobs in existence, with the numbers growing every day.[20] By 1999, the U.S. Bureau of Labor Statistics estimated there were 133 million employed workers in the United States, and the Bureau's statisticians used a methodology that almost always undercounted working Americans, because it did not allow for self-employment.

In fact, the computer had now started to perform one of the key functions of nineteenth-century managers, that of information transmission. A century earlier, the strategic goals of a company had to be passed on to the workforce orally through managers in meetings. Even after most workforces were literate, managers continued to function as primarily a conduit: They informed workers of strategic goals and related production or sales issues to the "top brass." Suddenly, computers now performed many of those functions. Employees could discern the corporate strategy from a web page, or send e-mails directly to their superiors. Sales and inventory data were automatically logged. The managerial revolution was ending or, at least, rapidly losing its character.

Buoyed by slimmer, more flexible companies, a second boom in the 1990s occurred. The market, rather than seeing weak companies, teetering with debt and ripe for foreign acquisition, found restructured firms made more efficient by raiders and competition. For the first time in decades, the boards of directors of major U.S. companies demanded that CEOs—not just faceless middle managers—be held responsible for company performance. At GM, Compaq, Kodak, Westinghouse, American Express, and IBM, boards revolted, no longer rubber-stamping their CEO's decisions. At GM, the board even separated the position of CEO from the position of chairman of the board when it fired Robert Stempel, a step that none of the other major companies took.

It was positive moves such as these that encouraged the optimists of the New Economy, while the corporate scandals and the dot-com bust convinced the pessimists that the New Economy was all smoke and mirrors. Under normal circumstances, the economy would have shaken off the dot-com bust, but the erosion of confidence brought about by CEO malfeasance further eroded trust, making a recovery more difficult. These problems were, ultimately, minor compared to the blow that was about to be delivered to the U.S. economy by terrorists on September 11.

THE DECLINE OF SAVING

During the boom, a variety of critics have argued for some time that traditional measures of savings had failed to capture the American experience. William Gale and John Sabelhaus have contended that traditional measures of savings in the United States, which put personal saving at one-half of one percent, are badly flawed. Such rates have not taken into account corporate retained earnings, net inflow of foreign savings, and above all, capital gains. Most of the decline in gross saving, they found, was offset by the acquisition of financial assets—which have appreciated—and with capital gains included, they wrote, "the household saving rate is the highest it's been in the last forty years."[21] Not surprisingly, entrepreneurial families save at even higher rates than everyone else, with much of their savings plowed back into their businesses.[22]

And even this savings is probably understated as well. Research in the *American Economic Review* showed that "intangible" capital accumulation in the stock market derived from quality increases in "installed capital."[23] No one can deny that the stock market, whether undervalued or not, has become a major part of the average American's financial picture. A 1997 Federal Reserve study found that the percentage of stock-owning families with incomes between $25,000 and $49,000—what anyone would agree constituted the "middle class"—increased by almost 50 percent from 1989 to 1995. The increase was greatest for those on the bottom end of the ladder.[24] Another way of looking at savings and standard of living is through recreational expenditures, and again, the story is much the same. Economics professor Dora Costa discovered that recreational expenditures indicate that real per capita growth from 1972 to 1991 may have been as much as 1.8 percent higher, which, of course, would filter into savings equations.[25]

UNORTHODOX AND UNUSUAL: PATHS TO ENTREPRENEURIAL ACHIEVEMENT

Arnold Schwarzenegger's name constituted only one barrier to his success. What was it that led a skinny Austrian kid with an unintelligible English accent to become the best bodybuilder in the world, a top American movie star, a well-respected businessman, and governor of California? While most people consider Schwarzenegger an actor—and many joke about his talent—he has approached his product with an entrepreneur's vision and faith. At first, he concentrated entirely on being the best bodybuilder in the world; and when he accomplished that, he studied acting and worked on his accent. Schwarzenegger (usually simply referred to as Arnold) carefully selected his roles, choosing those that had little dialogue, and at the same time picking movie vehicles that allowed him to display his (at the time) only asset, his physique. When offered the title role in what became the smash hit *Terminator*, Schwarzenegger realized that the cyborg character he portrayed would dominate the movie. He later tweaked scripts to make his accent believable, such as in *Red Heat*, where he played a Soviet cop, or in futuristic science-fiction films like *Running Man* and *Total Recall*. He parlayed his million-dollar paychecks into a real estate bonanza, and few in the business community doubt his capabilities when it comes to commerce. Then in 2003, the business executive transformed himself again, to become the enormously popular governor of California. Is Arnold Schwarzenegger an entrepreneur?

What about Michael Jordan? Although his 1980s basketball career comes to mind immediately, Jordan was much more than a basketball player, and indeed, Nike's Air Jordan shoe commercials emphasized that he was a "corporation." Think of all the hundreds of baseball, football, hockey, and basketball players who have received six- and seven-digit salaries for years, only to retire on a pittance. Michael Jordan earned $18-million-plus commissions from Nike; he also sold McDonald's hamburgers, cologne, and his own high-fashion line of ties. Jordan, like Schwarzenegger, realized that his image was his product. Is Michael Jordan an entrepreneur?

The very nature of entrepreneurs has expanded to include a variety of jobs and positions, and a new stair-step process whereby people leave jobs as employees and incrementally become entrepreneurs. This is especially true with university and government employees, where the perks are often lucrative and the free time more generous. Some companies have no employees at all, only "independent contractors" who are hired to perform a specific function for a company. An advertising firm, for example, may consist of only the owner, who pays artists and writers fees to develop the ads and contracts with an ad placement person to decide where the ad is to appear.

What has not changed is the rate at which entrepreneurs rise and fall, a dynamic that affects both individuals and firms. In the previous chapter, we discussed the rise of the VCR and movie rental stores, both of which had been largely replaced by 2007. The VHS videocassette format was obsolete, having given way to digital video disc (DVD) technology and digital video recorders (DVRs). Likewise, with the advent of satellite dish and cable movies on demand, video rental stores such as Hollywood Video and Blockbuster were disappearing. And the video arcades? They had been rendered obsolete by home game systems such as the Xbox (*Halo 3*, a game designed exclusively for the device, pumped Xbox maker Microsoft several points the week it was introduced). Portable video games and the Nintendo "Wii" console continued the revolution.

Only eleven of the top twenty-five businesses in 1989 were still ranked that highly a decade later.[26] It might surprise some to know that more than half of America's 500 richest people changed every year in the 1990s, or that one-third of the *Forbes* 400 wealthiest were off the list every ten years. Such is the rapid shifting of fortunes in America. The United States has always glamorized the "rags to riches" story, and always provided a means to achieve almost any dream. Income mobility has attracted immigrants to American shores for more than 200 years. And by 2007, there were more ways than ever to join the ranks of the "rich and famous," with entrepreneurship broadening to include athletes, academics, consultants, writers, movie stars, music personalities, and nonprofit foundation leaders, as well as traditional financiers, manufacturers, inventors, and even managers. Lines have blurred between employers and employees, between entrepreneurs and managers. Traditionally, entrepreneurs had to be "self-employed." Is that definition appropriate anymore, especially when people cross over through different situations frequently, and occasionally several times in one day? Michael Jordan, for example, may have been an "employee" when he played a two-and-a-half-hour basketball game for the Bulls, but when he promoted his ties and cologne during the postgame talk shows, he worked for his own company. Oprah Winfrey was technically an "employee" of the studios that purchased and broadcast her show, but her empire became so vast that she turned her image into a magazine ("O") and product brand and became the richest woman in the entertainment industry.

Still, critics point to lower participation rates among some ethnic groups—as if every ethnic group, with its own heritage and cultural background, should behave precisely the same and proportional to its numbers in the general population. Of particular concern to critics are African Americans. Surveys showed that blacks defined themselves as "self-employed" only one-fourth as often as whites and only one-half as often as Asians.[27] But for those groups with a history of low business participation, the crossover phenomena would be even harder to detect, because individuals themselves may identify with their "steady" job. In fact, the data diverges significantly when Jamaicans, Haitians, Dominicans, and more recently, African blacks are considered separately: Jamaicans had business participation rates of more than 21 percent, and Haitians, more than 15 percent, both percentages far above that of whites. A split has appeared between African-born blacks and

American-born blacks, with the immigrants achieving far faster rates of income growth and workforce participation as well as entrepreneurship.

Part of the dilemma for minorities has been to target a market. One approach, such as that taken by John H. Johnson, involved providing products aimed at, in Johnson's case, other blacks. Johnson, *Black Enterprise* magazine's "Entrepreneur of the Decade" in the 1980s, published *Ebony*, *Jet*, and *EM*, *Ebony Man*. Johnson Publishing Company was the largest U.S. black-owned business in 1987, with $175 million in sales, when Johnson was honored.[28] Whereas Johnson prospered by tailoring publications to the black community, the most popular businesses among the top-100 black-owned companies in America were auto dealerships, which had no special ethnic focus. In the mid-1980s, for example, two of the top-five black-owned firms in growth were auto dealerships.[29] And Reginald Lewis became one of the wealthiest Americans, as recognized by *Forbes*, by acquiring undervalued companies and making them into marketable commodities.[30] When he bought food-processing company Beatrice International for $1 billion in 1987, investors quickly knew it would be valuable: His earlier purchase of McCall Pattern Company had fetched a 90-to-1 return!

Still, differences in entrepreneurship between whites and blacks were striking. A 1993 study found 11.6 percent of white males were self-employed, as compared with only 3.8 percent of black men.[31] That ratio had remained constant over an eighty-year period and was a growing concern among policymakers. A 1999 study by Robert Fairlie found two important factors limited black entry into self-employment: lower start-up capital in the form of assets, and the probability of having a self-employed father.[32] Yet the quadrupling of current black asset levels would scarcely have any impact at all, while the father's self-employment status would be important. Obviously, the quickest way to affect increased numbers of self-employed black fathers is to increase the number of black fathers in the home, an issue that returns us to the critique of government welfare policies.

Debates about the "dependency mentality" imposed by slavery peaked in the 1960s and have shifted somewhat to evidence suggesting that New Deal/Great Society programs created a different type of dependency mentality—on the federal government. By the 1960s, civil rights legislation ended most segregation officially, although some social, cultural, and residential segregation continues to occur—some by deliberate design, some by personal choice. Of more lasting impact were the programs enacted by the federal government loosely termed "affirmative action" or "equal opportunity" programs. In their original form, equal-access laws specifically prohibited denying anyone a job or access to public programs on the basis of skin color. Over time, however, government used quotas to ensure that certain numbers of minority groups would be hired—a point vehemently renounced at the time of the adoption of such laws. The only way the federal agencies could guarantee proper "distributions" of outcome (not opportunity) was to institute quotas; and when business did not institute such quotas voluntarily, it opened itself to litigation from the government. By the 1980s, then, the solution to discrimination had become ... discrimination.

Meanwhile, welfare, designed (as proponents were fond of saying) to be a "hand, not a handout," quickly became a trap of its own. Welfare incentives tended to accelerate marriage dissolution and illegitimacy.[33] Reformers tended to focus on programs that emphasized working as a solution to receiving welfare, while the issue of marriage largely went unaddressed.[34] By the 1990s, studies had shown quite conclusively that welfare and illegitimacy were linked, and that illegitimacy further correlated strongly with low employment rates and poor work habits.[35] Government regulations designed to lift people out of poverty have in some cases specifically harmed minorities, as in the case of minimum-wage laws.[36] Other government regulations enacted on behalf of unions have limited the mobility of minorities into such occupations as beauty and hair care and taxi and transportation services. In some cases, as with the armed forces and school admissions, government has played an important role in ensuring equal access to public facilities. In the private sector, though, important breakthroughs occasionally had little to do with government. Jackie Robinson desegregated baseball because the Brooklyn Dodgers desperately wanted to beat the St. Louis Cardinals and needed to overcome the magic of Stan Musial. Certainly the Dodger organization had no more racial sensitivity than other clubs, and government did not mandate hiring minorities. Instead, the private sector, with its incentives for gaining a competitive edge, gave Jackie Robinson a chance.[37] And markets, even in the post–Civil War South, showed a propensity to be "color blind" if the return was high enough: Jennifer Roback, for example, found that Southern streetcar businesses were desegregating on their own (for profit) until local governments segregated them.[38]

Since most small entrepreneurs do not receive start-up capital from banks, but from friends and family, entrepreneurship remains the best opportunity for minorities to advance economically. Such entrepreneurship relies more heavily on the values a child inherits from family than on inherited financial assets. Studies have shown that family income only marginally affects children's life chances, especially once extremely basic needs are met, which is the case with most Americans in poverty. As Susan Mayer found, "the parental characteristics that employers value and are willing to pay for, such as skills, diligence, honesty, good health, and reliability, also improve children's life chances, independent of their effect on parents' income. Children of parents with these attributes do well even when their parents do not have much income."[39] An intact family can capitalize a business with its labor, but a broken family will find it much more difficult. As a result, minorities other than American-born blacks, with higher success rates of keeping families together, especially Asians and Jamaicans, have moved in to establish groceries, laundries, and other businesses in inner cities by using family labor.

Despite these hurdles, evidence suggests that American-born blacks have started to engage in entrepreneurship at higher rates. According to reports from *Black Enterprise* magazine, sales for the nation's top black-owned businesses rose almost 12 percent in 1995, outperforming both the *Fortune* 500 and the *Forbes* 400 lists, representing a revenue jump of almost 10 percent.[40] Black-owned firms stressed innovation—"striving to meet their entrepreneurial mission in ways that they may not have considered or attempted in the past," noted Alfred Edmond, Jr., the executive editor of *Black Enterprise*.[41] One of the businesses frequently owned by blacks is auto dealerships, where people such as former Detroit Lions running back Mel Fall have excelled. Still, entrepreneurship within the American-born black community has lagged behind other groups. One reason has been the high employment of blacks in nonprofit occupations. Working in a business—as opposed to working for a government agency or nonprofit firm—has been identified as a crucial component in the training of minority entrepreneurs.[42]

Achieving such training comes hard when up to one-half of the rising black middle class, according to one study, worked in some way for government at the state, local, or federal level. Even when blacks engaged in private enterprise, government often was a central client. For example, in 1987, the fastest-growing black business in America, Lawson National Distributing Company in Chicago, growing at an annual rate of 100 percent, made buses for the city of Chicago. Such dependence on the government as a client is detrimental to black-owned businesses, especially in an age when state and local governments are experiencing budget constraints. Overall, it may well be that black employment in the public sector constitutes the single largest impediment to black entrepreneurship since slavery.[43]

On the other hand, the tax cuts of the 1980s proved especially beneficial to blacks. The U.S. Civil Rights Commission found that the number of black-owned businesses rose at record rates during the period 1978–87, nearly doubling in the period that top capital gains tax rates were cut from 49 percent to 20 percent. Public policy, however, could only provide a framework for entrepreneurship. The creation of thriving businesses still required what it always has in America: faith, family, work, and service. Fortunately, as the American economy continued to boom in the 1990s, studies showed—to the surprise of many academics and perpetual advocates of more welfare—that the job market had attracted greater numbers of low-wage men into the workforce than ever before.[44]

It is not surprising, then, to find that outstanding black entrepreneurs like Herman Cain, the CEO of Godfather's Pizza, started with a firm spiritual grounding.[45] "My father never looked for a government program, a government handout," Cain recalled. Instead, Herman Cain saw his father work hard and heard his mother teach him about God. "Success," he remembered her saying, "is not a function of what you start with materially but what you start with spiritually." Cain grew up in a tiny duplex, sleeping on a fold-up cot in the kitchen with his brother. He shined shoes, waxed cars, and latched on to a job at Coca-Cola, where his father was a chauffeur. He put himself through Morehouse College, then worked as a civilian statistician for the U.S. Navy. Demanding more of himself than merely a comfortable life, Cain earned a master's degree at Purdue in computer science, and eventually worked as an analyst at Pillsbury. He knew, however, that the path from the computer division ended well below the top, and he met with a former boss, Win Wallin, by then the Pillsbury president, for advice. Boldly, Cain told the president he wanted his job. "I can't get to your job from where I am. What do you recommend?"

For many modern black youths steeped in the rebellious "gangsta" culture, what Cain heard—and did—next would have been unfathomable. Indeed, many would have said it constituted "acting white." Wallin told Cain he had to quit his position and go to another department, starting absolutely at the bottom and learning the operations from the ground up at the corporation's subsidiary, Burger King. Cain had to resign his title, give up a company car and privileges, and forgo stock options to flip burgers and cook fries. Understandably, Cain prayed about the decision, receiving assurance that he could do anything he put his mind to. Herman Cain joined the sixteen-year-olds at the Burger King assembly lines and front counters, mopping floors and cleaning toilets. But he persisted, learning the two-year program in nine months, impressing management so much that he was named a vice president of the Philadelphia region—perhaps, not coincidentally, the worst-performing region in the chain. Cain launched a restructuring program, restoring morale and turning the region into Burger King's best region in growth, sales, and profits at the end of four years.

Pillsbury had seen all that it needed to see: In 1986, at age 40, Cain was named president of the Godfather's Pizza chain of 911 stores. Like the Philadelphia Burger King, however, Godfather's had lost money. Cain chopped 300 locations, standardized menus, and sought advice from the local managers. In 1988, he formed a group of Godfather's executives to buy out the company for $50 million, putting his life's work on the line. Within two years, the value of the company had doubled, but Cain knew what made it work: "Service is the driving force in any restaurant business.... Our number-one rule is the customer is always right. Rule number two is, if he is not right, go back to rule number one." Cain conducted outreach programs to inner-city youth, trying to impress on them the potential for entrepreneurship. "Many blacks in America today show disdain for the food-service trade.... But I saw it as a chance to run something, to own something. Black people should get over the idea that serving people carries a stigma.... More than half of current restaurant owners began their careers in hourly positions like dishwashers and servers.... I just decided not to use segregation and racism and color as an excuse," he said.[46] After a failed run for a U.S. Senate seat in 2000, Cain hosted his own radio talk show and was in demand as a motivational speaker.

As the ranks of blacks in entrepreneurial positions swelled, women also have become entrepreneurs like never before. By 1997, according to one study, one out of every four American workers is employed by a female-owned business.[47] Sales in women-owned firms had risen 235 percent over a nine-year period, while employment nearly tripled. According to Julie Weeks, research director for the National Foundation for Women Business Owners, the influx of women into business schools had women "thinking of entrepreneurship right off the bat."[48] The report found service-sector businesses made up more than half of the female-owned companies while, surprisingly, the number of women-owned construction firms rose by 171 percent since 1987.

Female entrepreneurs also experienced impressive gains in the 1990s. Between 1997 and 2002, the number of women-owned businesses rose 14 percent to 6.2 million. Female businesses accounted for 28 percent of all privately owned businesses and employed more than 9 million people.[49] Women have benefited from the expansion of computer technology into the home, starting with desktop publishing operations and moving quickly into Internet stores and websites. Like black entrepreneurs, however, they also have appreciated the service aspect of business. Firms such as Patti-Maids and other house and office cleaning businesses have thrived, as have in-home day care facilities that require little start-up capital and have enormous, consistent demand.

Cable television and the Internet have made millionaires of women and minorities who found that they could market their products or expertise directly without going through a layer of supervisors. In the early 1990s, Susan Powter, the guru of diet "infomercials," and Tamilee Webb, who advertised a videotape series primarily on cable television that became memorable even if only for its title, "Buns of Steel," reached unimaginable heights for a once-fat divorcee and an aerobics instructor, respectively. Later in the decade, karate/kickboxer Billy Blanks marketed a best-selling program called "Tae Bo" to vault him into infomercial stardom.

TRADING AWAY OUR FUTURE?

During each of America's revolutionary business periods, where products and processes rapidly change, "gloomsters" appear to proclaim the demise of the U.S. economy. Jeffersonians cried that the British were defeating American merchants with unfair trade practices in the early 1800s. Populists warned about the demise of agriculture eighty years later. And in the 1980s, Japan was routinely held up as the single greatest threat to U.S. business. The success of Japan seemed so sudden that many concluded only forces outside the market could account for it. Scores of books championing Japan's MITI appeared, heralding the demise of American manufacturing and the eclipse of a free market economy by a "planned" economy. Companies rushed to adopt kaizen business techniques, with "quality circles" consisting of meetings of employees at all levels suggesting improvements in how the business operated. They adopted "just-in-time" manufacturing, where parts appeared at the loading dock just as they were needed on the assembly line, and developed a love affair with robotics. All this was a means of incorporating Japanese traits of success before our firms were buried by Mitsubishi, Toyota, and Nikon. Indeed, critics prophesied the death of the American computer industry as Japan's government-backed "artificial intelligence" effort ground under giants such as Microsoft and Sun Microsystems.

It never happened. Japan's economy went into the doldrums in the early 1990s and didn't begin to recover until 2006. Only recently has the truth become apparent: Japan achieved success in spite of its government's involvement, not because of it. A recent study of MITI, for example, concludes with a much different assessment of Japan's success, especially in the 1980s. Scott Callon, in *Divided Sun*, maintains that "whatever the validity of this notion of a cooperative and functional Japanese industrial policy, it is now seriously out of date."[50] Contrary to the view that the substitution of government industrial policy for market principles gave the Japanese an advantage, Callon concluded that "there are costs and there are dramatic failures in Japanese industrial policy, and these costs and failures appear to have increased *substantially* since Japan became an advanced industrialized economy" (italics in original).[51] Most analysts, some reluctantly, have blamed MITI and special "government relationships" with Japanese corporations for their collapse in the 1990s, and by 1998, virtually no policymakers held up Japan as a model for industrial policy. And as Callon pointed out, the Japanese government's policies may have killed its only hope of long-term competition—computers: Far from focusing the Japanese computer companies on exports, government subsidies had the perverse effect of turning them inward, to fight for an overpriced and profitable protected domestic market.

Wherever Japanese companies did take the lead from American firms—as in consumer electronics and automobiles—it was because the Japanese created more competitors, not fewer. Among the industries in which the Japanese prevailed, they "created three times as many shipyards, four times as many steel firms, five times as many motorcycle manufacturers, four times as many automobile firms, three times as many makers of consumer electronics, and six times as many robotics companies as the United States."[52] Often, Japan of the 1950s, 1960s, and 1970s resembled America in the same decades exactly one century earlier: At various times, the Japanese had fifty-three integrated steel firms, fifty motorcycle companies, twelve auto companies (compared to the "Big Three" in the United States), and forty-two makers of handheld calculators. As Japan surged ahead of America in robotics, it created 280 new robotics companies. In the area of video-cassettes, there were eight companies, as well as thirteen fax machine manufacturers and twenty copier companies. In contrast, a study by economists Richard Beason and David Weinstein indicated that Japan's most subsidized industries have not been its most successful.

The absolutely crucial role of competition in forging productive industries emerged as a powerful theme in the comprehensive study of international trade advantages by Michael Porter, *The Competitive Advantage of Nations.*[53] Examining the industries from ten nations (including the United States), Porter and his team identified those industries in which a nation had a significant international market position as of 1985. Overlap could exist—for example, both Japan and Korea had significant international market positions in shipbuilding—but predictably Singapore, the smallest of the ten nations, had the fewest competitive industries. Japan had the most. Porter's analysis differed from traditional approaches, though, when he argued that nations succeed in "clusters" of industries, connected through vertical and horizontal relationships, rather than in individual industries.

Among Porter's most important findings was the fact that his team found "few 'national champions,' or firms with virtually unrivaled domestic positions, that were internationally competitive. Instead, most were uncompetitive though often heavily subsidized and protected."[54] A notable exception to this rule in the United States was Boeing. Among all U.S. passenger jet manufacturers, the firm received only a small portion of its orders from the U.S. government for military planes. Facing competition from the heavily subsidized Airbus in

Europe, Boeing assumed a commanding lead by introducing the superior 777 jet and 787 Dreamliner (the first to be delivered by 2008). As nation after nation placed orders for the Boeing airplane, Airbus became almost unsustainable to the Europeans.

In virtually every other field, other than passenger jets, more competitors rather than fewer was the key to success. Japan, which was noted for its audio equipment, had twenty-five competitors in that field, and 112 in machine tools. In the United States, where soft drinks accompany virtually all fast-food meals, the two largest competitors, Coca-Cola and Pepsi, aggressively battle for the market, despite the fact that they are global competitors. Moreover, the presence of the two giants has not stopped a consistent stream of new soft drink firms from launching alternatives, such as Snapple. (Snapple was created by entrepreneurs in 1972 and purchased by international food giant Quaker Oats in 1994. In 2006, it was owned by Cadbury.) In some cases, such as the production of ceramic tiles in Italy, 30 percent of the world's production comes from a number of competitors in a single town.

Competition alone, however, will not ensure entrepreneurship. The business climate, including taxes, regulation, education, and public support for commercial ventures, must be favorable. Recent evidence suggests that, despite the high-tech promise of computers, basic education in reading and math makes a substantial difference in earnings—up to $30,000 a year for a high school graduate. Indeed, the authors of *Teaching the New Basic Skills* maintain that much of what accounts for a "wage gap" between college graduates and high school graduates can be learned before students even finish high school.[55] Wiring every classroom to connect to the Internet thus becomes far less important than learning to add, multiply, read, write, and speak in public. This was especially true in minorities: In a study called *Who's Not Working and Why*, the authors conclude that functional literacy is critical and virtually eliminates the racial divide in earnings.[56]

Not surprisingly, over the past twenty-five years, employment for less educated males has fallen. The number of jobs available to such males has actually increased, but the larger number of men seeking such jobs has depressed the wage pool. And despite an increasing supply of highly educated workers, the wages for those requiring a college education have actually gone up, due to the extremely high wages paid to the top tiers.[57] Furthermore, most evidence points to increasing premiums paid to those with advanced degrees.

WEAKNESS IN THE NEW ECONOMY

While the economy of the 1990s represented an unprecedented expansion, in fact as the decade ended, the bottom was about to fall out. As early as 1996, Federal Reserve Chairman Alan Greenspan warned about "irrational exuberance" in the stock market. Computer chips and Internet growth had been spectacular, but even the New Economy had to conform to economic realities. A researcher at AT&T Labs named Andrew Odlyzko echoed Greenspan's warning in October 1998 with a paper that debunked the notion that the Internet traffic was doubling every three months.[58] The real rate, he argued, was once a year. Companies sold investors on grand schemes of laying optical fiber cable, at the same time ignoring the difficulty of the "last mile" hookups—usually in urban areas—that were extremely expensive and complicated by the Baby Bells' ownership of these connections into the home. Ultrafast switches, known as routers, were absolutely essential, and many times more expensive than the cable. Revenues dried up. Industry stars overnight became dogs. Qwest posted a loss of $81 million in a single year. Level 3 Communications, founded in 1999 by James Crowe, was once building out its network at a pace of nineteen miles per day; its stock value climbed to $130 a share in 2000, then collapsed, with Level 3 shares dropping to $7 a year later. "We were in a hothouse environment where every plant, regardless of its strength, prospered," Crowe said. "Now, we are outside in a cold world."[59] Intel's Andrew Grove glumly said the industry was in "the Valley of Death."[60]

There was more to the tech collapse than merely overbuilding of the Web. First, most entrepreneurs were not like Jeff Bezos. Few had a business model, let alone a business model that made sense. Initially, it was just assumed that on-site advertising would support almost anything. But the revenues from ads and pop-ups proved shockingly below that which was anticipated. Without an alternative source of income, dot-coms disappeared like puffs of smoke. In November 2000, Pets.com became the first listed U.S. dot-com to fold (although its symbolic sock puppet dog survived into the next millennium), followed by E-toys a few months later. Second, few had factored in the powerful impetus the "Y2K" scare had provided the computer industry, wherein the flip-over from the digits 99 to 00 for the calendar year would cause massive crashes in software and operating systems on New Year's Eve

2000. In fact, there was no Y2K effect at all, precisely because most companies had spent heavily in 1998 and 1999 preparing for the changeover. That was the good news. The bad news was that the services of all those programmers were no longer needed, and the software was already purchased. Consequently, much of the late 1990s boom disappeared when Y2K came and went out with a whimper.

Third, like any bubble, the Internet boom took on a life of its own, with investors anxious to jump on the bandwagon before the parade ended. In the 1970s, Michael Milken had understood that Wall Street investment houses had greatly undervalued new start-up companies, so he provided junk bonds as a means to address the absence of venture capital. By the late 1990s, however, the wheel had turned 180 degrees, and most of the dot-com companies were drastically overvalued, often based on little more than a slick sales presentation and the magic of the Web's seemingly limitless expansion. One consultant noted that "branding and spin" had captivated venture capitalists, who "bought [into] it because none of them wanted to admit they didn't know what the hell it meant."[61]

Indeed, the exotic language of gigabytes and terahertz, of RAM and ROM and wireless, befuddled investors. Revolutionary change within the industry further obscured reality. "Who's to say if a concept wasn't viable? Neither was Windows, until it worked," was the rationale. For example, investors in one Southern California company, Pixelon, thought their technology genius, Michael Fenne, had developed live, streaming video in 2000. Fenne was given all the equipment he craved and a suite of offices large enough to keep his wife and toddler with him at work. After spending $15 million on a launch party in Las Vegas, the technology was revealed to be less than it seemed, and the genius was revealed to be a convicted embezzler from Virginia. Booming subscriber lists masked the fact that few venture capitalists or outsiders truly mastered the technology, and ironically one who had—writer George Gilder—completely missed the dot-com bust and damaged his reputation as a high-tech guru. Shortly after his book *Telecosm* came out in 2000 (after first being released, appropriately, online in segments in the late 1990s), Gilder began a technology newsletter largely designed to sell his services as an evaluator of cutting-edge technology stocks. Many of his picks were in corporate graveyards a few years later. Some of his ideas, such as his notion that PCs are becoming obsolete, and that virtually all functions will exist on the Web and be downloaded as needed, may still prove correct. As of 2007, however, the PC has not gone away, and although sales have slowed, there still appears to be a central place in the economy for hardware and PCs.

In the meantime, for those directly affected by the dot-com bust, a sense of shock set in. The Dow Jones dropped to 8,235 in September 2001, from a previous all-time high of 11,722 that January. Similarly, the NASDAQ dropped to 1,400, down from 5,000, and the FTSE Techmark bottomed at 1,064 from a high of 6,930 the previous November. In a single week in April 2000, U.S. markets lost $2 trillion in value! The aggregate numbers were even more telling for individuals: Amazon's Bezos, whose fortune had exceeded $10 billion in 1999, had fallen to number 293 on the *Forbes* richest list, at $1.5 billion.

CHAPTER 14

Americans and the
Global Market

A pall hung over once-hot technology regions. Silicon Valley nightclubs hosted employment parties where recently laid-off engineers and executives showed up with their resumes to "speed date" potential employers. "The 'pink slips' are falling like confetti," observed one reporter, as 10,000 Silicon Valley workers lost their jobs in December 2000 alone.[1] While the region hardly experienced the ghost town fate that befell some of the cattle towns of the 1800s, Silicon Valley nevertheless saw many of its brightest star companies lose their luster. Lucent, Cisco, Sun, Compaq (now Hewlett-Packard), and others all shuddered as their sales plummeted, stock value collapsed, and employment shrank. The Dow Jones dropped 349 points in April 2000, and the U.S. economy, drifting toward a recession, absorbed another blow with the "dot-com" bust. By the time the "bust" was over, companies had lost $750 billion in market value and 600,000 jobs.[2]

The American business sector, which seemed so confident and robust in the 1990s, suddenly flailed. As the Internet boom unraveled, a new threat developed.

Structural flaws in the economy, brought about by an emphasis on performance-based compensation, had produced a new type of corporate leader, obsessed with short horizons and stock value and with an incentive to show "profits," no matter how questionably they were measured. CEOs could no longer take years to rebuild a company—or to build one—but rather had to show instant returns. And they were well compensated, showered with massive stock-option plans, bonuses, and kickbacks related to stock performance. Forgotten were the lessons of titans such as Carnegie, whose companies never paid a dividend, because he poured his profits back into Carnegie Steel. Cornelius Vanderbilt had already proved that the stock-value-driven model did not work, and that one always had to pay attention to the product or service itself.

When combined with old-fashioned greed, the incentive system of the New Economy could be disastrous. One of the worst companies, Enron, was a Houston-based energy company that was ironically named by *Fortune* magazine as "America's Most Innovative Company" for six straight years. A supplier of electricity and natural gas, the company promoted derivatives as tradable financial instruments. Loved by its employees and shareholders, the company had opulent offices and lucrative retirement packages. Behind the curtain, however, Enron executives were involved in shady contracts in Central and Latin America. They had negotiated a controversial $3 billion contract in India, allegedly using political connections, and booked the sale without hope of payment. But the worst problems developed when the profit growth slowed and the financial department began hiding losses in "Raptors," new companies created specifically to get losing subsidiaries off Enron's books. Worse, the scandal involved the complicity of the accounting firm that audited Enron's books, Arthur Andersen & Co. In theory, the auditor is supposed to provide accurate information to the board of directors to prevent fraud, but in the case of Enron, Arthur Andersen helped cover up the "irregularities." At the peak of the dot-com collapse, Enron's troubles became public. The company filed for bankruptcy in December 2001, followed not long afterward by its accounting firm.

The Enron scandal proved to be only the tip of the failing corporate iceberg. Just six months after Enron went bankrupt, WorldCom filed for bankruptcy protection, making it the largest such filing in American history up until then. Bernard "Bernie" Ebbers, WorldCom's founder, was later convicted of fraud and conspiracy related to false reporting. His defense that he was too ignorant to assess the finance and accounting information seemed ludicrous in light of his accomplishments in building the company. Other scandals continued to emerge. Adelphia, the fifth largest cable company in the United States, fell apart in 2002, and two of its top officers were found guilty of skimming $100 million. Tyco International saw both its former chairman and chief financial officer indicted on charges of stealing $600 million from the company; it will forever be known as the company whose CEO bought a $6,000 shower curtain.[3] ImClone, a biopharmaceutical company, was rocked by insider-trading charges that ultimately involved Martha Stewart, the guru of household arts. Samuel Waksal was sentenced to seven years in prison, and Stewart served five months for perjury. Individually, any one of these scandals would have damaged confidence in an already-depressed economy. Collectively, they frightened investors and blackened business's image. One poll showed that 54 percent of Americans thought most corporate CEOs were not honest, and another showed 69 percent of respondents said self-policing procedures by audit companies did not work.[4] Yet when questions were personalized, people still retained a great deal of trust in their own companies: 89 percent said they trusted those who ran their own companies, and only 10 percent thought that what happened at Enron or WorldCom was representative of problems at "most" companies.[5]

The weaknesses allowing corporate scandals to occur had been concealed for several years by the astounding gains in the securities markets. In turn, the stock market reflected an underlying—and totally fantastic—rise in American assets that started in the Reagan administration and continued on through the 1990s. In 1989, the Dow Jones Industrial Average was at 2,144. At the beginning of 2000, it was 11,357. While it dropped to 10,646 in 2001, this phenomenal climb would end with one stunning day in U.S. history.

ECONOMICS OF TERRORISM

When nineteen hijackers flew two jumbo jets into the Twin Towers of the World Trade Center, then another into the Pentagon (with a fourth crashing in a Pennsylvania field) on September 11, 2001, the nation was under attack by terrorists. As the towers collapsed into dust, the loss of life, and the human impact of terrorism, was obvious to all.

Physical damage could be immediately seen in the smoking hole in the Pentagon and the rubble of what once were two great buildings in New York City (later followed by many more building collapses as collateral damage). More difficult to identify were the airplanes, which virtually vaporized. Researchers at the Milken Institute calculated that the total property damage amounted to between $10 billion and $13 billion.[6] Even the Milken researchers did not engage in the grisly work of producing actuarial tables to estimate the impact of human loss from the 3,000 dead, but statistics (such as those compiled for Vietnam or Civil War losses) suggest they would be profound. In the case of business, many of the nation's leading financial minds, for example, died in the towers. The aftermath of 9/11, however, added more losses to the totals. Airline and shipping revenues fell, the hotel and recreation industry temporarily shriveled, advertising revenues plunged as the networks went ad-free for days, and consumer spending dried up, totaling as much as $47 billion.[7] A sharp plunge in the stock market wiped out over $1 *trillion* in capitalization, while the subsequent "terrorist tax" involving the costs of additional sky marshals, new technology, and better airport security added another $41 billion to the 9/11 price tag.[8]

Even without factoring in the overall macroeconomic effects of a slowing economy, the researchers put the 9/11 butcher's bill at over $2 trillion, dwarfing the impact of the insured losses for such natural disasters as Hurricane Hugo in 1989 ($5 billion) or Hurricane Andrew in 1992 (almost $17 billion), or other terrorist acts, such as the Oklahoma City bombing in 1995 ($127 million). Placed in the context of U.S. GNP, 9/11 ranks alongside the 1993 "oil crisis" in severity, well below the economic impact of the Hawley-Smoot Tariff in 1930, and just above the economic harms of the Navigation Acts during the American Revolution.

The extent of al-Qaeda's economic damage only became apparent later. The New York Stock Exchange shut down immediately. When it reopened, the Dow Jones Industrial Index dropped 624 points.[9] Professional football games were canceled; nightclubs closed. By government order, the airlines were shut down, and with no planes flying, travel to recreation spots—even should anyone choose to go—dried up immediately. Rumors swirled that Osama bin Laden had speculated in airline stocks and had sold short. America was under a new kind of attack: economic warfare. All this occurred in the immediate aftermath of the dot-com bust and a recession President George W. Bush inherited from the last year of the Clinton administration

Yet remarkably, the economy regained its footing fairly quickly. The Dow Jones Industrial Index was up to its pre-attack level by early 2002.[10] George W. Bush's tax cuts spurred a recovery, the stock market rebounded, and job growth—always good—got better. More than 3 million jobs were added since 2000, despite the terrorism and slump. At its base, the American economy was still fundamentally healthy. New businesses continued to appear at record levels. Start-ups rose from about 200,000 per year in the 1970s to over one million per year by 2000, with more than 2.3 million new businesses launched each year between 1996 and 2000.[11]

EMERGING FROM THE INTERNET BUST

The 9/11 terrorist attack on the United States came at a time when the economy was worried that Internet companies were a "bubble" in the stock markets. While the market slowed only briefly after the attack, in fact, 2001 would turn out to be the last year that a company wanted to have "dot-com" as part of its name. Tom Gimple, founder of Tickets.com, put it this way during an entrepreneurship class lecture: "When I started the company, you had to have dot-com in the name. Now I would like to get rid of it."[12]

As 2002 began, weakness appeared in more and more of the dot-com companies. For one thing, the dot-com companies had developed a growth pattern that courted disaster. It often took a lot of money and talent to get these companies started. Start-ups with tech guys needed managers to get funding. Since they had no cash flow, they offered stock options to employees. The value of options is based on the value of the stock, so that encouraged short-term strategies. Even the consultants brought in at high pay to make up for lack of experienced managers could be paid partly in options. Eventually the initial public offering or sale to another company gave an exit opportunity to those who put money in early and also let employees exercise options and get cash. However, the value of the stock seemed to be based not on earnings, or even projected earnings, but instead on future growth of the company, which required ever more spending. This business model, which was like the 1920s Ponzi scheme, couldn't continue. Increasingly, earnings restatements, reorganizations, and business failures dominated the news.

Yet just as the "bubble" showed that all dot-com companies weren't above the time-tested requirement that business show a profit, so too the "bursting" of the bubble showed that plenty of profitable companies remained. For one thing, the technology continued to develop. After 2000, the focus shifted from consumer-oriented websites to business uses of the Internet, dubbed "business to business" (B2B). One trend was strategic extensions of inventory control. Staples could link your company's copy machine to the Internet to automatically send more paper to you when the copier tells the store it has made a certain number of copies. The extension of that is that Staples can also send more coffee and sugar for the company break room, based on the presumption that copy quantities can convert to the number of people on-site. Supermarkets began to scan every product purchased to not only have exact counts on inventory and sales profiles, but to automatically reorder products. So many retailers adopted the model that it was widely predicted that the consumer's own refrigerator would soon restock itself. In fact, Internet ordering from supermarkets has been available since 2000 with limited success, despite the failings of a doomed company called "Webvan" (although no refrigerators as yet seem to be using the Internet to reorder their own contents).

Internet use continued to grow, aided by the fact that the median price for a standard unit of fiber-optic capacity from Los Angeles to New York fell from $1.8 million in 2000 to $60,000 by 2005.[13] The Internet also became wireless, allowing workers to access it freely from virtually anywhere. So much information is available online that if anyone wants the answer to a question, they can search for it via the Internet. The search engine Yahoo!, developed in the 1990s, was joined by a rival, Google, and the term "Google it" has became part of everyday vocabulary. The company Google went public in 2004 and its stock was valued at the end of the first day of public trading at $128 billion. By 2006, the United States had an installed base of 172 million web surfers.[14] Soon, consumer users of the Internet were not only looking for information. Now they download music and, increasingly, videos to play on computers and mobile devices; they instant message (or "Twitter") and blog, and they create social networks to communicate with strangers or friends.

The Internet had become an internal tool for companies, too. By transferring information to the Internet, employees can access needed information from wherever they are. First came the personal digital assistant (PDA), introduced in the 1990s, that kept appointments and contact information handy for workers away from their computers. Appointment books could even be viewed by others, so bosses could see when all their employees were available for group meetings. The technology that had once offered such freedom from control was being used to reestablish corporate power over the "pyramid" of middle managers. After 2000, it became increasingly common for newer versions of these devices—called smart phones—to receive and send e-mail and allow direct access to the Internet, and while some companies and universities tried to regiment their employees using technology, most gave up and agreed to let the technology liberate their workers. By 2005, GPS was integrated into all the other functions. UPS and FedEx found the system useful so that their drivers could locate addresses, but it also allowed the companies to locate their trucks easily. Converged mobile devices that combine phone, PDA, and GPS functions are a continuing trend.

OUTSOURCING TO INDIA; CAPITALISM IN CHINA

The legacy of the "New Economy" was that it truly allowed new ways to do business—and not all of these changes would be perceived to be favorable to the U.S. economy. All the communication capacity resulting from the Internet boom has made new ways of doing business possible. For example, by 2003 if you needed a new laptop, you went online to Circuit City and selected one. The computer indicated that it was in stock at a nearby location. You place the order, with the plan to go to Circuit City to pick up the computer as soon as possible. But the credit card was not accepted! You call the help number displayed on the screen and explain the problem. "No problem," the soothing, only slightly accented voice assures you. "I will place the order for you." You just bought a computer from a salesperson at a call center in India, yet it was waiting for you at a store five miles from your house.

New telephone technology called "Voice over Internet Protocol" (VoIP) has allowed very inexpensive long-distance calling and enabled call centers, soliciting business or doing surveys, to be the first examples of outsourcing to India, where well-educated, English-speaking young people were anxious to train for the work. These individuals became so specialized that they developed different regional American dialects so they could appear to be local.[15]

Soon it emerged that the country with an extremely good educational system also had outstanding programmers. Technical support and computer programming were the next tasks added to the list of services that routinely were based in India. In 2003, the state of Indiana needed to upgrade its computer system that processed unemployment claims. An Indian consulting company won the bid by about $8 million, but never got to complete the job, due to politics.[16] But the outsourcing trend continued, nonetheless, and it wasn't long before virtually all programming was written in India. By 2002, it seemed there was no job that couldn't be done in India. With the time difference, executives in the United States could hire an executive assistant to work all night, crunching numbers or preparing reports. When the executive left the office, he could e-mail the work to be completed—for example, a PowerPoint presentation based on an attached outline. In India, the assistant arrives, completes a sophisticated presentation, and sends it back for final review. India seemed to have an inexhaustible pool of well-educated people, supplemented by another 2.5 million graduates from their colleges each year and homemakers who are gaining independence and respect by supplementing the family income.[17]

China was another place that seemed to have untouched possibilities. At first, American businesses thought of the one billion consumers there. Unfortunately, these consumers had only about $1 each a year in income. The market system in China was first launched as "trade zones." Although controlled by the government and marked by antiquated techniques and copyright piracy, the free trade zones succeeded so spectacularly at producing that they had to ban immigrants from other parts of the country. More zones had to be added and these zones broke free of control. By 2007, all urban areas sprouted factories overnight, making the simplest of products with the most primitive capital equipment. In the city of Lishui, there was a bazaar with product offerings from 30,000 local producers.[18] Foreign producers, although at first fearful of the still-centralized Chinese government, added more modern factories to the mix. Mercedes parts and Volkswagen Beetles were soon manufactured there.

Fortunately, despite the decline in American education and other burdens that still afflict business, the United States still has the most favorable business climate of any nation in the world, including the latest "threat" on the horizon, China. On the one hand, China has remained a highly controlled state, with political power firmly in the hands of the Communist Party. On the other hand, the government has permitted remarkably free trade in many parts of China, if not overtly, then with the wink of an eye. But Chinese markets, to the extent they are free, must still be disciplined by international economic laws, as the Chinese found out in 2007 when a pet food poisoning scare swept the United States and it was revealed that the basic ingredients in the foods had come from China. American consumers instantly abandoned Chinese products for safe brands, and the mystified reaction in China was predictable for those businesses not steeped in competition and in the tradition of pleasing consumers. The message was: No price is low enough if a product cannot be trusted.

Despite the hysteria over outsourcing American jobs to workers abroad, new studies suggested a limit to the type and number of functions that could be effectively transferred out of a sphere of influence where the main manufacturing/operations plant resides. In 2004, Dell Inc. made a splash by moving product support for business accounts from India back to the States.[19] U.S. Airways, Sears, Cingular, Comcast, and other companies also found that as more and more Indian employees were hired, what was gained in lower employee costs in India were often offset by increased errors, additional time and paperwork, and customer complaints.[20]

Meanwhile, compared to Europe, America remained a business mecca. Unemployment in Germany continued to hover at around 10 percent, and in Italy and France at 11 percent. A central factor in that performance is that the share of GDP absorbed by government remained lower in the United States than in any other advanced country except Japan, which trails by a small margin. Research at U.S. universities continued to lead the world, as evidenced by the 76 Nobel Prize Laureates named in chemistry, physics, and physiology/medicine between 1970 and 1989. In the 1970s, Americans took 57 percent of the Nobel Prizes in those fields; in the 1980s, the Americans' share had risen to 62 percent. Whatever the failings of the elementary educational system in the United States, its colleges still excel in the hard sciences. The University of California–Berkeley alone claimed more prizes than the former Soviet Union had in its entire history. Europeans complained about—but were helpless to stop—a continued "brain drain" to the United States. Policymakers in the European Union grew so concerned about the trend that they produced the "Barcelona Objective," a plan to have member nations devote 3 percent of their GDP to research.[21] Although more European students were getting degrees than their counterparts in the United States, and although a higher percentage of those degrees were in science and engineering (26 percent there to 17 percent here), the European Union employed fewer researchers (5.4 percent) than did the United States (8.7 percent).

A more important factor has been the continued (relatively) low taxation rates of the United States. Tracking the incredible increase in capital gains after the top marginal rate was cut from 70 percent in the early 1970s to 20 percent under Reagan, Warren Brookes found that gains reported by the top one percent of all taxpayers rose from under $20 billion in 1976 to $176.3 billion in 1986, while the amount of taxes paid by that group increased by a factor of eight. Between 1979 and 1986 alone, gains rose by 467 percent, and taxes paid rose by 305 percent. Tax cuts, in fact, have been identified as the leading cause of increasing participation in the labor force, adding 6 percent to 7 percent to the GDP between 1982 and 1989.[22] The "global economy" only further underscored the inability of governments to artificially bolster markets or pump up employment. Capital reacted instantly to shifts in government policy. Wealth, once created, is a lightning bolt that must touch ground somewhere, and it will ground with the most receptive point on the horizon.

INTO THE TWENTY-FIRST CENTURY

By September 2007, the once-depressed Dow Jones Industrials hit an all-time high of nearly 14,000 points. High-tech growth centers such as Silicon Valley had been joined by smaller, but vibrant, tech oases such as Boise, Idaho; Minneapolis–St. Paul, Minnesota; and Raleigh/Durham, North Carolina. Cities catering to high-tech businesses were leading America's growth, buoyed by continued rising productivity. While realism tempered some of the wildly optimistic expectations about cell phones and handheld media devices, their use continued to grow, if at a somewhat more sustainable pace than in the late 1990s. In June 2007, Apple introduced its touch screen iPhone with GPS, Internet connections, data storage, and a screen large enough to allow reasonable viewing of movies downloaded from the Internet. A million quickly sold, but, disappointed in these sales, Apple lowered the price from $599 to $399.

Again, it was George Gilder who predicted the paradigm shift. In his history of computers, *Microcosm* (1989), Gilder observed that the computer freed humanity from natural resources. Made of silicon and glass—essentially sand—computer chips increasingly got more powerful as they got smaller, marking a major departure from the industrial paradigm of "bigger is better." They also required little in the way of fossil fuels to produce. More relevant, Gilder argued, the computer, when used in conjunction with the modem, could transform the workplace itself into a tiny site employees only occasionally needed to visit from their primary places of work—their homes. That restored to individuals much of the autonomy they had ceded to managers over the previous 120 years. Automation performed most of the routine labor, causing work to be increasingly individual rather than collective, as a cog in an industrial machine.

As the cell phone became ubiquitous after 2000 and the favored method of communication became e-mail, it was young people particularly who combined the two into text messaging: short bursts of text sent over cell phone paths. By 2005, reaching age 12 meant having a cell phone. "Rents" (otherwise known as "parents"—the short length of text messages required reinvention of the English language) could call their kids from work, and the kids could send photos of the friends they were with, on the spot, from their phone. Technology continued to develop to allow workers to break away from big companies. In "Is It a Smartphone or a Laptop?" *BusinessWeek* surveyed new devices entering the market in 2007, such as the Palm Foleo, an inexpensive two-and-a-half pound computer with a ten-inch display and full Vista and Microsoft capabilities. "It's a companion to your phone and a companion to you," contended Palm founder Jeff Hawkins. While this particular product was not a success, a market clearly existed for larger phones or smaller computers. The 2008 Apple Airbook and the Sony 10″ screen laptop were other efforts to fill this demand.[23] These gadgets aimed to serve business professionals when they were away from their desks, or lower level employees who actually were not provided offices or desks at the company. That same year Sony had introduced a computer/cell phone at half the weight, but at a far higher price.

The implications for the restoration of individual freedom from government were also extensive. No longer could government automatically tax people through withholding if an ocean of consultant, work-at-home "free agents" dominated the economic landscape. While still possessing the terrifying potential to become Big Brother, the central government in a decentralized economy would lose much of its mission and power. Government—federal, state, and local—still retains an important influence over the economy in that it remains the only substantial sector for the growth of union jobs. Overall, union membership had dropped to under 15 percent of the U.S. workforce in the 1990s, but the proportion of all union members holding a government job has increased. This formidable alliance between organized labor, with its dues-rich pot of AFL-CIO funds, and politicians bent on government expansion poses severe problems for further improving the efficiency of government and, thus, the economy.

Big business was also losing ground in the United States. In 2006, the top-five American corporations in *Fortune* magazine's list of 500 corporations (Exxon Mobil, Wal-Mart Stores, General Motors, Chevron, and Ford Motor) generated total sales of $1.2 trillion, with Exxon Mobil alone generating $339 billion in sales, surpassing the GNP of many nations in the world.[24] But the influence of the large corporation has waned steadily since 1970, and between 1990 and 2006 the sales of the top five fell from 2.2 percent of GNP to 0.09 percent of GNP.[25] On an individual basis, although each of the five companies experienced rising sales, two of the five showed a percentage loss in profits since 2004. Put another way, the largest units of business have lost an increasing portion of the marketplace to entrepreneurial small businesses since 1990.[26]

THE ROLE OF THE ENTREPRENEUR

Of course, all that means is that more than ever, entrepreneurs remain the essence of enterprise. Small technology companies rise and fall like waves in the ocean, in the process generating fabulous new ideas and products before being absorbed, only to be replaced by new tech entrepreneurs. Even here, the old values pretty much are the same: Work hard, serve others, get married, save and invest, and, most important, break new ground. In 1972, Nolan Bushnell invented the world's first video arcade game, Pong. He started the first home video game machines, Atari, which he sold for $28 million in 1976. Adding food to fun, his "Chuck E. Cheese" franchise created a pleasant atmosphere for kids to have pizza parties. In 2007, his audience become adults and he was developing "uWink," a restaurant where customers place their orders via a touch screen on the table, and amuse themselves by remotely challenging other diners to contests played on the same screen.[27]

Kenneth Tuchman worked at a bicycle shop at age 13, then started importing puka shells "to meet women."[28] After selling used cars, he started working for his dad, where he learned that customers could not get answers to questions about air conditioners, roofing, and other systems they had purchased. In 1982, at age 22, he started TeleTech to handle customer questions and complaints for big companies, such as ITT, Herbal Life, and others. Despite completing only two years of community college, Tuchman, worth $1 billion, had attended "the university of life."[29]

Ted Schwartz, who founded APAC (All People Are Customers) TeleServices, handled 200 million phone calls a year, acting as a middleman to firms such as United Parcel Services. A college dropout, Schwartz sold airtime for a small Colorado radio station, beating the streets to drum up business. In 1973 he founded Radio America in Chicago, then in 1985, he secured a contract with Xerox, calling for subscriptions to the *Weekly Reader* through a phone bank he established. Worth more than $1 billion, Schwartz and his family owned the majority of stock in APAC.[30]

Or consider the phenomenal rise of the manicure/nail business in America. Whereas two decades earlier manicurists were confined almost entirely to exclusive hotels and corners of hair salons, the number of nail salons in the United States blossomed into a $6 billion industry—equivalent to video games—and more than 400 manufacturers made nail-related products.[31] With more than 239,000 people in the industry, manicurists and nail specialists represented a growth business that was not even listed in the Bureau of Labor Statistics in 1979. Nail stylists, while licensed, do not have to pass batteries of tests or EPA inspections, thus the industry came to provide employment for the newest and least educated of citizens, including those with limited knowledge of English. In Los Angeles County, for example, 80 percent of the more than 15,000 nail stylists were Vietnamese-born. Nail techni-cians make $20 an hour and work in air-conditioned, comfortable sur-roundings, although the work is often derided as one of the "low-wage jobs." Some manicurists do even better. Linda Troung was still a child when Vietnam fell to the communists, but she was old enough to remember that life. She married a local boy, but dreamed of living in the United States. When her son was born, she demanded that her husband escape and find a better life for her baby. She did not see her husband again for four years. He had managed to get to Germany and they saved enough money for her to join him. But her life in Germany wasn't what she wanted, and the family soon moved to the Vietnamese community in Orange County, California. Her husband got jobs in construction, and when her second child was old enough to go to school, Linda helped the family's finances by going to manicurist school, then work-ing part-time. This allowed them to buy a home in a more integrated neighborhood with excellent schools. As the children grew older, she worked longer hours, and when the owner of the tiny nail salon where she worked decided to retire, Linda mortgaged the home and bought the business. She bought new furniture, had her husband and son paint the walls, and soon was busy enough to move to a more spacious loca-tion. She moved again, creating the most upscale salon in the neighbor-hood, and then began to branch out. At age 45, she got an offer she couldn't turn down, sold the business, and retired.[32]

On the other end of the spectrum is Dennis Washington, a billion-aire who started out working at a gas station to buy his first car. Washington was diagnosed with polio, which at the time was an often fatal disease. He survived, only to be bounced around through several family members when his mother decided she did not want to take care of him.[33] Working construction in Alaska, Washington started his own business, pouring everything he and his wife could save into the con-struction firm. Convinced that the Anaconda copper mine in Butte, Montana, had potential, he purchased the closed mine for $5 million and was losing $800,000 a month when an English investor offered him $50 million for the property. Suspicious, Washington held on to the mine as the price of copper rebounded, making Washington a billion-aire. Washington then turned to philanthropy, setting up a 64,000-acre ranch for Young Life, a Christian ministry.

Not all successful entrepreneurs are uneducated, of course. UCLA engineering professor Henry Samueli got a government grant to research military broadband communications systems. Enlisting the help of his brilliant Ph.D. student Henry Nicolas III, he started Broadcom in 1991. Focusing on connections between devices, the company grew in cable modem sales. By 1997, Broadcom had $37 million in sales, but losses of $1.2 million. In spite of losses, the company's perceived role in the Internet revolution allowed it to go public in April 1998. The stock price leaped from just over $20 to $200 a share by January 1999, and the "Two Henrys" joined the list of America's billionaires, a list they remain on in 2008.[34] Henry Samueli bought the Anaheim Ducks in 2005. In 2007, the team won the Stanley Cup.[35]

Perhaps the most amazing story of entrepreneurship, one not captured in the *Forbes* 400, occurred in the least likely place with a tradition steeped in socialism: the Indian reservation. The Choctaw Indians in Mississippi had for decades operated like most other Indian tribes, receiving government aid, eschewing business enterprise, and eking out a living by farming. Then, in 1975, after a long campaign to give the Tribal Council executive authority over all activities, Chief Philip Martin led a drive to put private enterprise on an industrial park that the tribe had built with a seed grant from the government. Of 150 letters Martin sent to companies, only one respondent, a purchasing agent for the Packard Electric Division of General Motors, expressed interest. When George Gibbons, the purchasing agent, visited the site he was shocked, finding that the Choctaws had paved parking lots and cleared land for plant construction and electricity. A contract was finalized in which the Choctaws purchased component parts and assembled wire harnesses for instrument panels. Under the aegis of the MBCI (Mississippi Band of Choctaw Indians) economic development program, the tribe received a $1.3 million loan to build a 42,000-square-foot plant that turned out its first products in 1979. Within another two years, the Choctaws moved into greeting card manufacturing, raising money for a second plant for producing the cards. By that time, production at the original facility had expanded so much that still another facility was needed. Ford Motor, requiring the same electric harnesses as General Motors, signed a contract for $4.3 million worth of harnesses.

Previous generations of Choctaws had lived with unemployment rates of 75 percent. Under Chief Martin, unemployment fell below 20 percent—still too high by the standards of most capitalists, but an accomplishment of fantastic proportions given the tribe's history. Martin admitted that the tribe benefited from government minority status, but pointed out that its performance had to retain any customers once brought in by special privilege. Ford and Chrysler both gave Choctaw plants awards for quality in excellence. By 1993, the tribe had a portfolio of businesses: It was constructing circuit boards for Chrysler, Ford, Navistar, and AT&T, as well as operating the American Greetings card-making factory. Most of the businesses were owned by the tribe, accounting for more than $271 million in sales and making the tribe the tenth-largest business in the state. As U.S. Senator Ben Nighthorse Campbell noted, "Indians now see private enterprise as the best way out of poverty."[36] And, he could add, away from government dependence: Of the $90 million in capital investment in the MBCI projects, less than 4 percent came from the government. Employment reached 5,000 by 1995, with an additional 2,000 jobs coming on line with the opening of a new casino. Meanwhile, annual per capita income increased 201 percent between 1979 and 1990, while only 2.7 percent of household income came from welfare or other social assistance.[37] By 1999, the tribe and its affiliated enterprises employed 5,822 people, of whom 2,243 were Indian and paid wages of nearly $1 million.[38] Perhaps even more astounding, not only the Choctaws but (because of casinos) virtually all Indian reservations had started to display "help wanted" signs for the first time in their history.

Although the Choctaws were the most successful of the tribes, they were not alone. In Arizona, the Yavapais in Prescott took advantage of their proximity to the resort community to build a resort hotel, securing the assistance of Phoenix developer William Grace. With his help and a bond sale from the city of Prescott, the tribe completed a 160-room Sheraton hotel in 1988, later home to the first casino in the state. The tribe then leased some of the reservation to Grace, who built a shopping mall anchored by Wal-Mart. Only 130 miles away, the Ak-Chin tribe farms two-thirds of its 22,000-acre reservation, bringing in revenues of $10 million annually. Private enterprise had driven the unemployment rate to 3 percent, prompting the tribe to tell the local welfare office, "We have plenty of jobs," and asking them to send back any tribe members who came for welfare. In reclaiming their place in modern society and regaining their independence, several Indian tribes have decided instead of getting even to get rich.

Ultimately, if enterprise can thrive in a culture that has known little but government intervention and socialism for over a century; if college and high school dropouts can become millionaires; if most of the

400 richest Americans were not on the list a decade earlier; if elderly entrepreneurs like Lydia Pinkham with her tonics in the late 1800s and middle-aged failures like C. W. Post who developed a cereal company in the mid-1800s still providing popular breakfast over 100 years later, can found large-scale enterprises; if immigrants account for large segments of the most rapidly growing sectors of business; and if people can shake off failure after failure, lose it all, only to start again and demand nothing less than success from themselves, then truly business enterprise in the free market captures the essence of the American dream. In every case, faith was the key—faith in one's own creative powers, in the basic fairness and good judgment of consumers, and often in God.

As often is said of democracy, the free market is not perfect, and it is the worst system on earth except for all the others. The market certainly offers its share of degradation and evil, much of it available on cable television or over the Internet. Approached the right way, however—the way Adam Smith wanted his theory to be applied—the free enterprise system appeals to the most noble elements of the human character, requiring sacrifice, commitment, service to the wants and needs of others, and above all, hard work. It is anti-elitist in that the taste or view of the average citizen in purchasing products carries as much weight as the wealthiest blue blood. What the market does not care about is intentions. That accounts for much of the media and cultural hostility toward business, because a person can have no higher aspiration than to get rich and still be successful. In a society that celebrates feelings over actions, and deals more with intentions than results, entrepreneurs can seem removed. Even when acting out of noble motivations, most entrepreneurs disdain having to explain themselves to CNN or *Time* magazine, which accounts in part for the high visibility in the media of those few entrepreneurs who publicly champion their efforts for the environment, social justice, or animal rights.

Lest the reader be left with the impression that the United States has entered a "golden age" of entrepreneurship, a warning is in order. For all the freedoms that make possible economic growth, personal fulfillment, and business enterprise, many have come under attack in recent years. Attempts to regulate the Internet, censor television through government-imposed "V-chips," eliminate firearms under the guise that they are the cause of murders, destroy the tobacco industry, mandate entire products out of existence (e.g., Freon-based air conditioners, perfumes, and colognes) or regulate them so strictly that they become inaccessible (e.g., medical drugs) have already occurred. Federal departments have floated plans—again, under the best of intentions—to reduce auto emissions by having global positioning satellites transmit "kill" signals to auto engines that do not comply (while in use on the road!), or to censor free speech through campaigns that eliminate advertising of "unworthy" products. Already, a campaign is afoot against sport-utility vehicles (SUVs) on the grounds that they are too safe, and thus endanger others if they are involved in an accident, or that they use more than their "fair" share of gasoline. Still other discussions already have occurred in Congress to penalize companies (designated "bad companies") that do not reward their workers or provide childcare or offer other benefits that the government deems socially just, or even prevent (at taxpayer expense) a company from closing an unprofitable location.

The great danger is that most of the laws and regulations that permit such incursions of human freedom are carried out by government officials and supported by a media elite—those that economist Thomas Sowell calls "the anointed." As a class, that group fosters a deep-seated hostility to business enterprise and entrepreneurs—except for those few, like Ted Turner, who embrace their social agenda. An even worse danger is that the intrusion of those laws and regulations into American life occurs on an incremental basis, and that only when they become so completely reprehensible does the public respond. Meanwhile, attempts to rein in government, first by Reagan in the 1980s, and again by Congress in the 1990s, have met with only minor success.

Thus, the entrepreneurial adventure continues, confronted with new challenges to market freedoms. However, history is not progressive—it is not constantly improving toward perfection, as huge chasms in the material well-being of humanity attest. Therefore, the continued operations of free markets and the economic liberties enjoyed by entrepreneurs are not guaranteed, but must be maintained and protected.

Yet the market is resilient, and entrepreneurs relentless. Few places on earth offer the same opportunities for achievement as the United States, even with its growing restrictions. Americans still achieve, in part, thanks to low taxes, as compared with all the developed nations; the most favorable climate toward property rights in the world; and a vibrant class of entrepreneurs bent on accomplishments, regardless of the odds. Despite its handicaps, the United States offers a path to achievement, especially through business, that remains open for the ambitious and the talented, the hardworking, and the dreamers. Success is available for all who choose to embrace it. Larry Schweikart related the story of one of his former students, Marty Grunder, who at age 12 began mowing yards. He had a capital investment of $25 in a lawn mower and did yard work because "I liked plants and the idea of having a little money in my pocket."[39] That year—1981—Grunder's total sales came to $1,800, hardly placing him on the *Forbes* 400, but setting him on a career path far ahead of his high school contemporaries. Along with his brother Rich, Grunder started a two-man mowing operation in 1983 that used a small tractor, initiating a cycle that expanded the business steadily over time: "We would save money, buy equipment, save money, employ people, go to school, buy equipment…."[40] A $10,000 contract with a doctor's office complex solidified the seasonal nature of the business. Within three years of getting his driver's license, Grunder had a yard-cutting operation that had swelled to $19,000 in sales, and he and Rich had employed a friend.

Even then, Marty Grunder did not think of himself as a landscape artist, but instead envisioned a career in sports broadcasting. To that end, he attended the University of Dayton, continuing to run the business on the side. Working from seven in the morning to ten or eleven, then going to classes, then working again, Grunder maintained a hectic pace, but he also attracted attention. In 1989, *The New York Times* included him in a story on student entrepreneurs. When local papers picked up the story, his business took off. While in school, for a class assignment he had interviewed motivational speaker Zig Ziglar. That encounter helped convince him to devote himself full-time to his landscaping career. He also took on a partner, cousin Dave Rado, who impressed on Grunder the value of goodwill in marketing. As a result, Grunder's employees received rewards when they stopped to help motorists or performed acts of charity, providing testimony to the company motto, "Where Service Is Always in Season."

A self-taught horticulturist, Grunder learned as the business grew to trust his specialist-employees and to focus on delegating responsibility. He still motored from site to site, overseeing work and meeting clients to select the most appropriate shrub or bush for a yard; yet he well understood the necessity of moving beyond the direct daily involvement of the owner in field operations if the business was to reach the next echelon. One of the keys to landscaping in cold-weather climates is to manage the cyclical nature of the business. That prompted Grunder to move into snow removal, deck construction, and corporate landscaping. In 1993, Grunder Landscaping opened a 6,500-square-foot facility in Miamisburg, Ohio, and had a fleet of a dozen trucks, staffed by eighteen full-time and seven part-time employees. Once Grunder Landscaping boomed into a $4-million-a-year business, Marty found himself speaking before hundreds at the White House Conference on Small Business in Washington, D.C.[41]

For the entrepreneurial business to grow to the next level, it has to operate beyond the constant input of a single individual on matters of detail. That is why the story of Sam Walton, with whom we started chapter 12, is so appropriate. Walton managed to run a billion-dollar business like a local store. Ultimately, small entrepreneurs who want to see businesses grow must make that leap—enter the "Walton zone"—and expand outside the personal, daily control of the founder. It requires trust in subordinates, valuing their opinions and decisions. Grunder had a close network of assistants and partners; just as, on a different scale, Andrew Carnegie molded a core of trusted lieutenants who implemented his vision, developing a powerful management team. A. P. Giannini built a world-class banking institution on such simple principles that it took "professional" managers more than thirty years to forget them. Ray Kroc used franchising and strict product testing to expand McDonald's, finding a way to standardize quality control in such a way that franchisees could oversee the quality issues themselves. Lee Iacocca, for a brief time, was able to convince the entire vast corporate ships of Ford and Chrysler to follow his new course. Bill Gates, Steve Jobs, and Steve Wozniak all tapped into the hacker's mentality, offering their designers independence and creative outlets in return for new ideas.[42]

Yet Sam Walton, perhaps, was the master at entrepreneurial management of a giant corporation, walking into a store before hours in his Wal-Mart cap and congenially talking to the people upon whom the quality of the business rested: the employees. As he knew, computers could facilitate ordering and inventory control, management structures could improve efficiency in operations, but in the end it took vision, faith, and hard work to realize a dream. Even more, as Abe Karatz, Preston Tucker's right-hand man in the movie *Tucker*, observed, people who associate with entrepreneurs catch their dreams. The entrepreneur must be infectious, to the extent that employees "catch his dreams."

The dreamers are still out there. Mike Brown didn't plan on owning his own business when he started college as a business major, until his parents gave him a BMW 3 Series. He started to modify it, but had trouble finding the products and accessories he wanted on the Internet. "I [knew of] some good products, but … it was difficult to find them, in my opinion. So I thought this was an opportunity to do something I love, which is modifying my car, and to take these products that aren't being marketed as effectively as they could be and get them out in front of customers better. That was the whole mission of ModBargains—to find quality parts, things that I was installing in my own car, and start marketing them out to other car enthusiasts. So that was the beginning." By the time Brown was a college senior the company had $1 million a year in sales, leading to Brown's selection as the Global Best College Entrepreneur in 2007.[43]

Mike Brown would echo many entrepreneurs in his advice to other student entrepreneurs:

> I could start by saying that there's a common mistake that a lot of people make not only in entrepreneurship but also in life in general in choosing a career. Some people look at the marketplace and ask themselves, "Where can I make the most money?" instead of looking within themselves and asking, "What am I passionate about?" I truly believe that if you find something that you are passionate about and you work hard on it, that you are setting yourself up for success. I am passionate about cars. I enjoy waking up in the morning and I've got sixty or seventy e-mails from customers, waiting there to be answered. It's not like, "Oh, man, I've got to go to work today." Instead [I tell myself], "Sweet. I've got some people who are interested in modifying their cars. How can I help these people out?" If you can find something that you're passionate about and can turn into a business, then that is the best way to start.[44]

To the extent that America still leads the world in entrepreneurship and young people like Mike Brown are still around, America will still lead in business. Success in the competitive markets of the twenty-first century will not go to the nation that dominates existing technology, but the nation whose entrepreneurs break through into the next technologies and service ideas. The future belongs to those able to discern those businesses that no one else has even heard of today, and to invent those products not even thought necessary now. No one can do that better than American entrepreneurs. If the American past is a guide to our future, the entrepreneurs of the world will be seeking to catch our dreams.

THE CAROUSEL OF AMERICAN SUCCESS

While entrepreneurs have changed little over the history of the United States, the businesses they have succeeded in have changed a great deal. American businesses have always reflected the world in which they operated. In the seventeenth century, there were accepted routes of trade and products to trade. Explorers stretched these boundaries, finding tomatoes, potatoes, and vast new sources of gold and silver in the British American colonies. A hundred years later, tobacco growing and exporting was the source of wealth in the southern United States. Freedom from Britain brought about new opportunities to make furniture, hats, candles, and other goods for household use. The young republic began to trade with China, Mexico, and South America, making products once reserved for the rich more affordable.

Eli Whitney's invention of the cotton gin changed United States business again, by turning the South from a backwater into the nation's wealthiest section, yet that success sowed the seeds of the South's eventual eclipse by the more industrialized North. Ironically, it was Samuel Slater's textile factories that turned Whitney's invention in favor of the Yankees. Soon every New England river sprouted spinning mills, which evolved into factories producing thread and cloth. Moving products to market now demanded more rapid transit of the waterways, leading John Fitch, then Robert Fulton, to control steam-powered ships, and De Witt Clinton to link the Great Lakes region to New York with his Erie Canal.

It was inevitable that the free labor of Northern farms and industries would triumph over the slave-based system, and when it did, business changed. Railroads, once merely a competitor to canals, achieved dominance as they absorbed the capital funds that once poured into textile factories. Iron and steel, the building blocks of the railroads, took center stage as Andrew Carnegie produced the cheapest, best steel in the world. That same steel went into reapers, harvesters, and other farm equipment, lifting the United States to the top ranks of world food producers, then bringing with it a host of other packaged goods: cigarettes, cereals, cheese, beer, then paint and whiskey. Funding these newly emerging businesses was a powerful, dynamic financial system, led by people like J. P. Morgan.

The mechanical know-how and industrial base that built railroads and farm equipment laid the groundwork for automobile manufacturing after 1900. Henry Ford created the world's most popular car in the Model T. A necessary companion to the automobile industry—the oil industry—emerged to make the gas station a feature of the landscape. Consumers, with incomes rising from high-wage jobs, not only demanded automobiles but other conveniences as well. They got "sanitary packages," new retail systems, kitchen gadgets, and radios, and soon they even began to own their own homes, thanks to creative financiers such as A. P. Giannini.

Interrupted by the New Deal and the controls of a wartime economy, American business staged a revival in the 1950s. The budding airline industry of the 1920s, which had started by carrying mail, now hauled millions of passengers. Juan Trippe and other aviation magnates took command of the air, with trips shortened greatly by the introduction of jet engines. Shipbuilding techniques perfected under the pressure of war made America the world's ruler of the oceans. Postwar American consumers exerted their pent-up demand for autos, electronic appliances, televisions, and houses, encouraged by William Levitt's low-cost, mass-produced suburban homes.

Following fifteen years of explosive growth when the United States was the unchallenged world leader, the economy regrouped in the 1960s and 1970s. Government again exerted its influence over markets through environmental and consumer regulations. Inevitably, business and consumers chaffed at the predictable inflexibility of the controlled telephone, trucking, energy, aviation, and transportation industries. Yet even during a high tide of post-Depression government involvement in markets, individual entrepreneurs, such as Steve Jobs and Steve Wozniak, were revealing a future in which the personal computer would change the way people worked and played.

These forces were released in the Ronald Reagan supply-side 1980s. Deregulation allowed airlines and telephones to thrive; fiber-optic cable expanded the carrying capacity of telephone lines and brought new stations to television sets everywhere with cable.

Entrepreneurs started work on better delivery systems for telephone and television.

The proliferation of computers required the writing of vast amounts of software. It seemed like an endless source of jobs. From the 1980s to the 1990s, everyone wanted software, from kids playing games to large corporations wanting each department to have only a limited selection of information from the accounting department. In this New Economy, fewer resources were used to produce more goods. Outsourcing of programming functions to India and, a few years later, low-tech manufacturing to China further accelerated productivity.

Resources saved in one area create opportunities in another. Having ceded the lead in several industries—electronics, textiles, and even automotives, the American economy continued the entrepreneurial adventure by reinventing itself yet again, as the world's high-tech leader. Privately owned Boeing defeated its European rivals in head-to-head competition for the latest jets; American biomedical firms continued to dominate the world; and above all, the United States continued to develop new products and services at blinding speed.

In cycle after cycle, wave after wave, the entrepreneur remained the decisive figure of the American economy. Encouraged by reasonable taxes and low levels of regulation, boosted by Horatio Alger stories of entrepreneurial virtue, empowered by private ownership and contracts that have been held sacred by court after court, businessmen pushed and pulled the U.S. economy into world preeminence. And what an adventure it was.

The Recession Returns

By 2008, the American economy began to slow again. There was an obvious cause: The boom of the 1990s Internet businesses had been replaced by a real estate boom. Easy credit, especially for homeowners, fueled this boom and, like other booms, it fed on itself. Steadily rising prices became an end in themselves, as people began to purchase property more as investments than as a primary residence. Prices became unsustainably high. As the one-income homeowner became nearly obsolete, investors gobbled up homes that they rented out at a loss, hoping to recoup their losses with appreciation of the property. Television programs such as *Flip That House* became sensations. The record of previous real estate booms showed that some people could indeed make money in such a market, but after 2005, prices began to fall and many people found themselves "upside down" on their mortgages.

This happened quickly in the "subprime" mortgages. As housing prices rose after the mid-1990s lull, mortgage banking became a fast-growth industry. Mortgage banks borrowed large sums of money from banks, and then aggressively marketed loans to homeowners. Encouraged by the Bill Clinton administration, they developed new products to allow more people to own their own homes. Subprime mortgages allowed homeowners to borrow the full market price of their homes, or let borrowers make payments of interest only, or refinanced homes without the owners having to prove they still had the income to make the agreed-upon payments. Furthermore, the money borrowed did not have to be used for the house. Interest on these loans was tax deductible, even if used to buy a new car, send the kids to college, or just live less frugally. Consumer spending soared.

New Century Financial Corp. was one of the mortgage banks providing subprime loans in the early 2000s. In 2006, New Century alone made subprime loans totaling $2.4 billion.[1] The company's stock reached $51 a share in April 2006, but the stock collapsed in February 2007 and the company went into bankruptcy in April.[2] The New Century bankruptcy "put an exclamation point on the era of investing in securitized subprime debt. It's probably over for [the] time being," said Greg Hallman, a lecturer on real estate finance. "That market worked for as long as investment banks provided funding. [The banks] have cut the money off."[3]

The real estate boom was over. Housing price growth peaked in 2005. With the debt burden becoming frightening, new mortgages slowed. Housing prices still grew, but there were more and more predictions of declines. By midyear 2007, home prices declined across the nation, and the existing home market had a two-year backlog.[4] Slowing of the economy followed. Still, the economy seemed to be sliding down a fairly gradual slope. This situation changed rather quickly in September 2008. Suddenly the economy was in financial crisis. The first sign that the problems were not isolated came when Henry Paulson, then U.S. Secretary of the Treasury, seized Fannie Mae and Freddie Mac. Fannie Mae had started in 1938 as the Federal National Mortgage Company, a government agency that issued government-guaranteed bonds and used the funds to purchase mortgages from financially strapped banks. Fannie Mae purchased only home mortgages of small amounts for homes with specific requirements, so in 1970 Congress created Freddie Mac to do the same for larger "nonconforming" loans. Fannie Mae became a private company with no government guarantees on its loans in 1968, and Freddie Mac never had such guarantees, but Congress still often worried about the potential that the U.S. government would become liable if the bonds the companies issued defaulted. At the time, Fannie Mae and Freddie Mac were holding almost half of the mortgages issued in the United States. Paulson claimed that he was saving the housing market.

There is no doubt the mortgage market was troubled and deteriorating further. Delinquencies had been rising since May 2007. Still, as of

March 31, 2008, 30.1 million of the total loans serviced (98.83 percent) were current or less than sixty days delinquent.[5] By September, the total had risen dramatically.[6] Speculation mounted about whether Paulson would rescue the mortgage giants, as it had Goldman Sachs, or treat the companies as he had Bear Stearns, trying to force a sale for $2 a share when the stock was selling on the market at $12 a share.[7]

Increasingly, White House officials and Congress fretted that a full-scale 1930s-style "meltdown" of the economy was occurring. Chairman of the Federal Reserve, Ben Bernanke—who had spent much of his academic career studying the deflation-induced Great Depression—seemed determined not to permit a deflationary cycle. Congress likewise sought a financial bailout plan but the legislation was worded so as to give Paulson virtually dictatorial authority over spending the "relief" money. Paulson soon began changing the objectives of the program from saving the banks, to restoring the financial system, to stimulating economic growth. A flummoxed President Bush admitted that he had to jettison his free market principles to "save the economy."

In 2008, both Democratic presidential candidate Barack Obama and the Democratic House and Senate candidates ran and won on the issue of the economy, promising relief in the form of a massive economic stimulus package, which, by 2009, increased the U.S. national debt by trillions of dollars. The stock market remained unconvinced of recovery.

As usual, a failing economy has brought out weaknesses in businesses that had been easily hidden by growth. General Motors climaxed a twenty-year decline in sales with a 49 percent drop in 2008 and was generally assumed to be headed for bankruptcy. Ford and Chrysler (recently brought back to U.S. ownership) experienced drops nearly as devastating. A panicked rush of auto executives, traveling in private jets to Washington, D.C., to ask for federal loans resulted in public ridicule, although a more sedate journey two weeks later, this time with the executives driving their companies' hybrid vehicles, resulted in their obtaining some of the money earmarked for buying troubled securities.

Kids still rolled on their Heelys, not minding that the company's stock was, like that of most other companies, at a price less than one-third of its peak. Americans still consumed enough pizza to keep Michael Ilitch on the *Forbes* 400 list of richest Americans. H. Ty Warner's Beanie Babies fans had to slow their purchases, though, and even Pierre Omidyar's egalitarian eBay faltered, but both men had retired and were able to keep most of their wealth. In 2008, Bill Gates left the company he founded to focus on giving away the vast sums he had accumulated. His wealth was surpassed in 2007 by his friend Warren Buffett. Perhaps as compensation, Buffett rewrote his will to contribute most of his fortune to the Bill and Melinda Gates Foundation, its $36 billion making it the richest potential donor in the world.[8]

Many other entrepreneurs found their dreams undercut by falling GDP. The drop in the stock markets from 2007's high in the 14,000 range to below 8,000 at the beginning of 2009 caused most people's wealth to decline. As for the founders of high-tech Broadcom—Henry Nicolas and Henry Samueli—they probably wished to be back in their early entrepreneurial days when they were professor and former student. They were accused of backdating stock options granted to their employees, which had the effect of boosting the employees' compensation. Samueli pleaded guilty only to lying about his knowledge of the backdating, and received probation and a $12 million fine, but he left his active role in the company and was banned by the National Hockey League from contact with his team, the Anaheim Ducks. Nicolas promptly entered a drug treatment facility, delaying his prosecution, while shocking tales emerged of a "pleasure den" he had secretly carved out under his California suburban home.

There will always be mistakes and fraud in a free market system. The essence of such a system, after all, is the freedom to allow new ideas. Growth cannot occur without change. Shifting spending from private individuals to the government cannot repair the economy, as the Great Depression clearly illustrated. Nevertheless, by 2009, precisely such an unprecedented shift was under way. Entrepreneurship is an amazing phenomenon, though. It can emerge in any economy. Entrepreneurs are people who will seek out ways to serve any market and do it better than it has ever been done before. They have moved the American economy forward toward efficiently using its resources. The American entrepreneur remains one of the most resilient creatures on earth!

NOTES

CHAPTER 1

1. Michael E. Ross, "An Inventor's Lifelong Heeling Process: Heelys Are the Latest in Mobility," MSNBC.com, April 27, 2004, http://www.msnbc.msn.com/id/4354874/; "Skate Shoe Company Moves Along," http://bizjournals.com/dallas/stories/2005/02/28/story6.html; Bruce Freeman, "Sitting Back on Your Heels," ProLine Communications, Inc., http://prolinepr.com/html/adams.htm.

2. "Hot Growth Companies," *BusinessWeek*, June 4, 2007. By August 2007, Heelys, Inc.'s stock had slipped. As a Dallas eighth-grader described the situation: "They're old," quoted in "Can Heelys Regain Momentum?" *Wall Street Journal*, August 21, 2007.

3. Adam Smith, *An Inquiry into the Nature and Causes of the Wealth of Nations*, eds. R. H. Campbell and A. S. Skinner, 2 vols. (Indianapolis, IN: Liberty Classics, 1981).

4. Robert Heilbroner, with the assistance of Laurence J. Malone, *The Essential Adam Smith* (New York and London: W. W. Norton, 1986), 169.

5. Heilbroner, *The Essential Adam Smith*, 170.

6. Ibid., 168.

7. Recent assessments of the Catholic Church's position on "just price" appear in Robert B. Ekelund, Jr., et al., *Sacred Trust: The Medieval Church as an Economic Firm* (New York: Oxford University Press, 1996).

8. Frank H. Knight, *Risk, Uncertainty, and Profit* (New York: Augustus M. Kelly, 1964 [1921]), 363. Knight's italics.

9. Information about richest Americans is from "*Forbes* 400: The 400 Richest Americans," Forbes.com, http://www.forbes.com/lists/2006/54/biz_06rich400_The-400-Richest-Americans_land.html.

10. Say's theories can be found in Henry W. Spiegel, *The Growth of Economic Thought* (New York: Prentice-Hall, 1971), 260, and in C. Joseph Pusateri, *A History of American Business*, 2d ed. (Arlington Heights, IL: Harlan-Davidson, 1988), 6–7.

11. Jonathan R. T. Hughes, *The Vital Few: The Entrepreneurs and American Economic Progress*, 2d ed. (New York: Oxford University Press, 1986).

12. George Gilder, *Wealth and Poverty* (New York: Basic Books, 1981), 262.
13. George Gilder, *Recapturing the Spirit of Enterprise* (San Francisco: ICS Press, 1992).
14. Michael Novak, *The Spirit of Democratic Capitalism* (New York: American Enterprise Institute, 1982).
15. See, for example, Richard Heilbroner, *The Making of Economic Society*, 8th ed. (Englewood Cliffs, NJ: Prentice-Hall, 1989); Joseph Scotchie, ed., *The Vision of Richard Weaver* (New Brunswick, NJ: Transaction, 1995); and Daniel Bell, *The Cultural Contradictions of Capitalism*, 20th anniversary ed. (New York: Basic Books, 1996).
16. U.S. Census Bureau data, http://www.census.gov.
17. U.S. Census Bureau, "Number of Firms, Number of Establishments, Employment, and Annual Payroll by Employment Size of the Enterprise for the United States and States, Totals—2004." The total number of employees was 115 million, of which 56 million worked for the largest businesses.
18. Hang Nguyen, "Oakley's Jannard Signs Non-Compete Agreement," *Orange County Register*, June 24, 2007, http://www.ocregister.com/ocregister/money/7dayarchive/saturday/article_1741400.php.
19. Oakley, Inc., "Oakley History," http://oakley.com/innovation/history.
20. Max Weber, *The Protestant Ethic and the Spirit of Capitalism*, trans. Talcott Parsons (New York: Charles Scribner's Sons, 1958).
21. Ekelund, et al., *Sacred Trust*, passim.
22. Thomas Sowell, *Race and Culture: A World View* (New York: Basic Books, 1994).
23. Ibid., 47 and passim. Also see Sowell's *Economics and Politics of Race: An International Perspective* (New York: William Morrow, 1983).
24. Frederick K. C. Price, *High Finance: God's Financial Plan, Tithes, and Offerings* (Tulsa, OK: Harrison House, 1982). Price notes, for example, that as a tax collector, Matthew was well off financially, and that Peter, James, and John had fishing fleets with employees, and that apparently the disciples traveled with a considerable amount of cash on them because they needed a treasurer to hold the "bag," and that Judas stole from the bag for more than three years without anyone noticing.
25. William M. Ramsay, *St. Paul: The Traveler and Roman Citizen* (London: Angus Hudson, 2001).
26. Paul Johnson, *A History of Christianity* (New York: Atheneum, 1976), 195, 216.
27. Christine Rider, *An Introduction to Economic History* (Cincinnati, OH: South-Western Publishing, 1995), 37. Some of this interpretation is challenged by Ekelund et al. in *Sacred Trust*, who argue that the Church merely used economic doctrine to maximize its own monopoly status, but that process in turn fostered a heightened level of entrepreneurial activity.
28. Yahoo, Inc., "The History of Yahoo! How It All Started...," http://docs.yahoo.com/info/misc/history.html.
29. References for each of these stories will appear in the more developed sections discussing each individual throughout the book. In general, however, see Joseph J. Fucini and Suzy Fucini, *Entrepreneurs: The Men and Women Behind Famous*

Brand Names and How They Made It (Boston: G. K. Hall, 1985), as well as Robert Sobel and David B. Sicilia, *Entrepreneurs: An American Adventure* (Boston: Houghton-Mifflin, 1986).

30. Andrew Carnegie is number six, according to the *New York Times* ranking of the wealthiest Americans ever; see http://www.nytimes.com/ref/business/ 20070715_GILDED_GRAPHIC.html#.

31. J. P. Morgan is number twenty-four in the *New York Times* ranking of the wealthiest Americans ever.

32. John W. Nordstrom, *The Immigrant in 1887* (n.p.: privately printed, 1950); Everett Nordstrom, *A Winning Team* (n.p.: privately printed, 1985).

33. David S. Landes, *The Wealth and Poverty of Nations: Why Some Are So Rich and Some So Poor* (New York: Norton, 1999), 59.

34. Randall Fitzgerald, *When Government Goes Private: Successful Alternatives to Public Services* (New York: Universe Books, 1988).

35. Several sources discuss these trends, dissecting the data in different ways. See Henry R. Nau, *The Myth of America's Decline* (Cambridge: Oxford University Press, 1992); Ben Wattenberg, *The First Universal Nation* (New York: Free Press, 1991); and Edwin S. Rubenstein, *The Right Data* (New York: National Review, 1994). For current data, see the U.S. Department of Commerce, Bureau of Economic Analysis, http://www.bea.gov/newsreleases/national/gdp/gdpnewsrelease.htm.

CHAPTER 2

1. W. Elliot Brownlee, *Dynamics of Ascent: A History of the American Economy*, 2d ed. (New York: Alfred A. Knopf, 1979), 8.

2. C. Joseph Pusateri, *A History of American Business*, 2d ed. (Arlington Heights, IL: Harlan-Davidson, 1988), 40.

3. See James Burke, *Connections* (Boston: Little, Brown, 1978), 122–23, and Carlo Cipolla, *Guns, Sails, and Empires: Technological Innovations and the Early Phases of European Expansion, 1400–1700* (New York: Pantheon Books, 1965).

4. Rodney Stark, *The Victory of Reason: How Christianity Led to Freedom, Capitalism, and Western Success* (New York: Random House, 2005).

5. William H. McNeill, *The Pursuit of Power: Technology, Armed Force, and Society Since 1000 A.D.* (Chicago: University of Chicago Press, 1983).

6. Victor Davis Hanson, *Carnage and Culture: Landmark Battles in the Rise of Western Power* (New York: Anchor, 2002).

7. An excellent discussion of the explorers of this era appears in Esmond Wright, *The Search for Liberty: From Origins to Independence* (Oxford: Blackwell, 1995), 5.

8. Oliver Perry Chitwood, *A History of Colonial America*, 3d ed. (New York: Harper & Row, 1961 [1931]), 24.

9. Brownlee, *Dynamics of Ascent*, 15.

10. David Landes, *The Unbound Prometheus: Technical Change and Industrial Development in Western Europe from 1750 to the Present* (Cambridge: Cambridge University Press, 1969); Nathan Rosenberg and L. E. Birdsell,

How the West Grew Rich: The Economic Transformation of the Industrial World (New York: Basic Books, 1969).

11. Joel Mokyr, *The Lever of Riches* (New York: Oxford, 1990), 302.

12. McNeill, *Pursuit of Power*, passim.

13. Jack A. Goldstone, "Cultural Orthodoxy, Risk, and Innovation: The Divergence of East and West in the Early Modern World," *Sociological Theory* (Fall 1987), 119–35, quotation on 119.

14. Landes's *Unbound Prometheus* provides a classic study of these forces, as does Rosenberg and Birdsell's *How the West Grew Rich*.

15. E. L. Jones, *The European Miracle: Environments, Economics, and Geopolitics in the History of Europe and Asia* (Cambridge: Cambridge University Press, 1981), 149.

16. Jones, *European Miracle*, 148–49.

17. Christine Rider, *An Introduction to Economic History* (Cincinnati, OH: South-Western Publishing, 1995), 95.

18. Quoted in Wright, *Search for Liberty*, 119.

19. Edmund S. Morgan, *American Slavery, American Freedom: The Ordeal of Colonial Virginia* (New York: Norton, 1975).

20. See John M. Dobson, *A History of American Enterprise* (Englewood Cliffs, NJ: Prentice-Hall, 1988), 14. The most thorough discussion of tobacco prices during this period appears in Russell R. Menard, "Farm Prices of Maryland Tobacco, 1659–1710," *Maryland Historical Magazine* 68 (1973), 80–85; Jacob Price, "The Economic Growth of the Chesapeake and the European Market, 1697–1775," *Journal of Economic History* 24 (1964), 496–511; and John J. McCusker and Russell R. Menard, *The Economy of British America, 1607–1789* (Chapel Hill: Institute of Early American History and Culture and the University of North Carolina Press, 1985), especially ch. 6.

21. Patricia Irvin Cooper, "Tennessee Places—Cabins and Deerskins: Log Building and the Charles Town Indian Trade," *Tennessee Historical Quarterly* 53 (Winter 1984), 272–79.

22. Byrd quoted in John Spencer Basset, ed., *The Writings of Colonel William Byrd* (New York: B. Franklin, 1970 [1901]), 207–8; Pierre Marambaud, *William Byrd of Westover, 1674–1744* (Charlottesville: University Press of Virginia, 1971).

23. See James T. Flexner, *George Washington*, 3 vols. (Boston: Little, Brown, 1965–69).

24. See Larry Schweikart, "Antebellum Southern Bankers: Origins and Mobility," in *Business and Economic History*, ed. Jeremy Atack (Urbana, IL: Bureau of Economic and Business Research, 1985), 79–103, and "Entrepreneurial Aspects of Antebellum Banking," in *American Business History: Case Studies*, eds. C. Joseph Pusateri and Henry Dethloff (New York: Harlan-Davidson, 1987), 122–39. See Schweikart's *Banking in the American South from the Age of Jackson to Reconstruction* (Baton Rouge: Louisiana State University Press, 1987).

25. Nathaniel Philbrick, *Mayflower: A Story of Courage, Community and War* (London: Viking, 2006), 29.

26. Philbrick, *Mayflower*, 41, 43.

27. Ibid., 184.

28. See Bernard Bailyn, *The New England Merchants in the Seventeenth Century* (Cambridge, MA: Harvard University Press, 1979 [1955]).

29. Eric Jay Dolin, *Leviathan* (New York and London: W. W. Norton, 2007), 67.

30. Dolin, *Leviathan*, 35.

31. Ibid., 132–33.

32. Ibid., 205.

33. Keith L. Bryant, Jr., and Henry C. Dethloff, *A History of American Business*, 2d ed. (Englewood Cliffs, NJ: Prentice-Hall, 1990), 40.

34. Gerald Gunderson, *The Wealth Creators* (New York: Truman Talley Books, 1989), 37.

35. Jonathan R. T. Hughes, *The Vital Few: The Entrepreneur and American Economic Progress*, expanded ed. (New York: Oxford, 1986), 54.

36. Richard Walsh, "The Revolutionary Charleston Mechanic," in *Small Business in American Life*, ed. Stuart Bruchey (New York: Columbia University Press, 1980), 49–79.

37. Other instruments, similar to bills of exchange, were sight drafts, which were payable when they arrived back at the account on which they were drawn, and time drafts that had a specified pay date on them. For further information, see Larry Schweikart, ed., *Encyclopedia of American Business History and Biography: Banking and Finance to 1913* (New York: Facts on File, 1990), 64.

38. Dobson, *History of American Enterprise*, 24.

39. See "Paul Revere, Pioneer Industrialist," pamphlet, Revere Copper and Brass Incorporated, n.d., ca. 1957.

40. Esther Forbes, *Paul Revere and the World He Lived In* (Boston: Houghton-Mifflin, 1942; Sentry Edition, 1969), 377–97, 424, 481n, quoted in Bryant and Dethloff, *History of American Business*, 43.

41. "Paul Revere, Pioneer Industrialist," 5.

42. Thomas M. Doerflinger, *A Vigorous Spirit of Enterprise: Merchants and Economic Development in Revolutionary Philadelphia* (New York: W. W. Norton, 1986), 345.

43. Doerflinger, *Vigorous Spirit of Enterprise*, 351.

44. For a different approach to wealth, based on consumption patterns, see Carole Shammas, *The Pre-industrial Consumer in England and America* (Oxford: Clarendon Press, 1990), and Lois Green Carr, Russell R. Menard, and Lorena S. Walsh, *Robert Cole's World: Agriculture and Society in Early Maryland* (Chapel Hill: Institute of Early American History and Culture and University of North Carolina Press, 1991).

45. Jeremy Atack and Peter W. Passell, *A New Economic View of American History* (New York: W. W. Norton, 1994), 40–51; David W. Galenson, "The Market Evaluation of Human Capital: The Case of Indentured Servitude," *Journal of Political Economy* 89 (1981), 446–67; and Galenson's *White Servitude in Colonial America* (New York: Cambridge University Press, 1981); James Henretta, *The Evolution of American Society, 1700–1815: An Interdisciplinary Analysis* (Lexington, MA: D. C. Heath, 1973); and Alice Hanson Jones, *Wealth of*

a Nation to Be: The American Colonies on the Eve of Revolution (New York: Columbia University Press, 1980).

46. Alan Brinkley, *American History: A Survey*, 9th ed. (New York: McGraw-Hill, 1995), 50.

47. Louis B. Wright, *The Atlantic Frontier: Colonial American Civilization, 1607–1763* (Ithaca, NY: Cornell University Press, 1947), 221. See also the chapter in Hughes, *Vital Few*, on William Penn.

48. Bernard Bailyn portrayed this indecision as a crisis of confidence that contributed directly to the Revolution. See his *The Ideological Origins of the American Revolution* (Cambridge, MA: Harvard University Press, 1967).

49. An excellent discussion of these themes appears in Leo Strauss, *Natural Right and History* (Chicago: University of Chicago Press, 1953), as well as Ted V. McAllister, *Revolt Against Modernity: Leo Strauss, Eric Voegelin, and the Search for a Postliberal Order* (Lawrence: University of Kansas Press, 1996). On the relationship between business and religion at that time, see James D. German, "The Social Utility of Wicked Self-Love: Calvinism, Capitalism, and Public Policy in Revolutionary New England," *Journal of American History* 82 (December 1995), 965–98.

50. McCusker and Menard, *Economy of British America*, 362.

51. Ibid., 364. See also Robert A. East, *Business Enterprise in the American Revolutionary Era* (New York: Columbia University Press, 1938), and John T. Schlebecker, "Agricultural Markets and Marketing in the North, 1774–1777," *Agricultural History* 50 (1976), 21–36.

52. Jeremy Atack and Peter Passell, *A New Economic View of American History*, 2d ed. (New York: W. W. Norton, 1994), quotation on 62; Lawrence Harper, "Mercantilism and the American Revolution," *Canadian Historical Review* 23 (1942), 1–15; Robert P. Thomas, "A Quantitative Approach to the Study of the Effects of British Imperial Policy on Colonial Welfare," *Journal of Economic History* 25 (1965), 615–38; and Peter McClelland, "The Cost to America of British Imperial Policy," *American Economic Review* 59 (1969), 370–81.

53. See B. R. Burg, "Robert Morris," in Schweikart, ed., *Encyclopedia of American Business History and Biography: Banking and Finance to 1913*; and Clarence L. Ver Steeg, *Robert Morris, Revolutionary Financier* (Philadelphia: University of Pennsylvania Press, 1954).

54. Larry Schweikart, *America's Victories: Why the U.S. Wins Wars and Will Win the War on Terror* (New York: Sentinel, 2006).

55. George Gilder, *Wealth and Poverty* (New York: Basic Books, 1981), 29.

56. Charles Beard, *An Economic Interpretation of the Constitution* (New York: Macmillan, 1913).

57. Forrest McDonald, *We the People: The Economic Origins of the Constitution* (Chicago: University of Chicago Press, 1958).

58. Robert A. McGuire and Robert L. Ohsfeldt, "An Economic Model of Voting Behavior Over Specific Issues at the Constitutional Convention of 1787," *Journal of Economic History* 46 (March 1986), 79–111, and their earlier article, "Economic Interests and the American Constitution: A Quantitative Rehabilitation of Charles A. Beard," *Journal of Economic History* 44 (1984), 509–20.

59. Larry Schweikart and Michael Allen, *A Patriot's History of the United States: From Columbus's Great Discovery to the War on Terror* (New York: Sentinel, 2007).

CHAPTER 3

1. Mansell G. Blackford and K. Austin Kerr, *Business Enterprise in American History*, 2d ed. (Boston: Houghton-Mifflin, 1990), 59.

2. John M. Dobson, *A History of American Enterprise* (Englewood Cliffs, NJ: Prentice-Hall, 1988), 50.

3. See Daniel B. Klein and John Majewski, "Economy, Community, and Law: The Turnpike Movement in New York, 1797–1845," *Law and Society Review* 26 (1992), 469–512.

4. Cecilia Kenyon, "Alexander Hamilton, Rousseau of the Right," *Political Science Quarterly* 73 (June 1958), 161–78. See also Paul Goodman, "The First American Party System," in *The American Party Systems: Stages of Political Development*, eds. William Nisbet Chambers and Walter Dean Burnham (New York: Oxford University Press, 1967), 56–89.

5. Charles W. Calomiris, "Hamilton v. Hamilton: Lessons from History," *The International Economy* (December 1989), 244. For a different view, see John Steele Gordon, *Hamilton's Blessing: The Extraordinary Life and Times of Our National Debt* (New York: Penguin, 1998 [1997]).

6. Ron Chernow, *Alexander Hamilton* (New York: Penguin, 2004).

7. Douglas A. Irwin and Peter Temin, "The Antebellum Tariff on Cotton Textiles Revisited," *Journal of Economic History* 61 (September 2001), 777–805.

8. Views on Jefferson range from those who see him as auguring in a wave of individualistic capitalism under the rubric republicanism, to assessments of Jefferson as a conservative and a restrained student of Jean-Baptiste Say. See Joyce J. Appleby, *Capitalism and a New Social Order: The Republican Vision of the 1790s* (New York: New York University Press, 1984) for the first view, and M. L. Burstein, *Understanding Thomas Jefferson: Studies in Economics, Law, and Philosophy* (New York: St. Martin's Press, 1993) for the second. Burstein cites a single letter from Jefferson (February 1, 1804) to Say suggesting that he would never have blocked the natural growth of manufactures, based on the conclusion that nature sometimes permitted manufactures to arise.

9. Gary Walton and Hugh Rockoff, *History of the American Economy*, 10th ed. (Cincinnati, OH: Thomson/Southwestern, 2005), 144–45.

10. Jonathan Hughes and Louis P. Cain, *American Economic History*, 4th ed. (New York: HarperCollins, 1994), 87.

11. For a study of farming in America, see David B. Danbom, *Born in the Country: A History of Rural America* (Baltimore: Johns Hopkins University Press, 1995), esp. 72–73 in this context.

12. Hernando de Soto, *The Mystery of Capital: Why Capitalism Triumphs in the West and Fails Everywhere Else* (New York: Basic Books, 2000).

13. Several sources deal with Jefferson's concept of landownership and development. See, for example, Donald Jackson, *Thomas Jefferson and the Stoney Mountains: Exploring the West from Monticello* (Urbana: University of Illinois Press, 1981);

Merrill D. Peterson, *Thomas Jefferson and the New Nation* (New York: Oxford University Press, 1970). Also see Carl Edward Skeen, "Jefferson and the West, 1798–1808," in *Papers on the War of 1812 in the Northwest*, no. 7 (Columbus: Ohio State Museum, 1960).

14. Jeremy Atack and Fred Bateman, *To Their Own Soil: Agriculture in the Antebellum North* (Ames: Iowa State University Press, 1987), 124.

15. Robert C. Puth, *American Economic History* (Chicago: Dryden Press, 1982), 71; Edwin Perkins, *The Economy of Colonial America*, 2d ed. (New York: Columbia University Press, 1988). Also see Winifred Rothenberg, "The Market and Massachusetts Farmers, 1750–1855," *Journal of Economic History* 41 (June 1981), 283–314.

16. Michael F. Konig, "John Jacob Astor," in Larry Schweikart, ed., *Encyclopedia of American Business History and Biography: Banking and Finance to 1913* (New York: Facts on File, 1990), 13.

17. See Lewis Davids, "'Fur' Money and Banking in the West," in *Banking in the West*, ed. Larry Schweikart (Manhattan, KS: Sunflower University Press, 1984), reprinted from the April 1984 issue of *Journal of the West*.

18. John D. Haegar, "Business Strategy and Practice in the Early Republic: John Jacob Astor and the American Fur Trade," *Western Historical Quarterly* 19 (May 1988), 183–202; Hiram M. Chittenden, *The American Fur Trade of the Far West* (3 vols., New York: Francis P. Harper, 1902; 2 vols., Stanford, CA: Academic Reprints, 1954).

19. Konig, "Astor," 17.

20. Keith L. Bryant, Jr., and Henry C. Dethloff, *A History of American Business*, 2d ed. (Englewood Cliffs, NJ: Prentice-Hall, 1990), 204; Vivana A. Rotman Zelizer, *Morals and Markets: The Development of Life Insurance in the United States* (New York: Columbia University Press, 1979); and George A. Bishop, *Capital Formation through Life Insurance: A Study in the Growth of Life Insurance Services and Investment Activities* (Homewood, IL: Richard D. Irwin, 1976).

21. U.S. Bureau of the Census, *Historical Statistics of the United States: Colonial Times to 1970*, 2 vols. (Washington, DC: Government Printing Office, 1975), 1:22, 23; Puth, *American Economic History*, 133.

22. A provocative interpretation of these events appears in James Burke, *Connections* (Boston: Little, Brown, 1978), 145–51.

23. Robert S. Woodbury, "The Legend of Eli Whitney and Interchangeable Parts," *Technology and Culture* 2 (Summer 1960), 235–53; Robert A. Lively, "The American System: A Review Article," *Business History Review* 29 (March 1955), 81–96.

24. Puth, *American Economic History*, 190; Alfred Conrad and John Meyer, "The Economics of Slavery in the Antebellum South," *Journal of Political Economy* (April 1958), 95–130; D. Schaefer, "The Effect of the 1859 Crop Year upon Relative Productivity in the Antebellum South," *Journal of Economic History* (December 1983), 851–65.

25. Constance McLaughlin Green, *Eli Whitney and the Birth of American Technology* (Boston: Little, Brown, 1956).

26. Merrit Roe Smith, *Harpers Ferry Armory and the New Technology* (Ithaca, NY: Cornell University Press, 1977); and David Hounshell, *From the American System to Mass Production* (Baltimore: Johns Hopkins University Press, 1984).

27. Donald Hoke, "Product Design and Cost Considerations: Clock, Watch, and Typewriter Manufacturing in the 19th Century," in William J. Hausman, ed., *Business and Economic History*, 2d series, 18 (1989), 119–28, quotation on 120; for a deeper analysis, see Hoke's *Ingenious Yankees: The Rise of the American System of Manufactures in the Private Sector* (New York: Columbia University Press, 1989).

28. William B. Edwards, *The Story of Colt's Revolver: The Biography of Col. Samuel Colt* (Harrisonburg, PA: Stackpole, 1953); and Robert Sobel and David B. Sicilia, *Entrepreneurs: An American Adventure* (Boston: Houghton-Mifflin, 1986), 152.

29. Henry Barnard, *Armsmear: The Home, the Arm, and the Armory of Samuel Colt: A Memorial* (New York: C. A. Alvord, 1866), 276, quoted in William Hosley, *Colt: The Making of an American Legend* (Amherst: University of Massachusetts Press, 1996), 22.

30. C. Joseph Pusateri, *A History of American Business*, 2d ed. (Arlington Heights, IL: Harlan-Davidson, 1988), 157.

31. Hosley, *Colt*, 75.

32. See Allen S. Marber, "America's First Marketers: The New York Iron Merchants," in William Childs, ed., *Essays in Economic and Business History* 13 (1995), 83–96.

33. Jeremy Atack and Peter Passell, *A New Economic View of American History*, 2d ed. (New York: W. W. Norton, 1994), 189.

34. Material for this section comes from John W. Malsberger, "David Thomas," in *The Encyclopedia of American Business History and Biography: Iron and Steel in the Nineteenth Century*, ed. Paul Pascoff (New York: Facts on File, 1989), 333–36.

35. Samuel Thomas, "Reminiscences of the Early Anthracite-Iron Industry," *Transactions of the American Institute of Mining Engineers* 29 (1899), 901–28.

36. Ronald Zboray, "Literary Enterprise and the Mass Market: Publishers and Business Innovation in Antebellum America," in Edwin J. Perkins, ed., *Essays in Economic and Business History* 10 (1992), 168–72, quotation on 169. Also see Zboray's *A Fictive People: Antebellum Economic Development and the American Reading Public* (New York: Oxford University Press, 1992) and "Antebellum Reading and the Ironies of Technological Innovation," *American Quarterly* 40 (1988), 65–82; as well as John Tebbel, *A History of Book Publishing in the United States*. Vol. 1, *The Creation of an Industry* (New York: R. R. Bowker, 1972).

37. Zboray, "Literary Enterprise and the Mass Market," 170.

38. See, for example, Rosalind Remer, *Printers and Men of Capital: Philadelphia Book Publishers in the New Republic* (Philadelphia: University of Pennsylvania Press, 1996).

39. Moses Brown to T. Rogerson, November 11, 1810, quoted in Barbara M. Tucker, "Forms of Ownership and Management," in *American Business History: Case Studies*, eds. Henry Dethloff and C. Joseph Pusateri (Arlington Heights, IL: Harlan-Davidson, 1987), 60. Also see Tucker's book, *Samuel Slater and the Origins of the American Textile Industry, 1790–1860* (Ithaca, NY: Cornell University Press, 1984).

40. W. Elliot Brownlee, *Dynamics of Ascent: A History of the American Economy*, 2d ed. (New York: Alfred A. Knopf, 1979), 160.

41. Robert Sobel and David B. Sicilia, *The Entrepreneurs: An American Adventure* (Boston: Houghton-Mifflin, 1986), 65–71.

42. An overview of the structure of banking in this period appears in Schweikart, ed., *Encyclopedia of American Business History: Banking and Finance to 1913*, as well as Benjamin J. Klebaner, *Commercial Banking in the United States: A History* (Hinsdale, IL: Dryden Press, 1974); for a concise treatment of the historical interpretations and a survey of the literature, see Larry Schweikart, "U.S. Commercial Banking: A Historiographical Survey," *Business History Review* 65 (Autumn 1991), 606–61.

43. Among the sources dealing with these developments are Vincent P. Carosso, *Investment Banking in America: A History* (Cambridge, MA: Harvard University Press, 1975), and Fritz Redlich, *The Molding of American Banking, Men and Ideas*, 2 vols. (New York: Johnson Reprint Co., 1968 [1947]).

44. Edwin J. Perkins, *Financing Anglo-American Trade: The House of Brown, 1800–1880* (Cambridge, MA: Harvard University Press, 1975).

45. See the "Assigned estate William Johnston, 1851," in the William Johnston Papers, South Carolinian Library, Columbia.

46. J. Van Fenstermaker and John E. Filer, "Impact of the First and Second Bank of the United States and the Suffolk System on New England Money: 1791–1837," *Journal of Money, Credit, and Banking* 18 (February 1986), 28–40. Also see Fenstermaker's excellent monograph, *The Development of American Commercial Banking* (Kent, OH: Kent State University Press, 1965).

47. Donald R. Adams, Jr., *Finance and Enterprise in Early America: A Study of Stephen Girard's Bank, 1812–1831* (Philadelphia: University of Pennsylvania Press, 1978); Harry Emerson Wildes, *Lonely Midas: The Story of Stephen Girard* (New York: Farrar & Rinehart, 1943); and Gregory Hunter's essay, "Stephen Girard," in Schweikart, ed., *Encyclopedia of American Business History and Biography: Banking and Finance to 1913*, 221–24.

48. Steven Wheeler, "New York Stock Exchange," in Schweikart, ed., *Encyclopedia of American Business History and Biography: Banking and Finance to 1913*, 384–85; Robert Sobel, *The Big Board: A History of the New York Stock Market* (New York: Macmillan, 1970); Deborah S. Gardner, *Marketplace: A Brief History of the New York Stock Exchange* (New York: New York Stock Exchange, 1982).

CHAPTER 4

1. George Rogers Taylor, *The Transportation Revolution, 1815–1860* (New York: Holt Rinehart, 1962). Also see Guy S. Callender, "The Early Transportation and Banking Enterprises of the States in Relation to the Growth of the Corporation," *Quarterly Journal of Economics* 17 (1902), 111–62; Albert Fishlow, "Internal Transportation," in *American Economic Growth*, eds. Lance Davis, et al. (New York: Harper & Row, 1972), 468–547.

2. Sidney Ratner, James H. Soltow, and Richard Sylla, *The Evolution of the American Economy: Growth, Welfare, and Decision Making*, 2d ed. (New York: Macmillan, 1993), 110.

3. Albert Gallatin, "Reports on Roads and Canals," 10th Congress, 1st session, 1808, document no. 250, reprinted in *New American State Papers—Transportation* 1 (Wilmington, DE: Scholarly Resources, 1972).

4. *Historical Statistics of the United States—Colonial Times to 1970* (White Plains, NY: Kraus International Publications [U.S. Department of Commerce, Bureau of the Census], 1989), 1114–15.

5. Paul Johnson, *The Birth of the Modern: World Society, 1815–1840* (New York: HarperPerennial, 1991), 174.

6. Johnson, *Birth of the Modern*, 171.

7. Keith L. Bryant, Jr., and Henry C. Dethloff, *A History of American Business*, 2d ed. (Englewood Cliffs, NJ: Prentice-Hall, 1990), 94; John Stover, *Transportation in American History* (Washington, DC: American Historical Association, 1970); and Nathan Miller, *The Enterprise of a Free People: Aspects of Economic Development in New York State During the Canal Period, 1792–1838* (Ithaca, NY: Cornell University Press, 1962).

8. Joseph A. Durrenberger, *Turnpikes: A Study of the Toll Road Movement in the Middle Atlantic States and Maryland* (Valdosta, GA: Southern Stationery and Printing, 1931); William Hollifield, *Difficulties Made Easy: History of the Turnpikes of Baltimore City and County* (Cockeysville, MD: Baltimore County Historical Society, 1978); and Roger N. Parks, "The Roads of New England, 1790–1840" (Ph.D. dissertation, Michigan State University, 1966).

9. The *Palladium* quoted in Thomas S. Wermuth, "Rural Elites in the Commercial Development of New York: 1780–1840," in William J. Hausman, ed., *Business and Economic History* 23 (Fall 1994), 71–80, quotation on 76.

10. Wermuth, "Rural Elites," passim. Also see Thomas S. Wermuth, "To Market, to Market: Yeoman Farmers, Merchant Capitalists and the Transition to Capitalism in the Hudson River Valley, 1760–1840" (Ph.D. dissertation, Binghamton University, 1991).

11. Johnson, *Birth of the Modern;* Daniel B. Klein, "The Voluntary Provision of Public Goods? The Turnpike Companies of Early America," *Economic Inquiry* 28 (October 1990), 788–812, quotation on 790; David Beito, "From Privies to Boulevards: The Private Supply of Infrastructure in the United States during the Nineteenth Century," in *Development by Consent: The Voluntary Supply of Public Goods and Services*, eds. Jerry Jenkins and David E. Sisk (San Francisco: Institute for Contemporary Studies, 1993), 23–49; and David Beito. "'A Spirit of Rivalry in Road Building': Toll Roads in the Great Basin, 1852–1890" (paper presented at the Western History Association, 1994).

12. Christopher T. Baer, Daniel B. Klein, and John Majewski, "From Trunk to Branch: Toll Roads in New York, 1800–1860," in Edwin Perkins, ed., *Essays in Economic and Business History* 11 (1992), 191–209, quotation on 196.

13. Mansell G. Blackford and Austin Kerr, *Business Enterprise in American History*, 2d ed. (Boston: Houghton-Mifflin, 1990), 82.

14. Forest G. Hill, *Roads, Rails, and Waterways: The Army Engineers and Early Transportation* (Norman: University of Oklahoma Press, 1957).

15. James Willard Hurst, *Law and the Conditions of Freedom in the Nineteenth Century United States* (Madison: University of Wisconsin Press, 1964).

16. Jeremy Atack and Peter W. Passell, *A New Economic View of American History* (New York: W. W. Norton, 1994), 150; Carter Goodrich, *Government Promotion of American Canals and Railroads, 1800–1890* (New York: Columbia University Press, 1960), *Canals and American Economic Development* (New York:

Columbia University Press, 1961), and *The Government and the Economy, 1783–1861* (Indianapolis, IN: Bobbs-Merrill, 1967); Ronald E. Shaw, *Erie Water West: A History of the Erie Canal, 1792–1854* (Lexington: University of Kentucky Press, 1966); Ronald W. Filante, "A Note on the Economic Viability of the Erie Canal, 1825–1860," *Business History Review* 48 (Spring 1974), 95–102; and Peter L. Bernstein, *Wedding of the Waters: The Erie Canal and the Making of a Great Nation* (New York: W. W. Norton, 2005).

17. See B. R. Burg, "DeWitt Clinton," in *Encyclopedia of American Business History and Biography: Banking and Finance to 1913*, ed. Larry Schweikart (New York: Facts on File, 1990), 123–30.

18. Louis Hunter, *Steamboats on Western Rivers* (Cambridge, MA: Harvard University Press, 1949).

19. See Douglas B. Ball, *Financial Failure and Confederate Defeat* (Urbana: University of Illinois Press, 1991).

20. Atack and Passell, *New Economic View of American History*, 150–56.

21. Ibid., 155; Roger Ransom, "Social Returns from Public Transport Investment: A Case Study of the Ohio Canal," *Journal of Political Economy* 78 (September–October 1970), 1041–64, and his "Interregional Canals and Economic Specialization in the Antebellum United States," *Explorations in Entrepreneurial History* 5 (Fall 1967), 12–35.

22. Harold Evans, *They Made America: From the Steam Engine to the Search Engine: Two Centuries of Innovators* (Boston: Little, Brown, 2004).

23. Burton W. Folsom, *Myth of the Robber Barons* (Herndon, VA: Young America's Foundation, 1991), 2.

24. C. Joseph Pusateri, *A History of American Business*, 2d ed. (Arlington Heights, IL: Harlan-Davidson, 1988), 121–23; Erik Haites, James Mak, and Gary M. Walton, "Steamboats and the Great Productivity Surge in River Transportation," *Journal of Economic History* 32 (1972), 619–40; and their book *Western River Transportation: The Era of Early Internal Development, 1810–1860* (Baltimore: Johns Hopkins University Press, 1975); Jeremy Atack, et al., "The Profitability of Steamboating on Western Rivers: 1850," *Business History Review* 49 (Autumn 1975), 350–54; and Erik Haites and James Mak, "Ohio and Mississippi River Transportation, 1810–1860," *Explorations in Economic History* 8 (1970), 153–80.

25. Bryant and Dethloff, *American Business History*, 104.

26. Folsom, *Myth of the Robber Barons*, 2.

27. John G. B. Hutcins, *The American Maritime Industries and Public Policy, 1789–1914* (Cambridge, MA: Harvard University Press, 1941).

28. Folsom, *Myth of the Robber Barons*, 7.

29. Quoted in Wheaton J. Lane, *Commodore Vanderbilt: An Epic of the Steam Age* (New York: Alfred A. Knopf, 1942), 148; William E. Bennet, *The Collins Story* (London: R. Hale, 1957).

30. Folsom, *Myth of the Robber Barons*, 10. On the detrimental effects of the shipping subsidies, see Royal Meeker, *History of the Shipping Subsidies* (New York: Macmillan, 1905), 5–11; and Walter T. Dunmore, *Ship Subsidies: An Economic Study of the Policy of Subsidizing Merchant Marines* (Boston: Houghton-Mifflin, 1907), 92–103.

31. Lane, *Commodore Vanderbilt*, 124, 136.

32. John F. Stover, *American Railroads* (Chicago: University of Chicago Press, 1961), and his *Iron Road to the West* (New York: Columbia University Press, 1978).

33. James Hipp, "Matthias W. Baldwin," in *The Encyclopedia of American Business History and Biography: Railroads in the Nineteenth Century*, ed. Robert L. Frey (New York: Facts on File, 1988), 17–20.

34. John K. Brown, *The Baldwin Locomotive Works, 1831–1915* (Baltimore: Johns Hopkins University Press, 1995), 17.

35. John Steele Gordon, *The Scarlet Woman of Wall Street* (New York: Weidenfeld & Nicholson, 1988), 101.

36. John Majewski, "Who Financed the Transportation Revolution? Regional Divergence and Internal Improvements in Antebellum Pennsylvania and Virginia," *Journal of Economic History* 56 (December 1996), 763–88.

37. Nathan Rosenberg and L. E. Birdsell, Jr., *How the West Grew Rich: The Economic Transformation of the Industrial World* (New York: Basic Books, 1986 [1985]), 190.

38. *Bank of Augusta v. Joseph B. Earle*, 13 Peters 580 (1839); Eric Monkkonen, "Bank of Augusta v. Earle: Corporate Growth v. States' Rights," *Alabama Historical Quarterly* (Summer 1972), 113–30.

39. Edwin J. Perkins, "Nicholas Biddle," in Schweikart, ed., *Encyclopedia of American Business History and Biography: Banking and Finance to 1913*, 51–63.

40. Robert V. Remini, *Andrew Jackson and the Bank War* (New York: Norton, 1967), and, to a lesser extent, Thomas Govan, *Nicholas Biddle: Nationalist and Public Banker, 1786–1844* (Chicago: University of Chicago Press, 1959).

41. Traditional interpretations appear in Remini, *Andrew Jackson and the Bank War*, as well as Bray Hammond, *Banks and Politics in America from the Revolution to the Civil War* (Princeton, NJ: Princeton University Press, 1957), and Arthur Schlesinger, Jr., *The Age of Jackson* (Boston: Little, Brown, 1945).

42. Thomas Payne Govan, "The Fundamental Issues of the Bank War," *Pennsylvania Magazine of History and Biography* 82 (July 1954), 305–15, and *Nicholas Biddle: Nationalist and Public Banker, 1786–1844* (Chicago: University of Chicago Press, 1959); Walter Buckingham Smith, *Economic Aspects of the Second Bank of the United States* (Cambridge, MA: Harvard University Press, 1953).

43. Richard Timberlake, Jr., "The Specie Standard and Central Banking in the United States Before 1860," *Journal of Economic History* 21 (September 1961), 318–41, and his book, *The Origins of Central Banking in the United States* (Cambridge, MA: Harvard University Press, 1978); Peter Temin, *The Jacksonian Economy* (New York: W. W. Norton, 1969).

44. David Martin, "Bimetallism in the United States Before 1850," *Journal of Political Economy* 76 (May/June 1968), 428–42, and "Metallism, Small Notes, and Jackson's War with the B.U.S.," *Explorations in Economic History* 11 (Spring 1974), 227–47; Larry Schweikart, "Jacksonian Ideology, Currency Control, and 'Central' Banking: A Reappraisal," *The Historian* 51 (November 1988), 78–102.

45. Hugh Rockhoff, *The Free Banking Era: A Reexamination* (New York: Arno Press, 1975), and Arthur J. Ronick and Warren Weber, "New Evidence on the Free

Banking Era," *American Economic Review* 73 (December 1983), 1080–91, and their "Banking Instability and Regulation in the U.S. Free Banking Era," *Federal Reserve Bank of Minneapolis Quarterly Review* (Fall 1982), 10–19.

46. Peter Krass, *Carnegie* (Hoboken, NJ: John Wiley, 2002), and David Nasaw, *Andrew Carnegie* (New York: Penguin Press, 2006).

47. Charles W. Calomiris and Gary Gorton, "The Origins of Banking Panics: Models, Facts, and Bank Regulation," in *Financial Markets and Financial Crises*, ed. R. Glenn Hubbard (Chicago: University of Chicago Press, 1991).

48. Dan Rottenberg, *The Man Who Made Wall Street: Anthony Drexel and the Rise of Modern Finance* (Philadelphia: University of Pennsylvania Press, 2001).

49. John M. Dobson, *A History of American Enterprise* (Englewood Cliffs, NJ: Prentice-Hall, 1988), 120. A provocative, but flawed, interpretation of the "spin-offs" of railroads appears in Walt W. Rostow, *The Stages of Economic Growth* (Cambridge: Cambridge University Press, 1990).

50. W. Elliot Brownlee, *Dynamics of Ascent: A History of the American Economy*, 2d ed. (New York: Alfred A. Knopf, 1979), 203.

51. Peter Temin, *Iron and Steel in Nineteenth-Century America: An Economic Inquiry* (Cambridge, MA: MIT Press, 1964).

52. Pusateri, *History of American Business*, 134.

53. J. Wilson Newman, *"Dun & Bradstreet" Established in 1841 "For the Promotion and Protection of Trade"* (New York: Newcomen Society, 1956).

54. Gregory J. Millman, *The Vandals' Crown* (New York: Free Press, 1995), 104.

55. See "Growth of U.S. Postal Services, 1790–1860," in Ratner, Soltow, and Sylla, *Evolution of the American Economy*, 128, table 5-4; Alan R. Pred, *Urban Growth and the Circulation of Information* (Cambridge, MA: Harvard University Press, 1973), 80.

56. Richard R. John, *Spreading the News: The American Postal System from Franklin to Morse* (Cambridge, MA: Harvard University Press, 1995), and his "Private Mail Delivery in the United States During the Nineteenth Century—A Sketch," in William J. Hausman, ed., *Business and Economic History*, 2d series, 15 (1986), 131–43.

57. Culver H. Smith, *The Press, Politics, and Patronage: The American Government's Use of Newspapers, 1789–1875* (Athens: University of Georgia Press, 1977), 131.

58. Erik McKinley Eriksson, "President Jackson's Propaganda Agencies," *Pacific Historical Review* 7 (January 1937), 47–57.

59. John, *Spreading the News*, ch. 2, 39, for the 700 percent estimate.

60. Quoted in Robert J. Chandler, "Henry Wells," in Schweikart, ed., *Encyclopedia of American Business History and Biography: Banking and Finance to 1913*, 491–96, quotation on 493.

61. Chandler, "Henry Wells."

62. Robert Sobel and David B. Sicilia, *Entrepreneurs: An American Adventure* (Boston: Houghton-Mifflin, 1986), 234.

63. Jonathan Lurie, *The Chicago Board of Trade, 1859–1905* (Urbana: University of Illinois Press, 1979).

64. Raymond W. and Mary Lund Settle, *Saddles and Spurs: The Pony Express Saga* (Lincoln: University of Nebraska Press, 1955); Fred Reinfeld, *Pony Express* (Lincoln: University of Nebraska Press, 1966).

65. Raymond and Mary Settle, *Saddles and Spurs*, 94–112.

66. Susan E. Hirsch, "From Artisan to Manufacturer: Industrialization and the Small Producer in Newark, 1830–60," in *Small Business in American Life*, ed. Stuart Bruchey (New York: Columbia University Press, 1980), 80–99.

67. Stuart Blumin, "Black Coats to White Collars: Economic Change, Nonmanual Work, and the Social Structure of Industrializing America," in Bruchey, ed., *Small Business in American Life*, 100–121.

68. Susan Ingalls Lewis, "Female Entrepreneurs in Albany, 1840–1885," in William J. Hausman, ed., *Business and Economic History*, 2d series, 21 (1992), 65–73.

69. Clyde and Sally Griffen, "Business and Occupational Mobility in Mid-Nineteenth-Century Poughkeepsie," in Bruchey, ed., *Small Business in American Life*, 122–41.

70. Ralph W. Haskins, "Planter and Cotton Factor in the Old South: Some Areas of Friction," in *The Changing Economic Order*, eds. Alfred D. Chandler, Jr., Stuart Bruchey, and Louis Galambos (New York: Harcourt, Brace & World, 1968); Robert Davis, *The Southern Planter, the Factor, and the Banker* (New Orleans: n.p., 1871); Larry Schweikart, "Entrepreneurial Aspects of Antebellum Banking," in *American Business History: Case Studies*, eds. Joseph Pusateri and Henry Dethloff (New York: Harlan-Davidson, 1987), 122–38.

71. Lewis E. Atherton, "The Pioneer Merchant in Mid-America," *The University of Missouri Studies* 14 (April 1939); John G. Clark, *The Grain Trade in the Old Northwest* (Urbana: University of Illinois Press, 1966); David Dary, *Entrepreneurs in the Old West* (New York: Alfred A. Knopf, 1986); and John Haeger, "Economic Development of the American West," in *American Frontier and Western Issues: A Historiographical Review*, ed. Roger Nichols (New York: Greenwood Press, 1986).

72. Lewis Davids, "'Fur' Money and Banking in the West," *Journal of the West* (April 1984), 7–10; Lynne Pierson Doti and Larry Schweikart, *California Bankers, 1848–1993* (New York: Guinn Press, 1994), 11.

73. Material for Gail Borden comes from Joseph J. Fucini and Suzy Fucini, *Entrepreneurs: The Men and Women Behind Famous Brand Names and How They Made It* (Boston: G. K. Hall, 1985), 13–16.

CHAPTER 5

1. James K. Medbury, *Men and Mysteries of Wall Street* (New York: Fields, Osgood, 1870), 264–65, quoted in John M. Dobson, *A History of American Enterprise* (Englewood Cliffs, NJ: Prentice-Hall, 1988), 143; and Kenneth D. Acerman, *The Gold Ring: Jim Fisk, Jay Gould, and Black Friday, 1869* (New York: HarperBusiness, 1988), 2.

2. See Anthony Trollope's 1875 novel *The Way We Live Now* (New York: Penguin, 1995) for a realistic story of this type of fraud.

3. Robert Puth, *American Economic History* (Chicago: Dryden, 1982), 172.

4. Dobson, *History of American Enterprise*, 111.

5. For one analysis of the evolution of track gauge, see Douglas J. Puffert, "The Standardization of Track Gauge on North American Railways, 1830–1890," *Journal of Economic History* 60 (December 2000), 933–60.

6. Robert Sobel and David B. Sicilia, *Entrepreneurs: An American Adventure* (Boston: Houghton-Mifflin, 1986), 105–12.

7. See the *American Railroad Journal* 29 (May 3, 1856), 280, as well as Alfred D. Chandler, Jr., *Henry Varnum Poor: Business Editor, Analyst, and Reformer* (Cambridge, MA: Harvard University Press, 1956).

8. "Reports of the President and Superintendent of the New York and Erie Railroad to the Stockholders, for the Year Ending September 30, 1855," in *The Railroads: Pioneers in Modern Management*, ed. Alfred D. Chandler (New York: Arno Press, 1979), 34–36.

9. Dobson, *History of American Enterprise*, 116.

10. Alfred D. Chandler, Jr., *The Visible Hand: The Managerial Revolution in American Business* (Cambridge, MA: Belknap Press, 1977), 110–18.

11. Chandler, *Visible Hand*, 116–21. Fink's formulas and tables are reproduced on 119–20.

12. Chandler, *Visible Hand*, 134.

13. Quoted in William A. Croffut, *The Vanderbilts and the Story of Their Fortune* (Chicago: Bedford, Clarke, 1886), 75.

14. John Steele Gordon, *Scarlett Woman of Wall Street* (New York: Weidenfeld & Nicholson, 1988), 88.

15. Clifford I. Browder, *The Money Game in Old New York: Daniel Drew and His Times* (Lexington: University Press of Kentucky, 1986).

16. Gordon, *Scarlett Woman of Wall Street*, 90.

17. Ibid., 91.

18. *New York Herald*, October 9, 1867.

19. Maury Klein, *The Life and Legend of Jay Gould* (Baltimore and London: Johns Hopkins University Press, 1986), 39–40.

20. William Worthington Fowler, *Ten Years in Wall Street* (Ann Arbor: Michigan Historical Reprint, 2000), 506.

21. Charles Francis Adams, Jr., and Henry Adams, *Chapters of Erie* (Boston: Osgood, 1871).

22. Gordon, *Scarlet Woman of Wall Street*, 213.

23. Ibid., 125.

24. Ibid., 126.

25. See John Majewski's study of Pennsylvania and Virginia railroading in "Urban Investment versus Local Enterprise: Railroad Financing in Pennsylvania and Virginia, 1830–1860," William J. Hausman, ed., *Business and Economic History* 23 (Fall 1994), 92–101.

26. See Jac C. Heckelman and John Joseph Wallis, "Railroads and Property Taxes," *Explorations in Economic History* 34 (1997), 77–99.

27. Charles Calomiris and Larry Schweikart, "The Panic of 1857: Origins, Transmission, and Containment," *Journal of Economic History* 51 (December 1991), 807–34. For an opposing view, see James L. Huston, *The Panic of 1857 and the Coming of the Civil War* (Baton Rouge: Louisiana State University Press, 1987).

28. These developments are described in Larry Schweikart, *Banking in the American South from the Age of Jackson to Reconstruction* (Baton Rouge: Louisiana State University Press, 1987).

29. Stewart Holbrook, *James J. Hill: A Great Life in Brief* (New York: Alfred A. Knopf, 1955), 93; Albro Martin, *James J. Hill and the Opening of the Northwest* (New York: Oxford University Press, 1976), 366; and Burton W. Folsom, *Myth of the Robber Barons* (Herndon, VA: Young America's Foundation, 1991), 26–27.

30. Claire Strom, *Profiting from the Plains: The Great Northern Railway and Corporate Development of the American West* (Seattle and London: University of Washington Press, 2003).

31. Mansell G. Blackford and Austin Kerr, *Business Enterprise in American History*, 2d ed. (Boston: Houghton-Mifflin, 1990), 220.

32. Dobson, *History of American Enterprise*, 167.

33. Ibid., 162.

34. Oscar Lewis, *The Big Four: The Story of Huntington, Stanford, Hopkins, and Crocker, and the Building of the Central Pacific* (New York: Alfred A. Knopf, 1938).

35. Don L. Hofsommer, *The Southern Pacific, 1901–1985* (College Station: Texas A&M University Press, 1986); Neil C. Wilson and Frank J. Taylor, *Southern Pacific: The Roaring Story of a Fighting Railroad* (New York: McGraw-Hill, 1952); and James Marshall, *Santa Fe: The Railroad That Built an Empire* (New York: Random House, 1945).

36. On the effects of silver politics on the economy, see Milton Friedman, "The Crime of 1873," *Journal of Political Economy* 98 (December 1990), 1159–94.

37. For the differences among railroaders regarding business unanimity on the Interstate Commerce Act, for example, see Edward A. Purcell, Jr., "Ideas and Interests: Businessmen and the Interstate Commerce Act," *Journal of American History* 54 (December 1967), 561–78.

38. Albro Martin, "The Troubled Subject of Railroad Regulation in the Gilded Age—A Reappraisal," *Journal of American History* 61 (September 1974), 339–71.

39. Martin, *James J. Hill*, 296–97, 409–10, 537.

40. Among Chandler's numerous books on the railroads and the new forms of business, see especially *Strategy and Structure: Chapters in the History of American Industrial Enterprise* (Cambridge, MA: MIT Press, 1962).

41. Chandler, *Visible Hand*, 7.

42. See the introductory essay by Henry C. Dethloff and Keith L. Bryant, "Entrepreneurship," in *American Business History: Case Studies*, eds. Henry Dethloff and C. Joseph Pusateri (Arlington Heights, IL: Harlan-Davidson, 1987), 4–21, especially "The Manager as Entrepreneur."

43. "Lydia E. Pinkham and Her Vegetable Compound," in Sobel and Sicilia, *Entrepreneurs*, 193–96.

44. "Henry Steinway," in Joseph J. Fucini and Suzy Fucini, *Entrepreneurs: The Men and Women Behind Famous Brand Names and How They Made It* (Boston: G. K. Hall, 1985), 47–50; Rich K. Lieberman, *Steinway & Sons* (New Haven, CT: Yale University Press, 1995).

45. Clinton Woods, *Ideas That Became Big Business* (Baltimore: Founders, 1959), 33–34.

46. The following discussion is taken from "Elisha G. Otis," in Woods, *Ideas that Became Big Business*, 60–63.

47. Fucini and Fucini, *Entrepreneurs*, 58; Wayne Broehl, Jr., *John Deere's Company: A History of Deere and Company and Its Times* (New York: Doubleday, 1984).

48. Robert Sobel, *The Entrepreneurs: Explorations within the American Business Tradition* (New York: Weybright and Talley, 1974), 60.

49. Keith L. Bryant and Henry C. Dethloff, *A History of American Business*, 2d ed. (Englewood Cliffs, NJ: Prentice-Hall, 1990), 83.

50. See the discussion in Paul A. David, "The Mechanization of Reaping in the Antebellum Midwest," in *The Reinterpretation of American Economic History*, ed. Robert W. Fogel and Stanley L. Engerman (New York: Harper & Row, 1971), 214–27; Robert E. Ankli, "The Coming of the Reaper," in Paul A. Uselding, ed., *Business and Economic History* (1976), 1–24; and the chapter "Northern Agricultural Development Before the Civil War," in Jeremy Atack and Peter W. Passell, *A New Economic View of American History*, 2d ed. (New York: W. W. Norton, 1994), 274–98.

51. Alan L. Olmstead and Paul W. Rhode, "Beyond the Threshold: An Analysis of the Characteristics and Behavior of Early Reaper Adopters," *Journal of Economic History* 55 (March 1995), 27–57, and Olmstead's original piece, "The Mechanization of Reaping and Mowing in American Agriculture, 1833–1870," *Journal of Economic History* 35 (June 1975), 327–52.

52. C. Joseph Pusateri, *A History of American Business*, 2d ed. (Arlington Heights, IL: Harlan-Davidson, 1988), 83.

53. Cyrus McCormick, *The Century of the Reaper* (Boston: Houghton-Mifflin, 1931), 89–127. Also see Clarence H. Danof, *Change in Agriculture: The Northern United States, 1820–1870* (Cambridge, MA: Harvard University Press, 1969).

54. See William N. Parker and Judith L. V. Klein, "Productivity Growth in Grain Production in the United States, 1840–60 and 1900–10," in *National Bureau of Economic Research, Studies in Income and Wealth, vol. 30, Output, Employment, and Productivity in the United States after 1800* (New York: Columbia University Press, 1966), 533.

55. Jeremy Atack and Fred Bateman, *To Their Own Soil: Agriculture in the Antebellum North* (Ames: Iowa State University Press, 1987), passim.

56. David M. Potter, *The Impending Crisis, 1848–1861*, ed. Don E. Fehrenbacher (New York: Harper, 1976); Richard D. Brown, "The Missouri Crisis, Slavery, and the Politics of Jacksonianism," *South Atlantic Quarterly* 65 (Winter 1966), 55–72.

57. The most famous advocate of the "natural limits" theory, aside from Lincoln, was historian James G. Ramsdell. See Ramsdell's "The Natural Limits of Slavery Expansion," *Mississippi Valley Historical Review* 16 (1929), 151–71.

58. James L. Huston, *Calculating the Value of the Union: Slavery, Property Rights, and the Economic Origins of the Civil War* (Chapel Hill: University of North Carolina Press, 2002).

59. James L. Huston, *The Panic of 1857 and the Coming of the Civil War* (Baton Rouge: Louisiana State University Press, 1987), discusses the antebellum literature on these issues extensively. See, in particular, the efforts of the New York Children's Aid Society (*New York Daily Tribune*, October 26 and November 11, 1857) and John Commerford of the Land Reform Association (*New York Daily Tribune*, November 25, 1858, and July 21, 1859); George M. Weston, *Southern Slavery Reduces Northern Wages* (Washington, D.C., 1856); and issues of the Washington, D.C., newspaper *National Era*, esp. November 12, 1857.

60. See the Salem (Ohio) *Anti-Slavery Bugle*, November 7, 1857. Historians have challenged the idea that western lands maintained higher wages, including Fred A. Shannon, "A Post-Mortem on the Labor-Safety-Valve Theory," *Agricultural History* 19 (1945), 31–38, and Henry Littlefield, "Has the Safety Valve Come Back to Life?" *Agricultural History* 38 (1964), 47–49.

61. John Ashworth, *Slavery, Capitalism, and Politics in the Antebellum Republic*, 2 vols., *Volume 1: Commerce and Compromise, 1820–1850* (Cambridge: Cambridge University Press, 1995).

62. George Fitzhugh, *Cannibals All! or Slaves Without Masters*, ed. C. Vann Woodward (Cambridge, MA: Belknap Press, 1960 [1856]). The best exposition on the relationship between slavery and freedom in Fitzhugh's writings is Robert J. Loewenberg, *Freedom's Despots: The Critique of Abolition* (Durham: Carolina Academic Press, 1986).

63. "The Great Questions of National and State Politics," Speech of Hon. Nathaniel P. Banks, quoted in Eric Foner, *Free Soil, Free Labor, Free Men: The Ideology of the Republican Party Before the Civil War* (New York: Oxford, 1995), 62.

64. Foner, *Free Soil*, 63.

65. Richard Hofstadter, "John C. Calhoun: The Marx of the Master Class," in Sidney Fine and Gerald S. Brown, *The American Past: Conflicting Interpretations of Great Issues*, vol. 1, 3d ed. (London: Macmillan, 1970), 460–79.

66. Puth, *American Economic History*, 192.

67. Ulrich Bonnell Phillips, "The Economic Cost of Slave Holding in the Cotton Belt," *Political Science Quarterly* 20 (1905), 257–75; Charles Sydnor, *Slavery in Mississippi* (New York: Appleton-Century, 1933).

68. Kenneth Stampp, *The Peculiar Institution* (New York: Alfred A. Knopf, 1956).

69. Alfred Conrad and John Meyer, "The Economics of Slavery in the Antebellum South," *Journal of Political Economy* 66 (1958), 95–130, esp. table 9 on 107.

70. Fred Bateman, James Foust, and Thomas Weiss, "Profitability in Southern Manufacturing: Estimates for 1860," *Explorations in Economic History* 12 (1975), 211–31.

71. Fred Bateman, James D. Foust, and Thomas J. Weiss, "Large-Scale Manufacturing in the South and West, 1850–1860," *Business History Review* 15 (Spring 1971), 1–17, and papers by Bateman and Weiss alone, "Manufacturing in the Antebellum South," in *Research in Economic History*, vol. 1, ed. Paul Uselding (Greenwich, CT: JAI Press, 1976), and "Comparative Regional Development in Antebellum Manufacturing," *Journal of Economic History* 35 (1975), 182–208.

72. Bateman and Weiss, "Manufacturing in the Antebellum South," and their book, *A Deplorable Scarcity*, passim.

73. Richard K. Vedder, "The Slave Exploitation (Expropriation) Rate," *Explorations in Economic History* 12 (1975), 453–58; Robert W. Fogel and Stanley L. Engerman, *Time on the Cross: Evidence and Methods* (Boston: Little, Brown, 1974).

74. Atack and Passell, *A New Economic View of American History*, "How the Southern Slave System Worked," 326–54.

75. Robert W. Fogel, *Without Consent or Contract: The Rise and Fall of American Slavery* (New York: W. W. Norton, 1989), 77.

76. David L. Carleton and Peter A. Coclanis, "The Uninventive South? A Quantitative Look at Region and American Inventiveness," *Technology and Culture* 36 (April 1995), 302–26. Their study begins at 1870 and extends well into the twentieth century, and thus is not indicative of inventiveness in the antebellum period. Nevertheless, it uses regression analysis to suggest that the South was not less inventive because it was the South, but because it was a "frontier" or "periphery" region of the industrial Eastern seaboard. That, in turn, begs the question of why, as late as the 1870s, the South was a periphery.

77. Gavin Wright, *Old South, New South: Revolutions in the Southern Economy Since the Civil War* (New York: Basic Books, 1986), table 2.4 on 27.

CHAPTER 6

1. Larry Schweikart and Michael Allen, *A Patriot's History of the United States* (New York: Sentinel, 2004), for example, argues that many of these acts were unnecessary at best and tended to retard private investment at worst.

2. Charles A. and Mary Beard, *The Rise of American Civilization* (New York: Macmillan, 1927); Louis M. Hacker, *The Triumph of American Capitalism* (New York: Columbia University Press, 1940).

3. Jeremy Atack and Peter Passell, *A New Economic View of American History*, 2d ed. (New York: W. W. Norton, 1994), 363.

4. Robert Gallman, "Commodity Output, 1839–99," in *National Bureau of Economic Research, Trends in the American Economy in the 19th Century*, vol. 24, Series on Income and Wealth (Princeton, NJ: Princeton University Press, 1960).

5. Claudia Goldin and Frank Lewis, "The Economic Cost of the American Civil War: Estimates and Implications," *Journal of Economic History* 35 (June 1975), 304–9. Also see Peter Temin, "The Post-Bellum Recovery of the South and the Cost of the Civil War," ibid., 26 (December 1976), 898–907.

6. U.S. Department of Commerce, Bureau of the Census, Bicentennial Statistics (Washington, D.C.: Government Printing Office, 1976), 407; U.S. Department of Commerce, Bureau of the Census, *Historical Statistics of the United States: Colonial Times to 1970*, 2 vols. (Washington, D.C.: Government Printing Office, 1975), 1:456–520.

7. See Timothy W. Genion, Harvey S. Rosen, and Kirsten L. Willard, "Messages from 'The Den of Wild Beasts': Greenback Prices as Commentary on the Union's Prospects," *Civil War History* 41 (December 1995), 313–28.

8. This discussion is developed in Lynne Pierson Doti and Larry Schweikart, *Banking in the American West: From the Gold Rush to Deregulation* (Norman: University of Oklahoma Press, 1991).

9. Joseph F. Rishel, "Jay Cooke," in *Encyclopedia of American Business History: Banking and Finance to 1913*, ed. Larry Schweikart (New York: Facts on File, 1990), 135–43, quotation on 137; and the two biographies of Cooke, Henrietta M. Larson, *Jay Cooke: Private Banker* (Cambridge, MA: Harvard University Press, 1936), and Ellis Paxson Oberholtzer, *Jay Cooke: Financier of the Civil War*, 2 vols. (Philadelphia: Jacobs, 1907).

10. Richard Bensel, *Yankee Leviathan: The Origins of Central State Authority in America, 1859–1877* (Cambridge: Cambridge University Press, 1990), 94.

11. Bensel, *Yankee Leviathan*, 95.

12. Edward Hagerman, *The American Civil War and the Origins of Modern Warfare: Ideas, Organization, and Field Command* (Bloomington: Indiana University Press, 1988).

13. Bensel, *Yankee Leviathan*, 95.

14. See, for example, Louise B. Hill, *State Socialism in the Confederate States of America* (Charlottesville, VA: Historical Publishing, 1936), and Raimondo Luraghi, "The Civil War and the Modernization of American Society," *Civil War History* 18 (September 1972), 230–50, as well as Richard E. Beringer, et al., *Why the South Lost the Civil War* (Athens: University of Georgia Press, 1986).

15. Stanley Lebergott, *The Americans: An Economic Record* (New York: W. W. Norton, 1984), 243. Also see his "Why the South Lost: Commercial Purpose in the Confederacy, 1861–1865," *Journal of American History* 70 (June 1983), 58–74, and "Through the Blockade: The Profitability and Extent of Cotton Smuggling, 1861–1865," *Journal of Economic History* 41 (December 1981), 867–88.

16. Benjamin quoted in Mary A. DeCredico, *Patriotism for Profit: Georgia's Urban Entrepreneurs and the Confederate War Effort* (Chapel Hill: University of North Carolina Press, 1990), 27.

17. Robert A. Taylor, *Rebel Storehouse: Florida in the Confederate Economy* (Tuscaloosa: University of Alabama Press, 1995), 55.

18. Emory M. Thomas, *The Confederate Nation, 1861–1865* (New York: Harper Torchbooks, 1979), 207, 212.

19. Scott Nelson, "The Confederacy Serves the Southern: The Construction of the Southern Railway Network, 1861–65," *Civil War History* 41 (September 1995), 227–43, quotation on 243.

20. See Jeffrey Rogers Hummel, *Emancipating Slaves, Enslaving Free Men: A History of the American Civil War* (Chicago: Open Court, 1996).

21. Literature on this subject includes James McPherson, *Battle Cry of Freedom: The Civil War Era* (New York: Oxford University Press, 1988) and his *Ordeal by Fire: The Civil War and Reconstruction*, 2d ed. (New York: Alfred A. Knopf, 1992), and Roger L. Ransom, *Conflict and Compromise: The Political-Economy of Slavery, Emancipation, and the American Civil War* (Cambridge: Cambridge University Press, 1989), plus the numerous interpretations dealt with in the classic by Thomas J. Pressly, *Americans Interpret Their Civil War* (Princeton, NJ: Princeton University Press, 1954).

22. This argument is extended in Larry Schweikart, "Abraham Lincoln and the Growth of Government in the Civil War Era," *Continuity* (Spring 1997), 25–42.

23. Robert C. Kenzer, *Black Economic Success in North Carolina, 1865–1915* (Charlottesville: University Press of Virginia, 1989).

24. Gavin Wright, *Old South, New South: Revolutions in the Southern Economy Since the Civil War* (New York: Basic Books, 1986), 34.

25. Roger L. Ransom and Richard Sutch, *One Kind of Freedom: The Economic Consequences of Emancipation* (London: Cambridge, 1977), 84, and Robert C. Puth, *American Economic History* (Chicago: Dryden Press, 1982), 334.

26. Kenzer, *Black Economic Success*, 18, table 5.

27. Several sources provide excellent discussions of these developments, including Lebergott, *The Americans*, 241–68; Puth, *American Economic History*, 330–39; Gavin Wright, *Old South, New South: Revolutions in the Southern Economy Since the Civil War* (New York: Basic Books, 1986); Joseph Reid, "Sharecropping as an Understandable Market Response: The Postbellum South," *Journal of Economic History* 33 (March 1973), 106–30; and William Brown and Morgan Reynolds, "Debt Peonage Reexamined," *Journal of Economic History* 33 (December 1973), 862–71.

28. Theodore Rosengarten, *All God's Dangers: The Life of Nate Shaw* (New York: Alfred A. Knopf, 1974).

29. "Andrew Jackson Beard," in *A Salute to Black Scientists and Inventors*, vol. 2 (Chicago: Empak Enterprises and Richard L. Green), 6.

30. Juliet E. K. Walker, *Free Frank: A Black Pioneer on the Antebellum Frontier* (Lexington: University Press of Kentucky, 1983).

31. "Letter of Robert W. Cosgrove of the New York Central System Historical Society," *Detroit News*, March 20, 1996.

32. Time-Life, *African Americans: Voices of Triumph* (Alexandria, VA: Time-Life Books, 1993), 1:32.

33. Burton Folsom, "Real McCoy Showed Depth of *Black Enterprise*," *Detroit News*, February 28, 1996.

34. Robert C. Kenzer, "The Black Business Community in Post Civil War Virginia," *Southern Studies*, n.s., 4 (Fall 1993), 229–52.

35. Kenzer, "Black Business Community," 250, n58.

36. Stephen DeCanio, "Cotton Overproduction in the Late Nineteenth Century Agriculture," *Journal of Economic History* 33 (1973), 608–33, and his "Productivity and Income Distribution in the Postbellum South," *Journal of Economic History* 34 (1974), 422–46; Gavin Wright, "Cotton Competition and the Postbellum Recovery of the American South," ibid., 34 (1974), 610–35, and his *Old South, New South*, passim; and Robert A. McGuire and Robert Higgs, "Cotton, Corn, and Risk in the Nineteenth Century: Another View," *Explorations in Economic History* 14 (1979), 167–82.

37. Gavin Wright, "The Strange Career of the New Southern Economic History," *Reviews in American History* 10 (December 1982), 164–80; Donald B. Dodd and Wynelle S. Dod, *Historical Statistics of the South, 1790–1970* (Tuscaloosa: University of Alabama Press, 1973).

38. Henry Hudson, "The Southern Railway and Steamship Association," quoted in C. Vann Woodward, *Origins of the New South* (Baton Rouge: Louisiana State University Press, 1980 [1951]), 122.

39. Quoted in Woodward, *Origins of the New South*, 128.

40. John Samuel Ezell, *The South Since 1865* (New York: Macmillan, 1963), 141.

41. John M. Dobson, *A History of American Enterprise* (Englewood Cliffs, NJ: Prentice-Hall, 1988), 135.

42. Joseph J. Fucini and Suzy Fucini, *Entrepreneurs: The Men and Women Behind Famous Brand Names and How They Made It* (Boston: G. K. Hall, 1985), 102–5.

43. Dorrance quoted in Douglas Collins, *America's Favorite Food: The Story of Campbell Soup Company* (New York: Harry N. Abrams, 1994), 38. See also Alecia Swasy, *Soap Opera: The Inside Story of Procter and Gamble* (New York: Times Books, 1993).

44. Alfred Leif, *"It Floats": The Story of Procter and Gamble* (New York: Rinehart, 1958).

45. Robert Sobel and David B. Sicilia, *Entrepreneurs: An American Adventure* (Boston: Houghton-Mifflin, 1986), 214.

46. Sobel and Sicilia, *Entrepreneurs*, 74; Lewis F. Swift and Arthur Van Vlissington, *The Yankee of the Yards: The Biography of Gustavus Franklin Swift* (New York: A. W. Shaw, 1928).

47. Mary Yeager Kujovich, "The Refrigerator Car and the Growth of the American Dressed Beef Industry," *Business History Review* 44 (1970), 460–82.

48. "Armour & Company, 1867–1938," in N.S.B. Gras and Henrietta Larson, *Casebook in American Business History* (New York: F. S. Crofts, 1939), 623–43.

49. Sobel and Sicilia, *Entrepreneurs*, 77.

50. David A. Hounshell, *From the American System to Mass Production: The Development of Manufacturing Technology in the United States* (Baltimore: Johns Hopkins University Press, 1984), 82.

51. Alfred D. Chandler, *The Visible Hand: The Managerial Revolution in American Business* (Cambridge, MA: Belknap Press, 1977), 303.

52. Andrew B. Jack, "The Channels of Distribution for the Innovation: The Sewing Machine Industry in America," *Explorations in Entrepreneurial History* 9 (February 1957), 113–41, and Robert B. Davies, "Peacefully Working to Conquer the World: The Singer Manufacturing Company in Foreign Markets, 1854–1889," *Business History Review* 43 (Autumn 1969), 299–346.

53. Alden Hatch, *Remington Arms: An American History* (New York: Rinehart, 1956), 148.

54. Fucini and Fucini, *Entrepreneurs*, 18.

55. Sobel and Sicilia, *Entrepreneurs*, 62.

56. Stephen J. Pyne, *Fire in America: A Cultural History of Wildland and Rural Fire* (Princeton, NJ: Princeton University Press, 1982), 11.

57. Pyne, *Fire in America*, 26.

58. See W. E. Haskell, *The International Paper Company, 1898–1924: Its Origin and Growth in a Quarter of a Century with a Brief Description of the Manufacture of Paper from the Harvesting of Pulpwood to the Finished Roll* (New York: International Paper, 1924), 8–9.

59. Clinton Woods, *Ideas That Became Big Business* (Baltimore: Founders, 1959), 110.

60. Woods, *Ideas*, 313–14.

61. The classic biography of Carnegie is Joseph Wall's *Andrew Carnegie* (New York: Oxford University Press, 1970); see also Andrew Carnegie, *Autobiography of Andrew Carnegie* (Boston: Houghton-Mifflin, 1920); Peter Krass, *Carnegie* (Hoboken, NJ: John Wiley & Sons, 2002); and David Nasaw, *Andrew Carnegie* (New York: Penguin, 2006).

62. Stuart Leslie, "Andrew Carnegie," in *The Encyclopedia of American Business History and Biography: Iron and Steel in the Nineteenth Century*, ed. Paul Pascoff (New York: Facts on File, 1989), 47–71, quotation on 51.

63. Jonathan R. T. Hughes, "Andrew Carnegie," in *The Vital Few: The Entrepreneurs and American Economic Progress*, 2d ed. (New York: Oxford University Press, 1986), 237.

64. Hughes, "Carnegie," in *Vital Few*, 238.

65. Quoted in Leslie, "Andrew Carnegie," 61.

66. Ibid., 65.

67. Charles W. Baird, "Labor Law Reform: Lessons from History," *CATO Journal* 10 (Spring/Summer 1990), 175–209, quotation on 190.

68. Paxon quoted in Baird, "Labor Law Reform," 192.

69. Quoted in Leslie, "Andrew Carnegie," 69.

70. Oliver E. Allen, "Bet-a-Million," *Audacity* 5 (Fall 1996), 18–31.

71. Quoted in Burton W. Folsom, *Myth of the Robber Barons* (Herndon, VA: Young America's Foundation, 1991), 70. Much of this material comes from Robert Hessen, *Steel Titan: The Life of Charles M. Schwab* (New York: Oxford University Press, 1975), and Schwab's own *Succeeding with What You Have* (New York: Century, 1917).

72. *New York Times*, April 13, 1915.

73. Hughes, "J. P. Morgan," in *Vital Few*, 443.

CHAPTER 7

1. Carol Nackenoff, *The Fictional Republic: Horatio Alger and American Political Discourse* (New York: Oxford University Press, 1994), 7, 10.

2. "Horatio Alger" in the *Dictionary of American Biography* (New York: Charles Scribner's Sons, 1928), 178–79; Gary Scharnhorst and Jack Bales, *Horatio Alger, Jr.: An Annotated Bibliography of Comment and Criticism* (Metuchen, NJ: Scarecrow Press, 1981), as well as Scharnhorst's *Horatio Alger, Jr.* (Boston: Twayne Publishers, 1980).

3. These stories, and others, are related with glee by Matthew Josephson in his famous critique of American enterprise called *The Robber Barons: The Great American Capitalists, 1861–1901* (New York: Harcourt Brace, 1934), 338 and ch. 14, passim.

4. Edward Chase Kirkland, *Dream and Thought in the Business Community, 1860–1900* (Chicago: Quadrangle, 1964 [1956]), 32.

5. "Biltmore House: Explore a Real-Life Castle," http://www.biltmore.com/explore/house/house.shtml (accessed January 9, 2007).

6. Testimony from the "Report of the Committee [on Education and Labor] of the Senate upon the Relations between Labor and Capital, 1885," quoted in Kirkland, *Dream and Thought*, 6.

7. An excellent summary of farm attitudes and problems during this period appears in David B. Danbom, *Born in the Country: A History of Rural America* (Baltimore: Johns Hopkins University Press, 1995), ch. 7.

8. Jeremy Atack and Peter W. Passell, *A New Economic View of American History* (New York: W. W. Norton, 1994), 412.

9. Douglass C. North, Terry L. Anderson, and Peter J. Hill, *Growth and Welfare in the American Past*, 2d ed. (Englewood Cliffs, NJ: Prentice-Hall, 1974), 133.

10. Atack and Passell, *New Economic View*, 414; James Stock, "Real Estate Mortgages, Foreclosures, and Midwestern Agrarian Unrest, 1865–1920," *Journal of Economic History* 44 (1984), 89–105.

11. Robert F. Fogel and Jack Rutner, "The Efficiency Effects of Federal Land Policy, 1850–1890: A Report of Some Provisional Findings," in William Aydelotte et al., *The Dimensions of Quantitative Research in History* (Princeton, NJ: Princeton University Press, 1972).

12. Robert Higgs, "Railroad Rates and the Populist Uprising," *Agricultural History* 44 (1970), 291–97, esp. chart on 295.

13. Jeffrey Williamson, "The Railroads and Midwestern Development, 1870–1890: A General Equilibrium History," in *Essays in Nineteenth-Century Economic History*, eds. David Klingaman and Richard Vedder (Athens: Ohio University Press, 1975), 269–352.

14. Atack and Passell, *New Economic View*, 422.

15. Danbom, *Born in the Country*, 156–57 and ch. 7, passim.

16. Jack Blicksilver, *The Defenders and Defense of Big Business in the United States, 1880–1900* (New York: Garland, 1985), 137.

17. A well-argued exposition of this thesis appears in George H. Miller, *Railroads and the Granger Laws* (Madison: University of Wisconsin Press, 1971).

18. Jonathan Hughes and Louis P. Cain, *American Economic History*, 7th ed. (Boston: Addison Wesley, 2007), 306.

19. Danbom, *Born in the Country*, 151.

20. Milton Friedman, "The Crime of 1873," *Journal of Political Economy* 98 (December 1990), passim.

21. William Leach, *Land of Desire: Merchants, Power, and the Rise of a New American Culture* (New York: Pantheon, 1993), 59.

22. Henry M. Littlefield, "The Wizard of Oz: Parable on Populism," *American Quarterly* 16 (Spring 1964), 47–58; Hugh Rockoff, "The 'Wizard of Oz' as a Monetary Allegory," *Journal of Political Economy* 98 (August 1990), 739–60.

23. Clarence D. Long, *Wages and Earnings in the United States, 1860–1890* (Princeton, NJ: Princeton University Press, 1960), table a-10.

24. Atack and Passell, *New Economic View*, 536; Claudia Goldin and Robert Margo, "Wages, Prices, and Labor Markets before the Civil War," in *Strategic Factors in*

Nineteenth Century American Economic History, eds. Claudia Goldin and Hugh Rockhoff (Chicago: University of Chicago Press, 1992), tables 2A.1, 2A.2, and 2A.3.

25. C. Wright Mills, "The American Business Elite: A Collective Portrait," *Journal of Economic History: The Tasks of Economic History* 5 (December 1945), 20–44.

26. Quoted in Blicksilver, *Defenders and Defense of Big Business*, 60.

27. Frank W. Taussig and Charles S. Joslyn, *American Business Leaders: A Study in Social Origins and Social Stratification*, quoted in Blicksilver, *Defenders and Defense of Big Business*, 45.

28. Burton Folsom, "Like Fathers, Unlike Sons: The Fall of the Business Elite in Scranton, Pennsylvania, 1880–1920," *Pennsylvania History* 46 (October 1980), 291–309, quoted in Burton W. Folsom, *Myth of the Robber Barons* (Herndon, VA: Young America's Foundation, 1991), 57.

29. Lynne Pierson Doti and Larry Schweikart, *Banking in the American West: From the Gold Rush to Deregulation* (Norman: University of Oklahoma Press, 1991).

30. Statistics from this section are taken from a survey of railroaders in Robert L. Frey, ed., *The Encyclopedia of American Business History and Biography: Railroads in the Nineteenth Century* (New York: Facts on File, 1988), and Keith L. Bryant, Jr., ed., *The Encyclopedia of American Business History and Biography: Railroads in the Twentieth Century* (New York: Facts on File, 1988). Special thanks to Elizabeth Koslick, who conducted a detailed tabulation of all of these volumes. Two cautions are in order with the data from these volumes. First, some biographies only noted number of children without specifying sex, and some did not note if the men had any children at all. Second, some people were included in the *Encyclopedia* due to the spectacular nature of their failure or illegal activities (Charles Ponzi, for example).

31. William Leary, ed., *The Airline Industry* (New York: Facts on File, 1992).

32. William Miller, "American Historians and the Business Elite," in *Men in Business: Essays on the Historical Role of the Entrepreneur*, ed. William Miller (New York: Harper & Row, 1962), 309–28.

33. C. Wright Mills, "The American Business Elite: A Collective Portrait," in *Power, Politics, and People: The Collected Essays of C. Wright Mills*, ed. Irving Horowitz (New York: Oxford University Press, 1962), 110–39. Also see Reinhard Bendix and Frank W. Howton, "Social Mobility and the American Business Elite," in *Social Mobility in Industrial Society*, eds. Reinhard Bendix and Seymour Martin Lipset (Berkeley: University of California Press, 1959), 114–43.

34. Herbert Gutman, "The Reality of the Rags-to-Riches 'Myth,'" in Herbert G. Gutman, *Work, Culture, and Society in Industrializing America* (New York: Vintage, 1977 [1966]), 211–33, quotation on 232.

35. Quoted in Seymour Martin Lipset, "The Work Ethic—Then and Now," *Public Interest* (Winter 1990), 61–69, quotation on 63.

36. Quoted in Herbert G. Gutman, "Work, Culture, and Society in Industrializing America, 1815–1919," *American Historical Review* (June 1973), 531–88, quotation on 548.

37. Gutman, "Work, Culture, and Society," 559.

38. Daniel Aaron, *Men of Good Hope* (New York: Oxford, 1961), 58.

39. C. Joseph Pusateri, *A History of American Business*, 2d ed. (Arlington Heights, IL: Harlan-Davidson, 1988), 234. On Bellamy, see Joseph Dorfman, *The Economic Mind in American Civilization*, 5 vols. (New York: Augustus M. Kelley, 1969), 3:152, and Arthur E. Morgan, *Edward Bellamy* (New York: Columbia University Press, 1944), as well as Bellamy's "What 'Nationalism' Means," *The Contemporary Review*, July 1890.

40. Quoted in Joseph Dorfman, *Economic Mind in American Civilization*, 3:117.

41. Henry Demarest Lloyd, *Wealth Against Commonwealth* (New York: Harper & Bros., 1894); Ida M. Tarbell, *The History of the Standard Oil Company* (New York: Harper & Row, 1966); Allan Nevins, *Study in Power: John D. Rockefeller*, 2 vols. (New York: Charles Scribner's Sons, 1953).

42. Josephson, *The Robber Barons*, 1934.

43. Upton Sinclair, *The Jungle* (n.p.: Barnes and Noble Classics, 2008).

44. Material for this section comes from Joseph J. Fucini and Suzy Fucini, *Entrepreneurs: The Men and Women Behind Famous Brand Names and How They Made It* (Boston: G. K. Hall, 1985), 19–22, and James D. Robertson, *The Great American Beer Book* (Ottawa, IL: Caroline House Publishers, 1978).

45. "Jack Newton Daniel," in Fucini and Fucini, *Entrepreneurs*, 8–10.

46. "Dr. Thomas B. Welch," in Fucini and Fucini, *Entrepreneurs*, 69–72.

47. Frank Rowsome, Jr., *They Laughed When I Sat Down* (New York: McGraw-Hill, 1959); Nettie L. Major, *C. W. Post: The Hour and the Man* (Washington: privately printed, 1963).

48. Fucini and Fucini, *Entrepreneurs*, 106.

49. Pusateri, *History of American Business*, 251.

50. Alfred D. Chandler, *The Visible Hand: The Managerial Revolution in American Business* (Cambridge, MA: Belknap Press, 1977), 274–75.

51. Frederick W. Taylor, *The Principles of Scientific Management* (New York: Harper & Bros., 1915); historian Spencer Klaw quoted in Oliver E. Allen, "This Great Mental Revolution," *Audacity* 4 (Summer 1996), 52–61, quotation on 60.

52. Allen, "This Great Mental Revolution," passim.

53. Chandler, *Visible Hand*, 276.

54. W. Elliot Brownlee, *Dynamics of Ascent: A History of the American Economy*, 2d ed. (New York: Alfred A. Knopf, 1979), 319–40; Clarence D. Long, *Wages and Earnings in the United States, 1860–1890* (Princeton, NJ: Princeton University Press, 1960); Albert Rees, *Real Wages in Manufacturing, 1890–1914* (Princeton, NJ: Princeton University Press, 1961); Atack and Passell, *New Economic View of American History*, 542–43; Jeremy Atack and Fred Bateman, "How Long Was the Workday in 1880?" *Journal of Economic History* 52 (March 1992), 129–60; Robert Whaples, "The Great Decline in the Length of the Workweek" (working paper, University of Wisconsin–Milwaukee, 1988).

55. A useful review of labor history can be found in Melvyn Dubofsky, *Industrialism and the American Worker, 1865–1920* (Arlington Heights, IL: Harlan-Davidson, 1975); and Sidney Lens, *The Labor Wars: From the Molly Maguires to the Sitdowns* (Garden City, NY: Anchor Books, 1975).

56. Harold Livesay, *Samuel Gompers and Organized Labor in America* (Boston: Little, Brown, 1978).

57. Livesay, *Samuel Gompers*, passim.

58. Claudia Goldin, "Maximum Hours Legislation and Female Employment: A Reassessment," *Journal of Political Economy* 96 (1988), 189–205, and *Understanding the Gender Gap: An Economic History of American Women* (New York: Oxford University Press, 1990), and her work with Robert Margo, "Wages, Prices, and Labor Markets before the Civil War," in *Strategic Factors in Nineteenth Century American Economic Growth: A Volume to Honor Robert W. Fogel*, eds. Claudia Goldin and Hugh Rockoff (Chicago: University of Chicago Press, 1992), 67–104.

59. A useful review of this era appears in Samuel P. Hays, *The Response to Industrialism, 1885–1914* (Chicago: University of Chicago Press, 1957).

60. Thomas C. McCraw, *Prophets of Regulation* (Cambridge, MA: Belknap Press, 1984).

61. Albro Martin, *Enterprise Denied* (New York: Columbia, 1971), 44.

62. Martin, *Enterprise Denied*, 359.

63. Ida M. Tarbell, *The History of the Standard Oil Company*, ed. David M. Chalmers (New York: Norton, 1969), 27. The quotation is Henry Lloyd's, from his article in the *Atlantic Monthly*, quoted in Dorfman, *Economic Mind in American Civilization*, 3:117.

64. Margaret S. Creighton, *Rites and Passages: The Experience of American Whaling, 1830–1870* (Cambridge: Cambridge University Press, 1995).

65. Pusateri, *History of American Business*, 206.

66. Quoted in Folsom, *Myth of the Robber Barons*, 85.

67. J. W. Trowbridge quoted in Nevins, *Study in Power: John D. Rockefeller*, 1:132.

68. On the economic relationship between the falling prices of kerosene and the decline of whaling, see Alexander Starbuck, *History of the American Whale Fishery* (Secaucus, NJ: Castle Books, 1989); David Moment, "The Business of Whaling in America in the 1850s," *Business History Review* 31 (Autumn 1957), 261–91; Teresa D. Hutchins, "The American Whale Fishery, 1815–1900: An Economic Analysis" (Ph.D. dissertation, University of North Carolina, 1988).

69. Ron Chernow, *Titan: The Life of John D. Rockefeller, Sr.* (New York: Random House, 1998), is an authoritative and entertaining biography.

70. Quoted in Folsom, *Myth of the Robber Barons*, 84.

71. John D. Rockefeller, *Random Reminiscences of Men and Events* (New York: Doubleday, Page, 1909), 111.

72. See figures 1 and 2 in David Moment, "The Business of Whaling in America in the 1850s," 283. Admittedly, several factors were involved in rising prices for whale products, including some whaling fleet disasters and the effects of the Civil War.

73. Nevins, *Study in Power: John D. Rockefeller*, 2:76; 1:277–79.

74. Rockefeller, *Random Reminiscences*, 20.

75. Nevins, *Study in Power*, 1:672.

76. Ibid., 1:208.

77. Ibid., 2:29–30.

78. Rockefeller, *Random Reminiscences*, 22.

79. Folsom, *Myth of the Robber Barons*, 94.

80. Nevins, *Study in Power*, 1:328.

81. Stuart Bruchey, *The Wealth of the Nation: An Economic History of the United States* (New York: Harper & Row, 1988), 124.

82. Bruchey, *Wealth of the Nation*, 125.

83. Ibid., 132.

84. George E. Mowry, *The Era of Theodore Roosevelt and the Birth of Modern America* (New York: Harper & Bros., 1958), 55.

85. Louis Galambos and Joseph C. Pratt, *The Rise of the Corporate Commonwealth: U.S. Business and Public Policy in the Twentieth Century* (New York: Basic Books, 1988), 62.

CHAPTER 8

1. Robert Sobel and David B. Sicilia, *Entrepreneurs: An American Adventure* (Boston: Houghton-Mifflin, 1986), 166. See also Winifred C. Leland and Minnie Dubbs Millbrook, *Master of Precision* (Detroit, MI: Wayne State University Press, 1966).

2. Sobel and Sicilia, *Entrepreneurs*, 168.

3. Sobel and Sicilia, *Entrepreneurs*, 170.

4. Frederick Allen, *Secret Formula* (New York: HarperBusiness, 1994) 28–66; Mark Pendergast, *For God, Country, and Coca-Cola: The Unauthorized History of the Great American Soft Drink and the Company that Makes It* (New York: Collier, 1993).

5. For more on Wiley, see Jack High and Clayton A. Coppin, "Wiley and the Whiskey Industry: Strategic Behavior in the Passage of the Pure Food Act," *Business History Review* 62 (Summer 1988), 286–309.

6. W. Elliot Brownlee, *Federal Taxation in America: A Short History* (Cambridge: Cambridge University Press and the Woodrow Wilson Center Press, 1996), and his edited volume, *Funding the Modern American State, 1941–1945: The Rise and Fall of the Era of Easy Finance* (Cambridge: Cambridge University Press and Woodrow Wilson Center, 1996).

7. Stanley Lebergott, *The Americans: An Economic Record* (New York: W. W. Norton, 1984), 407.

8. Brownlee, *Federal Taxation in America*, 3–8.

9. Gerald Eggert, "Richard Olney and the Income Tax," *Mississippi Valley Historical Review* (June 1961), 24–25.

10. Quoted in Lebergott, *The Americans*, 407–8, originally taken from Edwin Seligman, *The Income Tax* (New York: MacMillan, 1911), 420.

11. Lebergott, *The Americans*, 408. Equally as telling as Lebergott's understatement is the subtitle of Elliot Brownlee's edited volume, "The Rise and Fall of the Era of Easy Finance"—easy because it was hidden. As might be predicted, some have complained that the tax system's failure was that it did not go far enough. In *Dimensions of Law in the Service of Order: Origins of the Federal Income Tax, 1861–1913* (New York: Oxford University Press, 1993), Robert Stanley argues

that the tax was a means of social control, symbolic but not truly redistributive. The Progressives—really "conservatives" in Stanley's view—forged a consensus to enact minor taxation as a means to enlist the support of lower classes for long-term domestic tranquility. In reality, however, the heaviest burdens after the income tax soared to new rate levels in the post–World War II period have been carried by the lowest-income class of workers, who have found themselves unable to avoid taxes with clever investments or shelters, escape it by relocating in other areas of the world, or often even pay it. By the 1990s, the average American worked almost half a year just to pay the federal income taxes—a far cry from the singing birds and sunshine envisioned by the congressman.

12. Wilson quoted in Burton W. Folsom, *Myth of the Robber Barons* (Herndon, VA: Young America's Foundation, 1991), 107–8; Andrew Mellon, *Taxation: The People's Business* (New York: Macmillan, 1924), 129; and Lawrence L. Murray, "Bureaucracy and Bipartisanship in Taxation: The Mellon Plan Revisited," *Business History Review* 52 (Summer 1978), 200–225.

13. For financial history, see Larry Schweikart, ed., *Encyclopedia of American Business History and Biography: Banking and Finance to 1913* (New York: Facts on File, 1990).

14. An analysis of the reform movements leading up to the Jekyll Island meeting are documented in several of the individual biographies in Schweikart, ed., *Encyclopedia of American Business History and Biography: Banking and Finance to 1913*, and its follow-up volume, *Banking and Finance, 1913–1989*, especially the essays on John Pierpont Morgan, Frank Vanderlip, Nelson Aldrich, George F. Baker, and others. An excellent technical assessment of the reformer's efforts on the banking system can be found in Eugene N. White, *Regulation and Reform of the American Banking System, 1900–1929* (Princeton, NJ: Princeton University Press, 1983); James Livingston, *Origins of the Federal Reserve System: Money, Class, and Corporate Capitalism* (Ithaca, NY: Cornell University Press, 1986); and Richard Timberlake, Jr., *The Origins of Central Banking in the United States* (Cambridge, MA: Harvard University Press, 1978).

15. Henry C. Dethloff, "Arsene P. Pujo," in Schweikart, ed., *Encyclopedia of American Business History and Biography: Banking and Finance to 1913*, 397–98.

16. Vincent P. Carosso, *The Morgans: Private International Bankers, 1854–1913* (Cambridge, MA: Harvard University Press, 1987). A brief but adroit summary of Morgan appears in Albro Martin, "John Pierpont Morgan," in Schweikart, ed., *Encyclopedia of American Business History and Biography: Banking and Finance to 1913*, 325–48, quotation on 347. Also see Jean Strouse, *Morgan: American Financier* (New York: Random House, 1999).

17. Morgan and Untermeyer quoted in Carosso, *The Morgans*, 632–33.

18. Carosso, *The Morgans*, 633.

19. Charles W. Calomiris and Carolos D. Ramirez, "The Role of Financial Relationships in the History of American Corporate Finance," *Journal of Applied Corporate Finance* 9 (Summer 1996), 52–72, quotation on 65.

20. W. Elliot Brownlee, *Dynamics of Ascent: A History of the American Economy*, 2d ed. (New York: Alfred A. Knopf, 1979), 379.

21. Milton Friedman and Anna J. Schwartz, *A Monetary History of the United States, 1863–1960* (Princeton, NJ: Princeton University Press, 1963).

22. The Federal Reserve's ineptness is cited as a problem in Barry Eichengreen, *Golden Fetters: The Gold Standard and the Great Depression, 1919–1932* (New York: Oxford University Press, 1992), although Eichengreen is careful to point out that no central bank successfully dealt with the gold standard, and thus blames the inflexibility of gold more than the government.

23. See the discussion of these various views in Larry Schweikart, "U.S. Commercial Banking: A Historiographical Survey," *Business History Review* 65 (Autumn 1991), 606–61.

24. U.S. Bureau of the Census, *Historical Statistics of the United States: Colonial Times to Present* (Washington, D.C.: Government Printing Office, 1975), 884, 887.

25. John M. Dobson, *A History of American Enterprise* (Englewood Cliffs, NJ: Prentice-Hall, 1988), 216; Steven Wheeler, "John Pierpont Morgan, Jr.," in Schweikart, ed., *Encyclopedia of American Business History and Biography: Banking and Finance, 1913–1989* (New York: Facts on File, 1990), 316–21; and John Douglas Forbes, Jr., *J. P. Morgan, Jr., 1867–1943* (Charlottesville: University of Virginia Press, 1981).

26. Johannes R. Lischka, "Armor Plate: Nickel and Steel, Monopoly and Profit," in Benjamin Franklin Cooling, ed., *War, Business, and American Society: Historical Perspectives on the Military-Industrial Complex* (Port Washington, NY: Kennikat Press, 1977), 43–58. Lischka concludes that monopoly profits did exist, but they were retained by the corporations for new plant expenditures and to bring the par value and paper value of the companies together, removing the large amounts of paper value that had been injected to create the corporations in the first place. Or, in other words, the monopoly profits only covered the risk taken by the entrepreneurs that made it possible for American ships to have armored plate at all!

27. William Gibbs McAdoo, *Crowded Years* (Boston: Houghton-Mifflin, 1931), 296–97, 304–9.

28. Marc Wortman, *The Millionaires' Unit: The Aristocratic Flyboys Who Fought the Great War and Invented American Air Power* (New York: Public Affairs, 2006), 47.

29. Keith L. Bryant and Henry C. Dethloff, *A History of American Business*, 2d ed. (Englewood Cliffs, NJ: Prentice-Hall, 1990), 290.

30. No biography of Schwab exceeds Robert Hessen's *Steel Titan: The Life of Charles M. Schwab* (New York: Oxford University Press, 1975), with the discussion of Schwab's war activities on 236–44.

31. Carnegie quoted in Hessen, *Steel Titan*, 244. Also see Larry Schweikart, *America's Victories: Why the U.S. Wins Wars and Will Win the War on Terror* (New York: Sentinel, 2007).

32. Bernard Baruch, *Baruch: The Public Years* (New York: Holt, Rinehart & Winston, 1960), quoted in Sidney Ratner, James H. Soltow, and Richard Sylla, *The Evolution of the American Economy: Growth, Welfare, and Decision Making*, 2d ed. (New York: Macmillan, 1993), 411.

33. Ratner, Solow, and Sylla, *Evolution of the American Economy*, 411.

34. David M. Kennedy, *Over Here: The First World War and American Society* (New York: Oxford University Press, 1980), 253; K. Austin Kerr, *American Railroad Politics, 1914–1920: Rates, Wages, and Efficiency* (Pittsburgh, PA: University of Pittsburgh Press, 1968).

35. Robert Higgs, *Crisis and Leviathan: Critical Episodes in the Growth of American Government* (New York: Oxford University Press, 1987).

36. Charles Whiting Baker, *Government Control and Operation of Industry in Great Britain and the United States During the World War* (New York: Oxford University Press, 1921), 3.

37. Sobel and Sicilia, *Entrepreneurs*, 16–20; Russell B. Adams, Jr., *King C. Gillette: The Man and His Wonderful Shaving Device* (Boston: Little, Brown, 1978); and Editors of News Front, *The 50 Great Pioneers of American Industry* (Maplewood, NJ: C. S. Hammond; New York: Year, Inc., 1964).

38. Adams, *King C. Gillette*, 23.

39. Sobel and Sicilia, *Entrepreneurs*, 204.

40. Harry E. Resseguie, "A. T. Stewart's Marble Palace: The Cradle of the Department Store," *New York Historical Society* 48 (April 1964), 131–62.

41. Bryant and Dethloff, *History of American Business*, 322–23.

42. See Harry E. Resseguie, "Alexander Turney Stewart and the Development of the Department Store, 1823–1876," *Business History Review* 39 (Autumn 1965), 301–22, and his "The Decline and Fall of the Commercial Empire of A. T. Stewart," *Business History Review* 36 (Fall 1962), 255–86. An excellent source for the story of most of the major retail giants is Robert Hendrickson, *The Grand Emporiums* (New York: Stein and Day, 1979).

43. Sobel and Sicilia, *Entrepreneurs*, 208.

44. Joseph H. Appel, *The Business Biography of John Wanamaker* (New York: Macmillan, 1930); Maury Klein, "The Gospel of Wanamaker," *Audacity* 4 (Summer 1996), 26–39, quotation on 27.

45. Klein, "Gospel of Wanamaker," 28.

46. Appel, *Business Biography of John Wanamaker*, 44

47. Ibid., 47.

48. Ibid., 80–81.

49. Godfrey M. Lebhar, *Chain Stores in America, 1859–1962* (New York: Chain Store Publishing Corp., 1963), and Tom Mahoney, *The Great Merchants* (New York: Harper & Bros., 1955).

50. Fucini and Fucini, "Washington Atlee Burpee," in *Entrepreneurs*, 5–8; Ken Kraft, *Garden to Order* (Garden City, NY: Doubleday, 1963).

51. Sobel and Sicilia, *Entrepreneurs*, 209–11.

52. Boris Emmett and John E. Jeuck, *Catalogues and Counters: A History of Sears, Roebuck and Company* (Chicago: University of Chicago Press, 1950).

53. Bryant and Dethloff, *History of American Business*, 325.

54. See Godfrey M. Leghar, *Chain Stores in America, 1859–1962*, 3d ed. (New York: Chain Store Publishing Corporation, 1963).

55. Norman Beasley, *Main Street Merchant: The Story of the J. C. Penney Company* (New York: Whittlesey House, 1948). For the story of a similar store, F. W. Woolworth, see John K. Winkler, *Five and Ten: The Fabulous Life of F. W. Woolworth* (New York: Robert M. McBride, 1940).

56. George Laycock, *The Kroger Story: A Century of Innovation* (Cincinnati, OH: The Kroger Company, 1983).

57. Thomas Hine, "The Packaging Made the Product ... and Remade the American Grocery Store," *Audacity* (Summer 1995), 28–31, quotation on 28.

58. Bryant and Dethloff, *History of American Business*, 186.

59. Stephen Fox, *The Mirror Makers: A History of American Advertising and its Creators* (New York: Vintage, 1985 [1984]), 50. See also Merle Curti's discussion of the way advertisers' views of the "nature of man" changed over time in his "The Changing Concept of 'Human Nature' in the Literature of American Advertising," *Business History Review* 41 (Winter 1967), 335–57.

60. Roland Marchand, *Advertising the American Dream: Making Way for Modernity, 1920–1940* (Berkeley: University of California Press, 1985).

61. Sobel and Sicilia, *Entrepreneurs*, 217–21.

62. Fox, *Mirror Makers*, 115.

63. Marchand, *Advertising the American Dream*, 18–19.

64. Fox, *Mirror Makers*, 106.

65. Bruce Barton, *The Man Nobody Knows* (New York: Bobbs-Merrill, 1925). A modern version of the book, using terminology tailored to the 1990s, is Laurie Beth Jones, *Jesus, CEO: Using Ancient Wisdom for Visionary Leadership* (New York: Hyperion, 1992).

66. Fox, *Mirror Makers*, 108.

67. Ibid., 109.

68. Joseph Turow, *Breaking Up America: Advertisers and the New Media World* (Chicago: University of Chicago Press, 19970, and Randall Rothenberg, "How Powerful Is Advertising?" a review of Turow's book in *Atlantic Monthly*, June 1997, 113–20.

69. Bryant and Dethloff, *History of American Business*, 134.

70. Burton Klein, *Dynamic Economics* (Cambridge, MA: Harvard University Press, 1977), table 3.

71. Sobel and Sicilia, *Entrepreneurs*, 172.

72. See "Henry Ford," in Jonathan R. T. Hughes, *The Vital Few: The Entrepreneurs and American Economic Progress*, 2d ed. (New York: Oxford University Press, 1986), 274–356.

73. Hughes, *Vital Few*, 274–355.

74. Ibid., 290.

75. Ford quoted in Hughes, *Vital Few*, 292.

76. Ford quoted in Sobel and Sicilia, *Entrepreneurs*, 174.

77. David E. Kyvig and Myron A. Marty, *Nearby History: Exploring the Past Around You* (Nashville: American Association for State and Local History, 1982), 1–2.

78. These and other Fordisms are detailed in Hughes, *Vital Few*, 306–23, and in Harold Livesay, *American Made: Men Who Shaped the American Economy* (Boston: Little, Brown, 1979), 159–82, as well as by his major biographers, Allen Nevins and F. E. Hill, in their three-volume work, *Ford: The Times, the Man, the Company* (New York: Scribner's, 1954); *Ford: Expansion and Challenge, 1915–1933* (New York: Scribner's, 1957); *Ford: Decline and Rebirth, 1933–1962* (New York: Scribner's, 1963). A much more critical work, Keith Sward, *The*

Legend of Henry Ford (New York: Rinehart, 1948), and a "court biography" appearing in W. A. Simonds, *Henry Ford* (Los Angeles: F. Clymer, 1946), provide different perspectives. A recent, very readable biography is Steven Watts, *The People's Tycoon: Henry Ford and the American Century* (New York: Alfred A. Knopf, 2005).

CHAPTER 9

1. Gordon Thomas and Max Morgan Witts, *The San Francisco Earthquake* (New York: Stein and Day, 1971).

2. Felice A. Bonadio, *A. P. Giannini, Banker of America* (Berkeley: University of California Press, 1994), 33–35.

3. Larry Schweikart and Lynne Pierson Doti, *Banking in the American West: From the Gold Rush to Deregulation* (Norman: University of Oklahoma Press, 1991), passim, and *California Bankers 1848–1993* (Needham, MA: Simon and Schuster, 1994), 82–83.

4. Paul Johnson, *Modern Times: A History of the World from the Twenties to the Eighties* (New York: Harper Colophon, 1983), 223.

5. John Kenneth Galbraith, *The Great Crash, 1929* (Boston: Houghton-Mifflin, 1955).

6. George David Smith, "Forfeiting the Future," *Audacity* 4 (Spring 1996), 25–39, quotation on 25.

7. George David Smith, *The Anatomy of a Business Strategy: Bell, Western Electric, and the Origins of the American Telephone Industry* (Baltimore: Johns Hopkins University Press, 1985); Robert W. Garnet, *The Telephone Enterprise: The Evolution of the Bell System's Horizontal Structure, 1876–1909* (Baltimore: Johns Hopkins University Press, 1985). Other discussions of Bell and his telephone appear in Robert V. Burce, *Bell: Alexander Graham Bell and the Conquest of Solitude* (Boston: Little, Brown, 1973), and John Brooks, *Telephone: The First Hundred Years* (New York: Harper & Row, 1975).

8. Smith, "Forfeiting the Future," 26.

9. Ibid., 28.

10. Robert Sobel and David B. Sicilia, *Entrepreneurs: An American Adventure* (Boston: Houghton-Mifflin, 1986), 248.

11. Garnet, *Telephone Enterprise*, 162.

12. Erik Larson, *Thunderstruck* (New York: Crown Publishers, 2006), weaves the Marconi story entertainingly with that of a London murderer whose escape was thwarted by a radio transmission.

13. C. Joseph Pusateri, *A History of American Business*, 2d ed. (Arlington Heights, IL: Harlan-Davidson, 1988), 270.

14. "David Sarnoff: U.S. Media Executive," The Museum of Broadcast Communications, http://www.museum.tv/archives/etv/S/htmlS/sarnoffdavi/sarnoffdavi.htm.

15. Erik Barnouw, *A Tower in Babel: A History of Broadcasting in the United States, vol. I, to 1933* (New York: Oxford University Press, 1950), 68–69; Elliot N. Sivowitch, "A Technological Survey of Broadcasting's 'Pre-History,' 1876–1920," *Journal of Broadcasting* 15 (Winter 1970–71), 1–20.

16. Sobel and Sicilia, "David Sarnoff: The Entrepreneur as Dreamer," *Entrepreneurs*, 253–63.

17. For an insightful look at the studio system and its effect on a Hollywood icon, see James S. Olsen and Randy Roberts, *John Wayne: American* (New York: Free Press, 1995). An investigation of the origins of the American movie industry appears in David Robinson, *From Peep Show to Palace: The Birth of American Film* (New York: Columbia University Press, 1996).

18. John M. Dobson, *A History of American Enterprise* (Englewood Cliffs, NJ: Prentice-Hall, 1988), 264–65, from Jack C. Ellis, *A History of Film*, 2d ed. (Englewood Cliffs, NJ: Prentice-Hall, 1985), ch. 9.

19. Ellis, *History of Film*, ch. 8; Margaret Ingels, *Willis Haviland Carrier: Father of Air Conditioning* (Louisville, KY: Fetter Printing, 1952).

20. Ellis, *History of Film*, 180; see also Tino Valio, *Grand Design: Hollywood as a Modern Business Enterprise, 1930–1939*, vol. 5, in *History of the American Cinema*, ed. Charles Harpole (Berkeley: University of California Press, 1995), for the decline in the business during the Depression.

21. Steven Watts, *The Magic Kingdom: Walt Disney and the American Way of Life* (Columbia and London: University of Missouri Press, 1997).

22. Gene Smiley and Richard H. Keehn, "Margin Purchases, Brokers' Loans, and the Bull Market of the Twenties," *Business and Economic History* 17 (1988), 129–42.

23. See Stanley Lebergott, *The Americans: An Economic Record* (New York: W. W. Norton, 1984), table 33.6, 442.

24. Robert Sklar, ed., *The Plastic Age, 1917–1930* (New York: George Braziller, 1970), 93.

25. Edwin J. Perkins, "Charles E. Merrill," in Larry Schweikart, ed., *Encyclopedia of American Business History and Biography: Banking and Finance, 1913–1989* (New York: Facts on File, 1990), 284, and Edwin J. Perkins, *Wall Street to Main Street: Charles Merrill and Middle-Class Investors* (New York: Cambridge, 2006).

26. Both Wilson and Fitzgerald quoted in Johnson, *Modern Times*, 222.

27. Johnson, *Modern Times*, 239.

28. Stuart Bruchey, *The Wealth of the Nation: An Economic History of the United States* (New York: Harper & Row, 1988), 144.

29. Harold G. Vatter, "The Position of Small Business in the Structure of American Manufacturing, 1870–1970," in Stuart Bruchey, ed., *Small Business in American Life* (New York: Columbia University Press, 1980), 142–68.

30. Vatter, "Position of Small Business," 150.

31. Ibid., quotation on 151.

32. Bert G. Hickman, *Growth and Stability of the Postwar Economy* (Washington, D.C.: Brookings Institution, 1960), and his "What Became of the Building Cycle?" in *Nations and Households in Economic Growth: Essays in Honor of Moses Abramovitz*, eds. Paul David and Melvin Reder (New York: Academic Press, 1973); Ben Bloch, Rendig Fels, and Marshall McMahon, "Housing Surplus in the 1920's?" *Explorations in Economic History* 8 (Spring 1971), 259–84; Lloyd J. Mercer and W. Douglas Morgan, "Housing Surplus in the 1920's? Another Evaluation," *Explorations in Economic History* 10 (Spring 1973), 295–304.

33. Johnson, *Modern Times*, 216.

34. Andrew Mellon, *Taxation: The People's Business* (New York: Macmillan, 1924), 9, 16–17, 79–81, 96–97, and his "Taxing Energy and Initiative," *The Independent* 112 (March 29, 1924), 168.

35. Gene Smiley and Richard H. Keehn, "Federal Personal Income Tax Policy in the 1920s," *Journal of Economic History* 55 (June 1995), 285–303.

36. Burton Folsom, Jr., *The Myth of the Robber Barons* (Herndon, VA: Young America's Foundation, 1991), 103–20.

37. Smiley and Keehn, "Federal Personal Income Tax Policy," passim.

38. David Beito, "Andrew Mellon," in Schweikart, ed., *Encyclopedia of American Business History and Biography: Banking and Finance, 1913–1989*, 267–282; and Dwight R. Lee, ed., *Taxation and the Deficit Economy: Fiscal Policy and Capital Formation in the United States* (San Francisco: Pacific Research Institute for Public Policy, 1986).

39. Sidney Ratner, James H. Soltow, and Richard Sylla, *The Evolution of the American Economy: Growth, Welfare, and Decision Making*, 2d ed. (New York: Macmillan, 1993), tables 18-7 through 18-10 on 444–45.

40. Donald McCoy, *Calvin Coolidge: The Quiet President* (New York: MacMillan, 1967), 392.

41. An excellent source on Coolidge, and one that explains why modern views of this great president have become so distorted, is Thomas B. Silver, *Coolidge and the Historians* (Durham: Carolina Academic Press, 1982).

42. James Bovard, *The Farm Fiasco* (San Francisco: Institute for Contemporary Studies, 1989), 13.

43. Lebergott, *The Americans*, 439.

44. Joseph S. Davis, *On Agricultural Policy* (Palo Alto, CA: Stanford University, 1938), 435; H. Thomas Johnson, *Agricultural Depression in the 1920s* (New York: Garland, 1985 [1961]), 213.

45. W. Elliot Brownlee, *Dynamics of Ascent: A History of the American Economy*, 2d ed. (New York: Alfred A. Knopf, 1979), 397.

46. Coolidge quoted in Murray Rothbard, *America's Great Depression* (Princeton, NJ: D. Van Nostrand, 1963), 202.

47. Lebergott, *The Americans*, 439.

48. Gene Smiley, *The American Economy in the Twentieth Century* (Cincinnati, OH: South-Western Publishing Co., 1994), 37, fig. 3.1.

49. See L. Milton Woods, *Sometimes the Books Froze: Wyoming's Economy and its Banks* (Boulder, CO: Boulder Associated University Press, 1985).

50. Bovard, *Farm Fiasco*, 22.

51. Joseph J. Fucini and Suzy Fucini, "James Lewis Kraft," in *Entrepreneurs: The Men and Women Behind Famous Brand Names and How They Made It* (Boston: G. K. Hall, 1985), 111–13; Arthur W. Baum, "Man with a Horse and Wagon," *Saturday Evening Post* 17 (February 1945), 14–15.

52. David B. Danbom, *Born in the Country: A History of Rural America* (Baltimore: Johns Hopkins University Press, 1995), 203.

53. Charles Calomiris has examined deposit insurance effects in "Is Deposit Insurance Necessary? A Historical Perspective," *Journal of Economic History* 50 (June 1990), 283–96; "Deposit Insurance: Lessons from the Record," *Economic Perspectives* 13 (May/June 1989), 10–30; and an antebellum comparison of systems in Charles Calomiris and Larry Schweikart, "The Panic of 1857: Origins, Transmission, and Containment," *Journal of Economic History* 51 (December 1991). Also see V. V. Chari, "Banking Without Deposit Insurance or Bank Panics: Lessons from a Model of the U.S. National Banking System," *Federal Reserve Bank of Minneapolis Quarterly Review* 13 (Summer 1989), 3–19.

54. See Carol Martel and Larry Schweikart, "Arizona Banking and the Collapse of Lincoln Thrift," *Arizona and the West* 28 (Fall 1986), 246–63; and Gerald P. O'Driscoll, Jr., "Bank Failures: The Deposit Insurance Connection," *Contemporary Policy Issues* 6 (April 1988), 1–12.

55. Secretary for George Wingfield to [cashier], Virginia City Bank, July 27, 1925, box 115, folder "1925," George Wingfield Papers, Nevada Historical Society, Reno, NV.

56. Larry Schweikart, "George Wingfield and Nevada Banking, 1920–1933: Another Look," *Nevada Historical Society Quarterly* 35 (Fall 1992), 162–76.

57. See William Frazer and John J. Guthrie, Jr., *The Florida Land Boom: Speculation, Money, and the Banks* (Westport, CT: Quorum Books, 1995).

58. Jeremy Atack and Peter W. Passell, *A New Economic View of American History* (New York: W. W. Norton, 1994), 606–7.

59. Charles Kindleberger, *The World in Depression, 1929–1939*, rev. ed. (Berkeley: University of California Press, 1986).

60. Several scholars have debated the "mind-set" of the Fed in the 1920s and early 1930s (see Smiley, *American Economy in the Twentieth Century*, ch. 6, for a thorough discussion of each). One interesting view, that the Fed was "captured" by the bankers, contends that the Fed sought to maintain its gold position, and thus tried to prop up bond prices. By so doing, the proponents of this view argue, the Fed did not undertake open market purchases sufficient to revive the economy. If true, however, this view provides a deadly critique of allowing government agencies to control the money supply at all, especially if the regulators can be captured so easily, and it hardly bolsters the authors' underlying presumption that "big government" is benign! See Gerald Epstein and Thomas Ferguson, "Monetary Policy, Loan Liquidation, and Industrial Conflict: The Federal Reserve and Open Market Operations of 1932," *Journal of Economic History* 44 (December 1984), 957–84, as well as the critique by Philip R. P. Coelho and G. J. Santoni, "Regulatory Capture and the Monetary Contraction of 1932: A Comment on Epstein and Ferguson," *Journal of Economic History* 51 (March 1991), 182–89.

61. Charles W. Calomiris and Joseph R. Mason, "Contagion and Bank Failures During the Great Depression: The June 1932 Chicago Banking Panic," *American Economic Review* 87 (December 1997), 863–83.

62. Milton Friedman and Anna Schwartz, *A Monetary History of the United States 1867–1960* (Princeton, NJ: Princeton University Press, 1963).

63. Jonathan Hughes and Louis Cain, *American Economic History*, 6th ed. (Boston: Addison Wesley, 2003), 462.

64. Stephen J. DeCanio, "Expectations and Business Confidence During the Great Depression," in *Money in Crisis: The Federal Reserve, the Economy, and Monetary Reform*, ed. Barry N. Siegel (San Francisco: Pacific Institute, 1984).

65. Smiley, *American Economy in the Twentieth Century*, 20.

66. Alfred D. Chandler, Jr., ed., *Giant Enterprise: Ford, General Motors, and the Automobile Industry* (New York: Harcourt, Brace & World, 1964), 3; Lester V. Chandler, *America's Greatest Depression, 1929–1941* (New York: Harper & Row, 1970), ch. 3; and David A. Shannon, ed., *The Great Depression* (Englewood Cliffs, NJ: Prentice-Hall, 1960).

67. Sobel and Sicilia, *Entrepreneurs*, 28–31.

68. Johnson, *Modern Times*, 247.

69. Pusateri, *History of American Business*, 288.

70. Charles Calomiris and Gary Gorton, "The Origins of Banking Panics: Models, Facts, and Bank Regulation," in *Financial Markets and Financial Crises*, ed. R. Glenn Hubbard (Chicago: University of Chicago Press, 1991); Douglas Diamond and Philip Dybvig, "Bank Runs, Deposit Insurance, and Liquidity," *Journal of Political Economy* 91 (June 1983), 401–18.

71. Richard Vedder and Lowell Galloway, *Out of Work: Unemployment and Government in Twentieth-Century America* (New York: Holmes & Maier, 1993).

72. Danbom, *Born in the Country*, 217.

73. Michael Darby, "Three and a Half Million U.S. Employees Have Been Mislaid: Or, an Explanation of Unemployment, 1934–41," *Journal of Political Economy* 84 (February 1976), 1–16.

74. Darby, "Three and a Half Million U.S. Employees Have Been Mislaid," 8.

75. Larry Schweikart and Michael Allen, *A Patriot's History of the United States: From Columbus's Great Discovery to the War on Terror* (New York: Sentinel, 2004), 568–70.

76. Schweikart and Allen, *Patriot's History of the United States*, 568.

77. Smiley, *American Economy in the Twentieth Century*, 136.

78. Bovard, *Farm Fiasco*, 26.

79. See, for example, Randall S. Kroszner and Raghuram G. Rajan, "Is the Glass-Steagall Act Justified? A Study of the U.S. Experience with Universal Banking Before 1933," *American Economic Review* 84 (September 1994) 810–32.

80. Barry Eichengreen, *Golden Fetters* (New York: Oxford University Press, 1992); John Maynard Keynes, *The General Theory of Employment, Interest, and Money* (New York: Harcourt Brace, 1936); Milton Friedman and Anna J. Schwartz, *A Monetary History of the United States, 1867–1960* (Princeton, NJ: Princeton University Press, 1963); Peter Temin, *Did Monetary Forces Cause the Great Depression?* (New York: W. W. Norton, 1976), and his *Lessons from the Great Depression* (Cambridge, MA: MIT Press, 1989); Richard H. Keehn and Gene Smiley, "U.S. Bank Failures, 1932–1933: A Provisional Analysis," *Essays in Business and Economic History: Selected Papers from the Business and Economic Historical Society Meetings, 1987*, vol. 6 (1988), 136–56; Jude Wanniski, *The Way the World Works* (New York: Touchstone, 1978); and W. Elliott Brownlee, *Dynamics of Ascent*, ch. 15. Historiographical summaries of the various views, showing the inability of any single "school" to explain the Depression, appear in Jeremy Atack and Peter Passell, *A New Economic View of American History from Colonial Times to 1940*, 2d ed. (New York: Norton, 1994); Smiley,

American Economy in the Twentieth Century, and, specifically to banking,
Larry Schweikart, "U.S. Commercial Banking: A Historiographical Overview,"
Business History Review 65 (Autumn 1991), 606–61.

CHAPTER 10

1. Paul Johnson, *Modern Times: A History of the World from the Twenties to the Eighties* (New York: Harper Colophon, 1983), 401–2.

2. Johnson, *Modern Times,* 401–2.

3. Ibid., 402.

4. Gary quoted in Edward Robb Ellis, *Echoes of Distant Thunder: Life in the United States, 1914–1918* (New York: Coward, McCann & Geohagan, 1978), 381.

5. John B. Rae, "Financial Problems of the American Aircraft Industry, 1906–1940," *Business History Review* 39 (Spring 1965), 99–114.

6. F. Robert van der Linden, *Airlines and Air Mail: The Post Office and the Birth of the Commercial Aviation Industry* (Lexington: University of Kentucky Press, 2002).

7. Robert Daley, *An American Saga: Juan Trippe and His Pan American Empire* (New York: Random House, 1980).

8. T. A. Heppenheimer, "The Only Way to Fly," *Audacity* (Spring 1995), 16–27, quotation on 27.

9. Van der Linden, *Airlines and Air Mail,* 31, 143, 150, and passim.

10. "The DC-3 Opens a New Era of Commercial Air Travel," in Frank McGill, ed., *Great Events in History: Business and Commerce Series,* 5 vols. (Pasadena, CA: Salem Press, 1994), 2:752–57, quotation on 753.

11. Richard Hack, *Hughes: The Private Diaries, Memos, and Letters* (Beverly Hills, CA: New Millennium Publishing, 2001), 246.

12. Peter Harry Brown and Pat. H. Broeske, *Howard Hughes: The Untold Story* (New York: Dutton, 1996), 93.

13. Donald L. Bartlett and James B. Steele, *Empire: The Life, Legend, and Madness of Howard Hughes* (New York: W. W. Norton, 1979), 105–60.

14. Mark S. Foster, *Henry J. Kaiser: Builder in the Modern American West* (Austin: University of Texas Press, 1989).

15. Johnson, *Modern Times,* 402; Mark S. Foster, "Giant of the West: Henry J. Kaiser and Regional Industrialization," *Business History Review* 59 (Spring 1985), 1–23.

16. John Morton Blum, *V Was for Victory: Politics and American Culture During World War II* (New York: Harcourt Brace, 1948), 115.

17. Bruce Catton, *The War Lords of Washington* (New York: Harcourt, Brace, Jovanovich, 1976).

18. Richard Overy, *Why the Allies Won* (New York: W. W. Norton, 1995), 2–4 and ch. 6, passim, makes these points.

19. Pusateri, *History of American Business,* 319.

20. Foster, *Henry J. Kaiser,* 254.

21. John A. Heitmann, "The Man Who Won the War: Andrew Jackson Higgins," *Louisiana History* 34 (1993), 35–40, quotation on 36. Also see his "Demagogue and Industrialist," *Gulf Coast Historical Review* 5 (1990), 152–62.

22. Heitmann, "The Man Who Won the War," 40.

23. Heitmann, "The Man Who Won the War," 42; Higgins Industries, *History in a Hurry: The Story of Higgins of New Orleans* (New Orleans, LA: Higgins Industries, 1945), 42.

24. Stuart Bruchey, *The Wealth of the Nation: An Economic History of the United States* (New York: Harper & Row, 1988), 181.

25. U.S. Census Bureau, *The Statistical History of the United States*, Series D-29-41 (New York: Basic Books, 1976), 132; Bruchey, *Wealth of the Nation*, 182.

26. Robert Higgs, *Crisis and Leviathan: Critical Episodes in the Growth of American Government* (New York: Oxford University Press, 1987), 230.

27. Nevertheless, small business survived, and of course, whenever feasible, tried to use the federal government for its own purposes. See Jonathan J. Bean, *Beyond the Broker State: Federal Policies Toward Small Business, 1936–1961* (Chapel Hill: University of North Carolina Press, 1996).

28. Johnson, *Modern Times*, 408; Gary Cross and Rick Szostak, *Technology and American Society: A History* (Englewood Cliffs, NJ: Prentice-Hall, 1995), 280–83.

29. Larry Schweikart, *America's Victories: Why the U.S. Wins Wars and Will Win the War on Terror* (New York: Sentinel, 2006).

30. Robert Sobel, *The Age of Giant Corporations: A Microeconomic History of American Business, 1914–1992*, 3d ed. (Westport, CT: Praeger, 1993), 158.

31. Sobel, *Age of Giant Corporations*, 156.

32. Jesse H. Jones, *Fifty Billion Dollars: My Thirteen Years with the RFC* (New York: Macmillan, 1951), 9.

33. Sobel, *Age of Giant Corporations*, 162.

34. Andrew A. Workman, "Manufacturing Power: The Organizational Revival of the National Association of Manufacturers, 1941–1945," *Business History Review* 72 (Summer 1998), 279–317.

35. Jonathan Hughes, and Louis P. Cain, *American Economic History* (New York: HarperCollins, 1994), 483.

36. Robert Higgs, "Wartime Prosperity? A Reassessment of the U.S. Economy in the 1940s," *Journal of Economic History* 52 (March 1992), 41–62.

37. Higgs, "Wartime Prosperity?" 53.

38. Richard Vedder and Lowell Galloway, *Out of Work: Unemployment and Government in Twentieth-Century America* (New York: Holmes & Meier, 1993), 157.

39. Thomas A. Bailey and David M. Kennedy, *The American Pageant*, 10th ed. (Lexington, MA: D.C. Heath, 1994), 893; Johnson, *Modern Times*, ch. 17.

40. "Japan's Economy," AsianInfo.org, http://www.asianinfo.org/asianinfo/japan/economy.htm.

41. John B. Rae, *The American Automobile Industry* (Boston: Twayne Publishers, 1984), 174.

42. Peter Duignan and L. H. Gann, *The Rebirth of the West: The Americanization of the Democratic World, 1945–1958* (Lanham, MD: Rowman & Littlefield, 1992), 110.

43. Keith L. Bryant and Henry C. Dethloff, *A History of American Business*, 2d ed. (Englewood Cliffs, NJ: Prentice-Hall, 1990), 341–43; Mira Wilkins, *The Emergence of Multinational Enterprise: American Business Abroad from the Colonial Era to 1914* (Cambridge, MA: Harvard University Press, 1970), 201–2.

44. See Mira Wilkins, *The Maturing Multinational Enterprise: American Business Abroad from 1914 to 1970* (Cambridge, MA: Harvard University Press, 1970), 201–2.

45. Bryant and Dethloff, *American Business History*, 352.

46. "William J. Levitt," *Time*, July 13, 1950.

47. Lynne Pierson Doti and Larry Schweikart, *Banking in the American West: From the Gold Rush to Deregulation* (Norman: University of Oklahoma Press, 1991), 160–61; and their "Financing the Post-War Housing Boom in Phoenix and Los Angeles, 1945–1960," *Pacific Historical Review* 58 (May 1989), 173–94; and Carl Abbot, "The Suburban Sunbelt," *Journal of Urban History* 13 (May 1987), 275–301.

48. Doti and Schweikart, "Financing the Post-War Housing Boom," 178; Larry Schweikart, *A History of Banking in Arizona* (Tucson: University of Arizona Press, 1982), ch. 6, passim.

49. Larry Schweikart, *That Quality Image: The History of Continental Bank* (Tappan, NY: Custom Book, 1987), 8–10.

50. Joseph J. Fucini and Suzy Fucini, *Entrepreneurs: The Men and Women Behind Famous Brand Names and How They Made It* (Boston: G. K. Hall, 1985), 99–101; Emmett Culligan, "Softeners Rented," *BusinessWeek* 28 (December 1946), 21; and G. Hamilton, "Hey Zeolite Man," *Northbrook (Illinois) Star* 26 (February 1976), 30–31.

51. Doti and Schweikart, *Banking in the American West*, ch. 5; Walter Buenger and Joseph Pratt, *But Also Good Business: Texas Commerce Banks and the Financing of Houston, Texas, 1886–1986* (College Station: Texas A&M University Press, 1986).

52. Fucini and Fucini, "Dan Gerber," *Entrepreneurs*, 66–69.

53. *Pioneers of American Business*, comp. Sterling G. Slappey (New York: Grosset & Dunlap, 1973 [1970]), 140–44.

54. "Tupperware!" *American Experience*, PBS.org, http://www.pbs.org/wgbh/amex/tupperware/timeline/timeline2.html (accessed May 29, 2007).

55. Larry Schweikart, "Business and the Economy," in *American Decades: The 1950s*, ed. Richard Layman (New York: Gale, 1994), 87; Carl Solbert, *Conquest of the Skies: A History of Commercial Aviation in America* (Boston: Little, Brown, 1979).

56. Several sources deal with Kaiser's run at the Big Three, including David Halberstam, *The Reckoning* (New York: Avon Paperbacks, 1986); Mark S. Foster, "Henry J. Kaiser," in *The Automobile Industry* (New York: Facts on File, 1989), 224–30; and James J. Flink, *The Car Culture* (Cambridge, MA: MIT Press, 1975).

57. Larry Schweikart and Michael Allen, *A Patriot's History of the United States: From Columbus's Great Discovery to the War on Terror*, paperback ed. (New York: Sentinel, 2006), ch. 18.

58. Kemmons Wilson, *The Holiday Inn Story* (New York: Newcomen Society, 1968).

59. John Crean with Jim Washburn, *The Wheel and I: Driving Fleetwood Enterprises to the Top* (Newport Beach, CA: John Crean, 2000).

60. Richard F. Weingroff, "Creating the Interstate System," U.S. Department of Transportation, Federal Highway Administration (FHA), http://www.tfhrc.gov/pubrds/summer96/p96su10.htm. See also *America's Highways 1776–1976* (Washington, D.C.: FHA, 1976); Mark H. Rose, *Interstate Express Highway Politics 1941–1989*, rev. ed. (Knoxville: University of Tennessee Press, 1990).

61. Ray Kroc and Robert Anderson, *Grinding It Out: The Making of McDonald's* (Chicago: Contemporary Books, 1977), 66.

62. Kroc and Anderson, *Grinding It Out*, 67.

63. Ibid., 75.

64. George Gilder, *Recapturing the Spirit of Enterprise* (San Francisco: CS Press, 1992), ch. 2.

65. Shane Hamilton, "The Economies and Conveniences of Modern-Day Living: Frozen Foods and Mass Marketing, 1945–1965," *Business History Review* 77 (Spring 2003), 33–60.

66. "Berry Gordy, Jr., the Gordy Family, and the Motown Record Corp.," in David Bianco, *Heat Wave: The Motown Fact Book* (Ann Arbor, MI: Pierian Press, 1988); Steve Chapple and Reebee Garofalo, *Rock 'n' Roll is Here to Pay* (Chicago: Nelson-Hall, 1977); Arnold Shaw, *Black Popular Music in America* (New York: Shirmer Books, 1986); and Randy Taraborelli, *Michael Jackson: The Magic and the Madness* (New York: L. Birch, 1991).

67. Quoted in Larry Schweikart, "Disneyland Opens," in *Great Events in History: Business and Economics* (Santa Monica, CA: Salem Press, 1994), 1058–63, quotation on 1059; Steven Watts, *The Magic Kingdom: Walt Disney and the American Way of Life* (Columbia: University of Missouri Press, 1997); Bob Thomas, *Walt Disney: An American Original* (New York: Simon and Schuster, 1976); Randy Bright, *Disneyland: Inside Story* (New York: Abrams, 1987).

68. By 1954, one-third of the world had also seen a Disney film. Janet Wasko, *Understanding Disney* (Cambridge: Polity, 2001), 22.

69. Bryant and Dethloff, *History of American Business*, 195.

70. "The 1939 World's Fair Introduces Regular U.S. Television," in McGill, ed., *Great Events in History: Business and Commerce Series*, 2:803–8. See also Albert Abramson, *The History of Television, 1880–1941* (Jefferson, NC: McFarland, 1987).

71. William H. Whyte, Jr., *The Organization Man* (New York: Simon and Schuster, 1955); Vance Packard, *The Hidden Persuaders* (New York: Packet, 1957). Also see Sloan Wilson, *The Man in the Gray Flannel Suit* (New York: Simon and Schuster, 1955).

CHAPTER 11

1. Sam Walton with John Huey, *Sam Walton: Made in America—My Story* (New York: Doubleday, 1992); Sandra S. Vance and Roy V. Scott, "Sam Walton and Wal-Mart Stores: The Remaking of Modern America," in *American Vistas, 1877 to the Present*, eds. Leonard Dinnerstein and Kenneth Jackson (New York: Oxford, 1995), 359–80.

2. John Huey, "Builders and Titans: Sam Walton," *The Time* 100 (December 7, 1988), http://www.time.com/time/time100/builder/profile/walton.html.

3. "Mary Kay Ash," in Joseph J. Fucini and Suzy Fucini, *Entrepreneurs: The Men and Women Behind Famous Brand Names and How They Made It* (Boston: G. K. Hall, 1985); Mary Kay Ash, *Mary Kay* (New York: Harper & Row, 1981); Robert L. Shook, *The Entrepreneurs* (New York: Harper & Row, 1980); and P. Rosenfield, "The Beautiful Make-Up of Mary Kay," *Saturday Evening Post* (October 1981), 58–63.

4. Dilip Mookherjee, "Decentralization, Hierarchies, and Incentives: A Mechanism Design Perspective," *Journal of Economic Literature* 44, no. 2 (June 2006), 367–90.

5. David Halberstam, *The Reckoning* (New York: Avon Paperbacks, 1988), 218.

6. All quotations from Halberstam, *The Reckoning*, 218–19.

7. "The Hunk of Junk Hall of Fame," *BusinessWeek* (September 3, 2007), 14.

8. Ralph Nader, *Unsafe at Any Speed* (New York: Grossman, 1965).

9. Michael Kinsley, writing in 1985 in the *Washington Post*, quoted in Halberstam, *The Reckoning*, 501.

10. B. Bruce-Briggs, *The War Against the Automobile* (New York: E. P. Dutton, 1977).

11. Edmund Contoski, *Makers and Takers* (Minneapolis, MN: American Liberty Publishers, 1997), 97.

12. Michael Fumento, *Science Under Siege: Balancing Technology and the Environment* (New York: William Morrow, 1993).

13. Robert Crandall, *Why Is the Cost of Environmental Regulation So High?* (policy paper, Center for the Study of American Business, Washington University, St. Louis, February 1992), 3.

14. Peter Asch, *Consumer Safety Regulation: Putting a Price on Life and Limb* (New York: Oxford University Press, 1988).

15. Gene Smiley, *The American Economy in the Twentieth Century* (Cincinnati, OH: South-Western Publishing Co., 1994), 381.

16. William Lilley III and James C. Miller II, "The New 'Social Regulation," *The Public Interest* 47 (Spring 1977), 49–61, quotation on 56.

17. C. Joseph Pusateri, *A History of American Business*, 2d ed. (Arlington Heights, IL: Harlan-Davidson, 1988), 326–28, quotation on 327.

18. Robert Sobel, *Age of Giant Corporations: A Microeconomic History of American Business, 1419–1992*, 3d ed. (Westport, CT: Praeger, 1993), 191.

19. Interviews with C. William Verity, February 1998; Larry Schweikart, *Marriage of Steel: The Life and Times of William and Peggy Verity* (New York: Simon and Schuster Custom Book, 1998).

20. See Hans G. Mueller, "The Steel Industry," in J. Michael Finger and Thomas D. Willett, eds., *The Internationalization of the American Economy, The Annals of the American Academy of Political and Social Science* 460 (March 1982), 73–82; Robert E. Baldwin, Barry Eichengreen, and Hans van der Den, "U.S. Antidumping Policies: The Case of Steel," in *The Structure and Evolution of Recent U.S. Trade Policy*, ed. Anne O. Kreuger (Chicago: University of Chicago Press for National Bureau of Economic Research, 1984), 67–103.

21. Mansell G. Blackford and K. Austin Kerr, *Business Enterprise in American History*, 2d ed. (Boston: Houghton-Mifflin, 1990), 430–31.

22. James L. Clayton, ed., *The Economic Impact of the Cold War* (New York: Harcourt, Brace, 1970), 242–43.

23. Jacques S. Gansler, *The Defense Industry* (Cambridge, MA: MIT Press, 1980), and *Affording Defense* (Cambridge, MA: MIT Press, 1989).

24. Jacques S. Gansler, "How the Pentagon Buys Fruitcake," *Air Force Magazine* (June 1989), 94–97.

25. Smiley, *American Economy in the Twentieth Century*, figures 15.2–15.9, on 358–65.

26. E. Anthony Copp, *Regulating Competition in Oil: Government Intervention in the U.S. Refining Industry, 1948–1975* (College Station: Texas A&M University Press, 1976), 192.

27. Robert L. Bradley, Jr., *Oil, Gas, and Government: The U.S. Experience*, vol. 1 (Lanham, MD: Rowman & Littlefield, 1996).

28. "Thomas J. Watson," IBM Archives, http://www-03.ibm.com/ibm/history/exhibits/chairmen/chairmen_3.html (accessed August 31, 2007).

29. Thomas J. Watson, *Father, Son & Co.: My Life at IBM and Beyond* (New York: Bantam Books, 1990).

30. George Gilder, *Microcosm: The Quantum Revolution in Economics and Technology* (New York: Simon and Schuster, 1989), 48.

31. Gilder, *Microcosm*, 68.

32. Michael Moritz, *The Little Kingdom: The Private Story of Apple Computer* (New York: William Morrow, 1984).

33. "Jobs and Wozniak Found Apple Computer," in *Great Events in History II: Business and Commerce Series*, 5 vols. (Pasadena, CA: Salem Press, 1994) 2:1611–15.

34. Pusateri, *History of American Business*, 353.

35. James Wallace and Jim Erickson, *Hard Drive: Bill Gates and the Making of the Microsoft Empire* (New York: Wiley, 1992), and Stephen Manes and Paul Andrews, *Gates: How Microsoft's Mogul Reinvented an Industry and Made Himself the Richest Man in America* (New York: Doubleday, 1993); Robert X. Cringeley, *Accidental Empires: How the Boys of Silicon Valley Make Their Millions* (Reading, MA: Addison Wesley, 1992).

36. William T. Youngs, "Bill Gates and Microsoft," in Youngs, ed., *American Realities: Historical Episodes, vol. 2, From Reconstruction to the Present*, 3d ed. (New York: HarperCollins, 1993), 285.

37. On Federal Express, see Robert A. Sigafoos, *Absolutely Positively Overnight!* (New York: New American Library, 1984).

38. Robert Sobel and David B. Sicilia, *Entrepreneurs: An American Adventure* (Boston: Houghton-Mifflin, 1986), 46.

39. Marc Levinson, *The Box: How the Shipping Container Made the World Smaller and the World Economy Bigger* (Princeton, NJ: Princeton University Press, 2006).

40. Interviews with C. William Verity, President, National Chamber of Commerce (1980–81), February 1998.

41. Seymour Martin Lipset and William Schneider, *The Confidence Gap: Business, Labor, and Government in the Public Mind* (New York: Free Press, 1983), 48–49.

42. Bureau of Labor Statistics, Consumer Price Index for All Urban Consumers, ftp://ftp.bls.gov/pub/special.requests/cpi/cpiai.txt (accessed September 13, 2007).

43. Bureau of Labor Statistics, ftp://ftp.bls.gov/pub/special.requests/lf/aat1.txt (accessed September 13, 2007).

44. Federal Deposit Insurance Corporation, *An Examination of the Banking Crises of the 1880s and Early 1990s* (Washington, D.C.: FDIC, 1997) 14–15.

45. Frederic Mishkin, *The Economics of Money, Banking and Financial Markets*, 8th ed. (Boston: Addison Wesley, 2006), 298.

CHAPTER 12

1. Louis Galambos and Eric John Abrahamson, *Anytime, Anywhere* (Cambridge: University of Cambridge, 2002), 34.

2. Galambos and Abrahamson, *Anytime, Anywhere*, 35.

3. Ibid., 19.

4. Ibid., 38.

5. Ibid., 40.

6. Ibid., 3.

7. Ibid., both quotes on 66.

8. Ibid., 74.

9. Ibid., 138.

10. Warren Brookes, "The Silent Boom," *The American Spectator*, August 1988, 16–19, which contained elements of his article, "The Media vs. the Economy," taken from the *Detroit News*, December 29, 1988.

11. John P. Hoerr, *And the Wolf Finally Came: The Decline of the American Steel Industry* (Pittsburgh, PA: University of Pittsburgh Press, 1988), 606–7.

12. Richard Preston, *American Steel* (New York: Prentice-Hall, 1991), 80.

13. Preston, *American Steel*, 80–81.

14. Ibid., 45–46.

15. Ibid., 74.

16. Larry Schweikart interview with Ken Iverson, June 8, 1995.

17. "Behind the Wheels," *Newsweek*, October 8, 1984, 62.

18. Lee Iacocca with William Novak, *Iacocca: An Autobiography* (New York: Bantam, 1984), 62.

19. John Bussey, "Lee Iacocca Calls Odometer Policy Dumb," *Wall Street Journal,* July 2, 1987.

20. Iacocca, *Iacocca: An Autobiography.*

21. For these and other outrageous suits brought through federal regulations, see James Bovard, "The Lame Game," *The American Spectator,* July 1995, 30–33, and his *Lost Rights: The Destruction of American Liberty* (New York: St. Martins, 1994).

22. Thomas D. Hopkins, "A Guide to the Regulatory Landscape," *Jobs & Capital* 4 (Fall 1995), 28–31.

23. S. Robert Lichter and Stanley Rothman, "Media and Business Elites," *Public Opinion* 4 (October/November 1981), 42–60, and their "Personality, Ideology, and World View: A Comparison of Media and Business Elites," *British Journal of Political Science* 15 (1984), 29–49.

24. George Gilder, *Wealth and Poverty* (New York: Basic Books, 1981), 101.

25. Ann Marsh, "Meet the Class of 1996," *Forbes* 400 (October 14, 1996), 100–295.

26. Lamm cited in Arthur Levitt, Jr., "In Praise of Small Business," *New York Times Magazine,* December 6, 1981.

27. Steven Solomon, *Small Business USA: The Role of Small Companies in Sparking America's Economic Transformation* (New York: Crown, 1986), 23.

28. Council of Economic Advisers, *Economic Report of the President, February 1985* (Washington, D.C.: U.S. Government Printing Office, 1985), 193.

29. See George Gilder, *Recapturing the Spirit of Enterprise* (San Francisco: ICS Press, 1992), ch. 6.

30. Material on Zabian is from Gilder, *Wealth and Poverty,* 53–54; material on Colangelo is from an unpublished history of the Phoenix Suns basketball team by Larry Schweikart and interviews with Colangelo.

31. Pyong Gap Min, *Ethnic Business Enterprise: Korean Small Business in Atlanta* (New York: Center for Migration Studies, 1988), 82; Alixa Naff, "Lebanese Immigration into the United States: 1880 to the Present," in Albert Hourani and Nadim Shehadi, *The Lebanese in the World: A Century of Emigration* (London: Taurus, 1992), 148. Also see Thomas Sowell, *Race and Culture: A World View* (New York: Basic Books, 1994).

32. Irwin Garfinkle and Robert Haveman, with the assistance of David Betson, U.S. Department of Health, Education, and Welfare, *Earnings Capacity, Poverty, and Inequality,* Institute for Research on Poverty Monograph Series (New York: Academic Press, 1977).

33. Allan Reynolds, "The Ominous Decline in Work Incentives," *Jobs & Capital* 3 (Fall 1994), 9–17, quotation on 13; Hilary Hoynes, "Welfare Transfers in Two-Parent Families: Labor Supply and Welfare Participation under AFDC-UP" (NBER working paper, no. 4407, July 1993).

34. Marsh, "Meet the Class of 1996," quotation on 100.

35. Thomas J. Stanley and William D. Danko, *The Millionaire Next Door: The Surprising Secrets of America's Wealthy* (Atlanta: Longstreet Press, 1996), 3.

36. Associated Press, "What Makes Jerry Jones Run?" January 25, 1996, in author's possession. See also Jim Dent, *King of the Cowboys* (Holbrook, MA: Adams Publishing, 1995).

37. Alec R. Levenson, "New Evidence on the Growth in Part-Time Employment," *Jobs & Capital* 3 (Fall 1994), 7–8.

38. Ben Wildavsky, "McJobs," *Policy Review* (Summer 1989), 30–37.

39. Peter Temin with Louis Galambos, *The Fall of the Bell System: A Study in Prices and Politics* (New York: Cambridge University Press, 1987), 346.

40. See Alan Stone, *Wrong Number: The Breakup of AT&T* (New York: Basic Books, 1989), and Theodore P. Kovaleff, "For Whom Did the Bell Toll: A Review of Recent Treatment of the American Telephone and Telegraph Divestiture," *The Antitrust Bulletin* 34 (Spring 1989), 437–50.

41. "AT&T Agrees to Be Broken Up as Part of an Antitrust Settlement," in Frank McGill, ed., *Great Events in History: Business and Commerce Series*, 5 vols. (Pasadena, CA: Salem Press, 1994), 5:1821–25.

42. Temin, *Fall of the Bell System*, chs. 2 and 7.

43. George Gilder, *Life After Television: The Coming Transformation of Media and American Life* (Knoxville, TN: Whittle Direct Books, 1990), 60.

44. Tom Peters, "A Sampling of Popular Misconceptions," *Washington Times*, September 8, 1988.

45. Michael Jensen, "Eclipse of the Public Corporation," *Harvard Business Review* (September–October 1989), 61–74; and Glenn Yago, *Junk Bonds: How High Yield Securities Restructured Corporate America* (New York: Oxford University Press, 1991).

46. Gilder, *Life After Television*, 69–72.

47. Ibid., 71.

48. See Temin, *Fall of the Bell System*, 347, as well as Peter W. Huber, *The Geodesic Network*, a 1987 report prepared for the Department of Justice on competition in the telephone industry.

49. James Coates, "New IBM Chief Clears for Battle," *Dayton Daily News*, June 25, 1995; Richard Thomas DeLamarter, *Big Blue: IBM's Use and Abuse of Power* (New York: Dodd, Mead, 1986).

50. "Study: New Trends Driving the PC Market," *Prodigy*, June 12, 1995.

51. Grove quoted in Karl Zinsmeister, "MITI Mouse: Japan's Industrial Policy Doesn't Work," *Policy Review* (Spring 1993), 28–35, quotation on 31.

52. Kenneth J. Bindas and Craig Houston, "'Takin' Care of Business': Rock Music, Vietnam, and the Protest Myth," *Historian* (November 1989), 1–23, quotation on 16.

53. James Lardner, *Fast Forward: Hollywood, the Japanese, and the Onslaught of the VCR* (New York: W. W. Norton, 1987), 59.

54. Gail DeGeorge, *The Making of a Blockbuster: How Wayne Huizenga Built a Sports and Entertainment Empire from Trash, Grit, and Videotape* (New York: Wiley, 1997).

55. Scott Allen, "Wayne Huizenga Biography," About.com, http://entrepreneurs.about.com/od/famousentrepreneurs/p/waynehuizenga.htm.

56. "Everybody's Talkin' at Us," *BusinessWeek* (May 22, 1995), 104–5, 108.

57. David Sheff, *Game Over: How Nintendo Conquered the World* (New York: Vintage Books, 1994), 5.

58. Interview with Ed Semrad, editor-in-chief of *Electronic Gaming Monthly*, June 28, 1995.

59. See "Video Game Timeline," *Electronic Gaming Monthly* (January 1988), 112–37, as well as other EGM issues that have provided a running history of the industry.

60. David Johnston, *Temples of Chance: How America, Inc. Bought Out Murder Inc. to Win Control of the Casino Business* (New York: Doubleday, 1992); Larry Schweikart, "Atlantic City Legalizes Casino Gambling," in *Great Events from History II: Business and Commerce Series, vol. 4, 1927–1980*, ed. Frank N. McGill (Pasadena, CA: Salem Press, 1994), 1600–05.

61. See Ira Magaziner and Robert B. Reich, *Minding America's Business: The Decline and Rise of the American Economy* (New York: Harcourt, Brace Jovanovich, 1982); Clyde Prestowitz, Jr., *Trading Places: How We Allowed Japan to Take the Lead* (New York: Basic Books, 1988); Lester Thurow, *The Zero-Sum Society* (New York: Basic Books, 1980); and Stephen Cohen and John Zysman, *Manufacturing Matters: The Myth of the Post-Industrial Society* (New York: Basic Books, 1987).

CHAPTER 13

1. Jeff Bezos in interview with Barry Libert of Anderson, http://www.fei.org/maga-zine/Exclusives/Libert-4-18-2k1.cfm. This interview appeared in its entirety in *Bisk Audio Financial Accounting & Management Report*, January 2001.

2. "Storewidth Peers," *Gilder Technology Report* 6 (December 2001), 1–7.

3. "Storewidth Peers," 5.

4. Ibid., 2.

5. In 1990, a British company called Instanet introduced the first fully computerized securities trading terminals, allowing brokers to bypass brokerage houses and further democratizing securities exchanges. See Robert J. McCartney, "Computer Network Lets Traders Bypass Exchanges," *Dayton Daily News*, July 8, 1990.

6. "Storewidth Peers," 2.

7. Joel Kotkin and Roxx C. DeVol, "Knowledge-Value Cities in the Digital Age," Milken Institute Study, February 13, 2001, 2, in authors' possession.

8. Laura Bischoff, "TransWave's Circling the Globe," *Dayton Daily News*, January 4, 2000; Jennifer Keller, "TransWave" (HST 370 seminar paper, 2000, in author's possession).

9. Remarks by Chairman Alan Greenspan, Haas Annual Business Faculty Research Dialogue, University of California, Berkeley, September 4, 1998.

10. "Rules of the Road: Governing Principles for the New Economy," New Economy Task Force Report, September 13, 1999, Progressive Policy Institute, http://www.ppionline.org/ppi_ci.cfm?contentid=1268&knlgAreaID=128&subse-cid=174.

11. "The History of Yahoo! How It All Started…," Yahoo Media Relations, http://docs.yahoo.com/info/misc/history.html.

12. A recent examination of the state of scholarship, by Richard John ("Elaborations, Revisions, Dissents: Alfred D. Chandler, Jr.'s *The Visible Hand* after Twenty Years," *Business History Review* 71 [Summer 1997], 151–200), despite updating

the discussion, fails to address the rather radical departures outlined by George Gilder and Walter Wriston, and the effects of those changes on the theory of the "visible hand." See also Dwight R. Lee and Richard B. McKenzie, "Countervailing Impotence," *Society* (November/December 1992), 34–40.

13. Stacey Tevlin and Karl Whelan, "Explaining the Investment Boom of the 1990s," *Journal of Money, Credit, and Banking* 35 (February 2003), 1–22.

14. Tom Farley, "The Cell-Phone Revolution," *Invention & Technology* (Winter 2007), 8–19.

15. Annalee Saxenian, "Lessons from Silicon Valley," *Technology Review* (July 1994), 42–51.

16. Michael Jensen, "The Modern Industrial Revolution: Exit and the Failure of Internal Control Systems," *Journal of Finance* 48 (July 1993), 831–80. Also see Michael Jensen, "Eclipse of the Public Corporation," *Harvard Business Review* (September–October 1989), 61–74.

17. Charles Y. Baldwin and Kim B. Clark, "Capital Budgeting Systems and Capabilities Investments in U.S. Companies after the Second World War," *Business History Review* 68 (Spring 1994), 61–74.

18. "Corporate Killers," *Newsweek*, February 26, 1996.

19. See, for example, "On the Battlefields of Business, Millions of Casualties," *New York Times*, March 3, 1996.

20. Michael Cox and Richard Alm, "The Churn: The Paradox of Progress," Dallas Federal Reserve Bank, 1992 Annual Report, May 1993, 11.

21. William G. Gale and John Sabelhaus, "The Savings Crisis: In the Eye of the Beholder?" *Milken Institute Review* (Third Quarter 1999), 46–56, quotation on 56; Shawn Everett Kantor and Price V. Fishback, "Precautionary Saving, Insurance, and the Origins of Workers' Compensation," *Journal of Political Economy* 104 (April 1996), 419–42.

22. William M. Gentry and R. Glenn Hubbard, "Entrepreneurship and Household Saving," 2000, draft paper in authors' possession.

23. Robert E. Hall, "The Stock Market and Capital Accumulation," *American Economic Review* (December 2001), 1185–1202.

24. Paul Gigot, "This Isn't What Marx Meant by Das Kapital," *Wall Street Journal*, March 19, 1999.

25. Dora L. Costa, "American Living Standards: Evidence from Recreational Expenditures," National Bureau of Economic Research, Working Paper No. W7148, May 1999.

26. "From GM to Cisco in Just Four Decades," *BusinessWeek*, February 7, 2000.

27. Statistics by Timothy Bates, "An Analysis of Minority Entrepreneurship" (1985), cited in Shelley Green and Paul Pryde, *Black Entrepreneurship in America* (New Brunswick, NJ: Transaction Publishers, 1990), 25. Also see Joel Kotkin, "The Reluctant Entrepreneurs," *Inc.*, September 1987.

28. "The Top 100," *USA Today*, May 6, 1987.

29. Harriet C. Johnson, "Fast-Growth Firm Makes Buses," *USA Today*, May 6, 1987.

30. Reginald F. Lewis and Blair S. Walker, *"Why Should White Guys Have All the Fun?" How Reginald Lewis Created a Billion-Dollar Business Empire* (New

York: John Wiley, 1995). When Lewis died of brain cancer, just six years after his purchase of Beatrice International, former Dallas Cowboy tight end Jean Fugett took over the management of the conglomerate.

31. Robert W. Fairlie, "The Absence of African-American Owned Business: An Analysis of the Dynamics of Self-Employment," *Journal of Labor Economics* 17 (1999), 80–108.

32. Fairlie, "Absence of African-American Owned Business," 103.

33. Edward D. Berkowitz, *America's Welfare State: From Roosevelt to Reagan* (Baltimore: Johns Hopkins University Press, 1991), 100–101.

34. Daniel Patrick Moynihan's report is reproduced in William L. Yancey and Lee Rainwater, *The Moynihan Report and the Politics of Controversy* (Boston: MIT Press, 1967). Also see Moynihan's *Maximum Feasible Misunderstanding* (New York: Free Press, 1969).

35. Stuart Butler, *Out of the Poverty Trap* (New York: Free Press, 1987), and Charles Murray, *Losing Ground* (New York: Basic Books, 1984). A different interpretation appears in William Julius Wilson, *The Truly Disadvantaged: The Inner City, the Underclass, and Public Policy* (Chicago: University of Chicago Press, 1987), and David T. Ellwood, *Poor Support: Poverty in the American Family* (New York: Basic Books, 1988). A somewhat middle ground is presented by Bradley R. Schiller, *The Economics of Poverty and Discrimination*, 5th ed. (Englewood Cliffs, NJ: Prentice-Hall, 1989).

36. Thomas Sowell has numerous books on this topic and other evidence about the nonimpact of racism on economic matters. See Thomas Sowell, *The Economics and Politics of Race, Knowledge, and Decisions, Ethnic America: A History* (New York: Basic Books, 1981), *Preferential Policies: An International Perspective* (New York: William Morrow, 1990), and *Race and Culture* (New York: Basic Books, 1994). Walter Williams's work is best captured in *The State Against Blacks* (New York: New Press, 1982). Other material can be found in George Gilder, *Wealth and Poverty* (New York: Basic Books, 1981), as well as Dinesh D'Souza, *The End of Racism* (New York: Free Press, 1995).

37. Steve Sailer, "How Jackie Robinson Desegregated America," *National Review* (April 8, 1996), 38–41.

38. Jennifer Roback, "The Political Economy of Segregation: The Case of Segregated Streetcars," *Journal of Political Economy* 46 (December 1986), 893–917.

39. Susan E. Mayer, *What Money Can't Buy: Family Income and Children's Life Chances* (Cambridge, MA: Harvard University Press, 1977), 2–3.

40. "Black Businesses Excel: Outperform *Forbes, Fortune* Top Companies," *Dayton Daily News*, May 7, 1996; "24th Annual Report on Black Business," *Black Enterprise* (June 1996), 103–95, and in the same issue, Eric L. Smith, "Is Black Business Paving the Way?" 194–206.

41. "Black Businesses Excel."

42. Green and Pryde, *Black Entrepreneurship in America*, 100; Carol Hymowitz, "Taking a Chance: Many Blacks Jump Off the Corporate Ladder to Be Entrepreneurs," *Wall Street Journal*, August 2, 1984.

43. Welfare remains an impediment to entrepreneurship, though, and not just in the United States. See "A German Who Offers Low-Pay Service Work Dismays Countrymen," *Wall Street Journal*, March 3, 1998.

44. Sylvia Nasar with Kirsten B. Mitchell, "Booming Job Market Draws Young Black Men into Fold," *New York Times*, May 23, 1999. See also William Freeman, "Area Economic Conditions and the Labor Market Outcomes of Young Men in the 1990s Expansion," in *Prosperity for All? The Economic Boom and African Americans*, eds. William M. Rodgers III and Robert Cherry (New York: Russell Sage Foundation, 2000). No sooner had the Freeman article come out than George W. Bush, a Republican, was elected president, and Freeman quickly hustled out articles explaining that the job gains of the 1990s were not "real."

45. The following material comes from Wallace Terry, "I *Chose* to Change My Life," *Parade* (October 13, 1996), 4–5.

46. All quotations from Terry, "I *Chose* to Change My Life."

47. "1 of 4 U.S. Workers Employed by Women," *Dayton Daily News*, March 27, 1996, quoting the National Foundation for Women Business Owners, "1996 Facts on Women-Owned Businesses," and Census Bureau data.

48. "1 of 4 U.S. Workers Employed by Women."

49. Nancy Michaels, "Women Entrepreneurs Growing in Numbers and Importance," *U.S. News & World Report*, June 26, 2003, http://www.score.org/m_pr_20.html.

50. Scott Callon, *Divided Sun: MITI and the Breakdown of Japanese High-Tech Industrial Policy, 1975–1993* (Stanford, CA: Stanford University Press, 1995), 2.

51. Callon, *Divided Sun*, 201.

52. George Gilder, *Microcosm: The Quantum Revolution in Economics and Technology* (New York: Simon and Schuster, 1989), 341.

53. Michael Porter, *The Competitive Advantage of Nations* (New York: Free Press, 1990).

54. Porter, *Competitive Advantage of Nations*, 117.

55. Richard J. Murnane and Frank Levy, *Teaching the New Basic Skills: Principles for Educating Children to Thrive in a Changing Economy* (New York: Free Press, 1996).

56. Frederick L. Pryor and David L. Schaffer, *Who's Not Working and Why: Employment, Cognitive Skills, Wages, and the Changing U.S. Labor Market* (Cambridge: Cambridge University Press, 1999), 45.

57. Pryor and Schaffer, *Who's Not Working*, 217–21.

58. Rebecca Blumenstein, "'Web Overbuilt': How the Fiber Barons Plunged the U.S. into a Telecom Glut," *Wall Street Journal*, June 18, 2001.

59. Blumenstein, "'Web Overbuilt.'"

60. "A Look Back to When PC Power Took Off," *USA Today*, August 8, 2001.

61. Andrew Gumbel, "In dot.com Valley, the 'Pink Slips' Are Falling Like Confetti," February 10, 2001, http://www.independent.co.uk/news/Digital/Update/2001-02/dotcom100201.shtml.

CHAPTER 14

1. Andrew Gumbel, "In dot.com Valley, the 'Pink Slips' Are Falling Like Confetti," February 10, 2001, http://www.independent.co.uk/news/Digital/Update/2001-02/dotcom100201.shtml.

2. Daniel Gross, *Pop! Why Bubbles Are Great for the Economy* (New York: Collins, 2007), 118–19.

3. "Timeline of the Tyco International scandal," *USA Today*, June 17, 2005, http://www.USAtoday.com/money/industries/manufacturing/2005-06-17-tyco -timeline_x.htm.

4. FoxNews/Opinion Dynamics Poll, July 2002, and Ipsos-Reid Poll, January 2002, both cited in Karlyn Bowman, "Sinking CEOs," *The American Enterprise* (October/November 2002), 61.

5. Gallup, June 2002, and NBC News/*Wall Street Journal*, July 2002, polls, cited in ibid.

6. Peter Navarro and Aron Spencer, "September 11, 2001: Assessing the Costs of Terrorism," *Milken Institute Review* (Fourth Quarter 2001), 17–31, chart on 19.

7. Navarro and Spencer, "September 11, 2001," 22.

8. Ibid., 24.

9. Dow Jones & Company, Historical statistics, www.Djindexes.com/mdsix (accessed June 14, 2007).

10. Ibid.

11. Jeffrey Timmons, *New Venture Creation: Entrepreneurship for the Twenty-First Century* (New York: Irwin/McGraw-Hill, 1999); Chris Edwards, *Entrepreneurs Creating the New Economy*, Joint Economic Committee Staff Report, Office of the Chairman, Connie Mack, November 2000, www.senate.gov/~jec; William Dennis, Jr., *Business Starts and Stops*, National Federation of Independent Business, January 2000.

12. Revenue for Tickets.com in 2001 was $56.1 million. Gimple left the company in 2002. In 2003, the company lost major clients to Ticketmaster and reported accounting problems. The company disappeared by 2004. See Jim Fickle, "Tickets.com Gets a Split from Baseball," *The OC Register*, January 9, 2003; "Bad News Comes in Fives," *The OC Register*, April 2, 2003; and "OC Bloomberg Index," *The OC Register*, April 6, 2003. The company name is owned by Ticketmaster.

13. Gross, *Pop! Why Bubbles Are Great for the Economy*, 121.

14. Ibid., 3.

15. One of Lynne Doti's students in California spent the summer at home in India selling snow removal equipment. He not only learned to speak as if he were from Minnesota, he became conversant with Green Bay Packers statistics, the nuances of ice hockey, and types of snow, which he had never seen.

16. Thomas Friedman, *The World Is Flat: A Brief History of the Twenty-First Century* (New York: Farrar, Straus and Giroux, 2005), 206.

17. Friedman, *The World Is Flat*, 31.

18. Peter Hessler, "China's Instant Cities," *National Geographic* 211, no. 6 (June 2007), http://ngm.nationalgeographic.com/2007/06/instant-cities/hessler-text.

19. Elizabeth Corcoran, "Dell Moves Outsourced Jobs Back to U.S. Shores," *Forbes.com*, April 28, 2004, http://msnbc.msn.com/id/4853511/.

20. Robert Haynes and Jeremy Crockford, "Bringing the Jobs Back Home," *Boston Globe*, April 13, 2007, http://www.boston.com/news/globe/editorial_opinion/ oped/articles/2007/04/13/bringing_the_jobs_back_home/.

21. Michael Woods, "Europe Slow in Stemming 'Brain Drain' to America," *Pittsburgh Post-Gazette*, October 20, 2003.

22. Allan Reynolds, "The Ominous Decline in Work Incentives," *Jobs & Capital* 3 (Fall 1994), 15.

23. Steve Hamm and Cliff Edwards, "Is It a Smartphone or a Laptop?" *BusinessWeek* (June 11, 2007), 56–57.

24. "The 2006 Fortune 500: Annual Ranking of America's Largest Corporations," *Fortune*, http://money.cnn.com/magazines/fortune/fortune500/full_list/ (accessed June 2007).

25. U.S. Department of Commerce, Bureau of Economic Analysis, National Economic Accounts, http://www.bea.gov/national/nipaweb/TableView.asp?SelectedTable=43&FirstYear=2006&LastYear=2007&Freq=Qtr (accessed June 2007).

26. "The 2006 Fortune 500."

27. Justin Ewers, "Moving Beyond Pong and Pizza," *U.S. News & World Report*, February 26, 2007.

28. Kenneth D. Tuchman, "400 Richest Americans," *Forbes*, 192.

29. Ibid.

30. "Ted Schwartz," *Forbes* 400, 188.

31. Virginia I. Postrel, "The Nail File," *Reason* (October 1997), 4–8.

32. Linda Troung is personally known to Lynne Doti.

33. Elliot Blair Smith, "Montana Billionaire's Legacy is Biggest Burden," *USA Today*, October 27, 1997.

34. "Broadcom Corporation: Company Profile," http://www.referenceforbusiness.com/history2/75/Broadcom-Corporation.html (accessed June 13, 2007); and "Broadcom: Company Fact Sheet," http://www.broadcom.com/company/factsheet.php (accessed June 13, 2007).

35. For more information on the ongoing case, see *The Orange County Register*, June 24, 2008. "Broadcom's Samueli pleads guilty to lying." "Dr. Nicholas and Mr. Hyde," *Vanity Fair*, November 2006.

36. Andrew E. Serwer, "American Indians Discover Money Is Power," *Fortune*, April 19, 1993, reprint from Choctaw tribe.

37. Peter Michelmore, "Uprising in Indian Country," *Reader's Digest*, November 1984.

38. Mississippi Band of Choctaw Indians are still thriving. See http://content.usatoday.com/topics/topic/Mississippi+Band+of+Choctaw+Indians (accessed March 9, 2009).

39. Marty Grunder, interviews with Larry Schweikart, various dates 1996; Carol Mattar, "Grunder Discovers Green in Landscaping," *Dayton Business Reporter* (October 1993), 4.

40. Mattar, "Grunder Discovers Green," 4.

41. Martin J. Grunder Jr., e-mail to Larry Schweikart, June 20, 2007.

42. The reverse also is true, as large corporations seek to maintain the entrepreneurial attitude. See L. D. DeSimone, et al., "How Can Big Companies Keep the Entrepreneurial Spirit Alive?" *Harvard Business Review* (November–December 1995), 183–92.

43. Daniel Jimenez, "The Best College Entrepreneurs of the Year," *Young Money* (February/March 2007), 12.

44. Jimenez, "Best College Entrepreneurs of the Year."

EPILOGUE

1. *Fortune 500* 2006, "New Century Financial Corp.," http://money.cnn.com/magazines/fortune/fortune500/snapshots/2551.html (accessed February 2, 2009).

2. Stanford Law School, Securities Class Action Clearinghouse, http://securities.stanford.edu/1037/NEW_01/ (accessed February 2, 2009).

3. "New Century files for Chapter 11 Bankruptcy: Troubled Subprime Mortgage to Cut 3,200 Jobs, Sell Servicing, Seek Funding While it Reorganizes," CNNMoney.com, April 3, 2007.

4. Standard & Poor's, "The S&P/Case—Shiller U.S. National Home Price Index Posts a Record Annual Decline in the Third Quarter of 2007," news release, November 27, 2007.

5. "Disclosure and Analysis of Fannie Mae and Freddie Mac Mortgage Loan Data for Full-Year 2007 and First Quarter 2008," Federal Housing Finance Agency Mortgage Metrics Report, September 24, 2008, 6.

6. FDIC reported on its website that for September 2008, $124 million in real estate loans of the total of more than $2 trillion, or nearly 6 percent, were on a nonaccrual basis.

7. JPMorgan Chase had an offer on the table for Bear Stearns at $8 to $12 a share, while Paulson forced the sale at $2, but large investors in the stock rebelled and the deal was completed at $10 a share. "Paulson's Freddie Fannie Fix," CNNMoney.com, August 22, 2008, http://money.cnn.com/2008/08/22/news/newsmakers/paulson.fannie.fortune/index.htm?postversion=2008082215. In March 2008, the Federal Reserve System loaned money to JPMorgan Chase bank to lend to Bear Stearns, after which the bank acquired Bear Stearns. Bank of America acquired Merrill Lynch in September 2008. Lehman Brothers declared bankruptcy on September 15, 2008, and the next day, the Fed made an $85 billion loan to AIG, which had insured securities backed by mortgages.

8. "Forbes 400: The 400 Richest Americans," Forbes.com, http://www.forbes.com/lists/2008/54/400list08_William-Gates-III_BH69.html (accessed February 9, 2009).

INDEX